Rediscovered Classics of Japanese Animation

Rediscovered Classics of Japanese Animation

The Adaptation of Children's Novels into the World Masterpiece Theater *Series*

Maria Chiara Oltolini

BLOOMSBURY ACADEMIC
NEW YORK • LONDON • OXFORD • NEW DELHI • SYDNEY

BLOOMSBURY ACADEMIC
Bloomsbury Publishing Inc, 1359 Broadway, New York, NY 10018, USA
Bloomsbury Publishing Plc, 50 Bedford Square, London, WC1B 3DP, UK
Bloomsbury Publishing Ireland, 29 Earlsfort Terrace, Dublin 2, D02 AY28, Ireland

BLOOMSBURY, BLOOMSBURY ACADEMIC and the Diana logo are trademarks of
Bloomsbury Publishing Plc

First published in the United States of America 2024
Paperback edition published 2025

Copyright Maria Chiara Oltolini, 2024

For legal purposes the Acknowledgements on p. viii constitute an extension
of this copyright page.

Cover design: Eleanor Rose
Cover image: A still from *Arupusu no shōjo Haiji* (*Heidi girl of the Alps*), 1974,
dir. Isao Takahata © Allstar Picture Library Limited / Alamy

All rights reserved. No part of this publication may be: i) reproduced or transmitted in any form, electronic or mechanical, including photocopying, recording or by means of any information storage or retrieval system without prior permission in writing from the publishers; or ii) used or reproduced in any way for the training, development or operation of artificial intelligence (AI) technologies, including generative AI technologies. The rights holders expressly reserve this publication from the text and data mining exception as per Article 4(3) of the Digital Single Market Directive (EU) 2019/790.

Bloomsbury Publishing Inc does not have any control over, or responsibility for, any third-party websites referred to or in this book. All internet addresses given in this book were correct at the time of going to press. The author and publisher regret any inconvenience caused if addresses have changed or sites have ceased to exist, but can accept no responsibility for any such changes.

Library of Congress Cataloging-in-Publication Data
Names: Oltolini, Maria Chiara, author.
Title: Rediscovered classics of Japanese animation : the adaptation of children's novels into the World Masterpiece Theater series / Maria Chiara Oltolini.
Description: New York : Bloomsbury Academic, 2024. | Includes bibliographical references and index. | Summary: "The first academic work to examine the Japanese World Masterpiece Theater (Sekai Meisaku Gekijô, 1969-2009), which popularized the practice of adapting foreign children's books into long-running animated series and laid the groundwork for powerhouses like Studio Ghibli."–Provided by publisher.
Identifiers: LCCN 2023031397 (print) | LCCN 2023031398 (ebook) | ISBN 9781501389900 (hardback) | ISBN 9781501389870 (paperback) | ISBN 9781501389894 (epub) | ISBN 9781501389887 (pdf) | ISBN 9781501389863
Subjects: LCSH: Animated television programs–Japan–History and criticism. | Television adaptations–Japan–History and criticism. | World Masterpiece Theater.
Classification: LCC PN1992.8.A59 O58 2024 (print) | LCC PN1992.8.A59 (ebook) | DDC 791.45/340952–dc23/eng/20230810
LC record available at https://lccn.loc.gov/2023031397
LC ebook record available at https://lccn.loc.gov/2023031398

ISBN: HB: 978-1-5013-8990-0
PB: 978-1-5013-8987-0
ePDF: 978-1-5013-8988-7
eBook: 978-1-5013-8989-4

Typeset by Deanta Global Publishing Services, Chennai, India

For product safety related questions contact productsafety@bloomsbury.com.

To find out more about our authors and books visit www.bloomsbury.com and
sign up for our newsletters.

CONTENTS

List of Figures vi
Acknowledgements viii

Introduction 1

1 Children's fiction in Japan: From the origins to the post-war 5

2 Japanese animation and children's literature 37

3 The roots of the *World Masterpiece Theater* 65

4 Framing the meisaku series 105

5 From *Anne of Green Gables* to *Akage no An* 183

6 From *A Little Princess* to *Shōkōjo Sēra* 215

Conclusions 245

Bibliography 255
Index 271

FIGURES

3.1a	Hyakkimaru and Dororo	81
3.1b	The final battle between Hyakkimaru and Lord Kagemitsu	82
3.2a	Moomintroll snatching his dad's rifle	83
3.2b	Moomintroll greets his best friend Snufkin	84
3.3a	Chianti transforms into a clumsy dragon	87
3.3b	Chianti and Zucco	88
3.4a	Rocky Chuck	92
3.4b	The woodchuck confronting his family	92
3.5a	Depth of field in *Heidi*	102
3.5b	Heidi's grandfather feels soothed	102
4.1a	Nello, Alois and Patrasche, running	111
4.1b	Marco crying	112
4.2a	Rascal washing his first sugar cube	116
4.2b	Perrine helping her mother	116
4.3a	Tom escorts Becky	119
4.3b	Ernest Robinson cures his son	119
4.4a	Lucy-May, Kate and Little	122
4.4b	Annette breaks Lucien's sculpture	122
4.5a	Katri reads the Kalevala	124
4.5b	Pollyanna hugs her aunt	125
4.6a	The March family	127
4.6b	Cedie plays the flute	127
4.7a	Captain Hook makes Wendy walk the plank	130
4.7b	Judy at John Grier orphanage	130
4.8a	Maria meets the Trapp Family	133
4.8b	Tembo, Murphy and Jackie are joined by Mickey	133
4.9a	Nan learns a lesson	135
4.9b	Funny chasing in *Tico*	136
4.10a	Romeo signs the contract	138
4.10b	John feeds Lassie	138
4.11	Vitalis encourages Remi	140
4.12a	Nan makes a hubbub	145
4.12b	Marco's mother	145
4.13a	Judy and Jervis confess to each other	147
4.13b	Remi and Mattia hug	148

4.14a   Katri between Pekka and Martti 149
4.14b   Sterling is comforted by Rascal 150
4.15a   Tom and Huck play 151
4.15b   Alfredo and Romeo 151
4.16a   Arthur Popple 153
4.16b   Lucien opens up with Peguin 154
4.17a   Pollyanna hit by a car 161
4.17b   The children's trafficker Antonio Luini 162
4.18   Nello's grandfather 163
4.19a   Perrine makes her own shoes 166
4.19b   Celebrating Flone's eleventh birthday 166
4.20a   Old Genoa 168
4.20b   John first meets Lassie 169
4.21   Maria confronts Yvonne 171
4.22a   Cedie prays with his mother 173
4.22b   A pastor blesses Remi 174
4.23a   Katri dreams 177
4.23b   Little Katri falls running after her mother 178
4.24   Flone and Tamtam 179
4.25a   Nanami and Tico 181
4.25b   Jackie finger-feeds Murphy 181
5.1a   Anne's arrival 197
5.1b   Anne's imagination 197
5.2   Anne and nature 202
5.3   A sense of distance 204
5.4   Anne and Marilla 207
5.5a   Anne at the beach 209
5.5b   Anne returns home 209
5.6a   First solemn vow 212
5.6b   Reconciliation 212
6.1a   Mr Burrow and Miss Minchin 228
6.1b   Sara at the Savoy hotel 229
6.2a   Sara prays 233
6.2b   Professor Dufarge encourages Sara 233
6.3a   Night studying 235
6.3b   King Alfred 236
6.4a   Sara is trapped 238
6.4b   Young Miss Minchin 239
6.5a   Ram Dass and his monkey 242
6.5b   Sara tells a story 242

ACKNOWLEDGEMENTS

Writing any book is a laborious task. It took a few years to convert my research into a publishing proposal and then to a book. Like some of the events described in the following chapters, the process was not a straightforward one. It involved several stops and starts, twists and delays – some personal, some professional. As a researcher, I come from both a traditional and non-traditional background. My perspective on animation history and children's fiction is no doubt influenced by my education in literary studies and modern philology, which made me somehow sensitive to textual and comparative analysis. Also working as a writer for children helped me understand how commercial animated series are devised today. This means that, as a freelancer, I lived the struggles of not having a permanent academic job. The consequent instability led to a number of hauls and setbacks, but also to a process of discovery, dedication and learning, which I always find stimulating.

This work is obviously not the last word on the *World Masterpiece Theater*. Being a TV project spanning across several decades and consisting of over twenty series, it would have been impossible for the present treatment to cover everything in an exhaustive way. Instead, I hope to offer readers a starting point from which to explore further the subjects of children's fiction and animation in the series of the programme and beyond. There were many ideas that did not make their way into this book, and which I hope will be the starting point for another study.

Much of this book was written in parallel with drafting scripts and teaching undergraduate students at Università Cattolica del Sacro Cuore in Milan. I am grateful for all the lively and challenging discussions with students and colleagues, which helped me to refine many of my ideas. Most of all, I would like to express my appreciation to Professor Armando Fumagalli, who believed in this project from the start.

While this book was in its proofreading phase, I had a chance to live near Tokyo for a few months. It was a great experience, which gave me the opportunity to see first-hand themes and features of Japan – like the importance of food culture or the pervasiveness of manga and anime, from the shelves filled with Moomin characters to Rascal the raccoon advertising laundry nets in the shops – as well as collecting information for future works. Further, I was able to visit the International Library of Children's

Literature. To them goes my appreciation for making available online part of their collection.

I have been very fortunate to begin my creative career at Calon, an independent television company based in Cardiff. There, my friend and colleague Andrew Offiler was (and has been since) a wonderful source of information on animation and he inspired me with his experience and wisdom. I also learnt a lot from Robin Lyons in terms of animation writing and production (how things work behind the scenes). Additionally, I had engaging discussions with my friends and colleagues Eleonora Fornasari and Andrea Baravelli, both fans of the *World Masterpiece Theater*. Many of these series have subtitles written by volunteers. Also thanks to them for making these series accessible to a broader audience.

I am delighted to be able to publish this book with Bloomsbury and I am grateful to all the editorial staff. In particular, it has been a pleasure to work with Erin Duffy, for the initial contact, and with Katie Gallof, Stephanie Grace-Petinos and Alyssa Jordan, respectively, the present editor and editorial assistants for the Film and Media Studies series, as well as with production manager Amy Brownbridge, designer Eleanor Rose and Vishnu Prasad, project manager at Deanta. I am extremely thankful for their patience as well as their encouragement as I worked through various revisions of this manuscript. My gratitude goes also to the anonymous peer reviewers who provided thought-provoking feedback on my work. While all errors in this book are my responsibility, any credit is a testament to the support of the people acknowledged here.

Lastly, I acknowledge members of my family, who have been a constant source of support during the writing of this book. My partner gave me confidence that I would not have had otherwise.

INTRODUCTION

The present work centres on the Japanese phenomenon of adapting Western literary works for children into Japanese animated series, considering the case of the 世界名作劇場, *Sekai meisaku gekijō*, or *World Masterpiece Theater* (from now on: *WMT*), a collection of TV-novels which started in the mid-1970s. Back then, forms of intermedia adaptation were not new to Japanese animation, as shown by the high proportion, today as yesterday, of anime series based on popular comics. It was not even the first time that a Japanese studio turned a foreign story into a domestically produced animation. However, masterpiece or *meisaku* series became an important staple of Japanese animation history, pioneering a style which left an imprint in the country and abroad. Due to the good reception of these early series and their successful exporting abroad, other companies began to do the same. Aside from triggering an international, albeit time-bound, phenomenon – in the mid-1990s the *WMT* interrupts, with episodic revivals in the early 2000s – these series are also interesting cases of linguistic, medial and cultural hybridizations. Given their literary origins, they can be analysed as palimpsests of several discourses. What were the reasons behind an adaptation choice? Why choose Western novels instead of Japanese children's fiction? How were the source texts interpreted, reshaped and visualized? Who was their core target, the Japanese or the overseas audiences? And what was the use value of these works? These are some of the questions that motivated my research.

In the last two decades, Japanese animation has attracted a growing number of researchers, whose insightful contributions have only been partly covered in this book. Europe has a vibrant scholarship on Japanese animated works and their reception abroad. For example, several Italian scholars theorized in terms of cultural resonance either to explain the global success of Japanese popular culture[1] or to create a map of its spread in Europe and in the United States, examining the connections between anime and Western

---

[1] Luca Raffaelli, *Le anime disegnate. Il pensiero nei cartoon da Disney ai giapponesi e oltre* [*Drawn souls. Schools of thought in cartoons from Disney to the Japanese and beyond*] (Latina: Tunué, 2018).

literature.² Some researchers, especially in the anglophone area, highlighted the need to integrate textual analysis and ethnographic perspective,³ as well as the ties with the industry, and the socio-historical situation.⁴ Others showed the importance of semiotics to illustrate mythological tropes and motifs embedded in Japanese animated movies.⁵

The goal of my research is to study how, and why, Western children's literature – mostly, but not exclusively written in English – was adapted for animation in the *WMT*. In doing so, I take a similar stance to cultural resonance when describing the ways in which Japanese creative output seemingly struck a chord with different audiences or eras. However, this approach tends to postulate forms of within-culture homogeneity, assuming, as Condry puts it, 'a static relationship between individuals and media or performance'.⁶ Hence, my primary focus will be on the evolving context bringing together the people, institutions, places and policies, which are relevant components in the realization of animation. In particular, I attempted to examine the phenomenon of novel-to-series adaptations from an interdisciplinary perspective – philologically, by paying attention to the reception of the source texts in Japan, and examining variants and continuity with the literary archetypes; historically, by reconstructing the mix of factors which led to the creation of the programme; and pedagogically, by focusing on the values and role models conveyed by the series. In addition, as a screenwriter for animation, I also tried to consider the diegetic choices and the technological possibilities which are typical of this language. In fact, my primary references have been screenwriting manuals and masterclass which are part of my training, and helped me grasp the practice, ideas and production styles of the audiovisual industry as both an artistic craft and a business.

It is worth noting that the animated series of *WMT* are often analysed in monographic studies on the famous Japanese directors Takahata Isao and Miyazaki Hayao. While the contribution of the future founders of Studio Ghibli cannot be overrated, and will be factorized in this work,

---

[2] For example, see: Marco Pellitteri, 'Ad est di Oliver Twist' [East of Oliver Twist], in *Con gli occhi a mandorla. Sguardi sul Giappone dei cartoon e dei fumetti* [*With almond-shaped eyes: Looking at Japan through its comics and cartoons*], ed. by Roberta Ponticiello and Susanna Scrivo (Latina: Tunué, 2005); Marco Pellitteri, *The Dragon and the Dazzle: Models, Strategies, and Identities of Japanese Imagination – A European Perspective* (Latina: Tunué, 2010). Interesting articles, often in the field of comparative studies, also appeared on the academic journal *Manga Academica*.
[3] Ian Condry, *The Soul of Anime: Collaborative Creativity and Japan's Media Success Story* (Durham: Duke University Press, 2013).
[4] Nobuyuki Tsugata, 'A Bipolar Approach to Understanding the History of Japanese Animation', in *Japanese Animation: East Asian Perspectives*, ed. Masao Yokota and G. Tze-yue Hu (Jackson: University Press of Mississippi, 2013).
[5] Yoshiko Okuyama, *Japanese Mythology in Film. A Semiotic Approach to Reading Japanese Film and Anime* (Lanham: Lexington Books, 2015).
[6] Condry, *The Soul of Anime*, 20.

approaching *WMT* series from a unique standpoint seems lopsided, and is likely to overshadow the mixed influences behind the project, as a collective activity spanning across four decades (vs Takahata and Miyazaki's five-year collaboration). Moreover, in spite of the title of the book, this is not a history of masterpieces. On the contrary, it tries to consider other voices within the animation world, taking into account also the adjacent sectors of advertising, TV production and children's books.

As the bulk of *WMT* series is adaptations from books written up to the 1910s (and beyond), the first chapter dives into the origins of Japanese translated children's literature, showing how Western novels contributed to the rise of modern juvenile fiction since the Meiji era, in the second half of the nineteenth century. This was a period of great modernization for the country, and practically its first chance to incorporate influences from abroad for more than two centuries. The chapter also explores the strategies employed by Japanese translators to adapt the source texts to their readership, the pendulum swinging between domestication and foreignization. The main publishing trends and reading habits of the first half of the twentieth century will also be investigated. Exploring the publishing world and general knowledge available in the decades prior to the *WMT* seems useful to grasp how certain titles acquired over time the status of 'masterpiece', thus drawing the attention of producers and broadcasters. Due to the high presence of female characters in *WMT* shows, information on the burgeoning girls' culture will be provided, as well as the Western values and role models which were disseminated through books and periodicals.

The second chapter focuses on Japanese animation and adaptation, taking stock of the scholarly discussion and explaining some technical specificities of the animated language. The main goal is to examine how the release of Western children's fiction, and, in the post-war, the cumulative import of foreign films based on children's books from America, impacted the adaptation practices of local animators. In particular, I will focus on the influence of Disney on Tōei and other studios that attempted to follow his footsteps. In order to fully encompass the role of the *WMT* series, some major events in the history of Japanese animation will be summarized here, together with the early stages of television, paying attention to the rise of the serial format and the other innovations introduced by Tezuka's revolution in the mid-1960s. Explaining the interchanging relations of his 'media mix' helps broaden discussion on the increasing importance of publicity and sponsors.

The third chapter explores the origins of animated masterpieces in the late 1960s, against the backdrop of contemporary animated series and genres. Different approaches to literary adaptation will be covered here, including adult animation for cinema, mainstream animation for export and outsourced animation for the United States. This will be helpful to contextualize the activity of Takahashi Shigeto, a former salesman who worked in the field of animated commercials, and his foundation of Zuiyō Enterprise in 1969, a studio for planning and later producing animated series for children. The analysis will thus concentrate on the relationships between the Zuiyō and the needs of the sponsor which allowed the production of *Calpis Theater*, the forerunner of *WMT*, for Fuji TV. This way, I intend to analyse the transition from early Calpis' series – but also the co-productions and collaborations undertaken by Takahashi – and the official *WMT* shows.

The fourth chapter showcases the *WMT* series per decade, providing a brief analysis of the single works up to the mid-1990s, in relationship with their original texts. This section will be followed by a transversal exploration of the diegetic strategies and core values which can be found in works of the project. In particular, I will try to identify tropes and motifs that can be more commonly found in *WMT* series, with a special emphasis on characterization, and pointing to the different purposes, production choices and cultural patterns, which were undertaken by the Japanese staff involved in order to suit the targeted audience and to accomodate the shows to the changing market conditions.

Keeping this analytical framework in mind, I will then move to the monographic part of this book. The fifth chapter is dedicated to Montgomery's *Anne of Green Gables* (1908), used as a basis for the TV series *Akage no An* (1979), directed by Takahata. After considering the structure of the novel and its main narrative aspects, the role of its protagonist in Japan will be taken into account since its first introduction in the post-war. Then the analysis returns to the animation, identifying Takahata's approach to the novel and his results. This way, the source text and the Japanese adaptation will emerge both separately, with their historical framework and cultural asset, and in connection, showing the interpolations between different medias and cultures.

A similar structure characterizes the sixth chapter, which revolves on the series *Shōkōjo Sēra* (1985) and its archetype *A Little Princess* (1905), by Burnett, discussing the parallelisms with the rereading of the story in Japan since its introduction in the late Meiji era. The original novel will be analysed in its constitutional ingredients, also considering its reception in Japan. The anime version, directed by Kurokawa Fumio, will consider the values circulating across these texts in Japan, showing at the same time the changes of style and tone that the *WMT* underwent in the 1980s.

Finally, a note on language: in the book, Japanese names are written in the Japanese style (surname and given name). The Hepburn system has been used to transcribe Japanese names and terms. Japanese characters are also used, to disambiguate translations or transliterations. Loan words follow their spelling in *katakana*, the writing system usually reserved for words of foreign origin. However, titles of animated works that are most frequently cited are rendered into English to assist readability.

1

Children's fiction in Japan:

From the origins to the post-war

When considering the amount of audiovisual media produced in Japan, it is easy to forget that there is a vastness of literary texts aimed specifically at children. So I was not surprised when I realized that Japanese children's literature is often invisible in international scholarly research. With the exception of some famous writers, who often got worldwide recognition thanks to the adaptation of their stories into other media, this is often uncharted material outside Japan. More academic attention has been devoted to translated children's books in Japan, especially in comparative and cultural studies. Both discourses – the one regarding Japanese juvenile fiction and the one on the impact of foreign books – provide interesting insights on the specific case of the *World Masterpiece Theater*, and how Japanese animation tackled adaptation from literature in general.

The following paragraphs are not meant to provide a complete historical overview of Japanese children's fiction. Instead, they try to focus on the connections between local narratives and translations of juvenile books, from the second half of the nineteenth century to the post-war. These materials, which the people involved in the animated adaptations of the *WMT* arguably assimilated during their formative years, had a great influence on their perception of non-Japanese (and specifically Western) children's fiction. Special attention will be dedicated to the publishing patterns and reading habits related to children's fiction, exploring how authors and books were canonized over time, achieving the status of classics. Also the cultural agencies behind juvenile literature, and its pedagogic aspects, will shed light on the construction of the TV series of the staple.

When did Japanese children's literature start?

There is evidence of Japanese literary texts and figurative art featuring young characters since the twelfth century, and especially in the Edo period (1603–1867).[1] These texts were probably read by children, but adults were often the primary recipients, as is the case of books on child-rearing. The first texts exclusively addressed to children appeared in the 1670s, more or less in the same period that children's literature was blossoming in Britain. These were primers on myths, legends, and folk tales in red bindings, hence were called 赤本 (*akahon* [red books]). In addition, more recent discoveries have demonstrated the existence of violent, non-didactic books for boys from the same period, redolent of Western nineteenth-century penny dreadfuls.[2] However, the size and capillarity of these publications seem difficult to define, so most scholars conventionally situate the birth of children's literature in the modern sense of the term in the Meiji era (1868–1912).

During these years, the situation of Japan radically changed, culturally if not politically. A new oligarchic government was installed in the country, whose aim was to transform Japan to a 富国強兵 (*fukoku kyōhei* [wealthy nation, strong military]). To do that, the oligarchs pursued a policy of reforms in all areas of the state, introducing, among other things, a compulsory school system for both sexes. The underlying mission was to create a merit-based education system controlled by the state, which would later be sustained by the future capable leaders at the top of this upbringing plan.[3] As a consequence, literacy rates rose to 70 per cent by the end of the Meiji period, but the spread of education was a slow process, relying as it did on localities for schooling expenses, while the government invested more resources in other sectors, such as defence and administration.[4]

Other slogans were 文明開化 (*bunmei kaika* [civilization and enlightenment]) and 和魂洋才 (*wakon yōsai* [Japanese spirit, Western technology]). In fact, after China's defeat in the Opium Wars with Britain, Japan recognized the stronger Western nations as models to follow, introducing Western-style political institutions, industry, economy and culture. After 200 years of isolation, Japanese literati were sent to the West to encourage emulation and learning, while not only Western scholars but

---

[1] Joan E. Ericson, 'Introduction', in *A Rainbow in the Desert. An Anthology of Early Twentieth Century Japanese Children's Literature*, trans. Yukie Ohta (New York: M. E. Sharpe, 2001), viii.
[2] Keller R. Kimbrough, 'Bloody Hell!: Reading Boys' Books in Seventeenth-Century Japan', *Asian Ethnology* 74, no. 1 (2015): 114.
[3] Patricia E. Tsurumi, 'The State, Education, and Two Generations of Women in Meiji Japan, 1868-1912', *English Supplement* 18 (2000): 3.
[4] Koji Taira, 'Education and Literacy in Meiji Japan: An Interpretation', *Explorations in Economic History* 8, no. 4 (1971): 373–4.

also 3,000 engineers and scientists were invited to Japan.[5] Many educators, writers and intellectuals absorbed Western customs and ideals. The demand for foreign goods increased too, with Western clothing, hats and umbrellas being adopted as more appropriate to the times.[6] In other words, for Meiji ideologues, Japan's Westernization equated with a modernization of the country.[7] This gradually created an infrastructure able to support the rise of children's literature.

The translation of Western children's fiction

Japan's modernization involved the assimilation of a variety of Western books, including literature.[8] Literary works from advanced Western countries, written in English, French, Russian and German, were translated in great numbers into Japanese, introducing new words, ideas and literary conventions. The translation of Western children's literature was part of this phenomenon, which peaked in the late 1880s and 1890s, influencing Japan's own production of children's fiction.[9] As children's literature had been thriving in the West for more than half a century, there was an abundance of texts available for translation, which was often performed with surprisingly little delay.[10] Also the few juvenile books which were already familiar to the Japanese, such as *Aesop's Fables* (whose first translation was published by Christian missionaries in 1593), were translated again and again, and permanently inserted in primary school textbooks for their moral lessons.[11]

In fact, while children's works were originally imported for adults to learn about Western culture, towards the end of the century there was a growing number of literate children in Japan, and translated Western books began

---

[5]David G. Wittner, *Technology and the Culture of Progress in Meiji Japan* (Abindgon and New York: Routledge, 2008), 28.
[6]Donald H. Shively, 'The Japanization of the Middle Meiji', in *Tradition and Modernization in Japanese Culture*, ed. Donald H. Shively (Princeton: Princeton University Press, 1971), 82.
[7]Elise K. Tipton and John Clark, 'Introduction', in *Being Modern in Japan: Culture and Society from the 1910s to the 1930s*, ed. Tipton and Clark (Honolulu: University of Hawai'i Press 2000), 7.
[8]Mino Saito, 'The Power of Translated Literature in Japan: The Introduction of New Expressions Through Translation in the Meiji Era (1868–1912)', *Perspectives* 24, no. 3 (2016): 418.
[9]Melek Ortabasi, 'Brave Dogs and Little Lords. Thoughts on Translation, Gender, and the Debate on Childhood in mid-Meiji', in *Translation in Modern Japan*, ed. Indra Levy (London: Routledge, 2010), 188.
[10]Judy Wakabayashi, 'Foreign Bones, Japanese Flesh: Translations and the Emergence of Modern Children's Literature in Japan', *Japanese Language and Literature* 42, no. 1 (2008): 242.
[11]Ho-Chi Beata Kubiak, 'Aesop's Fables in Japanese Literature for Children: Classical Antiquity and Japan', in *Our Mythical Childhood . . . The Classics and Literature for Children and Young Adults*, ed. Katarzyna Marciniak (Leiden and Boston: Brill, 2016), 195.

to cater to this readership for didactic purposes.[12] It is worth remembering that Japanese scholars developed their ideas on translation independently from Europe and America. Differently from the translation of foreign languages into English, which aims at hiding the translator's intervention (or, in Venuti's words, to make them invisible), this is easy to find in Meiji translations.[13] These ranged from loose translations, which substantially altered the originals, to a close sense-for-sense approach, though more rarely.[14] The two strategies, usually polarized by scholars as domestication and foreignization, played an important role in the diffusion of Western children's fiction, as they stemmed from different educational standpoints, namely, whether to close the cultural gap with the Japanese young readers (domestication) or to stress it, together with the novelties present in Western books (foreignization).[15]

Translations of children's literature from England, Germany, Denmark and France, and of a few key texts from other cultures, such as Greece and the Arab world, were serialized in burgeoning Japanese magazines.[16] These included fairy tales by Hans Christian Andersen or the Grimm Brothers, but also books by Jules Verne, Frances Hodgson Burnett and Lewis Carroll. Adaptations of European stories became a common feature, often circulating alongside more expensive line-to-line translations. Adaptations were in fact abridged translations, digests or Japanized retellings of Western stories, and, although usually overlooked by critics, they enjoyed large popularity among readers up to the immediate post-war.[17] As Sato notes, adapting foreign fiction for Japanese audiences was no easy task: it required specific skills, which contributed to the canonization of Western classics in Japan. In fact, the first book translated for children in Japan was an adaptation of Daniel Defoe's *Robinson Crusoe* (1719), a novel which originally catered to adults.[18]

---

[12] Wakabayashi, 'Foreign Bones, Japanese Flesh', 233.
[13] Danièle Allard, 'The Popularity of Anne of Green Gables in Japan – A Study of Hanako Muraoka's Translation of L.M. Montgomery's Novel and Its Reception' (Ph.D. diss., Université de Sherbrooke, 2002), 17–22.
[14] Peter Kornicky, 'Review of Adaptations of Western Literature in Meiji Japan by J. Scott Miller', *Monumenta Nipponica* 57, no. 3 (2002): 393.
[15] Wakabayashi, 'Foreign Bones, Japanese Flesh', 231.
[16] Ibid., 230.
[17] Motoko Sato, 'Japanese Adaptations of 19th Century and Early 20th Century Western Children's Literature', in *Reconstructing Cultural Memory. Translation, Scripts, Literacy, Proceedings of the XVth Congress of the International Comparative Literature Association 'Literature as Cultural Memory'*, ed. Lieven D'Hulst and John Milton, *Studies in Comparative Literature* 31, no. 7 (2000): 147–8.
[18] Wakabayashi, 'Foreign Bones, Japanese Flesh', 232.

Once upon a time a dog

Translators and adapters were especially keen on European fairy tales and folk tales, so it seems easy to understand why most children's fiction produced in Meiji Japan belonged to this genre.[19] Fairy tales are sources of entertainment and moral lessons, with a clear good-versus-bad dichotomy which suited the Confucian axiology of the Meiji government. Japanese readers were also used to the genre because Japan had its own tradition of medieval folk tales or 御伽草子 (*otogizōshi*), although these sounded outdated in the Westernized Meiji era.[20] Therefore, new children's stories were created on the model of German *Märchen*, by writer and translator 巖谷 小波 (Iwaya Sazanami) (1870–1933).[21] Iwaya wrote what is often regarded as the first example of modern children's literature in Japan, こがね丸 (*Koganemaru* [*A dog named Golden Boy*]) (1891), a novel-length tale stately addressed to children and teenagers.[22] It is the story of a dog taking revenge for his killed dad, mixing old tropes of local fiction, such as the theme of vendetta or the use of personified animal characters, with a narrative style that Iwaya considered as suitable for boys.

Koganemaru had a huge success in the 1890s – approximately 50,000 copies were sold, a high number for the time – becoming an instant classic among young readers.[23] However, it raised mixed reactions from contemporary intellectuals. In fact, despite Iwaya's interest towards German fairy tales, and his attempts to align his work to Goethe's animal story *Reinecke Fuchs* [*Reynard the Fox*] (1794), *Koganemaru* featured ritual suicides and other similarities with the samurai world, bespeaking the same past values which the Meiji government aimed to overcome.[24] It is also worth noting that *Koganemaru* was designed as the first book of a series called 少年文学叢書 (Shōnen bungaku senshō [Youth literature series]), by the large commercial publisher Hakubunkan, with 'shōnen bungaku' being Iwaya's translation of the German *Jugendschrift*. However, of the thirty-two volumes of the collection, most were translations of foreign works and biographies of important men. This seems to suggest the idea that, to some extent, European stories (and the values sedimented in them) resonated more with the zeitgeist than Japanese own cultural roots.

Koganemaru launched the career of its twenty-one-year-old author in the field of children's fairy tales or 御伽話 (*otogibanashi*), a word Iwaya coined

---

[19] Ortabasi, 'Brave Dogs and Little Lords', 191.
[20] L. Halliday Piel, 'Loyal Dogs and Meiji Boys: The Controversy Over Japan's First Children's Story, *Koganemaru* (1891)', *Children's Literature* 38 (2010): 214.
[21] Ibid., 209.
[22] Wakabayashi, 'Foreign Bones, Japanese Flesh', 240.
[23] Piel, 'Loyal Dogs and Meiji Boys', 211.
[24] For the press reactions to *Koganemaru*, see Piel, 'Loyal Dogs and Meiji Boys', 213–18.

around 1893.²⁵ His work 世界お伽話 (Sekai otogibanashi [World fairy tales]) (1899–1908) is a collection of 100 volumes of mostly European stories, freely retold by Iwaya. In other words, these were adaptations of Western fairy tales and folk tales, which became one of the main streams of Japanese children's literature.²⁶ Japanese tales were also rewritten in order to adapt to the times and to their new status as juvenile fiction. For example, Iwaya's 1894 retelling of 桃太郎 (Momotarō [Peach Boy]), the famous tale of a child born from a peach, portrayed the protagonist as a heroic leader and a loyal subject of the emperor, inserting nationalistic feelings which were welcome to the state.²⁷ The process of appropriating Japanese folk tales was anticipated, in the early Meiji period, by European residents who would publish them in English. However, Ericson notes a parallel between Iwaya in Japan and the brothers Grimm in Romantic Germany, as in both cases children's fiction coalesced into discourses of civic ethos and nation-building.²⁸

The birth of children's journals

What today is a competitive market in the hands of a few publishing giants began as a literary practice with educational purposes towards the end of the nineteenth century. Journals for adults and newspapers had already emerged at the beginning of the Meiji era, and often contained sections for children to read.²⁹ However, literary journals intended specifically for children started to be released in the late 1880s, when woodblock printing changed to printing by movable type – a new method which allowed mass production and commercialization – and, consequently, the Japanese script became easier to read, making literature more accessible to children.³⁰ In particular, the first major children's magazine in Japan was 少年園 (*Shōnen'en* [*Children's garden*]) (1888–95), published by the translator and science popularizer 山県悌三郎 (Yamagata Teisaburō) (1858–1940).

Shōnen'en was primarily targeted to elite boys, featuring scientific articles on a variety of topics, from mountaineering to military technology, the latter being predominant during the Sino-Japanese war.³¹ The underpinning idea

---

²⁵Wakabayashi, 'Foreign Bones, Japanese Flesh', 251.
²⁶Sato, 'Japanese Adaptations of 19th Century and Early 20th Century Western Children's Literature', 147.
²⁷Nona L. Carter, 'A Study on Japanese Children's Magazines 1888-1949' (Ph.D. diss., University of Pennsylvania, 2009), 49–50.
²⁸Ericson, 'Introduction', ix–x.
²⁹Carter, 'A Study on Japanese Children's Magazines 1888-1949', 54.
³⁰Ibid., 41–2.
³¹Ruselle Meade, 'Juvenile Science and the Japanese Nation: Shōnen'en and the Cultivation of Scientific Subjects', *Japan Review* 34 (2019): 122.

was to foster outdoor activities (hence the 'garden' in the title) as ventures of male heroism, following the example of Victorian magazines.³² At the same time, *Shōnen'en* would frequently publish adaptations of Western children's literature, such as *Aesop's Fables* or *Grimm's Fairy Tales*, which were very popular among readers, although the primal focus of the journal was on non-fiction essays.³³ The emphasis on science, patriotism and the importance of Western models were in line with the Meiji policy, setting the standard for the following flood of similar magazines. For instance, 小国民 (*Shōkokumin* [*Little citizens*]) (1889–95) was moulded on the American magazine *Harper's Round Table*, containing both educational articles and entertaining stories for elementary school children.³⁴ Journals also saw the contribution of important writers, including Iwaya, who founded, edited and contributed to 少年世界 (*Shōnen sekai* [*Children's world*]) (1895–1914), the most popular magazine of its day.³⁵

The overlapping roles of the people involved in children's journals were typical of this period, when author, editor and publisher were often the same person. However, whereas previous magazines had an artistic bent, lacking a profit-based rivalry, things changed with *Shōnen sekai*. Published by Hakubunkan, this was the first example of mass-circulated children's literature available in Japan, prioritizing entertainment fiction over education.³⁶ Western stories were serialized on its pages, as well as Japanese stories set in foreign countries, such as Iwaya's 新八犬伝 (*Shin hakkenden* [*The new biography of eight dogs*]) (1898), a revisitation of the epic novel 南総里見八犬伝 (*Nansō satomi hakkenden* [*The biography of eight dogs*]) (1814–42). Though preserving the Confucian values of the original – a story of virtue triumphing over vice, which also inspired *Koganemaru* – Iwaya created a tale of boys travelling to a South Sea island, with a mix of didacticism, adventure and imperialism which would influence children's fiction for decades.³⁷ In particular, after *Shōnen sekai*, popular literature became increasingly focused on fictional stories and visual culture, while artistic literature revolved around traditional Japanese folk tales.³⁸

---

³²Ibid., 115.
³³Carter, 'A Study on Japanese Children's Magazines 1888-1949', 54.
³⁴Ibid., 60–1.
³⁵Owen Griffiths, 'Militarizing Japan: Patriotism, Profit, and Children's Print Media, 1894-1925', *The Asia-Pacific Journal: Japan Focus* 5, no. 9 (2007): 590.
³⁶Carter, 'A Study on Japanese Children's Magazines 1888-1949', 64.
³⁷Griffiths, 'Militarizing Japan', 591.
³⁸Carter, 'A Study on Japanese Children's Magazines 1888-1949', 65.

The relation with women's and girls' culture

The proliferation of magazines was part of larger publishing trends towards a fragmentation of the market into diverse readerships. For example, in 1895 *Shōnen sekai* created a column for girl readers called 少女欄 (*shōjoran* [girls' section]), which eventually spun off as 少年世界 (*Shōjo sekai* [*Girls' world*]) (1906–33), a new magazine for girls in their early teens.[39] So, while the target 'child' was broken up into 'young child', 'child' and 'adolescent', children's magazines began to be segregated along gender lines.[40] This was made possible by the scholastic reforms of the Meiji era. After 1899 all girls' higher schools were administered by the government, fostering the 良妻賢母 (*ryōsai kenbo* [good wife, wise mother]) ideal of feminine behaviour.[41] As summarized in this slogan, young women were encouraged to manage the chores and home economy efficiently, and to educate their children. The underpinning idea was, to use the words of educator 中村 正直 (Nakamura Masanao) (1832–91): 'If the mothers are superb, they can have superb children, and Japan can become a splendid country'.[42] The concept was well received in Meiji Japan, because it built on the Confucian tenet that viewed family as the basis for the state.

However, the traditional Japanese household or 家 (*ie*) (a multigenerational system including extended and adopted family members) was restructured into a modern nuclear family under the influence of Westernization. This involved views on womanhood and child-raising. Notions that were already being challenged in the West, such as the Victorian angel in the house, loving and maternal, were welcomed in Japan as progressive role models for women. As mothers were expected to read stories to their offspring, women and children became a linked readership in Japanese journals.[43] In fact, some of the earliest cases of Western children's fiction were published in women's magazines. For instance, 小公子 (*Shōkōshi* [*The little lord*]) (1890–2), the first translation of Burnett's *Little Lord Fauntleroy*, was serialized on 女学雑誌 (*Jogaku zasshi* [*Women's education magazine*]) (1885–1904), a magazine for upper-middle-class women. The goal of the Meiji oligarchs was ultimately political – to shape Japan's future citizens as sons and daughters

---

[39]Hiromi Tsuchiya Dollase, *Age of Shōjo: The Emergence, Evolution, and Power of Japanese Girls' Magazine Fiction* (Albany: State University of New York Press, 2018), 19.
[40]Rachel Matt Thorn, 'Shōjo Manga – Something for Girls', *Japan Quarterly* 48, no. 3 (2001): 45.
[41]Deborah Michelle Shamoon, *Passionate Friendship: The Aesthetics of Girls' Culture in Japan* (Honolulu: University of Hawai'i Press, 2012), 30.
[42]Quoted in Sumiko Sekiguchi, 'Confucian Morals and the Making of a "Good Wife and Wise Mother": From 'Between Husband and Wife There is Distinction' to 'As Husbands and Wives be Harmonious'', *Social Science Japan Journal* 13, no. 1 (2010): 108.
[43]Ortabasi, 'Brave Dogs and Little Lords', 189.

of the nation – as is confirmed by the severe censorship laws on children's magazines.[44]

Even if schools and the media disseminated imperialistic values and were usually administered by men, they were a chance for women to improve their status. A growing number of women writers or 閨秀作家 (*keishū sakka*) entered the business in the Meiji era.[45] Some of them worked as translators and editors too, creating a communal sense between readers, who in turn were able to purchase magazines which they recognized as 'theirs'. Journals like *Jogaku zasshi* not only indoctrinated women about domestic responsibilities but also urged them to participate actively in society, fostering strong and independent behaviours.[46] The contradiction between women's submissive education and their enhanced agency, at home as well as producers and consumers of culture, is evident in the concept of 少女 (*shōjo* [girl]). As typical of modern industrialized countries, teenage girls emerged in Japan as a social category in the Meiji period.[47] However, while schools moulded girls as future brides-to-be, they also postponed their access to adulthood, cocooning them in a liminal space far from marriage and child-rearing.

Schoolgirls aged thirteen to eighteen were a small portion of the female population (in 1905, less than 5 per cent graduated from secondary school), mainly located in urban areas, among the middle and upper classes.[48] Though their number was meant to rise, girls attending exclusive all-female high schools became the perfect incarnation of the shōjo type. Equipped with desirable values of femininity, such as purity and refinement, schoolgirls were はいから (*haikara* [high collar]) (a slang term for everything new and modern) and fashionable icons, easily recognizable thanks to their stylish uniforms.[49] Idealized shōjo representations branched out to photography, manner guides, novels, magazines and much more. Both narratives and illustrations of the newborn 少女 文化 (*shōjo bunka* [girls' culture]) emphasized emotional interiority – significantly, the art of pre-war girls' magazines consisted of 叙情画 (*jojōga* [lyrical paintings]), featuring willowy

---

[44]Carter, 'A Study on Japanese Children's Magazines 1888-1949', 27.
[45]Yukiko Tanaka, *Women Writers of Meiji and Taishō Japan. Their Lives, Works and Critical Reception 1868-1926* (Jefferson: McFarland & Company, 2000), 5.
[46]Rebecca L. Copeland, *Lost Leaves. Women Writers of Meiji Japan* (Honolulu: University of Hawai'i Press, 2000), 9.
[47]Shamoon, *Passionate Friendship*, 2.
[48]Ibid., 30.
[49]Alice Freedman, 'Romance of the Taishō Schoolgirl in Shōjo Manga: *Here Comes Miss Modern*', in *Shōjo Across Media. Exploring 'Girl' Practices in Contemporary Japan*, ed. Jaqueline Berndt, Kazumi Nagaike, and Fusami Ogi (Cham: Palgrave Macmillan, 2019), 26–30.

girls with big eyes and dreamy expressions – which formed the basis of post-war 少女漫画 (shōjo manga [girls' comics]).[50]

The influence of Christianity

Although Confucianism had long been ingrained in the country, and anti-Christian feelings were still present in the Meiji period,[51] Christians, both Japanese and from the West, played an important role in the cultural landscape of the second half of the nineteenth century. The Harris Treaty (1858) allowed Americans of Protestant religion to come to Japan and erect churches, evangelizing the Japanese with their missionary activities.[52] Missionary schools were particularly influential on female education beyond the elementary level, teaching English and Japanese literature, home economics, sewing and music, with a clear Christian underpinning.[53] By the 1880s, these schools were thriving in Japan, and there were even plans of making Christianity the state religion.[54] In fact, Christianity met the interests of the upper classes, which equated religion with Western civilization. These included former samurai (such as the already recalled educator Nakamura) and authors, including the doyen of Meiji children's fiction, Iwaya.

Christianity had an impact on children's literature also through translation. Given the historical presence of Christianity in the West, even the more secular writers shared a background of religious practice and beliefs, which percolated into the Japanese translations. Moral commonalities with Confucianism, such as the clear-cut distinction between good and evil, or the importance of filial piety, arguably facilitated the acquisition. It is true that, to facilitate young readers, translations often domesticated texts replete with religious references. Significantly, out of the 200 fairy tales published by the Grimms, those with strong Christian overtones were commonly discarded by translators. However, Christian works were not excluded and could be used as means for proselytism. For example, John Bunyan's *The Pilgrim's Progress* was first translated into Japanese by 村上

---

[50]Mizuki Takahashi, 'Opening the Closed World of Shōjo Manga', in *Japanese Visual Culture. Explorations in the World of Manga and Anime*, ed. W. Mark MacWilliams (Abingdon: M.E. Sharpe 2008), 119.
[51]Richard L. Sims, *Japanese Political History Since the Meiji Renovation 1868-2000* (New York: Palgrave, 2001), 2.
[52]Shuma Iwai, 'Japanese Christianity in the Meiji Era: An Analysis of Ebina Danjo's Perspective on Shintoistic Christianity', *Transformation* 25, no. 4 (2008): 195–204.
[53]Margaret Mehl, 'Women Educators and the Confucian Tradition in Meiji Japan (1868–1912): Miwada Masako and Atomi Kakei', *Women's History Review* 10, no. 4 (2001): 580.
[54]Thomas John Hastings, 'Japan's Protestant Schools and Churches in Light of Early Mission Theory and History', in *Handbook of Christianity in Japan*, ed. Mark Mullins (Leiden: Brill, 2003), 111.

俊吉 (Murakami Shunkichi) (1847–1916), a renowned Christian writer and pastor, and released on the Christian weekly magazine 七一雑報 (*Shichi ichi zappō* [*Once in seven days general news*]) in 1877.⁵⁵

As Christian writers and translators were among the more enthusiastic promoters of children's books for pedagogic ends, Torigoe goes even further arguing that it was the Christians who brought modern children's fiction to Japan.⁵⁶ A remarkable example of Christian authors writing for women's and children's journals was Wakamatsu Shizuko, who translated canonical juvenile books such as *Little Lord Fauntleroy* and *Sara Crewe* (the novella inspiring *A Little Princess*). The above-mentioned women's magazine *Jogaku zasshi* was founded by the Christian educator 巌本 善治 (Iwamoto Yoshiharu) (1863–1942), Wakamatsu's husband, to promote Christian values. Meanwhile, through the filter of Western art and literature, new images of femininity and childhood circulated in the schools founded by foreign ministers, and these were consistent with Christian religion. For instance, the notion of 恋愛 (*ren'ai* [spiritual love]), or the Christian idea that divinely inspired feelings can lead to moral elevation – contrarily to the Buddhist condemnation of love as an expression of carnal lust – was incorporated in the budding romanticism of girls' culture.⁵⁷

The Taishō era and the birth of the dōwa genre

The dissatisfaction of Japanese intellectuals with the rigidity of the Meiji system paved the way for the changes occurring during the Taishō era (1912–26).⁵⁸ In these decades, Japan became relatively affluent. After winning the Sino-Japanese War and the Russo-Japanese War, the country was gaining the respect of the Western nations as a newly emerged competitor in the world of imperialism and war capitalism. A group of liberal leaders replaced the Meiji bureaucrats, setting the basis for a consumer-based society which welcomed also the more materialistic aspects of Westernization. Western clothes and food became widely popular, while townscapes were transformed with Western-styled buildings, cafés, ballrooms and theatres.⁵⁹ Discourses on 文化 (*bunka* [culture]) replaced 文明 (*bunmei* [civilization]) slogans,

---

⁵⁵Wakabayashi, 'Foreign Bones, Japanese Flesh', 234.
⁵⁶Quoted in Carter, 'A Study on Japanese Children's Magazines 1888-1949', 54–5.
⁵⁷Shamoon, *Passionate Friendship*, 146.
⁵⁸Elizabeth M. Keith, 'Kaneko Misuzu and the Development of Children's Literature in Taishō Japan' (M.A. diss., University of Hawaii), 18.
⁵⁹Kazuo Usui, *Marketing and Consumption in Modern Japan* (London: Routledge, 2016), 17.

fostering a Western-oriented lifestyle which, differently from the Meiji period, emphasized individualism, cosmopolitanism and self-cultivation.[60]

In this Indian summer, which has been compared to the Edwardian era,[61] a new tradition of children's fiction was born under the auspices of the 文壇 (*bundan* [literary establishment]), the close-knit network of Japan's writers, editors, critics and publishers. Sazanami's books were criticized for their old-fashioned ethos, as well as other children's works created in the Meiji period. Instead, in 1912, a group of elite, mostly university-educated literati formed the 少年文学研究会 (*Shōnen bungaku kenkyūkai* [Youth literature study group]), advocating an artistic approach to children's fiction.[62] These writers, who were often authors of adult fiction and poetry, were influenced by Western literary fairy tales or *Kunstmärchen*, such as Andersen's stories. They pioneered a genre that produced 童話 (*dōwa* [children's stories]), the most celebrated children's literature in modern Japan.

How were dōwa different from Meiji tales? While language and settings were archaic and fantastic in Meiji folk tales, dōwa used everyday language and were usually set in realistic, contemporary locations. Moreover, dōwa lacked happy endings and had a poetic style which mirrored Buddhist notions of impermanence,[63] whereas previous stories were impacted by Meiji nationalism, bearing traces of feudalistic ways of thinking. Dōwa writers, who had been exposed to Romanticism, were also keen on exploring individual perspectives – childhood as they had lived it and remember it. They considered their stories as a form of 純文学 (*jun bungaku* [pure literature]), in opposition to popular fiction. Ericson notes that, through the dōwa style, Japan's literary coteries began to set standards for children's fiction while losing grip on adult fiction, which became increasingly commercialized, due to the proliferation of popular journals.

The 'child-mind' movement and literary magazines

Dōwa authors were influenced by Western cultural movements, which in turn sparked new ideas and concepts. An example is the 童心主義 (*dōshin shugi* [child-mind principle]), a theory stemming from the Romantic myth

---

[60]Jordan Sand, 'The Cultured Life as a Contested Space. Dwelling and Discourse in the 1920s', in *Being Modern in Japan: Culture and Society from the 1910s to the 1930s*, ed. K. Elise Tipton and John Clark (Honolulu: University of Hawai'i Press, 2000), 99–100.
[61]Teruo Jinguh, 'Japan', in *International Companion Encyclopedia of Children's Literature*, vol. 2, ed. Peter Hunt (Abingdon: Routledge, 2004), 1109.
[62]Ericson, 'Introduction', x.
[63]Ibid., xi.

whereby children are pure-hearted and connected to nature. This notion, which contrasted with the importance attached to old age by Confucian ideology, mirrored contemporary social changes, such as the decrease of the family unit and the resulting major interest in children.[64] At the same time, the child-mind added a psychological dimension of longing for one's own hometown and childhood. A common adult construction, this nostalgia shared similarities with Edwardian literature, which also viewed childhood as an ideal age of bliss in contrast to the structures of civilization.[65] In Japan, which was transforming from an agriculture-based nation to an industrial economy, dōwa writers such as 小川 未明 (Ogawa Mimei) (1872–1961) believed that the purpose of children's stories was to re-create the simplicity of Japan's rural past, which was rapidly disappearing under the pressure of modernity.[66]

The child-mind principle found expression in 赤い鳥 (*Akai tori* [*Red bird*]), one of the most important literary magazines of the period, which heralded the dōwa movement of quality children's literature. The scope of *Akai tori* was, as stated in the inaugural issue, 'to preserve and develop the purity of children by gathering together the sincere efforts of the best writers and illustrators of today and encouraging the creative work of young writers for children'.[67] Published by the novelist 鈴木 三重吉 (Suzuki Miekichi) (1882–1936), with the cooperation of the poet 北原 白秋 (Kitahara Hakushū) (1885–1942), *Akai tori* featured short stories, illustrations and 童謡 (*dōyo* [children's songs]), and was supported by influential literary luminaries and artists, who had progressive ideas in the field of education, advocating for children's freedom and creativity.[68] *Akai tori* also solicited submissions of stories, poems and sketches from readers, fostering a connection with their young audience and publishing selected contents written for children by children.

Akai tori played an important role in the definition of children's literature as a work of art to express one's feelings. The underpinning idea was that dōwa works were not only for kids but also for adults who had not lost their 子供の心 (*kodomo no kokoro* [children's heart]), to use Ogawa's words.[69] This is confirmed by the number of adult subscribers to children's magazines

---

[64] Keith, 'Kaneko Misuzu and the Development of Children's Literature in Taishô Japan', 13–14.
[65] Adrienne Gavin and Davies Humphries, *Childhood in Edwardian Fiction: Worlds Enough and Time* (London: Palgrave Macmillan, 2009, 4.
[66] The connection between storytelling and the legacy of a pre-modern ethos paralleled the revived interest for folklore by ethnographer 柳田 國男 (Yanagita Kunio) (1875–1962). Ericson, 'Introduction', xii.
[67] Quoted in National Diet Library, 'Part 2 The Dowa Era: From the Launching of Akai Tori to the Pre-War', *Japanese Children's Literature* (2017). Available online: https://www.kodomo.go.jp/jcl/e/section2/index.html (accessed 28 February 2023).
[68] Keith, 'Kaneko Misuzu and the Development of Children's Literature in Taishô Japan', 26–7.
[69] Ericson, 'Introduction', xii.

and authors writing children's fiction. Dōwa-style children's stories and poetry became so popular that over sixty literary magazines were launched in Tokyo alone.[70] But most of these were mostly short-lived, shutting down after the outburst of the First World War. One reason seems to be that *Akai tori*'s utopian views, influenced by Romanticism and Idealism, were distant from the social issues of the time. The dōwa tradition enjoyed relative prosperity among the public, but was hugely successful among Japanese critics, who framed it as the last golden age of children's literature and contributed to its canonization.

Commercial children's magazines

The Taishō era represented both the swan song of literary journals and the harbinger of the success of commercial magazines for children in Japan. Magazine publishing and circulation skyrocketed in this period, with titles rising from 3,123 in 1918 to 11,118 in 1932.[71] This is not surprising, if we consider that a new middle class was born, with higher wages and culture. Almost 100 per cent of the Japanese completed elementary school, and a growing number had access to secondary education. Everybody could read magazines, especially if they were affordable in content and price. By 1920, commercial magazines reached every province of Japan, expanding beyond urban environments to cater peasantry.[72] They offered different types of literature (for women, for children, for rural or urban readers), and, as literary journals, took the response of the public into account, encouraging the readers to write to the editors, as well as to produce their own fiction.

Children's fiction was a large part of this industry. Children's magazines reached numbers unheard before, selling as many as 400,000 copies monthly, which far exceeded the publication rates of *Akai tori*. They featured mainstream fiction, often in the form of serialized stories, a type of narrative which would dominate the scene until the surge of manga (comic) magazines in the post-war. The authors were not children's specialists but writers for the masses, like 江戸川乱歩 (Edogawa Ranpo) (1894–1965), famous for his mystery novels. To some extent, the surge of Japanese commercial magazines is comparable to the spread of the feuilleton genre, which was incredibly successful in Western literature of the nineteenth century, and also appeared in newspapers or magazines.

One of the reasons for the popularity of such publications in Japan was that they would rarely question the cultural agenda promoted by the

---

[70]Keith, 'Kaneko Misuzu and the Development of Children's Literature in Taishō Japan', 30.
[71]Carter, 'A Study on Japanese Children's Magazines 1888-1949', 76.
[72]Ibid., 6–7.

state, adapting to the times.[73] However, by the late 1920s, works of the so-called 児童文学運動 (jidō bungaku undō [children's literature movement]) started to appear in commercial children's magazines.[74] This style was influenced by Japanese Proletarian literature, spreading leftist ideas which were increasingly opposed by the government. Proletarian writers portrayed realistic circumstances, criticizing the idealized and allegedly classist vision of childhood fostered by dōwa authors. It is worth noting that Japanese histories usually credit the dōwa tradition for the creation of modern children's literature, dismissing popular magazines and Proletarian fiction because of their scarce artistic quality and the way they privileged propaganda over contents. Nonetheless, commercial magazines were a driving force of the publishing media, and laid the foundations of Japanese magazines as we know them today. Also the realism of Proletarian literature had an impact on children's fiction, which is still indicated with the term *jidō bungaku*, though stripped of its political connotation.[75]

Success story: The case of Kōdansha

That commercial children's magazines could become massively popular is exemplified by the rise of Japanese publisher Kōdansha until the end of the Occupation. Founded in 1910 by 野間 清治 (Noma Seiji) (1878–1938), by 1930 Kōdansha published nine magazines with a total circulation of seven million.[76] Like modern-day manga magazines, its strategy was to cater to increasingly narrow demographics, publishing entertaining stories which were cheap and big in length. Other key factors were the inclusion of the peasantry as a readership and the compliance to the ideals endorsed by the state. Such a highly commercialized approach allowed Kōdansha to monopolize the industry of popular magazines, becoming strongly present in the children's area. In fact, Kōdansha launched 少年倶楽部 (*Shōnen kurabu* [Boys' club]) (1914–62), the most popular magazine of the pre-war and war period, targeting boys from the fifth grade of elementary (around ten to eleven years old) to the second year of middle school (around thirteen to fourteen years old).[77]

The goal of the magazine was to educate and entertain, prioritizing enjoyment over didacticism in order to appeal to readers.[78] For the same

---

[73]Ibid., 90–1.
[74]Ericson, 'Introduction', xiii.
[75]Ibid.
[76]Carter, 'A Study on Japanese Children's Magazines 1888-1949', 131.
[77]Karl Ian Uy Cheng Chua, 'Boy Meets World: The Worldview of Shōnen kurabu in the 1930s', *Japan Forum* 28, no. 1 (2016): 75.
[78]Ibid., 77.

reason, the magazine, which had started publishing short stories and poems, as artistic journals did, switched to serialized novels. Single instalments did not sell well, while serialization made stories addicting, hooking readers into compulsive purchase. An added bonus was that *Shōnen kurabu* came at a very affordable price: sixty sen, one sen being worth one-hundredth of a yen (a national newspaper cost around eight sen).[79] Contents spanned from entertaining stories of good triumphing over evil to success stories and comics. War stories became a feature in the war period, when the magazine was eventually taken over by the regime. The impact of *Shōnen kurabu*, which in the mid-1930s peaked a print run of over 700,000, was therefore as strong as schools when it came to disseminating nationalistic ideals.[80]

Illustrated children's fiction

Comics were among the main attractions of *Shōnen kurabu*, but the connection between children's fiction and illustration was not exclusive of commercial magazines. Artistic journals, too, attracted talented illustrators. But when did graphic arts become a feature of Japanese children's literature? According to scholars, 絵巻物 (*emakimono* [painted scrolls]) presumably addressed children as early as the twelfth century, as was the case of 鳥獣戯画 (*chōjūgiga* [animal scrolls]), humorous pictures of birds and animals.[81] By the eighteenth century, when colour woodblock printing and cheap bindings reduced book costs, 絵本 (*ehon* [picture books]) were pervasively published, and these could also reach children, borrowing from folk tales and classic literary compilations. By the 1910s, thanks to the new technologies imported from the West, all-in-colour children's magazines regularly published picture stories, and images became more important for the plot.[82] Children's manga also appeared, growing in popularity in the 1920s, while 写真小説 (*shashin shōsetsu* [photo-novels]) and stories created by still frame images from movies were common in the 1930s, in response to a general shift to realism in fiction.[83]

Visual storytelling has many advantages, which obviously transcend the scope of Japanese children's literature. Being fast to proceed and easy to remember, stories told by images allow for an efficient communication. Pictures carry important meanings without relying on the written text, and thus can be understood by less experienced readers such as small children.

---

[79]Carter, 'A Study on Japanese Children's Magazines 1888-1949', 138.
[80]Cheng Chua, 'Boy Meets World: The Worldview of Shōnen kurabu in the 1930s', 76.
[81]Ericson, 'Introduction', viii.
[82]Carter, 'A Study on Japanese Children's Magazines 1888-1949', 104.
[83]Ibid., 136.

At the same time, pictures can help build reading skills, connecting with the words on the page (which in Japanese are of pictographic origin). Being able to breach language barriers, illustrated children's fiction and comics escalated in the immediate post-war, during the American Occupation of Japan, as a sort of lingua franca.[84] Moreover, thanks to design features such as colour and shape, illustrated stories manage to spark a wide range of emotions, which make them particularly engaging. They can also create character types with embedded cultural agendas. For example, homogeneousness was common in children's representation in wartime magazines, while diversity became increasingly important in the illustrated fiction of the Occupation period.[85]

Children's manga (as manga in general) changed a lot over time, gaining in sophistication and popularity. Originally comics featured humorous contents with captions of text – a format which would survive until the 1950s, their average length consisting of four to eight frames per page. From the 1920s, dialogue bubbles were preferred to captioned manga, while in the 1930s long serialized instalments became the norm. These sold better than short stories, and could be reprinted as hardback books, like modern-day 単行本 (*tankōbon*) or collected editions of manga. As happened with commercial children's literature, the adoption of a serial format was a paradigm shift. Consequently, literary journals were gradually replaced by manga magazines, which would thrive in the post-war. In this period, Tezuka Osamu created a new type of comics, called ストーリー漫画 (*sutorī manga* [story comics]). These were complex stories which used cinema framing techniques, just like today's comics. A proliferation of genres would follow, and manga magazines became more competitive, strengthening their marketing strategies and their ties with other media.

Book sets for children . . .

Serialization was applied to several sectors of Japanese publishing, including book sets, which had a considerable impact on the way children's fiction and literature in general were intended in Japan. Books spreading across several volumes, later to be stacked as a set, were published as early as the seventeenth century, thanks to the advent of commercial printing.[86] Mass-produced book series were made available by improved printing technology from the 1920s and early 1930s, a period known as 円本時代

---

[84]Ibid., 137.
[85]Ibid., 210.
[86]Andrew T. Kamei-Dyche, 'The History of Books and Print Culture in Japan: The State of the Discipline', *Book History* 14 (2011): 275.

(*enpon jidai* [era of one-yen books]). In these years, publishers released some 200 collections of books of a few hundred pages each, named enpon from their low subscription fee – one yen per volume (or less), as much as a taxi ride.[87] There were different categories of enpon, which covered literature and other branches of knowledge, but their common feature was that they were intended for a general readership, offering significant cultural notions to Japan's burgeoning information-based society. In fact, as Keaveney points out, enpon took inspiration from the Harvard Classics series, first published in 1909 by Charles W. Eliot, the president of Harvard, who believed that anyone could achieve the benefits of a liberal arts education by reading world classics.[88]

The educational ends of enpon sets emerge from one of their most common formats, 全集 (*zenshū* [complete works]). These were comprehensive literary collections aimed at teaching either which texts were worth reading (in the case of miscellaneous anthologies) or what writers were worth following (in the case of single-author zenshū).[89] Vast zenshū projects coalesced into the enpon phenomenon from the start,[90] colonizing children's literature, and often generating intense competition between publishers. An example is the enpon war which pitted ARS against Kōbunsha and Bungei Shunjūsha.[91] In 1927 they started to release two zenshū series for children, 日本児童文庫 (Nihon jidō bunko [Japanese children library]), published by ARS, and 小学生全集 (Shōgakusei zenshū [Elementary school children's complete works series]), by Kōbunsha and Bungei. Important figures in children's education endorsed each book set. The novelist 菊池 寛 (Kikuchi Kan) (1888–1948) established Bungei, while the poet Kitahara (who, as seen, collaborated with *Akai tori*) was related to ARS, founded by his younger brother 鉄雄 (Tetsuo) (1887–1957).

Much to the advantage of the advertising agencies involved, the resulting rivalry was both commercial and cultural, to the point that the high expenses vexing ARS and Kōbunsha annihilated their profits, causing them

---

[87] Edward Fowler, *The Rhetoric of Confession: Shishosetsu in Early Twentieth-Century Japanese* (Berkley: University of California Press, 1992), 141.
[88] Christopher T. Keaveney, *The Cultural Evolution of Postwar Japan. The Intellectual Contributions of Kaizō's Yamamoto Sanehiko* (New York: Palgrave Macmillan, 2013), 95.
[89] Kiyoko Myojo, 'The Functions of Zenshū in Japanese Book Culture: Practices and Problems of Modern Textual Editing in Japan', *Variants* 10 (2013): 260.
[90] The enpon craze started in 1926, when Kaizōsha, a publisher in dire straits, issued a sixty-five-volume Gendai Nihon bungaku zenshū (Complete works of modern Japanese literature). The series sold 380,000 copies, an astronomical figure for the times, and more than ten similar zenshū sets were published in the following three years; Fowler, *The Rhetoric of Confession*.
[91] Sari Kawana, *The Uses of Literature in Modern Japan: Histories and Cultures of the Book* (London: Bloomsbury Academics 2018), 42.

to go bankrupt.⁹² The Great Kantō Earthquake (1923) has been invoked as a cause for the popularity of enpon sets, because thousands of books were destroyed during the calamity, including publishers stocks. Publishers had to dump prices to recoup their losses, making profits from higher volume of sales. As Kawana notes, 'the phenomenon becomes curious when taking into account contemporary working and living conditions for many, in which wages were stagnant (low disposable money) and living space was limited (less room for possession)'.⁹³ ARS and Kōbunsha-Bungei series consisted of seventy-six and eighty-eight volumes each. This made them incredibly vast collections for the smaller housing units which were becoming the norm in Japan – also because, one might infer, extra room had to be allocated to series for adults too. Besides, enpon were large books, mostly printed in a format 50 per cent bigger than today's paperbacks.⁹⁴

... and why they were popular

According to Kawana, the popularity of multivolume sets lies in the use value of literature as it was perceived among the reading public.⁹⁵ The long wave of the 'learning from the West' slogan, combined with the internationalism of the Taishō period, gave rise to a mass culture which absorbed Western forms of knowledge as part of Japan's modernization. These cultural imports included the notion of literature as comprising novels, drama and poetry – an art genre which did not exist as such in the country.⁹⁶ The definition of literature as an essential feature of education was also due to the influence of 教養主義 (kyōyōshugi [culturalism]), a Meiji philosophical movement which was still active in the enpon era, advocating the need for a broad, general knowledge as a means for self-enrichment.⁹⁷ Kyōyōshugi extolled the importance of 教養 (kyōyō [culture]), 修養 (shūyō [self-cultivation]) and 人格 (jinkaku [character development]), associating them with reading.⁹⁸

---

⁹²Between lawsuits, praises from the Ministry of Education and alleged subscriptions from the imperial family; Kawana, *The Uses of Literature in Modern Japan*, 42.
⁹³Kawana, *The Uses of Literature in Modern Japan*, 18.
⁹⁴Ibid.
⁹⁵Ibid., 48.
⁹⁶Gunilla Lindberg-Wada, 'Japanese Literary History Writing: The Beginnings', in *Literary History: Towards a Global Perspective: Volume 1: Notions of Literature Across Cultures*, ed. Anders Petterson (Berlin: Gruyter, 2006), 114.
⁹⁷Kawana, *The Uses of Literature in Modern Japan*, 37.
⁹⁸Influenced by German Neo-idealism, but also connected to Confucianism. See Kamei-Dyche, 'The History of Books and Print Culture in Japan: The State of the Discipline', 277; Leslie Pincus, *Authenticating Culture in Imperial Japan. Kuki Shuzo and the Rise of National Aesthetics* (Berkley: University of California Press, 1996), 34; Michiko Suzuki, *Becoming*

As a consequence, people were keen to acquaint themselves with Western thought and culture via literature as a sort of cultural duty.[99] Traces of these discourses can be found in the enpon campaigns, whose rhetorics capitalized on the values of culture and literature, connoting the act of buying (and owning) book sets as a form of intellectual achievement, which could be exhibited in the reader's house. Publishers particularly mythicized the idea of creating a 'home library' by giving away actual bookcases, or using them in promotional images, as was the case of ARS and Kōbunsha ('A Shōgakusei zenshū for the child you love' was the latter's slogan, associated to the picture of a neatly stored bookcase). Various enpon ads had also a political flavour, as they equated enpon to democracy, allowing subscribers to decide for what was worthy of a permanent collection.[100]

Nurtured by decades of educational policies and centuries of Confucian substrata, the yearning of Japanese readers for comprehensive literacy was channelled through a consumer activity during the enpon era. In the context of a burgeoning capitalistic nation, publishers promoted book sets as a means to obtain indispensable knowledges – complete knowledges, in the case of zenshū. This culture was made accessible to all social classes, commodified for the modest sum of one yen. Also, thanks to their elegant look, enpon came to be regarded as beautiful things and status symbols, to the point that vast collections were often unread, and used only to decorate one's living room.[101]

Series of classics

As book sets were wide-scale projects, for many writers they were a possibility of living by the pen, providing financial gain and literary success. Translators, publishers and editors benefitted from the enpon boom, too. Publishers and editors became particularly influential, given their role in creating hype through advertising and promotion.[102] Kikuchi's career is a clear example. Aside from editing the children's collection Shōgakusei zenshū, he founded his own publishing company and was also a prolific writer and translator. Perhaps the most evident legacy of the enpon age was the canonization and popularization of many literary works.[103] This is especially true for zenshū sets, whose texts were advocated as the best among the best, both by mass-

---

Modern Women: Love and Female Identity in Prewar Japanese Literature and Culture (Stanford: Standford University Press, 2010), 72.
[99]Myojo, 'The Functions of Zenshū in Japanese Book Culture', 259.
[100]Kawana, *The Uses of Literature in Modern Japan*, 40.
[101]Myojo, 'The Functions of Zenshū in Japanese Book Culture', 260.
[102]Kawana, *The Uses of Literature in Modern Japan*, 46.
[103]Myojo, 'The Functions of Zenshū in Japanese Book Culture', 260.

market publishers like Kōdansha and upstarts focused on the intellectual market like Iwanami Shoten.[104] Japanese and Chinese classics entered the zenshū canon, as well as a growing number of Western works. What about children's fiction? As Japan started to translate foreign children's books in the Meiji period, consequently developing its own tradition of stories and nursery rhymes, zenshū sets for children mirrored this process, disseminating tropes which would gain currency among readers, and future writers, in the years to come.

Zenshū for children were intended as an expression of a modern, wholesome culture – something bespeaking Western intelligence and social prestige. This was likely to appear as an appealing feature to parents, considering their role as gatekeepers of children's fiction.[105] According to a survey from 1927, wealthy readers were willing to sign up for two or three book series at one time,[106] which seems to suggest that subscribing for children's sets and for adult sets was not mutually exclusive. That the opinion of adults mattered is confirmed by the same zenshū authors, who would address parents in explaining the utility of a certain book or collection of books for children's education. For example, the illustrator and cartoonist 岡本一平 (Okamoto Ippei) (1886–1948), who cured a comic anthology for Shōgakusei zenshū, seems to cater to adults as he compares comics to おやつ (oyatsu [snacks]), not as nutritious as 主要食 (shuyō shoku [staple food]), but still important for children's 成長 (sēchō [growth]), implicitly justifying their presence in a zenshū.[107]

The same serial format which fostered book canonization with the enpon boom was employed by commercial magazines to hook readers into episodic stories, whose most successful examples were later published as single volumes – all generating separate incomes. This publishing practice was profitable for both parties, encouraging private ownership and multiple subscriptions through collections. At the same time, magazines and books were situated on a different level, the underlying idea being that only masterpieces, or proclaimed such, deserved a book edition. In this context, zenshū sets ticked all the boxes. As relatively cheap packaged commodities, they could be purchased by all. As lavishly illustrated materials, they were something to show off in your personal library. As collections of world

---

[104]Kamei-Dyche, 'The History of Books and Print Culture in Japan: The State of the Discipline', 278.
[105]Deborah Stevenson, 'Classics and Canons', in *The Cambridge Companion to Children's Literature*, ed. M. O. Grenby and Andrea Immel (New York: Cambridge University Press, 2009), 108–24.
[106]Kawana, *The Uses of Literature in Modern Japan*, 46.
[107]Ippei Okamoto, *Jidō manga shū* [Children's manga collection], Shōgakusei zenshū 23 (Tokyo: Kōbunsha, 1927), 2.

classics, they were must-have items which no cultivated individual could be without, in an age when knowledge was a moral feature of education.

Youth culture and zenshū

A closer look at the zenshū issued by ARS and Kōbunsha-Bungei can give us an idea of what was youth culture like in interwar Japan. The two series feature similar categories, the bulk of which is devoted to fiction, such as fairy and folk tales, poetry, myths and adaptations of classic stories. Literary works from Japan make up most of the selection by ARS, but foreign fiction is also well represented, covering over 30 per cent of the titles in both sets, and surpassing Japanese contents in Kōbunsha-Bungei. Together with foreign literature came a set of new literary genres and subgenres, such as novels and 探偵小説 (*tantei shōsetsu* [detective stories]). It is worth noting that, although the expression 世界 (*sekai* [world]) is employed in most cases, it is usually referred to 西洋 (*seiyō* [Western]) materials. For example, ARS's 世界童話集 (Sekai dōwa shū [World fairy tales collection]) contains mainly British and Russian tales, while roughly three-quarter of the titles in Kōbunsha-Bungei are from Europe (France, Germany, Italy, Spain, Netherlands).

Literary works appear to be chosen, and thus canonized, for their morality. For example, Kikuchi's preface to the Italian novel クオレ (*Cuore* [*Heart*]) (Shōgakusei zenshū 53) defines it as a 傑作 (*kessaku* [masterpiece]), because of its valuable 友情、正義等の教訓 (*yūgiō, seigi nado no kyōkun*) [lessons on friendship, justice, etc.].[108] This confirms a pattern started with Meiji translators, who also favoured Western works for their didactic values. Zenshū's vast catalogues allowed for a broader inclusion, with issues on Indian fairy tales (ARS), or African tales (Kōbunsha-Bungei), albeit these were a minority.[109] Informational non-fiction was also present in the form of encyclopaedic materials (mostly primers on scientific subjects which today would be classified as STEM, such as chemistry, mathematics etc.), texts about leisure activities, books on national features of Japan (from art to flora and fauna), dramatized historic events and biographies of important men. Furthermore, a handful of issues in each collection are atlas-like books on travels, in Japan and overseas.

---

[108] An abridged version of the preface is reported in Tomoko Bashomatsu, 'Shogakusei zenshū' [Elementary school children's complete works series], *Umineko* (2003). Available online: http://www.umi-neko.com/book/shougakuseizenshuu/shougakuseizenshuujyoukyuu.htm (accessed 28 February 2023).
[109] These are 印度童話集 (*Indo dōwa shū* [*Indian fairy tales collection*]) and a couple of stories in 世界童話集 (*Sekai dōwa shū* [*World fairy tales collection*]), respectively, issue 15 of ARS books and issue 10 of Kōbunsha-Bungei books.

The similarities between these collections reveal a consistency in terms of which texts would fit into an ideal children's library, that is, national and Western stories – be them anchored in history or fictional – as well as practical texts which encouraged some sort of interaction with the real world. However, there are also some differences between the artistic (ARS) and commercial (Kōbunsha-Bungei) approach to children's fiction. ARS seemed to privilege Japanese works, and poetry over prose, adorning its zenshū with exquisite illustrations and bindings, which is perhaps not surprising, considering its connections with the artistic circles of *Akai tori*. In turn, Kōbunsha-Bungei inserted a bigger proportion of informational non-fiction, advertising it as pivotal for a successful career. While Nihon jidō bunko featured adaptations of Western novels, which were released in dedicated anthological issues, Shōgakusei zenshū put greater emphasis on these contents by publishing them as separate books. These included stories which would achieve classic status, such as the English novel フランダースの犬 (*Furandāsu no inu* [*A Dog of Flanders*]) or 家なき子 (*Ie-naki-ko* [*Homeless child*]), a translation of the French novel *Sans Famille* [*Without family*], known in English as *Nobody's Boy*.[110]

Children's literature during the war

In the 1930s, at the beginning of the Shōwa era (1926–89), the enpon movement gave signs of saturation and eventually disappeared, after selling an estimated three million volumes.[111] The publishing field, which had turned into a capitalistic-oriented operation, became increasingly state-controlled. Ultranationalism intensified, while intellectuals started using the slogan 近代の超克 (*kindai no chōkoku* [overcoming modernity]), rejecting Westernization and supporting Japan's militarist expansion in Asia.[112] This cultural climate affected children's fiction. Between 1926 and 1937, Proletarian children's literature enjoyed a temporary success, with realistic 生活 童話 (*seikatsu dōwa* [lifestyle stories]) detaching from the poetic expression and idyllic innocence of the child-mind movement.[113] The preference for traditional Japanese materials resulted in the boom of 髷物 (*magemono* [historical fiction]), samurai novels set in feudal Japan

---

[110]These were published as, respectively, issues 26 and 54 of Kōbunsha-Bungei series.
[111]Keaveney, *The Cultural Evolution of Postwar Japan*, 105.
[112]John W. M. Krummel, 'The Symposium on Overcoming Modernity and Discourse in Wartime Japan', *Historická Sociologie* 13, no. 2 (2021): 85; Sims, *Japanese Political History Since the Meiji Renovation*, 180.
[113]Carter, 'A Study on Japanese Children's Magazines 1888-1949', 116.

and serialized in popular magazines.[114] Although Western fiction from the English-speaking world was ostracized, it did not vanish completely, as Ishihara notes analysing a samurai adaptation of Twain's *The Prince and the Pauper*, by the writer 大佛 次郎 (Osaragai Jiro) (1897–1973).[115]

In the years of the total war, when fascism took power in Japan and the scheme of Greater East-Asia Co-Prosperity sphere started to be put in action, children's literature was totally state-controlled. At the beginning of the second Sino-Japanese conflict (1937), the home ministry named children's literature as *shōkokumin bungaku* 少国民文学 (little citizens's literature), a political manoeuvre more than a linguistic one, which instilled the idea that children were loyal subjects of the emperor, spurring them to participate into the war.[116] Direct propaganda was fostered by publishing texts in line with Confucian values such as piety, loyalty and industriousness, as well as celebrating militarism and colonialism.[117] Although often overlooked by critics, 冒険小説 (*bōken shōsetsu* [adventure novels]), usually set in countries which Japan intended to conquer, and stories of jungle explorers á la Tarzan, became popular subgenres.[118] However, Japan's 'little citizens' were savvy consumers who looked out for literature which would suit their tastes. There is evidence that they would often reread magazines and enpon of the interwar period, zenshū libraries being often stored in the countryside where many of them were relocated.[119] Also, several children probably simply found pleasure in the mainstream entertainment provided by contemporary fiction, refusing the nationalistic messages to which they were nonetheless exposed.

Children's literature during the Occupation

At the end of the war, the conditions of the country were appalling, both for the consequences of the dropping of the bomb and the high death ratio of the soldiers and civilians during the war. In the Occupation period (1945–52), when the American General Headquarters (GHQ) governed Japan, isolating it from the world for a second time in its history, the country saw a number of epochal transformations and reforms, covering all areas of the state with the goal to extirpate militaristic and nationalistic values. With

---

[114]Tsuyoshi Ishihara, *Mark Twain in Japan. The Cultural Reception of an American Icon* (Columbia and London: University of Missouri Press, 2005), 37.
[115]Ibid., 37–52.
[116]Quoted in Hyoseak Choi, *Losing the War, Winning the Pooh: Ishii Momoko and the Construction of Contemporary Children's Literature in Postwar Japan*, MA Thesis (University of Toronto, 2017), 2.
[117]Ishihara, *Mark Twain in Japan*, 57.
[118]Kawana, *The Uses of Literature in Modern Japan*, 75.
[119]Ibid., 54–64.

the democratization programme performed by the Allies, a new wave of Americanization swept through the country, promoting wonderful images of the American lifestyle and culture. The growth of the publishing industry and of children's literature was part of this process.

Under the control of the Supreme Command for the Allied Powers (SCAP), a flood of foreign books that were curtailed during the war period were translated into Japanese – a total of 3,335 books were translated, the majority of which were American books.[120] General MacArthur was especially keen in the introduction of the 'Little House' series by Laura Ingalls Wilder (1867–1957), to give hope to young readers.[121] Tales of the Brothers Grimm, *Aesop's Fables* and Andersen's stories were frequently published, as well as non-fiction materials, such as ABC books or biographies of important American men.[122] Children's literature was directly employed as a means to encourage a positive reception of American values. Initiatives such as the 'Gift Book Program', whereby American children's books were exhibited in Japanese towns and given for free to local school libraries, served this purpose.[123] Consequently, references to the war and to the underside of American society were censored, while values that were dominant in Japan in the pre-war and war period, such as sacrifice and militarism, but also purity and elegance, came to halt.

A new genre of children's literature, known as 良心 (*ryōshin* [conscientious]), developed in the field of Japanese magazines. Aiming at fostering democratic ideals, it failed to provide entertaining storytelling, and this was why the movement was short-lived.[124] Also 無国籍童話 (*mukokuseki dōwa* [non-nation specific stories]) became common, as well as lifestyle stories in the fashion of Proletarian literature, but stripped from their political standpoint.[125] The preference for light-hearted entertainment accorded by the Allies resulted in the proliferation of children's manga magazines, whose sales escalated in the post-war, and eventually replaced pre-war literary journals.[126] Essentially a post-war phenomenon, comics responded to the demand of leisure and economically accessible entertainment of the period, peaking in 1947 with Tezuka's debut manga 新宝島 (*Shin takarajima* [*New treasure island*]), loosely based on Stevenson's novel. In the following years,

---

[120] Ishihara, *Mark Twain in Japan*, 62.
[121] Yuka Kajihara, 'An Influential Anne in Japan', in *The Lucy Maud Montgomery Album*, ed. Mc Cabe et al. (Fitzhenry & Whiteside: Toronto, 1999), 433.
[122] Carter, 'A Study on Japanese Children's Magazines 1888-1949', 207.
[123] Ishihara, *Mark Twain in Japan*, 63.
[124] Marnie K. Jorenby, 'About Face: The Transformations of the Hero in Post-War Japanese Literature for Youth' (Ph.D. diss., University of Wisconsin-Madison 2003), 81–2.
[125] Ericson, 'Introduction', xiii.
[126] Carter, 'A Study on Japanese Children's Magazines 1888-1949', 211–12.

manga would develop their own grammar, also through the renegotiation of Western stories and genres.

The second boom of book series

Book series of classics, which sank into stagnation in the previous decade, benefitted from the translation boom of the Occupation. For example, one of the most significant translation efforts of this period was Kōdansha's 世界名作全集 (Sekai meisaku zenshū [World masterpieces complete works series]) (1950–60), which consisted of 180 volumes, each one featuring a single novel, embellished with a binding, large cover illustrations and golden decorative frames. The same publisher released less sumptuous book series such as 講談社の絵本 (Kōdansha no ehon [Kōdansha's picture books]) (1946–58), following on an enpon format already popular during the war. As happened in burgeoning Japanese magazines, and in line with the past zenshū tradition, these publications tapped into the children's attraction for illustrated stories and collectible publishing patterns, fostering values and role models compatible with the educational agenda of the SCAP.

To give an idea of the size of the phenomenon, and the related capillary diffusion of stories and ideals, it seems useful to mention some titles. Aside from the above-mentioned World masterpieces series, several other multivolume sets for children started publication in 1950 alone, including Kōdansha's 世界名作童話全集 (Sekai meisaku dōwa zenshū [World masterpiece children's stories complete works series]) (60 volumes), Komine Shoten's 小学生文庫 (Shōgakusei bunko [Elementary school children's library]) (37 volumes), Poplar's 世界名作物語 (Sekai meisaku monogatari [World masterpiece stories]) (40 volumes) and Iwanami Shoten's 岩波少年文庫 (Iwanami shōnen bunko [Iwanami youth library]) (194 volumes), to name just a few. It is worth noting that Iwanami, which since the pre-war years had a reputation as an academic publisher, established the *bunko* or paperback format of publication, which remained a dominant model in Japanese publishing.[127] As Keaveney notes, bunko series, consisting of extremely compact, affordable and attractively designed books, can be considered as the 'true heirs' to the enpon boom of the pre-war and interwar period.[128] But which were the contents of post-war children's book sets, and how did they differ from pre-war series?

If we consider the composition of Kōdansha's Sekai meisaku zenshū, the impression is of a broad cultural variety, as books from peripheral countries are included, such as the epic poems *Lāčplēsis* (1888) and *The Knight in the*

---

[127]Kiyoshi Kojima, 'Iwanami Publishing House', in *The Encyclopedia of Contemporary Japanese Culture*, ed. Sandra Buckley (London and New York: Routledge, 2006), 223.
[128]Keaveney, *The Cultural Evolution of Postwar Japan*, 186.

Panther's Skin (XII century), respectively from Latvia and Georgia.[129] Books from the Middle East and Asia are present as well, but the majority of books are from English-speaking countries, with American or Anglo-American texts (44) and British texts (40) topping the list, followed by European novels from France (27), Germany (7), Russia (7) and Scandinavia (6). Japanese books are in fourth position (16), accounting for 10 per cent of the total, while there are only two Chinese works. Aside from being a minority, titles which can be labelled as Middle Eastern were often already ingrained in the Western canon, such as the *Arabian Nights* or the Bible. Conversely, among English-written works, there are many which today are scarcely remembered, such as *The Story of a Bad Boy* (1870), by the American writer Thomas Aldrich. There are also books which were adapted in Hollywood films, such as the Polish historical novel *Quo vadis* (1896) or the Swiss classic *Heidi* (1881).

In terms of literary genres, novels are the most numerous (138 titles), largely composed of children's fiction or adaptations of adult contents from the nineteenth century. Western girls' books are also increasingly represented, with newly translated classics, such as *Little Women*, and novels translated for the first time, like *Anne of Green Gables*. Biographies, folk tales and legends are present, though less numerous than in pre-war series, while stories from Africa or India, which were featured in past collections, are not on the list. The predominance of American titles seems in line with the trends of the Occupation, replenishing the local canon with American stories. In a similar way, the presence of (at least some) non-English books may be due to their circulation in the form of Hollywood movies, such as the Austrian novel *Bambi* (1923), by the Austrian writer Felix Salten.

The birth of contemporary children's literature

The policy of the Occupation had an effect on the reconstruction of contemporary children's literature in post-war Japan. Critics, scholars, teachers and writers formed in this period were guided to view Western juvenile fiction, which was already rooted in the country, as a landmark reference for Japanese culture. Practices fostered by the Allies, such as cultural exchange programmes, were conducive to forge positive relations between Japan and the United States, allowing children's authors to travel to America and Europe, creating connections with Western publishers and educators. Consequently, as in the Meiji period Japanese intellectuals were prompted to adopt Western science and technology, and in the war period

---

[129]In Kōdansha's collection these are issues 53 勇士ラチプレシス (*Yūshi rachipureshisu* [Hero Lāčplēsis]) (1954) and 113 虎の皮を着た勇士 (*Tora no kawa o kita yūshi* [Hero in tiger skin]) (1955).

they complied with the values of the regime, post-Occupation authors of children's fiction reshaped their tradition in order to fit the new standards. Whereas pre-war children's literature was mainly expressed in poetry, and war children's fiction was imbued with imperialistic themes and a clear Confucian underpinning, post-war children's fiction was prosaic and fun-oriented, electing the novel as its preferable form.

Editors of children's books, whose increasing importance dated back to the pre-war period, became authoritative voices and had a key role in cementing the emulation of the Western canon. The parable of 石井 桃子 (Ishii Momoko) (1907–2008) exemplifies these trends.[130] A writer of children's fiction herself, Ishii mostly worked as a translator (hence the paucity of information available on her activity in English scholarship) and as an editor for Iwanami, planning children's books such as the previously recalled multivolume series Iwanami shōnen bunko. In her book 子どもと文学 (*Kodomo to bungaku* [*Children and literature*]) (1960), co-authored with other five important figures in post-war children's literature, Ishii examined Japan's pre-war juvenile tradition comparing it to world fiction, a label which, as Choi shows, mainly refers to anglophone literature. In fact, most of the literary works quoted in the essay came from book lists recommended by American librarians and critics, whom Ishii met thanks to a Creative Fellowship issued by the Rockefeller Foundation.

The notion of a world canon equating to American and British literature seems consistent with the representation of English-language books in the translation boom. Conversely, the essay criticized Japanese dōwa authors such as Mimei on the assumption that anglophone literature was based on universal tenets, thus connoting Japanese fiction as a deviation from the norm. Choi points out that Ishii's views on children's literature were highly influential in Japan, as can be argued from the fact that the importance of dōwa authors was significantly reduced in the post-war. Ishii's ideas on translation and children's libraries had an impact on Japanese culture, too. For example, Ishii advocated for 完訳 (*kan'yaku* [complete translations]), which would become the standard in the field, downplaying the role of previous domesticating strategies.[131] As for children's libraries, Ishii imported the concept from the advanced American system, compounding the idea of libraries as democratic places for children to play and study.[132]

If we look at the titles included in Iwanami shōnen bunko, these seem to observe the guidelines set out in *Kodomo to bungaku*, presenting a similar scenario to Kōdansha's zenshū. Most books are novels (123), and books written in Great Britain (43) and in the United States (41), including works

---

[130]Choi, *Losing the War, Winning the Pooh*, 4–12.
[131]Ibid., 47.
[132]Ibid., 67.

by prominent children's educators, such as the historical novel *Meggy MacIntosh* (1930) by Elizabeth Gray Vining,[133] who tutored crown prince Akihito during the Occupation, as well as titles honoured with awards given by librarians, like the Newbery Medal. In total, titles from Europe represent the large majority (almost 70 per cent), several of which were translated for the first time into Japanese, such Erich Kästner's works, Gianni Rodari's tales, or Antoine de Saint-Exupéry's *Le petit prince* [*The little prince*] (1943). Japanese and Asian books are present in small numbers, accounting for, respectively, 4.6 and 5.2 per cent of the catalogue. As Choi notes, Iwanami's inclination towards foreign books is confirmed by the publisher's present output, which is still mainly composed of translated works.[134] The same logo of Iwanami, modelled on *The Sower* by Jean-François Millet, seems to bespeak a preference for Western 'masterpieces'.

Comparing the book lists of Iwanami shōnen bunko and Kōdansha's World masterpieces series (including Kōdansha's dōwa collection), they have in common about fifty works, a number which is deemed to rise if we consider authors featured in each series but with a different book choice, such as Lev Tolstoj, Andrew Lang and Selma Lagerlöf. To some extent, Kōdansha's sets appear more traditional, with a preference for older classics and commercially successful genres such as adventure or detection (Maurice Leblanc's 'Lupin' series is broken down in five issues), while Iwanami's selection is comprehensive of more modern and diverse publications, including soviet works and one African American book, *Popo and Fifina: Children of Haiti* (1932). The presence, in Iwanami's series, of a higher number of non-fiction works, such as biographies or exploration stories, is another variation, although Kōdansha, too, released thematic book series on similar topics, like 少年少女世界探検冒険全集 (Shōnen shōjo sekai tanken bōken zenshū [Boys and girls' world exploration adventures complete works series]) (1958).

Book series after the Occupation

There seems to be consistency with the choice of books included in Iwanami and Kōdansha sets, which were among the most numerous series of the post-war, and other book sets for children of the same period. For instance, almost all the books of 世界名作文庫 (Sekai meisaku bunko [World masterpiece library) (1951–6), a 140-volume series released by Kaisesha, were also part of either Kōdansha's or Iwanami's sets (or both), including orphan tales (significantly *Jane Eyre* is renamed 嵐の孤児 (*Arashi no koji*

---

[133]In Iwanami's series it is issue 36: メギー新しい国へ (*Megī atarashī kuni e* [*Meggy goes to a new country*]) (1952).
[134]Choi, *Losing the War, Winning the Pooh*, 46.

[*Orphan of the storm*]) in Kaisesha's series) and adventure stories, from classic *Treasure Island* to the Victorian novel *The Prisoner of Zenda*. Similar observations could be made for book collections released in the 1960s and 1970s. Poplar's fifty-eight-volume series 世界名作童話全集 (Sekai meisaku dōwa zenshū [World masterpiece children's stories complete works series]) (1963–5) and forty-volume 世界の名著 (Sekai no meicho [World famous books]) (1967–9) reproduce the same titles, writers and streams of Iwanami and Kōdansha, such as animal fiction (from Ernest Seton to Nikolaj Bajkov), or retellings of biblical episodes.

Shōgakukan's fifty-five-volume series 少年少女世界の名作 (Shōnen shōjo sekai no meisaku [Boys and girls' world masterpieces]) (1972–5) showcases another popular format for children's book sets, serializing stories according to their geographical origin, and including non-fiction contents such as biographies and historical accounts. For example, issue 12 is the third of eight volumes dedicated to America, featuring Burnett's novels *Little Lord Fauntleroy* and *A Little Princess*, Lofting's *The Voyages of Doctor Dolittle*, 海賊キッドなぞの宝 (Kaizoku Kiddo nazo no takara [*The mysterious treasure of Pirate Kidd*]) (probably a translation of Poe's short story 'The Gold-Bug'), a collection of local folk tales and a biography of President Kennedy. Other matches are historical stories (from Schiller's drama to the Christian novel *Ben Hur*), animal tales (especially dog stories) and exploration accounts (with a preference for mountaineering), aside from countless books by Verne, Montgomery, Bonsels, Ouida, Malot, Wyss, Alcott and other Western writers.

Considering that publishers such as Shōgakukan and Kōdansha were also active in the flourishing market of manga magazines, it is easy to understand why book sets were serialized multiple times with numerous thematic variations. For example, in 1949 Kōdansha started a collaboration with Disney which would last until today,[135] publishing series of picture books such as 講談社のディズニー絵本 (Kōdansha no Dizunī ehon [Kōdansha's Disney picture books]) (1961–4) and ディズニー名作童話全集 (Dizunī meisaku dōwa zenshū [Disney masterpiece fairy tales complete works series) (1969–70). Several girl-oriented book series were also released, such as Kōdansha's 世界少女小説全集 (Sekai shōjo shōsetsu zenshū [World girls' novels complete works series]) (1957–8), and this seems consistent with the growing number of girl characters in Western juvenile fiction. Although there are more book sets for children than this analysis can cover, it seems safe to say that a pattern was established in the post-war period – which was to be repeated in the following decades – of canonical writers and stories. As

---

[135]In particular, Kōdansha started to publish four Disney's picture books in 1950, including ミッキーマウス (*Mikkī mausu* [*Mickey Mouse*]); 'Dizunī to shuppan keiyaku' [Publishing contract with Disney] (2009), *Asahi Shimbun*, Reduced-size edition, February 20, No. 1051.

seen, the contents of these sets were impacted by the Occupation, favouring Western contents over Asian ones. At the same time, there was not a total hiatus from previous book series.

Traces of the home library culture advocated by Ishii can be found in pre-war zenshū-type publications, which encouraged book collection, fostering the notion of possessing knowledge as a form a moral enhancement. In addition, many titles included in post-war book sets arrived to Japan at the beginning of the twentieth century, if not earlier. Also, literary genres booming in the post-war such as adventure stories and science fiction were already popular in the war period, although connoted in a militaristic way, and had their roots in Meiji children's literature. Another sign of continuity is represented by the inclusion, in post-war book sets, of diverse materials other than American and British fiction. Albeit not preponderant, encyclopaedic non-fiction materials such as biographies and world histories were featured in modern book series, as well as contents from non-English-speaking countries. For example, Shōgakukan's geographic set included eight volumes on France, followed by Germany (6), USSR (5), Scandinavia (2), Southern Europe (1), China (2) and finally Japan with eight books – the same number as France, Britain and America. Children's fairy tales and folk tales, too, which were highly regarded since the Meiji period, were not discarded in post-war book series, in spite of the stronger emphasis on novels.

These considerations seem to suggest that the way children's culture was formulated in post-war Japan used a mix of influences from multiple sources. The impact of the Occupation was evident in the number of American and British books, praised by American and British librarians. Moreover, when Japanese book series tackled contents such as Greek mythology or world history, these were often the work of American or British authors, such as Hendrik Van Loon's *Story of Mankind* (1921–2). However, for Japanese translators and readers, book sets represented an opportunity to meet different cultures and books, which might have been popular in America, but were already ingrained in pre-war translated fiction, such as *Cuore*, by Edmondo De Amicis. The repeated inclusion of several titles in different book sets – *Heidi* got translated over 100 times – tells us of the impact these stories had on the Japanese children and youth.

2

Japanese animation and children's literature

Japanese animation has a long history. Originally a popular form of entertainment, it gained artistic recognition over time, and, together with manga, is considered a solid staple of Japanese visual culture. Critics and scholars have pointed out that animation is a mass art consumed by millions, a by-product of the emergence of capitalism and industrialization in a modern society such as Japan at the beginning of the twentieth century. The influences between Japanese animation and local entrepreneurs have also been stressed, envisioning anime as a result of cross-pollination between artistic expression and commercialization.

In recent years, a growing number of scholarly works in English have been issued, often in the form of thematic, cultural, social and historical analyses by European and American researchers, whose countries have been importing anime since the 1960s. Something similar has occurred in East Asia, despite the lower volume of empirical research. Due to the international interest in anime as a cultural good, albeit stemming from a rather small and fragile industrial structure – what has been defined as a cottage industry – the notion of Japanese animation as a form of soft power has been widely disseminated in academic sectors, in relation to the Cool Japan policy. Think of former premier 安倍 晋三 (Abe Shinzo) (1954–2022) in 2016, saluting Tokyo 2020 surrounded by popular icons of Japanese animation, like Hello Kitty and Captain Tsubasa, as part of the Olympic closing ceremony in Rio.

In general, the connection with children's fiction is not the first focus of anime scholars, also because Japanese animation has long been identified with a diverse targeting structure, differently from more mainstream animation forms, often born in the wake of Disney works. Moreover, Children's literature scholars in Japan have long preferred to focus on canonical works rather than fiction in other media, albeit catered to, and consumed by, children. After a short introduction on adaptation, this chapter will try to create a bridge between the two worlds, focusing on the historic roots of Japanese animation and how it customized literature for the small and the big screen, paving the way for the works of the *WMT*. In doing so, I include more dated studies among my secondary sources, and particularly Italian anime histories published in the 1990s. This is because they feature details that are not usually presented in recent literature, which, in turn, often points to these works as references. Note also that the chapter deals with preliminary (but not strictly essential) information regarding Japanese animation, so it can be skipped by readers who are either familiar with the topic, or primarily interested in the *WMT* case. It still provides some context, and could be useful to non-specialized audiences.

Adaptation and animation

Fiction and learning often go together. Storytelling not only provides entertainment and captures emotions but also generates meaningful patterns that help us understand the world we live in.[1] This is particularly notable in children's books, given the didactic approach traditionally associated with juvenile literature. Moving pictures, on both the big screen and the small screen, are always in need of stories, engaging viewers in ripples of effects. Therefore, it is not surprising that, in the age of mass media, the adaptation of verbal texts into visual ones is such a common and successful narrative technique[2] and a well-known practice in the mass media environment. In spite of the number of box-office hits and TV shows based on juvenile fiction, until recent years the area has received little critical attention.[3] From a theoretic point of view, discourses on adaptation, once framed 'in negative terms of loss',[4] call for a move beyond the fidelity-based approach that regarded literature as a superior authority. In fact, written sources and audiovisual works belong to different semiotic systems, thus presenting autonomous signification processes, but are close to each other in terms of diegetic structures and recipient inferences.[5]

Adaptation actually implies a more re-inventive effort than translation, demanding to interpret a text through a show-don't-tell strategy,[6] as well as to decode (and recode) sociocultural patterns embedded in a narrative that is

---

[1] Janice McDrury and Maxine Alterio, *Learning Through Storytelling in Higher Education: Using Reflection and Experience to Improve Learning* (London and New York: Routledge, 2003).
[2] Deborah Cartmell and Imelda Whelehan, *Adaptations: From Text to Screen, Screen to Text* (London: Routledge, 2005).
[3] Deborah Cartmell, 'Adapting Children's Literature', in *The Cambridge Companion to Literature on Screen*, ed. D. Cartmell and I. Whelehan (Cambridge: Cambridge University Press, 2007).
[4] Linda Hutcheon, *A Theory of Adaptation* (London: Taylor & Francis, 2012), 37.
[5] Armando Fumagalli, *I vestiti nuovi del narratore* (Milano: Il Castoro, 2004).
[6] Robert McKee, *Story: Substance, Structure, Style, and the Principles of Screenwriting* (New York: ReganBooks, 1997).

able to disseminate role models and beliefs.[7] Besides, in the field of children's fiction, discussions extend to the pedagogical and ideological underpinnings of the agencies involved.[8] Bearing in mind that formal, cultural, textual and contextual aspects are inextricably linked, I will use a plural methodology.[9]

If we consider adaptation for animation, there are distinctive factors to highlight. Not only screenwriting has different rules than writing a novel, as how-to books by story analysts and editors constantly remind us,[10] but animation is a language in itself, allowing a wide range of dramatic effects – from worldbuilding to camera movements.[11] Furthermore, being both a technology and an industrial process, animation involves a set of practical limitations, as well as economic and financial elements, in addition to the semiotic aspects of the literary passage into other media and formats. This seems especially important for Japan, where animated works based on popular manga are extremely common and commercially successful, although the adaptation of such texts has received less critical attention than other types of analysis. Something similar could be said for the anime of the *WMT*, which have often been mentioned in anime histories in relation to the future parable of Studio Ghibli, but have never been studied per se, and will be the object of the next chapters of this book.

Anime and animation

As Denison points out, there are various meanings associated to anime, depending on the context.[12] In Japanese texts, アニメーション (*animēshon* [animation]) and its shortened form アニメ (*anime* [animated cartoons]) are often used interchangeably. Historically, other terms have been used too, including 線画 (*senga* [line art]), 凸坊新畫帖 (*dekōbo shin gachō* [mischievous new pictures]), 魔術 (*majutsu* [magic]), 漫画映画 (*manga eiga* [cartoon films]), 動画 (*dōga* [moving pictures]) and テレビまんが (*terebi manga* [television cartoons]). However, 'anime' is the most common modern word to indicate animation made in Japan. It is also an umbrella

---

[7]George Gerbner et al., 'Growing up with Television: Cultivation Processes', in *Media Effects: Advances in Theory and Research*, ed. Jennings Bryant and Mary Beth Oliver (New York: Routledge, 2009).
[8]Benjamin Lefebvre, *Textual Transformations in Children's Literature: Adaptations, Translations, Reconsiderations* (New York: Routledge, 2013).
[9]Kamilla Elliott, 'Rethinking Formal-cultural and Textual-contextual Divides in Adaptation Studies', *Literature/Film Quarterly* 42, no. 4 (2014): 576–93.
[10]John Truby, *The Anatomy of Story: 22 Steps to Becoming a Master Storyteller* (NewYork: Faber and Faber, 2008); Bobette Buster, *Do Story: How to Tell Your Story so the World Listens* (New York: The Do Book Company, 2013).
[11]Jean Ann Wright, *Animation Writing and Development: from Screen Development to Pitch* (New York: Routledge, 2005).
[12]Rayna Denison, *Anime: A Critical Introduction* (London: Bloomsbury, 2015), 2.

term referring to different media and formats, such as TV series, theatrical movies, commercials and video games. Adding to the complexity is the fact that anime is genre-rich (according to a recent study, there are over 150 anime genres and subgenres[13]), and caters to different demographic niches. At the same time, especially in the Western world, there is a tendency to view anime as a genre, popularly connected to an audience of older kids and young adults. Anime has also become a transcultural phenomenon, which ignited imitation from other countries, blurring the boundaries between anime and animation.

This multiplicity is reflected in the scholarly approaches to anime, which range from textual to cultural analyses, and beyond. Considering that Japanese animation, and animation in general, is the product of modern printing and media technologies,[14] or, as Hu puts it, a latecomer industrial art,[15] particularly interesting is Lamarre's attempt to investigate the material processes of what he calls 'the anime machine'.[16] Lamarre focuses on cel animation, which is made by hand, and represents Japan's most common animation technique. In cel animation, a series of drawings are transferred or copied onto celluloid sheets (hence the abbreviation 'cel'), and coloured in. These images are then layered, photographed in sequence and projected fast enough to give the illusion of movement, that is, twenty-four frames per second. Most of the character movements can be rendered with twelve drawings per second, or 'on twos', as each drawing is reused two times. More sophisticated movements may require 'on ones', or twenty-four different drawings. You can also decrease the number of cels by animating 'on threes', shooting the same eight drawings for three times. The two poles of the process are called full and limited animation, and are often associated, respectively, with Disney's classic animation and Japan's anime.

However, these processes are not to be viewed as a geopolitical divide. Being the most traditional form of animation, cel animation is present everywhere in the world. Yet it is true that modern computer animation is now widespread in many countries, while most of Japan's anime still looks like cel animation, although digitalization has rendered the use of film stock almost obsolete.[17] In particular, Lamarre notes that the specificity of anime, or animetic animation, seems to lie in 2D compositing, or the editing of image layers, which have a flat, diorama-like style. For example, Lamarre

---

[13]Hyerim Cho et al., 'Facet Analysis of Anime Genres: The Challenges of Defining Genre Information for Popular Cultural Objects', *Knowledge Organization* 45 (2018): 484–99.
[14]Gilles Poitras, 'Contemporary Anime in Japanese Pop Culture', in *Japanese Visual Culture: Explorations in the World of Manga and Anime*, ed. Mark W. MacWilliams (London: Routledge, 2015), 49.
[15]Tze-Yue G. Hu, *Frames of Anime: Culture and Image-Building* (Hong Kong: Hong Kong University Press, 2010), 23.
[16]Thomas Lamarre, *The Anime Machine: A Media Theory of Animation* (Minneapolis: University of Minnesota Press, 2010).
[17]Hu, *Frames of Anime*.

mentions one sequence in スチームボーイ (*Suchīmubōi* [*Steamboy*]) (Otomo Katsuhiro, 2004), where the landscape elements look like cut out layers, or the panoramic scenes of several Miyazaki's movies, whose dynamism resides in the sliding planes of the animated images, rather than in simulating tridimensional movement. On the contrary, this is emphasized in cinematic animation, which creates a sense of depth and geometric perspective according to the Cartesian model. Think of the opening scene of Disney's *Pinocchio* (1940), where the multiplane camera allows to mimic the effect of a swooping crane shot, flying over, and through, the streets of a village.[18]

Animetic and cinematic animation are not mutually exclusive, nor, as said about the techniques of limited and full animation, are they typical of Japanese and American animation only. According to Lamarre, an advantage of considering the technical determinators of animation is that they challenge the 'Japan versus the West' dichotomic approach, which often underlies narrative or thematic analyses, reinforcing the myth of Japanese and Western unity. At the same time, it seems helpful to take contexts such as historic and biographical data into account, in order to prevent generalizing risks. For example, Lamarre's approach connects cinematism to violence and war, but Miyazaki's movies would fall into this category, as he also animates into the picture plane. Think of the sea in 紅の豚 (*Kurenai no buta* [*Crimson pig*]) (1992), internationally known as *Porco Rosso*, which is brilliantly animated so that it seems that we are flying over and into the picture. As anime and animation refuse a singular interpretation, it is worth factorizing technical, textual and cultural aspects.

Traditions of Japanese animation

In a similar way to what Lamarre notes about the animetic aesthetics of flatness, researchers and practitioners have identified parallels between Japan's animation and art, tracing connections with older traditions of visual storytelling. For example, 高畑 勲 (Takahata Isao) (1935–2018) viewed 絵巻物 (*emakimono* [picture scrolls]) as 'twelfth century animation', drawing attention to the similarities with animation, such as the use of contour lines or the consequential flow of the narratives.[19] Also, critics compared the flat composition of anime to 浮世絵 (*ukiyoe* [pictures of the floating world]), multicoloured woodblock prints which, from the seventeenth to the nineteenth century, portrayed the everyday life and

---

[18]Vanessa E. Greenwood, *Navigating Media Literacy: A Pedagogical Tour of Disneyland* (Bloomfield: Myers Education Press, 2020), 134.
[19]Isao Takahata, *Jūniseiki no animēshon: kokuhō emakimono ni miru eiga teki anime teki narumono* [*Twelfth century animation: seeing the cinematic and anime-like aspects in the national treasures, emakimono*] (Tokyo: Tokuma Shoten, 2008).

landscapes of Japanese towns.[20] Popular forms of entertainment, too, have been associated to anime, starting from 紙芝居 (*kamishibai* [paper play]), a street theatre for children, whereby a storyteller would tell a story pulling out a sequence of illustrated cards, especially in the 1940s and 1950s.[21] Japan's first animated series were actually criticized as 電動紙芝居 (*dendō kamishibai* [electric paper play]) for their limited movements.[22]

However, the closer we look at Japan's history of animation, the less homogenous the panorama appears. Especially prior to the advent of television, there were different techniques other than cel animation, including puppetry, cutout and stop motion. For example, animator 大藤 信郎 (Ōfuji Noburō) (1900–61) was famous for his experiments with *chiyogami* (cutout paper patterns) and silhouette animation, inspired by Lotte Reiniger's works. Hence, several anime scholars agree that the term 'anime' is not suitable to describe all Japanese animation, as it oversimplifies Japan's local animation production culture.[23] Aside from Ōfuji's independent artwork, Japan's early animation was commercialized as soon as in the 1920s and 1930s, creating ties with domestic film companies like Nikkatsu.[24] At the same time, pre-war animation was an assortment of small groups based around a senior animator, who would train a number of disciples in a sort of esoteric fashion.[25] To some extent, this situation has similarities with the modern day, despite the international impact of Japanese animation. There are around 800 small animation companies in Japan, with a bunch of larger studios, such as Tōei Animation, Production I.G, Sunrise and Kyoto Animation.[26]

Following on Tsugata, Steinberg approaches the variety of Japanese animation by dividing it into two main streams.[27] One is the 'anime-proper' tradition, which focuses on the relation between animation and manga, finding expression in the new medium of television. The other is the Disney-influenced axis, which favours the relation between animation and cinema,

---

[20]Dani Cavallaro, *Anime and Memory: Aesthetic, Cultural and Thematic Perspectives* (Jefferson: McFarland & Company, 2009), 20.
[21]Marc Steinberg, 'Immobile Sections and Trans-Series Movement: Astroboy and the Emergence of Anime', *Animation: An Interdisciplinary Journal* 1, no. 2 (2006): 190–206.
[22]Kaori Chiba, *Haiji ga umareta hi: terebi anime no kinjitō o kizuita hitobito* [*The day Heidi was born: people who built the landmark of television animation*] (Tokyo: Iwanami Shoten, 2017), 39.
[23]For example, see: Jonathan Clements, *Anime: A History* (London: The British Film Institute, 2013).
[24]Nobuyuki Tsugata, 'A Bipolar Approach to Understanding the History of Japanese Animation', in *Japanese Animation: East Asian Perspectives*, ed. Masao Yokota and Tze-yue G. Hu (Jackson: University Press of Mississippi, 2013), 27.
[25]Steinberg, 'Immobile Sections and Trans-Series Movement', 196.
[26]Association of Japanese Animation, 'Anime Industry Report 2022: Summary', 2023. Available online: https://aja.gr.jp/download/2022_anime_ind_rpt_summary_en (accessed 18 July 2023); although a bit dated, see also Ian Condry, *The Soul of Anime: Collaborative Creativity and Japan's Media Success Story* (Durham: Duke University Press, 2013), 1–35.
[27]Steinberg, 'Immobile Sections and Trans-Series Movement'.

and whose physical apparatus is the film theatre. Since the two traditions are characterized, respectively, by the use of limited and full animation, I will name them 'animetic' and 'cinematic', borrowing from Lamarre's terminology. Thus, the following paragraphs will explore how both traditions evolved historically, expanding on the way they tackled children's literature. In particular, I will argue that the animetic tradition favoured manga-to-anime adaptation, catering to specific niche demographics, while the cinematic tradition centred on children's literature for a mainstream audience. Also, it is worth keeping in mind that, as previously noted, there is no clear-cut distinction in the production of Japanese animation, in the sense that an animated work can be defined as purely cinematic or animetic, so there will be osmosis between the two groups.

Early Japanese animation

Japanese fairy tales, folk tales and legends were used as sources for animation since the Taishō era, when Japan's first animations were created. The earliest one to record, さるかに合戦 (*Saru kani gassen* [*The battle of the monkey and the crab*] (1917), was produced by Nikkatsu, Japan's oldest major, and directed by pioneer animator 北山 清太郎 (Kitayama Seitarō) (1888–1945). The film took inspiration from a Japanese fable where a crab, outwitted by a monkey, is vindicated by its children. Dozens of other shorts would follow, all realized with rudimentary techniques, and usually based on national classic stories, such as the already recalled Momotarō, 西遊記 (*Saiyūki* [*Journey to the West*]) – an ancient Chinese legend novelized in the sixteenth century, about a Buddhist priest and his fellow animal wards traveling to India, which would later inspire *Dragon Ball* – or 忠臣蔵 (*Chūshingura* [*The treasury of loyal retainers*]), a famous tale of vendetta where a group of masterless samurai avenge their lord, based on actual events of the Edo period.[28]

The existence of many film adaptations is not surprising, if we consider that fairy tales and folk tales came with many advantages. As seen in Chapter 1, the genre had long been popular in the country, where many traditional tales were rewritten and adapted as children's stories since the Meiji period. Being concise and entertaining by definition, fairy tales and folk tales translated well to the briefer formats available in the early days of animation. Besides, these stories are commonly familiar to the domestic audience, as they mirror

---

[28]Francesco Prandoni, *Anime al cinema: Storia dell'Animazione Giapponese 1917-1995* (Milano: Yamato Video, 1999), 4.

the ethos of a country.²⁹ Together with indigenous stories, also Western fables and fairy tales were often adapted into animation. Again, this process seems easy to predict, given the success of European *Märchen* in Japan, which welcomed them as a model for the burgeoning tradition of dōwa stories and nursery rhymes. The online archive of Tokyo's National Film Center includes titles inspired by Andersen, Aesop and the *Arabian Nights*, showing the influence of a well-established canon of translated fiction.

Though more rarely, recent Western juvenile books could also inspire early animated films, such as 難船ス物語 第壱篇 猿ヶ嶋 (*Nansensu monogatari daīppen sarugashima* [*Nonsense story: first episode – The monkey*]) (1930), a cutout short about a boy escaping from a deserted island inhabited only by monkeys, probably inspired by *Tarzan*.³⁰ This was the debut work of 政岡 憲三 (Masaoka Kenzō) (1898–1989), a former painter and a self-taught animator, who is remembered for numerous technical achievements, including the use of celluloid, which was employed in the United States since 1919. The brainchild of the American writer Edgar Rice Burroughs, *Tarzan* would appear in many post-war zenshū for the youth, but became a popular icon in Japan as early as in the 1920s, when the word 'Tarzan' was synonym with a general jungle setting for the audience, due to the enthusiastic reception of Hollywood silent films.³¹ So, while fairy tales and folk tales quickly gained currency among writers and animators, modern fiction, too, made its way into adaptation, and would provide increasingly more contents for the Japanese media.

Japanese animation during the war period

During the 1930s, as the Pacific War broke out, popular children's manga such as のらくろ (*Norakuro* [*Black stray*]), about a clumsy dog soldier, were adapted for animation as militaristic icons, similarly to what was happening with Disney's Donald Duck and other American characters overseas.³² Another source of inspiration came from the creatures of Japanese folklore, such as 狸 (*tanuki* [raccoon dogs]), animals native to Japan which are known in fables for their mischievous nature and ability to shape-shift. Tanuki are

---

²⁹Maria Tatar, 'What Is a Fairy Tale?', in *Teaching Fairy Tales*, ed. N. L. Canepa (Detroit: Wayne State University Press, 2019), 15–23.
³⁰Yasushi Watanabe, 'The Japanese Walt Disney: Masaoka Kenzo', in *Japanese Animation: East Asian Perspectives*, ed. Masao Yokota and Tze-yue G. Hu (Jackson: University Press of Mississippi, 2013), 101.
³¹Deanna T. Nardy, 'Tarzan and Japan: Racial Portraits of a Nation in Boy Kenya', in *Japanese Visual Media. Politicizing the Screen*, ed. Jennifer Coates and Eyal Ben-Ari (Abingdon: Routledge, 2022).
³²Prandoni, *Anime al cinema*, 12.

the protagonists of several shorts, such as 動絵狐狸達引 (*Ugoki-e kori no tetehiki* [Moving picture: Fox vs. raccoon dog]) (1933), where they engage in a prank battle with their natural enemy, a (samurai-disguised) fox. The director of the film, 大石 郁雄 (Ōishi Ikuo) (1901–44), was a teacher to many artists of the next generation, such as 芦田巌 (Ashida Iwao) (*c*. 1910–?). They both joined the Shadow Staff, a wartime film unit that made instructional movies commissioned by the Ministry of Army, including animation.[33] These animated works, too, shared some affinities with the folk-tale tradition, such as the use of animal characters. For example, 協力防空戦 (*Kyōryoku Bōkūsen* [Collaborative air defence]) (1942), directed by Ashida, explained how to act in case of bombings using a farm of anthropomorphic animals as location.

As the war escalated, the need for uniquely Japanese cartoons resulted in the propaganda movies 桃太郎の海鷲 (*Momotarō no umiwashi* [Momotaro's sea eagles]) (1941) and 桃太郎 海の神兵 (*Momotarō: Umi no shinpei* [Momotaro: Sacred sea warriors]) (1945), directed by Seo Mitsuyo (瀬尾 光世) (1911–2010), Masaoka's disciple, with the collaboration of his teacher. The film series revolved around the folk tale of Momotarō, the divine boy who defeats vicious demons with the help of his animal friends – a dog, a monkey and a pheasant. The Ministry of Navy, which commissioned these works, used a character known to all Japanese children to inoculate militaristic messages, transforming Momotarō in a patriot and a symbol of colonization, as happened in contemporary children's literature.[34] In particular, the animation contributed to canonize the custom of making animal characters especially cute, which helped to downsize the underpinning nationalist agenda, epitomizing Japan's idealization of the role of the country during the Pacific War.

Modern Japanese stories for children provided material for animation as well. A movie project based on Iwaya's *Koganemaru* started in 1941 and was later abandoned to produce films for the Army.[35] Instead, Masaoka's くもとちゅうりっぷ (*Kumo to chūrippu* [The spider and the tulip]) (1943), adapted from a fairy tale by the children's writer 横山 美智子 (Yokoyama Michiko) (1895–1986), was released in theatres. This work, the story of a ladybug who serendipitously escapes from an evil spider, is regarded as a landmark of Japanese animation for its naturalistic scenery and sheer animation. In spite of the Japaneseness of the film, other cultural influences are also palpable. It has been noted that Masaoka's spider resembles the Hollywood comedian Harold Loyd, as well as the blackface character played by Al Jolson in *The Jazz Singer* (1927).[36] In addition, stories about

---

[33]Jonathan Clements and Barry Ip, 'The Shadow Staff: Japanese Animators in the Tōhō Aviation Education Materials Production Office 1939–1945', *Animation* 7, no. 2 (2012): 189–204.
[34]Carter, 'A Study on Japanese Children's Magazines 1888-1949', 174–5.
[35]Prandoni, *Anime al cinema*, 14.
[36]Watanabe, 'The Japanese Walt Disney', 105.

insects were common in the shorts by Disney (*Bugs in Love*, 1932) and the Fleischers (*The Cobweb Hotel*, 1936), while translations of Jean-Henry Fabre's *Souvenirs entomologiques* (1879), a famous French textbook on insects, were often featured in Japanese book sets for the youth. Also the emphasis on depth of field, especially in the storm sequence, is close to Disney's cinematic animation in *The Old Mill* (1937).[37]

The influence of American films

What the foregoing seems to suggest is that the influence of the West, and especially of American cinema, was taking hold in Japan. Like children's literature, American animation was imported to the country, deeply impacting popular culture. American animated shorts were shown in Japanese theatres around 1930, during the transition to the talkies, proving widely successful. In this period, characters such as Mickey Mouse and Betty Boop became so popular that there were cafés named after them.[38] Critics praised the smooth movements and three-dimensional feel of American cartoons, criticizing Japanese animation for its flat look.[39] On the other hand, appraised animators such as Masaoka and Ōishi were compared to Disney for their skills, Ōishi's works being redolent of the *diableries* of the Fleischer brothers too. American animation became both a benchmark and a competitor for Japan's animation, which was more expensive to make, and therefore less appealing to distributors. Suffice to say that producing a film in Japan would cost as much as purchasing the rights for two movies of Mickey Mouse and Popeye.[40]

With the escalation of the war, American works, both literary and audiovisual, were banned by the fascist regime, including Disney movies produced after *Snow White and the Seven Dwarfs* (1937). However, the influence of American-style animation did not fade away. Seo notoriously took inspiration from *Fantasia* (1940), which was screened in secret at the Ministry of Navy, for the cute, humanized animal characters of his 'Momotarō' films.[41] American cartoons were also used for satire. For example, the poster of *Momotarō no umiwashi* shows Popeye and Betty

---

[37]Laura Montenero-Plata and Marie Pruvost-Delaspre, 'Shaping the Anime Industry: Second Generation Pioneers and the Emergence of the Studio System', in *A Companion to Japanese Cinema*, ed. David Desser (Malden: Wiley, 2022), 224.
[38]Akiko Sano, '*Chiyogami*, Cartoon, Silhouette. The Transitions of Ōfuji Noburō', in *Japanese Animation: East Asian Perspectives*, ed. Masao Yokota and Tze-yue G. Hu (Jackson: University Press of Mississippi, 2013), 89.
[39]Ibid., 90.
[40]Prandoni, *Anime al cinema*, 14.
[41]Ibid., 27.

Boop drowning, utterly defeated. Moreover, the military's investment in animation brought Japan's independent ateliers closer to a Disney-inspired Taylorist business model, fostering the use of cel animation as it was customary in the United States.[42] The same Ōfuji pursued American-style cel animation for a while, as happens in 空の荒鷲 (*Sora no arawashi* [*Eagles in the sky*]) (1938), a wartime movie where animal characters fight against giant clouds with the shape of Popeye.[43]

During and after the American Occupation, the American influence obviously grew stronger. American animated films were cumulatively released in Japan, from the short films by Terrytoons (*Mighty Mouse*) and Hanna & Barbera (*Tom & Jerry* and *Woody Woodpecker*) to feature films by Disney (*Snow White, Bambi, Pinocchio, Cinderella, Alice, Dumbo*) and the Fleischers (*Gulliver's Travels, Mr Bug Goes to Town*). These works enthralled Japanese viewers of all ages, including future animators and manga artists. Always a cinema buff, young 手塚 治虫 Tezuka Osamu (1928–89) reported to have seen over 365 films in a year, watching *Snow White* over fifty times, and *Bambi* over eighty times.[44] Future Ghibli founders Takahata and 宮崎 駿 (Miyazaki Hayao) (born 1941) were also greatly influenced by the energetic animation of the Fleischers, as noted for *Mr Bug Goes to Town* (1941).[45]

It is worth stressing that all these movies were either inspired by Western fairy tales or children's books, often featuring cute, anthropomorphic animal characters. Similarly to American imported animation, early postwar Japanese works revolved around animal stories and Western fairy tales, which were probably perceived as safer materials not to incur into the SCAP censorship. At the same time, these stories belonged to Japan's own literary tradition which canonized folk tales and fairy tales, both indigenous and of Western origin, as highbrow children's fiction. Significantly, the first animated work made after the war was Ashida's 昆虫天国 (*Konchu tengoku* [*Insect heaven*]) (1945), again on the fortunate theme of entomology, in which a butterfly is kidnapped by a spider and saved by a group of insects. A cartoon Pinocchio appeared in ちどり (*Chidori* [*Plovets*]) (1947), the first Japanese film mixing animation and live action, in which a little girl learns about parental care by seeing adult birds looking after their chicks.[46] In 1948, Ashida also directed バグダッド姫 (*Bagudaddo no hime* [*Baghdad's princess*]), Japan's first animated feature film based on the *Arabian Nights*,

---

[42]Hikari Hori, *Promiscuous Media. Film and Visual Culture in Imperial Japan, 1926–1945* (Ithaca: Cornell University Press, 2018), 203.
[43]Prandoni, *Anime al cinema*, 13.
[44]Frederik Schodt, *The Astro Boy Essays: Osamu Tezuka, Mighty Atom, and the Manga/Anime revolution* (Berkley: Stone Bridge Press, 2007), 59.
[45]'Komento' [Comment], *Ghibli Museum*, 10 October 2009. Available online: https://www.ghibli-museum.jp/batta/comment/ (accessed 7 February 2023).
[46]Clements, *Anime*.

another fantasy trope frequently borrowed by Hollywood cinema, as well as a recurring feature in children's literature since the Meiji era.

The Allies took a keen interest in the film industry[47] and actively supported the production of Japanese animated movies for propagandistic ends. In late 1945, under the auspices of the SCAP, the pioneer animator 山本早苗 (Yamamoto Sanae) (1898–1981) recruited about 100 people involved in animation production, including veterans Masaoka and Seo, to establish Shin Nihon Dōgasha, meaning 'new Japanese animation studio'.[48] This production company released shorts and cooperative projects with other film studios, incorporating values welcomed by the Occupation such as freedom and democracy.[49] For example, Masaoka's film すて猫トラちゃん (*Suteneko Tora-chan* [*Little Tora, the abandoned cat*]) (1947) featured an orphan kitten being adopted by a feline family – orphans and widows being tragically numerous in the period – against the backdrop of Western motifs like Christmas decorations and sunflowers, a typical American species. Although the name Tora (Tiger) is common for a cat in Japanese, it reminds the homonymous child character of 虎ちゃんの日記 (*Tora-chan no nikki* [*Little Tora's diary*]) (1929), a famous children's story by the novelist 千葉省三 (Chiba Shōzō) (1892–1975). Shōzō was the editor of 童話 (*Dōwa*), an influential literary magazine in the fashion of *Akai tori*, and it is possible that his legacy inspired Masaoka's work. Also Western tales about lonely children were adapted to screen by other companies, such as Andersen's 'The Little Match Girl', which inspired two silhouette movies in 1947.[50]

Tōei and the cinematic tradition

Masaoka's *Tora-chan* had a catchy operetta soundtrack (the composer scored many films of the period as well as doing classical compositions[51]) and was animated on one, sharing many similarities with the Silly Symphony's *The Three Orphan Kittens* (1935).[52] This short, on the adventures of three cats taking shelter in a house, experimented with the use of perspective for

---

[47]David Bordwell and Kristin Thompson, *Film History: An Introduction* (Boston: McGraw-Hill Education, 1995), 462.
[48]Hori, *Promiscuous Media*.
[49]Hu, *Frames of Anime*, 78.
[50]Maria Roberta Novielli, *Floating Worlds: A Short History of Japanese Animation* (Boca Raton: Taylor & Francis, 2018).
[51]Catherine Munroe Hotes, 'Tora-chan, The Abandoned Kitten (すて猫トラちゃん, 1947)', *Nishikata Film Review*, 5 June 2010. Available online: https://www.nishikata-eiga.com/2010/06/tora-chan-abandoned-kitten-1947.html (accessed 7 February 2023).
[52]Montenero-Plata and Pruvost-Delaspre, 'Shaping the Anime Industry', 237.

realistic effects prior to the invention of the multiplane camera,⁵³ which were emulated by Masaoka. However, the Japanese kittens look more anthropomorphic, with clothes and other human amenities, as in *The Milky Way* (1940), by Rudolf Ising, a former Disney animator who was more inclined towards 'warmth and cuteness' (in the film, three kittens dream to fly to the galaxy filled with dairy food).⁵⁴ More 'Tora-chan' films were directed by Masaoka in 1948 and 1950, all poorly received due to the appalling conditions of Japan in the immediate post-war, but much appreciated by the public for their cute look and cinematic quality. As was the case for Seo's works, they left a long-lasting imprint on future Japanese animation, anticipating 可愛い (*kawaii* [cute]) and 萌え (*moe* [crush for a fictional character]) styles of cuteness. But how could the cinematic style become so influential in the long run?

A turning point was when Nichidō Eigasha, as Nihon Dōga was renamed in 1952, released the colour short film うかれバイオリン (*Ukare baiorin* [*The merry violin*]) (1955). As the title seems to suggest, this work was probably based on the old English tale 'A Mery Geste of the Frere and the Boye', which is featured in several Japanese book series of the period, such as Kōdansha no ehon.⁵⁵ Since in the original story, a variation on the Pied Piper trope, a poor boy is awarded a magic violin that makes everyone dance, it is possible to imagine a musical animation on the fashion of Disney's *Silly Symphonies* and their accolades. The film was commissioned by the Educational Film Department of Tōei, a newly born film studio established in 1951, and the latest of Japan's film majors to emerge in the post-war. Happy with the results, its president, 大川 博 (Okawa Hiroshi) (1897–1971), asked Nichidō for another film, this time a feature based on a Chinese folk tale, the story of two star-crossed lovers, a boy and a beautiful princess who is actually a snake.

As is known, the movie was 白蛇伝 (*Hakujaden* [*White snake enchantress*]) (1958), Asia's first colour animated feature film,⁵⁶ which left a strong impression on generations of future animators, marking the beginning of Toei's own animation studio, Tōei Dōga. This was founded in 1956 by acquiring Nichidō, which was in dire straits.⁵⁷ Tōei's budget (the film cost over 40 million yen) and the presence of a group of skilled pre-war

---

⁵³Krystina Madej and Lee Newton, *Disney Stories: Getting to Digital* (Cham: Springer, 2021), 58.
⁵⁴Michael Barrier, *Hollywood Cartoons: American Animation in Its Golden Age* (New York: Oxford University Press), 300.
⁵⁵A book titled *Ukare baiorin*, illustrated by 嶺田弘 (Mineda Hiroshi) (1900–65) and written by 宇野 浩二 (Uno Kōji) (1891–1961), was published in this series in 1950.
⁵⁶Giannalberto Bendazzi, *Animation: A world History, Volume II The Birth of a Style – The Three Markets* (Boca Raton: CRC Press, 2016), 85.
⁵⁷Prandoni, *Anime al cinema*, 21.

artists, such as 森康二 (Mori Yasuji) (1925–92), a disciple of Masaoka, and 大工原章 (Daikubara Akira) (1917–2012), who cut his teeth with Ashida, played a key role in the success of *Hakujaden*. Nichidō's staff trained Tōei's new recruits – including young talents like 大塚康生 (Ōtsuka Yasuo) (1931–2021) – and showed them the ropes of cinematic animation, with realistic movements and multiplanar effects of depth. It is not by chance that the studio would later get famous as 'Tōei Dōga University', the title being only half humorous.[58] Former Nichidō's artists could also count on their expertise in creating stories for children, exploiting musical numbers, cute character designs and amusing gags.[59] In particular, the innocent look of the characters, the exotic setting and the use of comical animal counterparts in *Hakujaden* have been interpreted as a way for animators to renegotiate (and detach from) Japan's wartime cruelty.[60] At the same time, as seen, this style was in line with the cinematic tradition of Japan's American-inspired animation.

The Disney model

The idea of making animation based on children's fiction was not new, nor was the fascination for American animation. Already in 1955, the manga artist 横山 隆一 (Yokoyama Ryūichi) (1909–2001), who during the Occupation had been able to meet Walt Disney and visit his studio as a reporter for the *Mainichi shinbun*, founded Otogi Pro (from おとぎ, *otogi* [fairy tale]), a production company creating experimental animation based on fairy tales, both Japanese and from the world.[61] However, differently from Yokoyama's more authorial works (which raised concerns from distributor Toho), Ōkawa was the first to believe in the commercial power of Japan's animation and had ambitious plans to turn Tōei into the 'Disney of the East'.[62] His strategy focused on emulating Disney's business model and mission, producing feature-length animated films on an industrial basis, with modern technologies and catering to a general audience. These films would foster positive values close to the cultural agenda of the Allies, such as 'love for humanity' and 'ethics'.[63]

Tōei's promotion, too, mirrored Disney. In the original trailer of *Hakujaden*, Ōkawa addressed the viewers from his office, with models

---

[58] Clements, *Anime*.
[59] Montenero-Plata and Pruvost-Delaspre, 'Shaping the Anime Industry', 232.
[60] According to Hu, Tōei animators wanted to correct the country's image of *warui kuni* (bad country), by creating something new and comforting; Hu, *Frames of Anime*, 83–95.
[61] Bendazzi, *Animation*, 88.
[62] Condry, *The Soul of Anime*, 89.
[63] Hu, *Frames of Anime*, 90.

of the characters visible on his desk, introducing 'Toei Animation Studio' as a dream studio equipped with the latest state-of-the art technology. In 漫画映画のできるまで (*Manga eiga no dekiru made* [*How cartoon movies are made*]) (1959), a promotional video for the movie 少年猿飛佐助 (*Shōnen Sarutobi Sasuke* [*The boy Sarutobi Sasuke*]), we see Tōei's artists at work, copying the poses of real actors and animals. These strategies were also employed to promote current Disney films in the anthological TV series Walt Disney's *Disneyland* (1954–8). The parallels are even stronger if we look at the trailūr of *Saiyūki* (1960), which begins with a sequence mixing cel animation and live action where Goku, the monkey protagonist, knocks at Ōkawa's door and briefly interacts with his 社長 (*shachō* [president]), like Disney did with his cartoon characters since the TV series *Walt Disney Presents* (1958–61).

Tōei's domestication of Disney's practices also involved the use of classic stories as a base for animation. In fact, Tōei's early works were period films inspired by Japanese stories and legends. However, titles based on foreign children's literature, especially from the Western canon, increased after the film アラビアンナイト・シンドバッドの冒険 (*Arabian naito: Shindobaddo no bōken* [*Arabian nights: The adventures of Sinbad*]) (1962), again on a classic Arabic story. The preference for light-hearted entertainment and cute animal characters, usually designed by Mori, contributed to consolidate the international look of Tōei's movies. A successful example of this foreignization process was the film 長靴をはいた猫 (*Nagagutsu haita neko* [*Puss 'n Boots*]) (1969), a fairy-tale pastiche whose cat protagonist, Pero (from the name of the French author Perrault), would become Tōei's mascot. Even 太陽の王子 ホルスの大冒険 (*Taiyō no ōji Horusu no daibōken* [*Prince of sun: The great adventure of Hols*]), a feature film that marked Takahata's debut as a director, was originally set in Japan (the movie being based on a local puppet play, in turn derived from an Ainu myth), and later shifted to Scandinavia at the behest of Tōei bosses.[64]

International animation

Tōei's interest for Western narratives as sources for animation was consistent not only with the influence of Disney but also with the trends of Japanese children's fiction after the Occupation, a process facilitated by the fact that countless book series popularized fairy tales and children's novels from Europe and America since the pre-war years. Moreover, from the Disney

---

[64]Michelle Le Blanc and Colin Odell, *Studio Ghibli: The films of Hayao Miyazaki and Isao Takahata* (Harpenden: Kamera books, 2009), 42.

model stemmed Tōei's search for export and international cooperation, which would bring more profit and visibility to the Japanese studio.

As a matter of fact, works like *Nagagutsu o haita neko*, which was among the first Japanese animated movies to be released in theatres in several nations in Europe,[65] demonstrated that adaptations of classic Western stories could branch out to the overseas market, targeting children viewers who were already familiar with Disney (and Disney-like) mainstream literary-based animation. Tōei executives, who were especially interested in American investors, in the mid-1960s decided to devote a segment of the staff to American animated contract work.[66] An example of joint production is キングコング００１／７親指トム (*Kingu Kongu 00$^1/_7$ Oyayubi Tom* [*King Kong 00$^1/_7$ Tom Thumb*]) (1967), the first American cartoon outsourced in Japan,[67] mixing classic characters of the American spy cinema and English folklore for a children's audience (in the show, Kong is a kind ape who helps Professor Bond and his two kids, while 'Tom of Thumb' is a secret agent).

The American studio commissioning *King Kong*, Videocraft International (later known as Rankin/Bass), produced animation which was mostly made in Japan. Kimura notes that the process of outsourcing projects was favoured by the lower prices of animation production in the country, leading to bigger profits for Japan, but also to a flow of skills and techniques from the United States.[68] For example, according to 原 徹 (Hara Tōru) (1935–2021), the founder of Topcraft, which specialized in outsourced animation for the United States, for one feature film for the American market his company could receive five times more than the money spent for domestic animated films.[69] This exposed the Japanese staff to different production and adaptation processes, deepening their connection with American culture. In fact, shows by Rankin/Bass, differently from Disney, often dramatized famous American songs, as in *Rudolph the Red-Rosed Reindeer* (1964), or created modernized adaptations of Western children's books, as in *The New Adventures of Pinocchio* (1961), both animated by MOM Productions. This studio, established by the pioneer animator 持永 只仁 (Mochinaga Tadahito) (1919–99), was responsible for Animagic, or the 'herky-jerky' stop motion technique Rankin/Bass is remembered for.[70] So, to some extent,

---

[65] Jonathan Clements and Helen McCarthy, *The Anime Encyclopedia: A Guide to Japanese Animation Since 1917* (Berkeley: Stone Bridge Press, 2015).
[66] Hu, *Frames of Anime*, 94.
[67] Michal Daliot-Bul and Nissim Otmazgin, *The Anime Boom in the United States: Lessons for Global Creative Industries* (Cambridge, MA: Harvard East Asian monographs, 2020), 33.
[68] Tomoya Kimura, 'Business and Production: Development and Politics of Outsourcing', in *Japanese Animation in Asia: Transnational Industry, Audiences, and Success*, ed. Marco Pellitteri and Wong Heung-wah (Abingdon: Routledge, 2022), 74.
[69] Quoted in Ibid., 75.
[70] Kevin Sandler, 'Limited Animation 1947-1989', in *Animation*, ed. Scott Curtis (New Brunswick: Rutdgers University Prss, 2019), 100.

subcontracted works supported local production in animation techniques unsuitable for mass production, for their expensive and time-consuming schedules.

The birth of TV

It is worth noting that most Rankin/Bass productions consisted of holiday specials for American television, which were rarely aired in Japan. However, television became capillary diffused in Japan in the 1960s, when colour TV sets, together with car and air conditioners, symbolized the more comfortable lifestyle introduced by the economic boom and were commonly referred to as 三種の神器 (*san shuno shinki* [three sacred treasures]).[71] As happened in the United States ten years earlier, television was a major competitor for the big screen, causing a decline of cinema in the 1960s and 1970s.[72] Suffice to say that, of the over 8,000 theatres reported in Japan in 1960, more than 5,000 closed by 1975.

This had an impact on animation, including larger companies like Tōei, whose growing attention to foreign sales was certainly dependent on a turbulent internal situation. In fact, after *Hakujaden*, Ōkawa began to produce feature films at the pace of one per year, which meant harsher schedules – and a lot of unpaid overtime work – for the staff, leading to union battles that would continue up until the 1970s. These issues worsened in 1966, when, as a countermeasure against the rise of television, Tōei started to release three annual films, two in limited animation for the domestic market, and one in full animation with an eye for export, reinforcing the feeling among the staff that animators were factory workers rather than artists.[73] Another blow was given from the reorganization of the company in the early 1970s, under the presidency of 岡田 茂 (Okada Shigeru) (1924–2011), after the oil crisis prompted a restructuring of many industries. In order to cut corners, Tōei laid off employees and quit hiring, offering piecework instead of permanent contracts. A diaspora of talents would follow, either migrating to other studios or founding their own. This way, as Clements notes, Tōei 'was responsible for the training of the bulk of the anime industry, but in doing so they created countless enemies'.[74] At

---

[71] The definition comes from the Japanese Imperial Regalia (sword, mirror and jewel), legendary objects of divine origin symbolizing the Confucian values of valour, wisdom and benevolence. See Fred R. Schumann, *Changing Trends in Japan's Employment and Leisure Activities: Implications for Tourism Marketing* (Singapore: Springer, 2017), 35.
[72] Shunya Yoshimi, 'Japanese Television: Early Development and Research', in *A Companion to Television*, ed. Janet Wasko (Malden, MA: Blackwell, 2005), 541.
[73] Prandoni, *Anime al cinema*, 38.
[74] Clements, *Anime*.

the same time, the advent of the new media paved the way for the creation of different formats and types of productions, prompting Japan's studios to start a new chapter in the history of animation.

Tezuka and the animetic tradition

It seems safe to say that many aspects typically associated to Japanese animation today belong to the animetic tradition. This was heralded by Tezuka, one of the many rivals Tōei inadvertently raised.[75] A prolific self-taught mangaka (and graduated physician) who is often remembered as マンガの神様 (*manga no kami-sama* [god of manga]), his drawing speed was legendary, and by the 1950s he created almost 250 works, including magazine serials and book-form comics,[76] becoming the richest commercial artist of the Kansai region.[77] Tōei approached Tezuka because of this popularity, and had him storyboard and direct *Saiyūki*, a feature film based on his successful manga ぼくのそんごくう (*Boku no Songoku* [*My Songoku*]) (1952–9), which was in turn a retelling of the already mentioned Chinese story *Journey to the West*. The arrangement was convenient on both sides. While the idea of animating a narrative, which was (and still is) extremely famous all over Asia, was in line with Tōei's export aims, for Tezuka it was a chance to learn the ropes of animation. He had been highly impressed by the Chinese animated film *Tiě shàn gōngzhǔ* (*Princess Iron Fan*) (1941), an adaptation on the same subject of *Saiyūki* made by the Wan brothers, and set his goals on becoming an animator since he watched Seo's 'Momotarō' films. He was also an estimator of Disney animation, which was another point of contact with Tōei. Moreover, Tezuka's comics revealed the influence of Western juvenile fiction and Japanese classic stories, the same materials which Tōei chose as sources for animation.

Therefore it does not seem surprising that, aside from *Saiyūki*, Tezuka provided the concept for Tōei's feature わんわん忠臣蔵 (*Wanwan chūshingura* [*Woof-woof treasury of loyal retainers*]) (1963), a retelling of the samurai epic in which all the parts are played by dogs.[78] Both films did well in box offices, and *Saiyūki* was exported to the United States. However, the collaboration with the studio ended shortly after. There were practical reasons, such as Tezuka's conflicting schedules as a manga artist,

---

[75]Ibid.
[76]Helen McCarthy, *The Art of Osamu Tezuka God of Manga* (Lewes: Ilex), 248.
[77]Hu, *Frames of Anime*, 96.
[78]Johnatan Clements, 'The Curious Case of the Dog in Prime Time', in *Sherlock Holmes and Philosophy: The Footprints of a Gigantic Mind*, ed. Steiff Josef (Chicago and La Salle: Open Court, 2011), 310.

and the completion of his PhD, which resulted in delays for the production of *Saiyūki*.⁷⁹ Most importantly, Tezuka had different ideas on animation, and these collided with Tōei. For example, he suggested a non-happy ending for *Saiyūki*, a type of conclusion which was widely accepted in comics, but was vetoed by Tōei,⁸⁰ arguably because it went against the conventions of mainstream cinema.

This prompted Tezuka to found his own company, Tezuka Dōga Gaisha, in 1961. Drawn by his fame and artistic vision, many Tōei animators flocked to Tezuka's studio, later renamed as Mushi Production. If Tōei focused on sumptuous, Disney-style adaptations for a family audience, Tezuka aimed at producing original animation with less time, drawings and money. Significantly, Mushi's debut was an experimental film, ある街角の物語 (*Aru machikado no monogatari* [*Tale of a street corner*]) (1962), with a modernist design (the story is set in a fantastic street where characters from posters come alive), on the theme of life after ruins – a leitmotiv in Tezuka's works.⁸¹ This gained Mushi prizes and critical attention, but the costs were much higher than thought, a problem which Tezuka would have inherited for the next step he was planning: making animated TV series.⁸²

Inspired by Tezuka's own manga with the same name, 鉄腕アトム (*Tetsuwan Atomu* [*Iron arm Atom*]) started airing in 1963 on the commercial network Fuji Television, pulling in ratings of 27.4 per cent. The story revolved around the futuristic adventures of a child robot with 100,000 horsepower – and a golden heart – echoing a type of male-oriented fiction which was extremely popular in Japanese children's literature during the war period, though stripped of the imperialistic connotation. It was not new for a Japanese TV show to be based on a manga (the same *Atom* was adapted into a live action TV series in 1960), nor was *Atom* the very first animated TV series in Japan.⁸³ However, it was the first time that a Japanese studio made complex serialized animation for Japanese TV. To do so, Tezuka adopted practices that were not innovative per se, but the way they were assembled together proved that Japan's animation could be extremely profitable in the ancillary markets of merchandise and commercials, igniting the rise of animated TV series.

---

⁷⁹Prandoni, *Anime al cinema*, 22.
⁸⁰Natsu Onoda Power, *God of Comics: Osamu Tezuka and the Creation of Post-World War II Manga* (Jackson: University Press of Mississippi, 2009), 131.
⁸¹Prandoni, *Anime al cinema*, 28.
⁸²Clements, *Anime*.
⁸³おとぎマンガカレンダー (*Otogi manga karendā* [*Otogi manga calendar*]) (1961) was the first domestic animated series, consisting of three-minute shorts to explain various historical events; Clements and McCarthy, *The Anime Encyclopedia*, 388.

Atom's revolution

Tezuka's animetic revolution had much to do with the innovations he introduced as a manga artist. Tezuka's contribution to Japanese comics was twofold. Technically, he used cinema grammar and framing techniques, such as close-ups, angled perspectives and other linguistic elements which made manga increasingly closer to storyboards. Narratively, he is remembered as the father of the story manga, a genre revolving around serialized plots (as opposed to gag strips or political cartoons[84]), showing the unfolding of the action in chronological order to hook readers release after release. As seen, serialization was an international phenomenon by no means specific of Japanese comics, which inherited the publishing pattern and target diversification of pre-war popular journals. However, with Tezuka, manga achieved a level of sophistication that was absent in previous comics. This affected animation, since Tezuka chose his own comics as a basis to produce animated series. From his seminal series *Atom* descended the animetic style which would become the template for TV animation in the years to come.

Narratively, this established the practice of manga-to-anime adaptation, introducing manga genres and demographics to TV animation. *Atom* also contributed to shape the format of animated TV series, as consisting of long episodes of thirty minutes. Technically, rather than adhering to full animation, or the standards for quality animation set by Disney, Tezuka used limited animation to cope with small production budgets and short lead time of television, which needed weekly instalments, and therefore a more intense pace of work than cinema. Tezuka's goal was animating 'on three', with one cel for every three frames shot, for a total of 2,000–3,000 cels per episode, but in fact he managed to keep the number of drawings under 2,000 (only 900 at the extreme), compensating the reduced ratio with pans and zooms to give the illusion of movement.[85] Another widespread strategy was the バンクシステム (*banku shisustemu* [bank system]), or the re-use of frequent scenes (e.g. Atom flying).[86]

By turning comics into TV series, Tezuka created a system where his own characters were traveling across media. This is more remarkable if we consider that Tezuka had his own meta-narrative 'star system', or a group of stock characters that he would 'cast' to play different roles in different comics, creating a sense of unity and inside jokes.[87] He was also keen on using

---

[84] Dan Mazur and Alexander Danner, 'The International Graphic Novel', in *The Cambridge Companion to the Graphic Novel*, ed. Stephen E. Tabachnick (Cambridge: Cambridge University Press), 64.
[85] Schodt, *The Astro Boy Essays*, 67; Condry, *The Soul of Anime*, 104.
[86] Such scenes were saved and 'banked' for future use, hence the English loanword term employed by Tezuka; Clements, *Anime*, 131.
[87] Onoda Power, *God of Comics*, 66.

sponsors and merchandise as a way to promote his works and fund further animation production. *Atom* was sponsored by the confectionery company Meiji Seika, which produced chocolates with stickers of the character as gadgets. Other goods including toys, stationery materials, clothes and so on began to appear in the year of broadcasting, for a total of 700 products and over fifty companies involved.[88] This form of commercial exploitation, which groups together television, publishing and advertisement, is known as 'media mix' and represents one of Tezuka's most long-lasting innovations. The synergic relationship between different platforms allowed for an industrial production of TV animation, whose number would skyrocket in the following decades.

It is worth remembering that most of these measures were adopted for reasons of *force majeure*, and thus highly regretted by Tezuka. Hoping to make *Atom* more competitive, in his bid to Fuji Television he agreed to adhere to inhuman conditions, which forced Mushi to work day and night without stop.[89] He also sold the broadcasting rights for *Atom* cheaply, setting a precedent for the years to come.[90] Although Tezuka is often blamed for starting a harsh and low-waged system for animators, tight budget and schedules were a common issue even for Tōei and cannot be traced back to a single person.[91]

That said, *Atom*'s cultural importance is undeniable. After Tezuka, animated series based on comics became the norm up until today, when they represent 90 per cent of modern Japanese animation.[92] The popularity of comics acted as a catalyst for the anime boom of the following decades. Furthermore, *Atom* injected manga-inspired genres into television, such as science-fiction (and particularly ロボットアニメ, *robotto anime* [robot anime]), which were in turn indebted with trends of juvenile fiction started in Japan prior to and during the war period. From manga also descended the connection with highly targeted audiences. This implies that what started as a children-oriented format with *Atom* could be geared to other (and older) demographics. A cult series of the period, 巨人の星 (*Kyojin no hoshi* [*Star of the Giants*]) (1968), on the martial-like trainings of a baseball pitcher, catered to a more adult target, as the sponsor of the series (a pharmaceutical company promoting an energy drink) seems to demonstrate.[93]

---

[88] Prandoni, *Anime al cinema*, 32.
[89] Schodt, *The Astro Boy Essays*, 67.
[90] Tezuka sold the broadcasting rights for *Atom* at the same price as a telefilm (550,000 yen per episode), although the production cost per episode was higher for animation than live action (ca 2,700,000 vs 300,000 yen); Prandoni, *Anime al cinema*, 31.
[91] Condry, *The Soul of Anime*, 105.
[92] Mark W. MacWilliams, 'Introduction', in *Japanese Visual Culture: Explorations in the World of Manga and Anime*, ed. Mark W. MacWilliams (London: Routledge, 2015), 6.
[93] Clements, *Anime*, 139.

Japanese TV in the age of the economic boom

Which were the main features of the burgeoning Japan's television, and how did the new animated (and animetic) series fit into the schedule? Whereas in the 1950s Japanese television was a 街頭テレビ (*gaitō terebi* [open-air theater]), located in public places such as railways and department stores, in the 1960s the medium shifted from the outdoors to the home, bringing families together in the 'sacred space' of the living room or お茶の間 (*ochanoma*).[94] This went hand in hand with the emergence of different types of TV programmes, starting from American TV shows, which were convenient and produced with higher budgets than resource-poor Japan could afford. These series left a long-lasting impression on collective imagination with their positive portraits of Western lifestyles.[95] Aired in 1960 as 名犬ラッシー (*Meiken Rasshī* [*Famous Lassie*]), the American telefilm *Lassie* (1954) was particularly successful, bespeaking an already noted preference for animal and dog stories, while the sitcom *Bewitched* (1964–72), known in Japan as 奥さまは魔女 (*Okusama wa majo* [*My wife is a witch*]), popularized a female ideal of lovely but powerful housewives-witches, which would inspire the 魔法少女 (*mahō shōjo* [magical girl]) animation genre.[96]

Through the process of airing an interrupted flux of daily programming, television became quickly entrenched in daily life, which resulted in the creation of three main national time zones. These were the morning period (from 7.00 am to 9.00 am), prior to daily commuting to work or school; the midday period (between 11.00 am and 2.00 am); and the peak evening entertaining slot (from 7.00 pm to 10.00 pm), known as ゴールデンタイム (*Gōruden taimu* [Golden time]), the most expensive for TV advertisement, as it coincided with a moment of aggregation for the whole family.[97] Time zones were often gender-targeted, too. Male viewers were usually favoured during Golden time, which started with the news at 7.00 pm, followed by family quiz shows and baseball games, while after 8.00 pm it was the turn of variety programmes and drama. On the contrary, morning and midday slots shared a typically female audience, with women-oriented programmes

---

[94]Yoshimi, 'Television Advertising as Textual and Economic System', 543–52.
[95]Aaron Gerow, 'Japanese film and television', in *Routledge Handbook of Japanese Culture and Society*, ed. Victoria Lyon Bestor and Theodore C. Bestor, with Akiko Yamagata (London and New York: Routledge, 2011), 221.
[96]Akiko Sugawa-Shimada, 'Shōjo in Anime: Beyond the Object of Men's Desire', in *Shōjo Across Media. Exploring 'Girl' Practices in Contemporary Japan*, ed. Jaqueline Berndt, Kazumi Nagaike, and Fusami Ogi (Cham: Palgrave Macmillan, 2019), 184.
[97]Florian Kohlbacher and Michael Prieler, *Advertising in the Aging Society: Understanding Representations, Practitioners, and Consumers in Japan* (Basingstoke: Palgrave Macmillan, 2016), 25.

such as 連続テレビ小説 (*Renzoku terebī shōsetsu* [Serialized TV novels]) (short: *asadora*) on NHK, Japan's national broadcaster, or, on commercial stations, メロドラマ (*merodorama* [melodrama]) and ワイドショー (*waido shō* [talk shows]).

The flourishing format of domestic live-action series often consisted of adaptations of Japanese novels and famous stories, differing greatly according to their viewership. While *asadora* were six-month-long TV series, usually set in the period straddling the Second World War (the 1920s to the 1950s), and revolving around the life of kind but strong women who endure all for the sake of their family, the same NHK broadcast 大河ドラマ (*Taiga dorama* [Grand river drama]) on Sunday evenings (8.00 pm), historical dramas which would run for an entire year, set in the pre-modern world.[98] Both shows enjoyed large popularity, especially the high-brow *Taiga dramas*, which dramatized the era of Japan's unification – the imperialistic policy of the war period being conveniently obscured – contributing to spread values that were welcome in the middle class, such as national identity and entrepreneurial spirit.

In this context, it is also worth noting that female characters were increasingly represented in TV series. Mirroring the social changes affecting Japanese families in the 1960s, when the majority of men were more and more distant from home because of the long working hours, mother-centred plots became frequent particularly on commercial stations, with women appearing either as 頼母子母 (*tanomoshi haha* [reliable mothers]) or as 耐える女 (*taeru onna* [suffering women]), had they chosen or not to remain within the domestic sphere.[99] Although the dominant message of TV dramas was arguably 'Home is the woman's castle', the growing importance of female viewership seems to suggest that broadcasters had started to give serious consideration for female tastes to get good ratings.[100]

Domestic TV series for children

One of the reasons why no one prior to Tezuka tried to serialize animation for television was that animated TV series already existed and were broadcast in the country since the mid-1950s. These were American

---

[98]Yoshimi, 'Television Advertising as Textual and Economic System', 554; Philip Seaton, 'Taiga Dramas and Tourism: Historical Contents as Sustainable Tourist Resources', *Japan Forum* 27, no. 1 (2015): 83.
[99]Hilaria M. Grössman, 'New Role Models for Men and Women? Gender in Japanese TV Dramas', in *Japan Pop: Inside the World of Japanese Popular Culture*, ed. Craig Timothy J. (London and New York: Routledge, 2015), 208.
[100]Yasuko Muramatsu, 'Gender Construction Through Interactions Between the Media and Audience in Japan', *International Journal of Japanese Sociology* 11 (2002): 73–9.

cartoons, such as the Fleischer Brothers' *Superman* (the first animated series shown in Japan in 1955), *Popeye*, and the Hanna and Barbera shows *Huckleberry Hound* and *The Flintstones*.[101] Thirty minutes of Tōei-style 'on two' cinematic animation could require up to 100 staff members, an estimated period of six months and a budget of 30 million yen,[102] while imported American cartoons would cost slightly over ¥100,000 for the same duration.[103] So, it seems easy to understand why purchasing animated series from the United States sounded more reasonable than producing them. As a matter of fact, thirty-five foreign animated works arrived in Japan by 1962, airing on weekends at 6.00 pm and catering to an audience of children.[104]

Considering the above, to put Tezuka's animated series in the schedule was not an obvious choice. On the one hand, American cartoons such as Hannah and Barbera's shows were in limited animation, showing that Tezuka followed an already accepted technique, although contemporary Japanese animators were not keen on it for its alleged 'poor quality'.[105] On the other hand, *Atom* was something that Japanese TV had never seen before, and had to compete with ready-made American cartoons and already established viewing habits of Japanese children close to primetime territory. While American cartoons consisted of five-to-ten-minute slapstick comedies, *Atom*'s episodes were more than twice the length. This allowed for a more complex exploration of stories and characters, touching on dramatic themes such as discrimination and condemnation of war (although plots would become repetitive later on, with the pressure of meeting weekly deadlines).

Also the domestic production of live-action TV series was initially hindered by American TV series, which in 1959 were twice as many than those created in Japan.[106] How did the situation change so that both Tezuka-style animation and Japan's live-action drama could raise the

---

[101] Northrop Davies, *Manga and Anime Go to Hollywood* (New York and London: Bloomsbury Academic), 188.
[102] This being calculated on Tōei's ninety-minute feature films, which could need up to 300 animators, a working period of one year and a half, and a budget of 60 million yen; Yasuo Yamaguchi, *Nihon no anime zenshi: sekai o seishita Nihon anime no kiseki* [*The complete history of anime: how Japanese animation conquered the world*] (Tokyo: Ten Books, 2004), 75.
[103] Saya Shiraishi, 'Doraemon Goes Abroad', in *Japan Pop. Inside the World of Japanese Culture*, ed. Craig Timothy J. (London and New York: Routledge, 2015), 298.
[104] Yasuo Kameyama, 'Kokusan terebi anime shirīzu to nipponteki bijinesu moderu no tanjō' [*Domestic TV animation series and the birth of a Japanese business model*], *Minna no Animegaku*, 2002, 7 January 2022. Available online: https://min-ani.com/kameyama_0002/ (accessed 7 February 2023).
[105] Jonathan Clements, 'Tezuka's Anime Revolution in Context', *Mechademia* 8 (2013): 215.
[106] Alexander Zahlten, 'Before Media Mix: The Electric Ecology', in *A Companion to Japanese Cinema*, ed. Desser David (Malden: Wiley, 2022), 485.

interest of local broadcasters? Aside from Tezuka's slashing prices down, what proved that the operation could be profitable was 月光仮面 (*Gekko kamen* [*Moonlight mask*]) (1958), a TV series featuring Japan's first live-action superhero, a mysterious selenite sent to Earth to protect humanity from evil, following into the footsteps of the American Superman.[107] An anticipator of the 特撮 (*tokusatsu* [special effects]) genre, this show was extremely low budget (Gekko kamen's motorbike was often the most expensive prop of the show). Nonetheless, its white-cloaked protagonist became a favourite among children, switching from a daily ten-minute format to a thirty-minute series aired every week on Sunday evening. The successful serialization of *Gekko kamen*, pulling ratings over 60 per cent, had an effect on children's publishing, with weeklies increasingly replacing monthly manga magazines, while the involvement of the advertising company Senkosha, the creator of the series, paved the way for Tezuka's media mix.[108]

Animation and advertising

Already before the advent of animetic series, there was a strong connection between Japanese animation, publicity and storytelling, and this facilitated the rise of highly commercialized approaches to TV animation. As early as in the Taishō period, Yamamoto's animation studio adapted a famous Aesop's fable in his 教育お伽漫画 兎と亀 (*Kyōiku otogi manga usagi to kame* [*Educational fairy-tale cartoon: the hare and the tortoise*]) (1924), a one-reel children's entertainment sponsored by Morinaga Milk Chocolate.[109] The birth of television, as a popular vehicle for advertising, resulted in the creation of TV commercials. These often utilized animation to clearly show brands and products in a period when pictures were black and white and of poor resolution.[110] In the same years, animation was entrenched in TV advertising in other countries as well. In 1953, when Japan's first animated commercial was aired (featuring a cartoon rooster and clock by the watch manufacturer Seikō), American researchers were testing the efficacy of animation in TV ads, for example, for illustrating intangibles.[111] Moreover, animated shorts for advertising were screened in cinemas in Europe and

---

[107]Clements Jonathan and Motoko Tamamuro, *The Dorama Encyclopedia: A Guide to Japanese TV Drama Since 1953* (Berkley, California: Stone Bridge Press, 2003), 200.
[108]Zahlten, 'Before Media Mix'.
[109]Clements, *Anime*, 40.
[110]Chiba, *Haiji ga umareta hi*, 24.
[111]The president of Schwerin Research Corporation mentioned the idea of brightness in cleanser commercials, which can be conveyed through animated sparkling effects; Horace S. Schwerin, 'Cartoons, Used Well, Can Fill Big Niches', *The Billboard*, 10 October 1953: 7.

America already in the 1940s.[112] However, Japan's animated ads played a key role in the development of animation as a mass art, prompting the production of televisive contents prior to animetic series.

One of Japan's leading producers of animated commercials was the video department of Nippon Television Co. (later known as TCJ, Television Corporation of Japan), established in 1952 with the support of several zaibatsu families, as an import company specializing in TV sets. It is interesting to note that, a few years before Ōkawa, TCJ founder 梁瀬次郎 (Yanase Jirō) (1916–2008), aimed at becoming 日本のディズニー (*Nihon no Dizunī* [Japan's Disney]) and starting a 新しい文化 (*atarashī bunka* [new culture]) in Japanese television,[113] probably taking Disney's contemporary expansion into the new media as a model. As Tōei would do, TCJ turned to a production company of veteran animators, Ashida Manga, to achieve skilled staff members, as well as instructors for their new recruits. Clements notes that Ashida Manga was the top studio of the 1950s, working under contract for American broadcasters and turning down applications from future celebrities like Tezuka and Ōtsuka.[114] Despite TCJ's plans to acquire it, Ashida Manga stayed independent[115] and was forgotten overtime, as it worked mainly in advertising, which is not usually covered in anime histories. However, several of its employees chose to move to TCJ, passing on a know-how that dated back to the pre-war period. TCJ also poached members from Nichidō such as Yabushita and 上金史明 (Kamigane Fumiaki).

This pool of talents is probably the reason why Tezuka spent a couple of weeks at TCJ, after his collaboration with Tōei and before the production of *Atom*.[116] TV commercials were still an uncharted territory for animators, thus fostering experimentation with different techniques. In particular, former Ashida Manga's members such as 大西 清 (Onishi Kiyoshi) (1934–2014) and 西島 行雄 Nishijima Yukio (*c.* 1930–1990s?) made advertising in American-style limited animation, with a modernist look redolent of UPA shows. For example, starting from 1958, Onishi animated a series of commercials for Torys whiskey, featuring アンクルトリス (*Ankuru Torisu*

---

[112] John McDonough and Karen Egolf (eds), *The Advertising Age: Encyclopedia of Advertising* (Chicago: Fitzroy Deaborn Publishers, 2002), 82.
[113] Kosei Ono, 'Takahashi Shigeto, Nihon ni okeru terebi CM to TV anime no sōsō ki o kataru (TCJ kara zuiyō e no rekishi)' [Takahashi Shigeto talks about the early days of TV commercials and TV animation in Japan (history from TCJ to Zuiyo)], *Kyōto seika daigaku kiyōdai* [*Journal of Kyoto Seika University*] 26 (2004): 191.
[114] Clements and McCarthy, *The Anime Encyclopedia*. To give an idea of the popularity of the company, Chiba notes that when Tezuka applied for the job in 1947, there were other 200 candidates; Chiba, *Haiji ga umareta hi*, 35.
[115] Reportedly because of Ashida's opposition; Ono, 'Takahashi Shigeto', 193.
[116] Ono, 'Takahashi Shigeto', 195.

[Uncle Torys]), a bald salary man which is still the advertising character of the brand. The same Onishi was posthumously inserted in the Creators Hall of Fame by the ACC Tokyo Creativity Awards, Japan's prestigious festival of the Asian Cultural Council.[117] It is interesting to note that their short length, together with the burgeoning status of television as an open theatre, made TCJ's commercials narrative-rich, and closer to American cartoons in tone and style. In other words, TV animated advertising initially led the market of limited animation, pioneering animetism in an age when Disney's cinematic tradition was the main model for Japan.

Sponsors for animation

The awareness that exposure to televised animated stories could generate profit grew stronger when Tezuka introduced the manga-to-anime adaptation process. The success of *Atom* demonstrated that a popular children's show could have an impact not only on the publishing market (the sales for Tezuka's comics escalated after the series was aired) but also on the sales of its sponsor's products ('Atom' chocolates sold so well that Meiji struggled to keep up with demand). The benefits of the 'image alliance', whereby the interest for story's characters is boosted by their increased visibility, resulted in grouping television, manga, merchandise and product sponsorship.[118] This is even more relevant if we consider that animated series initially targeted children, a privileged audience for selling character-related products. In fact, one of the advantages of the キャラ (*kyara*), or character-based system that still perdures in Japan,[119] is the use of beloved protagonists as ageless testimonials of virtually any item, mirroring the sponsor's brand image as well.

As a production company specialized in commercials, TCJ had connections with different sponsors and soon started to produce animated series with their endorsement, such as 鉄人28号 (*Tetsujin 28-go* [*Iron man no. 28*]) (1963), sponsored by Meiji's competitor Glico, and エイトマン (*Eito man* [*Eight man*]) (1963–4), supported by Marumiya Food Industry. However, TCJ animators did not use exclusively limited animation for manga-to-anime adaptations. In fact, the first work commissioned by TCJ to Ashida Manga was the short 蜜蜂マーヤの冒険 (*Mitsubachi Maya no bōken* [*The adventures of Maya the honeybee*]) (1954), based on Waldemar

---

[117]*Dai 5-kai kurieitāzu dendō* [5th Creators Hall of Fame], ACC Awards, 2017. Accessible online: https://www.acc-awards.com/pantheon/2015.html (accessed 23 February 2023).
[118]Shiraishi, 'Doraemon Goes Abroad', 299–300.
[119]Steinberg, 'Immobile Sections and Trans-Series Movement', 39–40.

Bonsels' children's story, which was translated several times into Japanese since 1925.[120] The animation, which won a special prize at the first edition of the Asia-Pacific Film Festival,[121] seems to suggest that prestigious animation from Western fiction was also on the list. These works would start gaining attention in the following years.

---

[120]Kiyoto Fukuda and Toshiko Yamanushi, *Nihon jidō bungeishi* [*History of Japanese children's literature*] (Tokyo: Sanseido, 1983), 434.
[121]Shinichi Sano, *Nihon eiga wa, ima – sukurīn no uragawa kara no shōgen* [*Cinema of Japan now: a testimony from behind the screen*] (Tokyo: TBS Britannica, 1996), 145.

3

The roots of the *World Masterpiece Theater*

The creation of the *WMT* was not a straightforward process, but a layered phenomenon. The project started with a single sponsor and was carried out by the same studio for over two decades, and yet was the fruit of different creative skills and intuitions which evolved through the years, depending on the staff involved, the needs of sponsors and broadcasters and the changes in the public. Also, the way literature was addressed mutated consistently according to these variables. There are various paths that have been traced, interrupted or took a different route along the way. While the previous chapter delved into the roots of animated adaptations of children's literature in Japan, this chapter will try to cast a light on the productive and creative processes that led to the foundation of the *WMT*, focusing on the situation of Japanese animation in the late 1960s and early 1970s.

Japanese animation in the late 1960s

In this period, TV animation was the latest trend and a profitable venture for the entertainment market. Modelled on the success of *Atom* and other pioneering series, which were based on comics and supported by pervasive marketing campaigns, more popular manga were animated for television, giving life to a differentiation of genres.[1] These included robot stories, magical girls, スポ根 (*spokon* [sport tenacity]) series and adaptations of ギャグ漫画 (*gyagu manga* [gag comics]), often created by the manga artist duo 藤子 不二雄 (Fujiko Fujio), and following the adventures of funny

---

[1] Prandoni, *Anime al cinema*, 50.

creatures, like the endearing ghost of オバケのQ太郎 (*Obake no Kyūtarō* [*Q-Taro the ghost*]) (1965), and their human friends. To have an idea of the success of gag anime, suffice to say that the sales of Fujiya chocolates, *Q-Taro*'s sponsor, surpassed Meiji while Shōgakukan, which published the manga, built a new ten-storey office building in Tokyo, quickly nicknamed オバQビル (*Obakyū biru* [Oba-Q building]).[2] Other fortunate serializations belonged to the 妖怪 (*yōkai* [ghosts]) boom, which usually renegotiated monsters stories of the Japanese folklore for a juvenile audience.

The growing demand of TV series prompted the creation of new animation studios, mostly located in the Tokyo area and close to Tōei studios in Nerima, a ward in western Tokyo.[3] Some companies gathered professionals from adjacent fields, such as TCJ (which, as seen in Chapter 2, was specialized in animated commercials) or Tokyo Movie, born from the rib of a puppet animation studio. Also comic artists, who were struggling to keep up with the new schedules of weekly magazines, founded their own companies, like Tatsunoko, established by the 吉田 (Yoshida brothers), and Fujiko Fujio's Studio Zero. The drive to produce animation could come directly from the broadcasters, which were ready to follow the example of Fuji TV with *Atom*. For instance, Tokyo Movie (later renamed Tokyo Movie Shinsha) was set up to create ビッグX (*Biggu Ekkusu* [*Big X*]) (1964), a superhero series commissioned by TBS. More studios sprouted per effect of the diaspora of talents from Tōei as well as Mushi, which was in bad shape due to the rising problems of Tezuka's administration. This also meant a continuation of the master-disciple relations (and attached transmission of expertise) which were typical of pre-industrial animation, as veterans tended to move to other studios with younger animators.

Since the animated series created in the wake of *Atom* were mostly on the animetic side, with manga-based adaptations animated on three, and ingrained in a media mix system, Tōei rapidly adapted to the times, igniting highly influential genres of TV animation such as the already recalled mahō shōjo, spokon and yōkai. Tōei maintained features of its cinematic style, starting from the tendency to bowdlerize stories for a mainstream, typically children's audience, differently from other studios (as early as in 1963, TCJ produced 仙人部落, *Sennin buraku* [*Hermit village*], the first animated series for adults). Urged by the crisis of cinema, in 1967 Tōei also initiated the practice of screening re-edited episodes of TV series as a side to one of its feature films.[4] These shows, known as 東映まんがまつり (*Tōei manga matsuri* [*Tōei manga festival*]), became a fixture during holidays, capitalizing

---

[2]Shiraishi, 'Doraemon Goes Abroad', 299.
[3]Saburo Murakami, *Anime in TV. Storia dei cartoni animati giapponesi prodotti per la televisione* [*TV anime. A history of Japanese cartoons for television*] (Milano: Yamato Video, 1998), 17.
[4]Prandoni, *Anime al cinema*, 38.

on successful animated series, and using cinema as an advertising medium for television.

This context was the starting point for the *WMT*, which gathered professionals from different walks of life, as well as technical and aesthetic influences from several studios. The idea of serializing classic stories coincided with a new stream of Japan's animation. No one was making novel-based animation in this period – at least, not for television.

Animated classics for children and adults

As seen, Tōei's theatrical production started with adaptations of popular stories, in the attempt to create a brand image comparable to Disney's and penetrate foreign markets. However, Ōkawa originally focused on Asian contents, shaping a trajectory which continued in the TV shows released by the studio. Note that 狼少年ケン (*Ōkami shōnen Ken* [*Wolf boy Ken*]) (1963), Tōei's first animated series, was an original concept redolent of *Tarzan* and *The Jungle Book*,[5] created by Tezuka's disciple 月岡 貞夫 Sadao Tsukioka (1939).[6] Rudyard Kipling's *Jungle Books* (1894–6), which were in turn among the sources of *Tarzan*, were first translated into Japanese on the pages of the juvenile magazine *Shōnen sekai* as early as in 1899, and this bespeaks Tōei's preference for classic children's books.[7] However, the following TV series produced by the studio were based on popular comics, as Tezuka did. The same animetic formula was applied to Tōei's 'class B' movies, which were produced for domestic release starting from サイボーグ009 (*Saibōgu 009* [*Cyborg 009*]) (1966). Based on a manga by 石ノ森章太郎 (Ishinomori Shōtarō) (1938–98), this film launched the appealing trope of a heroic team fighting against the forces of evil, and Ishinomori's fortune in the world of TV animation.

Adaptations from Western literature were redirected to Tōei's more fluidly animated, and potentially exportable, 'class A' theatricals. Titles of this group included stories of the Western juvenile canon, such as アンデルセン物語 (*Anderusen monogatari* [*Andersen story*]) (1968), ちびっ子レミと名犬カピ (*Chibikko Remi to meiken Kapi* [*Little Remi and the famous dog Kapi*]) (1970), and the already recalled 'Puss 'n Boots' series. Apart from *Remi*, an adaptation of the French novel *Sans Famille*

---

[5]Ibid., 34.
[6]Technically, the same *Ken* followed the innovations of manga-style limited animation, skilfully using still frames and exaggerated movements; Yamaguchi, *Nihon no anime zenshi*, 85.
[7]Mikako Ageishi, 'How Translated Literature Shaped Education in Modern Japan: The Reception of Walter Scott and Rudyard Kipling', *Kushiro Ronshū: Hokkaidō kyōiku daigaku Kushiro-kō kenkyū kiyō* [*Journal of Hokkaido University of Education at Kushiro Campus*] 50 (2018): 48–9.

(1878), fairy and folk tales were numerically more common (e.g. *Anderusen monogatari* is a musical blending of the writer's romanticized childhood with some of his most famous tales). This seems in line with decanted trends of translated children's fiction in Japan, with Western fairy tales being assimilated first, and ushering several zenshū book sets. Significantly, Tōei's last class A film, どうぶつ宝島 (*Dōbutsu takarajima* [*Animal treasure island*]) (1971), was a zoomorphic retelling of Stevenson's classic story, returning to the constantly utilized topos of animal stories with moral teaching and geared to a children's audience.

In this same period, there were also attempts to create animated adaptations of foreign stories for older demographics. When the film distributor Herald (now Kadokawa Herald Pictures) proposed to create adult animation suitable for export, Tezuka, notably dissatisfied with the standardization of children's TV series, seized the opportunity.[8] Various storylines from the West were taken into account (Tezuka was especially interested in Goethe's *Faust*), the choice falling on the *Arabian Nights*, whose latest re-translation by 大場 正史 (Ōba Masafumi) (1914–69) caused a sensation in the post-war, as it emphasized the pornographic elements of the oriental original.[9] The result was 千夜一夜物語 (*Senya ichiya monogatari* [*One thousand and one nights*]) (1969), the first part of a triptych known as アニメラマ (*animerama*), crasis of animation, cinerama (a popular widescreen technology), and drama. These films featured non-linear narratives and experimental animation. For example, in *Senya ichiya monogatari* there is a 3D model of Baghdad similar to the Fleischers' sets, while sex scenes are evoked through abstract images.

Like Tōei's class A films, Mushi's animerama boasted high production values (800 animators from twenty different studios worked on the film) and exotic locations deemed to make them palatable for the overseas markets. They also proved that animation could tackle eroticism and adult humour.[10] However, their overall poor reception at the box office, eventually bankrupting Mushi and forcing Tezuka to retire, confirmed the status of children's animation as a play-safe strategy for producers and distributors.

The origin of 'world masterpieces'

In 1977, following the tradition of adapting classic stories for the big screen, Tōei started to produce fairy-tale-based movies crowned with the

---

[8] Prandoni, *Anime al cinema*, 45.
[9] Rayna Denison and Stefanie Van de Peer, '1001 Nights and Anime: The Adaptation of Transnational Folklore in Tezuka Osamu's *Senya ichiya monogatari / A Thousand and One Nights* (1969)', *Open Screens* 4, no. 4 (2021): 2.
[10] Onoda Power, *God of Comics*, 137.

title 世界名作童話 (*Sekai meisaku dōwa* [World masterpiece fairy tales]). However, it was not the first time this expression was used. Aside from being a recurring title for the fairy-tale issues of numerous zenshū books since the pre-war period, in 1967 TCJ produced the animation アルプスの少女 (*Arupusu no shōjo* [*Girl of the Alps*]), a five-minute test for a longer project called 世界名作シリーズ (*Sekai meisaku shirīzu* [World masterpiece series]). This work, a trailer adaptation of the Swiss novel *Heidi*, was an idea of 高橋 茂人 (Takahashi Shigeto) (1935–2015), the former sales manager of TCJ's TV commercial production. He had been transferred to the animation department halfway through the production of *Tetsujin 28*, with the stated aim to make profits.[11] In fact, as was the case with *Atom*, broadcast rights were sold at a very low price to the TV station, TCJ being only a subcontractor producer. This created a pattern whereby animation studios were constantly at a loss in spite of the good ratings of their TV series.

Takahashi, who had a background in law, was keenly aware of the revenue-generating potential of copyright, and started to work as a planning manager as well, negotiating with the original authors of manga-based animated series such as サスケ (*Sasuke*) (1968–9), an adaptation of the ninja story by 白土三平 (Shirato Sanpei) (1932–2021).[12] However, he personally disliked the increasingly edgy contents which serial animation was taking up from manga genres, such as 番長 (*banchō* [juvenile delinquents]) stories, for he assumed animation had to cater to children. Hence the idea of turning educative children's books into animation. As seen, TCJ produced a short on the German story 'Maya the Bee' as early as in 1954, but it was an isolate experiment to take over Ashida Manga, the following works released by the studio being TV ads and series of the animetic type. The same pilot for *Heidi*, which did not develop into a show (although it was commercialized as a Flexi disc), conformed to the standards of the period. *Heidi*'s character – a work of TCJ's new recruit 芦田豊雄 (Ashida Toyō) (1944–2011), who would later design the 'magical girl' Minky Momo – has braids and sparkling eyes like the first Licca-chan, Japan's most famous doll, also designed in 1967 by the shōjo manga artist 牧 美也子 (Maki Miyako) (born 1935).[13]

Especially *Heidi*'s Alpine set felt 違和感 (*iwakan* [incongruous]) to Takahashi, since it was drawn by people who never saw the European locales

---

[11]Ono, 'Takahashi Shigeto', 196.
[12]Ibid., 196–7.
[13]The similarity has been noted by the collector who uploaded on YouTube the tracks of the Flexi disc: RICMANIA, 'Sekai meisaku dōwa 14 – Arupusu no shōjo', 26 December 2017, Available online: http://ricmania.com/index.php?module=blog&act=printview&eid=10698&date=2017-12 (accessed 17 February 2023). However, TCJ Heidi's look is consistent with shōjo manga traditional style since the 1950s, as in the seminal works by the artist 高橋真琴 (Takahashi Makoto) (born 1934).

for real.¹⁴ As Chiba explains, the reason why Takahashi was so interested in carefully reproducing the atmosphere of the West was rooted in his childhood, which he spent in Beijing and then in the French Concession in Tianjin, due to his father's job at the North China Film Company.¹⁵ Founded in 1939, this was one of the several film companies which operated in areas under the occupation of the Japanese empire, distributing movies in line with the Pan-Asian values.¹⁶ However, while Japan was plunging into war, progressively eliminating foreign culture (except for the books written in the countries of the Axis), Takahashi grew up in an international environment, cocooned in the affluence of extraterritoriality. In this sort of Chinese Switzerland, he experienced European architectures and designs, because foreign concessions were close to each other and filled with Western-style buildings.

Takahashi did not view these sites, some of which dated back to the Opium Wars, as a humiliating colonial legacy, as they must have appeared to the Chinese. Instead, he enjoyed learning Western customs such as dining etiquette and eating German-style sausages, French bread and Swiss cheese. He also read children's fiction available in Japan such as translated children's novels, *Heidi* being one of his favourites.¹⁷ The impression is that Takahashi, as a Japanese child, saw only the cultural value of concession history, almost as if they were part of a world fair showcasing admirable Western icons, which would shape his idea of 'masterpiece'.

Modern classics: The case of *Moomin*

As in the case of Tōei, Takahashi's idea of 'masterpiece' as a cultural product of the West was indebted to the zenshū tradition, which contributed to disseminate foreign children's stories, defining them as the best of the best. This holds particularly true for the post-war period, when Japanese scholars, translators and authors of children's fiction established Western juvenile literature as a model to follow, under the auspices of the GHQ. In this context, it is possible to imagine why young Takahashi, who returned to Japan with his mother towards the end of the war, became even more engrossed in Western culture. Whereas the experience of the conflict was a culture shock, exposing him to the harsh reality he had been sheltered from in Tianjin, the Occupation brought about what he loved about the West: children's literature and fairy tales, often fully translated for the first time. In

---

¹⁴Quoted in Chiba, *Haiji ga umareta hi*, 42.
¹⁵Ibid., 6–10.
¹⁶Hideaki Fujiki, *Making Audiences: A Social History of Japanese Cinema and Media* (New York: Oxford University Press, 2022), 218–19.
¹⁷Chiba, *Haiji ga umareta hi*, 8.

fact, as seen in Chapter 1, the domesticating approach which was used in the pre-war and war period was abandoned for more faithful and foreignizing translation techniques.

Like other people of his generation, who joined animation in the most serendipitous ways,[18] Takahashi entered Nippon Television/TCJ almost by chance, mistaking it for the Japanese broadcaster Nippon TV. It was in 1956, when he was still a job-hunting student from Keio University.[19] The company was young and lively and Takahashi moved up quickly, learning by doing what today could be defined as a producer's work.[20] While TCJ was a stimulating environment for cutting his teeth on animation, as well as a starting point to connect with sponsors and advertising agencies, Takahashi had his own views on copyright management, which were largely ignored by the company. However, when it came to the pedagogic aspects of animation, he used to overlook the importance of TV series, and even considered them in a negative light, according to the widespread notion whereby videos, differently from books, are likely to kill children's imagination.[21]

The production of the animated series ムーミン (Mūmin [Moomin]) (1969) marked a turning point. This was based on a collection of children's books, published in Sweden between 1945 and 1971 by the Finnish author Tove Jansson (1914–2001). These books told the adventures of a family of trolls living in harmony with nature. Takahashi, who was especially fond of fairy tales from Northern Europe, saw the novels at Maruzen, a bookstore specialized in foreign-language books, following the advice of one of his assistants.[22] Takahashi was intrigued by Jansson's hippo-like creatures, and thought they had potential for animation. His intuition was confirmed after talking with an editor of Kōdansha, the publisher of the 'Moomin' series in Japan, who informed him that around 5,000 copies had been purchased by university study groups of Children's literature.[23] It is worth noting that 'Moomin' books were not yet popular in the country, being first translated into Japanese only a few years before with the title たのしいムーミン一家 (Tanoshī Moomin ie [The fun Moomin family]) (1964). However, the local boards of education, child education specialists and teachers endorsed the publication, recommending it as a reading for primary schools.[24]

---

[18]As is known, several future celebrities of Japan's animation who were born in the war period had no formal artistic background, such as Miyazaki (graduated in economics), Tezuka (medicine), Takahata (French literature), being animation still a young business.
[19]Ono, 'Takahashi Shigeto', 190–1.
[20]Chiba, Haiji ga umareta hi, 28.
[21]Ono, 'Takahashi Shigeto', 199.
[22]Ono, 'Takahashi Shigeto', 198; Chiba, Haiji ga umareta hi, 44.
[23]Ono, 'Takahashi Shigeto', 199.
[24]Hideko Mitsui, 'Uses of Finland in Japan's Social Imaginary', in Reflections on Imagination: Human Capacity and Ethnographic Method, ed. Mark Harris and Nigel Rapport (London: Routledge, 2016), 163.

Takahashi's enthusiasm for *Moomin* prompted him to start planning the animation. He wrote a letter to the Finnish writer, enclosing sample cels drawn by the colour designer 一色 弘安 (Isshiki Hiroyasu) and others, and was ready to fly to Europe to negotiate the contract in person.[25] Predictably, the idea was coldly received at TCJ. Not only was *Moomin* not a hit among children (while TCJ's shows were all based on very famous comics) but producing an animated adaptation of foreign copyrighted fiction was unheard of in Japan, and TCJ refused to pay for the overseas royalties. Even pre-war book collections of translated books were probably often published without the permission of the original authors, a process that Kawana compares to modern 'fansub' culture,[26] and, when in the post-war the Allies prodded Japan to revise copyright laws according to the Berne Convention,[27] animation maintained its preference for fairy tales, being conveniently in public domain.

The foundation of Zuiyō Enterprise

Takahashi had no intention of dropping his project. When, in March 1969, the animation department of TCJ became an independent company, TCJ Dōga Center (later renamed as Eiken), he took the opportunity to leave and establish his own studio, Zuiyō Enterprise.[28] Zuiyō was specialized in planning and managing copyright sales of TV shows, taking on outsourced work from Tokyo Movie and TCJ.[29] As a producer, Takahashi was involved in the TV series 忍風カムイ外伝 (*Ninpū Kamui gaiden* [*The legend of Kamui the ninja*]) (1969), another ninja story by Shirato, who reportedly was very pleased with the work Takahashi did with *Sasuke*, and only trusted him for the adaptation.[30] According to Ono's interview, Takahashi made a good impression because he discussed things with the mangaka, struggling to stick to his style and themes, in a period when authorial rights were still vague. For example, Tōei's feature film *Watari Ninja Boy* (1966), based on Shirato's manga ワタリ (*Watari*), left the mangaka very disappointed, as it

---

[25]Chiba, *Haiji ga umareta hi*, 45.
[26]Kawana, *The Uses of Literature in Modern Japan*, 192–3.
[27]Choi, *Losing the War, Winning the Pooh*, 50.
[28]This was also because TCJ's new president, 村田 英憲 (Murata Hidenori) (born 1928), who had been the former director of the animation division, had a different philosophy from his. In Ono's interview, Takahashi explained that Murata did not share his ideas on copyright, thwarting his attempts to negotiate rights with authors and broadcasters; Ono, 'Takahashi Shigeto', 198.
[29]Clements, *Anime*, 194.
[30]Ono, 'Takahashi Shigeto', 209–10.

bowdlerized his work – a marxist story of class rebellion – for a children's audience. Instead, Shirato was happy with the way Takahashi handled *Ninpū Kamui gaiden* and drew a logo for Zuiyō as thanks.

Takahashi intended to apply the same rigorous approach to the adaptation of *Moomin*, so he spent his liquidation from TCJ to fly to Stockholm and discuss an agreement with Jansson. It is worth noting that Zuiyō's policy to おとなとこどもが共に楽しめるものを作る (*otona to kodomo ga tomoni tanoshimeru mono o tsukuru* [create something that adults and children can enjoy together]) came into focus in this occasion.[31] One anecdote told by Takahashi sheds a light on this issue.[32] On the flight to Sweden he met a Swedish boy with his father on their way back from America. Much to Takahashi's surprise, what the child enjoyed most during his trip was *Tetsujin 28*, which was known to American kids as *Gigantor*. Although Takahashi probably ignored that the TCJ series was substantially altered in the American version,[33] this made him realize that Japanese animation could have a great influence on the children of the world, and thus must be devised carefully.

The meeting with Jansson was successful, so Takahashi could start to plan the production of the TV series *Moomin* (1969–70), which was taken over by Tokyo Movie with its affiliation A Pro, founded by Tōei's veteran 楠部 大吉郎 (Kusube Daikichiro) (1934–2005). Much has been said on this work, which was never released elsewhere than in Japan, nor has been rebroadcast there, allegedly because Jansson sent a claim to voice her disappointment.[34] The same Takahashi described the experience as a culture shock, due to the differences in beliefs and behaviours between the two countries, which obviously affected the show.[35] However, it is interesting to observe that Takahashi wanted to respect the original (his friendship with Jansson would last until her death in 2001), but purposely allowed the staff to make changes in the adaptation. The settings, which in the original stories changed depending on the book, had to become one in the animation to avoid contradictions.[36] Plot construction and characters also deviated from

---

[31] Ibid., 204.
[32] Ibid., 199.
[33] *Gigantor*, which eclipsed *Atom*'s popularity in America in the late 1960s, modified the concept whereby the robot protagonist was a Japanese army to use against the Allies during the Second World War; Fred Ladd with Harvey Deneroff, *Astro Boy and Anime Come to the Americas. An Insider's View of the Birth of a Pop Culture Phenomenon* (Jefferson: McFarland & Company, 2009), 48.
[34] Chiba, *Haiji ga umareta hi*, 51.
[35] For example, Takahashi was shocked to hear that, to Jansson, the fun of catching butterflies was not in the actual catch, but in the chase itself; Ono, 'Takahashi Shigeto', 200.
[36] Ono, 'Takahashi Shigeto', 201.

those in the books. Ōtsuka, who was appointed as the character designer, drew Moomins with longer legs to make them easier to animate.³⁷

This seems to suggest that Takahashi was aware of the specific strategies, in terms of worldbuilding and narrative rationalization, required by television. Moreover, by minimizing Japanese elements, Takahashi's goal was to create a series for a global market.³⁸ This attitude seems to resonate with the way children's series are conceived now by the Western animation industry. However, the project was hard to sell in Japan. Nobody believed in its potential, except Takahashi and Calpis, the sponsor of the series, whose parable and mission had much in common with Zuiyō's take on animation.

Between East and West: The history of Calpis

Now a wholly owned subsidiary of Asahi, the beer company, Calpis Co. Ltd. is Japan's largest manufacturer of fermented lactic beverages.³⁹ These include the homonymous drink, which is branded in English-speaking countries as Calpico and is perhaps as iconic as Coke in many Asian communities.⁴⁰ Calpis is derived from the fermentation of milk by lactobacilli, has a mildly yogurt-like flavour and is considered beneficial to human health. In fact, the founder of the company, 三島 海雲 (Mishima Kaiun) (1878–1974), during his youth travelled to Mongolia, where the sour milk which nomads drank daily deeply improved his digestion, and this resulted in launching Calpis in 1919.⁴¹ Initially a costly treat for special occasions, in the mid-1960s Calpis became an ordinary commodity and one of Japan's most popular beverages.⁴² This success had something to do with the Westernization of the country since the Meiji period, when milk consumption was encouraged among the Japanese 'to make their bodies strong' – a policy which continued with the Americanization of the post-war years.⁴³ The same diffusion of

---

³⁷Ibid.
³⁸Chiba, *Haiji ga umareta hi*, 51.
³⁹*Factbook: Asahi Group*, Asahi Group Holdings (2017), 10. Available online: https://www.asahigroup-holdings.com/en/ir/pdf/2017_2q_factbook.pdf (accessed 18 July 2023).
⁴⁰Andrew Chau and Bin Chen, *The Boba Book. Bubble Tea and Beyond* (New York: Clarkson Potter, 2020), 128.
⁴¹'History', *Calpis*, 2006. Available online: https://www.calpis.co.jp/english/outline/outline1.html (accessed 17 March 2023).
⁴²'Nippon ronguserā kō. Carupisu: Oishī omoide o tsukutte 84-nen' [Thoughts on Japan's long-selling products. Calpis: 84 years of making delicious memories], *COMZINE* (July 2003). Available online: https://www.nttcom.co.jp/comzine/no002/long_seller/index.html (accessed 17 March 2023).
⁴³*Factbook: The History of Milk in Japan*, Japan Dairy Association (2020), 2–11. Available online: https://www.j-milk.jp/report/study/h4ogb400000011y2-att/h4ogb40000003f7e.pdf (accessed 18 July 2023).

soft drinks in Japan was related to the activity of European traders in the nineteenth century.[44]

As a businessman educated in the Meiji era, Mishima was determined to improve society through his commercial activity (significantly, he distributed his beverages for free to the victims of the Great Kantō Earthquake[45]), mixing world culture – Western but also from mainland China – and Japan's own traditions. The same word 'Calpis' is a crasis of Calcium, which scholars of the Taishō period began to associate with milk, and the Sanskrit *sarpís*, one of the five stages of making ghee (clarified butter), which was said to be a cure for all ailments, and was used as a metaphor for Buddha's teachings.[46] This attitude is reflected in the philosophy of Calpis – to promote the health of body and mind – and its promotional campaigns, which since the start had an international feel, though being targeted domestically. For example, early Calpis posters had a modernist art style and were created by Western painters or Western-style Japanese painters, such as 伊原宇三郎 (Ihara Usaburo) (1894–1976). It is worth noting that the posters made in Europe were the winners of a wide-scale competition (over 1,400 entries) sponsored by Calpis to help German, French and Italian artists after the First World War, introducing innovative models and styles to Japanese art.[47] This way, Mishima's advertising coalesced into sponsorship activities which were in line with his mission of contributing to society.

Calpis publicity reveals how the brand of the company evolved over time. The posters of the Taishō period featured adult characters, usually women dressed in Western fashion, with the tagline 初恋の味 (*hatsu koi no aji* [the taste of first love]), a synesthetic association to Calpis bittersweet flavour. The foreignizing quality of this type of advertising is evident in Calpis trademark character, a 黒ん坊 (*kuronbō* [black man]) minstrel in hillbilly clothing consuming the white drink, which the company would use for years without racist intents.[48] Designed by the German Otto Dünkelsbühler (1898–1977), this was another sign of Western influence, from modernism's fascination with primitive art to the stereotype of the black as a comic jester, which was ingrained in Japan since the Meiji period.[49] Also the packaging

---

[44]Michael Ashkenazi and Jeanne Jacob, *Food Culture in Japan* (Westport: Greenwood Press, 2003), 74.
[45]Masashi Matsumoto, *20 Seiki terebi dokuhon sekai meisaku gekijō taizen* [20th century TV reader World masterpiece theater encyclopedia] (Tokyo: Dōbunshoin, 1999), 149.
[46]William Edward Soothill and Lewis Hodous, *A Dictionary of Chinese Buddhist Terms* (Delhi: Motilal Banarsidass 1977), 115.
[47]S. Richard Thornton, *Japanese Graphic Design* (London: Lawrence King, 1991), 39.
[48]Millie Creighton, 'Soto and uchi "Others": Imaging Diversity', in *Japan's Minorities. The Illusion of Homogeneity*, ed. Michael Weiner (New York: Routledge 1991), 223.
[49]John Russell, 'Race and Reflexivity: The Black Other in Contemporary Japanese Mass Culture', in *Rereading Cultural Anthropology*, ed. George E. Marcus (Durham: Duke University Press, 1992), 303.

of Calpis bottles – white polka dots on a blue background (now blue on white) – communicated positive feelings, as it represented the starry sky of 七夕 (*Tanabata* [Evening of the seventh]), a summer festival celebrated on July 7, the day when Calpis was first marketed, conveying the idea of a refreshing drink.[50]

'Mother and child' advertising: *Calpis Manga Theater*

While the colours and design for Calpis were inspired by the Milky Way – which, according to a Chinese legend, separates the stars of two celestial lovers who reunite once a year on Tanabata – it is also suggestive of objects (milk), practices (wishing on stars) and patterns (polka dots) often associated to juvenile innocence. Mishima attached growing importance to children consumers, holding a nursery rhyme contest for elementary school students as early as 1923, with 'Akai tori' Kitahara Hakushū and other prominent authors of children's poems as judges.[51] In the Shōwa period, Calpis became a typical children's drink.[52] In 1963, for the forty-first anniversary of the company, Mishima launched the campaign 「カルピス」ひなまつりプレゼント (*Carupisu hinamatsuri purezento* [Calpis girls' festival gift]), targeting preschoolers. This programme is still active and coincides with a Shintō festival, 雛祭り (*Hinamatsuri* [Girls' festival]), which falls on March 3, when girls display beautiful doll sets, traditionally inherited from their mothers and grandmothers, and toast with 白酒 (*shirozake* [white sake]), a mild liquor with a milky colour. In a similar way, Calpis provides children with their beverages and, starting from 1982, small picture books created by established Japanese children's writers, the full versions being available in bookstores.[53]

Such operations show that Calpis consciously cherry-picked national festivities which were consistent with its brand image, creating a connection with quality children's education. This was anchored in Mishima's body and mind policy, resonating with the core values of Calpis according to his founder, namely, おいしい (*oishī* [delicious]), 滋養 (*jiyō* [nourishment]),

---

[50]Milk cartons, too, are often coloured blue and white, a typical association with 'cool' and 'milk'; Peter Stensel, *Design & Technology. Design for Life* (Singapore: Pearson Longman, 2007), 93.
[51]Jun Ikushima, *Inryō gyōkai no paionia supiritto* [*Pioneer spirit in the beverage industry*] (Tokyo: Fuyo Shobo, 2009), 59.
[52]Mami Aoyagi, 'Karupisu wa "hatsukoi no aji" to kotaeru Shōwa sedai mo igai to shiranai "7 / 7 Karupisu no hi"' ['7 July Calpis day' that even the Shōwa generation, who would answer Calpis is 'the taste of first love,' surprisingly doesn't know], *Okāsan Daigaku*, 6 July 2019. Available online: https://www.okaasan.net/mjreport/41572/ (accessed 18 March 2023).
[53]'"Karupisu" hinamatsuri purezento [Calpis girls' festival gift], *Asahi*, 2023. Available online: https://www.asahiinryo.co.jp/peace/hinamatsuri/ehon/ (accessed 18 March 2023).

安心感 (*anshinkan* [sense of security]) and 経済的 (*keizaiteki* [economical]).[54] The 母子 (*boshi* [mother and child]) niche was particularly relevant, as mothers typically dealt with child-rearing, administering products addressed to their sons – hence the need to strengthen Calpis connotation as a healthy drink suitable for children. This is evident in the advertising strategies of the 1960s, when, aside from launching several family oriented campaigns, Calpis started to include wholesome personalities such as the baseball player Nagashima Shigeo (長嶋 茂雄) (born 1936), already a national hero at the time.[55] Moreover, events such as the Olympic Games of 1964 prompted the spread of television as a home practice, so Calpis publicity expanded from printed media to TV commercials and shows.

As seen, female viewers became increasingly important for television in this decade. Given the interest of Calpis for targeting mothers, the company co-sponsored several TV series for women, such as 肝っ玉かあさん (*Kimottama kāsan* [*Courageous mom*]) (1968–72) or ありがとう (*Arigatō* [*Thank you*]) (1970–5). Created by the female producer 石井 ふく子 (Ishī Fukuko) (born 1926), these shows were home dramas, a Japanese TV genre focusing on family stories,[56] and were part of a successful evening programme, TBS木曜8時枠の連続ドラマ (*TBS mokuyō 8 ji waku no renzoku dorama* [*TBS Thursday 8:00 TV slot of serial drama*]). As a consequence, Calpis sales skyrocketed, and, in 1969, this allowed the company to sponsor its own TV programme, カルピスまんが劇場 (*Carupisu manga gekijō* [*Calpis Manga Theater*]).[57] It was a long-awaited achievement for Calpis. Being the sole sponsor meant taking its marketing campaign to the next level, providing airtime for commercials, but also elaborate stories to fit Calpis's corporate image.

The strand consisted of animated series broadcast by the commercial station Fuji TV (CX). As is the case with other private broadcasters, Fuji TV is integrated in a media conglomerate that also owns a newspaper company, and started airing sportive television contents to attract high ratings.[58] However, in the late 1960s and 1970s, the channel differentiated its production to cater to a family audience. Until the mid-1980s, Fuji TV adopted the slogan 母と子のフジテレビ (*haha to kodomo no Fuji terebi* [mother and children Fuji TV]), implying that television had to be fun if it

---

[54]Ikushima, *Inryō gyōkai no paionia supiritto*, 75.
[55]'"Karupisu ® no sekigyokutekina hansoku katsudō to terebi CM no kaishi' ["Calpis ® aggressive promotional activity and the start of Tv commercials], *Asahi*. Available online: https://www.asahiinryo.co.jp/entertainment/asahiinryohistory/pdf/brand/calpis/%E3%82%AB%E3%83%AB%E3%83%94%E3%82%B904_221221.pdf (accessed 18 July 2023), 9.
[56]Grössman, 'New Role Models for Men and Women?', 208.
[57]Matsumoto, *20 Seiki terebi dokuhon sekai meisaku gekijō taizen*, 150.
[58]Donna Wong, Isamu Kuroda and John Horne, 'Sport, Broadcasting, and Cultural Citizenship in Japan', in *Sport, Public Broadcasting and Cultural Citizenship. Signal Lost?*, ed. Jay Scherer and David Rowe (New York and Abingdong: Routledge, 2014).

was to be enjoyed.⁵⁹ Hence the channel became famous for its animation, variety programmes and dramas for the young. It was the same that aired *Atom* and other fortunate works, representing a perfect match for Calpis-themed publicity. Still, Calpis wanted to detach from contemporary Japanese animation, which often came from comics and live-action series or films, and, as such, could tackle a wide range of contents for increasingly diverse demographics. While most animated series favoured comical entertainment and fighting heroes, Calpis aimed at offering didactic shows for children, which would gain the approval of an already retained female audience, potentially expanding to the whole family. This is confirmed by the time slot of the programme, which was aired every Sunday at 7:30 pm, in appealing primetime territory, and during one of the few moments in the week when all family members gathered in front of the TV. The target is also evident in the title choice, which changed to カルピスこども劇場 (*Carupisu kodomo gekijō* [*Calpis children theater*]) in 1975, and to カルピスファミリー劇場 (*Carupisu famirī gekijō* [*Calpis family theater*]) in 1978.

Calpis brand building and animation: *Dororo*

As seen in Chapter 2, Japanese animetic TV series of the 1960s were fruitful assets for their sponsors, which exploited the popularity of beloved characters to promote their own products. At the same time, through the conduit of advertising and television, Japanese companies were interested in producing visual contents which aligned with their brand image. In this respect, it has been noted that Japanese advertising tends to be media-oriented rather than marketing-oriented, conveying a set of positive values which resonate with the audience without hard-selling products.⁶⁰ This kind of soft marketing, which attempts to intrigue viewers in the most creative ways, is evident in the practice of TV sponsorship, a frequent phenomenon by no means limited to Japanese animation. For example, the same title for *Calpis Theater* was redolent of themed programmes such as 東芝日曜劇場 (*Toshiba nichiyō gekijō* [*Toshiba Sunday theater*]) (aired since 1956) or 近鉄金曜劇場 (*Kintetsu kinyō gekijō* [*Kintetsu Friday theater*]) (1961–7), sponsored, respectively, by Japan's oldest producer of electronic products and one of the major railway companies of the country. Both programmes were hosted by TBS, a channel with which Calpis already collaborated and featured serial adaptations of Japanese novels.

---

⁵⁹Brian Moeran, *A Japanese Advertising Agency. An Anthropology of Media and Markets* (New York and Abingdong: Routledge, 2007).
⁶⁰Jason Xiao, 'When Advertising Meets Japan', *Medium*, 24 June 2019. Available online: https://medium.com/@zx548/why-japanese-advertising-stands-out-6488158d5e10 (accessed 21 March 2023).

This is even more relevant if we consider that the idea to create a 'Calpis Theater' was suggested by 加藤菊造 (Katō Kikuzō) (1930–?), an employee of the advertising agency Dentsu, which worked for Calpis.[61] The 1960s were a period of rapid economic growth, and Dentsu was on its way to become a large communications company, expanding to the TV advertising market.[62] Katō, who had been transferred to the parent company in Tokyo from Dentsu Hokkaido branch, already experienced the impact which animation characters could have on the consumer habits of children and families. For example, he cured the advertising for バンビキャラメル (*Banbi kyarameru* [Bambi caramel]), a line of toffee sweets produced by the Hokkaido-based confectioner Ikeda Seika, which in 1952 had obtained to use Disney's famous fawn as a trademark character, consequently becoming a big hit among children.[63] This happened over ten years before *Atom* was aired, and, to some extent, represented a forerunner of Tezuka's media mix. So it is perhaps not surprising that the first show of the *Calpis Theater* was a twenty-six-episode series based on どろろ (*Dororo*) (1969), a manga by Tezuka which had been serialized between 1967 and 1968.

Albeit belonging to the yōkai genre, *Dororo* did not feature the funny monsters and light-hearted comedy which were popular at the time. Instead, this is a period drama set in feudal Japan, telling the adventures of a masterless samurai, Hyakkimaru, whose body parts were stolen by demons, and his friend Dororo, a cheeky boy thief (actually a girl in disguise, a common theme in Tezuka's works). *Dororo* includes Faustian motifs (Hyakkimaru's father, Lord Daigo, makes a deal with the demons, sacrificing his son in exchange for power) and bold social themes (Hyakkimaru's discrimination for his physical diversity, but also his fight against his father to free the farmers from their oppressor). Such mature contents, redolent of Shirato's coeval opus, were probably among the reasons why the manga, originally published in a boys' magazine, was discontinued before Tezuka could explore Dororo's maturation into a young woman.[64] However, the comic was still ongoing when Calpis and Fuji TV requested an adaptation to Mushi, which started production in April 1968. It was a chaotic period for Tezuka's studio, which was increasingly straying from its founder, looking

---

[61]Hitsurō Hamada, 'Katō Kikuzō to Eiki no seishun fu (3)' [Katō Kikuzō and Eiki's youth records (3)], *Dentsu*, 13 December 2016. Accessible online: https://dentsu-ho.com/articles/4737 (accessed 21 March 2023).
[62]Dentsu Integrated Report, 'Overview of the Dentsu Group', 2019, 5. Available online: https://www.group.dentsu.com/en/sustainability/reports/2019/about/glance.html (accessed 18 July 2023).
[63]Hamada, 'Katō Kikuzō to Eiki no seishun fu (2)' [Katō Kikuzō and Eiki's youth records (2)], *Dentsu*, 11 December 2016. Accessible online: https://dentsu-ho.com/articles/4736 (accessed 21 March 2023).
[64]Clements and McCarthy, *The Anime Encyclopedia*, 159.

for new and commercially successful ways of making animation. Would *Dororo* help raise the fortunes of the company?

From national folk tales to Western fairy tales

The choice of *Dororo* as the starting point for the *Calpis Theater* can be read as an indicator of the policy behind this TV programme. Aside from the intermediation of Dentsu, with Katō's ideas being close to Tezuka's media mix strategy, *Dororo* is a story imbued with themes drawn from Buddhism and Japanese folklore, which were ingrained in local children's literature since the Meiji period. An example in *Dororo* is the Shintō motif of 異常誕生 (*ijiō tanjō* [abnormal birth]), folk tales on children born with some kind of impairment (often healed in the end of the narrative), embodying otherness and exceptionality.[65] Another common literary trope is the 貴種流離譚 (*kishu ryūri-tan* [legend of a wandering noble]), coming-of-age stories for the youth where noble-born protagonists undergo a series of trials, to some extent similar to Campbell's Hero's Journey.[66] These were probably appealing traits for Calpis, as they illustrated a connection to celebrated forms of juvenile fiction. Not only Japanese folk tales and myths were commonly inserted in children's book sets but they had also been adapted by Tōei, in the attempt to emulate Disney. Since Calpis had set its goals on creating wholesome animated stories for the young, this seems to suggest a parallel with Ōkawa's studio and the cinematic tradition of Japan's animation.

Another contact point with Tōei is in the way the *Calpis Theater* purposely bowdlerized contents for a juvenile audience. In fact, as pointed out in the previous paragraph, *Dororo* dwelled on subjects which were much darker than those expected by Calpis. Both sponsor and TV station must have been aware of this, as the choice of shooting the show in black and white (when most series were already produced in colour) was dictated by the need to dilute the sight of bloody battles.[67] A puppy dog wearing a traditional hat, Nota, was added to the cast as a travelling companion for Dororo and Hyakkimaru as well as a comical sidekick, reminiscent of the cute, anthropomorphic animals of Tōei's films. Moreover, Calpis and Fuji TV intervened halfway through the series to revise the format and make it more palatable for children. This resulted in a number of changes, including the opening (from a rebellious march to Dororo running playfully on village

---

[65] Okuyama, *Japanese Mythology in Film*, 134–5.
[66] This structure is also typical of national legends, such as those told in the 古事記 *Kojiki* [*Records of ancient things*], a chronicle dating back to the VIII century; Okuyama, *Japanese Mythology in Film*, 137–9.
[67] 'Dororo', *Mushi Production*, 2018. Available online: https://www.mushi-pro.co.jp/2010/09/どろろ/ (accessed 23 March 2023).

FIGURE 3.1A *Mushi Pro's animators created a smooth motion for Hyakkimaru and Dororo's walk cycle in* Dororo's *ending credits sequence.*

roofs) and the narrative style (less scary monsters and more emphasis on Dororo as the central character).[68] Also the 冠 (*kanmuri* [title of the programme]) began to appear from Episode 14, with the words for 'Calpis Manga Theater' morphing into the new title of the series, どろろと百鬼丸 (*Dororo to Hyakkimaru* [*Dororo and Hyakkimaru*]), incorporating what was easily perceived as a protagonist.

Although not very successful in terms of ratings, *Dororo* boasted a degree of complexity which was ahead of its time, allowing it to become a cult series in later years. *Dororo*'s adult flavour had something to do with its staff, such as directors 杉井 ギサブロー (Sugī Gisaburo) (born 1940), a collaborator of Tezuka's animerama, and 出崎統 (Dezaki Osamu) (1943–2011), who would direct the dramatic spokon あしたのジョ (*Ashita no Jō* [*Tomorrow's Joe*]) (1970). However, while these animetic shows were not geared towards children, *Dororo*'s graphic violence was at odds with the target which Calpis had in mind, mismatching the sponsor's brand image. This prompted a change of route of the *Calpis Theater* right after its start. Hence Takahashi's project came into play. When he worked for TCJ, he was involved in the production of commercials for both Dentsu and Calpis.[69] It was the advertising department of Calpis that trusted Takahashi's idea of making animated adaptations of Western stories, supporting the production of *Moomin* – provided, as will be recalled, by Tokyo Movie – as the

---

[68]'Dororo', *Mushi Production*. See also the useful Wikipedia page in Japanese: https://ja.wikipedia.org/wiki/どろろ_(アニメ) (accessed 23 March 2023).
[69]Ono, 'Takahashi Shigeto', 202.

FIGURE 3.1B *The final battle between Hyakkimaru and Lord Kagemitsu, possessed by demons (Episode 26). In the previous scene, Hyakkimaru tells Dororo that he knows she is a girl, hoping she will become a happy mother in the future.*

second work for the *Calpis Theater*. Again, this was a similarity with Tōei, whose theatricals were increasingly based on Western stories, with a good reception abroad and domestically. Note that the other work on slate was a possible adaptation of ハレンチ学園 (*Harenchi gakuen* [*Shameless school*]) (1968–72), the famous manga by 永井 豪 (Nagai Gō) (born 1945), much criticized by teachers and Parent-Teacher Associations (PTAs) for inserting eroticism in boys' comics. This facilitated the choice of *Moomin* as more suitable to represent the sponsor, also considering Calpis' historic openness to westernization, and the superior quality afforded to western children's literature by contemporary critics.

Once upon a time in Scandinavia: *Andersen stories*

In spite of the modest expectations of the broadcaster – a person from Fuji TV said that, had they got double-digit ratings, he would have walked upside down in Ginza, Tokyo's luxury district[70] – the adaptation of *Moomin* gradually gained popularity. Ratings were not exceptional (from 10 to 15%), but established a basis for the future of *WMT*.[71] The positive outcome pleased Calpis, which had initially commissioned twenty-six episodes (or two クール, *kūru* [courses], one course being a Japanese broadcast unit of thirteen episodes scheduled for three months), as in *Dororo*. So the sponsor

---

[70]Ibid.
[71]'Mūmin' [Moomin]. *Asahi gurafu zōkan* [*Asahi Graph special edition*], 15 March 1978, 63.

FIGURE 3.2A *Moomintroll snatching his dad's rifle in* Moomin *(Episode 5). Note that the moral of the episode is against violence, as Moomintroll learns from Snufkin, a wise wanderer who just arrived in town.*

asked for an extension to cover a full year of programming, hence the production switched from Tokyo Movie – which by then had made plans for starting another series, ルパン三世 (*Rupan sansei* [*Lupin III*]) (1971) – to Mushi.[72] It was an uncommon move for a show already on air, and a source of confusion for both viewers and creators of the series. Especially Mushi's staff faced many problems as they kept the series going for another thirty-nine episodes, introducing adjustments to bring it closer to the original. Nonetheless, the troubled production did not prevent *Moomin*, which ran from October 1969 to March 1970, to become a favourite in Japan and the first step towards a popular franchise, accounting for a spin-off series, 新ムーミン (*Shin Mūmin* [*New Moomin*]) (1972), always delivered by Mushi and the second work of the *Calpis Theater*,[73] and, in the 1990s, a co-production series, a movie and several ads.[74]

One of the reasons why *Moomin* stories struck a chord in the heart of the audience was the positive values that, in the 1960s and early 1970s, Japan associated with 北欧 (*Hokuō* [Northern Europe or Scandinavia]).[75]

---

[72]Chiba, *Haiji ga umareta hi*, 51.
[73] For more information on the series, see Toadette, 'Rintarō, "New Moomin" (1972), and the Last Days of Mushi Pro', *On the Ones*, 23 March 2023. Available online: https://ontheones.wordpress.com/2023/03/23/rintaro-new-moomin-1972-and-the-last-days-of-mushi-pro/ (accessed 24 March 2023).
[74]Liisa Vähäkylä, *Nordic Animation: Balancing the East and the West* (Abingdon: CRC Press, 2023).
[75]Mitsui, 'Uses of Finland in Japan's Social Imaginary', 170–3.

FIGURE 3.2B *Moomintroll greets his best friend Snufkin, who helped him in secret in* New Moomin *(Episode 4). In this series, Moomintroll's pointed ears and rounded eyes are closer to Jansson's original drawings.*

Envisioned as a set of small but strong and modern nations, Scandinavia embodied a model which Japan aspired to emulate since the Meiji era, thus drawing the interest of Japanese politicians, sociologists and educators. The desired qualities attached to Hokuō, which are reflected in Takahashi's passion for Nordic culture, allow to cast a light on the reception of *Moomin* as a wholesome piece of entertainment. The broadcasting slot for *Moomin* was another key factor, suggesting an atmosphere of domestic bliss.[76] This was also because the years sandwiched between Japan's poor post-war and the bubble economy have been retrospectively regarded as an idyllic past, still unharmed by the effects of industrialization – hence the widespread vision of *Moomin* as part of the comfortable lifestyle of the middle class. A similar idealization concerned Moominvalley, the forest where Moomins live (which in fact, after the burst of the bubble, was framed in terms of ecological awareness in the Japanese media[77]).

The success of *Moomin* paved the way for the third series of the *Calpis Theater*, アンデルセン物語 (*Anderusen monogatari* [*Andersen stories*]), again based on a corpus of Scandinavian fairy tales, the first to be translated into Japanese in the Meiji era.[78] Produced by Mushi and planned by Zuiyō,

---

[76]Ibid., 163–4.
[77]Ibid., 167.
[78]Katsumi Hayano, 'Hans Christian Andersen Research Situation in Japan', *Andersen SDU*, 1993. Available online: https://andersen.sdu.dk/forskning/konference/tekst.html?id=9730 (accessed 24 March 2023); Toshihiko Satō, 'Hans Christian Andersen's "The Improvisator" in

the show started airing in January 1971 and consisted of fifty-two episodes, a yearly set which would become the norm for the programme.[79] As seen, Andersen's literary works were hugely popular in Japan and had been repeatedly adapted for cinema, most recently by Tōei, which probably made them look like a safe bet for a TV series. Takahashi also felt that Andersen's tales were easier for small children to understand.[80] In addition, a framing device was used whereby a couple of 妖精 (*yōsei* [fairies]), Chianti and Zucco, travel to the fairy-tale world, collecting cards which materialize with good deeds. Although they rarely interact with the main plot, these characters create a connection with the young audience, breaking the fourth wall and voicing the moral of a story. For example, in みにくいあひるの子 (*Minikui ahiru no ko* [*The Ugly Duckling*]) (Episodes 1–2), Chianti empathizes with the protagonist, who is discriminated for his look, deciding to help him. Note that, as a rule of thumb, the animation stayed true to the original narratives, but often expanded them to cover two-to-four episodes, stressing relatable themes such as motherly love. Think of the pilot, where mother duck sincerely cares for her adoptive son, pretending not to recognize him as a swan only to let him free to live his life – a very different reading from Disney's homonymous *Silly Symphony* (1939).

Zuiyō's formula for TV animation

While working on *Andersen stories*, Mushi was torn by internal dissensions and rising debts. On the one hand, the momentary success of Tezuka's animerama inspired hope for the future of adult animation.[81] On the other hand, a growing number of animators started questioning Tezuka's skills as president, producing TV series unrelated to his comics, as was the case with the two *Moomin* series and *Andersen stories*. As a consequence, these shows increasingly display Zuiyō's – rather than Mushi's – ideas on animation, foreshadowing a number of practices which were later adopted for *WMT*.

Andersen stories denotes Takahashi's interest in the adaptation of Western (namely Scandinavian) fairy tales and his goal of creating animation for an international audience. In fact, the series was released in Europe and the Middle East by the American company Paramount Television, with 植村伴次郎 (Uemura Banjiro) (1929–2019), the head of the Japanese

---

Japan', *Museum Odense*, 1 January 1963. Available online: https://museumodense.dk/artikler/hans-christian-andersens-the-improvisator-in-japan/ (accessed 24 March 2023).
[79]Matsumoto, *20 Seiki terebi dokuhon sekai meisaku gekijō taizen*, 49.
[80]Ono, 'Takahashi Shigeto', 14.
[81]Prandoni, *Anime al cinema*, 58.

distributor Tōhokushinsha, as executive producer.⁸² In line with Takahashi's approach to foreign fiction, the writing is generally faithful to the original – which implies maintaining Andersen's often tragic ends – however, for the same purpose of marketing the series for a global public, references to religion were removed in the adaptation. So, while the stories of the Danish author featured overt Christian themes, these are typically eschewed in *Andersen stories* in favour of other cultural markers. For example, 沼の王の娘 (Numa no ō no musume [The Marsh King's Daughter]) (Episodes 21–23), a long tale of the animal groom type (an Egyptian princess is kidnapped by a frog king in Denmark, and a cursed child is born from their union, who will marry an Arabian prince), kept the exotic elements of the source text, eliminating the protagonist's conversion, death and final going to Heaven. Other disturbing premises were completely refurbished, as in 赤いくつ (Akai kutsu [The Red Shoes]) (Episodes 42–43), originally a gruesome story about vanity and repentance, which is transformed into a light-hearted comedy in the animation.⁸³

The mitigation of the serious aspects of Andersen's stories is also indicative of the importance attached to comic relief. In the series this is provided by Chianti and Zucco, whose insouciant behaviour always gets them into trouble, giving way to slapstick fun. Further gags stem from their clashing personalities, Chianti being romantic and dreamy, Zucco, laid-back and ironic.⁸⁴ Consider that, in terms of structure, these situations convey horizontality to a highly vertical series, the show being an omnibus of thirty-one fairy tales. The presence of shorter and often self-contained storylines is suggestive of a young audience, diverging from Mushi's recent attempts to cater older demographics. This is reflected in the way the series mixed a simple and colourful style redolent of children's illustrations – as happened in Tōei's films for the same target – and certain characters with a more adult attire. Think of the female protagonists of 'The Marsh King's Daughter', whose edgy look recalls the sexy heroines of Tezuka's animerama. It is worth noting that Chianti and Zucco, the most manga-like characters of the series, were designed by the comic artist and researcher 牧野 圭一 (Keīchi

---

⁸²Uemura, who is credited in the English opening titles of the series, in 1961 founded Tōhokushinsha Film Corporation (TFC), originally a dub house for foreign TV programmes such as Bewitched. Since the mid-1960s, TFC also represented the British distributor ITC Entertainment in Japan, becoming involved in film production and licensing; 'Banjiro "Banji" Uemura 1929-2019', *Videoage*, 22 October 2019. Available online: https://www.videoageinternational.net/2019/10/22/watercooler/banjiro-banji-uemura-1929-2019/ (accessed 4 April 2023).
⁸³The series preserved the high concept of the tale (a pair of red shoes able to dance on their own), eliminating the attached moral (a girl is punished for her sins by dancing in her red shoes until she dies) and horror beats (when chopped off, the girl's feet never stop dancing).
⁸⁴Fun fact: the voice actors for Zucco and Chianti were the same who played the sly thief Lupin III and his love interest Fujiko Mine in the first animated series of *Rupan sansei*.

FIGURE 3.3A *Chianti transforms into a clumsy dragon to chase off the cats who were after the Ugly Duckling in* Andersen stories *(Episode 1).*

Makino) (1937–2022), while the other characters were created by 関 修一 (Seki Shūichi) (born 1946), a promising animator who would collaborate on many *WMT* shows.[85] This also reveals how works planned by Zuiyō were influenced by artists from different studios, as both Seki and Keīchi were former TCJ employees.

Cuteness is another ingredient in Zuiyō's series. Chianti and Zucco's appearance is emblematic of this, being reminiscent of anthropomorphic piglets, with little snouts, big eyes and fluffy hair. As observed, cute cartoon characters were typical of Disney's opus, which left an imprint on both the animetic and cinematic traditions of Japanese animation. Note how Chianti, as a shapeshifter fairy, is able to morph into several funny creatures without losing her definable features, recalling the memorable transformations of Merlin and Madam Mim in *The Sword in the Stone* (1963). Aside from their merchandising potential – which, as we will see, would be a reason for conflict between Calpis and Zuiyō – the presence of little and endearing characters was a contact point with the sponsor. In fact, together with the theme of motherly love, the series focused on childlike protagonists, even when the original featured grownups or adolescents, to suit the younger audience which Calpis aimed to reach. Likewise, romance is portrayed as a budding friendship sanitized from eroticism, in line with Calpis brand image of innocence and the catchphrase 'the taste of first love'. For example, in プシケ (Pushike [Psyche]) (Episode 49), a loose adaptation

---

[85]Chiba, *Haiji ga umareta hi*, 53.

FIGURE 3.3B *Chianti and Zucco are moved to tears by the sad story of the 'Little Match-selling Girl' (Episode 52).*

of the homonymous tale, dramatically directed by Dezaki, a sculptor kid falls in love with a girl of the same age, rejecting her feelings when she is transformed into a grownup goddess. Young companions could also be added from scratch in the series, as happens in マッチ売りの少女 (Matchi uri no shōjo [The Little Match Girl]) (Episode 52).

From Europe to America: *Yama nezumi Rocky Chuck*

Zuiyō did not only engage with retellings of traditional fairy tales from the Western canon. As was the case with the 'Moomin' shows, the company was also keen on making animation based on modern-day children's literature from the West. In fact, for the next series of the *Calpis Theater*, the choice fell on the work of Thornton W. Burgess (1874–1965), a prolific Massachusetts author of animal fables. These were regarded as favourites in America, where they had been published daily on the syndicated newspaper column 'Bedtime stories' since 1910, for a total of 70 books and 15,000 tales.[86] A selection of twenty Burgess's animal books was released in Japan in 1969, by the children's publisher Kin'nohoshisha.[87] As seen, animal stories held a special place in local children's fiction, with book series constantly featuring

---

[86] Paul O'Neil, 'Green Meadow. At 86, Thornton W. Burgess Endures as Classic Tale-teller', *Life*, 14 November 1960, 113.
[87] Fukuda and Yamanushi, *Nihon jidō bungeishi*, 418.

Aesop's Fables as well as fictionalized but believable accounts of nature such as Seton's. The preference for this genre is exemplified by the first translation (in any language) of Beatrix Potter's 'The Tale of Peter Rabbit' (1902), which appeared in 1906 in a Japanese farm magazine.[88] Note that it was from Potter, who was roughly contemporary with Burgess, that he borrowed the name Peter Rabbit for one of his characters, all of which he tried to portray in a realistic manner, detaching from the anthropomorphic style of the British writer-cum-illustrator.[89]

Burgess's body of work was well suited to Zuiyō's approach to animation. This had become substantially important by 1972, when Mushi was close to bankruptcy and thus no longer able to run the business, so Takahashi established a subsidiary of Zuiyō Enterprise, Zuiyō Eizō, for animation production.[90] In terms of exportability, optioning an American property meant a concrete chance for the company to reach English-speaking countries, a much courted market since Tōei's first theatricals. From an educational standpoint, which was also of great importance for both Zuiyō and the sponsor, Burgess's stories ticked all the boxes, as they taught children about wildlife (the author quoted biologists and zoologists, including the same Seton, among his sources[91]), without neglecting moral lessons. Moreover, as Jansson's *Moomin*, these stories boasted pretty illustrations and a nature-friendly message, Burgess himself being a conservationist.[92] Last but not least, his attitude towards the depiction of reality was another contact point. Burgess made sure to convey true facts about nature, but took some liberties when creating a fictional world which could feel safe for children ('What Does Old Man Coyote Eat?' was a reviewer's salacious comment, pointing to the avoidance of death in his stories[93]). This had a connection to what Connor calls the cinematic quality of Burgess's prose,[94] where predators perpetually chase their prey to no avail, as in Hannah and Barbera slapstick cartoons.

A mix of realism and stylized traits characterized also 山ねずみロッキーチャック (*Yama nezumi Rokkī Chakku* [*Rocky Chuck the mountain rat*]) (1973), the animated adaptation of Burgess's tales and the first series produced by Zuiyō. By then, the studio was an old one-storey

---

[88]Wakabayashi, 'Foreign Bones, Japanese Flesh', 242.
[89]Diane Speare Triant, 'The Curious Tale of Peter Rabbit', *Cape Cod Life*, November/December 2018. Available online: https://capecodlife.com/the-curious-tale-of-peter-rabbit/ (accessed 7 April 2023).
[90]Chiba, *Haiji ga umareta hi*, 55.
[91]Thornton W. Burgess, *The Burgess Animal Book for Children* (Mineola: Dover Publications, Inc.), vi.
[92]Burgess' characters were reproduced on a plethora of goods, including tin, stickum paper, ceramic, cracker dough and jewellery; O'Neil, 'Green Meadow'.
[93]Quoted in Kathleen-Marie Connor, 'Beyond the Words of a Storyteller: The Cine-semiotic Play of the Abject, Terror and Community in the Anti-hunting Trilogy of Thornton W. Burgess', PhD thesis (Ottawa: University of Ottawa, 2007), 237–8.
[94]Ibid.

building in Asagaya, a residential area of Tokyo.⁹⁵ As Chiba explains, it was almost by chance that Zuiyō's employees had been poached from other companies, later contributing to several works of WMT. For instance, 中島 順三 (Nakajima Junzō) (1938–2022), a still-life photographer with some experience in animation, joined Zuiyō with the idea of making commercials, a project which Takahashi was considering to take on but did not concretize.⁹⁶ Nakajima was thus redirected to *Rocky Chuck*, debuting as an animation producer. What followed was a sort of chain reaction. For the position of planning manager, Nakajima brought in 佐藤昭司 (Satō Shōji) (born 1938), a fellow student at Nihon University College of Art who was also in the animation field. In turn, Satō persuaded his friend 遠藤 政治 (Endō Masaharu) (born 1933), who cut his teeth at Mushi, to get involved as a director and character designer. Formerly a comic artist, Endō was keen on drawings animals, and thought that the show would be perfect for Mori. The legendary animator was unsatisfied with the new trends of Tōei – which, as seen, was more and more focused on animetic TV shows – so, after sixteen years of work, transferred to Zuiyō, where he served as animation director from Episode 12 of *Rocky Chuck*.⁹⁷

As *Moomin*, *Rocky Chuck* told the everyday adventures of a group of friends that live in harmony with nature, with a slow tempo and a nod to young viewers. Mori's trademark cute style enhanced Endō's animal sketches, ensuring a cuddly feel which lacked in the original. Think of the drawings by Harrison Cady (1877–1970), Burgess's official illustrator, which look closer to the tradition of satirical cartoons. Mori also gave uniformity to the animation, striving for smooth movements with a realistic effect. Note that, differently from other funny animals designed by Mori, such as those in Tōei's TV series ハッスルパンチ (*Hassuru Panchi* [*Hustle Punch*]) (1965), Zuiyō's show displayed lifelike animals – in spite of their whimsical anthropomorphic clothes – and a breathtaking attention to detail. The realistic characters and the episodic plot of *Rocky Chuck* were faithful to the source texts, and so was the location – an overall safe world where the occasional dangers have little to no consequences to the lives of the protagonists. However, the adaptation selected one book (*The adventures of Johnny Chuck*, 1913) among Burgess's numerous works, concentrating on a central character, renamed Rocky and changed to a mountain rat, the woodchuck species being absent in Japan.⁹⁸

---

⁹⁵Chiba, *Haiji ga umareta hi*, 119.
⁹⁶Ibid., 56.
⁹⁷Seiji Kano, '"Arupusu no shōjo Haiji" de Takahata enshutsu ga mezashita mono' ['What director Takahata aimed for in "Heidi girl of the Alps"'], *BS anime yawa*, vol. 7, 1 April 2008, 137. According to Kano, it was Ōtsuka who introduced Mori to Takahashi. However, Chiba notes that it was the insistence of Endō and Satō to win over Mori to Zuiyō; Chiba, *Haiji ga umareta hi*, 57.
⁹⁸Peter Oehlkers, 'Johnny Chuck in Japan', *Thornton W. Burgess Research League*, 8 March 2010. Available online: https://twbresearchleague.blogspot.com/2010/03/johnny-chuck-in-japan.html (accessed 10 April 2023).

This allowed to create a more horizontal series, gradually detaching from the verticality of *Moomin* and *Andersen stories*.

International childishness for Calpis and Zuiyō

In a period when animated series for children were highly influenced by American TV shows, with slapstick comedy and self-contained episodes, *Rocky Chuck*'s realism was a first. Also the circular movement of the narrative, which begins when spring arrives and ends in winter, conveyed a sense of authenticity, stressing seasonal changes and other markers of a cyclic notion of time. These cultural preferences, which would be maintained in future works of *WMT*, fitted well to the coming-of-age scheme of the main plot, where an adventurous little chuck wanders in search of a new home. Note that, whereas Burgess's Johnny is described as a gutsy teenager, Zuiyō's Rocky is a lively and enthusiastic child, as other protagonists of the *Calpis Theater*, and the ideal public of the programme. Rocky's characterization resonates with values traditionally associated with childhood in Japan, where preschoolers and elementary school students are expected to be 元気 (*genki* [energetic]), their noisy exuberance being encouraged by educators as 子供らしい (*kodomo-rashī* [child-like]).[99] Johnny's braveness and his need to settle down as a proper grownup are emphasized in the series, raising the stakes for Rocky. In fact, differently from Johnny, who was already living alone at the beginning of the story, Rocky has a loving family that cares for him. So, when Sister South Wind invites him and his brothers to stand on their own feet and go living in the 広い世界 (*hiroi sekai* [wide world]) (Episode 2), the challenge is even higher as it means leaving their nest and relatives behind.

Aside from being a twist on the original (Rocky moves to the Green Forest, while Johnny lives in the Meadows, as a real chuck would do), Rocky's striving for independence looks poles apart from the indulgent parent-child relation known as 甘え (*amae* [passive love]). Instead of allowing mama chuck to nurture Rocky, papa chuck seems aligned with the American educational standpoint whereby children must be trained to be separated from their family, cultivating their individuality and freedom to choose on their own.[100] This is more relevant if we consider the similarities between Rocky Chuck and the advertisement which Dentsu created for Calpis in the same period. A popular commercial of 1971, which was awarded at ACC Festival for television, featured a little girl of about four, タミーちゃん

---

[99]Catherine C. Lewis, *Educating Hearts and Minds: Reflections on Japanese Preschool and Elementary Education* (New York: Cambridge University Press, 1995), 49.
[100]Merry White, *The Japanese Educational Challenge. A Commitment to Children* (New York: Simon & Schuster, 1988), 41.

FIGURE 3.4A *Rocky Chuck facing the challenges of the outside world on his own (Episode 2). Note the realistic falcon versus Rocky's anthropomorphic look.*

FIGURE 3.4B *The woodchuck confronting his family before leaving his nest. Rocky has decided to go live in a bigger forest, and his father approves (Episode 2).*

(Tamī-chan [little Tamī]).[101] In the advert, Tamī answers the phone in lieu of her (apparently absent) mother, and engages in a playful mimicry of an adult, fidgeting on the spot and sipping the milky drink, then licks her

---

[101]"Karupisu "hahaoya Tamī-chan to denwa"' [Calpis 'Mother little Tamī on the phone"], *Broadcast Library*, 2023. Available online: https://www.bpcj.or.jp/search/show_detail.php?program=150600 (accessed 10 April 2023).

lips in typical childish fashion. A similar pattern was followed in another advert where Tamī looks home alone, humming to herself while dressing up. These narratives, which represented childhood as combining the values of cuteness, liveliness and self-reliance, acquired an international flavour in Calpis contemporary commercials starring the American music group the Osmonds.

The Osmonds were a band from Utah whose pop ballads enjoyed great popularity in the early 1970s, especially with young girls.[102] Moreover, they were a large Mormon family who saw music as an evangelical mission, and their squeaky-clean image tapped into the public's yearning for traditional values which would be questioned in later years.[103] This made them a good fit for the Calpis' brand, and even more so after 1970, when 土倉 冨士雄 (Dokura Fujio) (1908–1983), the former vice president and a fervent Christian, became the head of the company.[104] Hence, when the Osmonds toured Japan in 1970, they were invited to promote Calpis in a series of commercials, which proved incredibly successful.[105] These depicted heartwarming scenes of family life (being at home, companionship of siblings, outdoor leisure, etc.), in which all the Osmonds – patriarch George and grandmother Laverne included – sang catchy tunes and often danced together, suggesting that Calpis was good for the whole family. Whereas some adverts were parent-oriented, for example, featuring mom and dad relaxing while kids were out, it was little Jimmy Osmond to take the spotlight, saying the punch line 'Calpis'. As happened in Tamī's commercials, the emphasis was on Jimmy's peppy but responsible behaviour, with a notable difference: blond and cherubic, Jimmy bespoke foreign as he was shown playing pirates on a yacht, or in a ranch with his brothers, epitomizing Japan's fascination for the American way of life.

There seems to be a consistency between the Calpis' adverts and the shows of the *Calpis Theater*, especially if we consider that they were aired in the same time slot.[106] Both displayed the nuclear family as a safe haven and wholesome images of Western lifestyle, offering a conceptualization of

---

[102]The group drew inspiration from wholesome boy singers such as Paul Anka, but also from the bubblegum pop and synchronized dance of the Jackson 5; Arie Kaplan, *American Pop: Hit Makers, Superstars, and Dance Revolutionaries* (Minneapolis: Twenty-First Century Books, 2013), 18.

[103]Lynita K. Newswander, Chad B. Newswander, and Lee Trepanier, 'Mormonism', in *The Routledge Companion to Religion and Popular Culture*, ed. John C. Lyden and Eric Michael Mazur (Abingdon and New York: Routledge, 2015), 503.

[104]Keiei chōsa kenkyūkakai [Management research institute], *Nihon o sodateru shidōsha no kiroku: keizai-hen* [*Memoirs of leaders who nurture Japan: economy*] (Tokyo: Keiei chōsa kenkyūkakai, 1973), 237; Kazuyoshi Oshima, 'Dokura Fujio', *Patrasche.net*, 20 May 2010. Available online: http://www.patrasche.net/nello/human/09.html (accessed 10 April 2023).

[105]Donny Osmond, *Life Is Just What You Make It: The Autobiography* (London: Orion, 2006), 73.

[106]Matsumoto, *20 Seiki terebi dokuhon sekai meisaku gekijō taizen*, 150.

childhood as energetic and looking forward to grow up. In addition, as seen for *Rocky Chuck*, the Osmonds' commercials had a seasonal progression (from spring to winter), with different settings according to the time of year, as Calpis can be served cool or warm. This cemented the equation between Zuiyō's animation, Calpis' branding and the mainstream audience of the *Calpis Theater*.

Co-producing animated series with the West: *Vicke*

While Calpis' commercials were produced for Japanese consumption, *Rocky Chuck* was exported worldwide. The series was released in English by the American distributor ZIV International, and then sold to over twenty countries from the four continents. Consider that, from the 1960s, Japan had started to penetrate the Western markets, aided by the nation's currency exchange rate, which was pegged artificially high to make Japanese goods cheaper abroad.[107] The European countries were particularly receptive to Japanese animation, as a ready-to-use packet (dubbing costs excluded) to fill the ever-increasing television slots.[108] For example, *Rocky Chuck* was aired in Austria, Italy, the Netherlands, Poland, Portugal, Romania, Spain and West Germany.[109] So it is perhaps not surprising that Zuiyō started to collaborate with Europe, where local companies could benefit from Japan's know-how and affordable prices, engaging in international co-production. Differently from outsourced animation, co-production implies cultural and historical ties between the countries that team up for collaboration, granting access to the partner's domestic market, as well as allowing tax breaks or other benefits.[110] As self-explanatory as it may sound, animation is an expensive business, and co-production between different countries is still among the most common practices of animation production in Europe.

As a result, Zuiyō's Euro-Japanese TV series took advantage of animation as a transnational language to adapt successful books known in Japan and abroad. Among these, 小さなバイキング ビッケ (*Chīsana baikingu Bikke* [*Little viking Vicke*] (1972–4) was the first co-production

---

[107]Louis G. Perez, *Tokyo: Geography, History, and Culture* (Santa Barbara: ABC-CLIO, 2019), 88.
[108]Marco Pellitteri, 'Cultural Politics of J-Culture and "Soft Power": Tentative Remarks from a European Perspective', in *Mangatopia: Essays on Manga and Anime in the Modern World*, ed. Timothy Perper and Martha Cornog (Santa Barbara: ABC-CLIO, 2011), 223–4.
[109]'Fables of the Green Forest: Release info', *IMDb*, 2023. Available online: https://www.imdb.com/title/tt0408436/releaseinfo/?ref_=tt_dt_aka#akas (accessed 12 April 2023).
[110]Stephen Follows, 'Which Countries Most Commonly Team up to Create Film Co-productions?', *Stephen Follows: Film Data and Education*, 22 April 2019. Available online: https://stephenfollows.com/most-frequent-co-producing-nations/ (accessed 14 April 2023).

between the Federal Republic of Germany and Japan.[111] Written by the Swedish author Runer Jonsson (1916–2006), the inspiring work was a series of novels called *Vicke Viking*, on a small but clever Norse boy, whose first book was published in 1963.[112] It was, again, a Scandinavian story, and an interesting twist on the Viking lore (Vicke hates violence despite being the child of a fearless warrior), released in Japan in 1967 as the first instalment of the multivolume set 少年少女新しい世界の文学 (*Shōnen shōjo atarashī sekai no bungaku* [Boys and girls' new world literature]). Vicke reached the peak of popularity in West Germany, where it won the local *Kinderbuchpreis* (Children's Book Award) in 1965. This is why ZDF, Germany's public broadcaster, approached Zuiyō to make an animated adaptation of Jonsson's book.[113] In fact, Josef Göhlen, who was the head of ZDF's juvenile department, was looking for a way to create affordable but reliable animation for the Western market, compromising with Disney's high-quality production values.[114] This resulted in a joint venture between Zuiyō, ZDF, ORF (an Austrian public broadcaster) and the majors Beta and Taurus Film, owned by the West German media mogul Leo Kirch, the largest film distributor in Europe.[115]

Vicke had a lot in common with the works of the *Calpis Theater*, starting from its staff. Initially commissioned to Mushi, the series was created by Zuiyō's newly constituted pool of talents, with Seki adapting the German design for animation and 斎藤 博 (Saitō Hiroshi) (1936–2015), a former animator, directing the show. Like Seki, the producer 大場伊紘 (Ōba Yoshihiro) (born 1943) was an ex-TCJ member, who joined Zuiyō since the making of *Moomin*, while Saitō transferred to the company with Endō for the production of *Rocky Chuck*. As Calpis' shows, the series had a yearly format and catered to children, with a horizontal arc (Vicke travelling the world with his father's crew) and an episodic scheme, which stressed universal values such as problem-solving and pacifism. The protagonist is a model child who always saves the day using his imagination rather than brute force. Vicke's girlfriend, Ylvi, allowed identification from female

---

[111]Verena Doker-Tobler, 'Zeichentrickfilm und Comics aus medienpädagogischer Sicht' [Film animation and comics from a media education perspective] in *Comics and Visual Culture. Research Studies from ten Countries*, ed. Alphons Silbermann and H.-D. Dyroff (München: K.G. Saur, 1986), 250.
[112]Mary Ørvig, *Children's Books in Sweden, 1945–1970: A Survey* (Vienna: Austrian Children's Book Club, 1973), 21.
[113]Chiba, *Haiji ga umareta hi*, 54.
[114]Kerstin Eßer, 'Kinderprogramm ist Zeichentrick' [Children's programming is animation], in *Handbuch Medienerziehung im Kindergarten. Teil 1: Pädagogische Grundlagen* [*Handbook of Media Education in Kindergarten. Part 1: Pedagogical basics*], ed. Christine Feil et al. (Opladen: Leske + Budrich, 1994), 391.
[115]Leonie Naughton, *That Was the Wild East. Film Culture, Unification, and the 'New' Germany* (Ann Arbor: The University of Michigan, 2002), 54.

viewers, while character representation had an international flavour, mixing Norse typical iconography (the Vikings wear idiosyncratic hornet helmets and flails) and recognizable everyday behaviours (Vicke's family life with a supportive mom and an impulsive dad), as happened in the comic strips of another famous Viking of the period, Hägar the Horrible (1973).[116] Last but not least, *Vicke* was based on a Western book which, though not being a classic, had a strong premise and potential for intermedia storytelling, as *Moomin* and *Rocky Chuck*. The underlying idea is that Zuiyō's shows, aside from building on the fame of renowned classics, attempted to create new 'masterpieces' through animation. As we will see, a similar polarity can be found in the production of the *Calpis Theater* and the future *WMT*.

Heidi: A Japanese show for Europe?

Vicke was neither the first nor the last case of Euro-Japanese co-production. Already in 1969, the French company Telcia Films approached Eiken to create the animated series *Oum, le dauphin blanc* [*Oum the white dolphin*] (1971), whose dolphin protagonist would become the mascot for Nestlé's Galak brand of chocolate.[117] This paved the way for future collaborations whereby European networks and studios co-produced and/or sponsored animated series physically made in Japan, such as *Barbapapa* (Holland/Japan, 1974), *Calimero* (Italy/Japan, 1972–5) and *Maya the Honeybee* (Austria/Japan, 1975–6), the latter being created by Zuiyō (and later Nippon Animation).[118] These series displayed a distinctive standardized style which Iglesias calls 'animesque', impacting the reception of Japanese animation in Europe.[119] Moreover, the features highlighted for *Vicke* – a strong vertical structure on the problem/solution formula, a relatable child protagonist, the delivery of educational but not preachy messages, and the adaptation of an appealing literary property – are consistent not only with the *Calpis Theater* but also with the way animated co-productions are currently devised in Europe, especially in their hunt for licensed (and licensable) characters and stories. So it is perhaps not surprising that the above-mentioned co-productions underwent several remakes in the last few decades.

---

[116]The child brain of the American cartoonist Dik Browne (1917–1989); Tristan Mueller-Vollmer and Kirsten Wolf, *Vikings: An Encyclopedia of Conflict, Invasions, and Raids* (Santa Barbara: ABC-CLIO, 2022), 78–9.
[117]Pierre Faviez, *La Télé: un destin animé* [*TV: an animated destiny*] (Paris: Société des Écrivains, 2010), 16. The French show was probably inspired by the American *Flipper* (film and series), which was in turn an aquatic take on Hollywood's most famous dog Lassie.
[118]Bendazzi, *Animation*, 363.
[119]José Andrés Santiago Iglesias, 'The Anime Connection. Early Euro-Japanese Co-Productions and the Animesque: Form, Rhythm, Design', *Arts* 7, no. 4 (2018): 5.

These include アルプスの少女ハイジ (*Arupusu no shōjo Haiji* [*Heidi girl of the Alps*]) (1974), which recently inspired a CGI remake (2015) and a theatrical film from Belgian Studio 100, on slate for 2024.[120] The sixth series of Calpis' programme, *Heidi* is the most famous work produced by Zuiyō and a frequent source of discussion in anime studies, due to Takahata and Miyazaki's contribution to the show as, respectively, director and layout artist.[121] After cutting their teeth at Tōei, Ghibli's future founders moved to A Pro, the animation division of Tokyo Movie, where they participated to the aborted adaptation of *Pippi Långstrump* [*Pippi Longstocking*] (1945). A similar operation to the works of the *Calpis Theater*, *Pippi* also saw the involvement of Satō, Zuiyō's planner, who seems to be behind Takahata's invitation to Zuiyō.[122] As seen, *Heidi* was Takahashi's second attempt to adapt the novel by the Swiss author Johanna Spyri (1827–1901), which told the adventures of a little orphan girl left in the care of her grandfather, living in the Swiss Alps. The book was originally published in two parts between 1880 and 1881, focusing on Heidi's life on the mountains and her forced move to Frankfurt as a companion for a rich, wheel-chaired girl called Clara. Sponsored by the same German film studios co-producing *Vicke*,[123] which progressed in parallel with *Heidi*, the series was well received in Europe, where its high levels of artistry, and the presence of a classic story belonging to the Western canon, contributed to the massive import of Japan's animation in the following years.

As other 'animesque' shows, *Heidi* appears concocted to appeal to Europe.[124] Takahashi, who had a passion for mountaineering, paid for a ten-day trip of ロケハン (*roku han* [location hunting]) in Switzerland (where he had been several times) and Germany, so that the main staff working on *Heidi* could 見て感じて (*mite kanjite* [see and feel]) the real settings of the novel.[125] The underlying policy was, once again, of faithfulness to the original text, which Takahashi aimed to reproduce as ていねいに、リアルに (*teirei ni, riaru ni* [carefully and realistically]) as possible.[126] This also meant respecting Western communication signs such as proxemics and dining etiquette, as

---

[120]Sadhana Bharanidharan, 'Studio 100 Locks in More Distribution for its Heidi pic', *Kidscreen*, 24 October 2022. Available online: https://kidscreen.com/2022/10/24/studio-100-locks-in-more-distribution-for-its-heidi-pic/ (accessed 14 April 2023).
[121]For example, see Raz Greenberg, *Hayao Miyazaki: Exploring the Early Work of Japan's Greatest Animator* (London: Bloomsbury Academic, 2020).
[122]Chiba, *Haiji ga umareta hi*, 62.
[123]Bendazzi, *Animation*, 363 n90.
[124]Iglesias, 'The Anime Connection', 59.
[125]Chiba, *Haiji ga umareta hi*, 73; Kaoru Uda, 'On Location with Heidi's Japanese (Grand) fathers', *Swissinfo*, 17 September 2019. Available online: https://www.swissinfo.ch/eng/culture/anime-heidi_on-location-with-heidi-s-japanese--grand-fathers/45230948 (accessed 13 April 2023).
[126]Quoted in Ono, 'Takahashi Shigeto', 204.

well as other cultural specificities.[127] A similar approach concerned music and background sounds – which Takahata regarded as equally effective and falling within the scope of directing[128] – hiring professional yodel singers and recording real Swiss cowbells.[129] On a technical level, the search for realism made *Heidi* a strongly cinematic show. For example, character designer 小田部 羊一 (Kotabe Yōichi) (born 1936), another former Tōei's member who transferred to Zuiyō with Takahata and Miyazaki, reported that every episode consisted of 6,000 to 8,000 cels, despite directives to shoot on threes.[130] As is known, the demand for fidelity did not apply to religious issues (in the book, it is Christian faith to help both Heidi to overcome difficulties and Clara to grow stronger), which Takahashi was keen on erasing to cater to non-Christian countries such as the Middle East.[131] In fact, in his words, 外国の物語を日本人の手で作るとしたら、やっぱりアニメしかない (*Gaikoku no monogatari o nihonjin no te de tsukuru to shitara, yappari anime shika nai* [if you want to make a foreign story with Japanese hands, then animation is the only way]), which seems suggestive of animation's transnational potential.[132]

Cultural anthropology as entertainment

While it seems clear from the above that *Heidi* was intended not only for Europe but also for a global audience, it is worth pointing out the way in which the series situated itself in the output of the *Calpis Theater*, on the one hand, and, on the other, how it was geared to the Japanese public. In fact, even Euro-Japanese co-productions had an impact on domestic viewers (think of *One Piece*'s mangaka 尾田 栄一郎, Oda Eiichirō, whose passion for pirates started watching *Vicke* as a child[133]), which were of primary importance for Calpis, as the sole sponsor of the programme in Japan. In this respect, the choice of Spyri's novel seems not casual. Differently from

---

[127]To have an idea of *Heidi*'s philological attention to detail, suffice to say that producer Nakajima would check on flowers depicted in a scene to make sure they were the exact specimens growing there in a given season; Chiba, *Haiji ga umareta hi*, 73.
[128]Isao Takahata, *Eiga o tsukurinagara kangaeta koto* [*Thoughts while making movies*] (Tokyo: Tokuma Shoten, 1991), 13–15.
[129]Quoted in Ono, 'Takahashi Shigeto', 206.
[130]Remember that the average was ca. 3,000 cels per episode; Clements, *Anime*, 149.
[131]Quoted in Ono, 'Takahashi Shigeto', 207.
[132]Quoted in Chiba, *Haiji ga umareta hi*, 72.
[133]Misaki C. Kido, 'Interview: Eiichiro Oda', *Viz*, 2 April 2012. Available online: https://www.viz.com/blog/posts/interview-eiichiro-oda-466 (accessed 14 April 2023). A cameo of *Vicke* also appears in the work of the mangaka 幸村誠 (Yukimura Makoto) (who, like Oda, was born in the mid-1970s); see Maxime Danesin, 'Beyond Time & Culture: The Revitalisation of Old Norse Literature and History in Yukimura Makoto's Vinland Saga', *Mutual Images* 2 (2017): 185–217.

Burgess's tales and *Moomin*, *Heidi* was already a classic and one of the most important books of world literature, with a transnational circulation of around 60 million copies.[134] It was also a very popular title in Japan, where it was first introduced in 1920 by the female writer and translator 野上弥生子 (Nogami Yaeko) (1885–1985), as a part of the multivolume collection 世界少年文学名作集 (Sekai shōnen bungaku meisaku shū [World masterpieces of youth literature collection]), and then translated over 100 times, including book sets and stand-alone publications.[135] In particular, *Heidi* was integrated in local girls' fiction as early as 1925, when *Arupusu no shōjo* [*Alpine girl*] was serialized on the pages of 少女の友 (*Shōjo no tomo* [*Girl's companion*]), one of the most influential magazines in spreading cutesy images of girlhood.[136] Hence Japanese translations and illustrations framed *Heidi* as a shōjo narrative, verbalizing it in the title and stressing the friendship between Heidi and Clara.[137]

The fact that *Heidi* was a girls' story was also among the reasons why it was met with some resistance from Fuji TV, due to the scarcity of female protagonists – and their allegedly poor appeal – in animated series of the early 1970s.[138] Still, the sponsor's main target audience were mothers and children, so it seems easy to understand why Calpis was eager to endorse the project. It is perhaps less intuitive to expect that Takahashi and Takahata, by then two men in their late thirties, both claimed to be very fond of Spyri's novel. In fact, what probably influenced *Heidi*'s squarely positive reception was its alpine location. As will be recalled, mountaineering was a staple of boys' literature since the pre-war period, with wholesome accounts of international climbing expeditions being frequently added in journals and book collections. Moreover, Swiss permanent neutrality and pristine nature were key factors not only to explain the success of the animation in the years of the oil crisis (1973–4), communicating the idea of a country unscarred by the war and by the effects of industrialism,[139] but also to account for the stability of the novel in the canon of translated children's fiction, similarly to what happened for *Moomin*. In any case, if the gamble paid off – with ratings boosting up to 26 per cent, dedicated 'Heidi' stamps being issued by

---

[134]Peter Büttner, 'A Tour Through the Translation History of Johanna Spyri's "Heidi" with Special References to the Hebrew Editions from 1946 to Today' [Paper presentation], *Heidi from Japan: Anime, Narratives, and Swiss Receptions*, Zurich, 29–31 August 2019.
[135]Yoshiko Akamatsu, 'Japanese Readings of Anne of Green Gables', in *L.M. Montgomery and Canadian Culture*, ed. Elizabeth Epperly and Irene Gammel (Toronto: University of Toronto Press, 1999), 203.
[136]Carter, 'A Study on Japanese Children's Magazines 1888–1949', 68.
[137]Takashi Kawashima, 'Translation History of Heidi in Japan – A Story for Girls?' [Paper presentation], *Heidi from Japan: Anime, Narratives, and Swiss Receptions*, Zurich, 29–31 August 2019.
[138]Chiba, *Haiji ga umareta hi*, 65.
[139]Ibid., 21.

the Japan Post and fans of the series flocking to Switzerland[140] – it was due to the efforts of a highly skilled and dedicated staff, starting from Director Takahata.

Note that Takahata regarded an animated adaptation of *Heidi* as challenging on many levels. He voiced his worries to Zuiyō's president, including the lack of ファンタジー (*fantajī* [fantasy]) in the novel.[141] His number-one concern was the following: why making an animation of an everyday story which 実写映画でやるべき (*jissha eiga de yaru beki* [should be done in a live-action film]). This was a sensible question, because animation is not only costly and time-consuming but allows you to explore impossible worlds, angles and gags.[142] Unsurprisingly, many series of the period privileged magical or science-fiction settings, and the same shows of the *Calpis Theater* were retellings of fairy tales or fables. Where Takahata and Takahashi's goals converged, though, was in the creation of a 良心的作品 (*ryōshin-teki sakuhin* [conscientious work]).[143] For the director, this implied a 百八十度転換 (*hyakuhachijūdo tenkan* [180-degree change]) from traditional storytelling, which is based on the scheme 'conflict and resolution', to place 実生活 (*jisseikatsu* [real life]) and 'childishness' at the heart of the series, as he explained in a memo for his staff.[144] By doing so, Takahata's formula coalesced into Calpis's child-centred narrative, conveying in turn a new mode of narration. As future Ghibli producer 鈴木敏夫 (Suzuki Toshio) (born 1948) puts it, *Heidi* pioneered the use of 'cultural anthropology as entertainment', showing the lifestyle and habits of a Swiss child in a documentary-like fashion.[145] This also implied a detour from *Heidi*'s shōjo connotation. Heidi's sketches are a good reference to show her increasing realism – and progressive infantilization – from a braided and elegant girl (as she was often depicted in Japanese illustrations of the book) to a short-haired and chubby child, whom, by the way, Kotabe saw as quintessentially Japanese, wondering why it was so well-received abroad, where the character was usually coded as European.[146]

Being part of an already established programme, *Heidi* obviously incorporated several tropes of Calpis' shows, such as the presence of boy and girl protagonists. This was made possible by making goatherd Peter into a more likeable character than in the novel (where he gets jealous of all the attention Heidi pays to Clara and intentionally breaks her wheelchair, something that does not happen in the adaptation), tuning in to the already

---

[140]Prandoni, *Anime al cinema*, 64.
[141]Kano, '"Arupusu no shōjo Haiji" de Takahata enshutsu ga mezashita mono', 136.
[142]Paul Wells, *Understanding Animation* (Abingdon and New York: Routledge, 1998), 37–8.
[143]Kano, '"Arupusu no shōjo Haiji" de Takahata enshutsu ga mezashita mono', 138.
[144]Quoted in Ibid.
[145]Quoted in Condry, *The Soul of Anime*, 148.
[146]Uda, 'On Location with Heidi's Japanese (grand)fathers'.

recalled notion of children as naturally good and lively. Another common motif was the use of cute but realistic animals. Think of Joseph, a big St Bernardo that has no equivalent in the original, which was proposed by Takahashi as a means to soften the stern look of Heidi's grandfather.[147] Albeit not as anthropomorphic as previous characters of the *Calpis Theater*, Joseph grows on Heidi and helps her on several occasions, bespeaking a kinship between animals and humans which would be strengthened in future series. Where the series left the most lasting legacy on *WMT* was in its struggle to portray reality, which would also motivate Takahata and Miyazaki's own careers.[148] Realism was pursued at all levels, from the mise-en-scene, through the practice of location scouting, to animation and directing techniques, with camera movements such as pans and crane shots, to create depth and evoke feelings of awe for a beautiful landscape.[149] These elements made *Heidi* a cinematic series and gained currency in the following shows.

From Zuiyō to Nippon Animation

The almost ethnographic description of foreign locales was a driving factor for the success of these series, igniting Japan's fascination with the exotic, or, in Takahata's words, 憧れのヨーロッパ (*akogare no Yōroppa* [longing for Europe]).[150] Food culture was regarded as especially important for this purpose. For example, the numerous scenes in which Heidi eats cheese melted on a piece of bread over the fire made a big impression on Japanese children of the time, with Emmental becoming popular as 'Heidi cheese'.[151] Even greater emphasis was placed on psychologic realism, which, according to Takahata, was pivotal to make the audience 感じ (*kanji* [feel]) as if they were part of the story.[152] The director viewed empathy as particularly relevant in long-running series, a format allowing for elaborate characters' arcs impossible in a movie.[153] Hence the diffusion, after *Heidi*, of a strongly horizontal narrative and characters with nuanced personalities, instead of a clear-cut 'heroes versus villains' scheme. *Heidi*'s anti-dramatic structure was partly inherited from the Western novel, where Heidi, as other literary

---

[147] Chiba, *Haiji ga umareta hi*, 127.
[148] Hu, *Frames of Anime*, 119–23.
[149] Chiba, *Haiji ga umareta hi*, 113.
[150] Quoted in Chiba, *Sekai meisaku gekijō shirizu memoriaru bukku. Amerika & warudō-hen* [World masterpiece theater memorial book. America and the world] (Tokyo: Shin Kingensha, 2009), 323.
[151] Prandoni, *Anime al cinema*, 67.
[152] Quoted in Chiba, *Sekai meisaku gekijō shirizu memoriaru bukku. Amerika & warudō-hen*, 321.
[153] Ibid., 321–2.

FIGURE 3.5A *Depth of field in* Heidi *(Episode 3). The frame is part of a musical montage in which Heidi and Peter take goats up the mountains.*

FIGURE 3.5B *Heidi's grandfather feels soothed by her cheerful presence as he prepares gooey Swiss cheese by the fire (Episode 2).*

children, was portrayed as a benignant influence on her surroundings, rather than a source of conflict.[154] At the same time, the humanism of the series seems in line with Japan's post-war renegotiation of Western ideals, as happened in the domestic genre of *ryōshin* or conscientious literature.

---

[154]Wendy Barry et al. (eds), *The Annotated Anne of Green Gables* (New York: Oxford University Press, 1997), 12.

As is known, the downside of making high-quality TV animation was the amount of work which bordered on inhuman. A highly centralized approach was adopted whereby Takahata and his closest collaborators, Kotabe and Miyazaki, had complete control over all stages of the workflow.[155] This provided consistency of animation, but also delays and debts. For example, Miyazaki was in charge of creating layouts (detailed design drawings), checking on the backgrounds, postures and movements of the characters for six or seven key animators per day.[156] By then a talented animator in the shadow of Takahata, Miyazaki talked of the difficulties of learning foreign customs and the 'abnormal tension in the air' during production.[157] According to Mori, who saw finishing director 小山 明子 (Koyama Akiko) sleeping in the office for weeks, nobody worked as hard as people at Zuiyō, jokingly calling it アニメ症候群 (*anime shōkōgun* [anime syndrome]).[158] This was even more remarkable if we consider that, when production started in December 1973, gradually gathering more and more colleagues from Tōei, such as colour designer 保田 道世 (Yasuda Michiyo) (1939—2016) and background artist 井岡 雅宏 (Ioka Masahiro) (1941—85), the studio moved to a bigger building in Seiseki Sakuragaoka (still in the outskirts of Tokyo), but working conditions remained appalling, with no heating system nor arranged facilities for the animators.[159]

As Chiba notes, this resulted in a rising distance between Takahashi, who had an office in central Tokyo and spent one-third of the year trying to sell *Heidi* overseas, and his employees.[160] In addition, although Calpis was certainly pleased with the sensation *Heidi* caused in Japan, commissioning themed advertising for the TV programme[161], the dilution of religious references in the series did not completely align with Dokura's policy. In summer 1974, the president of Calpis asked Zuiyō for an adaptation of *A Dog of Flanders*, which in Japan enjoyed a great popularity as a Christian novel.[162] Takahashi, who had already made plans to start working on another

---

[155]Chiba, *Haiji ga umareta hi*, 100–1.
[156]Quoted in Matsumoto, *20 Seiki terebi dokuhon sekai meisaku gekijō taizen*, 197; See also Takayoshi Yamamura, 'Travelling Heidi: International Contents Tourism Induced by Japanese Anime', in *Contents Tourism and Pop Culture Fandom: Transnational Tourist Experiences*, ed. Takayoshi Yamamura and Philip Seaton (Bristol: Channel View Publications, 2020), 62–84.
[157]Miyazaki Hayao, *Starting point: 1979-1996*, transl. by B. Cary and F. Schodt (San Francisco: VIZ Media, 2010), 329.
[158]Yasuji Mori, *Mogura no uta – animētā no jiden* [*Song of a mole: autobiography of an animator*] (Tokyo: Tokuma Shoten, 1984), 149–50.
[159]Chiba, *Sekai meisaku gekijō shirizu memoriaru bukku. Amerika & warudō-hen*, 120.
[160]Ibid., 120–1.
[161]In 1974 they won an excellence award for a commercial featuring Janet Lynn, a famous American figure skater, waltzing on ice in a pristine mountain setting; *Broadcast Library*. Available online: https://www.bpcj.or.jp/search/show_detail.php?program=150976 (accessed 15 April 2023).
[162]Oshima, 'Dokura Fujio'.

Swiss story, based on the mythical figure of William Tell, did not agree. What followed was, in Mori's words, a チンプンカンな出来事 (*chinpunkanna dekigoto* [incomprehensible affair]):[163] while Takahashi was on a business trip abroad, the production elements of the studio were rebranded as Nippon Animation, with a new president, 本橋浩一 (Motohashi Kōichi) (1930–2010). Takahashi decided to drop the project in order to keep the series going – something that would have been impossible without Calpis's funds – but his company continued to exist as a distributor, and, after a lengthy trial, maintained the copyright for *Heidi* and the previous shows of the *Calpis Theater*.[164] The transition to Nippon Animation was smoothed by Motohashi's 働きものの庶民的な (*hataraki mono no shomin-teki* [hardworking and unpretentious]) attitude.[165] He got on well with Katō – the Dentsu manager, who had an extensive influence on the campaign for the *Calpis Theater*, was of a similar age and from the same Hokkaido town as Motohashi[166] – and took the reins of the programme, bringing it to a new phase.

---

[163] Mori, *Mogura no uta – animētā no jiden*, 148.
[164] Chiba, *Sekai meisaku gekijō shirizu memoriaru bukku. Amerika & warudō-hen*, 140–1.
[165] Mori, *Mogura no uta – animētā no jiden*.
[166] Hitsurō Hamada, 'Katō Kikuzō to Eiki no seishun fu (3)' [Katō Kikuzō and Eiki's youth records (3)], *Dentsu*, 13 December 2016. Accessible online: https://dentsu-ho.com/articles/4737 (accessed 21 March 2023).

4

Framing the meisaku series

The present chapter attempts to shed light on the animated series which were produced after the transition from Zuiyō to Nippon Animation, and thus branded (or rebranded) as the official *WMT* series. For reasons of space, the analysis will be limited to the works released up until 1996, when the programme was suspended for ten years. After a panoramic introduction on the activity of Nippon Animation, the first paragraphs are meant to provide a general overview on *WMT* shows (with the exception of *Akage no An* and *Shōkojō Sēra*, which will be treated in dedicated chapters), paying attention to their relations with the source texts, but also to the adaptation choices undertaken during production, and the evolving scenario of the sponsors. The second part shifts the focus on the *WMT* as a whole – what Clements calls 'meisaku anime'[1] – seeking to explore some of their tropes and conventions from a narrative standpoint. Trying to delineate these features seems helpful to understand how *WMT* series work, and whether there is consistency among them, which will hopefully be conducive to open discussion on further studies.

From *Calpis Theater* to *World Masterpiece Theater*

Nippon Animation was a latecomer in the Japanese animation scene. However, having absorbed the productive elements of Zuiyō and Calpis' sponsorship, the studio was able to manage a solid plan of releases, with an average of four animated series per year in the time period considered, plus

---

[1] Clements, *Anime*, 150.

some TV specials and feature films, usually created by editing footage from popular shows, according to the already recalled formula pioneered by Tōei. It is interesting to note that, among the works for television, there are also series on the animetic side, such as はいからさんが通る (*Haikara-san ga tōru* [*Here comes Miss modern*]) (1979), based on the famous shōjo manga by 大和 和紀 Yamato Waki (born 1948). Even so, most series were either adapted from Western books for children, such as ジャングルブック・少年モーグリ (*Janguru bukku shōnen Mōguri* [*Jungle book boy Mowgli*]) (1989), or trying to replicate their settings and plot devices through original works. An example is 若草のシャルロット (*Wakakusa no Sharurotto* [*Charlotte of the young grass*]) (1977), a series for girls which is set in Quebec and has a heartbreaking feuilleton-like story.[2] This seems to suggest that Nippon Animation modelled its policy on the *Calpis Theater*, this being the most prominent programme produced by the company.

The Japanese *Sekai meisaku gekijō*, or *World Masterpiece Theater*, recalls the *Masterpiece Theatre* TV series anthology aired in the United States from 1971. The title began to appear after 1979, when *WMT* series started to be provided jointly by Calpis and Kao Soap (now Kao Group), one of Japan's leaders in personal care, cosmetic and hygiene products. In fact, Calpis business was gradually deteriorating under the influence of contemporary anti-milk campaigns, which claimed that dairy beverages were bad for children's teeth.[3] This caused Calpis to quit its sponsorship from 1980. In the following years, the sponsors for the programme were Ajinomoto (1983–4), Japan's largest producer of seasonings, which had just expanded into processed food products,[4] and, since 1984, House Foods (now House Food Corporation), another big brand of condiments and instant food products. House's sponsorship, which lasted until 1993, was the longest after Calpis and was supplanted by NTT (Nippon Telegraph and Telephone), a telecommunications company. As Matsumoto notes, these brands (with the exception of the last one, NTT) catered to a public of housewives and children,[5] evoking wholesome domestic values as in the tradition indicated by Calpis. For example, Kao's brand focuses on beauty and cleanliness,[6] while House in 1980 adopted the slogan 楽しい家庭料理の世界をひろげるハウス食品 (*Tanoshī katei ryōri no sekai*

---

[2]Note that, as will be discussed later, *Little Women* is known in Japan as *Wakakusa monogatari*, so the 'Wakakusa' in the title of the series is suggestive of a classic of American literature for girls.
[3]Matsumoto, *20 Seiki terebi dokuhon sekai meisaku gekijō taizen*, 151.
[4]Roger Simon Farrell, *Japanese Investment in the World Economy. A Study of Strategic Themes in Internationalisation of Japanese Industry* (Cheltenham and Northampton: Edward Elgar Publishing, 2008), 116.
[5]Matsumoto, *20 Seiki terebi dokuhon sekai meisaku gekijō taizen*.
[6]'Changes to the Kao logo', *Kao Corporation*. Available online: https://www.kao.com/global/en/corporate/purpose/logo-symbol/logo_mark/ (accessed 18 April 2023).

o *hirogeru Hausu shokuhin* [House Food that enlarges the world of fun home cooking]),⁷ tapping into the local interest for exotic dishes, which abounded in the programme since the times of *Heidi*.

Thus, the role of sponsors was of paramount importance for *WMT*. Starting from Calpis, which aimed at promoting a humanist business model, the programme became synonym with high-quality animation for a mainstream audience. This is the reason why *WMT* has often been compared by the staff to NHK *Taiga drama*, which are among the most important events of Japan's TV year.⁸ The other sponsors inherited this positive connotation, using *WMT* series as a form of publicity, and benefiting from their favourable airtime (dinnertime, probably the best moment for food commercials). It is worth noting that, especially in the 1970s and early 1980s, sponsors were the only institutions able to plan annual series, as was the case with *WMT*, ensuring a more reliable budget. For example, *Haikara-san ga tōru* ended early due to disappointing ratings,⁹ but this did not happen with *WMT* shows until the mid-1990s. The power of sponsors also explains the foundation of Nippon Animation – and the parallel retreat of Zuiyō – as a way to keep *Heidi* going by meeting Calpis' demands, to the advantage of the television channel and advertising agencies involved. Hence the only way to tell a 'meisaku' series from other shows produced by Nippon Animation is to look at its broadcasting period, which was paid by the sponsor. To make a rough comparison, as manga demographics are defined by their magazines, TV series have been labelled as 'meisaku' when aired on Fuji TV as a part of the *WMT* programme.

How were *WMT* series conceived? According to Satō, the planning phase usually started in May or June, preparing a proposal with ten to fifteen possible titles to submit to the TV station.¹⁰ To get new ideas, every year Satō attended the Bologna Children's Book Fair,¹¹ a leading event for publishing and the exchange of editorial rights.¹² Fuji TV would inquire about several aspects, including the popularity of the books and the appeal of the main characters for the targeted audience. This narrowed down the list to three, the final choice being up to the sponsor. Then the series went into production. Producers were responsible for determining the budget and pipeline of the show,¹³ as well as negotiating with the TV channel, especially

---

⁷'Kaisha no ayumi' [History of the company], *House Foods*. Available online: https://housefoods.jp/company/information/history.html (accessed: 18 April 2023).
⁸Seki in Chiba, *Sekai meisaku gekijō shirizu memoriaru bukku. Amerika & warudō-hen*, 333.
⁹Prandoni, *Anime al cinema*, 86.
¹⁰Quoted in Chiba, *Sekai meisaku gekijō shirizu memoriaru bukku. Amerika & warudō-hen*, 334.
¹¹Ibid., 335–6.
¹²Nippon Animation had stands at MIPCOM too, a massive trade show in Cannes; 'Nippon Animation Co., LTD', *Variety*, 11 October 1989, 119.
¹³Quoted in Matsumoto, *20 Seiki terebi dokuhon sekai meisaku gekijō taizen*, 198.

in case of delays. Considering that each episode had to be delivered a week prior to the broadcast (in the late 1970s, Nippon Animation churned out five thirty-minute episodes per week[14]), while Takahata's works were not ready until the day before, it seems easy to guess why he was so grateful to producer Nakajima, who handled this with Fuji TV without weighing on the creators.[15] According to 松土 隆二 (Matsudo Takaji) (born 1947), another veteran producer who joined Zuiyō for *Rocky Chuck* and worked on several *WMT* shows, the most important task was hiring the crew: each *WMT* director had a distinctive style, and this obviously influenced the final product. Note that, together with the director, the scenario writer was appointed, their roles being equally important in *WMT* series. This was something new for Japanese animation of the time, where directors typically altered scripts according to their own taste. As we will see, things changed with *WMT* series, establishing a close collaboration between screenwriters and directors.

Nippon Animation, adaptation and children's culture

Although Zuiyō's series did not enter the meisaku canon, there are several touch points between Zuiyō and Nippon Animation's activity. From Zuiyō, Nippon Animation derived talents and their realistic approach to animation, but also the target audience of children and mothers, the practice of sending creators location-hunting abroad and the interest in reaching international markets. Nippon Animation continued on Zuiyō's path of co-producing series with German and Austrian companies, such as ピコリーノの冒険 (*Pikorīno no Bōken* [*Piccolino's adventure*]) (1976), an adaptation of *Pinocchio* (here called Piccolino, Italian for 'little'). Nippon Animation also partnered with other European studios, creating series like アニメ80日間世界一周 (*Anime 80 nichi kan sekai isshū* [*Around the world in 80 days animated*]) (1983), a zoomorphic retelling of Verne's novel, co-produced with the Spanish studio BRB International, and 冒険者 (*Bōkensha* [*Adventurer*]) (1991), a biopic on the life of Cristoforo Colombo, jointly provided with Spain, Italy and Switzerland for Columbus Quincentenary.[16] Both Zuiyō and Nippon Animation were involved in the adaptation of more recent, and

---

[14]'Busy Nippon Animation', *Variety*, 4 May 1977, 100.
[15]Quoted in Chiba, *Sekai meisaku gekijō shirizu memoriaru bukku. Amerika & warudō-hen*, 324.
[16]The studios involved were Sociedad Estatal Quinto Centenario (Spain), the Italian company Doro Tv Merchandising Srl (now Mondo TV), which was also a distributor, and Abdabra Cinematographique SA (Switzerland); 'Nippon Animation Co., LTD', *Variety*, 7 October 1991, 13.

thus copyrighted, Western materials. For example, Nippon Animation made リトル・ルルとちっちゃい仲間 (*Ritoru Ruru to chitchai nakama* [*Little Lulu and her little friends*]) (1976), based on the comic strips (and eponymous sassy heroine) published in America in the 1930s and 1940s. Last but not least, as was the case with Zuiyō, Nippon Animation produced vertical series of the educational type, including shows with animal characters, as in the skein シートン動物記 (*Shīton dōbutsuki* [*Seton's animal chronicles*]) (1977–9), based on the animal stories by Ernest Seton (1860–1946).

This seems to suggest that Nippon Animation expanded on Zuiyō's activity in a way that was consistent with post-war children's culture circulating through the media of book collections, rather than manga magazines. As multivolume sets for children, Nippon Animation serialized primarily Western stories, new and old, spanning across different literary genres with what today would be called an edutainment attitude. This resonated with the formula used by Japanese book series, holding together the edifying purposes of pre-war enpon, and the Anglo-American views of children's literature as more fun-oriented, welcomed in Japan after the Occupation. So Nippon Animation produced TV shows on the fields of animal stories, fairy tales and Japanese classics (as well as fictional works from different countries other than the English-speaking world) – all strands covered by book series. Examples are the already mentioned *Seton's animal chronicles*, グリム名作劇場 (*Gurimu meisaku gekijō* [*Grimm masterpiece theater*]) (1988), and 住友生命 青春アニメ全集 (*Sumitomo seimei seishun anime zenshū* [*Sumitomo youth classics complete works series*]) (1986), an anthology sponsored by a life insurance company. Aside from indicating a filiation from zenshū series, these collections represented an attempt to iterate the *WMT* project, though they did not last as much. Another major influence for Nippon Animation was Japan's cinematic tradition, which was in turn inspired by American animation, and eased by the diaspora of Tōei's talents. In fact, several adaptations by Nippon Animation were based on books that already received Disney's seal of approval. Think of 未来少年コナン (*Mirai shōnen Konan* [*Future boy Conan*]) (1978), loosely inspired by *The Incredible Tide* (1970). The author, Alexander Key (1904–79), was an already famous writer of juvenile books in America, with Disney making a film of his novel *Escape to Witch Mountain* in 1975.[17]

How about contemporary adaptations of similar materials created by other companies? Examples are まんが世界昔ばなし (*Manga sekai mukashi banashi* [*Manga world famous tales*]) (1976–9), a 127-episode series

---

[17]To some extent, Nippon Animation even tried to replicate the American Rankin-Bass formula of making adaptations of songs, as in 風の中の少女金髪のジェニー (*Kaze no naka no shōjo kinpatsu no Jenī* [*The girl in the wind: Jeanie with the light brown hair*]) (1993), which was inspired by the homonymous song by Stephen Foster (1826–64), but was actually a biopic on the life of the American composer.

co-produced by Dax International and TBS, or *Sekai meisaku dōwa* (1977–82), Tōei's already recalled fantasy film series. These works seemingly capitalized on the same literary tradition which informed *WMT* (in fact, several episodes of the TBS series were adaptations of books chosen by Nippon Animation as well), but they did so by appropriating an adjacent area of children's literature – that of popular tales – which was not prioritized in the output of Nippon Animation. That the common ground was book collections of the zenshū type seems confirmed by the wide range of stories selected by Dax International, spanning from biographies of famous people to mythology and classics. Another operation that was probably influenced by the *WMT* project was まんが日本昔ばなし (*Manga Nihon mukashi banashi* [*Manga traditional folk tales from Japan*]) (1975–94), a TV programme co-produced by Group Tac and the network MBS (Mainichi Broadcasting System), which conceived its thirty-nine series as an educational project for children.[18] While I cannot go into the material analysis of these works here, it is worth noting that adaptations of this kind gravitated around the meisaku phenomenon, but conveniently differentiated their offer by producing variations on a specific theme (fairy tales and folk tales), through the format of theatricals (Tōei) and miscellaneous anthologies (Dax International/Group Tac).

フランダースの犬 (*Furandāsu no inu* [*A Dog of Flanders*]) (1975)

Ouida's sad story about a friendship between a boy named Nello and his dog Patrasche moved Japanese readers since 1906, when it was first translated by 日高善一 (Zen'ichi Hidaka) (1879–1956), a Christian pastor.[19] The British novel was critical towards religion, a simple formula for many European countries according to the Victorian writer, whose goal was raising awareness of animal rights.[20] Yet Zen'ichi was impressed by the spiritual values of the book and translated it with the purpose of educating Japanese children in the Christian faith. This interpretation would inform many future editions of the novel, over eighty including those featured in book collections.[21] Considering that Calpis' president Dokura was a Christian, and that Nello works as a milk seller, an occupation redolent of the product sponsored in those years, it seems less surprising that the animation has a clear

---

[18] Hu, *Frames of Anime*, 108.
[19] Kazuyoshi Oshima, 'Hidaka Zen'ichi bokushi' [Pastor Hidaka Zen'ichi], *Patrasche.net*, 26 January 2004. Available online: http://www.patrasche.net/nello/human/06.html (accessed 1 June 2023).
[20] Natalie Schroeder and Holt Shari Hodges, *Ouida the Phenomenon. Evolving Social, Political, and Gender Concerns in Her Fiction* (Newark: University of Delaware Press, 2008), 9.
[21] Within the time frame 1900–75, there are eighty-four entries for 'A Dog of Flanders' in the book collections of Tokyo's National Diet Library; see https://ndlonline.ndl.go.jp/.

FIGURE 4.1A *Nello, Alois and Patrasche, running under butterbur-like leaves in the opening titles of* Flanders. *Sunflowers denoted Westernized locations also in Masaoka's short film* Tora-chan.

Christian underpinning to accomodate Calpis' wishes. This clearly emerges in the finale, when Patrasche and Nello are carried by the angels in the sky (Dokura drafted a beat of the scene himself), although producer Nakajima wanted to avoid the death of the main characters, as was generally the case with Hollywood adaptations of the book. Religious framework aside, the series partly aligned to Zuiyō's formula, with a couple of kind protagonists (ten-year-old Nello and a little girl of eight, Alois), a cute animal character (in the animation, Patrasche is a non-philological St Bernardo, not a real Bouvier des Flanders, probably to match Joseph's success in *Heidi*) and realistic settings, made possible by a scouting trip overseas. Like Takahata, director 黒田 昌郎 (Kuroda Masao) (born 1936) believed in the importance of empathy for characterization, turning Nello into a simple and responsible child (rather than a genial teenager), and toning down Ouida's description of poverty, perceived as distant from contemporary children. European motifs are often interwoven with Japanese cultural markers: think of Nello and Alois in the opening, dressed in typical Dutch fashion, but using large leaves as umbrellas, just like コロポックル (*koropokkuru* [people under butterbur leaf]), Ainu mythological little people.

母をたずねて三千里 (*Haha o tazunete sanzen ri* [*3000 leagues in search of mother*]) (1976)

Edmondo De Amicis's *Cuore* (1886), a novel structured as a diary of an elementary school boy, was a bestseller in Italy and had a large circulation

FIGURE 4.1B *Marco crying when his mother leaves (*Sanzen ri *– Episode 1). Stories of children separated from their mothers were common in post-war Japanese fiction for the young.*

in Japan. Since its first appearance in 1902, when three adaptations were published by the children's poet 杉谷 代水 (Sugitani Daisui) (1874–1915) and the novelist 原 抱一庵 (Hara Hōitsuan) (1866–1904), *Cuore* was included in several book series for the youth, canonizing its status as a children's classic.[22] As was common in Meiji translations, these early versions heavily domesticated the original work, often focusing on its educative setting, which would inspire another series by Nippon Animation, 愛の学校クオレ物語 (*Ai no gakkō Kuore monogatari* [*The story of Cuore, school of love*]) (1981). The monthly tale 'Dagli Appennini alle Ande' [From the Apennines to the Andes], one of the short parables told by the schoolteacher every month, had a parallel publishing history, at times surpassing the novel in popularity. In fact, the story of Marco Rossi, a child from Genoa who travels 3,000 leagues in search of his mother – this is the meaning of the Japanese title, a 里 (*ri*) corresponding to around three kilometres – touched on a sensitive theme for Japanese drama. When *Sanzen ri* was selected for adaptation, Takahata embarked on the project with a team of longtime collaborators. The director was intrigued by *Cuore*'s symbolic meaning for post-unification Italy, a period of strong nation-building which De Amicis idealized in an egalitarian, strictly non-religious way (in the book, no reference is made to Christian festivities despite Italy's Catholic culture). On the surface, the *WMT* show replicated *Heidi*'s formula. Marco's design was modelled

---

[22]On *Cuore*'s Japanese adaptations, see Sato, 'Japanese Adaptations of 19th Century and Early 20th Century Western Children's Literature', 149–51.

after his Swiss cousin, with a cute little monkey as a travelling companion – suggested by Dentsu's advertisers as a source for merchandising – and a sweet best friend, Fiorina, supporting him in times of difficulty. However, the series featured a classic period drama structure – the 股旅もの (*matatabi mono* [tales of wandering gamblers]), which deals with the adventurous journey of a travelling hero – while a scouting trip to Argentina and Italy allowed for a lifelike recreation of exotic settings only sketched in the novel. Influenced by neorealist cinema, the series also featured an unconventional cast of characters, a grey area where heroes are not always good, and enemies can be occasionally kind. According to Takahata, this was the first animated series featuring a 'human' protagonist.[23]

あらいぐまラスカル (*Araiguma Rasukaru* [*Rascal the raccoon*]) (1977)

Rascal: A Memoir of a Better Era (1963) is an autobiographical children's book by Sterling North (1906–74), in which the American writer recounted his childhood with his four-legged friend, a raccoon named Rascal. Set in Wisconsin at the turn of the century, the novel is a coming-of-age story that blends the author's life and the recent history of the United States, with the First World War, the Spanish flu and the burgeoning industrialization putting an end to the Gilded era. The book was endorsed by teachers and librarians, winning several awards, including a Newbery Honor,[24] and was so popular that in 1969 Disney released a live-action film based on it. The story was introduced in Japan in 1964, but neither the book nor the movie gained extensive fame in the country. Suffice to say that the edition used for the series, published by Kadokawa Bunko in 1976, was already out of print by the time of the adaptation.[25] Nippon Animation reunited the same team of *Rocky Chuck* – another American story with animal characters – starting from director Endō, who strongly believed in the potential of the project.[26]

---

[23]In Takahata's words: 私たちは、ここでおそらくはじめて、"主人公"たる資格に欠けた"人物"と"社会"を主人公にしたアニメーションをつくりあげたのだと (Watashitachi wa koko de osoraku hajimete, 'shujinkō' taru shikaku ni kaketa 'jinbutsu' to 'shakai' o shujinkō ni shita animēshon o tsukuri ageta noda to [this was probably the first time that they created an animated series featuring a 'human being' and a 'society' that lacked the typical features of a standard 'protagonist']); quoted in Namiki Takashi (ed.), *Il mondo di Marco – Kotabe Yōichi e 'Dagli Appennini alle Ande'* [*Marco's world – Kotabe Yōichi and 'From the Apennines to the Andes'*] (Tokyo: Istituto Italiano di Cultura, 2016), 29.
[24]The Newbery and Caldecott Awards, *A Guide to the Medal and Honor Books* (Chicago and London: American Library Association, 2001), 49.
[25]Quoted in Chiba, *Sekai meisaku gekijō shirīzu memoriaru bukku. Amerika & warudō-hen*, 338.
[26]Quoted in Chiba, *Sekai meisaku gekijō shirīzu memoriaru bukku. Yōroppa-hen* [*World Masterpiece Theater Memorial Book. Europa*] (Tokyo: Shinkigensha, 2010), 357.

The series also marked the debut of scriptwriter 宮崎 晃 (Miyazaki Akira) (1934–2018), who expanded on Takahata's cinematic take on realism by creating a boy-centred bildungsroman with a positive protagonist, lifelike side characters and a dramatic plot. Although war is not mentioned in the series (Sterling's elder brother who was fighting at the front is eliminated in the script), tragedies happen anyway: Sterling's mother dies after a long illness, and his father has to face serious troubles at work when the family farm is destroyed by a typhoon. Supported by his friends, and made stronger by the cathartic separation from Rascal, Sterling in the end is a 'Nello' who manages to survive, leaving his hometown for Milwaukee to fulfil his studies. But the real star of the series was Rascal, whose cute design was copiously reproduced in merchandise (Calpis offered plush toys prizes at the time of airing).[27] This also infamously triggered the import of thousands of raccoons, an alien and invasive species in Japan.

ペリーヌ物語 (*Perīnu monogatari* [*Perrine story*]) (1978)

The French writer Hector Malot dedicated the novel *En Famille* [*Amongst Family*] (1893), known in English as *Nobody's Girl*, to his daughter, Lucie.[28] Years before she had been the first reader of Malot's *Sans Famille*, which combined a typical orphan narrative with a travel novel for boys. The new story was a fortunate variation, catering to girl readers with an innovative female protagonist, Perrine. The book had a large circulation in Japan from 1917, when a university professor specialized in French law, 五来 素川 (Gorai Sosen) (1875–1944), translated it for the first time as 雛燕 (*Hina tsubame* [*Swallow chick*]),[29] swallows being a symbol of familial love in the country.[30] After the success of *Heidi*, *Perrine* allowed to introduce a positive and dynamic heroine in the series of *WMT*. As *Little Lord Fauntleroy*, the book pointed to the appalling conditions of the poor working in factories, proposing a sort of enlightened capitalism as a solution. On this basis, it seems easy to guess why Takahata, a member of the Communist Party, refused to direct the adaptation, which was placed in

---

[27]Matsumoto, *20 Seiki terebi dokuhon sekai meisaku gekijō taizen*, 29.
[28]Bianca Pitzorno, 'Prefazione – Un regalo per Lucie' [Preface – A gift for Lucie], in *In Famiglia*, ed. Hector Malot (Adriano Salani Editore, 2017).
[29]The novel was originally serialized for 新少女 (*Shin shōjo* [*New girl*]) and then published in book form; Sosen Gorai, *Hina tsubame*, *Fujin no tomo* [Housewife's companion], December 1917, 3–4.
[30]Haruo Shirane, *Japan and the Culture of the Four Seasons* (New York: Columbia University Press, 2013), 118.

the hands of Saitō.[31] Another complication was that most of the staff was working on *Conan*, Miyazaki's first series and the first animation funded by NHK, and this hampered production. Even Miyazaki Akira was offered to join, but declined because he was not keen on science fiction, working on *Perrine* instead.[32] *Perrine* was Saitō's first work as a meisaku director, and told the adventures of a thirteen-year-old girl traveling almost 150 kilometres across Europe to find her grandfather, a factory owner and her only surviving relative. Seki, also at his debut as a character designer for *WMT*, coined a sombre-style fitting for Perrine. An extraordinary orphan in the novel, in the series she is a model of intelligence and determination, who manages to overcome any obstacle – and Miyazaki's well-paced plot provided many – until she is recognized as the true heir of the Paindavoine family. Perrine's mother, Marie, dies early in the book (Chapter III), but passes away towards the midpoint of the series (Episode 21). This made it possible to expand the format to a full fifty-three episodes, an unbeaten record for *WMT*, exploring the relationship between mother and child, as well as hinting at racial prejudices (Marie is half Indian, and initially despised as such by Perrine's grandfather). Marie's testament of love encompasses the moral of the series, which is of wholesome humanism: as the narrator explains in the epilogue, kindness creates more kindness, if one learns to care for others and treat them as friends.

トム・ソーヤーの冒険 (*Tomu Sōyā no bōken* [*The adventures of Tom Sawyer*]) (1980)

When Mark Twain's juvenile fiction arrived to Japan, at the end of the nineteenth century, *The Adventures of Tom Sawyer* (1876) was not on the list. His ironic depiction of American society was too anti-authoritarian for the tastes of the Meiji reformers, who preferred more traditional narratives such as Twain's *The Prince and the Pauper*.[33] Moreover, neither Tom nor his best friend Huckleberry Finn are edifying characters, the first one being a professional liar, while 'the juvenile pariah of the village' (Chapter VI) steals and smokes, not to mention that the main plot revolves around a murder.[34] Of course, there is much more to the novel than meets the eye, in primis, a sharp critique of slaveholding and bigotry, but also a joyful ode to boyhood,

---

[31] Quoted in *Kyarakutā dezain wandārando perīnu monogatari seki shūichi* [*Character design wonderland Perrine story Seki Shūichi*] (Tokyo: Tokyo Shoseki, 2019), 51.
[32] See: Chiba, *Sekai meisaku gekijō shirizu memoriaru bukku. Amerika & warudō-hen*, 329; Matsumoto, *20 Seiki terebi dokuhon sekai meisaku gekijō taizen*, 36.
[33] Ishihara, *Mark Twain in Japan*, 14.
[34] Mark Twain, *The Adventures of Tom Sawyer* (Hartford: The American Publishing Company, 1884).

FIGURE 4.2A *Rascal washing his first sugar cube in a bowl of milk* (Rascal – Episode 11). *During the scouting trip for the series, a real raccoon family was filmed as a reference for Rascal's design, which was originally sketched by Mori.*

FIGURE 4.2B *Perrine helping her mother as they drive through the Alps* (Perrine – Episode 13). *Due to production delays, no location hunting was scheduled for this show, but art director Ioka painted beautiful background illustrations.*

which Tom, an imaginative orphan kid, fully embodies. So, when the book was translated by the juvenile writer 佐々木邦 (Sasaki Kuni) (1883–1964) in 1919, Tom was the first bad boy of Japanese translated literature, purposely domesticated to make it more palatable for the audience.[35] The *WMT* series gathered part of the team who worked on *Perrine* and *Rascal*, including director Saitō, character designer Seki and scriptwriter Miyazaki. To reframe Tom as a positive hero, the adaptation portrays him as a carefree boy – one who gladly skips class to go hunting wild pigs or playing pirates – whose flaws are counterbalanced by a set of desirable qualities: intelligence, loyalty and a heart of gold. Problematic issues such as violence or slavery are lightened, yet not completely eliminated, while the fictitious town of St Petersburg is charmingly recreated thanks to a scouting trip to Hannibal, Missouri. Although Seki used the illustrations by the American Norman Rockwell (1894–1978) as a reference,[36] Huck seems inspired by Jimsy's design (*Conan*), conveying a natural impression of a wild boy. Note that Tom's crush on Becky is maintained in the series, turning the girl into a recurring and more affirming character than in the book. Fun fact: the creative staff, who would often come up with ideas of pet characters for merchandise, suggested an alligator – a common species in Mississippi River – for *Tom*, but did not get producer Matsudo's seal of approval.[37]

家族ロビンソン漂流記 ふしぎな島のフローネ (*Kazoku Robinson hyōryū ki fushigi na shima no Furōne* [*Family Robinson castaway story: Flone of the mysterious island*]) (1981)

The popularity of *WMT* was slowly declining: while average viewer ratings exceeded 20 per cent in the mid-1970s, these dropped to around 15 per cent in the days of *Tom*.[38] So, the 1981 series represented a change of direction for the programme. The choice fell on perhaps the most translated Swiss book ever: *Der Schweizerische Robinson* [*Swiss Robinson*] (1812), the story of a family of immigrants – father, wife and four sons – who are shipwrecked on a desert island in the East Indies. Written by the parson Johann David Wyss (1743–1818) as an educational tale for his children, the novel was clearly indebted to Defoe, using a castaway story as a framework

---

[35]Ishihara, *Mark Twain in Japan*, 22.
[36]Quoted in Chiba, *Sekai meisaku gekijō shirizu memoriaru bukku. Amerika & warudō-hen*, 329.
[37]Quoted in Matsumoto, *20 Seiki terebi dokuhon sekai meisaku gekijō taizen*, 199.
[38]Unless otherwise specified, the ratings for *WMT* series are quoted from: Kenji Miyazaki, 'Kataritsugu oyako kiete "Sekai no meisaku" wa hyōgaki' ['Parents and children who pass down their stories disappear and the "World masterpiece" is ice age'], *Asahi Shimbun*, Tokyo morning edition, 1997 March 27, 27.

to provide lessons in science and natural history, but also to pass on moral teachings such as good behaviour and domesticity.[39] Edited and illustrated by Wyss's sons, the *Robinsonade* underwent innumerable translations and was adapted into different media. In Japan, it was first published in 1922 by Hakubunkan's 少年探偵冒険叢書 (Shōnen tantei bōken sōsho [Boys' detective adventure series]), and circulated in several anthologies since then, where it frequently appears as 家族ロビンソン (*Kazoku Robinson* [*Family Robinson*]), echoing the English title *Swiss Family Robinson*.[40] In 1960, the book was successfully adapted into a Disney film, later released in Japan as 南海漂流 (*Nankai hyōryū* [*Adrift in the South Sea*]), and still popular today, the house-on-a-tree built by the Robinsons being a regular attraction at Tokyo Disney Resort. The *WMT* staff included director Kuroda, designer Seki and art director Ioka, who was famous for his pictorial landscapes since the days of *Heidi*.[41] The trio was sent with producer Matsudo on a scouting trip to New Caledonia, Vanuatu Islands and Australia.[42] Flone, the eponymous heroine, is a tomboyish girl of ten who has no equivalent in the novel – though a couple of American TV series already introduced a female child in the main cast[43] – and keeps a cute couscous as a pet. Drama is added in the form of the challenges that a life in the wild entails, but the adaptation is generally light in tone, the focus being on a cosy family atmosphere. Special emphasis is given to Robinson patriarch, an exemplary father and a resourceful man who always manages to help his family, though his profession (a physician, instead of a pastor) implies a more secular view than the original.

南の虹のルーシー (*Minami no niji no Rūshī* [*Lucy of the southern rainbow*]) (1982)

With *Flone*, the *WMT* programme rose to an average rating of almost 19 per cent, so Nippon Animation repeated the experiment in 1982. Like the previous series, *Lucy* tells the story of a family of immigrants on their way to Australia, from the point of view of a little girl, allowing for a realistic depiction of everyday life in an exotic setting. However, this time the

---

[39]Jackie C. Horne, *History and the Construction of the Child in Early British Children's Literature* (Abingdon and New York: Routledge, 2016), 36–40.
[40]For other editions of the book, see Takashi Amemiya, 'Johann David Wyss', *Ameqlist.com*, 2023. Available online: https://ameqlist.com/sfw/wyss.htm (accessed 1 June 2023).
[41]See Chiba, *Haiji ga umareta hi*, 107.
[42]Kaori Chiba, *Sekai meisaku gekijō e no tabi* [*A Journey to the World Masterpiece Theater*] (Tokyo: Shinkigensha, 2015), 48.
[43]Produced in 1974 (Canada: Kleinburg and Freemantle) and 1975 (USA: Irwin Allen and 20th Century Fox).

FIGURE 4.3A *Tom escorts Becky to Saint Louis while visiting his aunt in Arkansas (Tom Sawyer – Episode 42). The trip gives life to sweet and funny narrative beats about young love.*

FIGURE 4.3B *Ernest Robinson cures his son Franz, blinded by a poisonous insect (Flone – Episode 13). While Ernest sees Franz's surviving as a miracle, the boy gives in to despair, embodying confrontational adolescence.*

inspiration came from a newly published novel, *Southern Rainbow* (1982), which planner Satō discovered at Bologna Children's Book Fair.[44] The book was written by Phyllis Piddington (1910–2001), a retired Australian schoolteacher,[45] and had yet to be translated into Japanese at the time of production. The *WMT* staff was expecting something like Ingalls's 'Little House' books, which enjoyed revamped popularity thanks to the airing of the American series on NHK.[46] But they were disappointed to find out that the Australian novel was different from the American saga, as it described the struggles of a poor family to start a farm in Adelaide, without giving much information about their life as settlers. The same scouting trip was of great interest for the creators of the series to discover Australian luscious nature and Aboriginal culture, but told them very little about the historic background of the frontier era.[47] Therefore, scriptwriter Miyazaki took his own route in the adaptation, where he introduced a number of subplots and a turning point in which Lucy May – a child of seven and a charming animal lover, equally intrigued by wild beasts and insects – loses her memory and is looked after by a rich couple, her final recognition leading to a happy end. Appointed as the director of the series, Saitō gave life to a realistic group of characters, each one with a distinctive personality. The cast also includes numerous animals, starting from Little, a dingo puppy trained by Lucy May. While the Robinsons are an ideal community with a heroic father figure, the Popples are not always successful in tackling their problems. Especially Arthur Popple, the head of the family and perhaps the real protagonist of the story, often acts stubbornly to fulfil his dreams of having a farm, but in the end realizes that the happiness of his sons is the most important thing.

アルプス物語わたしのアンネット (*Arupusu monogatari watashi no Annetto* [*Alps story my Annette*]) (1983)

Despite the similarities with *Flone*, *Lucy* was not just as successful, with average ratings slightly above 14 per cent. So, for the following meisaku series, Nippon Animation moved back to a beloved scenery since the times of *Heidi* – the Swiss Alps. As happened in 1974, the inspiring work was a children's novel with a strong religious underpinning, *Treasures of the Snow* (1950), which had been turned into a movie in 1980. The author of

---

[44]Quoted in Chiba, *Sekai meisaku gekijō shirizu memoriaru bukku. Amerika & warudō-hen*, 335.
[45]'Phyllis Piddington', *AustLit*, 10 May 2007. Available online: https://www.austlit.edu.au/austlit/page/A14717 (accessed 1 June 2023).
[46]Matsumoto, *20 Seiki terebi dokuhon sekai meisaku gekijō taizen*, 76.
[47]Chiba, *Sekai meisaku gekijō e no tabi*, 51–2.

the book, Patricia St. John (1919–93), was a British missionary nurse and a prolific novelist, who wrote it for young readers 'to learn the meaning of forgiveness'.⁴⁸ A Japanese translation was released in 1959, and, years later, planner Satō found it in a Christian bookstore.⁴⁹ The concept appealed to a top executive of Fuji TV, who was Christian, so the project was put into production. Set in the village of Rossinière, where St. John lived as a child, the story of a Swiss girl, Annette, and her friend Lucien might sound idyllic, but the parallels with *Heidi* stop here. In fact, after much bickering between each other, Lucien gets back at Annette by threatening the thing she loves the most: her little brother Dani. When an accident occurs which leaves the child lame for life, Lucien will have to face the guilt, while Annette finds herself incapable of forgiving him, in a crescendo of dramatic situations until the happy ending. Former animator 楠葉 宏三 (Kusuba Kōzō) (1948–2018), who already collaborated with Zuiyō and was now at his debut as a *WMT* director, did not eschew from the core themes of the novel – sin and repentance – providing a new change in direction for future meisaku series, where hatred and anger would be depicted in a graphic and emotional way. Things are made more intense by a multifaceted couple of protagonists, with Annette being a dual shōjo character (a motherly figure for Dani and a top student at school, but also an impulsive, vengeful girl), and Lucien as the real hero of the story, maturing from a lazy kid into a brave young man when he faces a blizzard only to interest a renowned physician in Dani's case. The series was the last work which saw the collaboration of art director Ioka, who fell ill during location scouting in Lausanne.⁵⁰

牧場の少女カトリ (*Makiba no shōjo Katori* [*Katri girl of the meadows*]) (1984)

In 1984, Nippon Animation adapted the novel *Paimen, piika ja emäntä* [*Shepherd, maid and mistress*] (1936), by Auni Nuolivaara (1883–1972), a Finnish teacher. Followed by two sequels, the literary saga largely drew on the real experiences of a woman from Langelmäki (Western Finland), retold by her daughter Kustaava Helander (1873–1948), an acquaintance of Nuolivaara.⁵¹ The book was praised for its ethnographic descriptions of rural life, winning a prize in an international competition, and was

---

⁴⁸Patricia St. John, *Patricia St. John Tells Her Own Story* (Kingston Broadway: Kingsley Press, 2008), 68.
⁴⁹Chiba, *Sekai meisaku gekijō shirīzu memoriaru bukku. Yōroppa-hen*, 361.
⁵⁰Quoted in Matsumoto, *20 Seiki terebi dokuhon sekai meisaku gekijō taizen*, 201.
⁵¹Seija Pessi, 'Paimen, piika ja emanta, kotizeutuhistoriaa Längelmäeltä' [Shepherd, maid and mistress, local history from Längelmäki], *Tampereen seudun sukututkimusseura Vuosikirja* XIX, no. 2 (1998): 77–8.

FIGURE 4.4A *Lucy May (in red), her sister Kate and Little sigh over their sister Clara's reunion with her fiancé (Lucy – Episode 32). Note how large mouths, typical of Seki's design, are effective in expressing the emotions of the characters.*

FIGURE 4.4B *Annette breaks Lucien's sculpture out of spite (Annette – Episode 29).*

translated into Japanese in 1952 by 森本ヤス子 (Morimoto Yasuko) (1902–98) for Kōdansha's World masterpieces series.[52] In the 1930s, a time of great interest in Scandinavian lore, Yasuko's husband had published the first complete translation of the *Kalevala*, the Finnish national epic. In post-war

---

[52]Chiba, *Sekai meisaku gekijō shirīzu memoriaru bukku. Yōroppa-hen*, 264.

Japan, Nuolivaara's story was simplified to cater to a young readership, emphasizing the role of the protagonist, a diligent young girl who works hard to become independent, climbing the social ladder from poor shepherd to housemaid of a rich family. In the meisaku series, director Saitō and scriptwriter Miyazaki altered the source material even more, moving the time frame to the beginning of the twentieth century, and linking Katri's fate to Finland's national history. So, Katri is separated from her mom at the outbreak of the First World War, when communications between Germany (where the woman works as a maid) and Finland stop. Then, the girl is encouraged to study by Akki, an activist of the Finnish Independent Movement. Finally, mother and daughter are reunited in 1917, when the country separates from Russia. This way, Katri's tale becomes the coming-of-age story of a strong-willed, clever heroine who improves her conditions through education, as touted in Japan since the Meiji period. However, visiting real farms in Lappeenranta (south-east Finland) pushed the staff to mitigate the tragic undertones of the original work, casting light on Katri's everyday life in a traditional Finnish community.[53]

愛少女ポリアンナ物語 (*Ai shōjo Porianna monogatari* [*The story of Pollyanna, girl of love*]) (1986)

By 1985 ratings had started to slump, but the following WMT series, *Shōkōjo Sēra* (see Chapter 6) was a big success. The show was based on a classic of children's literature, and increased interest in creating adaptations of famous works such as *Pollyanna* (1913) and *Pollyanna Grows Up* (1915). Written by the American Eleanor H. Porter (1868–1920), the books revolved around a fortunate trope: a kind orphan girl who does her best in spite of her poor means, and has a benevolent influence on her surroundings. *Pollyanna* was made into several movies, including a Disney film (1960) which contributed to the popularity of the novel in Japan.[54] Here *Pollyanna* was introduced in the same 1913, but became popular after 1939, when it was translated by the famous writer Muraoka Hanako (see Chapter 5), whose version was the basis for the animation.[55] Directed by Kusuba, the series emphasizes Porter's dramatic plot, in which Pollyanna is sent to live with her acrimonious aunt Polly, playing her 'glad game' even when she loses the use of her legs. While in the book Pollyanna's sunny nature and her aunt's dry humour coexist in a humorous counterpoint, the tone of the adaptation is strongly emotional,

---

[53]Chiba, *Sekai meisaku gekijō e no tabi*, 67.
[54]Matsumoto, *20 Seiki terebi dokuhon sekai meisaku gekijō taizen*, 120.
[55]Mio Bryce, 'Pollyanna: Transformation in the Japanese Context', in *Eleanor H. Porter's Pollyanna: A Children's Classic at 100*, ed. Roxanne Harde and Lydia Kokkola (Jackson: University Press of Mississippi, 2014), 228–32.

FIGURE 4.5A *Katri reads the Kalevala with her dachshund Abel* (Katri – Episode 14). *Katri is constantly shown studying, from the Bible to fairy tales and arithmetics.*

and big emphasis is placed on Polly as she finds herself transformed by her niece's love – hence the title of the show – into a maternal figure. The protagonist's age is lowered in the series (from eleven to eight years old), renegotiating the character as a little child. This seems connected to her chatty and self-centred behaviour, which can be perceived as inappropriate for a puberal girl in Japan.[56] So, despite Porter's Pollyanna turns twenty by the end of the story, getting married to her friend Jimmy, the *WMT* heroine never grows old, which, according to Kusuba, added to her appeal among children viewers.[57] Pollyanna's childishness is also suggested by her cute design, a work of 佐藤 好春 (Satō Yoshiharu) (born 1958), who already served as an animation director for *Annette*. It was Kusuba's idea to portray Pollyanna in overalls,[58] a type of garment which, too, connotes her as a very young girl.

愛の若草物語 (*Ai no wakakusa monogatari* [*Love story of the young grass*]) (1987)

With average ratings above 17 per cent, *Pollyanna* was the top-ranked *WMT* show of the 1980s, encouraging the production of another series based on a

---

[56]Ibid., 236.
[57]Quoted in Chiba, *Sekai meisaku gekijō shirizu memoriaru bukku. Amerika & warudō-hen*, 325.
[58]Quoted in Chiba, *Sekai meisaku gekijō shirīzu memoriaru bukku. Yōroppa-hen*, 354.

FIGURE 4.5B *Pollyanna hugs her aunt Polly in the garden, tended by old Tom (Pollyanna – Episode 6). The playful colour palette, with 'up' colours expressing Pollyanna's fun and spontaneity, counterbalances the sad tone of her story.*

famous work: *Little Women* (1868). At the time, the semi-autobiographical novel by Louisa May Alcott (1832–88) was very popular in Japan, especially among elementary and junior high school girls,[59] and already inspired two animated adaptations by Tōei and Kokusai Eigasha in the early 1980s. The book first appeared in 1906 as 小婦人 (*Shōfujin* [*Little ladies*]), by the novice translator 北田秋圃 (Kitada Shūho), and was repeatedly translated since then.[60] Future titles include 四少女 (*Yon shōjo* [*Four girls*]) (1923), 四人姉妹 (*Yon shimai* [*Four sisters*]) (1934), and the title still in use today, *Wakakusa monogatari* (1934), a lyric metaphor to indicate the freshness of youth.[61] Screenwriter Miyazaki and director Kurokawa Fumio took a detour from the original narrative, creating several subplots which could fit in a series. For example, the animation starts with Marmee and her four daughters escaping the Civil War, allowing for a reconstruction of the Battle of Gettysburg which is absent in the novel. The insertion of war acted as a prequel and a catalyst for the story, allowing to characterize the protagonists by putting them into an extreme situation. According to Kurokawa, this was pivotal to portray them as a close-knit family, where each member reacts

---

[59] Yuko Katsura, 'Red-Haired Anne in Japan' [Canadian Children's Literature], *Littérature canadienne pour la jeunesse* 34, no. 5 (1984): 58.
[60] Hiromi Tsuchiya Dollase, 'Shōfujin (Little Women): Recreating Jo for the Girls of Meiji Japan', *Japanese Studies* 30, no. 2 (2010): 248.
[61] Akamatsu, 'Japanese Readings of Anne of Green Gables', 202.

to the events in their own way.⁶² Note that Kurokawa did not finish the novel – he read Muraoka's translation and found it 読みにくい (*yominikui* [illegible]) – but really enjoyed the homonymous Hollywood film (1949), with Elisabeth Taylor playing the role of Amy. He, too, placed the youngest March at the centre of the series, which seems to suggest a core target of small children, as in *Pollyanna*. However, the focus of the show is on everyday life and its little incidents, exploring the different personalities of the March sisters and their interactions as in a stage play. This appears enhanced by the exquisite style of designer Kondō, who was especially keen on sensitive portrayals of girls since his work for *Akage no An*.

小公子セディ (*Shōkōshi Sedi* [*Little prince Cedie*]) (1988)

For the next work of the project, Nippon Animation selected another classic of English literature, *Little Lord Fauntleroy*, by the same author of *A Little Princess* (see Chapter 6). The rags-to-riches story of Cedric, an American boy who discovers to be an English aristocrat, was first translated into Japanese in the Meiji era, and strongly influenced the taste of local fiction for kind children and loving mothers, a characterization which seems reflected in the idealized audience of the *WMT* franchise. Directed by Kusuba, the series marked the return to a male protagonist after years of female leads, and to a more faithful rendition of the book, which was written by 石森 史郎 (Ishimori Fumio) (born 1931), a screenwriter with a full-fledged experience in the Japanese entertainment business, from melodramatic theatricals to tokusatsu TV series.⁶³ Minor changes occur in the adaptation, the first of which concerns the father of the main character, who is still alive at the beginning of the series, raising the stakes for Cedie (a name chosen for copyright reasons, Cedric being trademarked in Japan by Nissan for a luxury car⁶⁴). Once again, the bulk of the narrative centres on Cedie's relationship with his mother ('Dearest') and his cantankerous grandfather, emphasizing the boy's American connotation – including an apocryphal passion for baseball – but also his angelic gentleness and morality. The bright colours of the show, designed by Koyama, contribute to its charm, while Cedie's pretty appearance, work of the artist 美知代 桜井 (Sakurai Michiyo), was modelled after the British actor Mark Lester, who starred in the 1971 film *Melody*, a

---

⁶²Quoted in Chiba, *Sekai meisaku gekijō shirīzu memoriaru bukku. Yōroppa-hen*, 342.
⁶³Brett Homenick, 'Memoirs of an Iconoclastic Screenwriter! Fumio Ishimori on His Scriptwriting Career in Japanese Film and Television', *Vantage Point Interviews*, 2020. Available online: https://vantagepointinterviews.com/2021/05/18/memoirs-of-an-iconoclastic-screenwriter-fumio-ishimori-on-his-scriptwriting-career-in-japanese-film-and-television/ (accessed 1 June 2023).
⁶⁴Matsumoto, *20 Seiki terebi dokuhon sekai meisaku gekijō taizen*, 136.

FIGURE 4.6A *The March family after their house is bombed (*Wakakusa *– Episode 6). They will leave for Newcord, a fictitious town replacing the original Concord, which was already used as a setting in* Pollyanna.

FIGURE 4.6B *Cedie plays the flute to help his friend Eric, whose mother is poor and ill (*Cedie *– Episode 2). Cedie's emotional theme, which is repeated in the clou moments of the series, is based on the Scottish folk song 'Anne Laurie'.*

young love comedy which was a hit in Japan.⁶⁵ Both Koyama and Sakurai, who was also an animator for Studio Ghibli, were involved in the *WMT* since the days of Zuiyō. As for *Wakakusa*, *Tom* and *Flone*, *Cedie* is among the few *WMT* series which was exported to the English market. Even so, the episodes reached a minimum of forty-three (versus the over fifty of the previous decade), a number which would constantly decrease in the following years.

ピーターパンの冒険 (*Pītā Pan no bōken* [*The adventures of Peter Pan*]) (1989)

The 1980s ended with a series based on a renowned English novel, the third in a row released by Nippon Animation. Since 1921, *Peter Pan and Wendy* (1911), by James Barrie (1860–1937), had been frequently translated into Japanese by several children's authors, including Kikuchi, Ishī and writers in the circles of juvenile literary journals, a success incremented by Disney's wholesome adaptation (1953).⁶⁶ The meisaku series was planned to commemorate the twentieth anniversary of the programme since the creation of *Moomin*,⁶⁷ and yet, it represented a curious case in the history of *WMT*. Not only the plot of the show takes consistent liberties from the book but it is the only meisaku series belonging to the fantasy genre. So, The Boy Who Would Not Grow Up and the Darling children are transported in a whirlwind of magical adventures, between pirates, fairies and evil witches, plus cameo appearances of Rascal the raccoon, which in 1989 became the trademark character of Nippon Animation,⁶⁸ just like Tōei's cat Pero, another animal mascot designed by Mori. With its light-hearted entertainment – in this decade, the slogan of Fuji TV was 楽しくなければテレビじゃない (*tanoshiku nakereba terebi janai* [it is not TV if it is not fun]) – the series attempted to detach from classic *WMT* shows, breathing new life into a programme that started to feel the weight of years. This was made possible by putting together a staff of veterans – director Kuroda joined the project in the Zuiyō era – and new talents, such as the animation director and character designer 中村 たかし (Nakamura Takashi) (born 1955), who worked on *AKIRA* (1988) and gave the series a new steampunk look. The pilot, an hour-long special consisting of two episodes, wowed viewers with the cinematic quality of the animation, using over 20,000 cels to render the

---

⁶⁵Quoted in Chiba, *Sekai meisaku gekijō shirīzu memoriaru bukku. Yōroppa-hen*, 348.
⁶⁶'Otogi ehon seiyō no issun-bōshi Pītā Pan' [The fairy-tale picture book of Peter Pan, the famous western issun-bōshi] *Ōsaka furitsuchūō toshokan*, 28 November 2015. Available online: https://www.library.pref.osaka.jp/site/jibunkan/pi-ta-pan.html (accessed 8 June 2023). Issun-bōshi is a small character of Japanese fairy tales who never grows bigger.
⁶⁷Matsumoto, *20 Seiki terebi dokuhon sekai meisaku gekijō taizen*, 145.
⁶⁸Quoted in Chiba, *Sekai meisaku gekijō shirīzu memoriaru bukku. Yōroppa-hen*, 347.

flying characters smoothly[69] (versus the customary 6,000 to 8,000 cels of a thirty-minute episode). The action-packed incipit in Hook's boat in the sky is also emblematic of the tone of the show, the first one by Kuroda to target a male audience. Note that the series was sold to Great Britain, Peter Pan's home country, the English market proving to be more and more interested in Japanese animation.[70]

私のあしながおじさん (*Watashi no Ashinaga ojisan* [*My uncle Long-legs*]) (1990)

Based on the epistolary novel *Daddy-Long-Legs* (1912), by the American Jean Webster (1876–1916), this series represented another change in style for the *WMT* programme, which in the 1990s would increasingly cater to girls. The Pygmalionesque story of orphan Judy and Jervis, her wealthy tutor (and future crush), was first translated into Japanese in 1919 by the humour writer 東 健而 (Azuma Kenji) (1889–1933), and up until the 1980s is recorded as a favourite reading among junior school girls.[71] Director 横田 和善 (Yokota Kazuyoshi) (1950?–2011), who started his career as a storyboard artist for *Heidi*, lowered the age of the protagonist at the beginning of the series, exploring her maturation from her puberal years to her graduation from high school. In line with Judy's connotation as a teenager, much room is dedicated to her awkward feelings of being alone in the world and trying to hide her past as an orphan girl, which is not so important in the book. At the same time, the series follows Judy as she makes friends with her roommates, shy Sally and snobbish Julia, showing their realistic experiences as they grow up. As is often the case with meisaku shows, life events can be tough and exacerbated (in the pilot, young Judy satirizes the hypocritical charity of the rich ladies who visit the orphanage) but are never truly traumatic, conveying a positive message: in the end, Judy realizes that her misadventures shaped her into the independent young woman and writer she is. This is where Japan's ideal of doing one's best coalesced with a depiction of America as the country of dreams and democracy. The archetype of the plot being a variation on the Cinderella trope, romance has a rising importance in the second half of the show, when the protagonist becomes a valedictorian student and discovers to be in love. A number of shōjo-like beats will follow, such as Judy being torn between her feelings for Jervis and a more fraternal affection for Jimmy, respectively, Julia and Sally's uncle and brother.

---

[69]Quoted in Ibid.
[70]Matsumoto, *20 Seiki terebi dokuhon sekai meisaku gekijō taizen*, 146.
[71]Tsuchiya Dollase, *Age of Shōjo*, 153.

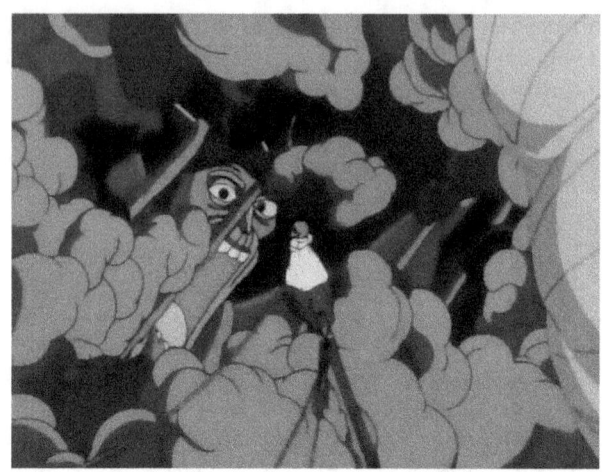

FIGURE 4.7A *Captain Hook makes Wendy walk the plank in the incipit of* Peter Pan *(Episode 1). Neverland's floating island shares similarities with Miyazaki's film* 天空の城ラピュタ *(Tenkū no shiro Rapyuta [*Laputa – Castle in the sky*]) (1986).*

FIGURE 4.7B *Judy at John Grier orphanage (*Ashinaga *– Episode 1). Seki's reference for the design was Pippi Longstocking, another ebullient orphan, while Judy's dreamy nature recalls the protagonist of* Akage no An, *the most popular red head of WMT.*

トラップ一家物語 (*Torappu ikka monogatari* [*Trapp family story*]) (1991)

WMT approached the biopic genre for the first time adapting *The Story of the Trapp Family Singers* (1949), an autobiography by the Austrian Maria Kutschera (1905–87). The true story of a novice nun who was sent as a tutor to support the Baron von Trapp with his children, inspired several adaptations, from a German film in 1956, to the Broadway musical *The Sound of Music*, which premiered in 1959, and the homonymous American movie (1956) directed by Robert Wise.[72] Due to its enduring popularity, the Hollywood version became a reference for the meisaku series, which combined a much loved setting – the Alps, though the protagonists eventually emigrated to America to escape war – with a feel-good story about music and family, as Calpis did two decades before with the Osmond brothers commercials. Director Kusuba and screenwriter しろやあよ (Shiroya Ayo) tried to follow the book more closely, downplaying the role of romance, which was pivotal in the movie, and placing family life at the heart of the series. So, while Maria becomes a mother to the seven Trapp children and a wife of the Baron, every family member is portrayed sympathetically in a rotation of dedicated episodes. Resilience is another key theme, showing Maria's sad backstory (not covered in the film) and her ability to overcome any obstacle, but also her Christian faith and positive influence on people. In fact, Maria embodies the perfect teacher, capable of empathizing with kids as well as empowering them. The trademark realism of *WMT* does not shy away from harsh historical events (the children are forced to do the Nazi salute at school, and a Jewish doctor acquainted with the Baron is deported), nor from sensitive themes (Kusuba was particularly happy with the way Shiroya handled Episode 22, describing the delicate interaction between Maria and Hedwig, the Baron's eldest daughter, who has menarche[73]).

大草原の小さな天使 ブッシュベイビー (*Daisōgen no chīsana tenshi busshu beibī* [*Little angel of the Savannah bushbaby*]) (1992)

This series is an adaptation of *The Bushbabies* (1965), the only children's novel by William Stevenson (1924–2013), a Canadian author of non-fiction books largely based on his travels around the world as a foreign

---

[72] Martin Kich and Aaron Barlow, *Pop Goes the Decade. The Sixties* (Santa Barbara: Greenwood, 2020), 6–8.
[73] Quoted in Chiba, *Sekai meisaku gekijō shirīzu memoriaru bukku. Yōroppa-hen*, 349.

correspondent.⁷⁴ Set in Kenya, where he once lived with his family, the book was optioned for an MGM live-action movie in 1969, and then published in Japan as カバの国への旅 (*Kaba no kuni e no tabi* [*Journey to the land of the hippopotamus*]) (1971). Planner Satō selected it as a candidate as early as 1983, perhaps due to the popularity of 少年ケニヤ (*Shōnen Kenya* [*Kenya boy*]) (1961), a manga that had been adapted multiple times to other media.⁷⁵ With original drawings by Mori, the proposal had better luck in the 1990s, providing an action-oriented narrative with spunky protagonists, as was the case with *Peter Pan*. Written by Miyazaki and directed by 鈴木孝義 (Takayoshi Suzuki) (born 1951), who started his career at Nippon Animation in the late 1970s, the meisaku series featured a new continent (Africa) and a new time frame (the 1960s), telling the story of Jackie, a thirteen-year-old English girl living in Nairobi, and Murphy, her bushbaby pet, in the days when Kenya declared its independence from Britain. While the first half of the series revolves around a well-established trope of *WMT* – the friendship between children and animals – with Jackie looking after Murphy as the puppy grows up, the two spend the rest of the show on the run to avoid leaving Africa, in a succession of adventurous situations. Also the visual style balances a retro and modern feel. Whereas 加藤 裕美 (Kato Hiromi) (born 1964), at his debut as a character designer, gave a cute manga look to Jackie and Murphy, the other characters were designed by Seki, always an advocate for a realistic representation of humanity. This is particularly evident in the treatment of Black characters, such as Tenbo, Jackie's father's collaborator and a precious friend for Jackie during her escapade. In addition, the animal characters were sketched by the Chinese artist 譚小勇 (Tan Xiao-Yong) (born 1955), who in the 1990s illustrated several materials related to the *WMT*, such as pamphlets and picture books.⁷⁶

若草物語 ナンとジョー先生 (*Wakakusa monogatari Nan to Jō sensei* [*Story of the young grass: Nan and teacher Jo*]) (1993)

Bushbaby was a moderate success, which prompted Nippon Animation to produce a sequel of a meisaku series that was positively received a few years before, *Wakakusa*. The new show, an adaptation from Alcott's *Little Men* (1871) – which was in turn a continuation of *Little Women* – was aired

---

⁷⁴'William Stevenson, Author of A Man Called Intrepid, Dies', *CBC News*, 27 November 2013. Available online: https://www.cbc.ca/news/entertainment/william-stevenson-author-of-a-man-called-intrepid-dies-1.2442847 (accessed 3 June 2023).
⁷⁵Matsumoto, *20 Seiki terebi dokuhon sekai meisaku gekijō taizen*, 177.
⁷⁶Chiba, *Sekai meisaku gekijō shirizu memoriaru bukku. Amerika & warudō-hen*, 282.

FIGURE 4.8A *Maria meets the Trapp Family* (Trapp – Episode 3). *Although Maria's pose matches Julie Andrews in the Hollywood film, Seki gave the character a more youthful look.*

FIGURE 4.8B *Tembo, Murphy and Jackie are joined by her schoolmate Mickey* (Bushbaby – Episode 25). *While on the track of dangerous poachers, Tembo is wrongly accused of kidnapping Jackie.*

with the avant title *Ai no wakakusa monogatari* as a promotional gimmick, using the same voice actors who worked on the previous show.[77] However, it was a completely different work, following the life of Jo March as a loving mother and educator at Plumfield school, where she encourages her students to find their individual talents, in line with the pedagogic views of the author's father, the teacher Amos Bronson Alcott (1799–1888), but also with the policy of *WMT* since the days of *Flanders*. Being a school story, the series has an episodic progression in which, as happens in *Trapp*, children are given ample space. In particular, the eponymous Nan is a tomboyish girl from a wealthy Boston family, who has much in common with young Jo. A minor character in the novel, she is the real heroine of the series, which begins in the form of a memoir as adult Nan, now a fine young lady and a skilled physician, comes to visit the place where she grew up. Directed by Kusuba, the series marked the return to the *WMT* of Satō Yoshiharu, who had worked for Studio Ghibli since the making of となりのトトロ (*Tonari no Totoro* [*My neighbour Totoro*]) (1988). As the animation director and character designer of the 1993 series, his contribution enhanced the quality of the animation, which prioritized simple lines and a round look, giving *Nan to Jō* a distinctive Ghibli vibe. Especially the animation of children living and playing in nature, a recurring theme in *WMT* series, provided plenty of opportunities to render their movements in a cinematic way,[78] showing their full-body figures without relying exclusively on extra-diegetic voice-overs and close-up camera angles.

七つの海のティコ (*Nanatsu no umi no Tiko* [*Tico of the seven seas*]) (1994)

For the twentieth anniversary of the official *WMT* series since the making of Flanders, the idea was to create an adventure show with a marine location, on the model of Verne's novels (*Two Years' Vacation* and *Twenty-Thousand Leagues Under the Seas* were also among candidates).[79] However, when an acquaintance of the planning department of Fuji TV, 広尾明 (Hirō Akira) (born 1958), pitched his story, Nippon Animation took a chance on producing a meisaku which was not an adaptation but an original work.[80] The scenario, which was novelized during the airing of the series, is set in modern times and recounts the journey of a Japanese-American girl,

---

[77]Quoted in Ibid., 327.
[78]Matsumoto, *20 Seiki terebi dokuhon sekai meisaku gekijō taizen*, 184.
[79]Quoted in Chiba, *Sekai meisaku gekijō shirīzu memoriaru bukku. Amerika & warudō-hen*, 335.
[80]Ibid., 303.

FIGURE 4.9A *Nan learns a lesson (*Nan to Jō *– Episode 2). Jo prompted her to use her love for nature observation to introduce herself to the class – a first step towards self-directed learning.*

Nanami, and her dad Scott, a biologist, in search of a legendary luminous whale. For the first time, a *WMT* series features an extra-large pet, an orca named Tico (perhaps influenced by the recent *Free Willy* franchise), following the protagonist wherever she goes. Between underwater sites and pirate's treasures, the show blends classic tropes of boys' literature and elements of contemporary anime. Especially Nanami's fantastic abilities (she can communicate with whales and dive deeper than humans) recall the heroine of ふしぎの海のナディア (*Fushigi no umi no Nadia* [*Nadia of the mysterious seas*]) (1990–1), a popular science-fiction show directed by 庵野秀明 (Anno Hideaki) (born 1960) for Gainax. In fact, according to Nippon Animation's producer 余語 昭夫 (Yogo Akio), the goal was to give a fresh look to the *WMT*, without breaking with tradition.[81] Hence the presence of well-entrenched ingredients of the programme, such as the portrayal of family life on the Peperoncino (Italian for 'chilli pepper', a top product sold by House Food), the boat where Nanami lives or the positive characterization of Scott, in a period when father absence was widely discussed in Japan. As was the case with *Nan to Jō*, the series saw the contribution of Ghibli talents who already worked for Nippon Animation: mecha elements were supervised by 片渕 須直 (Katabuchi Sunao) (born 1960), who was knowledgeable about aviation history, while water was

---

[81] Quoted in Murakami, *Anime in TV*, 167.

FIGURE 4.9B *Funny chasing in* Tico *(Episode 2). Nanami and Al, the Italian engineer (and chef) of the Peperoncino, help Thomas, a runaway kid who will later join their crew.*

rendered with animation techniques by the background artist 山本 二三 (Yamamoto Nizō) (1953–2023).[82]

ロミオの青い空 *(Romio no aoi sora [Romeo's blue sky])* (1995)

The *WMT* switched to more traditional contents with the adaptation of *Die schwarzen Brüder* [*The black brothers*] (1940–1), a novel written by the German-born Kurt Held (aka Kurt Kläber, 1897–1959) and his wife Lisa Tetzner (1894–1963), a couple of Nazi-opponents who emigrated to Switzerland.[83] Their book thus popularized the sad fate of poor children in the mid-nineteenth century, when they were sold to work as chimney sweeps in Milan. A producer discovered the story at the Bologna's Children's Book Fair in 1981 and the project had been on slate since then,[84] finally going into production in the 1990s, after *Bushbaby* and *Tico* proved that meisaku series not based on classics could be successful. The animation maintained the social criticism of the original, showing the cruelty of child labour with

---

[82]Ibid.
[83]Verena Rutschmann, 'Zwei Ausstellungen im Schweizerischen Jugendbuch-Institut: Meta Heusser-Schweizer (1797-1876) und Kurt Kläber/Held (1897-1959)', in *Kinder- und Jugendliteratur-forschung 1997/98* [*Children's and Youth Literature Research 1997/98*], ed. Hans-Heino Ewers et al. (Stuttgart: Springer-Verlag, 1999), 10.
[84]Matsumoto, *20 Seiki terebi dokuhon sekai meisaku gekijō taizen*, 212.

director Kusuba's trademark intensity, but placed more emphasis on the positive attitude of Romeo, an orphan boy who sacrifices himself for the sake of his adoptive family and keeps his spirits high even in the darkest times. A common topic since the Calpis era, the theme of hope emerged clearly in the title, with Romeo's blue sky, an idea of scriptwriter 島田満 (Shimada Michiru) (1959–2017), indicating the children's view from inside a chimney, and their longing for a better future.[85] Kusuba's goal was to create a boys' drama about friendship on the model of *Tom Sawyer*, adjusting the target audience of the novel – technically a young adult – for a junior age group.[86] However, the romantic aspects of the plot, starting from the heartwarming relation between Romeo and his best friend Alfredo, were popular with older female viewers, who would later flood the market with self-published comics about the two. This was also due to Satō Yoshiharu's beautiful character design, inspired by photos taken during the scouting trip for *Heidi*, and by Mori's sketches for the first proposal of the series.[87] A tribute to the veteran animator, who had recently passed away, appears in Episode 20 (Uncle Theo), a filler episode that was prepared in advance to meet the needs of the TV station. In fact, baseball matches were aired in alternation with the show, which was expected to provide extra episodes in case of a sudden cancellation.[88]

名犬ラッシー (*Meiken Rasshī* [*Famous dog Lassie*]) (1996)

A total of forty-five episodes had been planned for *Romeo*, but the show ran for only thirty-three episodes, the increasingly sporadic airing of WMT probably affecting its low ratings. The following series was even less successful, despite being based on a famous original, the novel *Lassie Come-Home* by the British Eric Knight (1897-1943). The story of Lassie, a faithful collie who travels hundreds of miles to be reunited with her owner, Joe, was well received in post-war Japan, when the 1943 MGM movie adaptation and the American TV series were released in the country. Not only Western dog shows were particularly numerous in the 1950s and 1960s, featuring canine stars such as Rin-Tin-Tin or Lassie, but also tales about friendly dogs were a big genre in Japanese literature, including translated fiction along the lines of *A Dog of Flanders*. So, *Lassie* had long been considered for a WMT serialization, which was meant to reach the primary audience of the

---

[85] Quoted in Chiba, *Sekai meisaku gekijō shirīzu memoriaru bukku. Yōroppa-hen*, 350.
[86] Quoted in Matsumoto, *20 Seiki terebi dokuhon sekai meisaku gekijō taizen*, 98.
[87] Quoted in Chiba, *Sekai meisaku gekijō shirīzu memoriaru bukku. Yōroppa-hen*, 355.
[88] Quoted in Ibid., 351.

FIGURE 4.10A *Romeo signs the contract to sell himself as a chimney sweep (Romeo – Episode 4). The series opens with a sense of tragedy, as Romeo's adoptive father is injured in a fire, and his family plunged into debts.*

FIGURE 4.10B *John feeds Lassie (Lassie – Episode 2). With his father and mother working all day, John is a responsible child who knows how to look after himself – and his newly adopted puppy.*

programme – children and mothers.[89] Director Katabuchi created a meisaku series that was poles apart from *Romeo*. In fact, *Lassie* has a peaceful atmosphere and cute characters with a rounded and stunted shape, work of the character designer and animation director 森川 聡子 (Morikawa Satoko) (born 1956), who would use a similar style in the Ghibli film 猫の恩返し, *Neko no ongaeshi* [*The cat's repayment*] (2002), known in English as *The Cat Returns*. Set in Depression-era Britain, the series has vivid colours and bucolic landscapes typical of the English countryside, detaching itself from the Hollywood version, which was filmed in California in black and white. The series also incorporated contemporary indicators such as modern technology and a family life where both the parents have a waged job, with the mother of the protagonist – christened John, perhaps to avoid confusion with Jo March – working as a nurse. As in *Bushbaby*, half of the series focused on John and Lassie's bonding, while the other half was meant to be an on-the-road drama: during hard times, John is forced to give Lassie to the owner of the local coal-mine, but the dog returns to her home in Yorkshire. Due to the cancellation of the series after Episode 25, Lassie's journey was relatively anti-climatic, lasting only two episodes.

家なき子レミ (*Ie-naki-ko Remi* [*Homeless child Remi*]) (1996–7)

Because *Lassie* was discontinued in August, the next meisaku series was aired from September, which was unusual for a *WMT* show.[90] As *Lassie*, *Remi* was based on a classic, Malot's novel *Sans Famille* (1878). The book, about the adventures of a foundling who is sold to a travelling musician, was meant to impart moral lessons as well as instructive information on French history and geography. Such educational values were clear to Gorai, who also translated *En Famille*, and first introduced Malot's work in the late Meiji era as a 家庭小説 (*kaitei shōsetsu* [family novel]) suitable for the children of decent families.[91] Future versions took a free approach to the original, often stressing the theme of looking for one's lost mother, as in the 1940s adaptation by the children's writer 荻江 信正 (Minami Yōichirō) (1893–1980). Something similar could be said of the *WMT* series, which made meaningful changes to the source material, the most evident of which is the gender swap of the main character, who is a boy in the novel and a girl in the animation, presumably to repeat the success of previous shows with female leads. Directed by Kusuba and partly written by Shimada, who

---

[89]Matsumoto, *20 Seiki terebi dokuhon sekai meisaku gekijō taizen*, 221.
[90]Ibid., 229.
[91]Sato, 'Japanese Adaptations of 19th Century and Early 20th Century Western Children's Literature', 149.

FIGURE 4.11 *Vitalis encourages Remi to keep moving forward (*Remi *– Episode 13). Themes of love and resilience resonate in the soundtrack, the ending song being incorporated in the fabric of the episode.*

had recently worked on *Romeo*, the series returned to more pathetic modes of narration, where a kind and lovable protagonist has to face terrible circumstances with hope. This is evident in the teachings that Remi learns from Vitalis, her guide and adoptive father. According to planner Satō, Remi's cute look and big eyes were inspired by the style of shōjo manga, a request of Fuji TV.[92] The series also takes a romantic turn after Episode 14, when Remi goes to Paris and makes friends with other orphan kids. The budding love story between Remi and Mattia, a bad boy with a golden heart, is a novelty of the show, allowing to reframe events of the book in a new perspective. Yet, *Remi* suffered ratings slumps and ended in less than six months, bespeaking the changing trends in the animation industry. While there were two adaptations of *Sans Famille* (a Tōei film and a TMS TV series) in the days of *Perrine*, in 1996 TV Tokyo aired *Neon Genesis Evangelion*, an innovative work which incorporated many postmodern themes. After *Remi*, *WMT* went on hiatus for a decade before reopening in the 2000s.

The series and the novels

Differently from Takahashi, who aimed at making animated adaptations of fairy tales, mostly from Northern Europe, the series of the *WMT* were

---

[92]Quoted in Chiba, *Sekai meisaku gekijō shirīzu memoriaru bukku. Amerika & warudō-hen*, 364.

based on Western novels. As seen in Chapter 1, Western fiction was deeply entrenched in Japanese fiction, especially thanks to the translation boom that followed the Occupation, which emphasized forms of literature connected to the English-speaking world such as prose over poetry, and novels over short tales. These patterns seem to be confirmed by the works chosen for the *WMT*, which in most cases had already been translated into Japanese, and often serialized in multivolume collections for the youth. It is remarkable that more than half-titles (fourteen out of twenty-three) were present in perhaps the most exemplary book series of the post-war, Kōdansha's World masterpieces, whose selection was consistent with other anthologies for children. This is suggestive of the impact that such publications had on the generations that grew up in the post-war years, and would later join the domestic media industry.

If we look at the geographic origin of the works behind the *WMT* series considered here, the majority of them (eleven) are adapted from European books, followed by American books (nine), Anglo-American books (two) and one Oceanian story. However, a more granular analysis shows that the majority of books used as a basis for the programme were from the United States (seven), followed by Great Britain (five, plus two Anglo-American works), France (two), Switzerland (two), Canada, Italy and Australia (one).[93] A preference for English-speaking territories seems to be confirmed by the fact that, even when the source books were not written by Anglo-Saxon writers, many of them have been adapted into Hollywood movies, including Disney films. These adaptations were at times so notorious to overshadow the books by which they were inspired. In fact, works such as the musical *The Sound of Music*, or Hollywood first colour version of *Little Women*, were quoted as main references by the meisaku staff. *WMT*'s shifting ideas about location and identity are also manifest if we consider that the representation of foreign locales was a common feature of the literary texts as well. For example, *Treasures of the Snow* is a British portrayal of Switzerland, *Die Schwarzen Brüder* was published in Switzerland, but was written by German writers and largely takes place in Milan, while the Italian 'Dagli Appennini alle Ande' is partly set in Argentina. These (re)imagined places were invested with different cultural meanings, contributing to define the way meisaku series addressed the exotic.

Note that not all *WMT* series were based on famous stories, nor had undergone renowned adaptations in other media, be they in America

---

[93]The classification is as follows: United States (*Little Women, Little Men, Tom Sawyer, Daddy Long-Legs, Pollyanna, Trapp Family Singers, Rascal, Bushbabies*), Canada (*Anne of Green Gables*), Anglo-American (*Little Lord Fauntleroy, A Little Princess*), Great Britain (*A Dog of Flanders, Peter Pan, Lassie Come-Home, Treasures of the Snow*), France (*Sans Famille, En Famille*), Switzerland (*Der Schweizerische Robinson, Die schwarzen Brüder*), Italy ('Dagli Appennini alle Ande'), Finland (*Paimen, piika ja emäntä*), Australia (*Southern Rainbow*).

or elsewhere in the world. As seen, Satō deliberately tried to produce adaptations of recent Western books, periodically travelling to world fairs, just as modern-day producers and broadcasters for animation would do. The same Fuji TV was interested in creating new projects long before the production of *Tico*.[94] The case of *Lucy*, a show based on a book that was not yet published at the time of production, is emblematic of this trend. It is also worth noting that *WMT* series were often released in book form at the time of broadcasting, by publishing houses such as Gakken, Takeshōbo and others, at times contributing to the rediscovery of lesser-known or half-forgotten titles. Think of the inspiring novel for *Bushbaby*: in 1991, Shinchōsha published a new edition for the launch of the series, because the princeps was already out of print when the company developed the adaptation.[95] This seems to indicate that canonization could also work the other way around, from animation to publishing. For example, in 1987 Kadokawa started to publish 世界名作アニメ全集 Sekai meisaku anime zenshū [World masterpieces animated complete works series], a collection of twenty-five volumes with illustrations from their animated version. To some extent, *WMT* series closed the circle on adaptation, repackaging animated works based on Western stories as a literary classics. In fact, Kadokawa's zenshū set included series which were not part of the *WMT* programme, the meisaku label conveying an allure of prestige to the entire output of Nippon Animation.

Main characters

Be they famous literary works already known in Japan, or brand-new concepts, the titles selected for adaptation had to mirror the values of the *WMT* programme. This emerges clearly in the choice of the main characters. As it is easy to guess, this is among the most important decisions in fiction, and was an object of constant discussion between the parties involved in the creation of meisaku series, because it had to connect sponsors (Calpis, Ajinomoto . . .), broadcaster (Fuji TV) and production company (Nippon Animation). As seen, in terms of audience profiling, *WMT* series were catered to a domestic audience of families, with a core target of children and mothers. At the same time, these shows were conceived with an eye for export from the start. This means that *WMT* protagonists had to be universally appealing. It sounds almost tautological, but in order for the public to like them, main characters should be likeable. What makes a character likeable has to do with many aspects, concerning the visuals and

---

[94]Matsumoto, *20 Seiki terebi dokuhon sekai meisaku gekijō taizen*, 192.
[95]Ibid., 179.

the writing of the show. More specifically, from a narrative standpoint, among the most pivotal aspects are what Wayne Booth calls the practical interests, which pertain to the moral sphere of characterization.[96]

To some extent, moral features depend on the culture of the recipients of the show. For example, a hardworking attitude and a strongly empathetic nature are framed as good traits in *WMT* series, in line with Japan's cultural framework. However, speaking in terms of a mainstream public, and excluding parodies, one tends to like kind characters, in spite of (or precisely because) of their flaws, and to dislike vicious ones. This is one of the reasons why *WMT* protagonists are mainly morally good characters, with peaks of saintlike ones. Antiheroes, which appeal to more sophisticated niches, are therefore excluded from the project, although there are cases when the protagonists (from a narrative point of view) are apparently presented as the villains of the show. For example, according to director Kusuba, the protagonist of *Annette* is Lucien, the boy who causes the main incident of the story, and repents afterwards. It is also important to stress that, since the time of its inception, *WMT* directors generally refused the idea of a 'good versus bad' scheme, favouring a more varied construction of characters. This means that clear-cut villainous characters are rare in *WMT* series, which in turn emphasize the effects of one's milieu.

Aside from being likeable, main characters should be relatable for the public, prompting identification among a varied audience of adults and children, whose gender and age composition changed over the years, as did social values and beliefs. For meisaku series, this seemed to have resulted in an increasingly greater number of female protagonists of different ages, spanning from five to eighteen years old. Boys characters were predominant in the first years of the *WMT*, but later decreased in number, with a total of eight protagonists. On the one hand, a majority of female characters is an interesting factor to consider for the representation of femininity and its exposure in the media. On the other hand, *WMT* protagonists are typically surrounded by a vast cast, and flanked by at least one friend of the opposite sex, engaging different targets and offering diverse role models that are consistent with the cultural agenda of the programme.

WMT female characters

WMT girl protagonists encompass several qualities, the most represented of which is kindness. Being kind to others (including animals) is always framed as a sign of nobility regardless of one's status, though it can be conducive to

---

[96]Wayne Booth, *The Rhetoric of Fiction* (Chicago and London: The University of Chicago Press, 1983), 133–4.

climb the social ladder. As we will see in Chapter 6, Sara Crewe is portrayed as a saint, and this is among the reasons why she will become as rich as a princess. Lucy May is offered to be adopted by a wealthy family because of her gracious persona. Remi is a model of compassion and gentleness for everyone she meets, persuading her friends in Paris to quit pickpocketing and start working together instead, before being identified as a noble girl. Even more insouciant girls, like Judy, Jackie or Anne, are good at heart and this makes them likeable.

As observed for the notion of childhood in Calpis' programmes, kindness is associated to a natural vitality, which makes female characters look cheerful and bubbly at various degrees. As in Western girls' and children's literature, these features enable *WMT* girls to become healing figures, instilling love and vitality in those around them. This also means that they have little story arc in terms of character development, epitomizing what screenwriters may call traveling angels.[97] Travelling angel stories are a sub-genre of comedy in which a flawless protagonist enters a community in trouble, helps inhabitants fix things, then moves on.[98] For example, Pollyanna makes her stern aunt Polly caring for her, ultimately turning her into a mother figure, while Katri brings love and warmth to the farms where she works. Other features, often overlapping with each other's, are perseverance, a thirst for knowledge and a tomboyish attitude or look. Clever characters are particularly frequent, and their thirst for knowledge is generally rewarded by adults. For instance, in her busy life as a cowherd girl, Katri spends every moment she can reading books. A hardworking spirit is also underlined as a positive trait. Think of Perrine becoming a factory-worker to gain the trust of her grandfather. Also Judy is eager to get a part-time job to be independent, although she has a tutor who provides for her education.

Masculine girls or 御転婆 (*otenba* [tomboy]) are especially insightful because of their age composition. Younger characters often define themselves as otenba, and are commonly accepted as such, portraying nonconformist models of behaviours in the early 1980s and 1990s. Lucy May and her sister Kate are spirited girls who love to explore and play pranks. Flone is athletic and full of bravado, while Jo wows her sisters talking with confidence about allegedly male topics, such as war. However, the older a female character gets, the more feminine she is expected to be. For example, boy-looking Jo will grow into a sensible teacher in *Nan to Jō*. Annette – a self-declared otenba who does not step away from a fight – is encouraged to act more like an 女の子 (*onnanoko* [girl or young woman]) by her great aunt, who gives her a mirror as a token of grooming (Episode 13). The case of Annette

---

[97]It is not by chance that many of them are also travellers: think of Perrine, Lucy or Remi, just to name a few.
[98]Truby, *The Anatomy of Story*.

FIGURE 4.12A *Otenba Nan makes a hubbub at her first day of school (*Nan to Jō *– Episode 1). Note the similarities with the protagonist* 魔女の宅急便 *(*Majo no takkyūbin *[The witch's express home delivery service]) (1989), known in English as* Kiki's Delivery Service, *where Satō worked as key animator.*

FIGURE 4.12B *Marco's mother with her family and a neighbour (*Sanzen ri *– Episode 1). Character designer Kotabe wanted her to emit the energy of a woman working hard to support her family.*

is quite interesting, because she is the only meisaku heroine to represent negative justice, holding a grudge against Lucien and trying to seek revenge for her crippled brother. Aware of these problematic aspects, director Kusuba purposely decided to stress Lucien's positive arc instead. However, Annette's descending parable is by no means not sugarcoated. For example, when she throws Lucien's carving in a gravine, her malicious gesture is emphasized by the use of slow motion (Episode 17).

Although there are villainous women in *WMT* series, most adult female characters display the same qualities of *WMT* girls, except their tomboyishness. Adult women are usually framed as feminine, kind and motherly from the start, or becoming such during the series. The latter development is what often makes them the protagonists in the shadow of the shows, be they the biologic parent of the protagonist, a close relative or an adoptive parent. For example, former nun Maria Kutschera leaves the convent to become Baron Von Trapp's wife and a mother to his large family. This conveys an embedded narrative that kindness and motherhood (and, to some extent, married life) are a female character's desirable status. Single women do exist, but they are often framed as deviation from the norm, at times through light-hearted comical portrayals, and without obliterating their potentially motherly nature. Think of Ms Sloane (*Ashinaga*), who is practically the girl dorm's mother, and a friend for Judy, in spite of the gags about her not being married.[99]

In general, mothers are among the most important characters of *WMT* shows, in line with the importance of mother-children relationships in Japanese popular fiction. Especially in older series, mothers can take part in the journey of the protagonists and establish the moral of the show. Perrine's mom is a clear example, encouraging her to believe in humanity and compassion. Visually, *WMT* mothers are usually portrayed as matronal and maternal, their solid figure contrasting with the cuteness of *WMT* girls. However, like their daughters, *WMT* mothers are hardworking, independent and, to some extent, empowered. Think of Marco's mom who works in Argentina to provide for her family. They can look timid, but they become protective and strong when it comes to helping their sons, like Flone's mother when facing the wolves that try to attack her children (Episode 13).

Sometimes *WMT* shows feature a young female protagonist growing up in the second half of the series. This is the case of coming-of-age stories, such as *Akage no An* or *Ashinaga*. More commonly, older girls are featured in the cast as sisters or close relatives of the protagonist. Think of cousin Mary in *Tom Sawyer*, first child Meg in *Wakakusa*, or Lucy May's older sister Clara. A recurring trait of these characters is that they express a gentle

---

[99] A recurring joke in the show involves male adults calling her 奥さん (*okusan* [wife]) by mistake, in spite of her non marital status.

model of femininity and romantic desires, making them perhaps the most invested in shōjo narratives. This is especially true in the 1980s and early 1990s, when romance was gradually ingrained in meisaku series. Albeit generally quieter than their younger sisters, *WMT* young women are also active characters who are not solely interested in love but look forward to their self-realization through work and education, embodying more modern models of femininity than their mothers. So, Sterling's older sisters go to college and drive cars, Clara in *Lucy* finds a job as a baker, and Mary in *Tom Sawyer* works as a nurse for the village's doctor, a story absent in the original.

WMT younger girls are always flanked by a male friend, and their relationship is often framed in terms of puppy love. Somehow redolent of Calpis' tagline ('the taste of first love'), these pairings achieved an increasingly romantic taste, as seems indicated by the presence of the word 'shōjo' in several titles of the staple, or of other terms connected to girls' literature, for example, 愛 (*ai* [love]) in *Pollyanna* and *Wakakusa*. However, there is a clear demarcation between women and older girls, who are allowed to experience romance in their life – and institutionalize it through wedding – and younger girls, whose friendship is always innocent and devoid of erotic elements. Think of Katri, whose loveliness places her at the heart of several funny skirmishes between her friends Martti and Pekka, who are protective towards the girl and childishly jealous of her company.

At the same time, later meisaku shows inoculated more tension in these dynamics, revealing a focus on relational interactions redolent of shōjo

FIGURE 4.13A *Judy and Jervis confess to each other (Ashinaga – Episode 34). This was the first kissing scene in a meisaku series, the following frame coyly cutting to the shadows of the characters.*

FIGURE 4.13B *Remi and Mattia hug when he saves her from an abandoned mine, a twist on the original book (Remi – Episode 22). Touched by Remi's kindness, Mattia is the character that changes the most in this arc of the series.*

sensitivity. This holds particularly true for *Romeo* and *Remi*, perhaps the most 'shōjo' among *WMT* shows. By changing the protagonist of the novel into a girl, and her friend Mattia into her love interest, *Remi* creates a young love story – the meisaku way. Where the series is especially effective is in expressing the emotions of the characters, portraying several heartwarming moments between the two without relying on teen drama clichés, such as an unrequited love or a secret crush. On the contrary, Remi and Mattia talk openly of their dreams and desires, and this makes them more realistic, in spite of the melodramatic events that occur to them.

Older women are also of great importance in *WMT* shows. Grandmothers and aunts can either be biologic relatives of the protagonist or not, but they are usually framed as positive mentors for the young. Actually, a special connection seems to unite the youngest and the oldest characters of *WMT*, as often they are both without a family and somehow alone in their journey. However, old women possess the knowledge the *WMT* girls need most. Think of Annette's aunt (her grandmother in the original book), whose religious faith informs the morals of the show, or Gunilla, a travelling weaver who shares her expertise with Katri. Old ladies or 小母さん (*obasan*) can appear as cantankerous and insular at first, like Aunt Martha in *Wakakusa* (named Josephine in the book). They might also have a masculine look, like Aunt Roquerie in *Perrine*. But they show a motherly nature when their help is needed.

In general, *WMT* shows featured a variegated cast, ranging from more traditional to quirky attitudes, and paving the way for a diverse representation of female characters on the media landscape. Models of femininity seem to be aligned to educational agenda of the period. Given that women and children were originally the core audience of the programme, female characters are portrayed in a relatable way, embodying aspirational and socially acceptable ideals that were consistent with the changing times. *WMT* shows up to the mid-1980s often feature wise and good mothers, framing tomboyishness and romanticism as a temporary status in the life of the female characters. Instead, *WMT* female characters in the late 1980s and 1990s retain some of their youthful features in adult life. Think of Maria, who is compared to a child by Baron Von Trapp for her sunny temperament, or Cheryl in *Tico*, a spoiled heiress and the only woman of the Peperoncino's crew. Despite being of the same age as Maria, Cheryl looks more like a girl, who certainly becomes nicer over time (and seems to have feelings for Nanami's father), without this transforming her into a wife or mother by the end of the series.

WMT male characters

As is the case for meisaku heroines, *WMT* male characters represent an observatory to analyse the representation of masculinity in the series of the programme. *WMT* male protagonists share many of the qualities of their female counterparts, which seem consistent with the portrayal of children in Japanese juvenile literature. So, the majority of them are characterized as children who are kind, diligent and protective towards others, be they

FIGURE 4.14A *Katri between Pekka (left), a cowherd, and Martti, the son of a wealthy family* (Katri – Episode 12). *The boys help the girl on several occasions; for example, Martti takes her place when she is ill, and Pekka finds a new job for her when she needs it.*

FIGURE 4.14B *Sterling is comforted by Rascal after his mother's funeral* (Rascal – Episode 14). *As happened in the final of* Flanders, *the scene is accompanied by the hymn 'Nearer, my God, to Thee', evoking feelings of hope in troubled times.*

relatives or strangers. When he loses his job, Nello works in secret and does his best not to cause his grandpa any worries. In *Lassie*, John does the housework when his mother returns tired from work. Male heroes are also ready to buckle up when tragedy strikes (which happens quite often in *WMT* shows), their fortitude finding expression in an enduring gentleness. Examples are Sterling facing his mother's death and quietly trying to move on or Romeo practically selling himself as a chimney sweep. This is matched with a sort of chivalrous maturity when they engage with their girlfriends. It also finds expression in the almost orphic relationship several male characters have with animals and music. Think of angelic Cedie playing the flute or Sterling being a friend to all animals.

The characterization of male children is also indebted to their source novels and the literary genres to which they belonged, though adapted to the policy of *WMT*. An example is the bad boy narrative, which was imported in Japan from America. So, Tom and Huck are somewhat bowdlerized in the 1980 meisaku series, but they are still portrayed as naughty children – with the heart in the right place – compared to other shows of the programme. Lucien is also realistically characterized as a problem child, dedicating ample space to his experience of bullying and being bullied. Something similar happens with the characterization of Werner, the middle son of Baron Von Trapp, who feels neglected and will overcome this thanks to the help of his family, in a dedicated mini arc of *Trapp* (Episodes 17–18). In later *WMT* series, bad boys tend to appear more frequently, taking on shōjo undertones, and evolving into positive characters during the course of the series. Think

FIGURE 4.15A *Tom and Huck play aboard the steamship to Arkansas (*Tom Sawyer *– Episode 42). Their friendship is emphasized by the boys' frequently moving in synch, a legacy of Miyazaki's style of animation.*

FIGURE 4.15B *Alfredo and Romeo in Locarno, Switzerland, before heading off to Milan (*Romeo *– Episode 4). Romeo bravely dives in the river to retrieve Alfredo's belongings, stolen by a street urchin.*

of Mattia going through a full arc of transformation – from street thief to aspiring violinist – in *Remi*. Boys' friendship is deeply explored in *Romeo*, displaying a complexity of feelings which borders on the romantic. Director Kusuba even changed the name of the protagonist from Giorgio to Romeo, as a reference to Shakespeare's *Romeo and Juliet*, one of the most well-known tragedies and love stories of all times.

Older youths, such as brothers, cousins or friends of the main character, also play a major role in *WMT* series. In particular, adolescent boys of thirteen to sixteen years old are framed as boys of an appropriate age to explore themes such as one's vocation or intergenerational tensions, even when there is no trace of this in the original books. Usually, older boys face a conflict with adults, nurturing desires that are far from what is expected of them. However, older boy characters come to terms with these feelings when a reality check makes them understand whether their aspirations are feasible or not. For example, Franz, Robinson's eldest son, wants to become a musician but decides to leave with his family for Australia, although he knows that his dream is likely not to come true in that context. Also Ben, Lucy May's older brother, would like to become a physician in spite of his limited means. In the end, Franz is able to study music abroad, while Ben has to give up on his dreams for the sake of his family, without conveying a sense of this being a tragic decision. The underlying implication seems to be that personal aspirations are framed as subject to negotiation, family harmony being the most important value.

WMT adult men, in a parallel way to WTM women, are characterized as father figures and represent the hidden protagonists of many *WMT* shows. Together with *WMT* mothers, fathers are traditionally presented as the pivot of the family and a model for the young. As seen, father Robinson in *Flone* is a skilful man who helps his family survive and bring civilization on a desert island. Even though this already happens in the novel, the show modernizes the character by turning him into a professional physician, thus realistically skilled in many scientific fields. In general, the role of fathers seems amplified in *WMT* series, giving them character depth and dedicated backstories. Think of Marco's dad who works for a medical practice helping the poor of his town in *Sanzen ri*, a narrative thread that is absent in the original story. However, fathers are not always perfect, their adult persona sometimes preventing them from expressing their feelings, a gap which is usually filled by mothers. An example is Romeo's foster father, whose love for his son is made clear by Romeo's mother (Episode 2). A father's staggering role is also reflected in the ups and downs of their family. In this sense, one of the most interesting characters is Lucy May's father, who has a perfectly circular inner journey. Mr Popple starts as an enthusiastic man at the beginning of the series, slowly falling into a spiral of alcohol and depression when his dreams to become a farmer are hindered by bureaucracy, and finally gets back to the top when he manages to buy a land for his farm. Significantly, this career advancement is marked by (and made possible by) the man's claiming his status as a father when he searches Lucy May and does not accept her being adopted by others.

As *WMT* women, men, too, can be turned into father figures by the kindness and love of healing younger characters in meisaku series. Think

FIGURE 4.16A *Arthur Popple decides to stop drinking and resume his work (Lucy – Episode 39). This apparent victory is followed by a dramatic twist (Lucy May's disappearance), raising the stakes for the character.*

of grumpy Mr Pendleton in *Pollyanna*, who finds himself able to love again, and eventually to adopt an orphan kid, thanks to the protagonist's good influence. Older characters can also belong to this category, such as Vitalis in *Remi*, or Perrine's and Cedie's ill-tempered grandpas. Moreover, grandfathers and uncles are generally good mentors for the young. Think of Peguin, an old man who carves wood for a living and sparks inspiration in Lucien, or Uncle Noel, a travelling craftsman who helps Nello become aware of his love for drawing. The underlying idea is the wholesomeness of work learnt by experience with people who mastered a skill.

Male characters with a shaded personality exist in meisaku series, and are more frequent than female characters in the same role. However, they are typically portrayed as complex figures, in line with the realistic representation of humanity in the series of the programme. For example, in *Sanzen ri*, the puppeteer Peppino forces his young daughters to work, but he also helps Marco during his journey. Even the most melodramatic *WMT* series are usually opaque in their rendition of evil characters. Mr Cojez is narratively characterized as an antagonist for Nello in *Flanders*, but also as a caring father who repents himself in the finale.[100] An exception is Gaspard in *Remi* (named Garofoli in the book), a brutal man in Paris who treats homeless children

---

[100]Director Kuroda's original intention was to depict Patrasche's first owner, who beats him without mercy, in a less villainous way, underlining that using dogs to carry carts was normal at the time.

FIGURE 4.16B *Lucien opens up with Peguin about his guilt feelings* (Annette – Episode 22). *The old man, who also has a troubled past, gives him a carving knife to help him move on and cultivate his talents.*

like slaves to squeeze their money, redolent of Dickens' Fagin in *Oliver Twist*. However, director Kusuba created ambiguous characters in other meisaku series, so this might also depend on the haste-making of the show.

Although less numerically present in the leading roles of the show, male characters are therefore as represented and narratively consistent as female characters. Their role in family stories seems to have been tailored to match the taste of the public, suggesting a more variegated viewership than mothers and children. As for the female cast, the representation of male figures changed with time, including diverse father figures, especially in the second half of the staple. Think of the more laid-back attitudes of Jackie's father in *Bushbaby*, or Nanami's father in *Tico*. These are youthful-looking men who express themselves quite freely, bespeaking less austerity than fathers in older shows. In the 1990s, there are also sterner father figures such as Georg in *Trapp*, who is much less humorous than the homonymous character in the Hollywood film. This seems to suggest that *WMT* fathers, together with the behavioural patterns they reflected, were rapidly changing. However, their role was never questioned in the programme, which purposely highlighted their importance in the families represented in the shows.

Stories and style

Strongly connected with the characters, and just as effective at generating empathy, are the stories narrated in the shows. Even if *WMT* series are based on Western novels, which in turn featured recognizable narrative patterns and archetypes, transforming them into a different format was no easy task. According to Kusuba, what made it especially 苦しかった (*kurushikatta* [hard]) was the fact that every show came with its own set of characters and adventures, differently from other long-running series such as ドラえもん (*Doraemon*) (1979–2004), the brainchild of the 'gag manga' duo Fujiko Fujio.[101] In fact, *WMT* series were adaptations from different books (which were not always meant for children to begin with), and, as such, they neither ensured a prolific concept to create vertical episodes nor usually provided enough contents to cover an annual show. Over the years, in order to maintain consistency in the programme, the staff involved followed the example set by earlier *WMT* series, acknowledging the pioneering role of the directors Takahata and Kuroda. Also, as seen, the series were concocted to match the demands of sponsors and TV station, which had their own agenda, and this obviously influenced the adaptation choices. But how were meisaku series any different from contemporary animation, and how did the screenwriters tackle the issue in the diegetic practice?

The basic narrative of *WMT* series revolves around young protagonists, who, as Satō puts it, 苦労しながらいわゆる感動的にやっていく (*kurōshinagara iwayuru kandōteki ni yatteiku* [in spite of the difficulties manage to get on in a so-to-speak emotional way]).[102] To some extent, this could be the premise for any story, which has been connected to a character overcoming obstacles and stirring emotions since Aristotle. While directors certainly had an impact on *WMT* series for their realistic vision and cinematic storytelling skills, screenwriters became increasingly important after Miyazaki Akira joined the project in the mid-1970s. Significantly, popular anime genres of the time, such as the gag manga, implied that directors, who were often former animators, would modify the scripts to incorporate visual comedy into the shows, as Saitō recalls doing with 天才バカボン (*Tensai Bakabon* [*Genius Bakabon*]) (1975–7). However, when Saitō started working in tandem with Miyazaki, he discovered that 脚本通り描いてみると、意外と楽なんですね (*kyakuhon-dōri kaite miru to, igaito rakuna ndesu ne* [it is surprisingly easy to draw according to the script]).[103] Writing for animation usually comes with its own set of rules, among which a priority is visualization, rendering stories through images rather than 'talking heads'.[104] Nevertheless, the reason

---

[101]Quoted in Chiba, *Sekai meisaku gekijō shirīzu memoriaru bukku. Amerika & warudō-hen*, 326.
[102]Ibid., 364.
[103]Quoted in Chiba, *Sekai meisaku gekijō shirīzu memoriaru bukku. Yōroppa-hen*, 365.
[104]Paul Wells, *Basics Animation 01: Scriptwriting* (Switzerland: AVA Publishing SA, 2007), 178.

why Miyazaki's scripts were so fitting for *WMT* series was, paradoxically, that they did not follow the standards for Japanese animation.¹⁰⁵

Miyazaki's career started in traditional live-action cinema at the Shochiku studios, where his name is credited since the late 1960s in several films by 山田 洋次 (Yamada Yōji) (born 1931), one of Japan's most popular and prolific directors.¹⁰⁶ Shōchiku was famous for the importance attached to screenplay, which was usually downplayed by earlier directors, and virtually nonexistent until the late 1910s. On the contrary, all apprentice directors at Shōchiku were expected to learn the ropes of screenwriting before moving on to filmmaking.¹⁰⁷ In particular, the Shōchiku style emphasized character development, which had to be depicted realistically. Famous filmmakers of the golden age of Japanese cinema, such as 小津安二郎 (Ōzu Yasujiro) (1903–63), epitomized this style with their stories centred on everyday life and female-oriented family drama.¹⁰⁸ Considering that the *WMT* series were adaptations of realistic novels with a big ratio of female characters, it seems reasonable to see a consistency with contemporary live-action TV series as well as Shōchiku cinema. In fact, Miyazaki's meisaku scripts focused on the construction of complex characters, with the plot being functional to their psychological growth.

Segueing on Takahata's approach to animation, which avoided manga-based tropes and exaggerations, Miyazaki's style contributed to consolidating the style of *WMT* in a realistic way. Therefore, though narrating exceptional events, meisaku episodes focused on storylines that arise from everyday life, privileging themes such as friendship or love between children and parents. Also, Takahata's interest in lifelike representations of humanity probably left an imprint on the *WMT*, which, as seen, featured several characters with antiheroic qualities, communicating a sense of natural complexity. However, differently from Takahata's vision of childhood, which became increasingly less idealized, the representation of the 子供の心 (*kodomo no kokoro* [child's mind]) in *WMT* series used characters that are almost too good to be true, able to inspire feelings of kindness and empathy in others, including viewers. This positive spin, highlighting the best in humanity, emerges in the quiet and slow-paced shows directed by Saitō, as well as in more emotionally loaded series. For example, in the seven adaptations directed by Kusuba, who started working for *WMT* as an assistant director in *Akage no An*,

---

¹⁰⁵Kindly note that, unfortunately, I have no access to the actual scripts written by Miyazaki, so my observations are based on published interviews and the watching of *WMT* series.
¹⁰⁶'Miyazaki Akira (1934-2018)', *IMDb*. Available online:https://www.imdb.com/name/nm0594496/ (accessed 19 April 2023).
¹⁰⁷Isolde Standish, *A New History of Japanese Cinema. A Century of Narrative Film* (New York and London: Continuum, 2005), 77.
¹⁰⁸Joo Woojeong, *The Cinema of Ozu Yasujiro. Histories of the Everyday* (Edinburgh: Endinburgh University Press, 2017), 212.

tragic situations are often radically emphasized, with dramatic developments that create a strong emotional hook for the audience. This does not diminish the realistic feel of *WMT* series, given the more nuanced characterization of the other characters surrounding the protagonist.

Of course, *WMT* shows have been created by different teams and in a time frame of more than two decades, which implies a rotation of scenario writers and directors, who did not always follow the same scheme. For example, more insights on the relation between realism and melodrama will be provided in Chapter 6. The following paragraphs explore a set of techniques and tropes that seem to inform the rhetorics of adaptation behind *WMT*.

Faithfulness

The post-war diktat that Japanese translations should be as faithful as possible to the original seemed to have lingered on *WMT* adaptations. In fact, though several titles were available in multiple editions, the creative staff usually chose those that were regarded as the most faithful translations. An example is *Perrine*, which is based on 家なき娘 (*Ie-naki-ko* [*Homeless girl*]) (1941), by 津田 穣 (Tsuda Yutaka) (1910–55), because it was the only complete translation of *En Famille* (unsurprisingly published by Iwanami).[109] In addition, meisaku series tended not to stray from the source texts, even when this led to unpalatable narrative choices. Think of the numerous deaths in the series of the programme, starting from Nello and Patrasche's tragic end. Fidelity also implied a careful reconstruction of sociocultural situations that could be perceived as alien by the Japanese audience, be it making cheese on the Swiss Alps as with Annette and Lucien or scraping hemp in a Finnish farm with Katri. Actually, as the practice of scouting trips demonstrated, such foreignizing aspects were a source of charm for the domestic viewers in an age of rampant Westernization, when the economic miracle was gradually allowing tourism overseas. Also, as already observed for the Zuiyō era, a faithful rendition of foreign cultural scripts was conducive to making the shows easier to export to the international markets.

However, *WMT* series were not always faithful to the original novels, in terms of both characters and story developments. This holds especially true for series based on works which were relatively new or intended for a different target. As seen, Miyazaki had to modify *Lucy*'s original story, adding subplots and twists to pep up a bleak scenario. Actually, one of the reasons why meisaku adaptations seem to have aged well in comparison to other series lies in their

---

[109]Matsumoto, *20 Seiki terebi dokuhon sekai meisaku gekijō taizen*, 39.

attempt to create stories that could work for a yearly format, reflecting the spirit of the source texts (or what was perceived as such), rather than being philologically faithful to them. This attitude resulted in several strategies. One was pioneered in *Heidi*, and consisted in the ethnographic use of real life – human more than Western – as a source of entertainment. A corollary of this is an increased effect of fidelity. *Katri*'s documentary-like narrative seems suggestive of a faithful adaptation in spite of the many differences from the Finnish saga, which begins in the mid-nineteenth century, dedicating more space to Katri's adult life. Another strategy is the identification of a general subject to be used as a compass to rearrange the narrative materials in the series. For example, Kuroda identified family as the core theme of *Flone*. This is why the series starts with an introduction of the Robinsons in their native home in Switzerland, instead of beginning with a shipwreck as in the novel. So, as a general rule, meisaku series favoured faithfulness, but attached even greater importance to realistic coherence.

Changes

WMT series consisted of weekly episodes of around twenty-five minutes each that would run for the whole year, decreasing in number only towards the end of the programme. This means that Western books for children, typically short in length, had to provide materials for fifty episodes or more. So, all *WMT* series underwent a number of expansions and additions in terms of characters, narrative and worldbuilding. When possible, additions were taken from books belonging to the same literary tradition as the original novel or written by the same writer. For example, a few storylines in the series *Tom Sawyer* were inspired by other books by Twain, such as *Tom Sawyer Abroad* (1894), for the scenes in which Tom and Huck fly on a hot-air balloon (Episode 37), or the memoir *Roughing it* (1872) for Episode 32, in which St Petersburg is affected by a sudden gold rush. Finding such adjacent narratives was relatively easy for European and American stories, but was unfeasible for *Lucy*, due to the lack of a canon of Australian children's classics. Given its thematic proximity to frontier literature, the series was promoted as the Australian version of *Little House on the Prairie*, whose TV adaptation was popular on NHK at the time.

Additions also concerned the pantheon of characters, which is always richer than in the source books. This is because the long duration of the format allowed to create ensemble casts that grew throughout the series, pushing it forward with additional story arcs. Children characters served an important diegetic function, as friends of the protagonist who give life to realistic childlike interactions. This trend is clear since the days of *Flanders*. Whereas the novella features the orphan protagonist and a few other characters (all adults except for him and his romantic interest, Alois), the series has over thirty characters. These include Nello's friends George and Paul, a spunky kid and his toddler brother, who, according to director Kuroda, were pivotal to create a 子ども社会 (*kodomo shakai* [children society]) around Nello, as well as changes of scene, since the boys frequently move from their village to Antwerp.[110] Another function of additional characters is the exploration of different subplots. Think of Judy's friends Sally and Julia, whose roles are expanded in *Ashinaga*, providing a number of narrative complications.

Note that Nello's age is lowered in *Flanders*, which portrays him as a ten-year-old boy, and Alois as a little girl of eight, despite being a fifteen-year-old in the original book. The rejuvenation of the main characters recurs in most *WMT* series and seems conducive to close the gap with the audience, bringing the protagonists as close as possible to the age of the children viewers. Even the age of the eldest meisaku heroine, Maria, was lowered from twenty-one to eighteen years old in the adaptation, putting the Von Trapp children at the heart of the series. That of age lowering is a convenient device also to treat the theme of friendship between boys and girls in a traditional way, for it allows to skim romance until age makes it socially appropriate. So Nello and Alois are good friends, not star-crossed lovers, while Maria and Judy are made the youngest possible not to lose the hook with the viewers, but still old enough for marriage.

Entralacement

Differently from contemporary TV series for children, which usually have a vertical structure (a storyline starts, develops and ends within the same episode), *WMT* shows mix verticality and horizontality, or self-contained adventures with ongoing narratives that continue from one episode to the other. Typically, *WMT* horizontal storylines have a serious tone and are interspersed with light-hearted vertical plots that provide comic relief. Horizontality also implies that, if a story is set up, there will be a pay-off afterwards. This is especially evident with side characters who have an impact on the main plot, and whose uncompleted narrative threads may disappear for long periods, but are eventually resurrected before the end of the show. This narrative device, which is rooted in the tradition of European literary sagas since the Middle Ages, and can be found in the structure of the novel-feuilleton as well as in the long-running soap-opera format, is in part a by-product of the adaptation. However, *WMT* series actively reproduced this narrative form even when the original book did not. For example, Perrine is forced to sell her donkey Palikare, and they will be reunited in the end of the show, as happens in the novel. But, in the same series, Perrine

---

[110]Quoted in Chiba, *Sekai meisaku gekijō shirīzu memoriaru bukku. Yōroppa-hen*, 345.

also meets again her friend Marcel, a circus boy who makes only a brief appearance in the book.

In meisaku series, adults' and children's narratives are closely interwoven, in line with the mainstream audience of the shows. This is a major difference from today's animation for kids, in Japan as in the rest of the world, where adult characters are often virtually absent or have limited agency. Recurring genres in *WMT* adult narratives are drama and romance. *Lucy* is an example: think of the protagonist's eldest sister Clara and her boyfriend John, a sailor whom she met on her journey to Australia, who go through several ups and downs before getting married towards the end of the show. The tone of this storyline is highly dramatic, and would not look out of place in a live-action series for women.

Just like adult characters are amply represented in meisaku series, where they play the role of teachers or guides for the young protagonists, adults can also help viewers navigate multistrand plots as voice-over narrators, often encompassing the moral of the shows. Extra-diegetic or external adult narrators are more frequent in early *WMT* series, and usually replace the literary omniscient, revealing authoritative information about the inner world of the characters, or summarizing events not shown in the animation. It is worth noting that, unlike literary texts, *WMT* narrators can be male or female, and this provides various effects, such as creating a critical distance from the narrative (see Chapter 5). Moreover, from the 1980s onwards, *WMT* series started to feature children narrators belonging to the fictional world. Examples are Kate (*Lucy*), Amy (*Wakakusa*) or Judy (*Ashinaga*). This has the additional consequence of telling the story from an unusual angle, as narrators are not always the protagonists of the show. Conversely, when narrators are absent, as happens in *Shōkōjo Sēra* (see Chapter 6), this emphasizes the feeling of immediacy and realism of a multistrand narrative, making it more cinematic.

From pillar to post

WMT stories have a calm pace, but this is not to say there is no room for plot progression. In fact, meisaku characters often have to endure dramatic situations going from bad to worse, this obviously being more effective when the protagonists are unaware of their fall. Due to the usually long format of *WMT* shows, many of these misadventures are invented from scratch. Think of *Wakakusa* starting out in the middle of the war. With their house being torn down, the protagonists are left penniless – a storytelling device to magnify their basic needs and desires. Moreover, by introducing characters and storylines that are absent in the book, *WMT* series manage to raise the stakes for the protagonist, iterating a positive message of hope. This is what happens in the first seventeen episodes of *Perrine*, which portray a positive view of humanity, a theme that runs through all the series of the programme.

For example, Perrine's encounter with a cantankerous old man reveals that he is actually a kind grandpa looking after his orphan nephew (Episode 5).

Another constant in *WMT* storytelling is an apparent quietness which is just preparing for the tempest to strike. In *Tom Sawyer*, Tom and Huck's seeing the murder of Dr Robinson, an early incident in the novel (Chapter IX), happens towards the end of the series (Episode 38), after a number of pacific episodes. This is a plot twist that injects tension in the narrative, engaging the viewers in a compelling way due to a sudden emotional change. Again, Pollyanna might save a little robin bird from a motorcar, but right after she gets hit by a car. Katri's grandparents are ready to sell one of their few cows but this gets eaten by a bear. Especially in older *WMT* shows (with the notable exception of *Flanders*), these tragic turns of fortune are often presented in an apparently uneventful way, where there is no need for sentimentality. From the mid-1980s, the melodramatic use of pathos in *WMT* series is equally effective in its emotional impact on viewers. For example, Pollyanna's overhearing her fate (Episode 21) – another recurring trope in the series of the programme – is among the most intense moments in the show, but the plain death of Sterling's mother in *Rascal* is by no means less dramatic. Note that, when pillar-to-post stories evolve into rags-to-riches narratives, antagonists can get what they deserve in a sort of karmic way, but they are frequently forgiven by the protagonists. Their emotional fluctuations also prove that there is no clear-cut distinction between heroes and villains.

FIGURE 4.17A *Pollyanna hit by a car (*Pollyanna *– Episode 21). The scene, an example of Kusuba's emotional directing, is filmed from the point of view of Pollyanna's friend Jimmy, the camera zooming in on her seemingly dead body with a jump cut.*

FIGURE 4.17B *The children's trafficker Antonio Luini finds himself unable to hit Romeo after the boy saved his life (*Romeo *– Episode 6). Emotionally complex villains such as Luini, renamed* 死神 *(shinigami [god of death]) in the series, are typical of* WMT.

Juxtaposition

As a rule of thumb, meisaku series revolve around children with good character traits, such as always being honest and kind to others. In order to present them as positive role models, juxtaposition is probably the most-used rhetorical device in *WMT* shows, placing the protagonist side by side with a dissimilar character. This helps bring out their differences, casting a light on the superior qualities of the protagonist and making them dear to the audience. Think of Remi arriving at Gaspard's house, and being the only child who refuses to steal. Particularly powerful effects can be obtained with contrasts, which create antithetical couples of characters. An example is the encounter between the March sisters and their cousin David in *Wakakusa* (Episode 12), an original character who takes advantage of their elderly aunt Martha. There are different levels of opposition between the March family and David: they are a close-knit group and he is alone; they are women and he is a man; they are kind and generous, while he is stingy and dishonest; they are poor and he is wealthy. This drives the audience to sympathize with the main characters, orienting their moral reading of the show.

Juxtaposition and antithesis are even more impactful on viewers when they concern moral opposites, for example, showing a good character being abused in a melodramatic way. This has the practical effect of stimulating feelings such as pity or admiration in the audience. For example, Katri is unfairly punished when she leaves her post on the order of her master's wife

(Episode 8). Tender-hearted Remi is also cruelly beaten by Gaspard when she tries to defend her friends. Similar polarization strategies can be used with parallel storylines, to stress the dramatic irony of the events told, for example, through cross-cutting editing. So, fortune seems to favour Mr Popple just as his daughter Lucy May goes missing (Episode 39). Similarly, Romeo is about to win a climbing competition when his father's crops are destroyed by fire (Episode 1). These scenarios evoke contrasting emotions and introduce dramatic plot developments, such as Mr Popple realizing his flaws as a father, and Romeo's hard times in Milan. It is also worth noting that juxtaposition is not limited to stress the positive attributes of the protagonist but of other characters as well. For example, *Flanders* pits Mr Cojez against Nello's grandfather for their opposite sensitivities, putting the latter one in best light. So, while Mr Cojez thinks that artists like Nello are idlers, putting him off, his grandpa believes they have the power to stir emotions (Episode 37).

Digressions

Temporary detours from the main narrative are fairly frequent in meisaku series. Digressions can be viewed as both a consequence of the multistrand structure of *WMT* shows and an effect of their educational agenda. In fact, they often take the form of retellings of historical events, novels or popular fairy tales, narrated by a character belonging to the world of the show. To distinguish them from the events of the series, these sequences are marked by a distinctive visual style, usually consisting of montages of still frames

FIGURE 4.18 *Nello's grandfather encourages him to follow his dream (*Flanders – Episode 38*).*

and attached voice-over narrator, as in the tradition of the Japanese paper theatre. However, digressions are fully integrated in the shows. As a story within the story, a digression might have a connection with the culture of the country in which the series takes place. For example, father Robinson tells his sons about Marie Antoinette being delivered to France as a royal bride when they are travelling down the Rhine (*Flone* – Episode 3). Fabry, Perrine's friend and confidant, gives her a copy of *Les Misèrables*, a classic of French literature, and tells her the story of Jean Valjean (Episode 28). Note that Hugo's character has much in common with Perrine, as they both assume a new identity for a good cause (Perrine uses the pseudonym Aurelie until the end of the narrative).

Digressions can also be used in juxtaposition to the protagonist, reflecting their wishes in a metaphoric way. Think of Katri reading 'The Ugly Duckling', and realizing that she, too, wants to become a swan, studying to become a teacher or a nurse (Episode 30).[111] In another different case historic events can take place in the same time of the narrative, thus being represented in the fictional world of the series, such as the Nazi invasion of Austria in *Trapp* (Episode 36). Last but not least, digressions include flashbacks, which in *WMT* are particularly frequent and thematically consistent. In fact, meisaku characters tend to trip down memory lane, remembering about meaningful past experiences that contrast with their current situation. Think of Katri's memories about her arrival at Raikkola farm when she is about to leave it (Episode 24). As it is easy to guess, this narrative technique is common in literature and films, having the additional benefit of providing filler content. However, *WMT* recollections often show scenes that have not been animated before, thus suggesting a poignant narrative function. An example is Aunt Polly recalling her happy childhood with her sister, who died when Pollyanna was little (Episode 14). These moments deal with dramatic changes, but communicate a sense of consciousness that change is inevitable in the passage of time, leaving the characters with feelings of 物の哀れ (*mono no aware*, or the 'gentle sadness') for the impermanence of things.

Realism and everyday life

In spite of their horizontal narratives being mostly dramatic, as was the case for their literary sources, *WMT* series are rooted in a realistic tradition, and, as such, they usually avoid fabulous or fantastic elements. As seen, this

---

[111]Other times, fairy-tale tropes are indirectly evoked in meisaku series. Think of Perrine being invited to live at her grandfather's castle (Episode 41), which seems suggestive of two French literary tales, the 'Beauty and the Beast' (for their polarised temperaments and Vulfran's isolation) and 'Cinderella' (for her status advancement).

resulted in the creation of characters that have both good and bad traits, not mere villains or knights in shining armour, with an embedded humanistic message. The old saying 'don't judge a book by its cover' could describe many episodes and characters of these shows. Think of Perrine, who finds friends in the most unexpected places and people, who are often apparently unsympathetic and yet hide a heart of gold. It is also true that *WMT* protagonists are meant to be morally edifying, in line with the educational style of the programme. This might make them seem less realistic, especially for modern standards of storytelling, which are often set on more morally ambiguous characters. Thus, what helps to convey a sense of realism in *WMT* series is the way they provide faithful depictions of daily life. By showing the characters immersed in real world, as they experience slice-of-life situations that feel familiar to the audience, *WMT* series engage the viewers emotionally, casting routine – which in meisaku shows is social and harmonious by definition – in a positive light.

In practical terms, this led to insert beats which, in today's commercial animation, would be slashed immediately at the pre-production stage. Think of Rascal eating sugar cubes that dissolve in water, or the Robinsons watching baby turtles as they hatch (*Flone* – Episode 21). The latter scene, with all the turtles going towards the sea, leaves the family in awe, showing the extraordinary in the ordinary of everyday life. The recurring beats in which the characters share a meal together are another example, with aesthetically pleasing plating redolent of 盛り付け (*moritsuke*), the Japanese art of food arrangement. Certainly a slow tempo was a convenient device for *WMT* series to maximize their contents, given their long-running format. However, the little things of everyday life might not mean much in terms of story progression, but they mean a lot for characterization, allowing the viewers to recognize *WMT* characters as human. Think of Nello's grandfather realizing that he is about to die, and yet performing mundane tasks such as helping his nephew to Antwerp, or playing hopscotch, because everyday life comes with a sense of accomplishment (*Flanders* – Episode 41). The underlying assumption is that, differently from the Hollywood tenet that narratives should be emotional rollercoasters, it is lifelike characters, and a consistent description of their fictional world, to hook viewers and foster empathy. In turn, this is connected to the educational values at the heart of the programme: teaching audiences that life can be troublesome, but you do not need much to be happy.

Western world

Perhaps the most evident feature of *WMT* is their careful representation of Western countries. As foreignizing translations, meisaku adaptations emphasized the cultural differences of foreign texts, including national traditions and specificities. So, in *WMT* shows, it is common to find picturesque images of Western landscapes, architectures, social habits,

FIGURE 4.19A *Perrine makes her own shoes* (Perrine – Episode 30). *The girl and her dog Baron, an original character and a source of comic relief, live by themselves in a hut in the forest, embracing a radically simple way of living.*

FIGURE 4.19B *Landing up on a desert island does not stop the Robinsons from settling into a daily routine and celebrating Flone's eleventh birthday (*Flone – Episode 31*). Luscious food moments have been a staple of the programme since the days of* Heidi.

costumes and customs, all reproduced with fine attention to detail. *WMT*'s foreignization seems related to its grounding in realisms, both partly descending from Takahata's anthropological working method since the time of Zuiyō. Over twenty years later, meisaku series were still aligned to the standards set back then. Think of Romeo arriving in Milan (Episode 7). In spite of the tragicness of the situation (it is explained that chimney sweeping shortened a child's life span), Romeo is welcomed by panoramic views on the city's most representative monuments, such as La Scala, the Duomo and Galleria Vittorio Emanuele. This kind of visuals was intended to educate the audience, conveying information about life in the West. For example, when John is searching for Lassie's mom (Episode 3), a stop by the canal is a chance to show how canal locks work in England. This is probably also the reason why the popularity of meisaku series gradually decreased in the 1980s, as documentaries and tourism abroad became increasingly available.

However, *WMT* shows are something more than postcards of exotic locations allowing to travel vicariously to the West. In fact, the adaptations privileged countries that had a special meaning for post-war Japan. Series such as *Ashinaga* or *Tom Sawyer* contain compelling descriptions of the American dream of freedom and democracy, which in turn appear enhanced by the beautiful locations of the United States. In a similar way, European settings, with their rich cultural heritage and historical sites, communicated a myth of nations unscarred by the war. This is evident in the numerous Swiss alpine landscapes in the series of the programme, usually portrayed as safe havens. Think of the Robinsons fondly remembering their life in Switzerland, singing yodels while living on an inhospitable island (*Flone* – Episode 28). The way Western spaces are presented in the *WMT* was also affected by the needs of production and scripting. For example, thanks to a scouting trip to Belgium, director Kuroda and his crew realized that Antwerp, where *A Dog of Flanders* originally takes place, had been heavily urbanized since the nineteenth century. This is why, for the *WMT* series, they took inspiration from the medieval town of Bruges and the close village of Damme.[112] They also inserted hills in the typical Dutch plains, arguably because it is more effective to portray depth in a layered scene with separate foreground and background elements. This created an effect of cinematic animation.

Combining original characteristics and deliberately invented features is typical of *WMT* locales. The outcome is an apparent realism, which achieves verisimilitude by creating worlds that look truer than the real ones. To some extent, this seems connected with the notion of 憧れのパリ (*akogare no Pari* [the Paris of our dreams]), or Japan's fantasized fascination with

---

[112]Chiba, *Sekai meisaku gekijō e no tabi*, 8–10.

FIGURE 4.20A *A glimpse of old Genoa while Marco runs through the streets of the town to deliver a letter (*Sanzen ri *– Episode 3). Scriptwriter Furukawa was also from a vibrant port city, Yokohama.*

Europe. Several scholars identified this trope in the films by Miyazaki,[113] who probably influenced the *WMT*, as well as being influenced by it. In meisaku series, the underlying message is a positive portrait of the West and the values it embodied. *Lassie* is an interesting example. On the one hand, the animation arbitrarily recreated Greenall Bridge, a (fictional) Yorkshire village where the story starts and ends, using materials collected during a past scouting trip to Haworth (see Chapter 6).[114] On the other hand, the coal mines and terraced houses of the series were inspired by *How Green Was My Valley* (1941), a famous Hollywood movie (which in turn was filmed in a replica Welsh town in California). The nostalgic feeling of the film seems to be reflected in *Lassie*, which also deals with the tensions between modernity and memories of a blissful past. In particular, the bucolic representation of a close-knit community is redolent of the rustic simplicity expressed in the series of the programme since the days of *Moomin*.

Family

One of the most recurring theme in *WMT* is a positive description of family life. A cosy nuclear family is usually presented as an ideal and the norm in

---

[113]See: Helen McCarthy, *Hayao Miyazaki: Master of Japanese Animation. Films, Themes, Artistry* (Berkeley: Stone Bridge Press, 1999); Dani Cavallaro, *The Animé Art of Hayao Miyazaki* (Jefferson: McFarland & Company, 2006).
[114]Chiba, *Sekai meisaku gekijō e no tabi*, 118–20.

FIGURE 4.20B *John first meets Lassie in a meadow (*Lassie *– Episode 1). The aerial view allows to see the clash of old and new, with a flock of sheep passing by modern machines.*

meisaku series, which reflect patterns and structures of traditional family stories from Western children's literature up to the twentieth-century, where accidents in the family are treated as means for plot development.[115] So, *WMT* characters either live in a loving family, usually with several brothers and sisters, who have to face some sort of trial, or look forward to connect to their relatives, embarking on a quest to find them. Significantly, even when a family is disrupted by dramatic events, a new family is built by the end of the narrative. Remi has to leave her family, and will both find an adoptive father and her real mother, but also a group of siblings and a boy she loves. In *Sanzen ri*'s finale, Marco and his mother return to Genoa, where the Rossi family is reunited. Lucien's father died before he was born, but his mother and sister take care of him, and he finds a father figure in old Peguin who teaches him to work. In larger family groups, family becomes the heart of the show as a place where everyone is different, but there is also help and affection.

Note that the nuclearization of family is a modern phenomenon that goes hand in hand with industrialization.[116] Historically, Western ideas and Confucian tenets coalesced into the notion of Japanese household, which merged aspects of the feudal *ie* (a corporate entity including non-kin and

---

[115]Kimberly Reynolds, *Children's Literature: A Very Short Introduction* (New York: Oxford University Press, 2011), 85–95.
[116]Fumie Kumagai, 'Families in Japan: Beliefs and Realities', *Journal of Comparative Family Studies* 26, no. 1 (1995): 140.

blood relations), and the ideology of the Meiji era, when the whole state was viewed as one family for nationalistic reasons. This helps frame the representation, in *WMT* series such as *Katri*, of tightly knit communities, where distant relatives, servants and workers form part of the same clan. Meisaku families are seen as a unit that can face all kinds of adversities, often openly stating their rhetoric. Think of the Robinsons finding the corpse of a castaway man, connecting his death to the fact that he was alone while they are a family of five, which is pivotal to their survival (*Flone* – Episode 35). There are many moments in which *WMT* families act as a whole, facing difficult situations together or celebrating a good turn of events. Series like *Lucy* suggests that no family is perfect but this does not make them less valuable, if they prioritize the values of peace and harmony. This is clear when *Lucy* juxtaposes the Popples with the Pettywells to exemplify how and how not to conduct family life, the latter being a wealthy couple who is never happy precisely because of the non-harmonic relations between its members. Over the years, meisaku series also incorporated sociocultural changes in the way in which families are depicted. So, the protagonist of *Tico* has a single parent and an elective family of close friends. However, the *WMT* tends to feature orphan stories in lieu of divorce or other causes of parental absence, thus the traditional role of family is never questioned.

Education

Family is also the place where education is passed on. Learning is closely connected with virtue in the Japanese value system,[117] so it is no surprise that meisaku series, whose target audiences were young children and their mothers, showcase ideal models of instruction, rooted in indigenous and borrowed ideas about childhood and pedagogy. Juxtaposition encourages viewers to compare different examples of education by contrasting parents (or parent figures) who take diametrically opposite views on the matter. For example, in *Rascal*, Sterling's understanding dad emerges as a positive character in comparison with his friend Oscar's father, who is initially framed negatively for his authoritarian ways (Episode 1). The role of family and school in a child's education is emphasized by the fact that parents in *WMT* shows are often professional teachers, like Jo (*Nan to Jō*) or Maria (*Trapp*). *Trapp* is perhaps one of the series that best epitomizes a full range of pedagogical methods, introducing three types of educators. Matilda, the old housekeeper of the Von Trapp family, is cold and punishing, while Yvonne, the noblewoman that the Baron initially plans to marry, is a laissez faire, who occasionally shows affection but little control or correction of

---

[117]White, *The Japanese Educational Challenge*, 51.

FIGURE 4.21 *Maria confronts Yvonne, the Baron's fiancée, about little Agathe von Trapp's education (*Trapp *– Episode 28). The child snatched a pair of scissors, and Maria is determined to teach her that they can be dangerous.*

problematic attitudes. Instead, the protagonist embodies what is presented as the best approach – a warm relationship that is attentive to children and does not skirmish from play, but can be authoritative when responsibility must be taught.

In general, the series of the programme favour an emotional style of teaching, or ウェット (*wetto* [wet, soft-hearted]), as it is described in Japan in opposition to ドライ (*dorai* [dry, unemotional]), another English loan word to indicate more rational and Western-like practices.[118] Rigid disciplinarians are often comically portrayed, as happens with professor Dobbins in *Tom* or professor Melnore in *Ashinaga*. In line with the Japanese notion of childhood, where cheerfulness and physical energy are commonly desired traits (see Chapter 3), good educators in *WMT* use free play to allow children to act 'like children'.[119] In this context, empathy is regarded as the most important thing, and learning as a process whose efficacy can be measured by emotional engagement rather than skills or knowledge. Think of Flone, who is physically punished for going alone in the forest, but not when she does the same to rescue a goat, because she showed thoughtfulness and consideration (Episode 30). Emotionally loaded narratives are also a vehicle for edutainment, often via meta situations such as school lessons. For example, Judy learns about the classics of children's literature at high school

---

[118]Lewis, *Educating Hearts and Minds*, 207.
[119]As in Ibid., 49.

(*Ashinaga* – Episode 6), and so do the viewers. What captures the interest of the audience is Judy's love for learning combined to her sad backstory, which she transfigures in a moving family essay.

Christianity

For their transnational reach and non-manga style, one might assume that meisaku series are 無国籍 (*mukokuseki* [culturally odourless]) shows.[120] For instance, Bryce considers Pollyanna's Christian identity unusual, because religious references were removed in *Heidi*.[121] However, the treatment of religion in *Heidi* was an exceptional case rather than the norm, and seems more reflective of Takahashi's policy at Zuiyō. On the contrary, Nippon Animation did not erase country-specific cultural markers (at least, not all and not always), but often emphasized them in a positive way. This is the case with the representation of Christianity in the programme. In general, characters in meisaku series are portrayed as Christian. This implies a set of ideas and practices, such as openly voicing their confidence in the Divine Providence, praying to God in topic moments, or going to mass. Religious characters are described in a good light, including nuns and priests. Many of these elements were incorporated from Western literature, but there are cases in which Christian faith is given more space in the adaptations than in their source novels. Think of Sterling's daily interactions with the local pastor, or Remi being helped by a priest on her way to Paris, which are original features of the animation. Even the least pious among meisaku protagonists, like Judy in *Ashinaga*, or those that embody a satirical critique of religion, such as Tom Sawyer, seem to share an anthropologically Christian way of life, underlying the difference between bigotry and more genuine forms of spirituality.

Christians are a minority in Japan, but the presence of Christian religion in *WMT* series appears as a connection point with its impact on children's literature in the country (see Chapters 1 and 6). Bryce notes that Pollyanna's being the daughter of a missionary plays a key role in eliciting the sympathy of the viewers, because missionaries are typically depicted as benevolent helpers outside the social hierarchy.[122] This conveys a sense of realism to the story of an orphan girl who finds herself crossing class barriers. When Christian themes are ingrained in the source novels, meisaku series tried to make them understandable to the domestic audience. Kusuba explained that Annette deliberately associates Christian teachings with the more

---

[120] As in Koichi Iwabuchi, *Recentering Globalization. Popular Culture and Japanese Transnationalism* (Durham and London: Duke University Press 2002), 33.
[121] Bryce, 'Pollyanna', 240.
[122] Ibid.

FIGURE 4.22A *Cedie prays with his mother (Cedie – Episode 3). The pious scene is emphasized by cross-cutting to the old Earl of Dorincourt railing against his son's wedding with a commoner.*

universal topic of the 子ども同士や親子の愛 (*kodomo dōshi ya oyako no ai* [love between children and between parents and children]).[123] Moral commonalities of this kind, which are salient in – but obviously not exclusive of – Christian faith, probably contributed to its favourable perception in the context of mainstream animation. At times, the Christian aspects of *WMT* shows may come off as contrived. Think of the Robinsons piously burying their donkey when the old animal dies (*Flone* – Episode 45). Nevertheless, aside from expanding themes already present in the books (in *Flone*'s case, the Swiss family's burying their dog in Chapter XVII), Christian imagery bespeaks Westernization in shows that were supposed to have a foreign flavour. A wholesome Christian framework was also consistent with Calpis, which served as a sponsor for the longest period of time in the history of programme.

Nature

Ideas about nature, which are central to every culture, have been frequently explored in Japanese animation, and are the focus of many studies on Ghibli films, usually in connection with Shintō animistic worship.[124] Also

---

[123]Quoted in Chiba, *Sekai meisaku gekijō shirīzu memoriaru bukku. Yōroppa-hen*, 348.
[124]For example, see Shoko Yoneyama, 'Miyazaki Hayao's Animism and the Anthropocene', *Theory, Culture & Society* 38, no. 7–8 (2021): 251–66.

FIGURE 4.22B *A pastor blesses Remi before she leaves for Paris (*Remi – Episode 14*)*.

WMT series are deeply connected to nature, but their general underpinning is different from environmentalist animation,[125] except from more recent shows such as *Tico*, which delves into overtly ecological narratives. As noted, the portrayal of foreign (usually Western) locales implied a realistic mise-en-scene, which served as a value of authenticity. Their careful portrayal of natural settings seems to be conducive to make the adaptations acceptable overseas, but also to pique Japan's interest for the exotic. Such a foreignizing gaze is evident in meisaku background art, which has a painterly look and feel that recall Western classic landscape paintings. At the same time, the way in which these shows tend to present nature appears to be consistent with Japan's historic identity as an agrarian site. So, as observed for Zuiyō's fascination for Scandinavian and Alpine scenery, which in turn was reflective of trends occurring in Japan since the pre-war period, meisaku series are likely to frame nature in positive terms, showing the beneficial effect it has on the main characters.

In general, meisaku protagonists receive healing and comfort from their proximity to nature. Lucien feels at ease in the woods, which soothes his worries and anxiety (*Annette* – Episode 16). Perrine turns a hut into her home because nature provides her with all the things she needs: fish, cereals, even fibres to make shoes. In *Tico*, Nanami is at one with the ocean. This is a recurring theme in the series of the programme, and seems reinforced

---

[125] As in Deirdre M. Pike, *Enviro-Toons: Green Themes in Animated Cinema and Television* (Jefferson: North Carolina: McFarland & Co., 2012).

by their attention to seasonal changes, a long-ingrained cultural narrative of Japan (see Chapter 5). Details such as flowers blossoming in spring or beautiful foliage colours in autumn would feel even more realistic because *WMT* shows were broadcast all year long, so the time frame of the narratives could match the audience's real-life experience. It is worth noting that, despite its idyllic connotation, nature in *WMT* is neither considered as mystical entity nor a final destination, but is put into service of human needs, for civilization is deemed more important. Think of Perrine, who instilled in her grandpa the will to create a phalanstery-like town, or the Robinsons struggling to leave their island in spite of their pleasant memories there. This also seems to suggest that nature is not viewed as opposed to urban life. The arrival of modernity can be problematic, particularly in earliest shows, but is usually equated with progress and opportunities. For example, Katri finds out that women can become doctors in cities, and this kindles her aspirations (Episode 29).

Dreams

Characters in *WMT* dream big and have high hopes for the future. From a narrative standpoint, this is useful to delineate strong storylines, which coincide with the protagonist's attempts to pursue their goals. Nevertheless, real dreams, daydreams and nightmares in meisaku series are just as interesting. What makes them fascinating is the fact that, with the exception of *Peter Pan* and *Tico*, dream sequences are usually the only source of fantasy in the context of the programme. As noted, there seems to be consistency in the shows that suggests a preference for realistic fiction, perhaps aligning with their Christian framework, which typically avoids representations of magic. More specifically, dreams in *WMT* seem to have one main function, as they provide comic relief in dramatically loaded narratives. Similarly to digressions, these beats may feature a different visual style, as well as integrate fairy-tale tropes and imagery. For example, Flone dreams of being a princess of a faraway land, with a fancy dress and a Prince Charming suitor (Episode 24), or of going under the sea in a seashell (Episode 31), evoking the story of 浦島太郎 (Urashima Tarō), the folk-tale character that visited the sea kingdom.

Moreover, dream sequences have frequently a distinctive, surreal taste, giving life to trippy situations which, too, soften the tone of the plot. Life is tough for Nello, but seeing a shooting star sparks his imagination, so constellations turn into beautiful paintings, expressing his love for drawing (*Flanders* – Episode 14). Flying animals appear in Katri's dreams when she has fever, and when the March family is on house hunt, Jo dreams of wandering in a maze castle in the clouds (*Wakakusa* – Episode 12). Fantastic elements of this kind are often located towards the end of an episode, leaving the viewers with an 'up' feeling, but they are common in the musical openings as well (see Chapter 6). Dreams have also another purpose, as they may show the protagonist's hidden fears or unhealed scars. Nightmarish sequences can more often be found at the beginning of an episode, and, although less numerous, they have an impact in setting the mood of a story. For example, both Lucien and Annette's feelings of guilt symbolically materialize in their sleep, with the first one being haunted by the sound of crutches (Episode 17), and the latter seeing a double self repeating her misdeeds over and over again (Episode 29).

Alone

One of the most frequently used words in meisaku series is probably 一人ぼっち (*hitoribocchi* [all alone]). In fact, *WMT* main characters are often forced to live on their own, either because they have been separated from their family, or they are orphans. As is known, orphan protagonists are ubiquitous in fiction, from epic characters such as Romulus and Remus to modern-day icons like Harry Potter. From a historical perspective, this is due to the high presence of orphans in the past ages, including post-war Japan. However, especially in children's literature, orphans represent a symbol of otherness, as well as of the possibility for one to reinvent themselves, because they begin with a clean slate, not having parents to influence them for good or evil.[126] This offers a number of practical advantages for storytelling. When isolated, a character has primal needs which anyone can understand. Think of how many *WMT* series feature a lonely young character in search of a family, friends or love, mirroring the human yearning for building new relationships. Moreover, an orphan can be seen as a quintessential outcast, who is free to break the rules and leave their place, making it easier for them to answer the Call of Adventure, as in the archetypal Hero's Journey.[127] Last but not least, being alone and vulnerable, orphan characters are more likely to engage the sympathy of the public.[128]

This effect is boosted by *WMT*'s rhetoric of empathy. Not only meisaku orphans are transported in a miserable condition in spite of their kindness and good intentions but it is the same reactions of the other characters, who feel pity for them, to instruct the responses of the viewers. That the audience is openly encouraged to care for the protagonists is clear in the terms chosen to describe them, such as 可哀想に (*kawaiisōni* [poor thing]),

---

[126]Melanie A. Kimball, 'From FolkTales to Fiction: Orphan Characters in Children's Literature', *Library Trends* 47, no. 3 (Winter 1999): 561.
[127]Christopher Vogler, *The Writer's Journey* (California: Michael Wiese Productions, 2007).
[128]Marion Gymnich, 'The Orphan in the Victorian Novel', in *The Orphan in Fiction and Comics Since the 19th Century 2018*, ed. Gymnich et al. (Newcastle: Cambridge Scholars, 2018), 20.

which stresses a sense of loneliness and dejection.[129] Something similar could be said for hitoribocchi, instead of the more factual 一人 (*hitori* [by oneself]). Here is where, once again, the Japanese ideals on childhood are helpful to assess the dramaturgic role of *WMT* characterization. 'All alone' characters are generally portrayed as stoic and rarely weepy. They do not complain about their issues, no matter how hard life can be. Such a brave personality, which is particularly emphasized in earlier series, reflects a set of appreciated values in Japanese children's education, such as 健気 (*kenagesa* [child's brave and best effort]), or the bold act of enduring something beyond your possibilities, stimulating empathy in older and more experienced people.[130]

In other words, hitoribocchi characters make for the perfect protagonists for the richly dramatic narratives of *WMT*, where they emerge as doing their best or 頑張る (*gambaru* [to persist]) (see Chapter 6) in the lowest peaks of their arcs, positively impressing the domestic public. This also means that, to some extent, solitude is welcomed as a positive state if associated to self-discovery and cultivation, another feature regarded as important in Japanese children's fiction. However, as observed for the images of childhood in the advertising strategy of Calpis, *WMT* characters unite these and other expected behaviours with values that are closer to Western education, such as their individualism and wish to be independence. So, meisaku characters, too, look eager to provide, grow up, and get a job, in spite of their physical

FIGURE 4.23A *Katri dreams of Abel and a cow flying in the sky (*Katri *– Episode 9).*

---

[129]Bryce, 'Pollyanna', 232.
[130]Ibid., 237–8.

FIGURE 4.23B *Little Katri falls while running after her mother who is leaving, a recurring scene in WMT series (Katri – Episode 1). The music, largely based on Jean Sibelius' work, underlines the emotional departure in connection with issues of character's development and nation-building.*

and psychological immaturity. Think of Judy, who becomes a private tutor even if Jervis is against it (*Ashinaga* – Episode 27), while Katri wants to be a cowherd although her grandpa thinks that she is too little (Episode 1). Still, this does not obliterate the childlike nature of the characters, which is made manifest in their cute innocence. Children will be children – this seems to be the underlying message of the shows – even if they work hard and are wise beyond years.

Ethnicity

Considering current standards, there is certainly little diversity in the way meisaku series describe ethnicity. This seems partly due to the influence of the source novels, which are selected from an era in which white authors and characters where almost exclusively represented in publishing. In particular, as Stevenson notes, 'the boom in multicultural literature hasn't been reflected in the pantheon of the classics, and the classics section may now be the whitest spot in the bookstore'.[131] Even

---

[131]Deborah Stevenson, 'Classics and Canons', in *The Cambridge Companion to Children's Literature*, ed. M. O. Grenby and Andrea Immel (Cambridge: Cambridge University Press, 2009), 108–24.

FIGURE 4.24 *Flone and Tamtam, another castaway (Flone – Episode 42)*. The friendship with an Australian Aborigine boy, whose family was killed by white people, problematizes the colonial myth represented by the Robinsons.

in the most recent books chosen for adaptation, such as *Bushbaby* and *Lucy*, which are set in Africa and Australia, the protagonists are Western. However, a closer look reveals a less monolithic scenario. In fact, there are several cases where characters of different ethnic backgrounds are featured in *WMT*. Although Injun Joe adheres to Twain's unequivocally evil characterization (which makes him a great antagonist), non-Caucasian characters are usually framed in a positive light. An example is Tenbo in *Bushbaby*. Designer Seki notes that he is 黒人でかっこいい (*kurojin de kakkoī* [black and cool]),[132] so that he often steals the scene, albeit being a side character.

Original characters can also be ethnically diverse, thematizing issues such as slavery, colonialism and racism. Tom helps a Black man to escape to the north of the country, where slaves can be free (Episode 33). In *Wakakusa*, too, the March women put themselves in danger to save John, a fugitive black slave (Episode 2). Moreover, Hannah, 'who [. . .] was considered by them all more as a friend than a servant' (Chapter II), is turned into a black woman in the animation. Although Japanese Hannah may look like a mimicry of Mammy, the devoted maid of *Gone with the Wind*, Marmee makes it clear that she is no slave, reassuring her when southern soldiers force black people

---

[132]Quoted in Chiba, *Sekai meisaku gekijō shirizu memoriaru bukku. Amerika & warudō-hen*, 333. It is worth remembering that *Bushbaby* also represents main characters with diverse body types, such as Jackie's friend-enemy Mickey, a sturdy kid and not particularly handsome.

to join them (Episode 3). Sterling, who is keen on boxing, is appalled to find out that Martin Miller, a black champion, is discriminated in the ring for the colour of his skin (*Rascal* – Episode 8). Younger characters belonging to other ethnic groups seem to emphasize these topics in a more relatable way for the audience. For example, when Flone meets Tamtam, a maori child, he is initially wary of her because white men killed his family (Episode 38). So, even though diversity was not the focus of *WMT*'s educational agenda, these series convey a message of fraternity for all humans, which are envisioned as different but united by moral commonalities. Think of Lucy May making friends with indigenous Australians, for they share the same love for nature and animals.

Animals

Part of the appeal of *WMT* is its animal characters, which are omnipresent in the series of the programme, especially in the works that depict wildlife. In fact, *WMT* protagonists are usually accompanied by a pet (at times more than one), who is also their friend. These can be as common as domestic dogs or cats – think of Lassie or *Wakakusa*'s kitty Milky Ann – but are more often unusual pets which represent the location of the series. For example, ermines like Klaus (*Annette*) or Piccolo (*Romeo*) are typical of the mountains, which is the home of their owners, while Tico is an orca and obviously stands for a nautical fiction. What seems to unite these characters is the fact that they are often original additions of the series, where they display intelligent behaviour and act as allies of the main character, as well as sources of comic relief. Meisaku animals may be kind and clever, but are by no means as anthropomorphized as the talking animals that abound in children's fiction. As noted for *Heidi* and *Rocky Chuck*, this is much indebted in Mori's design and animation techniques, which balanced realism and cuteness (see Chapter 3). The lovely look of pets was pivotal for merchandise since the days of Calpis. Plush toys were sold or given out as prizes at the time of broadcasting, sending bottle caps of Calpis beverages or other products. However, it was the production studio – first Zuiyō, then Nippon Animation – which owned the commercial rights, hence the sponsor did not make any direct profit except for the value of advertisement.[133]

Moreover, in line with the policy of *WMT*, pets played a key role in shaping the reception of the main characters – and their role models. In fact, as Bryce puts it, in *WMT* the relationship between children and their animal friends is used to illustrate children's innocence, an idealized quality in Japanese education.[134] So, animal-friendly attitudes are framed in a positive manner, and are instrumental for the audience to tell a good conduct from a

---

[133]Matsumoto, *20 Seiki terebi dokuhon sekai meisaku gekijō taizen*, 150–1.
[134]Bryce, 'Pollyanna', 239.

FIGURE 4.25A *Nanami and Tico (Episode 3). The orca, which was rescued by Nanami's father when Nanami was born, will become her best friend and the protagonist of a moving story arc.*

FIGURE 4.25B *Jackie finger-feeds Murphy like a mother (*Bushbaby *– Episode 2).*

malicious one. Lucy May and Flone go as far as refusing to eat meat or putting their life in danger to save animals. It is worth noticing that vegetarianism was not widespread, and this applies to both the narrative time and the early 1980s in Japan.[135] A particular way in which *WMT* children are shown

---

[135] Even characters like Tom, who in the book handles dead cats and mice, is made more respectful in the animation, where his squabbles with aunt Polly's cat are reduced to occasional gags.

taking on responsibilities for their animals is the puppy training. This is a topic story arc in which they rescue, feed and bond with a pet. Think of Lucy May training a stray dingo puppy to become a shepherd dog. Empathy is encouraged since their first encounter, usually by juxtaposition (the animal's scary-looking mother is killed, but the little one is harmless and cute). A series of heartwarming beats follows, including attempts to give milk to the puppy. This adds to the sweet characterization of the protagonists, hinting at the public of mothers and children. If an animal belongs to the wild, the protagonist in the end sets it free in an emotional scene.

5

From *Anne of Green Gables* to *Akage no An*

The animated series *Akage no An* [*Red-haired Anne*], based on the Canadian novel *Anne of Green Gables* (1908), represented Takahata and Miyazaki's major work before leaving Nippon Animation, and Kondō's debut as an animation director and character designer. Consisting of fifty episodes of twenty-five minutes each, the series was aired on Fuji TV from 7 January 1979 to 30 December of the same year, being the first to be crowned with the *WMT* logo. Albeit not as successful as other *WMT* series of the decade (average ratings were about 16.2 per cent, versus the 21.8 per cent of *Sanzen ri*, directed by the same Takahata[1]), it is still considered a classic in Japan.[2]

The narrative, a coming-of-age story centred on a high-spirited orphan girl, matches with Takahata's growing interest in exploring the boundaries between childhood and adulthood, a theme which would characterize much of his later works, from おもひでぽろぽろ (*Omoide poro poro* [Shedding of tears in remembrance]) (1991), internationally known as *Only Yesterday*, to かぐや姫の物語 (*Kaguya-hime no monogatari* [*The Tale of the Princess Kaguya*]) (2013). However, re-imagining the world of the novel was very challenging for the staff, with a production schedule that became infamous for its harsh conditions, especially due to Takahata's centralized approach and notorious perfectionism.

This chapter examines *Anne of Green Gables* and *Akage no An*, focusing on the animated adaptation as a transmedial and a transcultural process, set against the backdrop of Anne's popularity in Japan from the 1950s. To do so, a prior analysis of the novel, contextualized within Montgomery's

---

[1]Ishihara, *Mark Twain in Japan*, 92 n5.
[2]Matsumoto, *20 Seiki terebi dokuhon sekai meisaku gekijō taizen*, 42.

life and fiction, seems useful. A number of variants between the series and the source text will be highlighted, concentrating on the episodes that point either to the emergence of original cultural patterns or to the influence of the director's personal agenda on the making of the series.

Lucy Maud Montgomery

Lucy Maud Montgomery (1874–1942) is one of the best known Canadian writers. Originally from Prince Edward Island, the smallest province of Canada, she was wed to a Presbyterian minister, and became a professional novelist for contemporary American periodicals. Her parable as an author started at sixteen, when one of her poems was published on the Charlottetown *Daily Patriot*. Six years later, in 1896, she received her first payment for a story. Increasingly confident in her talent, she would then turn to novels and sagas. At her death, she left a rich corpus of 22 books and over 500 short stories, without mentioning her vast poetic production, which includes typically Romantic themes, such as nature, ethics and love.[3] In spite of her growing fortune as a writer, Montgomery's private life was full of struggles – a stillbirth in 1914, the imminent threat of war, a number of lawsuits with her first publisher over royalties and her husband's mental illness. She maintained an impeccable reputation as a fine lady author and a minister's wife, but her personal troubles emerge in the duality of her writings. Whereas her fiction is positive and amusing, her journals are painful and critical, providing an alternative portrait of the author as she coped with her daily issues.[4]

Montgomery's fame among her contemporaries (not only her books sold really well but they were also propelled by generally favourable reviews all over the English-speaking world) has long been ignored by the critics. Differently from other canonized texts of the period, the survival of her works depended almost entirely on a loyal readership, including librarians and school teachers.[5] Nevertheless, since the 1980s, a new generation of scholars has tried to assess the influence of her literary output, recognizing her as one of the first authors to create a more realistic, child-oriented fiction for

---

[3] John Ferns, 'Rainbow Dreams: The Poetry of Lucy Maud Montgomery', *Canadian Children's Literature/Littérature Canadienne pour la jeunesse* 42 (1986): 28–9.
[4] Susan Drain, 'Montgomery [married name Macdonald] Lucy Maud', *Oxford Dictionary of National Biography*, 23 September 2004. Available Online: https://www.oxforddnb.com/display/10.1093/ref:odnb/9780198614128.001.0001/odnb-9780198614128-e-58988?rskey=DWttNS&result=1.
[5] Mary Rubio, 'Subverting the Trite: L.M. Montgomery's Room of Her Own', Canadian Children's Literature/Littérature canadienne pour la jeunesse, No. 65, 1992, 10–13.

young girls.⁶ In particular, Montgomery's past label as a sentimental writer has been contested by feminist researchers such as Mary Rubio, Gabriella Åhmansson or Elizabeth Epperly, who describe her works as embedded with subliminal instances of rebellion, especially after the publication of her selected journals. Her novels can also be related to the reformist novel tradition of her time and to the educational changes taking place in Canada towards the turn of the century. The following paragraphs are devoted to *Anne of Green Gables*, Montgomery's first novel and one of the most read Canadian book of all times.⁷

The novel

Even though Montgomery left several accounts of her writing of *Anne of Green Gables*, the genesis of the book seems to be dated in the spring of 1905.⁸ While looking through a notebook collecting her 'ideas for plots, incidents, characters and descriptions', she found a 'faded entry' jotted down a decade before: 'Elderly couple apply to orphan asylum for a boy. By mistake, a girl is sent to them.' She started drafting her story to make a serial for a Sunday School paper, but Anne felt so 'real' that she decided to write a book about her. After being rejected by four publishers, the typescript of *Anne of Green Gables* was finally accepted by L.C. Page & Co. and put into print in 1908. It was an instant best-seller, skyrocketing its author and setting, Prince Edward Island, to international fame. To imagine the great success of the novel, suffice to say that, in five years, it would go into thirty-two printings, and has never gone out of print.⁹ Up until today, it sold more than 50 million copies and has been translated into thirty-six languages.

Such a favourable outcome was also the basis for an eight-volume saga on the same characters, which Montgomery, as a freelance author living by her pen, wrote for over thirty years.¹⁰ The original novel has also been adapted multiple times in different media, including two theatricals in Montgomery's lifetime – a silent film believed to be lost and a 1934 RKO talkie – and the longest-running musical in Canadian history. The theatre

---

⁶Clarence Karr, *Authors and Audiences: Popular Canadian Fiction in the Early Twentieth Century* (Montreal and Kingston: McGill-Queen's University Press, 2000), 130.
⁷Douglas Baldwin, 'L.M. Montgomery's Anne of Green Gables: The Japanese connection', *Journal of Canadian Studies/Revue d'études canadiennes* 28, no. 3 (1993): 124.
⁸L. M. Montgomery et al., *The Annotated Anne of Green Gables* (New York: Oxford University Press, 1997), 9.
⁹Ibid., 10.
¹⁰In addition to *Anne of Green Gables*, the series is composed by the following titles: *Anne of Avonlea* (1909), *Anne of the Island* (1915), *Anne of Windy Poplars* (known as *Anne of Windy Willows* in the British and Australian markets, 1936), *Anne's House of Dreams* (1917), *Anne of Ingleside* (1939), *Rainbow Valley* (1919) and *Rilla of Ingleside* (1921).

play, commissioned by the Charlottetown Festival in 1965, is performed every year during summer, and was a reference material for the Japanese series. Then, in the 1980s, the novel inspired various TV adaptations directed by Kevin Sullivan and produced by CBC (Canadian Broadcasting Corporation), Canada's public channel, including an animated series in 2000–2021. More recently, the same broadcaster co-produced with Netflix three seasons of *Anne with an E* (2017–19), a loose adaptation created by Canadian Moira Walley-Beckett, who incorporated darker aspects of Montgomery's life into the series.

Set in the late nineteenth century, the plot follows the archetypal story, much common in Western children's fiction, of an orphan girl with a charming personality who brings happiness and love in the world she lives in, incorporating fortunate tropes such as the fish out of the water and the rag-to-riches narratives. In fact, eleven-year-old Anne Shirley's life changes when she is adopted by the elderly brother and sister Matthew and Marilla of Avonlea. They sent for a boy to help them run their farm, Green Gables, and are astonished when a girl turns up in his place. Kind-hearted Matthew adores Anne from the start, but her temperament and talkativeness perplex Marilla, who nevertheless grows on her over time. At the end of the story, Anne gives up her college scholarship at Queen's Academy to stay with Marilla, who is becoming blind and has recently lost her brother.

The novel is written in third-person omniscient and mainly from the perspective of her protagonist, with almost three-quarters of the book devoted to her childhood, while only a quarter examines her teenage phase and maturation into a young woman, from fourteen to sixteen years old. The diegetic rhythm starts as slow-paced (Chapters I–XV), becomes increasingly episodic (XVI–XXIX) and finally speeds up, covering more than three years in less than seven chapters (XXX–XXXVII). Instead of being shown in medias res, the events are usually described as expected (before) or reported (afterwards) by the characters, the filter of Anne's voice adding a tone of intimacy to her recalled adventures.

Another frequent device is humour. Beyond the comedic value of the story, the narrator's verbal wit watermarks the whole novel, counterbalancing Anne's hyper-sensibility and the strict moral code of Avonlea. Both the non-linear plot progression and often intrusive narrator have been regarded as proofs of the 'oral quality' of Montgomery's storytelling.[11] Moreover, unlike other Sunday School-paper stories of the same period, the novel is not 'written down' to a child reader. On the contrary, the style is rich and flowery, with long naturalistic descriptions and a wide range of literary allusions.

---

[11]Rubio, 'Subverting the Trite', 20–2.

The characters

A character-driven story, characterization plays a pivotal role in the novel. Anne is an all-round, fascinating heroine, combining typically girlish traits with a strong, charismatic personality, a feature that much fiction contemporary to Montgomery tends to relegate to male leads. On the one hand, she is 'feminine to the core' (Chapter XV). She loves pretty things (be they poetry or puffed sleeves) and values beauty the most. On the other hand, as her red hair suggests, she is a hothead who speaks her mind without being concerned about the consequences, and can smash a slate on handsome Gilbert Blythe, the most popular boy of her grade, only because he dared to call her 'carrots' (Chapter XV). An optimist by nature, she does not brood over misfortunes but seeks to improve her conditions using her vivid imagination. She is also a great storyteller, with a passion for theatre (hence her overly dramatic way of talking) and a long list of quirks, like naming flowers and pretending they are alive.

What makes Anne a thoroughly empathetic protagonist is a mixture of flaws and virtues. Anne shows a remarkable presence of mind when she saves a child's life from croup (Chapter XVIII), but proves to be extremely gullible when she buys hair dye from a travelling peddler, turning her hair green and not black as claimed (Chapter XXVII). These contradictions add depth and humanity to the character, drawing sympathy from the reader. In narrative terms, Anne's imperfections give her somewhere to go, helping to outline her transformation arc throughout the novel. In fact, she perfects herself by learning from her mistakes. For instance, the hair dye incident teaches her to curb her vanity.

Anne's growth also depends on the life lessons she receives from the adults around her. In particular, a number of female figures have a great influence on her education. The main focus is on her elderly guardians, the Cuthberts, who look like the most improbable couple to bring up a child. They are brother and sister, both unmarried, already advanced in years, and have little experience with kids, not to mention their original plan was to co-opt an orphan boy as a farmhand, for utilitarian purposes only. The two characters change consistently throughout the story, embracing Anne's love and learning to love her back as if they were her real parents. In this respect, they come to constitute a nuclear family.

Like Heidi's grandfather, old Matthew has a reputation of being a hermit and spends most of the time working the land at Green Gables, although he is just painfully shy and has a terror for 'all women except Marilla and Mrs. Rachel' (Chapter II). These qualities have a comical connotation that elicits the sympathy of the reader, and will not prevent the bubbly protagonist to grow on him, creating a heartwarming paternal relationship. Whereas her brother is kind and caring, Marilla has become stern and resolute with age: she knows that duty comes first, whatever the circumstances, and is a severe ruler of her thoughts and behaviour, always managing to keep her emotions in check. However, with her sarcasm and witty remarks, Marilla is the perfect counterpart to Anne's flowery speech, creating a hilarious back-and-forth, which alone provides much of the comic relief of the story. Also, the narrator does not fail to note that there is a heart of gold underneath this cold exterior, and a great capacity to love: humanity is what makes her pass beyond stiff Calvinist doctrine and utilitarianism, forging the character-reader connection.

Marilla's common sense and good manners collide with Anne's inventiveness and free spirit. Little by little, the woman mellows and learns to live more lightly, getting accustomed to the role of mother. In some ways, it is the real love story of the book: not Anne's slowly falling for her ex-rival Gilbert, who is rather a friend than a romantic partner, but Marilla's growing fondness for the adopted girl. In this sense, Marilla Cuthbert can be regarded both as Anne's nemesis and as the hidden protagonist of the novel. She is the first important character introduced to the reader (Chapter I), and changes as much as Anne, if not more, as she gradually becomes a caring parent and an emotionally open person. Marilla's inner journey is punctuated by her increasingly frequent laughing and reaches its climax after Matthew's death (Chapter XXXVII), when she finally manages to voice her feelings for whom she sees as a daughter ('I love you as dear as my own flesh and blood and you've been my joy and comfort ever since you came to Green Gables').

Other important figures for Anne are sweet Mrs Allan, the reverend's companion; Miss Stacy, a volitive new teacher in the village school; and, to some extent, the notorious busybody Rachel Lynde, an industrious woman and a skilled dressmaker. All these women are well integrated in the Avonlea community, thus providing different models and advice for her upbringing. In particular, Miss Stacy embodies an idealistic, progressive kind of teacher, who encourages sport activities, recitations and 'field days' to study nature in the open air. Miss Stacy also acts as a mentor and is an aspirational figure for Anne, who will decide to pursue the teaching career to follow her footsteps.

Themes

From a cinematographic perspective, Anne could be defined as a travelling angel (see Chapter 4). As noted, Anne is a rescuer and an agent of change. It is true that she is not, to quote the Disney's version of Mary Poppins (one the most famous incarnations of this trope), 'practically perfect in every way', and instead of leaving Avonlea at the end of the novel, she will be integrated within its social fabric. But neither the 'tall, serious-eyed girl' of the last chapters nor Anne the teacher, wife and mother of the sequels is half as intriguing as the starry-eyed, eleven-year-old orphan who arrives at Green Gables. The bulk of the novel is devoted to Anne as a child, and can be viewed as an ode to girlishness, thematizing the shift from puberty to adolescence, in relation to the dualism between one's individuality and society's call to conformity.

Other themes addressed in the book include nature (lovingly described as a friendly cosmos, endowed with spirituality), home and family (given orphaned Anne's need to belong to someone who loves her), imagination as a positive value to foster through adulthood (because of its power to shape one's life), authentic religiousness as sincere ethics (against false moralism and bigotry), the importance of higher female schooling (in order for women to determine their own path) and the age-old conflict between a romantic outlook and the real world, with comedic effects. It is also worth remembering that, while early juvenile fiction is usually moralistic and written from an adult perspective, at the dawn of the twentieth century Montgomery is part of the first generation of writers that openly rejects didacticism, trying to approach her subject from a child's viewpoint.[12] In line with the modern recognition of children's mischief as normal and healthy, she sets her goals to pure entertainment, which comes closer to her personal sense of humour.[13]

Anne in Japan

Anne of Green Gables has been hugely successful in Japan – on the order of Harry Potter huge – soon becoming a safe bet for publishers. About seventy versions of the novel, issued by sixteen different publishers, have been released over the years: only Shinchōsha sold more than 2.5 million copies, and it is estimated that the book has been read by more than 13 million people in the country.[14] The integration into Japanese pop culture of the novel resulted in a myriad of by-products, including books about pot-pourri, herbs, quilting, sewing, Western cuisine, gardening and photographs of Prince Edward Island.[15] While many Japanese had the chance to travel to Prince Edward Island, forms of touristic fandom could be experienced in Japan as well. In fact, pretty much like famous anime characters and other stars of Japanese pop culture, Montgomery's heroine inspired fashion, cafes, restaurants and a theme park in Hokkaido.

Anne's status as a pop cultural icon was also made possible by the endorsement of the novel by children's critics and educators. The novel

---

[12] Baldwin, 'L.M. Montgomery's Anne of Green Gables', 125.
[13] Karr, *Authors and Audiences*, 130.
[14] Katsura, 'Red-Haired Anne in Japan', 57; Baldwin, 'L.M. Montgomery's Anne of Green Gables', 124; Akiko Uchiyama, 'Akage no An in Japanese Girl Culture: Muraoka Hanako's Translation of Anne of Green Gables', *Japan Forum* 26, no. 2 (2014): 210.
[15] Akamatsu, 'Japanese Readings of Anne of Green Gables', 206.

appears on the annual list of books recommended by the Ministry of Health and Welfare, while almost all libraries have copies of the novel, which is considered as a classic reading for young girls, together with *Little Women*.[16] An analysis of Japanese children's reading tendencies from 1955 to 1980 – so compatible with the reading habits in the country at the time of broadcasting – indicates it as one of the most popular titles among high junior school girls.[17] In fact, the novel was entrenched in local girls' fiction or shōjo shōsetsu. As seen, Western stories played a pivotal role in shaping Japanese girls' culture. According to Uchiyama, Anne makes for the perfect shōjo heroine, with her refined language and close friendship with her neighbour Diana.[18] The red-haired girl is also well-known for her emotional outbursts, romantic spirit and often melodramatic reactions, all common ingredients in shōjo narratives.

Note that *Anne* arrived in Japan relatively late, ten years after Montgomery's death. It was translated during the war by 村岡 花子 (Muraoka Hanako) (1893–1968), a female writer, the novel being a parting gift of a Canadian friend of her, Miss Loretta Shaw (1872–1940), forced to leave Japan during the years of ultranationalism. Muraoka's translation was then published in 1952, the last year of the Occupation, with the title *Akage no An* [*Red-haired Anne*], a suggestion of the publisher Mikaba Shōbō, the concept of 'gables' being too unfamiliar for Japan.[19] Black hair were still ranked as a criterion of beauty, so Japanese girls could relate to Anne's wish for her hair to be 'black as the raven's wing' (Chapter II). According to translator Taniguhi Yumiko, 'what made Hanako Muraoka most famous was [the translation of] *Anne of Green Gables*, and at the same time, what made this book most famous was the name of Muraoka'.[20] Muraoka was the eldest daughter of a couple of Methodists Christians and studied at a private girls' school established by the Woman's Missionary Society of the Methodist Church of Canada in 1884.[21] Exposed

---

[16] Judy Stoffman, 'Anne in Japanese Popular Culture', *Canadian Children's Literature (Littérature canadienne pour la jeunesse)* 91–92 (1998): 60; Yoshiko Akamatsu, 'The Continuous Popularity of Red-Haired Anne in Japan: An Interview with Yoshiko Akamatsu', in *Anne Around the World: L.M. Montgomery and Her Classic*, ed. Jane Ledwell and Jean Mitchell (Montreal and Kingston: McGill-Queen's University Press, 2013), 37.
[17] Katsura, 'Red-Haired Anne in Japan', 58.
[18] Uchiyama, 'Akage no An in Japanese Girl Culture', 213.
[19] Ibid., 210; Allard, 'The Popularity of Anne of Green Gables in Japan', 41.
[20] Quoted in Yoshiko Akamatsu, 'The Japanese Translation of The Blythes Are Quoted, Anne's Days of Remembrance: An Analysis of Its Characteristics, Style and Publication', *Nōtteorudamu Seishin joshi daigaku kiyō gaikoku-go gaikoku bungaku-hen* [Notre Dame Seishin University's Bulletin of foreign languages and literature] 38, no. 1 (2014): 5.
[21] Yoshiko Akamatsu, 'During and After the World Wars: L.M. Montgomery and the Canadian Missionary Connection in Japan', *The Looking Glass: New Perspectives on Children's Literature* 18, no. 2 (2015). Available online: https://ojs.latrobe.edu.au/ojs/index.php/tlg/article/view/647 (accessed 18 April 2023).

to a culture not far from Montgomery's, Muraoka discovered her love for English literature and became a teacher. She got married to a member of the Presbyterian Church, and began translating many classics of juvenile Western literature, such as パレアナの青春 (*Pareana no seishun* [*The youth of Pollyanna*]) in 1930.

Anne of Green Gables was Muraoka's most fortunate translation and a booster for her career. As Allard notes, it is a fluid translation, in which the work of the translator becomes invisible, a strategy that she adopts for two reasons: her desire to introduce Canadian customs to Japan, and make the book easily accessible to her young readers. This leads to a series of changes, which range from cultural adaptations and transformations, but also drastic reductions and omissions, turning Montgomery's book into 'somewhat of a 'Japanese novel' [. . .] about a Canadian story'.[22] The most significant change was in the pace of the last eight chapters. Here, Anne's growth into a young woman, her life at Queen's Academy, the references to Matthew's financial problems and his subsequent death are massively reduced. The narrative rhythm, which was already fast in the original novel, speeds up, and even if the major plot points are kept, crucial steps such as Anne's grieving for Matthew and Marilla's self-discovery as a maternal figure, are completely lost.

Aside from Muraoka's fame and the already recalled role of international collaborations with the Allies, which injected a high number of American books on the market, other contact points between Montgomery's novel and Japanese culture have been highlighted by scholars, including the importance of naturalistic descriptions, or the group spirit of a close-knit community such as Avonlea. Moreover, myths about young and talented orphans are common in Japan – think of 'Peach Boy' Momotarō. Anne is also a positive girl who finds her place in the world levelling the problematic facets of her personality: a case of moral progress that could fit well within the Confucian ethics, while her vitalism and mystical embrace of life shared some similarities with zen culture.

The issue of faithfulness

The adaptation of *Anne of Green Gables* into an animated series was a layered and complicated process. As was the case for many adaptations of the *WMT*, which reflected well-entrenched opinions of children's critics of the post-war period, the approach adopted by Takahata was admittedly faithful to the 原作 (*gensaku* [original work]). This is confirmed by his choice to use

---

[22] Allard, 'The Popularity of Anne of Green Gables in Japan', 67.

as a reference 神山妙子 Kamiyama Taeko's translation of the novel, which was published by Shingakusha in 1974.[23] Significantly, this was a school text and a less popular edition than Muraoka's, but it was regarded as the most faithful version of Montgomery's classic. According to Somers, Takahata's attitude was dictated by his need to interpret Anne's story correctly. In fact, as stated in one of his memoirs, the director seemed not to be able to understand Anne's behaviour and feelings, thus facing the job with a certain concern.[24] For the same reason, Miyazaki would have said アンは嫌いだ (*An wa kirai da* [I don't like Anne]), dropping the series after fifteen episodes. Yet, it is important to remember that Takahata held different views on the novel. In fact, he pointed out the differences between Montgomery's work and other adaptations he directed for the *WMT*, recognizing Anne as an adolescent girl, not an 大人から見た理想像じゃない (*otona kara mita risōzō janai* [idealized figure from an adult's point of view]). As such, some features of her personalities, namely her feisty temper and tartness, may appear as if 可愛げがない (*kawaige ga nai* [lacking charm]) if compared to the kind-hearted children inhabiting other famous shows, but Takahata viewed them as typical of a puberal child growing up.[25]

Note that Takahata juxtaposed his vision of childishness to Anne viewed as a shōjo, which was, in turn, another conceptualization of girlhood. However, as done in previous meisaku series, Takahata aimed at portraying Anne as a real human being, offering his personal take on the shōjo narrative. In particular, Takahata repeatedly advocated for the comedic value of Montgomery's work, which he defined as a ユーモア小説 (*yūmoa shōsetsu* [humour novel]) and, in another interview, a 傑作 (*kessaku* [masterpiece]) of girls' fiction precisely for its ability to connect to a wide, multigenerational audience.[26] According to the director, the funny interactions between Anne's romanticism and Marilla's down-to-earth attitude should be read in this light, creating an amusing effect by representing them both 客観的 (*kyakkanteki* [objectively]) in the animation.[27] That Takahata intended to transmit a feel of authenticity seems to be confirmed by his reading *The Scotch*, a memoir by John Kenneth Galbraith (1908–2006), in which the Canadian-American economist describes the temperament of the Scottish community where he

---

[23]Matsumoto, *20 Seiki terebi dokuhon sekai meisaku gekijō taizen*, 49.
[24]Emily Somers, 'An no shinjō [Anne's Feelings]. Politeness and Passion as Anime. Paradox in Takahata's Akage no an', in *Textual Transformations in Children's Literature. Adaptations, Translations, Reconsiderations*, ed. Benjamin Lefebvre (New York and Abingdon: Routledge, 2013), 155.
[25]Isao Takahata, 'Akage no an o kataru Takahata Isao kantoku' [Director Takahata Isao talks about Red-haired Anne], *Ghibli Museum*, 2010. Available online: https://www.ghibli-museum.jp/anne/kataru/takahata/006227.html (accessed 18 April 2023).
[26]Takahata, *Eiga o tsukurinagara kangaeta koto*, 97.
[27]Quoted in Chiba, *Sekai meisaku gekijō shirizu memoriaru bukku. Amerika & warudō-hen*, 125.

grew up in Ontario. The book portrayed the people of Avonlea from an anthropologically consistent perspective.[28]

In other words, Takahata grasped the 'shōjoness' of the protagonist, embracing at the same time the sense of realism which Montgomery infused in her narrative. On the one hand, this was in line with the trademark double audience of *WMT*, or the mother and child advertising/TV which had started with Calpis a decade before. On the other hand, Takahata did not reject Anne's emotions, and was more concerned with other practical aspects of the adaptations, such as the fact that the novel was dialogue-heavy. For example, he was aware that creating humour なかなか言葉の内容だけで伝えるのは無理なんです (*nakanaka kotoba no naiyō dake de tsutaeru no wa murina ndesu* [is quite difficult to convey only through words]). This is the reason why he was eager to exploit every humorous beat present in the original story, whose initial episodic progression fitted well in the structure of a series. He also went as far as to say that the animation was 僕の一番の功績 (*boku no ichiban no kōseki* [perhaps (his) best achievement]).[29]

While faithfulness was a paramount feature, it allowed some room for variations, when this served a narrative purpose. We will develop this observation in the rest of the chapter.

The style

For Takahata, viewing Anne as a shōjo character did not equate with the iconography of contemporary girls' fiction. It is worth remembering that, in spite of the rise of the Forty-Niners, a group of female mangaka who tackled bold themes and complex narratives, and the subsequent critical acclaim gained by shōjo manga, in the late 1970s and early 1980s girls' comics returned to light-hearted school comedies focusing on emotions and romance. This style, known as 乙女ちっく (*otomechikku* [maidenesque]), was characterized by frilly girls with unrealistic body proportions and items bespeaking a refined model of Westernization, such as cotton dresses, straw sun bonnets, herbal tea and Victorian houses.[30] Due to his realistic position, Takahata strongly detached from this shōjo style, in his attempt to create a more mainstream bildungsroman about an impish girl growing up into a fine young lady. The director was very exigent with Kōndo for Anne's character design. His sketches are emblematic of Takahata's desire to make the character increasingly less cute, and more realistic. In fact, Kōndo's early

---

[28]Ibid., 203.
[29]Takahata, 'Akage no an o kataru Takahata Isao kantoku'.
[30]Thorn, 'Shōjo Manga', 6.

drawings are consistent with the shōjo connotation of Anne in Japan, with starry eyes and a coy look.[31]

The same struggle to create a realistic shōjo aesthetics can be observed in the fluctuations of the character design throughout the series, with Anne changing from a skinny girl with a big head and a wide forehead (as she is described in the book) to a more proportioned and softer look when she gets fifteen, and a junoesque figure towards the end of the series. This also implies an attention to changes in the colour palette, work of colour designer Yasuda, who collaborated with Takahata since the times of *Hols*. According to Takahata, she also struggled to represent Anne realistically, checking the shade of her dress so as to reproduce the impression of the washed-out clothes an orphan would use.[32]

The adaptation strategies

On a narrative level, the animation had to transform thirty-eight chapters into fifty episodes of around twenty-five minutes each. This obviously implied a number of changes. The strategies adopted for the adaptation were the following. First, as trivial as it might sound, most of the work concerned visualizing what in the book is only evoked through dialogue or description. In other words, the events had to be shown, not just told. Anne's excited monologues were transformed into full-length episodes, exploiting every image in the original book to illustrate the protagonist's fantasies or reveal her and other characters' feelings. Camera angles and shots help to convey emotions, while an authoritative male voice-over replaces the third-person omniscient, providing access to a character's mind, but also objective distance, in line with Takahata's realistic approach and his departure from shōjo culture. In this respect, visualization of PEI's sceneries was obviously made easier by a scouting trip in the summer of 1978, involving Takahata, Kōndo and producer Nakajima, stopping in Ontario and then visiting PEI by car. This was a chance to collect important references for the animation, such as the typically red roads of the island, or traditional apple juice pressing in a museum of local history in Toronto.[33]

Other devices which can be traced in the conversion from novel to series are editing, expansion and addition of story beats, while omissions are very rare. Editing allows to shift, merge or summarize events which are already present in the original book, but are linearized chronologically in the animation. These changes often bring new meaning to the story, which at times hint at cultural differences or at the underlying educational policy.

---

[31]Takahata, 'Akage no an o kataru Takahata Isao kantoku'.
[32]Ibid.
[33]Chiba, *Sekai meisaku gekijō e no tabi*, 36–7.

Expansions and additions, too, can be indicators of the Japanese context, stressing themes and behaviours that are perceived as particularly relevant for the audience, such as the apology culture or the notion of thoughtfulness. In addition, given the long-running format of the series, these strategies allow to stretch the original fiction to cover a longer period of time. The following paragraphs will try to break down the process of adaptation into its constitutional phases, analysing the strategies used in several parts of the narrative, and their effects on the series, starting from the pilot.

The pilot

Both in literature and visual media, the beginning of a story is essential to capture the attention of the public, setting the expectations for the upcoming plot, therefore enclosing information on the genre to which a text belongs. Let's consider the first two chapters of the novel and the pilot of the series in comparison. Montgomery's book opens in medias res, with the introduction of Mrs Lynde, the local gossip and a secondary character, as she notices Matthew Cuthbert, who is known as 'the shyest man alive' and a bit of a recluse, driving in a buggy out of town. Then Mrs Lynde goes to Green Gables to seek an explanation, and Marilla gives her the shocking news that they adopted a boy and her brother has gone to fetch him. Note that Mrs Lynde's traditionalist nature is evoked by contrast through the image of an intricate brook which flows of the woods of Green Gables, foreshadowing Anne's future arrival and bubbling creativity.[34] From a diegetic perspective, this incipit provides readers with a clear set-up of what is about to happen (Avonlea's peaceful community is going to clash with an exceptional outsider), in the form of a turn of events (Matthew's surprising conduct, which disrupts Mrs Lynde's routine), hooking readers with a question (who will the adopted orphan be?), which are answered in the following chapter. Here, a new turn of event happens (Matthew finds Anne, a little talkative girl, and brings her home), which stimulates further curiosity (will the Cuthberts accept a girl instead?), while no information is given on the socio-historical framework.

The construction of the pilot is emblematic of the narrative strategies employed in the series. In line with the exotic taste of *WMT* series, a geographical contextualization is added to the story, with the camera panning on PEI's coastlines, gulfs and rural landscapes, which serves as a backdrop for Anne's arrival on a boat from Canada. Note that, whereas in the book the protagonist appears in Chapter II, her trip being only briefly described in

---

[34]'. . . Not even a brook could run past Mrs. Rachel Lynde's door without due regard for decency and decorum' (Chapter I).

Anne's direct speech to Matthew, the series shows the main character from the very beginning, as she travels towards a new home, leaning against the deck of the ship, and then looking around in the port. The visual introduction of Anne allows to forge an earlier connection with the protagonist, emphasizing her curiosity and imaginative nature through silent close-ups, interspersed with long and extreme long shots on the world she is about to enter. The audience is guided by the voice-over male narrator. Verbal indications on place and time, as well as touches of characterization, are conveyed in a very stylized tone, creating a sort of dramaturgic distance – a device that seems rooted in the storytelling tradition of Japanese popular culture, such as kamishibai.

The following sequence, featuring Matthew in his best suit while driving a buggy, paraphrases the initial paragraphs of Chapter II, just before Anne's introduction. Plot stages are thus edited so that Chapters I and II become one narrative, using cross-cutting to juxtapose three scenes with different settings: Matthew driving to meet Anne, Anne traveling to Avonlea, and Mrs Lynde going to Marilla. Again, the narrator provides some hints of characterization, but Matthew's timid nature also emerges from his embarrassed reaction as two women salute him by the roadside, and he has to nod at them, according to the etiquette. This way, the rearranged story beats follow a chronological logic, infusing visual dynamism into the story. In particular, Mrs Lynde's discussion with Marilla has a greater impact on viewers, because the beat is merged with Matthew's first encounter with Anne, which originally takes place in Chapter II. By bringing forward what constitutes the story's inciting event, thus revealing that the orphanage sent an eleven-year-old girl by mistake before the Cuthberts find out about it, the pilot increases the fun of two worlds colliding (Matthew's paralysing shyness versus Anne's exuberant temper) and reinforces the hook: Will Matthew and Marilla accept Anne, even if she is not a boy?

To a certain extent, a negative answer is expected here – a sort of Refusal of the Call – given the polar dichotomy between Anne's explosive personality and the Cuthberts' old-fashioned attitude. Yet, the viewer is gradually driven closer to Anne as they look at her waiting for Matthew, playing near the railway or simply looking around curiously. Although these beats do not contribute to story progression (and would probably be cut in a modern-day adaptation), they characterize Anne as an inquisitive little girl – one that can never get bored – creating a slow tempo and adding realism to the scene. Moreover, Anne's creative flair and sense of wonder do not only transpire from her dialogue lines but are powerfully visualized in a dream sequence. So, as Anne describes the cherry tree where she would have slept, had Matthew not come for her, cherry blossoms turn into a shower of petals surrounding the two characters. This offers an insight into the inner world of the character, revealing her unique mindset and the influence she has over anyone who meets her. Everything contributes to create an empathetic connection with Anne.

FIGURE 5.1A *Anne's arrival in Prince Edward Island (Episode 1). A flowery outline, redolent of decorative ornaments of book covers, introduces the main characters. Similar extra-diegetic devices are used to frame the title of the programme.*

FIGURE 5.1B *Anne's imagination overflows in real life, baffling Matthew (Episode 1).*

Shiftings

The position of a passage in the original book can be shifted alongside the story for reasons of clarity, characterization or narrative consistency. An interesting example is in Chapter VIII, when Anne sees a chromolithograph entitled 'Christ Blessing Little Children'. Anne stares at the picture and strongly empathizes with a little girl in the background, who looks sad and lonely compared to the other children, but still hoping for Christ's blessing. When Anne starts making comments on Jesus, Marilla quickly chides her for being irreverent. The dialogue is located at Green Gables, just after Marilla's horrified realization that Anne is unable to pray (Chapter VII). Even so, the girl repeatedly demonstrates a genuine, albeit naive, spirituality, the aforementioned scene thus representing one way to underline the gap between Anne's unorthodox sensitivity and Marilla's stern morality.

This beat is shown later on in the animation, for it is merged with the contents of Chapter XXII, when Mrs Allan, the new minister's wife, invites Anne for tea (Episode 23). Not only the action unfolds in a different place but also in a different time (fourteen chapters later, that is, towards the middle of the series), when Anne has already settled in her new home. Moreover, she has just got acquainted with Mrs Allan, who becomes for her a life model and a spiritual guide.[35] Both in Chapter XXII and in Episode 23, the theme is the importance of finding a balance between spontaneity and etiquette. Anne is nervous that she will forget her manners, but Marilla encourages her not to worry about it, trying to imagine how she could please Mrs Allan instead.

The struggle between acceptable behaviour and impulsive abandonment, or the need for social acceptance, is a relatable issue in Japan, while the image of 'Christ Blessing Little Children' can be perceived as more suitable for a minister's manse than a private house. Being Christianity a minority in the country, the target viewers would probably take sides with Anne's pantheistic faith, without grasping the reasons for Marilla's reproaches. So it is reasonable to assume that the scene is relocated in Episode 23 for reasons of consistency. Here, religion stands for the framework in which the story takes place (the minister's manse), the focus shifting to protocol-related discourses, whereas the presence of a Christian icon helps to explore Anne's relationship with Mrs Allan. Unlike Marilla, the young woman listens carefully to what the girl has to say, proving herself to have great empathetical skills, and consequently a high level of aspiration for the main character. This way, the series remains philologically faithful to the book, showing how, under Mrs Allan's guidance, religion can be a joyful experience. At the same time, Mrs Allan's understanding attitude provides a positive reading of Anne's spontaneous behaviour.[36]

---

[35] Anne meets Mrs Allan in Chapter XXII, which in the adaptation is turned into a couple of episodes (23–24).
[36] It is interesting to note that something similar happens in Takahata's adaptation of *Heidi*, when the protagonist visits the Sesemanns' Cabinets of curiosities in Frankfurt (Episode 28). Here Heidi sees a painting representing an elderly man holding a little lamb, and a youth on his knees, on a mountain background. The subject of the picture (graphically modelled on Giovanni

Imagery

Another effective strategy for visualization is the use of what story consultant Bobette Buster would call gleaming details, singular images which are able to capture 'both the emotion and the idea of the story at once', thus connecting with the audience.[37] An example is the representation of アイドルワイルド (Aidoruwairudo [Idlewild]), a beautiful meadow in the wood where Anne and Diana play together. In the novel, the place is introduced via direct speech in Chapter XIII, when Anne tells Marilla about it, and is adapted for television in Episode 10. Montgomery's description lingers on the suggestive natural background, which is maintained in the layout of the series. Anne's creativity is also explored, for the place is transfigured by her sense of wonder: this way, a wood of birches can become a house, 'big stones, all covered with moss', are turned into seats, and wooden boards are used as shelves. A reference to a shard of Mrs Barry's broken lamp, which becomes part of Idlewild's 'parlour' and is promptly renamed by Anne as 'fairy glass ... full of rainbows – just little young rainbows that haven't grown big yet'.

In the animated series, the fairy glass is introduced straightaway, as a trigger for Anne's imagination. The episode starts with Anne and Diana looking for some bric-à-brac to build a playhouse in the wood, foreshadowing the notion of Idlewild as a secret place just for the two of them. The girls are walking in the fields, when they notice something sparkling in the grass – a gleaming detail indeed. Anne's speculations about it being a ダイヤモンド (daiyamondo [diamond]) belonging to the 小人たち (kobitotachi [dwarves]) transport the viewers into a fantasy world, outlining their expectations for the story to come. Whereas any realistic information on the object is entrusted to practical Diana, who reveals it is a fragment of a lamp, Anne calls it a 妖精の鏡 (yōsei no kagami [mirror of sprites]), making up a fairy tale which appears on the opalescent surface of the shard for Diana to watch. This story is already present in the book, providing a fantastic, Anne-like explanation of the origin of the mirror.[38]

Segantini's work) is not verbalized in the series, but it is clearly based on a passage of the novel in which the evangelical parable of the Prodigal Son is mentioned, namely an illustrated book that Clara's grandmother gives Heidi in Chapter X. Even though other Christian contents are diluted in the animation, with a final secular conversion of Heidi's grandfather to community life and his consequent return to society, this biblical quotation is preserved by Takahata, albeit shifted alongside the story and turned into a mere painting, probably because of the visual power of the iconography, and the director's stated faithfulness to the source text. In particular, the image makes Heidi think about her grandfather, given the resemblance of him with the elderly figure in the painting (Father God), thus alimenting her wish to go back to the Alps.

[37] Bobette Buster, *Do Story: How to Tell Your Story so the World Listens* (San Francisco, CA: Chronicle Books, 2018), 33.

[38] In the novel, Anne says to Marilla: 'it's nice to imagine the fairies lost it one night when they had a ball, so we call it the fairy glass.' In the animation, Anne provides further details on

In the same episode, when Anne proposes to Diana that they keep the mirror, so every night the sprites will come to see it, a butterfly fluttering by turns into a fairy, peeping at the shard and then disappearing off screen, without the two friends noticing it. The beat only lasts a few seconds, and has no equivalent in the original novel, but it is enough to convey a feel of subtle magic, as is often the case with *WMT* dream sequences. Soon afterwards, when Anne and Diana move to Idlewild and start playing grownups, we see them having tea on a wooden board, laid with broken China dishes, and then watching the world through the coloured wrappers of their chocolate bonbons. The beauty of the scene lies in the lifelike representation of an ordinary experience, poetically transfigured by details.

Expansions

As a general rule, the scenes described in the book are usually expanded in the series, given the greater length of the episodes and the slow tempo of Takahata's directing. The expansions can be read as essential tools that have several effects on the audiovisual narrative. Whereas Montgomery's prose, especially in the first half of the novel, sparkles with fun and childlike adventures (only to slow down when it comes to naturalistic descriptions), the series has a quiet, meditative tone, and a considerable amount of time to dive in the plot, dilating those beats which are either perceived as more relevant to the story or considered as very close to the Japanese sphere of values.

These expansions may cover different areas, such as the pervading presence of nature, which, as Allard notes, seemingly hit a sensitive chord in Japanese readers – and their educators – since the times of Muraoka's translation.[39] In the animation, this is used as a means to emphasize Anne's sensitivity. An example is in Episode 6, when Anne is told that she will stay at Green Gables. In Chapter VIII, which is the basis for the episode, Montgomery simply describes Anne as crying because of her happiness. The rest of the chapter is devoted to Marilla trying to teach Anne how to pray, after her debacle in the previous chapter. The animation seems to isolate the beat in which Anne is sitting in front of a 'jugful of apple blossoms she had brought in to decorate the dinner-table' and build on it half of the episode, which is dedicated to tell how Anne comes to pick those flowers, and why.

A vivid naturalistic scenery is visualized behind her, expressing her excitement. Anne hears a voice calling for her: it comes from the plants of

---

the fairy ball, explaining for example how the sprites disappeared in a hurry when the cock crowed, while images of tiny, childlike sprites, hanging from a flower bud and softly glowing in the dark, appear on the shard.

[39] Allard, 'The Popularity of Anne of Green Gables in Japan', 81.

Green Gables, something the protagonist mentions in Chapter IV, when the girl notes, 'everything seems to be calling her: "Anne, Anne, come out to us. Anne, Anne, we want a playmate!"'. In the series a number of beats are interwoven, with Anne looking at the cherry trees, dancing barefoot in the garden, saluting the trees of the forest, lying on the flowery grass, hugging the trunk of a birch tree, smelling a bunch of lilacs, flying a fern in the sky, dipping her toes in a river, looking at the sun glimpsing through the foliage and blowing dandelion seeds in the air. Meanwhile, the music soars and a song starts, giving voice to the friendliness of the natural elements, in parallel with Anne's loneliness and wish to belong to someone.[40] Then Anne reaches Matthew in the fields, and after giving him the good news (and a big hug), she plucks a twig of apple blossom and returns home. Here, Marilla scolds her for her tardiness, but looks with interest at Anne's putting the flowers in a vase, not without forgetting to ask her if she cleaned her feet before coming in. Home decoration with wildflowers is attributable to the late nineteenth-century fashion for including flowers and plants in the domestic style, but is also redolent of the Japanese art of flower arrangement or 生花 (*ikebana* [living flowers]). It is interesting to note that, after putting the flowers in a vase, Anne and the Cuthberts have tea, another ritual moment, often linked to ikebana, which contributes to connote Anne's very first day at Green Gables as a special day.

Seasonal transitions

The passing of seasons, which finds ample space in the book, is also emphasized in the series, where this is suggestive of life as a cycle and the changes occurring to the characters. For instance, let's consider the beginning of Episode 20, which is significantly entitled 再び春が来て (Futatabi haru ga kite [Spring is coming again]), and translates into pictures the first half of Chapter XX. In the book, Montgomery's narration starts with a reference to the 'beautiful capricious, reluctant Canadian spring', mentioning several plants which are typical of PEI. The same blossoming flowers and trees are shown in the series, with Anne and Diana watching them in awe. However, the very beginning of the episode stages the seasonal transition from winter to spring, isolating a number of iconic details which are not included in the

---

[40]This is the first of three stanzas with the same pattern: 花と花とは目くばせしている / 蝶とつぼみはやくそくしている / わたしだけ / ひとりぼっちでみつめている / だれかとだれかと話したいのに (Hana to hana to wa mekubase shite iru / Chō to tsubomi wa yakusoku shite iru / Watashi dake / Hitoribocchi de mitsumete iru / Dare ka to dare ka to hanashi shitainoni' [Flowers and flowers are exchanging looks / Butterflies and buds are making a promise / Only I / I'm watching all alone / I want to talk with someone]).

FIGURE 5.2 *Anne's almost pantheistic embrace with nature (Episode 6).*

source text: the icy icicles hanging on the window at school, shining in the sun or the snow sliding off the roof of the school with a big thump.

The animation slightly deviates from the model, setting the scene during ある六月の朝のこと (*aru rokugatsu no asa no koto* [a certain morning of June]), as the narrator explains. Anne is still in bed, asleep under the covers. Filtering through the leaves, the sunlight creates elegant shadows on the ceiling. This is the first thing Anne notices when she wakes up. With a smile, Anne opens the window, gazing at the lovely view outside, which is filmed in subjective camera. What immediately leaps to the eye is a beautiful cherry tree, the Snow Queen, as Anne named it back in Episode 2. Shortly it will be revealed that Anne is so cheerful today because it is the anniversary of 'the turning point in [her] life': her arrival at Green Gables. In fact, as viewers may recall, the above-mentioned scene faithfully replicates, in tone, setting and stage directing, Anne's first morning with the Cuthberts.

Even though this is not the main point of Chapter XX, the event is given a greater importance in the adaptation, where it is placed as a conclusion of the first arc of the story, which focuses on Anne's childhood. The series consequently employs seasonal changes as a metaphor for the growth of the protagonist, with angles and stage directing which convey the idea that life comes in a circle: a year has passed, and everything is あの日と同じだは (*ano hito onajida wa* [the same as that day]), as Anne says while looking out of the window. And yet, as the story goes on, the cyclicality of nature contrasts with Anne's changes. In spite of her daily incidents, the protagonist has matured and so has Marilla, who thanks to Anne is beginning to learn how to love, and be loved.

Empathy

Expansions also concern cultural scripts that may be perceived as more relatable to Japan's behavioural patterns, starting from a diegetically relevant treatment of empathy. An example can be found in Episode 4, when Anne's sad backstory is revealed. As happens in the novel, where the action unfolds in Chapter V, Anne and Marilla are on their way to Mrs Spencer to understand why she brought home a female orphan instead of a male one. In an attempt to fill the awkward silence, Marilla asks Anne about her past. The girl is reluctant to talk, rather choosing fantasy over reality. But Marilla wants facts, so Anne briefly recounts her past misadventures, of how her parents died and she was placed in several foster families, until she was sent to the orphanage. Anne admits that she received little schooling, and read voraciously to satisfy her curiosity. However, what really draws the reader's attention here is that the protagonist is not putting into words: in all probability, a cycle of improper parenting and child abuse, as can be deduced by her agitated conduit.

In the series, this is dilated into a full scene, emphasizing Anne's distress in a dramatic way. First, Anne's refusal to talk is clearly shown, as can be seen from a comparison between her hesitation in the novel and curt rebuff in the episode. Then a beat is added where a woman approaches the buggy and wonders why Marilla has a girl with her, when Mrs Lynde is telling people she adopted a boy. Marilla explains there's been a mistake, to which the woman pitifully replies she is sorry for that. The conversation goes on for a short while, with the woman commenting again on Anne's sad fate as if the girl wasn't there. The camera zooms on Anne's tensed expression, to make the audience understand that these words are hurting her sensitivity, until she leaps out of the buggy, much to Marilla and the woman's astonishment. A considerably long beat follows, showing Anne sitting on a fence in silence and Marilla looking at her small figure from the buggy: the distance between the two characters, both physical and psychological, is underlined by the alternating point of view of the shots, while a quiet, melancholic soundtrack goes with the slow flow of the surrounding nature – the tall grass, waving in the breeze; the drifting of the clouds.

Finally, Anne looks up to the sky and reunites with Marilla, both of them apologizing to each other. Coming from a woman of few words, Marilla's apology sounds particularly impressive, with her acknowledgement of Anne's feelings. Only now Anne's tale actually begins, visualized through flash-backs and a montage of still frames. Various elements help to convey the sadness of the story, such as the chromatic palette (with the bright colours of the Shirleys' house turning to the sepia pictures about Anne's adoptive families), and the seasonal change (from the spring of Anne's birth to the winter of her arrival to the orphanage). Marilla saying 'sorry' to Anne can be framed into the Japanese notion of apology, which does not presuppose

FIGURE 5.3 *Takahata's directing conveys a sense of distance (Episode 4).*

the component 'I did something bad (to you)'.[41] What matters is the need to say publicly that someone feels bad for any kind of trouble caused to someone else, voluntarily or involuntarily. As other series of *WMT*, the underpinning educational agenda seems to lie in anticipating and preventing other people's bad feelings.

Additions

Another strategy to implement the original contents is represented by the use of additions – beats or scenes varying length, without correspondence in the novel, blended in with the main plot so that they are virtually undetectable for the audience. In terms of characterization, additions can introduce important characters that in the book appear in a less memorable way. For example, in Episode 24, when Anne meets Miss Stacey, who pays her a visit while she is recovering from a sprained ankle, at first, we see bed-forced Anne daydreaming about the new teacher, seeing the faces of the women of Avonlea before her. Then Diana presents Miss Stacy as a fine young lady with blue eyes, curly hair and the largest puff-sleeved clothes Avonlea has ever seen. She is also described as having a kind, yet firm, temper. A short comical digression is added, in which shy and elusive Matthew stumbles in Miss Stacy in town, being forced to interact with such a strong-willed lady. A final gag follows when Anne exchanges Miss Stacy for Marilla as she

---

[41]Anna Wierzbicka, *Semantics: Primes and Universals* (Oxford and New York: Oxford University Press, 1996), 530.

knocks the door. This builds up a sense of expectation and curiosity towards Anne's favourite teacher.

Consistently with the poetics of *WMT*, additions can provide information of Canadian history and geography, as seen in Episode 1. They also contribute to establish a sense of Canadianness in sequences involving food preparation and cookery. Original sequences are inserted concerning new recipes that Marilla imparts to Anne, as in Episode 15, when the girl bakes brownies. Additions may have no diegetic impact on the main story, but are useful to convey certain moods or feelings, representing an occasion to insert small details of everyday life. In this sense can be viewed the frequent domestic beats illustrating farming life, with Anne and Marilla getting the eggs out in the yard, Matthew harvesting or a mother cat and her kittens wandering around the garden of Green Gables, giving life to little visual gags. These insertions communicate a sense of somber life and rusticity.

Other times, additions are inserted to clarify concepts which are often self-explanatory in the book, but appear less familiar to the domestic audience, such as references to Greek-Roman mythology, Christian religion and Anglo-Saxon literature. This looks more significant if we consider the quotations in the novel from works of British authors such as Robert Burns, Walter Scott and others. This literary palimpsest, which was probably easy to decipher for contemporary adult readers of Montgomery, is difficult to uncover today. Most of the allusions hidden in the narrative do not survive in the animation, unless they play a relevant role for the plot. This is the case of 'An Unfortunate Lily Maid' (Chapter XXVIII/Episode 31), based on Arthur Tennyson's retelling of an Arthurian legend. In the series, the sequence begins with Anne's voice telling about the knights of Camelot. The viewers are transported in one of her dream sequences, displaying a different visual style closer to book illustration. Then, the real setting of the episode is shown (the river where Anne and her friends are fishing), in a humorous contrast between romantic fantasies and simple everyday life. Information on the Knights of the Round Table is provided by Anne's tale and dialogues with her friends, which are conducive to make the viewers understand the meaning of the game, foreshadowing the humorous aspect of Gilbert's rescuing her.

Other times the animation inserts allusions to Western literary works which are not mentioned in the book, but seem to play a narrative role in the series. For example, in Chapter XXXIII/Episode 40, Anne is invited to recite as a professional, together with a famous elocutionist, at White Sands hotel. The book focuses on Anne's inner world, describing her stage frights, and her recovery when she sees Gilbert in the crowd, being still firm in her the resolution not to act ridiculous in front of him. Nothing is said about the poem she is reciting, leading the Japanese staff to insert a poem at their discretion. The choice falls on a monologue rearrangement of Cordelia's lines in *King Lear* (IV, 4, 2516–38). Not only Shakespeare is a classic Western author, but in Montgomery's novel there are several quotations from his works. Moreover, Cordelia is a princess who dies a tragical death because of her father's madness. Honest and kind-hearted, she is the personification of virtue and filial love, which leads her to sacrifice herself for the sake of her family. Despite being a spurious addition, the association of Anne to the British princess creates a parallel between the two characters, underlining the protagonist's growth into a mature, sensible young woman. Cordelia has also something in common with girls' fiction, which is full of kind, strong-willed heroines of this kind, and with Anne's imagination, being the name of one of her alter egos since the beginning of the story.

Additions can be short and matched with other strategies, but no less powerful. An example concerns Anne's grieving for Matthew the night after his departure (Episode 47). As happens in the book (Chapter XXXVII), this beat is located in a point of no return for the narrative, made more intense by the previous climax (Anne has just been awarded a scholarship, much to the delight of the Cuthberts). The series expands on this contrast, adding an idyllic incipit on the daily life at the farm, which is juxtaposed with the dramatic plot twist (Matthew's sudden stroke). The realistic dilation of what follows – the wake arrangements, which also bespeak the religious framework of the series – occupies half of the episode, but it is the final sequence, an addition, that delivers the strongest emotions. To render Anne's shock, to the point that she is not able to cry until 'the recollection of the day came over her like a wave of sorrow', the animation visualizes her memories as she falls asleep by the windowsill. While the camera slowly zooms in on Anne's face, we cross-cut to different shots associated with Matthew (his wagon, the empty stable, the boots lying near the sofa etc.), revealing Anne's realization, in a sort of Kuleshov effect, that the man is gone. Then the music stops and Matthew appears, iterating his affection for Anne before entering a dark tunnel, obviously metaphoric of death, with purple flowers redolent of the ones that Anne placed in his coffin. This dream is conducive to convey Anne's feelings of love and being loved for/by her adoptive family, another key theme of the book, which also emerges clearly when the girl finally breaks up on Marilla's shoulder.

The second arc: Anne's maturation

In Montgomery's novel, the early chapters are mostly devoted to daylong childhood adventures, from cooking accidents to social gaffes, laying the basis for Anne's well-rounded characterization, and build on the comedy side of the plot. But after the protagonist's stay in Charlottetown (Chapter XXIX), and her realization that she prefers the countryside to the city, an 'epoch in Anne's life' is over. The second half of the story thus begins in Chapter XXX, starting a new arc that focuses on her growth into a young woman. As seen, this is matched by Montgomery's narrative becoming increasingly

FIGURE 5.4 *Marilla and Anne's heartfelt hug (Episode 47). As Matthew calls the girl his* 娘 *(*musume *[daughter]), Marilla, too, realizes to be a mother for Anne.*

elliptic. This is why the number of additions and expansions grows as the series progresses, while, until Chapter XXX, there is a minor gap between the literary work and the anime, because of the episodic structure of the first thirty chapters of the novel. The adaptation thus expands Anne's major plot points, introducing a number of significant additions and expansions, as in the case mentioned in the previous paragraph.

The treatment of Chapter XXX is emblematic of this approach. In the book, a lot is at stake here. First, a dialogue between Marilla and Anne communicates the news of Miss Stacy inviting her to prepare for the entrance exam to Queen's Academy, where she will be able to fulfil her dream – to study to become a teacher. Then Miss Stacy's class of advanced students is formed, with Anne and Diana being separated for the second time. Meanwhile, her rivalry with Gilbert escalates, for Anne now regrets causing tension, but it is the boy's turn to treat her coldly. Anne works passionately for the whole year, but when lessons are over, she locks away her books to 'let [her] imagination go riot' for her 'last summer as a little girl'. A final discussion between Marilla and Mrs Lynde informs the readers of Matthew's worsening health condition, and Lynde's change of heart about Anne, who has grown into a 'real smart girl'. In other words, Chapter XXX comprises many storylines and important themes for the main narrative, which has now reached a turning point.

The animated series splits the chapter into three episodes (33–35), with additions and expansions being particularly numerous in the last two. Anne spending the afternoon with Diana, an event which is recalled by Marilla at the beginning of the chapter, becomes the opening scene of Episode 33.

Then Anne and Diana's school paths drifting apart (to which is dedicated one short paragraph in the book) and Anne's suffering as if she 'tasted the bitterness of death' at seeing her friend alone cover the first half of Episode 34. Moreover, Montgomery's often non-linear plot is also readjusted to fit in a cause-and-effect structure. Especially Matthew's bad spell of heart is illustrated in a separated beat, in the midpoint of this episode, foreshadowing relevant developments for the main plot.

Other changes are obtained through visualization, conveying important information on the main characters and the world they live in effective non-verbal communication. In this sense, some of the most iconic moments are concentrated in Episode 35, consisting of pure visual scenes with little to no dialogue. In the first half of the episode, after school ends, Anne sits on the back of Matthew's wagon, her petite figure barely noticeable as they ride off towards Green Gables. The long shot emphasizes the beauty of the layout, which is also the vanishing point, located in the centre of the image. Anne and the wagon are seen in perspective and decreasing in size as they approach Green Gables, suggesting her physical and emotional connection to her new home. Anne sitting on the wagon is a visive rhyme that appears later in the series, as a means to stress the joy of farming life and working in contact with nature, another theme idealized by Takahata.

The emotional potential of visual storytelling is made even clearer in the second half of the episode, when Anne and Diana go playing on the beach. The scene comes at the end of a triptych of episodes which take place in autumn and winter, the cold seasons serving as a background for Anne's anxious realization that Diana will take a different path from hers. Therefore, the following scenes are deemed to make a deep impression on viewers. Anne and Diana running barefoot on the beach, with their straw hats on, as they look for seashells, become at one with the surrounding nature. The white sand, the cry of seagulls in the blue sky and the waves rolling onto the shore, are equally significant as the human characters, often filling the scene with their powerful presence. This vibrant seaside layout contrasts sharply with the previous scenery, both in terms of composition, colour palette and elaborated animation of water, thus giving the viewers a deep sense of visual satisfaction, after two episodes dominated by grey and leaden winter.

Girls' education and *omoiyari*

Another interesting aspect of the adaptation that emerges from the Episodes 33–35, is the attention paid to themes which are relatively unimportant in the novel, but acquire a different connotation in the series, resonating with a diverse cultural framework. For example, wide space is given to the dramatization of the concept of 思いやり (*omoiyari* [fellow feeling]), a basic pillar of Japanese communication and social psychology. The

FIGURE 5.5A *Anne at the beach (Episode 34). Note the evolution of Anne's character design and chromatic palette.*

FIGURE 5.5B *Anne returns home on Matthew's wagon (Episode 35).*

idea of omoiyari is a combination of 'altruism, sympathy, empathy and prosocial behaviour',[42] and is described by cultural anthropologist Lebra as 'the ability and willingness to feel what others are feeling, to vicariously experience the pleasure or pain that they are undergoing, and to help them

---

[42]Kazuya Hara, 'The Concept of Omoiyari (Altruistic Sensitivity) in Japanese Relational Communication', *Intercultural Communication Studies* XV, no. 1 (2006): 25.

satisfy their wishes . . . without being told verbally'.[43] The word is often found on signs bearing a school motto or at police stations, and is one of the qualities most commonly ascribed to a good person.[44] The education guidelines for teachers in Japan provides further proof of this, encouraging a 思いやりの心 (*omoiyari no kokoro* [compassionate heart]) as the key for harmonious group relations, hence the importance of this virtue for the moral development of the child.[45]

Omoiyari-based behaviours are fostered on several occasions throughout the adaptation and in *WMT* series in general. It is thematized in Episode 34, where Anne discovers that she will continue her studies, but her best friend will not, because her parents do not intend to send Diana to college. Both in the book and in the series, this seems 'nothing short of a calamity' to Anne, because she assumed they would study together. However, in the series, Anne ruminates on the matter for quite a long time, first with Diana, trying to persuade her to join Queen's class, then at the end of the day with Marilla. When Anne blames the Barrys because 'they did not even take Diana's feelings into consideration', Marilla corners her by turning her point of view upside down: 'Do you really understand Diana's feelings? Does Diana really want to be a teacher like you? (. . .) I think you must have blamed her too much, and that's why she can't tell you how she really feels'.[46]

The animation not only dedicates half of an episode to what in the novel is completed in a single paragraph (expansion) but also emphasizes the need to be considerate of others in a truly empathetic way, adding a new scene to tackle the issue from the perspective of omoiyari. As Anne's educator, it is Marilla's responsibility to help the protagonist recalibrate her omoiyari mindset, moving from a concern for another person to the experience of perceiving the world through someone else's eyes. In other words, Anne is requested to adopt an empathetic attitude, instead of a

---

[43]Takie Sugiyama Lebra, *Japanese Patterns of Behavior* (Honolulu: University of Hawaii Press, 1976), 38.
[44]According to a survey conducted in Japanese and Anglo-Australian society in Australia in 1992, asking to compile a list of ten words describing the personal qualities one most values, omoiyari is the third most commonly appearing word; Catherine Travis, 'Omoiyari as a Core Japanese Value: Japanese-Style Empathy?', in *Speaking of Emotions: Conceptualization and Expression*, ed. Angeliki Athanasiado and Elzbieta Tabakowska (Berlin: Mouton de Gryyter, 1998), 56.
[45]The first listed in these guidelines, put out by the Japanese Ministry of Education, is 'Omoiyari no kokoro o taisetsuni shimashō' ('Let's treasure the heart/mind of the omoiyari'); quoted in Travis Ibid.
[46]あんたこそダイアナの気持ちが分かっているのか？ ダイアナは本当にあんたと同じように先生になりたいと思っているのかね (. . .) きっとあんたがあんまり責めるものだからダイアナ本当の気持ちを打ち明けられなく (Anta koso Daiana no kimochi ga wakatte iru no ka? Daiana wa hontōni anta to onajiyōni sensei ni naritai to omotte iru no ka ne? (. . .) kitto anta ga anmari semeru mono dakara Daiana hontō no kimochi o uchiake rarenaku).

sympathetic one.[47] Omoiyari implies a 'sense of oneness' with the target of the omoiyari action,[48] making an effort to accept their vision of things, even when they might differ from the helper's one. In the series, when Anne stands her ground because she is eager to continue studying with Diana, Marilla reminds her that, no matter how good their intentions, 誰も自分の生き方を他人に強制することはできないんだよ (*dare mo jibun no ikikata o tanin ni kyōsei suru koto wa dekinai nda yo* [no one can force others to live their own way of life]). This is especially important as omoiyari appears only in conflict situations, in order to have good human relations, in the context of a group-oriented life.[49] In fact, Anne's recognizing Diana's feelings allows her to enhance their relationship, resulting in a new friendship vow, which recalls the one in Chapter XII.

Anne and Diana's first solemn vow is represented in Episode 9, set in the lush greenery of the Barry's garden in spring bloom. In Episode 34, Anne's gestures are repeated in the same location. This time, however, it is late autumn and the garden is bare, the seasonal change revealing the circular structure of the story and mirroring the emotions of the characters. The barren landscape, which is visually opposite to what seen in Episode 9, tells the viewer that time has passed, and the little girls are now gone to another stage in their life. Similarly, the second solemn vow, with the tilled soil in the background, seems to indicate that Anne and Diana's friendship will flourish again and grow with them, resting on a firmer ground of trust and mutual comprehension.

Diana's reframing

A high sensitivity to others has been linked to another Japanese cultural pattern, or the tendency to withhold explicit display of feelings.[50] This is related to the dualism between 本音 (*honne* [true inner feelings]) and 建前 (*tatemae* [public moral standards]).[51] Tatemae refers to anything that can be outwardly expressed, according to common sense or socially accepted conduct, whereas honne is connected with a person's heart and senses,

---

[47]On the differences between the concepts of sympathy and empathy, see, for example, Douglas Chismar, 'Empathy and Sympathy: The Important Difference', *Journal of Value Inquiry* 22 (1988): 257–66.
[48]Lebra, *Japanese Patterns of Behavior*, 115.
[49]Hara, 'The Concept of Omoiyari (Altruistic Sensitivity) in Japanese Relational Communication', 27.
[50]Cliff Goddard and Anna Wierzbicka, 'Discourse and Culture', in *Discourse as Social Interaction. Discourse Studies: A Multidisciplinary Introduction*, vol. 2, ed. Teun A. Van Dijk (London: SAGE, 1997), 239.
[51]Takashi Naito and Uwe P. Gielen, 'Tatemae and Honne: A Study of Moral Relativism in Japanese Culture', in *Psychology in International Perspective: 50 Years of the International Council of Psychologists*, ed. Uwe P. Gielen et al. (Swets & Zeitlinger Publishers, 1992), 161–2.

FIGURE 5.6A *Anne and Diana's first solemn vow (Episode 9).*

FIGURE 5.6B *Anne and Diana's reconciliation (Episode 34).*

which cannot be discussed in public. The reason for such a self-restraint lies in the emphasis on preventing displeasure, since it is believed that voicing out facts can hurt other people's feelings. It is easy to see that Anne's way of expressing herself is antithetical to this ethnography of speaking. Young Anne talks a lot, giving voice to her emotions free from the shackles of social conventions. She can be extremely confrontational, and as such, she does not always relent easily to inscribed hierarchal patterns of authority.[52]

---

[52]Somers, 'An no shijō [Anne's Feelings]', 159.

Conversely, Anne's 'bosom friend' is an amiable girl who sticks to the rules and always obeys her parents without complaining. In other words, Diana is a pretty normal girl, if not the epitome of ordinariness. Her subordinate position in the novel emerges clearly from Chapter XXX, when the girl is not allowed to join Miss Stacy's class of advanced students. However, Diana's not going to college can be seen as an implicit criticism of Barrys's views on female higher education. As Montgomery often embeds subversive counter-texts to challenge the society of her times,[53] it is possible to assume that she is claiming the right of women to education, a strong and too often neglected aspect of her fiction.[54]

Unlike Montgomery, the series is not critical of Diana's parents, nor of their narrow-minded views on schooling. However, Diana's silence on the matter is interpreted as a form of indirect communication, expressing a polite refusal in front of Anne's repeated insistence. In fact, the series makes it clear that the girl does not enjoy studying as much as Anne, but decides not to tell her because she is afraid of disappointing her. This is an original addition, and to some extent, allows to read Diana as a more relatable character for Japan. Keen on avoiding conflict and conforming to the norm, her personality is closer to the Confucian ideals of harmony and peace of mind, different from Anne's emotional outbursts and explosive temper. She is also turned into a more complex and multifaceted character, worthy of interest as much as the protagonist's strong individualism.

This reframing of Diana is an example of variation from the novel. It is worth mentioning that this same character is involved in two more such instances, as detailed below.

First, in the series, Diana is visually associated to *Alice in Wonderland*, which enjoyed great popularity in Japan. In Episode 8, Diana shows Anne a copy of the novel, quoted again in Episode 10, when the girls imagine seeing the White Rabbit on their way to Idlewild, and in Episode 41, when Diana gifts the book to Anne before her leaving for Charlottetown. The usage of Carroll's imagery expands on a hidden reference in the book, where the narrator says that Marilla is 'as fond of morals as the Duchess in Wonderland' (Chapter VIII). In the adaptation this minimal quote is turned into a symbol of Anne and Diana's friendship and childhood, instead of a token of Marilla's strictness.

Dually, in just one instance, there is a case where a chapter in the book is almost completely omitted. This is Chapter XX, where Anne and Diana imagine that the woods between their houses are haunted. One possible explanation is that, while this narrative has a comical undertone in the book, in the animation it would have acquired a nightmarish connotation, due to the stronger impact of visualization on the audience.

---

[53]Rubio, 'Subverting the Trite', 8.
[54]Karr, *Authors and Audiences*, 134.

These examples are suggestive of *WMT*'s take on faithfulness as a process subject to negotiation. Whereas a passing reference to Alice is reframed into a visual rhyme, an entire sequence (the 'Haunted Woods') is discarded for seemingly dramaturgic reasons, as it would have connoted imagination in a negative way, using fantasy elements in a typically realistic programme.

6

From *A Little Princess* to *Shōkōjo Sēra*

小公女セーラ (*Shōkōjo Sēra* [*Little lady Sara*]) is a meisaku series consisting of forty-six episodes, aired from 6 January 1985 to 29 December of the same year. Based on the children's classic *A Little Princess*, the animation was a great success in Japan, influencing the style and productive choices behind the adaptation of following *WMT* shows starting from *Pollyanna*. A composite team of talents worked on the project, including Kurokawa, at his debut as a director for a *WMT* series, producer Nakajima and veteran Mori, who was in charge of layout composition. The series also capitalized on the popularity of the original work in Japan, where the book had been translated since the Meiji period, becoming a staple of local girls' fiction. The first paragraphs of this chapter offer information on the original novel, focusing on the publication of *A Little Princess* and its reception across media, with an emphasis on its role for Japanese translated literature. In the analysis of the adaptation process, special attention will be devoted to the variants in the characterization of the main characters, and the repositioning of the narrative genre of the story, also in reference to the contemporary developments of the *WMT* programme.[1]

Frances Hodgson Burnett

Frances Eliza Hodgson (1849–1924) was a prolific author who left a corpus of 44 novels and over 100 short stories. Originally from the industrial town

---

[1] This chapter has also been partly published as the following: Maria Chiara Oltolini, 'Children's Fiction and Anime: The Case of Shōkōjo Sēra', *Journal of Screenwriting* 12, no. 3 (2021): 287–305, https://doi.org/10.1386/ josc_00068_1.

of Manchester, after the death of her father she immigrated to Knoxville, Tennessee. Here she started her publishing career when she was still a teenager, publishing stories as a means to support her mother and siblings. In 1873 she married Swan Burnett, and continued to write to add income to the family finances while her husband studied medicine. A professional author living by her pen, Burnett profited from the recent developments of the American publishing system, where penny magazines became popular as reading material for an increasingly larger part of the population. Due to her literary fame, Burnett was able to conduct a lavish lifestyle, entering the elite society whose affairs were accounted in newspapers. She frequently travelled back to England, which she considered her true home, and was in touch with renowned writers and artists, such as Henry James.

The accounts of Burnett's life and character, so hounded by the press in her time, were often biased. According to her modern biographers, Burnett's personal life was marred by sadness and anxiety. She suffered from various illnesses, probably brought on by the pressures of her career, her unhappy weddings (she divorced twice) and, most of all, the death of one of her sons, Lionel, in 1890. To assuage her sorrow, Burnett turned to Christian Science and the New Thought, spiritualist movements which were common among the Anglo-American upper-class circles, centring on themes such as the power of the human mind, the importance of a positive attitude and a general belief in metaphysical healing.[2] The interest in spirituality and the occult would leave an influence on her vast production, including Burnett's fairy tales, a much frequented genre until her death.

The critical reading of Burnett's works changed over years, and so did her public reception. In a study of Victorian children's authors, Marghanita Laski (1915–88) wrote that Burnett's main contribution to children's literature consisted of three books: *Little Lord Fauntleroy* (1886), *A Little Princess* (1905) and *The Secret Garden* (1911).[3] In fact, today Burnett is best remembered for her children's novels, but she also wrote romantic adult books, most of which were steady sellers in her days, and later fell into oblivion. It is worth noting that Burnett started out publishing juvenile stories when she was already an established author, thanks to the success of *Little Lord Fauntleroy*, whose protagonist was based on her son Vivian. The story, initially serialized on the famous American children's magazine *St. Nicholas*, was dramatized for the stage by Burnett herself. This practice was a common one for the writer, who had been fond of acting since her early childhood, foreshadowing the multiple adaptations of her novels into other media.

---

[2]Gertchen Gerzina, *Francis Hodgson Burnett* (London: Chatto & Windus, 2004), 89.
[3]Marghanita Laski, *Mrs. Ewing, Mrs. Molesworth, and Mrs. Hodgson Burnett* (New York: Oxford University Press, 1951), 81.

The novel

Among Burnett's children's books, *A Little Princess* has the most extended textual evolution, from a serialized novella (1887–8), to a stage play (1902), to a novel (1905), exemplifying the writer's habit of presenting her fiction in different forms, all generating a separate income.[4] Although this scheming had practical reasons, including Burnett's playwriting practice as a way to secure theatrical rights for her works,[5] such a full-fledged exploration of the story was beneficial to the final narrative.[6] This is about a rich child who becomes a poor orphan, and the trials and tribulations that she endures at the hands of others. The only daughter of a British millionaire, Captain Ralph Crewe, and a French woman, who died when she was born, Sara grew up in India as a little princess. Back to England, she becomes the show pupil of a boarding school in London, but when her father dies, leaving her without a penny, she is forced to work as a servant. In the end her fate changes again, and Sara's fortune is restored thanks to the unexpected help of Mr Carrisford, her late father's friend and business partner. However, everybody realizes that Sara has always been a princess in her heart, with her kindness, grace and imagination.

The urtext of the book is *Sara Crewe, or, What Happened At Miss Minchin's*, a short novella (less than eighty text pages), which Burnett started in 1885, during the serialization of *Little Lord Fauntleroy*, and finished in 1886. It appeared then in *St. Nicholas* and achieved a good success,[7] encouraging Burnett to adapt it into the play *A Little Unfairy Princess*, which opened in London's Shaftesbury Theatre, and, without 'Unfairy' in the title, in the Criterion Theatre in Broadway. Although her plays were received with little enthusiasm in Britain, Burnett's reputation as a playwright was thriving in New York, and Edward L. Burlingame, an editor at Scribner's, suggested her to make a longer version of *Sara Crewe*. With the play still running on both sides of the Atlantic, the publisher was expecting Christmas sales to be particularly strong.[8] Put into print in 1905, *A Little Princess: Being the Whole Story of Sara Crewe Now Being Told for the First Time* was more than three times the length of *Sara Crewe*, and reached a new generation of readers.

---

[4]Gerzina, *Francis Hodgson Burnett*, 234.
[5]Ann Thwaite, *Waiting for the Party: The Life of Frances Hodgson Burnett, 1849-1924* (London: Faber and Faber, 1994).
[6]Janice Kirkland, 'Frances Hodgson Burnett's Sara Crewe Through 110 Years', *Children's Literature in Education* 28, no. 4 (1997): 191–203.
[7]*Sara Crewe* has been printed approximately forty times prior to Burnett's death, either as a stand-alone book or as coupled with other writings; Johanna Elizabeth Resler, 'Sara's Transformation: A Textual Analysis of Frances Hodgson Burnett's Sara Crew and A Little Princess' (MA diss., Indiana: Indiana University, 2007), 21.
[8]Thwaite, *Waiting for the Party*, 206–7.

A Little Princess became a bestseller – suffice to say that, since 1905, it has been printed over 140 times[9] – and, as observed for *Anne of Green Gables*, was initially appreciated as much by adults as by children, due to a lack of rigid codification of juvenile fiction. While Twain praised Montgomery's work, the Earl of Crewe endeared to Burnett by taking special pride in claiming Sara as a relation.[10] From a diegetic perspective, the story blends modern features such as colonial and postcolonial tropes – in primis, the use of British colonies as a device for plot development[11] – with the traditional genres of the fairy tale and the moral exemplum,[12] typically short, anecdotic stories where a saintly child protagonist has a beneficial influence on those around them, for example, being able to effect instant conversions in others. Both genres were popular in Victorian England, conveying cultural values welcome to the middle class, and deeply influenced Burnett's writing. The world of the novel is a stylized nineteenth-century boarding school in London, with its upstairs-downstairs social architecture, dominated by director Miss Minchin.

It is worth noting that Burnett, too, was a talented orphan who achieved success after being reduced to poverty, so it is no surprise that themes such as fall from grace and reversal of fate are common in her fiction. In particular, *A Little Princess* has a perfectly circular rags-to-riches structure, with Sara belonging to the fertile archetype of Cinderella. In fact, like the classic tale canonized by Perrault and the Grimms, Burnett's novel describes the struggles of a patient heroine and her final triumph. In both cases, it is not the protagonists but the people around them who change, ultimately recognizing their royal stature.[13] However, Sara plays an active role in her redemption, using imagination and sympathy to cope with life's difficulties.[14] This topic is closely related with that of hardship as a trial: Sara proves to be a princess in passing through misfortunes without losing any of her goodwill. The underlying message is that, if you have high morals and work hard, you can change your destiny, because – in this as in other books by the same author – kindness always pays off, and true nobility lies not in titles but within oneself.

---

[9] Resler, 'Sara's Transformation', 22.
[10] Thwaite, *Waiting for the Party*, 165.
[11] Jonah Ruskin, *Mythology of Imperialism* (London: Random House, 1971), 17–18.
[12] Phyllis Bixler Koppes, 'Tradition and the Individual Talent of Frances Hodgson Burnett: A Generic Analysis of Little Lord Fauntleroy, A Little Princess, and the Secret Garden', *Children's Literature* 7 (1978): 191.
[13] Ibid., 193.
[14] Elisabeth Rose Gruner, 'Cinderella, Marie Antoinette, and Sara: Roles and Role Models in A Little Princess', *The Lion and the Unicorn* 22 (1998): 163–87.

The characters

As a heroine, Sara is poised halfway between the unfortunate and virtuous children of Victorian literature and the more lifelike characters of Edwardian fiction, or, to use Frye's terminology,[15] between high mimetic and low mimetic modes of characterization. On the one hand, she is endowed with a set of superior (high mimetic) qualities that make her almost too perfect to be true. Like Cinderella, Sara is a princess by nature, with a noble, sympathetic soul which leads her to help the needy and the oppressed. This emerges clearly in the end of the story (Chapter XIX), when Sara returns to a bakery where she bought buns in the midpoint of the novel, giving them to Anne, a beggar child hungrier than she was. Now that the girl has been employed there, Sara is happy to pass her mission on to her: to give bread to the hungry children, spreading generosity in the world – a theme dear to Burnett. In addition, as observed for *Anne of Green Gables*, Sara epitomizes a common myth in contemporary children's fiction: that of exceptional orphans who are light-bearers and a force of nature for their surroundings, questioning the values of a narrow-minded community with their positive cultural attributes.

At the same time, Sara has realistic (low mimetic) traits. She is 'a child full of imaginings and whimsical thoughts' (Chapter II), bookish and sharply clever. She gets 'snappish' when someone disturbs her reading time (Chapter VI), and her temper flares at pettiness or hypocrisy. Significantly, for her will to fight for justice, her father compares Sara to a knight in shining armour (Chapter III). As Anne Shirley, Sara is repeatedly described as 'queer' (the term occurs over thirty times in the book), while with her 'brown' hands (Chapter IX), green eyes and black hair, she does not have a classic princess looks either. A born storyteller, she is good-natured and empathetic, using her resources to help her friends. She teaches French to school dunce Ermengarde, soothes crybaby Lottie and comforts a poor maid, Becky, satisfying her hunger for food and stories. These features, and her ability to adapt to difficult situations holding on to her ideals ('I am a prisoner in the Bastille', she tells to herself in Chapter VIII, when Miss Minchin confines her to the attic), draw Sara close to archetypal personalities such as the Peacemaker (9w1) in Enneagram, or the Sage (INFJ), the rarest personality in the Myers-Briggs Type Indicator.

Just like her schoolmates are fond of Sara because she is 'wonderful and different from anyone else' (Chapter III), her rivals despise her for the same reason. Sara's nemesis at school is Lavinia, a spiteful girl who is among the eldest and richest students, who is jealous of Sara's magnetic

---

[15]Quoted in Maria Nikolajeva, 'The Changing Aesthetics of Character in Children's Fiction', *Style* 35, no. 3 (2001): 430–53.

persona. However, the main conflict is between Sara and Miss Minchin. A sort of Dickensian villainess, the headmistress is a calculating woman who fawns over Sara for her money and shows her true colours when the girl loses it all. Forced to earn her living as a student-teacher, Sara is starved, overworked and forbidden to socialize with other children, but always strives to behave like the little princess her father called her. This way, she learns to overcome adversity and eventually reunites with a family friend who makes her wealthy again. On the contrary, Miss Minchin seems to be punished by the events, as there is no doubt that in the end Sara will enrol to another school, undermining her reputation. This is especially clear in the play, which omitted the bakery scene to show Sara's rebuff to Miss Minchin when she asks her to go back to her.[16]

Sara's animal friends – the sparrows on the roof, the rat Melchisedec and his family in the attic, Ram Dass's monkey and Boris the dog (a present by Mr Carrisford) – also deserve a mention. Sara establishes a natural understanding with them, and in turn they are a source of strength for her.

The adaptation choices

Being a story of hope with a resilient protagonist, *A Little Princess* seems especially suitable for the *WMT* brand, which selected educative books from the Western tradition, usually set in non-magical universes, and replete with positive role models for the young. In particular, a growing number of *WMT* series featured strong and kind heroines facing hard times with optimism and determination, from the seminal *Heidi* (1974) to *Katri* (1984). In particular, among the meisaku shows produced prior to *Sara*, seven out of ten had female protagonists, which were constant since the times of *Flone* (1981), a family story starring a young heroine that is absent in the original book. The appealing location of the novel – Victorian London with glimpses of India – also seemed to work to the advantage of the series, which would have been the first of the programme to take place in Britain.

These aspects must have been clear to Satō, the director of the planning department of Nippon Animation. As will be recalled, Satō was responsible for proposing adaptation options such as the British novel *Treasures of the Snow* (1950), and the Finnish novel *Paimen, piika ja emäntä* (1927). However, the resulting animated series *Annette* (1983) and the above-mentioned *Katri* received a lukewarm reaction compared to previous shows.

---

[16]The new ending highlights Sara's self-possession and resolution: 'Minchin: [. . .] Will you not do your duty to your poor papa and come home with me? Sara: (steps forward) No, I will not. You know why I will not go home with you, Miss Minchin, you know – (this spoken quietly, steadily, and politely, looking squarely at her)'; quoted in Kirkland, 'Frances Hodgson Burnett's Sara Crewe Through 110 Years', 195.

This seems to indicate that the popularity of *WMT*, which still represented the jewel in the crown of the studio's output, was slowly declining in Japan. In fact, Japanese animation went through many changes in the early 1980s. Every day over six new anime were aired on television, hitting the record of forty-four series per week.[17] Many of these works were manga-based romantic comedies like うる星やつら (*Urusei Yatsura* [*Those noisy, annoying people from star Uru*]) (1981), where a sexy alien in tiger-striped bikini falls in love with a human student. These shows, specifically aimed at Japanese teenagers, were very different, in tone and genre, from the more generalist series of the *WMT* anthology.

In order to fit into an increasingly saturated scene and raise a stagnant audience, a new meisaku formula was needed. Theoretically, *Katri* had potential to succeed. It focused on the daily life of a hardworking heroine in Scandinavia, a beloved setting since the times of the pre-*WMT* series *Moomin*. Moreover, Miyazaki Akira and Saitō Hiroshi, respectively, the screenwriter and director of the series, had worked in tandem on other meisaku shows, following in the footsteps of Takahata and Miyazaki's anthropological approach with their character-driven, slow-paced animation. However, *Katri*'s inspiring novel, which gained momentum in post-war Japan, was much less popular in the 1980s. This was a deliberate decision by Satō, who was まだ知られていない名作を開拓しようと挑戦していたんです (*mada shira rete inai meisaku o kaitaku shiyō to chōsen shite itandesu* [still trying to develop a meisaku that was not well-known yet]).[18] The strategy did not come without risk, given that *Katri* was in danger of being cancelled halfway through due to its low ratings.[19] Thus it was essential to select a famous novel for the future series. Burnett's *The Secret Garden* had long been a candidate, yet the choice fell on *A Little Princess*.

To better understand this move and its significance for the adaptation, the following paragraph centres on the arrival of Burnett's works in Japan within the context of translated children's fiction.

Mrs Burnett goes to Tokyo

As seen, Western children's literature had been entrenched in Japanese collective imagery long before the creation of *WMT* series, thus problematizing the relation between such texts and the originals, but also a simplistic East-versus-West historical approach. Children's books and fairy tales from Europe, America and the Middle East were translated into Japanese for both

---

[17]Murakami, *Anime in TV*, 81.
[18]Quoted in Chiba, *Sekai meisaku gekijō shirīzu memoriaru bukku. Yōroppa-hen*, 361.
[19]Ibid., 341.

instructive and entertaining ends. Because of the cultural differences in the source texts, Meiji translators would either alter the originals to make them familiar to their readership or privilege fidelity to stress their novelty, the pendulum swinging between strategies of domestication and foreignization. Repeatedly published in magazines and book series, Western juvenile fiction contributed to promote, consciously or not, new vistas in terms of content, style and values, igniting the rise of local children's and girls' literature.

The Japanese reception of Burnett's works epitomizes these trends. *Little Lord Fauntleroy*, the novel that shot her into stardom, was first translated into Japanese by Wakamatsu Shizuko as *Shōkōshi* [*The little lord*] (1890), achieving instant success. One of the first recognized women translators of her time and a fervent Christian,[20] Wakamatsu purposely domesticated the book for a Japanese audience, but emphasized foreign ideals that she held dear, including the Romantic notion of the child as an innocent creature and the Victorian archetype of femininity as angelic and maternal.[21] To some extent, such tenets were consonant with Meiji 'good wife, wise mother' ideology, but Wakamatsu situated them in a religious perspective.[22] Similar considerations apply to her translation of Burnett's novella *Sara Crewe*, the first example of girls' literature published in Japan.[23]

Typically glossed in English as 'adolescent girl', the term *shōjo* was introduced when the reforms of the Meiji State, and the influence of missionary institutions, led to an expansion of female schooling, and to the emergence of a new readership of girls. A cultural construct rather than a social entity, shōjo representations of girlhood populated Japanese magazines in the form of serialized novels and comics, building on (and evolving from) the imported tradition of Western children's classics like *Little Women*, *Pollyanna* or *Heidi*.[24] Sara belonged to this family of gentle but strong female leads, which branched out to different media and formats, inspiring generations of Japanese girls with a set of desirable attributes of femininity. Whereas *Shōkōshi* canonized Burnett as a writer of uplifting fiction for the young, Wakamatsu's セイラ・クルーの話 (*Sēra Kurū no hanashi* [*The story of Sara Crewe*]) (1893–4) portrayed a 一風変わった (*ippu kawatta* [queer girl]) that posed a challenge to Meiji mores.[25] A more

---

[20]Yoshiko Takita, 'Wakamatsu Shizuko and "Little Lord Fauntleroy"', *Comparative Literature Studies* 22, no. 1 (1985): 1–8.
[21]Rebecca L. Copeland, *Woman Critiqued: Translated Essays on Japanese Women's Writing* (Honolulu: University of Hawai'i Press, 2006).
[22]Ortabasi, 'Brave Dogs and Little Lords', 192–3.
[23]Kazuko Taneda, 'Fūgawarina shōjo "shōkōjo" no hensen: Wakamatsu Shizuko kara itō sei made' [Transformation of 'Queer' (the otherness in) Little Princess: Transition of 'Shokojo' from Wakamatsu Shizuko to Itoh Sei], *Fuji joshi daigaku kokubungaku zasshi* [Fuji Women's University Japanese literature magazine] 99–100, no. 3 (2019): 21–37.
[24]Dollase, *Age of Shōjo*.
[25]Taneda, 'Fūgawarina shōjo "shōkōjo" no hensen'.

complex heroine than her official successor, the protagonist of *Sara Crewe* is both gentle and incredibly stubborn when it comes to defend her morals, a quality not associated with the 'good wife, wise mother' ideal.

As has been observed, Wakamatsu's Sara strived to maintain the low mimetic quirks of Burnett's Sara, but the early translators of the novel, which was released in English five years after Wakamatsu's death, would domesticate the character in accordance with the conservative agenda of contemporary publishers and educators.[26] The most translated girls' story prior and after the war, when the Occupation forces fostered the massive publication of American juvenile fiction, *A Little Princess* – named 小公女 (*Shōkōjo*) after Wakamatsu's seminal translation *Shōkōshi* – was repackaged in countless variations, disseminating a new image of Sara that accentuated her motherly nature and spirituality, at the expenses of her resoluteness and tenacity.[27] Such renegotiation of Sara as a 'good and wise' princess, eventually rewarded with a serendipitous twist of fate, shared similarities with the plot of numerous Japanese girls' comics up until the 1960s,[28] while implicitly stressing the destructive power of an antagonist who is also a career woman.[29]

Writing Sara for animation

Considering Burnett's well-established reputation in the country, the timely translation of her children's books into Japanese and the classic status rapidly achieved by *A Little Princess* as a shōjo novel, as well as its domestication across the decades, the confidence of Nippon Animation in the adaptation of *A Little Princess* seems clear. Director Kurokawa, who had already worked on several unofficial meisaku series since アラビアンナイト シンドバットの冒険 (*Arabian naito: Shindobaddo no bōken* [*Arabian nights: The adventures of Sinbad*]) (1975), Nippon Animation's take on 'Sinbad the Sailor', was aware of the importance of the project, not only for the company but also for himself: with the ratings of the programme getting as low as *hitoketa* (single-digit) in *Katri*, had *Sara* been a failure his debut in *WMT* would have been detrimental to his career.[30] As an anime

---

[26]Taneda, 'Fūgawarina shōjo "shōkōjo" no hensen'; Asuka Toritamari, '"Shōjo" wo sagashite: "Shōkōjo" ni miru risō no shōjo' [Looking for the 'Girl': the Ideal Girl in 'A Little Princess'], *Machikaneyama ronsō. Bunka dōtai-ron-hen* [*Machikanaeyama essays. Cultural dynamics*] 46 (2012): 39–57.
[27]Toritamari, 'Shōjo' wo sagashite'.
[28]Mizuki Takahashi, 'Opening the Closed World of shōjo manga', in *Japanese Visual Culture: Explorations in the World of Manga and Anime*, ed. Mark W. MacWilliams and F. L. Schodt (Abingdon and New York: Routledge, 2015), 114–36.
[29]Toritamari, 'Shōjo' wo sagashite'.
[30]Chiba, *Sekai meisaku gekijō shirīzu memoriaru bukku. Yōroppa-hen*, 341.

director, he had full control over the series and was responsible for the most crucial creative decisions since the early stages of pre-production.[31] This was especially true for Nippon Animation, which inherited Takahata's centralizing model in the Zuiyō era.

On a narrative level, as will be recalled, *A Little Princess* displays a paradigmatic Cinderella plot, that is, a basic storyline that easily translates into film. Burnett herself negotiated for a silent movie starring Mary Pickford in 1917, and various adaptations would follow ever since, including a film with genius child actress Shirley Temple (1939), a BBC TV series (1987) and a Japanese drama (2019). In almost all cases, great liberties were taken with the original book. A typical Hollywood move was making Sara reunite with her father, wounded but alive, in the end of the story, to tone down the tragicness. The novel also posed a number of diegetic limitations. The chronological framework is an example, spanning about six years starting with Sara's arrival at Miss Minchin's school at the age of seven, a fairly long time for an adaptation. Besides, the story time is discontinuous, going very fast in the first chapters (Chapters I–IV), and slowing down after the inciting incident (Sara's fall from grace when her father suddenly dies, in Chapter VII), although other characters seem unaffected by the increasing pace: for example, Lavinia, Sara's rival at school, is thirteen at the beginning, and still a schoolgirl at the end of the book.

Most importantly, a novel consisting of nineteen chapters (267 pages in the princeps) had to be turned into forty-six thirty-minute episodes, something that obviously implied a set of changes and additions, as was often the case in the *WMT* programme. The small, almost all-female cast – nineteen characters including extras – was also a challenge, compared to the rich universes of other meisaku series, which usually featured plenty of characters (*Katri* had more than sixty), and two children of different sex as a leading couple. The same location left little room for the animation to explore lifestyle and attractions of a foreign country, a typical ingredient of *WMT*, as the story takes place mainly in internals, at Miss Minchin's school. Besides, although Burnett knew London well, and visited it on three different trips to England in the 1870s, around the same time she was writing *Sara Crewe*, neither the novella nor the final book provides a lifelike portrayal of the town, which is used as a conventional setting. According to Burnett's critics, the writer drew on some of her experiences in her hometown, Manchester, where she and her siblings attended a 'Select Seminary for Young Ladies and Gentlemen' but was more interested in creating fantasy stories than in realism, which was so important at the beginning of her career.[32]

---

[31] Condry, *The Soul of Anime*.
[32] Thwaite, *Waiting for the Party*, 96.

To cope with these issues, the series was conceived as a one-year storyline, with new arcs and a full-fledged exploration of Sara's parable, visualizing her trials as well as British world-famous locales in a more dramatic way. This was made possible by a scouting trip to England in 1984, when Kurokawa and other members of the staff had a chance to visit London, but also the historic sites of York and Haworth, Yorkshire, the latter being the home of the Brontë sisters.[33] The cast of the novel was expanded to include 56 characters, more than one-third of them being male: these include Sara's best friend Peter, a funny kid with a nose for bargain that has no equivalent in the book. As it is common in meisaku series, a number of animals was also introduced as a source of comic relief.

'Sara is not the main character'

The issues mentioned above – a long time frame, the relative paucity of narrative material, a small cast, the vagueness of the worldbuilding – were common for meisaku adaptations and can be traced back to the roots of WMT, due to the vast plots and meticulous settings needed by long-running seriality. Nonetheless, in his interviews, Kurokawa claimed that Sara's real problem lied elsewhere, i.e., in the characterization of the main character.[34] According to the director, Burnett's protagonist was 少女は、自分では行動を起こさない少女なんです (*shōjo wa, jibun de wa kōdō o okosanai shōjona ndesu* [a girl who doesn't do anything of her own volition]) and 肝心の主人公が動いてくれない (*kanjin no shujinkō ga ugoite kurenai* [a main character (that) doesn't take action]), which would make it hard to propel the plot forward. Kurokawa was also aware that, in the novel, セーラの心の動きが書かれている (*Sēra no kokoro no ugoki ga kakareteiru* [Sara's innermost feelings are described]), which seems 文学はそれでいい (*bungaku wa sore de ii* [fine for literature]), but アニメーションでそれを表現するのは難しい (*animeshōn de sore o hyōgen suru no wa muzukashī* [difficult to express in animation]).[35] It is worth emphasizing that the expression *kokoro ugoki* literally means 'movements of the heart', implying a verbal-centred approach where the narrator has access to Sara's soul, and tells her story rather than showing it.[36] For all these reasons, it would be unlikely for a heroine like Sara to 見る人に共感を得られる (*miru hito ni kyōkan o erareru* [gain the sympathy of the viewers]) in the series,

---

[33]Chiba, *Sekai meisaku gekijō e no tabi*, 70.
[34]Unless otherwise stated, all the Japanese quotes in the following paragraphs are taken from the interviews to Kurokawa included in the booklets of the 1999 DVD collection of the series: Fumio Kurokawa, 'Little Princess Sara staff interview', *Shōkōjo Sēra*, DVD booklets (Japan: Bandai Visual Co., LTD, 1999).
[35]Quoted in Chiba, *Sekai meisaku gekijōeshirīzu memoriaru bukku. Yōroppa-hen*, 341.
[36]On the difference between 'show' and 'tell', see, for example, McKee, *Story*.

because she simply was not active enough to create any ドラマ (*dorama* [drama]).

In other words, Kurokawa regarded Sara as a very reluctant heroine, whose static persona was unsuitable as a source of dramatic conflict. He and 中西 隆三 (Nakanishi Ryūzō) (1932–2013), the scriptwriter of *Sara*, discussed the topic and, before the production started, proposed the following to the staff: 主人公はセーラではない。主人公はミンチン先生 (*Shujinkō wa Sēra de wanai. Shujinkō wa Minchin sensei* [Sara is not the main character. Miss Minchin is the main character]). Even though adult characters often played a pivotal role in the series of the staple and were usually (but not exclusively) presented as helpers for the young protagonists, this was the first time that a meisaku show gave such prominence to a clear-cut antagonist. Moreover, by rephrasing Sara's story from Miss Minchin's point of view, director and scriptwriter were deliberately inserting a new theme in the adaptation, and a rather unusual one for a series primarily aimed at children, as they chose to focus on 女の性 (*on'na no saga* [the spirit of a woman]) or 女の嫉妬 (*on'na no shitto* [female jealousy]). As a consequence, Miss Minchin's envy for Sara – a real princess in rags and tatters – is made much more explicit than in the book, as well as her vexations against the girl when she becomes poor, and thus a hindrance to pursuing her business.

The idea of swapping the narrative perspective was also instrumental to encourage the audience to side with Sara, whose extraordinary kindness is heightened by contrast with Miss Minchin's envy. On the one hand, just like Burnett's character, Minchin *sensei* looks poles apart from Sara: a greedy opportunist, she is servile with the rich, and domineering when it comes to people under her, including her servants and maids. On the other hand, as the real protagonist of the series, Miss Minchin is an anti-heroine, a あたりまえの人間 (*atarimae no ningen* [normal person]) who 学院の経営に心を砕いて生きている (*gakuin no keiei ni kokoro o kudaite ikite iru* [puts her heart and soul into running her institute]), to the point of making this her only aim in life. She is also given a sad backstory that is absent in the book: after losing her parents at the age of ten, she worked as a servant while studying at a charity school, in order to support her little sister. This is only revealed towards the end of the series (Episode 40), which adds to the tragicness of the character. This way, Sara comes to represent all that the headmistress has never been: a little lady at the beginning of the story, and, after her fall from grace, a sweet girl who does not give in to violence, while Minchin's condition as a businesswoman ultimately hardened her heart.

The pilot

Let's consider the pilot series, which is emblematic of the changes explained above. In this episode, Sara and her father arrive to Miss Minchin's school. Captain Crewe wants to be sure that everything is settled to welcome his daughter, used to the warmth of the South, in cold, foggy London. As usual for *WMT* works, plenty of lifelike background sceneries are displayed here, introducing the world in which the adaptation takes place. In the first scenes, the subjective camera shows a boat approaching the white cliffs of Dover, and then, after a series of pans and establishers, we see a carriage riding through the town, allowing for a detailed reconstruction of London in the 1880s. Through the use of the POV shots and other forms of visual storytelling, the viewer is guided in the story in a realistic way, without the voice-over narrator, which was typical of earlier meisaku shows, breaking the suspension of disbelief. Note that such a realistic feeling contrasts with the atmosphere of the novel, which starts 'Once on a dark winter's day' (Chapter I), conveying a sense of fairy-tale vagueness. It also diverges from the mood of the opening titles, which feature Sara in several fantastic settings. Starry-eyed and surrounded by flowers as a romantic shōjo character, Sara has unnatural blue shades in her hair, and is able to fly in the sky like the protagonist of a magical girl series. Only the music, an emotional arrangement by the composer 樋口康雄 (Higuchi Yasuo) (born 1952), connects the two sequences, evoking the idea of a serious and touching series.

Once the historical framework is set, and so is the atmosphere of the show, the story can actually begin. Significantly, the first character we meet is not Sara, as happens in the book, but Miss Minchin, the shadow protagonist, as the scene shifts to her school, somewhere near Waterloo station[37] – again, a real location. Mr Barrow, Mr Crewe's solicitor, is inspecting the room that the headmistress prepared for Sara, making severe comments on everything being not good enough for a princess. Ironically, he is the first one to call Sara so, but he will be also the one to confiscate Sara's possessions when her father dies, pushing Miss Minchin to exploit the girl as a servant, which, to some extent, makes him the real villain of the series. Note that, while Mr Barrow is talking with her, Miss Minchin's image is shown as mirrored in a lamp, or on other reflective surfaces. This is a visual rhyme which will be repeated in the series, evoking the main theme (female jealousy) through the classic trope of the symbolic mirror, as an indicator of one's hidden desires or duality. But the fairy-tale style of the opening, which in turn is derived from the book, seems not completely obliterated, with the mirror bespeaking another well-known jealous character: Snow White's stepmother.

In the first scenes featuring Sara, the viewers see her from behind, after a slow pan on the theatre of her hotel in Westminster, the Savoy – a realistic addition of the series – and an establishing shot on her large suite. The girl is leaning onto the balcony balustrade, looking at the town beneath her. Other details seem to carry a metaphoric meaning, such as Sara's juxtaposition with a parrot in a cage, foreshadowing her future condition at Miss Minchin's. Characterization also emerges from the dialogue between

---

[37]Chiba, *Sekai meisaku gekijō e no tabi*, 70.

Sara and her father. While in Chapter I Sara is described as an 'original child' with a 'mysterious little voice' and 'a queer old-fashioned thoughtfulness in her big yes', in the animation she sounds more angelic and submissive. In the following beat, she visits London as a true princess: on a beautiful carriage. Again, Sara is portrayed while looking outside, this time out of the window of the vehicle, with a cross-cut editing showing her alternatively from the front and backwards. This is another leitmotiv of the animation, bespeaking Sara's meditative nature and tendency to daydreaming. In addition, the brief dialogue between Sara and her father as they indicate the Big Ben and other sights of the city becomes a convenient device to provide educational information, in line with the touristic vein of *WMT*, and to characterize Sara as a bookworm, who has already read all about London.

Sara's outfit, too, seems to have a function in defining her character. In the pilot, she wears a burgundy dress with rich embroidery on the front, a light-yellow overcoat and fur hat to match. It is worth noting that Sara changes clothes quite often in the first arc of the series, sometimes even in the same episode. Considering the efforts of animating characters with different clothes, and thus different designs, this seems a reasoned choice, suggestive of Sara's genteel status. Instead, Ralph Crewe, who in the book is represented as a young man with a boyish attitude, looks much more of an adult in the animation, as is typical of the father figures in *WMT* series. Tall and elegant, Mr Crewe does not talk much, but has an air of authority, which appears softened by his love for Sara. The relationship between the two, which in the original it tinged by a cheerful note, here is depicted in more mature terms, as if Sara, after her mother's premature death, had a

FIGURE 6.1A *Mr Burrow and Miss Minchin reflected in a lamp (Episode 1).*

FIGURE 6.1B *Sara at the Savoy hotel (Episode 1).*

vicarious function as an angel in the house, according to the renegotiation of the character in Japan.

The way Sara is welcomed at school also detaches from the original. In the series, Sara is intrigued by the French lessons she overhears from the outside of the building, a hint of the fact that the teacher will become a supportive character. However, in the book, Sara is not enthusiastic about Miss Minchin's institution since the very beginning, and, being a perceptive child, she foresees that the headmistress has a harsh personality just by looking at her 'ugly' furniture ('the very armchairs seemed to have hard bones in them', reveals the omniscient narrator in Chapter I). Here, as is often the case with popular fairy tales, the notion of ugliness has a moral connotation, bespeaking of the antagonist's real nature. On the contrary, in the series the school is a plain Victorian house, mainly modelled after the hotel where the Japanese staff stayed in York,[38] without allusions to Miss Minchin's evilness. Besides, Sara gives Miss Minchin long inquisitive stares, but does not voice her disappointment as Burnett's Sara does.

Although surprised at Mr Crewe's fabulous gifts for his daughter, Miss Minchin is careful not to breathe a word about her disappointment. She shows her true colours only when young Peter offers his services in lieu of his father as the future driver of Sara's carriage. As seen, Peter is a character invented for the animation, and has a sad backstory. His mother is ill, and his father suffers from an injury. So, Peter, being reliable and independent as many *WMT* kids,

---

[38]Ibid., 71.

is eager to work to help his family. Miss Minchin tries to dismiss him, but Sara convinces his dad so that the boy can have the job. The scene is built to raise empathy: the viewers are likely to feel compassion for Peter's dramatic situation, just as Sara does, siding with the protagonist. At the same time, Miss Minchin's point that Peter is too young to drive a carriage is not completely dismissed. The woman is certainly not depicted as a positive role model, but her introductory behaviour sounds, if not sensible, more redolent of a rigid disciplinarian like Miss Rottenmaier in *Heidi*, rather than of a mere hideous villain. This ambiguity will be deepened throughout the series.

The episode ends with Sara promising her father that she will study hard and do her best until she will be able to go back to India as his companion, a declaration of intents which adds to her inner maturity. Mr Crewe's encouragement leads Sara to suppress her feelings in order not to worry him. Such abnegation is a trademark of the character, and albeit echoing the omoiyari attitude discussed for *Akage no An*, it will be given a clear Christian connotation in the series, as will be seen in the following paragraphs.

From soldier to saint

Contrary to Miss Minchin, Sara in the series becomes a fully high mimetic character, taking to the extremes the great kindness of Burnett's characterization. As happens in the book, Sara's best friends (Ermengarde, Lotti and Becky) have typified personalities, which are conducive to highlight her virtues. Sara is a patient tutor for the bottom of the school (Ermengarde), a motherly figure for an orphan child (Lottie), and a friendly equal to a lowly maid (Becky). However, differently from the novel – where, at times at least, Sara has to suppress her anger – Japanese Sara totally lacks emotions of rage. This is even more remarkable if we consider the major length of the animation, and the consequent higher number of trials for the girl to go through. As the theme of the series is 'female jealousy,' it is Sara's flawless personality that fuels the dramatic tension, stirring up a violent reaction in those who envy both her wealth and white soul, including Miss Minchin and Lavinia, the rich girl revered by all students. Diegetically, this creates a loop of teasing and pressure on Sara, with them trying in vain to break her spirit in a spiralling climax of abuse.

It is worth mentioning that, in the 1980s, many Japanese viewers recognized these aggressive behaviours as 虐め (*ijime* [bullying]), a hot topic in the media, where concerns arose about the competitive nature of the national educational system.[39] Kurokawa was quite disappointed with this

---

[39] Kaori Okano and Motonori Tsuchiya, *Education in Contemporary Japan. Inequality and Diversity* (Cambridge: Cambridge University Press, 1999), 194.

reading of the show: some fans even sent him threatening letters containing razorblades to セーラをいじめるな (*Sēra o ijimeru na* [stop bullying Sara]) while 僕たちの考えたテーマを正しく理解している人は、そうそういないんじゃないか (*bokutachi no kangaeta tēma o sei ku rikai shite iru hito wa, sō sō inai n janai ka* [very few people fully understood the theme (he and Nakanishi) came up with]). Nonetheless, Sara's attitude towards violence is certainly tackled from a new angle in the adaptation. In the novel, when Sara is transformed from princess to pauper, she uses her imagination to soldier on, making a comparison between her situation and that of Marie Antoinette in prison. An emblem of resistance to vulgar tyranny rather than a tyrant herself, Sara's romantic portrait of the French queen is functional to representing her innate nobility against Miss Minchin's ignoble cruelty.[40] Although all of this is visualized in the series, Japanese Sara's non-violent conduct is consistent with her Christian faith.

In fact, a main difference between the book and the adaptation is that the first, as is often the case in Edwardian children's fiction,[41] has no clear religious framework (significantly, with her exemplary role and all her difficulties, Burnett's Sara never prays), while the latter depicts Sara as a model Christian, who periodically goes to church, is often seen in prayer, and makes other people pray for her too (e.g. a helpful dressmaker crosses himself and invokes God to assist her). Remember that, in writing her novel, Burnett was influenced by spiritualistic movements of her time. In particular, Sara's optimism and her success story share affinities with Burnett's fascination for the New Thought, an American movement which stressed the importance of positive thinking as conducive to happiness, healing and wealth. This is evident, although embedded in the fairy-tale trope of coincidence, as Sara 'supposes' to find a coin in the ground, just to see it a moment later (Chapter XIII).

This beat, which is placed at the lowest point of Sara's narrative arc, is dramatized differently in the series, where Sara brings the coin to church as a donation (Episode 23). Realizing that she is poor and kind, a benevolent priest – a recurring character created for the animation – tells her that the coin has been dropped by God for someone with a 心が美しい (*kokoro ga utsukushī* [beautiful heart]) to find it. This gives a Christian taste to the following scene in which Sara breaks bread with a poor child, as well as a shōjo connotation to the character through a word choice bespeaking a gentle model of femininity. Sara's saintly superiority to worldly things reaches its zenith in the finale: whereas Burnett's book ends with Sara's being adopted, and nothing is said about Miss Minchin's school (although it is assumed it will fall to ruin), Japanese Sara forgives all her past torturers,

---

[40] Gruner, 'Cinderella, Marie Antoinette, and Sara'.
[41] Gavin and Humphries, *Childhood in Edwardian Fiction*.

announcing that not only she will be attending Miss Minchin's institute again, but she will also support it with a large donation (Episode 46).

At the same time, Sara's almost martyr-like virtue to endure hardships seems to overlap with the Japanese cultural concepts of *kenagesa* and *gambaru*, or the restless effort to overcome obstacles. An important value in children's education, persistence is fostered since pre-school in Japan, as it is considered superior to one's innate abilities.[42] The reason behind this is that work of any kind is regarded as requiring 100 effort; therefore a person may be valued by the degree of commitment he or she invests in that activity.[43] In the series, Sara is invited to *gambaru* (resist) by numerous adults who share a pedagogical role in her life, including her father (Episodes 1–2), her French teacher, Mr Dufarge (Episodes 26–27), and the dressmaker (Episode 34). Such figures are all present in the book, but none of them stimulates Sara as much as what happens in the series. Conveniently located at key points of the narrative, this form of encouragement often occurs at the end of an episode, taking over the function of a moral epilogue.

From storyteller to teacher

Further evidence of the greater emphasis placed by the adaptation on the idea of 'doing one's best,' can be found in Sara's devotion to study. Whereas Burnett's Sara is blessed with a sort of superior intelligence, which requires virtually no effort for her to achieve, Japanese Sara, as she begins to work as a servant, is forced to study at night, falling asleep at her desk (Episode 25). Sara's condition, which must have looked familiar to many Japanese viewers, closely recalls that of 二宮 尊徳 (Ninomiya Sontoku) (1787–1856), a famous philosopher of the nineteenth century, and a moral exemplar portrayed in countless statues in local schoolyards, who was himself an orphan child and completely self-taught, studying when he wasn't working for his uncle. The notion that 勉強 (*benkyō* [learning]) is a form of self-refinement is particularly relevant in Japan[44] and concurs to define Sara as a morally good character. This way, her peculiar passivity, attributed either to Western religious beliefs or to a Japanese cultural pattern, comes to embody a positive role model, able to inspire nurturance and indulgence in the good characters of the series.

The greater attention paid to Sara's erudition is matched with a marginalization of her narrative abilities, which in the series are mostly placed at the service of her educative function. This is clear when Sara, as a student-teacher, tells her pupils the story of Alfred the Great, king of

---

[42]Lewis, *Educating Hearts and Minds*, 48.
[43]White, *The Japanese Educational Challenge*, 34.
[44]Ibid., 51.

FIGURE 6.2A *Sara prays at church (Episode 15). The church was modelled after St James Piccadilly Church, which was close to the market where Sara goes shopping for Miss Minchin.*

FIGURE 6.2B *Professor Dufarge encourages Sara to be brave (Episode 27). Lavinia prompted Miss Minchin to fire the teacher because he favoured Sara in class.*

the Anglo-Saxons in the ninth century, slapped by a peasant woman who ignored his true identity. Burnett's Sara figures out for herself to be in a similar situation as the nobleman: her trained politeness, which prevents her from being violent, is what makes her a royal, but Miss Minchin, just like the peasant woman, is incapable to see through her tattered look (Chapter

XI). Also, Sara is amused at the thought of Miss Minchin's ignorance, and even breaks into a little laugh when the woman boxes her ears, stunning the headmistress with her genteel, yet cutting, words:

> 'I will beg your pardon for laughing, if it was rude [. . .] but I won't beg your pardon for thinking'. [. . .] 'I was thinking what would happen if I were a princess and you boxed my ears – what I should do to you. And I was thinking that if I were one, you would never dare to do it, whatever I said or did. And I was thinking how surprised and frightened you would be if you suddenly found out'. She had the imagined future so clearly before her eyes that she spoke in a manner which had an effect even upon Miss Minchin. It almost seemed for the moment to her narrow, unimaginative mind that there must be some real power hidden behind this candid daring.

Whereas the book seems to stress that Sara is not only a born princess, but also a gifted storyteller whose imagination allows her to rebel against oppression, the latter element appears less evident in the series, which focuses on Sara's role as an educator, albeit more vulnerable than Burnett's character, and unable to defend herself (Episode 26). More specifically, Miss Minchin enters the room where Sara is doing her class and hits her on the cheek – so hard that the girl falls on the floor – scolding her for 遊ばせる (*asobaseru* [playing]) with the students. It is Mr Dufarge who comes to her rescue, praising Sara as a 素晴らしい先生 (*subarashī sensei* [wonderful teacher]) and explaining how お話 (*ohanashi* [telling stories]) is 授業を楽しく為にわ必要なことですよ (*jugyō o tanoshiku suru ni wa hitsuyōna koto desu yo* [necessary to make classes enjoyable]). The man also sees the parallel between Sara and the king, pointing it out to Miss Minchin: he is sure she would have never hit her, if Sara were the same *musume* (daughter or girl) she was before. It is worth noting that musume's elitist meaning as 'girl of a good family' adds to the shōjo aura of the character, who avoids confrontation, and needs to be helped by a righteous male teacher that is liable to undermine Miss Minchin's authoritarian ways.

Between realism and melodrama

As seen, Sara had been planned out to raise the ratings of *WMT*, providing a change in direction from prior shows. This resulted, among other things, in choosing Kurokawa and Nakanishi as members of the staff, professionals who were experts in adaptations of Western stories, but had not yet been closely involved in the *WMT*. In particular, scriptwriter Nakanishi was credited in seven series by Nippon Animation, including the final episode of *Flanders*, the most tragic work of *WMT*. But he also had an expertise in crime films (usually dealing with yakuza, or Japanese organized crime syndicates), and in local 怪獣映画 (*kaijū eiga* [strange beast movies]), like ゴジラ (*Goijra* [*Godzilla*]) (1984). Albeit humorously, the same Kurokawa noted how Nakanishi, who had long worked for Nikkatsu, the oldest film studio in Japan, was used to portray a 男の世界 (*otoko no sekai* [male world]), which was at odds with *Sara*'s feminine themes. However, Nakanishi's extensive frequentation of action-packed narratives, together with Kurokawa's creative decisions, seem to have left a mark on *Sara* in terms of writing style and genre conventions.

On the one hand, Sara's misadventures are magnified in the series. This had a twofold function: first, to inoculate tension and accelerate the rhythm of the story; second, to strengthen the audience's attachment to Sara by stressing her moral qualities. For the same reason, Sara's enemies are more vicious than in the book, tormenting her in an escalation of cruelty, while new arcs are added in the adaptation, including cliff-hangers, suspense, last-minute rescues and other compelling plot devices typical of melodrama.[45] To some extent, this also applies to Victorian literature, which abounded with suffering orphans and inspired Burnett's book in the first place. But Sara's trials are pale in comparison with her miserable condition in the series, if we

FIGURE 6.3A *Sara wakes up on her desk after a night studying (Episode 25).*

---

[45] John Mercer and Martin Shingler, *Melodrama: Genre, Style and Sensibility* (London and New York: Wallflower, 2004).

FIGURE 6.3B *The story of King Alfred told by Sara (Episode 26).*

consider that, in what we can call the 'all is lost' moment[46] (Episode 35), the girl has to face, in chronological order: a severe illness, a malicious servant accusing her of faking it, a drunken doctor visiting her, and Miss Minchin blaming her for causing troubles, because she has been diagnosed with a deadly disease. None of this happens in the novel, with the effect of linking the Japanese character closer to the damsel-in-distress melodramatic trope.

On the other hand, to meet the expectations of the *WMT* programme, Sara displays a careful representation of a foreign world for the viewers to enjoy not only as a form of exoticism, but also as an educative show. This is evident in the numerous British locales portrayed in the series, such as the churches where Sara prays, or Becky's hometown in the countryside. These are locations that had been seen in real life by the Japanese staff, including art director 川本征平 Kawamoto Shōhei (born 1938),[47] and add to the realism of the adaptation. So, the viewers may recognize St Paul Cathedral (Episode 2) and St James Church in Piccadilly (Episodes 15–23), while Hayworth inspired Becky's village (Episodes 29–30). Even the expensive toys for Sara's birthday (Episode 11) are from Hamleys, a famous toy shop, and her doll's house looks like a small-scale reproduction of Windsor Castle. It is worth saying that, as was customary for meisaku series, the level of factual truth is subject to several limitations to meet the needs of the story. For example, Miss Minchin's Seminary is conveniently located next to St

---

[46] As in Snyder Blake, *Save the Cat!: The Last Book on Screenwriting That You'll Ever Need* (Studio City: Michael Wiese Productions, 2005), 86.
[47] Chiba, *Sekai meisaku gekijō e no tabi*, 74.

James Park, which is actually in Westminster, and the same school building mixes different ambients visited by the crew in York.[48] The Savoy is a real hotel in London and one of the most glamorous in the world, but it did not open until 1889, while the events of the animation are dated 1880 (Episode 1). To emphasize Sara's pitiable situation, the series goes to the point of showing a Queen's Guard leaving his sentry box in front of Buckingham Palace to help the girl when she falls in the heavy rain (Episode 21).

However, as usually happened in *WMT* adaptations, these poetic licenses do not undermine the verisimilitude of the show. In fact, an ethnographic approach watermarks the whole series, hidden (or exhibited) in several little details of everyday life, e.g., the lamplighter swathed in mist (Episode 10), or Sara holding a teapot with a tea-cosy (Episode 29). This emerges clearly if we consider Sara's ups-and-downs as a maid of all works, which are visualized and expanded in the animation. Here, the girl is repeatedly shown struggling with her everyday chores, such as serving at table, cleaning the rooms or washing dishes, but also delivering mails, collecting the coal and carrying heavy baskets of food in any weather. This stresses her hardships, as well as give us a glimpse of daily life in the Victorian age. Moreover, various Western festivities are incorporated to the main plot, as is the case of May Day (Episode 10), Halloween (Episode 41) and Christmas (Episode 46). Especially the last episode, where Sara forgives Miss Minchin, attaches a Christian meaning to the finale, with the girls singing もろびとこぞりて (Morobito kozorite [Joy to the World]) in front of a painting of the Nativity, which seems modelled on the German painter Matthias Grünewald's Isenheim altarpiece (*c.* 1515).

The overall realistic portrait of London, which almost becomes a character on its own, departs substantially from the book. This blends well with Kurokawa's directing, showing both the upper-class circles, and the poor people behind them. In fact, whereas Becky is Sara's only connection with the lower class in the novel, Sara meets a completely new arena of street kids, shops and open-air markets (such as Covent Garden, where the girl is often sent shopping), offering a chance to depict a composite society. Another note of realism in the series lies in the ambivalent characterization of Miss Minchin. According to Kurokawa, 彼女の置かれた環境が、彼女の性格をそうさせてしまったんです (*kanojo no oka reta kankyō ga, kanojo no seikaku o sō sa sete shimatta ndesu* [her personality was moulded by her environment]), which makes her different from Sara. While the girl in the series never changes (at least, not in terms of character development) because she is a purely good shōjo type, who will always remain innocent and young in the eyes of the viewers, a mercantile world changed Miss Minchin, turning her into a businesswoman who does

---

[48]Ibid.

not prioritize goodness, in spite of Sara's forgiving her in the end (Episode 46). In this light, Sara can be interpreted as a travelling angel who, contrarily to the trope's conventions, has no impact on her troubled community. This makes the narrative universe of the adaptation an ambiguous place, which is both melodramatic and painfully realistic, in the way it seems unaffected by Sara's silent acts of kindness.

Fairy-tale motifs

Although Sara is mostly connoted with teaching, fairy-tale motifs are scattered throughout the series. This seems to depend on the importance of storytelling in the novel, which explores the theme deeply, making clear that Sara's ability to tell stories is by far her best quality. Not only stories, being a source of hope, help her in troubled times, but Sara 'adored telling them,' seeing and living 'with the fairy folk' (Chapter V). Initially ostracized for their lack of explicit morals, fairy tales were gradually institutionalized as children's fiction, becoming an integral part of Victorian fantasy. They acquired a special meaning for Burnett, serving as a bulwark against the difficulties of the world.[49] In fact, from a narrative perspective, *A Little Princess* has a fairy-tale structure (the same term 'fairy' occurs twenty-two times). Fairy tales depict fantastic aspects of the human world, usually invisible to anyone except the protagonist, who is presented as a young,

FIGURE 6.4A *Sara is trapped in the stable when Lavinia and her minions inadvertently cause a fire (Episode 41).*

---

[49]Gerzina, *Francis Hodgson Burnett*, 112.

FIGURE 6.4B *Young Miss Minchin and her sister (Episode 40).*

pleasant character in the act of undertaking a quest. The happy ending, which rewards the deserving and punishes the transgressors, ratifies the moral propriety of the universe. Likewise, kind-hearted Sara falls from grace and then sees her fortune restored as a result of cosmic justice.

Although there are no supernatural elements, a plethora of marvellous coincidences take place in the book. This is evident in the second half of the story, where Mr Carrisford and Ram Dass serve as pseudo-magical agents. In particular, Ram Dass's plan of making Sara's visions come true creates a series of fantastic situations (e.g. a scrumptious meal appearing from nowhere) that can be linked to fairy-tale tropes. Sympathetic animals, such as the mice in Sara's attic, are also typical of fairy tales. To some extent, *A Little Princess* can be thus considered an Edwardian fairy tale. Blurring the edges between realism and fantasy, it relocates a classic plot in a modern setting, with exotic characters in lieu of magicians, serendipities as supernatural trappings and make-believe as magic. Fairy tales are also directly mentioned in the book, such as the *Arabian Nights* – which are linked to Captain Crewe's affair with diamond mines (Chapter IV), and to Ram Dass's transforming Sara's garret in a comfortable place (Chapter XIV) – and a story about a mermaid princess, read by Sara to her schoolmates, sparking Becky's interest (Chapter V).

In the animation, too, fairy-tale motifs have a narrative function and give life to dedicated mini-arcs, taking on a similar role as dream sequences in *WMT* shows. Fairy tales are typically associated with fantasy, which is conveyed through audiovisual codes including different directing styles, music, or changes in the design of both characters and background art. For example, let us consider the treatment of the Cinderella archetype, which, as seen, underpins the original novel. On a macro level, the series maintains this narrative structure, with the protagonist achieving power and wealth, losing it all and gaining it back in the finale. Real changes are introduced on a micro level, when the focus shifts from princess Sara to the scullery maid Becky. In fact, Becky is explicitly compared to Cinderella since the day she arrives in London in Episode 6, titled 灰かぶりベッキー (Hai-kaburi Bekkī [Becky, Covered in Ash]), drawing inspiration from the book, where her face is always described as 'smudgy' (Chapter V). Moreover, in the series the girl comes from a fictional village called Ashfield, a symbolic name suggestive of Cinderella.

The association is made clearer in the scene where Becky is scolded for listening to Sara's story while she is replenishing the fire (Chapter V/Episode 8). While Burnett's Sara tells a story about mermaids, the animation replaces this with 'Cinderella', which seems to imply a thematic choice. In line with the characterization of Sara as a knowledgeable student, the girl explains the German etymology of the name シンデレラ (*Shinderera* [Cinderella]), which means 灰かぶり娘 (*hai-kaburi musume* [girl covered in ashes]). The fairy tale is visualized in a series of still frames, alternating with Becky's working routine. On the one hand, this story within a story visually differentiates from the rest of the show, featuring a distinctive visual style, in which it is possible to recognize Mori's hand, and a sepia-shaded colour palette. On the other hand, the viewers are guided to spot the similarities between Becky and Cinderella, which is also the reason why the servant girl finds herself hooked in the tale.

In the series, Sara can also be associated with Cinderella (e.g. Episode 3), but she is mostly connected with another story, Andersen's 'The Little Match Girl' (1845). This fairy tale is evoked at various key points of the series which have no direct equivalence in the book. The first one to quote it is Donald Carmichael, the youngest son of Mr Carrisford's solicitor, who gives Sara alms because she reminded him of the Danish character, which leads to a dedicated fairy-tale sequence (Episode 18). Meanwhile, a cross-cutting editing shows Sara – hungry, weak and overworked – who walks around the city, between luxury houses and shops, until she sways and falls to the ground, surrounded by general indifference. Again, the audience is actively driven to recognize the parallels between Sara's condition and the tragic fairy tale. The adaptation takes this one step further, when, later in the series, Sara eventually leaves Miss Minchin's school and becomes a real match girl (Episode 43). Just like the protagonist of Andersen's story, she tries to sell matches in the street on a freezing winter's day, shivering and covered in snow. The music underlines the sadness of the moment, as the emotional theme of the opening (花のささやき, Hana no sasayaki [Whisper of a flower]) is repeated here, casting a light on Sara's thoughts and desires.[50]

---

[50]The ending lines in the song seem especially poignant: 私だって幸せほしいけど / 他にもっと　大事なものがある / それが愛か　優しい心かは / 生きてみれば　わかると思う

Why insert the Danish fairy tale in the animation? There seems to be a three-fold explanation for this reference. First, both Andersen's story and the animation tackle similar themes, telling about the dreams and hopes of a suffering young girl. Second, as seen, Andersen's tales enjoyed special fame in Japan since the Meiji period, being traditionally associated to children's fiction. Third, Burnett's novel features a number of motifs that, intentional or not, can be easily interpreted as influences from Andersen, such as Sara's mermaid story and Ram Dass's magic, which is redolent of the consoling visions of 'The Little Match Girl'. Fairy tales can also be evoked in a number of additional motifs. For example, when she tries to calm Ermengarde, who is afraid of rats, Sara tells a fantastic story about them (Episode 17). Lotte, too, when feeling sad for Sara's reversal of fate, has a bad dream mixing images from 'Little Red Riding Hood' and 'Snow White' (Episode 16).

An unsatisfying ending?

The ending is perhaps the most important part of a classic narrative structure. Set-ups are paid off, conflicts are solved, battles are over and the main character has changed in the process. This is very clear in fairy tales. After a number of trials, the hero returns to the ordinary world, while the villain is punished for his or her evil deeds. The audience sighs with relief: the story is over, and be it happy or tragic, a good ending always feels right for that plot, just like the glass slipper fits Cinderella's foot. However, as a product of the Edwardian age, Sara has neither a Fairy Godmother nor a Prince to help her, but she can count on other allies, including an Indian gentleman who will adopt her and make her rich. Obviously there is no romance involved, but it is assumed that Carrisford and Sara will live happily ever after as father and daughter, while Miss Minchin's school will fall to ruin.

The series preserves a similar 'Deus ex Empire' narrative device as in novel,[51] but introduces a number of changes that seem to alter the meaning of the finale. This is particularly relevant if we consider that, in visual storytelling, a good ending has an impact on the audience. The viewers are left with a physical image which will stick with them for a very long time, epitomizing the sense of what they have seen. The finale of the animation covers the last three episodes (Episodes 44–46), following the last three

---

(Watashi datte shiawase hoshī kedo / Hoka ni motto daiji na koto ga aru / Sore ga ai ka yasashii kokoro ka wa / Ikite mireba wakaru to omō [Even if I want happiness, too / There are other, more important things / Is this love? Is this a kind heart? / As long as I can move on, I think I will find out]).

[51] Ariko Kawabata, 'The Story of the Indian Gentleman: Recovery of the English Masculine Identity in A Little Princess', *Children's Literature in Education* 32, no. 4 (2001): 291.

FIGURE 6.5A *Ram Dass and his monkey pay a visit to Sara's attic (Episode 31). Ram Dass, who will embellish Sara's room when the girl is ill, is presented as a prince from the* Arabian Nights.

FIGURE 6.5B *Sara tells a story to Ermengarde, who is afraid of mice, to put her at ease (Episode 17). Note the similarities between Meru's family, designed by Mori, and the characters of* Rocky Chuck.

chapters of the book (XVII–XIX), but intervenes on the events narrated, their chronological order and their duration in time. In particular, Sara's reversal of fate occurs in Chapter XVII/Episode 44, with the girl returning Ram Dass's monkey to her neighbour, and being saluted as the child that

Carrisford and Carmichael were looking for the whole time. Episode 45 is dedicated to Miss Minchin and Amelia finding out the truth about Sara. In the book, Sara and Carrisford are present, while Carmichael explains that the girl has just inherited a fortune. When Miss Minchin tries and turns this around, flattering Sara so that she will return to her, the protagonist looks her 'steadily in the face' and gives her a firm no. Miss Minchin faces Amelia's meltdown, and a letter from Sara brings the news to the students.

In the series, the revelation is split into different scenes. First, Carmichael tells Miss Minchin about Sara in the presence of Carrisford. After the woman's timid suggestion that Sara will reward her for her help, she is confronted with the girl, covered with diamonds, as she is descending a staircase with Ram Dass and other servants following her. Taken aback by the surprise, the headmistress falls to her knees, uttering ダイヤモンドプリンセス (*daiyamondo purinsesu* [diamond princess]), while the camera angle underlines her lower position. Soon after, a letter is delivered at Miss Minchin's school, a pay-off of Sara's writing to the police to have news about his father (Episode 19). Intrigued, Lavinia urges Amelia to read the letter, so that everyone discovers the truth before Miss Minchin's arrival. A long beat follows with the woman staggering in the street and falling in the snow. Then comes Amelia's emotional outburst, which causes Miss Minchin to start crying uncontrollably. This way, the animation implements the dramatic tension by reproducing the final twist several times, causing a massive ripple effect on Miss Minchin's persona, who eventually appears in all her weakness. This is a major change from what happens in the novel, where the headmistress only looks baffled by Amelia's flare-up.

The variants are greater in Episode 46. Whereas in the book the curtain has fallen on Miss Minchin and her school (except from Becky, who becomes Sara's personal attendant), the last episode opens with the students putting up the Christmas decorations. Miss Minchin and Amelia have swapped roles, the first one looking sad and apathetic, and the latter busy with the celebration. Then, Carrisford announces that Sara will be attending Miss Minchin's school again, albeit residing at his house, and will donate 100,000 pounds to it. Everyone rejoices, so that Lavinia and her minions are willing to change sides. After the party, where Miss Minchin's servants make an appearance dressed up as Santa Claus, Sara and Carrisford go for a carriage ride. When they reach the bun's lady, it is her adoptive father, not Sara, who suggests that the bakery can give bread to the hungry kids, offering to cover the expenses. Finally, Sara, Carrisford and Becky leave for India, where they will stay for a few months to sort out some formalities about Sara's inheritance. Amelia, Miss Minchin, the students, Peter and others have all come to say goodbye, while Lavinia will return to America, teasing Sara that in ten years she will be the wife of the president of the United States. While the ship is sailing, a close-up on Sara reveals that she has tears in her eyes, followed by a musical montage on her difficult journey.

What happens here is a circular ending. Sara on the boat, her ride through the town with a father figure and the party at school, are just a few of the narrative threads that are paid off in the finale. However, whereas in the book it is assumed that Miss Minchin and her lot will be punished by fate, in the series they are all forgiven – and even rewarded – by Sara. In addition, Sara does very little to win her battle, acting like nothing happened until the very end. This can be disappointing for the viewers, whose narrative expectations are set on heroes making their own choices. It is worth stressing that, in the series, the villains receive no moral sanction for their wickedness, but are treated generously, while, in a classic story, the public would expect to see that the antagonists are defeated as a form of social justice. Significantly, in the Grimm's version of the tale, Cinderella's stepmother and sisters are made blind. Even if we look at this from Miss Minchin's perspective, there is no way to know for sure if the character changed by the end of the story, or if she is just behaving hypocritically. According to director Kurokawa, it is highly improbable that Miss Minchin has repented for her actions. In a similar way, it seems difficult to think that Lavinia will suddenly become friendly after having tormented Sara for the whole series.

Even though Sara chooses not to take revenge on her adversaries, at some points in the series a sort of karma seems to be at work, penalizing the villains for their evil deeds, as is often the case with *WMT* shows. For example, Molly, one of Miss Minchin's servant, hurts her foot while stealing Ram Dass's dinnerware from Sara's garret, and her companion James hits his finger while blocking up Sara's window (Episode 39). Something similar happens when Peter accidentally – and providentially – dirties with soot Lavinia's and Miss Minchin's rooms, as well as the kitchen where Molly and James work (Episode 37). Since the troubles involved are never serious, these little incidents can be viewed as a source of comic relief, but also as a way to offer a form of punishment for perceived injustice, without affecting Sara's gentleness. In fact, while the paucity of these occasions makes it difficult to ponder their effective weight in a series dominated by dramatic tones, what is consistent throughout the episodes, including the finale, is Sara's characterization as a Christian figure, who always behaves kindly and forgives her persecutors. In this light, her financial support to Miss Minchin's school seems to show her saintlike superiority to worldly things, as well as her passion for study and teaching, which are emphasized in the animation.

CONCLUSIONS

Some interesting aspects emerged from the analysis of the *WMT* case, which are detailed below. First, the adaptation of children's fiction into Japanese animation was facilitated by a number of factors. As happens in audiovisual media, children's fiction in Japan has been usually intended as a multisensorial experience, provided by sounds (words) and images (illustration). This resulted, as observed in Chapter 1, in the frequent intersections between literature, illustrated books and comics, rather than in parallel developments between texts of different forms.

Strictly connected to this formal element is the opposition between what has been variously defined as high, proper or pure literature, and other commercial types of fiction, entertainment-oriented and so deemed to be inferior in artistic excellence and moral teachings, which were considered as important elements in children's fiction. Another distinction between high and low literature was the physical publication of children's stories in books in the first case and magazines in the latter. While books are meant to stay, and thus bigger in format and lavishly illustrated, magazines are ephemera which are supposed to be discarded after reading. This contributed to shape the perceived value of children's books as literature of quality.

Both high and low forms of children's fiction were interested by the adoption of the same mode of publication: seriality. Serialization commodified cultural products such as books and comics, pushing boundaries between art and commerce. Especially the enpon phenomenon, and the related rise of multivolume book sets for children, stimulated book collection and competition between publishers. As the examination has shown, many Western texts appeared in these anthologies, popularizing stories, genres and reading patterns, in the wake of the Westernization policies pursued in Japan. In particular, the widespread diffusion of zenshū, or 'complete works', was linked with their promotion as a form of moral and cultural enrichment, taking advantage of the demand for comprehensive knowledge among the general public.

To some extent, serialization made books similar to magazines, and vice versa. Children's magazines were stored and re-read over time. Artistic journals, which saw the participation of renown novelists and poets, have been highly regarded by critics of children's literature. Moreover, as happened with serial novels in the West, literary instalments and manga encouraged consumption of increasingly longer forms of fiction while the best stories or 'masterpieces' would be later published in book form, blurring the lines between media.

That series and classics could go together seems like a relevant topic for the understanding of meisaku animation, and even more so if we take the positive connotation of Western books into account. Recently developed and readily available, Western children's literature became a benchmark in Japan since the Meiji period. As such, it was widely translated and repackaged in the increasingly diversified publishing formats available: stand-alone publications, magazine serializations and book series. The corollary of this was the circulation of ideas and ideals of childhood, motherhood, education and morals, which were conveyed by Western children's literature. As seen, the connection between children and female-oriented fiction led to the rise of girls' culture in Japan. This helped explain the dual target of the *WMT* and the representation of shōjo characters in the series of the programme.

As indicated in this research, there is consistency between the titles included in the *WMT* and in Japanese book series, particularly those published after the Occupation. Although the influence of American culture cannot be framed as a mere top-down phenomenon, the GHQ played a key role in fostering children's books from the English-speaking world. Their definition as classics was endorsed by post-war publishers, teachers and children's specialists, from the critical work of Ishii Momoko, chief editor of *Iwanami shōnen bunko*, to the large popularity of Kōdansha's book collections. This way, Western, and especially English, stories and characters left a legacy on generations of children, and on the way they would see children's literature, which is pivotal in understanding the positive view of the *WMT* among the gatekeepers of children's fiction – creators and families.

The linkage between children's fiction and animation became clear when we considered Japan's animation landscape prior to the *WMT*. In Chapter 2, a closer look at the animated works produced in the first fifty years of Japan's animation showed that fairy tales and folktales were a source of inspiration up to the war period. This mirrored a parallel situation, described in Chapter 1, whereby Taishō and early Shōwa writers and publishers valorized Japanese children's tales, or dōwa, as a form of highbrow literature. Conversely, in the post-war, it was Western fiction from the anglophone area that provided increasingly more contents for animation, creating a favourable context for the emergence of the *WMT*.

The influence of American cinema and television is another important factor. Hollywood film adaptations, which were released after the war, contributed to the hegemony of Western children's literature. This assisted our evaluation of meisaku series, which dramatized Western novels that had been often adapted by American filmmakers. The implication is that adaptations made in the United States either maintained or guaranteed the canonical status of the children's books on which the American films were based.

This holds especially true for American animation. As seen, Japanese animators started to emulate Disney and the Fleischer brothers as early as in the 1930s, experimenting with adaptations of children's stories and animal fables, both Japanese and from the West. American cinematic school, which aimed for smooth, realistic movements and an illusionistic sense of depth, was equated with quality animation and promptly imitated. Japanese animation also absorbed the anthropomorphic characters of Disney and the Fleischers, with their round and cute style, while subcontracted animation played a part in revealing the export potential of Western children's culture.

All these aspects appeared strongly entwined in the early production of Tōei, one of Japan's majors and the starting point for many talents in the post-war animation industry. The analysis has shown that Tōei set an exemplar which was partly taken up by meisaku animation. This model was highly cinematic and indebted to Disney, whose venture by then had already eclipsed the Fleischers. First, Tōei's movies were morally edifying, fun-oriented and suitable for mainstream audiences. Second, they adopted Disney's trademark cuteness and fluidity of motion, as internalized by Nichidō's veteran animators. Third, they gradually dismissed adaptations of classic Asian narratives in favour of famous stories from the West, which could be more easily marketed overseas.

The most obvious difference between Tōei's output and meisaku animation was in media and format: the first consisted of theatrical films and the latter, TV series. As a matter of fact, television needed more intense and fast-paced schedules than cinema. This is why animation cascaded to Japanese television through the conduit of commercials and animetic serials, be they imported American cartoons or manga-to-anime adaptations á la Tezuka. In particular, this research delved on the ties between advertising and TV series, where contents and budgetary restraints had to do, respectively, with sponsorship requirements and the choice of a limited animation technique (less drawings per second), in spite of the singular agendas of the animators. The analysis also found that there were other studios which aimed at replicating Disney's success, though specializing in television animation. An example was the establishment of TCJ and its attempt to take over Ashida Manga, which recalled the relation between Tōei and Nichidō.

The influence of TCJ, Tōei and other Japanese companies within the *WMT* was further investigated in Chapter 3, which reconstructed the context where the project was born. This provided a deeper insight into the ways that adaptation of Western fiction transitioned from theatrical to television production. In particular, the study indicated the key role of former TCJ member Takahashi and his studio, Zuiyō, in forging a link between children's literature and animated series for international young audiences. His venture benefitted from two factors: the interest of Western studios for outsourcing and co-producing animation with Japan, exploiting the country's affordable workforce and know-how, and the investment from domestic advertising agencies and sponsors in funding and promoting TV series for children.

This is where the involvement of Calpis came into play. Founded by a Meiji industrialist who epitomized the idealism of the day and Japan's openness to Westernization, Calpis became the sole sponsor of the *Calpis Theater*, a TV programme consisting of animated series for the company's double target – children and mothers. The analysis shed new light on the relations between Calpis and Zuiyō, Dentsu and Fuji TV, which served, respectively, as the show's planner/producer, advertiser and broadcaster. All these companies contributed in determining the future *WMT* – as the project was renamed after Calpis quitted its sponsorship – impacting its creative decisions, educational policy and media mix. For example, the evaluation of Calpis' corporate image, in relation to the animated series and the commercials aired during the programme, strengthened the idea that the *Calpis Theater* was a form of branded entertainment.

When considering its approach to adaptation, it could be argued that the *Calpis Theater* paralleled the trajectory of Tōei's early animation, turning to Eastern stories first, and then to Western children's literature. This might have been incidental, and yet allowed for re-circulation of ideas on children's literature which were popular in the post-war, when the generations of people who worked on the project came of age. So, the *Calpis Theater* started as entrenched in local stories (*Dororo*) to welcome Western fairy tales and novels. The study also pointed out to Japan's fascination with the Scandinavian model, well attested in series such as *Moomin* or *Andersen stories*, and to the frequent use, in the discourse on the programme, of the word *ryōshin*, or conscientious, echoing the homonymous literary genre and demanding that children's fiction could (and should) communicate edifying values. All this came with a particular representation of the child as playful and independent, which displayed points in common with Western-inspired education and the already recalled critical reading of children's literature in the post-war.

The findings of this investigation complemented those of earlier studies that focused on Takahata and Miyazaki's frequentation of the *WMT*. The study explored their long-lasting contribution as well as that of the various talents which animation, as a collaborative business, implied. These initially came from the animetic lineage (Mushi, Tokyo Movie and TCJ), and then from Tōei's ranks, shaken up by the changes brought on by television. In particular, Mori passed on a tradition of cute but realistic design, especially in the treatment of animal characters, shaping the style of animators such as Kotabe and Seki. From Takahata and Miyazaki came the anthropological attention to Western customs and the lifelike portrayal of the emotions of the characters. This demonstrated that a show like *Heidi*, though being a quantic leap from previous series, did not arise from a vacuum. Instead, it was the result of an assortment of influences and probably Japan's first attempt to make cinematic animation for an increasingly animetic media.

The push towards export and co-production emerged as a dividing line between the works of the *Calpis Theater* produced by Zuiyō first and then by Nippon Animation. In fact, Takahashi aimed at reaching a global audience and attracting foreign, namely European, companies for joint production. The study identified a number of strategies in Zuiyō's shows that are still employed in modern-day international animation, such as the adaptation of Western children's books, typically belonging to the literary tradition of one of the partners involved. Using simplified narratives with a vertical structure is also common, as they can easily generate episodes for long-running formats (significantly, there were two series of *Moomin* in the *Calpis Theater* and two seasons of *Vicke*). Other practices are the homogenization of cultural specificities, such as religion, to bridge the differences between countries and assist relatability, and the use of anthropomorphized animal characters, as is the case in popular fables.

Conversely, the analysis clarified the reasons why only the meisaku series created after *Heidi* have been labelled as official. The study indicated the primary importance, for Calpis, of Japan's domestic audience and of the moral, especially Christian, aspects of Western children's fiction. These demands differed greatly from the globalizing approach described above, and allowed to view the establishment of Nippon Animation, and Zuiyō pulling out of the project, as a compromise solution to accommodate the needs of the sponsor, whose financial support was pivotal for the funding of the shows.

The observations made in Chapter 4 helped to determine the continuity and change in the *WMT* after the shift from Zuiyō to Nippon Animation. The research confirmed the momentousness of the programme within the context of Nippon Animation's production history, highlighting the connection with children's literature as a defining feature of the other shows delivered by the company. As seen, Nippon Animation incorporated and formalized strategic decisions such as location scouting, which Zuiyō pioneered in *Heidi* and added to the documentary feel of the *WMT*. Interestingly, the studio also engaged in co-productions with the European industry and adaptations of fairy tales in TV series outside the *WMT* programme. This suggested that some aspects of Zuiyō's transnational animation were consciously removed from the *WMT* series, to the advantage of their domestic orientation and underlying ideals to bring Western literature to a new generation of Japanese.

The chapter explored the process of creating a *WMT* series from an idea to production, helping to shed some light on the development stage and on the ways in which the network, sponsor, writers and producers worked together to further develop the programme. This provided some evidence for the power of the network and sponsors on creative activities such as the choice of material for adaptation or the style to use. For instance, the study showed that the late insertion of elements typical of shōjo manga, both in terms of character design and narrative tropes, was driven by the demands of Fuji TV, arguably to increase the ratings of the shows. On the contrary, requests for series explicitly catering to boys, such as *Peter Pan*, were few and an exception. This indicated the growing importance of girls as a target audience for the *WMT*.

Chapter 4 also delved on the meisaku approach to the so-called 'classics'. As the analysis demonstrated, in spite of the globalizing label *World Masterpiece Theater*, the 'world' in the title stood for the Western, especially anglophone, countries, as in Ishii's prestigious critique of children's literature. Moreover, although they are usually glossed as 'masterpieces', not all shows of the programme were adaptations of literary classics. In fact, the study found that Nippon Animation's planners and producers would often search for new novels, visiting international fairs or bookstores in search for inspiration. Proposing titles of famous children's books was more common, due to their well-established reputation, when the broadcaster noted a decline in viewing. In both cases, canonization remained the bottom line of the WTM – to create modern classics or to perpetuate texts which had a prominent place in Japanese children's reading.

Further, this chapter identified the tight collaboration between screenwriters and directors of the *WMT* as an innovative factor in the animation landscape, highlighting the influential role played by screenwriter Miyazaki Akira in the cinematic construction of the series of the programme. This raised provoking questions about the relation between the *WMT* and Japanese live-action films, especially realistic comedies and melodramas of the golden age of Japanese cinema, which could be matter for future studies. Another interesting area for research is the comparative examination of the proposals, scripts and storyboards created for the *WMT*. Access to these sources would improve our understanding of the various steps of the pre-production process, as well as the formatting and structural rules of screenwriting, and how they impacted animation.

Drawing on a corpus of twenty-three TV series, the analysis addressed some of the rhetorical devices and storytelling elements that were distinctive of the *WMT*, including strategies of characterization, narrative tropes and recurring themes. Realism, in particular, emerged as a prominent feature. Components such as the mix of overarching and episodic plots, the representation of everyday life, the insertion of objective narrators or the accuracy of geographical and historical referents, all suggested a sense of reality and authenticity. Similar effects were pursued visually, in the character design and animation techniques, as demonstrated, for example, by the presence of animal characters with lesser degrees of anthropomorphism. Likewise, when the series did alter factual reality, for example by creating pastiches of Western locales, it was usually for reasons of narrative coherence.

This aesthetic of place has often been associated with Studio Ghibli's founders' interest in European culture, and calls for further research on the ways Japanese translated literature and the *WMT* romanticized aspects of the Western world during the nineteenth and early twentieth centuries.

As seen, meisaku series also assimilated topics that are often to be found in children's literature, including negotiation of gender and parental roles. Especially the relationship between mothers and their children was consistently thematized through common narratives, such as the search or longing for someone's mother, and archetypal arcs in which women transform into loving mothers. In addition, the study indicated the ways in which *WMT* characterization dealt with the rapidly changing notions of femininity and masculinity, presenting good fathers and mothers, but also exemplary children, as positive models within the context of a Christian nuclear family. The claim of the book that there was a continuity between Calpis' original commercials, with their wholesome values and conceptualization of the child, and the *WMT* should be read in this light.

Although meisaku series might appear as the epitome of the traditional bourgeois order, which was reproduced in many Western classics in the first place, the analysis pointed to interesting variations on the paradigm, such as the inclusion of characters of different ethnic and social background, or the depiction of alternative family units. *WMT* families varied in degree of complexity and were certainly conventional in many aspects, but the analysis showed that their functioning was portrayed in realistic terms, with the perks and underlying tensions of family life.

Ultimately, the chapter clarified how a truthful representation of emotions and feelings played a pivotal role in fostering identification from viewers, and even more so given their distance from the characters, both on the cultural level (because of the exotic nature of the location) and on the ontological level (because of the idealization of the characters). In a similar way, the *WMT* series emphasized the more universal – and thus easily understood – values of Christian religion, such as love, hope or kindness, to the benefit of the programme's educational stance.

From the rhetoric of empathy of the *WMT* also came the tendency to use a slice-of-life approach to narration, emphasizing the humanity of the characters through the lyrical description of their daily lives, or, conversely, to prioritize plot-driven stories with highly emotional, and at times sentimental, twists. These diegetic modes were addressed in greater detail in the last two chapters. In Chapter 5, the comparative study of *Akage no An* and *Anne of Green Gables* helped to assess the impact of Director Takahata's realistic animation in the series of the *WMT*. Conscious of the Japanese codification of the novel as a staple of girls' literature, Takahata departed from the stylized cuteness of contemporary shōjo imagery to shift the focus on the real love story of the narrative – that between Anne and her adoptive mother Marilla. By recreating a lifelike relationship between a bubbly teenager and a pragmatic woman, the adaptation aimed to reproduce Montgomery's humour and her ability to speak to an audience of children and adults.

The series exemplified Takahata's faithfulness to the Western novel in his particular choice of adapting from a literal rather than free translation. As seen, the assumption that complete or literal translations would more accurately preserve the ideas of the writer was consistent with Ishii's principles on children's literature in the post-war. In fact, the first and most famous translation of *Anne of Green Gables* in the country, by Muraoka Hanako, was a free translation, which domesticated, and considerably shortened, the source text. The analysis examined the ways in which Takahata interpolated the novel, demonstrating his awareness of the specific strategies that writing for different media entails. This was evident in the way he introduced additions and edited the order of the narrative to realistically emphasize the girl's coming-of-age arc and the importance of a life in touch with nature, themes that would later shape his cinema. The study also indicated how parenthetical sequences in the book were given relevance and framed differently in the animation, revealing the influence of cultural patterns dominant in Japan. For example, the characters are often encouraged to adopt thoughtful or omoiyari attitudes, given the value of empathy for prosocial behaviours in the country.

Chapter 6 explored a different narrative mode in *Shōkojo Sēra*, the adaptation of *A Little Princess*, showing how and why it managed to set a template for future meisaku series. In particular, the analysis delved on the ways in which the series detached from Burnett's novel. A first major change was in the genre of the story, with melodrama replacing the original mixture of fairy tale and moral exemplum. In fact, by Director Kurokawa Fumio's own admission, the show had intense plot developments and a gripping pace. The study identified this style as indebted to screenwriter Nakanishi Ryūzō's vast experience in hard-boiled movies. This was conducive to elicit strong emotional reactions, raising the audience of the programme without affecting the historical reliability of the series. In addition, the adaptation offered a peculiar resemantization of the main character, Sara Crewe. While what makes Burnett's Sara an active heroine is an apparent inertia – a princess's ideal implying a moral superiority to violence – the Japanese staff identified her as a passive protagonist. This posed a series of diegetic challenges for adaptation, including a lack of dramatic tension.

In this context, the research showed the effectiveness of Kurokawa's strategy to retell the story from the point of view of the villain of the novel, focusing on a new theme (female jealousy) and exacerbating the trials that Sara has to face. This way, the protagonist was turned into a damsel-in-distress, with a set of desirable attributes of femininity that were in line with its renegotiation in the context of shōjo literature. Also in this case, the approach to the adaptation shared similarities with the domesticating and foreignizing strategies used by Japanese translators of Western children's books. For example, Sara's cleverness is one of her natural talents in the book, but became a moral signifier of her learning efforts in the series, according to the special meaning attached to studying in Japan. Again, Sara's self-discipline, associated to the notion of persevering (*gambaru*) in the animation, stretched to encompass a religious connotation in her foreignizing portrait as a model Christian. This seems particularly relevant considering that *A Little Princess* had an unclear spiritual underpinning, but Christian beliefs and behaviours were extensively represented in the *WMT*, adding to the positive perception of the characters.

In summary, this study tried to outline how the *WMT* engaged with different literary genres and conventions, the role of translated children's fiction, the authorship of the creators involved, the agenda of producers and sponsors, as well as various cultural patterns and socio-historical circumstances in Japan. All in all, as proved by the changes introduced in the adaptations, the *WMT* appeared as a creative reworking rather than a pedestrian mimicry of Western stories and the animated heirs of the zenshū tradition, serializing highbrow literature for a general audience on the popular media of television. In this context, it seems likely that the renegotiation of the source texts was an effect of the programme-specific approaches to children's content, not necessarily corresponding with Japan's contemporary culture or discourses on childhood. Nonetheless, *WMT* producers, directors and screenwriters had their own vision on the subjects of the series, which circulated in the programme year after year, impacting the panorama of Japanese animation.

For example, as seen in Chapter 4, the characterization of girls in the *WMT* was much indebted to the Western narrative tradition of orphan girls exerting a positive influence on their surroundings. As such, *WMT* girls combined naturalized notions of femininity, including more challenging ideas such as the tomboy figure, which contributed to the increased visibility and variety of female characters in Japanese animation. This seems confirmed if we consider the initial resistance of Fuji TV to green-light series focusing on girls in the 1970s and the network's later requests for series of the same type to be produced.

There are still many uncharted areas to explore. One of the difficulties I encountered in working on this book was that the *WMT* was a vast project spanning across several decades, which makes it difficult to gauge it in its entirety. Other series of the programme, including the latest ones which are not discussed here, are worth being addressed in monographic detail. This could help better grasp the relation between translated children's fiction and Japanese animation, particularly regarding the significance of classics for today's young audience. For instance, further investigation on the culture of translation of European and American children's fiction in Japan, and particularly on the influence of the ideas expressed by Ishii at Iwanami Shoten, may cast light on the adaptation choices and techniques behind the making of Ghibli films.

The same considerations hold true for the TV series that did not belong to the *WMT*, though being based on Western books, both recent and classical. These works were often international co-productions and, as such, could be interesting case studies for research on several aspects of the collaboration – from the pooling of financial resources to the approach to cultural particularities, to the relations between the parties involved. This could be beneficial to comprehend whether or not it is possible to speak of a genre for the *WMT* and its accolades, following on Iglesias's insightful observations on the 'animesque' style of animation.

Future studies could continue to explore the ties between the *WMT* and commercials, looking for the ways in which television marketed animation as forms of publicity since the days of Ashida Manga, whose intriguing history has only been partly covered in anime studies. The role of Calpis and other food companies that sponsored the programme is an interesting topic, given the importance of food representation in *WMT* series. Publishing and merchandising, which gained prominence among the marketing mix related to the *WMT*, could also be the starting point for other analyses on the ways its characters traveled across media.

The reception of meisaku (and meisaku-inspired) series seems equally worthy of study. Interviews and focus groups could be useful tools to understand how viewers perceived themselves as an audience for the *WMT*, in Japan as in the rest of the world. Future research should test whether *WMT* works are still relatable for today's children and adults, considering the advantages and drawbacks of broad-audience mainstream versus niche-oriented animation. Moreover, the popularity of *WMT* shows in Europe, Asia and the Middle-East, on the one hand, and, on the other, the scarce presence of the *WMT* in the English-speaking countries, where the majority of the novel chosen for adaptation were conceived, call for further discussion on the positioning, influence and understanding of the meisaku phenomenon in these contexts.

Whatever path the reader intends to take, I hope this book has been a helpful companion.

BIBLIOGRAPHY

Ageishi, Mikako. 'How Translated Literature Shaped Education in Modern Japan: The Reception of Walter Scott and Rudyard Kipling'. *Kushiro Ronshū: Hokkaidō kyōiku daigaku Kushiro-kō kenkyū kiyō* [*Journal of Hokkaido University of Education at Kushiro Campus*] 50 (2018): 45–51.

Akamatsu, Yoshiko. 'Japanese Readings of Anne of Green Gables'. In *L.M. Montgomery and Canadian Culture*, edited by Elizabeth Epperly and Irene Gammel, 201–12. Toronto: University of Toronto Press, 1999.

Akamatsu, Yoshiko. 'The Continuous Popularity of Red-Haired Anne in Japan: An Interview with Yoshiko, Akamatsu'. In *Anne around the World: L.M. Montgomery and Her Classic*, edited by Jane Ledwell and Jean Mitchell, 216–27. Montreal and Kingston: McGill-Queen's University Press, 2013.

Akamatsu, Yoshiko. 'The Japanese Translation of The Blythes Are Quoted, Anne's Days of Remembrance: An Analysis of its Characteristics, Style and Publication'. *Nōtorudamu Seishin joshi daigaku kiyō gaikoku-go gaikoku bungaku-hen* [Notre Dame Seishin University's Bulletin of foreign languages and literature] 38, no. 1 (2014): 1–9.

Akamatsu, Yoshiko. 'During and After the World Wars: L.M. Montgomery and the Canadian Missionary Connection in Japan'. *The Looking Glass: New Perspectives on Children's Literature* 18, no. 2 (2015). Available online: https://ojs.latrobe.edu.au/ojs/index.php/tlg/article/view/647.

Allard, Danièle. 'The Popularity of Anne of Green Gables in Japan - A Study of Hanako Muraoka's Translation of L.M. Montgomery's Novel and Its Reception'. PhD diss., Université de Sherbrooke, 2002.

Aoyagi, Mami. 'Karupisu wa 'hatsukoi no aji' to kotaeru Shōwa sedai mo igai to shiranai "7 / 7 Karupisu no hi"' ['7 July Calpis day' that even the Shōwa generation, who would say Calpis is 'the taste of first love,' surprisingly doesn't know about]. *Okāsan Daigaku*, 6 July 2019. Available online: https://www.okaasan.net/mjreport/41572/ (accessed 28 February 2023).

Ashkenazi, Michael and Jeanne Jacob. *Food Culture in Japan*. Westport: Greenwood Press, 2003.

Association of Japanese Animation. 'Anime Industry Report 2022: Summary'. 2023. Available online: https://aja.gr.jp/download/2022_anime_ind_rpt_summary_en (accessed 18 July 2023).

Baldwin, Douglas. 'L.M. Montgomery's Anne of Green Gables: The Japanese Connection'. *Journal of Canadian Studies/Revue d'études canadiennes* 28, no. 3 (1993): 123–33.

'Banjiro 'Banji' Uemura 1929-2019'. *Videoage*, 22 October 2019. Available online: https://www.videoageinternational.net/2019/10/22/watercooler/banjiro-banji-uemura-1929-2019/ (accessed 4 April 2023).

Barrier, Michael. *Hollywood Cartoons: American Animation in Its Golden Age*. New York: Oxford University Press, 2003.
Bashomatsu, Tomoko. 'Shōgakusei zenshū' [Elementary school children's complete works series]'. *Umineko*, 2003. Available online: http://www.umi-neko.com/book/shougakuseizenshuu/shougakuseizenshuujyoukyuu.htm (accessed 28 February 2023).
Bendazzi, Giannalberto. *Animation: A World History, Volume II The Birth of a Style – The Three Markets*. Boca Raton: CRC Press, 2016.
Bharanidharan, Sadhana. 'Studio 100 Locks in More Distribution for its Heidi Pic'. *Kidscreen*, 24 October 2022. Available online: https://kidscreen.com/2022/10/24/studio-100-locks-in-more-distribution-for-its-heidi-pic/ (accessed 14 April 2023).
Booth, Wayne. *The Rhetoric of Fiction*. Chicago and London: The University of Chicago Press, 1983.
Bordwell, David and Kristin Thompson. *Film History: An Introduction*. Boston: McGraw-Hill Education, 1995.
Burgess, Thornton W. *The Burgess Animal Book for Children*. Mineola: Dover Publications, Inc., 2012.
Burnett, Frances Hodgson. *Sara Crewe or What Happened at Miss Minchin's*. New York: Charles Scribner's Sons, 1891.
Burnett, Frances Hodgson. *A Little Princess*. New York: Charles Scribner's Sons, 1937.
Buster, Bobette. *Do Story: How to Tell Your Story so the World Listens*. New York: The Do Book Company, 2013.
'Busy Nippon Animation'. *Variety*, 4 May 1977.
Büttner, Peter. 'A Tour through the Translation History of Johanna Spyri's 'Heidi' with Special References to the Hebrew Editions from 1946 to Today' [Paper presentation], *Heidi from Japan: Anime, Narratives, and Swiss Receptions*, Zurich, 29–31 August 2019.
Carter, Nona L. 'A Study on Japanese Children's Magazines 1888–1949'. PhD diss., University of Pennsylvania, 2009.
Cartmell, Deborah. 'Adapting Children's Literature'. In *The Cambridge Companion to Literature on Screen*, edited by Deborah Cartmell and Imelda Whelehan. Cambridge: Cambridge University Press, 2007: 167–80.
Cartmell, Deborah and Imelda Whelehan. *Adaptations: From Text to Screen, Screen to Text*. London: Routledge, 2005.
Cavallaro, Dani. *Anime and Memory: Aesthetic, Cultural and Thematic Perspectives*. Jefferson: McFarland & Company, 2009.
'Changes to the Kao Logo'. *Kao Corporation*. Available online: https://www.kao.com/global/en/corporate/purpose/logo-symbol/logo_mark/ (accessed 18 April 2023).
Chau, Andrew and Bin Chen. *The Boba Book. Bubble Tea and Beyond*. New York: Clarkson Potter, 2020.
Cheng Chua Karl Ian Uy. 'Boy Meets World: The Worldview of Shōnen kurabu in the 1930s'. *Japan Forum* 28, no. 1 (2016): 49–67.
Chiba, Kaori. *Sekai meisaku gekijo shirizu memoriaru bukku: Amerika & warudō-hen* [World masterpiece theater memorial book. America and the world]. Tokyo: Shinkigensha, 2009.
Chiba, Kaori. *Sekai meisaku gekijō shirīzu memoriaru bukku. Yōroppa-hen* [World masterpiece theater memorial book. Europe]. Tokyo: Shinkigensha, 2010.

Chiba, Kaori. *Sekai meisaku gekijō e no tabi* [A journey to the World masterpiece theater]. Tokyo: Shinkigensha), 2015.
Chiba, Kaori. *Haiji ga umareta hi: Terebi anime no kinjitō o kizuita hitobito* [The day Heidi was born: People who built the landmark of television animation]. Tokyo: Iwanami Shoten, 2017.
Chismar, Douglas. 'Empathy and Sympathy: The Important Difference'. *Journal of Value Inquiry* 22 (1988): 257-66.
Cho, Hyerim et al. 'Facet Analysis of Anime Genres: The Challenges of Defining Genre Information for Popular Cultural Objects'. *Knowledge Organization* 47, no. 1 (2020): 13-30.
Choi, Hyoseak. *Losing the War, Winning the Pooh: Ishii Momoko and the Construction of Contemporary Children's Literature in Postwar Japan*. MA Thesis, University of Toronto, 2017.
Clements, Jonathan. 'The Curious Case of the Dog in Prime Time'. In *Sherlock Holmes and Philosophy: The Footprints of a Gigantic Mind*, edited by Josef Steiff, 307-16. Chicago and La Salle: Open Court, 2011.
Clements, Jonathan. *Anime: A History*. London: The British Film Institute, 2013.
Clements, Jonathan. 'Tezuka's Anime Revolution in Context'. *Mechademia* 8 (2013): 214-26.
Clements, Jonathan and Barry Ip. 'The Shadow Staff: Japanese Animators in the Tōhō Aviation Education Materials Production Office 1939-1945'. *Animation* 7, no. 2 (2012): 189-204.
Clements, Jonathan and Helen McCarthy. *The Anime Encyclopedia: A Guide to Japanese Animation Since 1917*. Berkeley: Stone Bridge Press, 2015.
Clements, Jonathan and Motoko Tamamuro. *The Dorama Encyclopedia: A Guide to Japanese TV Drama Since 1953*. Berkley: Stone Bridge Press, 2003.
Condry, Ian. *The Soul of Anime: Collaborative Creativity and Japan's Media Success Story*. Durham: Duke University Press, 2013.
Connor, Kathleen-Marie. *Beyond the Words of a Storyteller: The Cine-semiotic Play of the Abject, Terror and Community in the Anti-hunting Trilogy of Thornton W. Burgess*. PhD thesis, University of Ottawa, 2007.
Copeland, Rebecca L. *Lost Leaves. Women Writers of Meiji Japan*. Honolulu: University of Hawai'i Press, 2000.
Copeland, Rebecca L. *Woman Critiqued: Translated Essays on Japanese Women's Writing*. Honolulu: University of Hawai'i Press, 2006.
Creighton, Millie. 'Soto and Uchi "Others": Imaging Diversity'. In *Japan's Minorities. The Illusion of Homogeneity*, edited by Michael Weiner. New York: Routledge, 1991: 211-238.
Dai 5-kai kurieitāzu dendō [5th Creators Hall of Fame], ACC Awards, 2017. Accessible online: https://www.acc-awards.com/pantheon/2015.html (accessed 23 February 2023).
Daliot-Bul, Michal and Nissim Otmazgin. *The Anime Boom in the United States: Lessons for Global Creative Industries*. Cambridge, MA: Harvard East Asian monographs, 2020.
Danesin, Maxime. 'Beyond Time & Culture: The Revitalisation of Old Norse Literature and History in Yukimura Makoto's Vinland Saga'. *Mutual Images* 2 (2017): 185-217.

Darling-Wolf, Fabienne. 'The "Lost" Miyazaki: How a Swiss Girl can be Japanese and why it Matters'. *Communication, Culture & Critique* 9, no. 4 (2016): 499–516.

Davies, Northrop. *Manga and Anime Go to Hollywood*. New York and London: Bloomsbury Academic, 2015.

Denison, Rayna. *Anime: A Critical Introduction*. London: Bloomsbury, 2015.

Denison, Rayna. 'Hayao Miyazaki's European Animation: From European Literary Influences to Nostalgic Re-imaginings'. *Wasafiri* 35, no. 2 (2020): 67–73.

Denison, Rayna and Stefanie Van de Peer. '1001 Nights and Anime: The Adaptation of Transnational Folklore in Tezuka Osamu's *Senya Ichiya Monogatari/A Thousand and One Nights* (1969)'. *Open Screens* 4, no. 4 (2021): 4–8.

Dentsu Integrated Report. 'Overview of the Dentsu Group'. 2019. Available online: https://www.group.dentsu.com/en/sustainability/reports/2019/about/glance.html (accessed 18 July 2023).

'Dizunī meisaku dōwa zenshū' [Disney masterpiece fairy tales complete works series]. Tokyo: Kōdansha, 1969–70.

'Dizunī to shuppan keiyaku' [Publishing contract with Disney]. *Asahi Shimbun*, Reduced-size edn, No. 1051, 20 February 2009.

Doker-Tobler, Verena. 'Zeichentrickfilm und Comics aus medienpädagogischer Sicht' [Film animation and comics from a media education perspective]. In *Comics and Visual Culture. Research Studies from ten Countries*, edited by Alphons Silbermann and H.-D. Dyroff, 248–53. München: K.G. Saur, 1986.

Dollase, Hiromi Tsuchiya. *Age of Shōjo: The Emergence, Evolution, and Power of Japanese Girls' Magazine Fiction*. Albany: State University of New York Press, 2019.

'Dororo'. *Mushi Production*, 2018. Available online: https://www.mushi-pro.co.jp/2010/09/どろろ/ (accessed 23 March 2023).

Drain, Susan. 'Montgomery [married Name Macdonald] Lucy Maud (1874–1942)'. *Oxford Dictionary of National Biography*, 23 September 2004. Available online: https://www.oxforddnb.com/display/10.1093/ref:odnb/9780198614128.001.0001/odnb-9780198614128-e-58988?rskey=DWttNS&result=1 (accessed 18 July 2023).

Elliott, Kamilla. 'Rethinking Formal-Cultural and Textual-Contextual Divides in Adaptation Studies'. *Literature/Film Quarterly* 42, no. 4 (2014): 576–93.

Ericson, Joan E. 'Introduction'. In *A Rainbow in the Desert. An Anthology of Early Twentieth Century Japanese Children's Literature*, translated by Yukie Ohta, 362–71. New York: M. E. Sharpe, 2001.

Eßer, Kerstin. 'Kinderprogramm ist Zeichentrick' [Children's programming is animation]. In *Handbuch Medienerziehung im Kindergarten. Teil 1: Pädagogische Grundlagen [Handbook of Media Education in Kindergarten. Part 1: Pedagogical basics]*, edited by Christine Feil et al. Opladen: Leske + Budrich, 1994.

'Fables of the Green Forest: Release Info'. *IMDb*, 2023. Available online: https://www.imdb.com/title/tt0408436/releaseinfo/?ref_=tt_dt_aka#akas (accessed 12 April 2023).

Factbook: Asahi Group. Asahi Group Holdings, 2017. Available online: https://www.asahigroup-holdings.com/en/ir/pdf/2017_2q_factbook.pdf (accessed 18 July 2023).

Factbook: The History of Milk in Japan. Japan Dairy Association, 2020. Available online: https://www.j-milk.jp/report/study/h4ogb400000011y2-att/h4ogb40000003f7e.pdf (accessed 18 July 2023).

Farrell, Roger Simon. *Japanese Investment in the World Economy. A Study of Strategic Themes in Internationalisation of Japanese Industry*. Cheltenham and Northampton: Edward Elgar Publishing, 2008.

Faviez, Pierre. *La Télé: Un destin animé [TV: An animated destiny]* Paris: Société des Écrivains, 2010.

Ferns, John. 'Rainbow Dreams: The Poetry of Lucy Maud Montgomery'. *Canadian Children's Literature/Littérature Canadienne pour la jeunesse* 42 (1986): 29–40.

Follows, Stephen. 'Which Countries Most Commonly Team up to Create Film Co-productions?'. *Stephen Follows: Film Data and Education*, 22 April 2019. Available online: https://stephenfollows.com/most-frequent-co-producing-nations/ (accessed 14 April 2023).

Fowler, Edward. *The Rhetoric of Confession: Shishosetsu in Early Twentieth-Century Japanese*. Berkley: University of California Press, 1992.

Freedman, Alice. 'Romance of the Taishō Schoolgirl in Shōjo Manga: *Here Comes Miss Modern*'. In *Shōjo Across Media. Exploring "Girl" Practices in Contemporary Japan*, edited by Berndt Jaqueline et al. Cham: Palgrave Macmillan, 2019: 25–48.

Fujiki, Hideaki. *Making Audiences: A Social History of Japanese Cinema and Media*. New York: Oxford University Press, 2022.

Fukuda, Kiyoto and Toshiko Yamanushi. *Nihon jidō bungeishi [History of Japanese children's literature]*. Tokyo: Sanseido, 1983.

Fumagalli, Armando. *I vestiti nuovi del narratore [The narrator's new clothes]*. Milano: Il Castoro, 2004.

Gavin, Adrienne and Andrew Humphries. *Childhood in Edwardian Fiction: Worlds Enough and Time*. London: Palgrave Macmillan, 2008.

Gerbner, George et al. 'Growing up with Television: Cultivation Processes'. In *Media Effects: Advances in Theory and Research*, edited by Jennings Bryant and Mary Beth Oliver, 43–68. New York: Routledge, 2009.

Gerow, Aaron. 'Japanese Film and Television'. In *Routledge Handbook of Japanese Culture and Society*, edited by Victoria Lyon Bestor et al., 213–25. London and New York: Routledge, 2011.

Gerzina, Gertchen. *Francis Hodgson Burnett*. London: Chatto & Windus, 2004.

Goddard, Cliff and Anna Wierzbicka. 'Discourse and Culture'. In *Discourse Studies: A Multidisciplinary Introduction, Vol. 2: Discourse as Social Interaction*, edited by Teun A. Van Dijk, 231–57. London: SAGE, 1997.

Greenberg, Raz, 'Giri and Ninjo: The Roots of Hayao Miyazaki's 'My Neighbor Totoro' in Animated Adaptations of Classic Children's Literature'. *Literature/Film Quarterly* 40, no. 2 (2012): 96–108.

Greenberg, Raz. *Hayao Miyazaki: Exploring the Early Work of Japan's Greatest Animator*. London: Bloomsbury Academic, 2020.

Greenwood, Vanessa E. *Navigating Media Literacy: A Pedagogical Tour of Disneyland*. Bloomfield: Myers Education Press, 2020.

Griffiths, Owen. 'Militarizing Japan: Patriotism, Profit, and Children's Print Media, 1894–1925', *The Asia-Pacific Journal: Japan Focus* 5, no. 9 (2007).

Grössman, Hilaria M. 'New Role Models for Men and Women? Gender in Japanese TV Dramas'. In *Japan Pop: Inside the World of Japanese Popular Culture*, edited by Timothy J. Craig, 207-21. London and New York: Routledge, 2015.

Gruner, Elisabeth Rose. 'Cinderella, Marie Antoinette, and Sara: Roles and Role Models in A Little Princess'. *The Lion and the Unicorn* 22, no. 2 (1998).

Hamada, Hitsurō. 'Katō Kikuzō to Eiki no seishun fu (2)' [Katō Kikuzō and Eiki's youth records (2)], *Dentsu*, 11 December 2016. Accessible online: https://dentsu-ho.com/articles/4736 (accessed 21 March 2023).

Hamada, Hitsurō. 'Katō Kikuzō to Eiki no seishun fu (3)' [Katō Kikuzō and Eiki's youth records (3)], *Dentsu*, 13 December 2016. Accessible online: https://dentsu-ho.com/articles/4737 (accessed 21 March 2023).

Hara, Kazuya. 'The Concept of Omoiyari (Altruistic Sensitivity) in Japanese Relational Communication'. *Intercultural Communication Studies* XV, no. 1 (2006): 24-32.

Hastings, Thomas John. 'Japan's Protestant Schools and Churches in Light of Early Mission Theory and History'. In *Handbook of Christianity in Japan*, edited by Mark Mullins, 101-24. Leiden: Brill, 2003.

Hayano, Katsumi. 'Hans Christian Andersen Research Situation in Japan'. *Andersen SDU*, 1993. Available online: https://andersen.sdu.dk/forskning/konference/tekst.html?id=9730 (accessed 24 March 2023).

'History'. *Calpis*, 2006. Available online: https://www.calpis.co.jp/english/outline/outline1.html (accessed 24 March 2023).

Hori, Hikari. *Promiscuous Media. Film and Visual Culture in Imperial Japan, 1926-1945*. Ithaca: Cornell University Press, 2018.

Hu, Tze-Yue G. *Frames of Anime: Culture and Image-Building*. Hong Kong: Hong Kong University Press, 2010.

Hutcheon, Linda. *A Theory of Adaptation*. London: Taylor & Francis, 2012.

Iglesias, José Andrés Santiago. 'The Anime Connection. Early Euro-Japanese Co-Productions and the Animesque: Form, Rhythm, Design'. *Arts* 7, no. 4 (2018).

Ikushima, Jun. *Inryō gyōkai no paionia supiritto* [*Pioneer spirit in the beverage industry*]. Tokyo: Fuyo Shobo, 2009.

Ishihara, Tsuyoshi. *Mark Twain in Japan. The Cultural Reception of an American Icon*. Columbia and London: University of Missouri Press, 2005.

Ishikawa, Kazuko. 'Message'. *Nippon Animation*, 2021. Available online: http://www.nipponanimation.com/message/ (accessed 14 April 2021).

Iwabuchi, Koichi. *Recentering Globalization: Popular Culture and Japanese Transnationalism*. Durham: Duke University Press, 2002.

Iwai, Shuma. 'Japanese Christianity in the Meiji Era: An Analysis of Ebina Danjo's Perspective on Shintoistic Christianity'. *Transformation* 25, no. 4 (2008): 195-204.

'Iwanami shōnen bunko' [Iwanami youth library]. Tokyo: Iwanami Shoten, 1950-70.

Jinguh, Teruo. 'Japan'. In *International Companion Encyclopedia of Children's Literature*, vol. 2, edited by Hunt Peter, 1108-14. Abingdon: Routledge, 2004.

Joo, Woojeong. *The Cinema of Ozu Yasujiro. Histories of the Everyday*. Edinburgh: Endinburgh University Press, 2017.

Jorenby, Marnie K. 'About Face: The Transformations of the Hero in Post-War Japanese Literature for Youth'. PhD diss., University of Wisconsin-Madison, 2003.

'Kaisha no ayumi' [History of the company], *House Foods*. Available online: https://housefoods.jp/company/information/history.html (accessed 18 April 2023).

Kajihara, Yuka. 'An Influential Anne in Japan'. In *The Lucy Maud Montgomery Album*, edited by Mc Cabe et al., 432–38. Toronto: Fitzhenry & Whiteside, 1999.

Kamei-Dyche, Andrew T. 'The History of Books and Print Culture in Japan: The State of the Discipline'. *Book History* 14 (2011): 270–304.

Kameyama, Yasuo. 'Kokusan terebi anime shirīzu to nipponteki bijinesu moderu no tanjō' [Domestic TV animation series and the birth of a Japanese business model], *Minna no Animegaku*, 7 January 2022. Available online: https://min-ani.com/kameyama_0002/ (accessed 7 February 2023).

Kano, Seiji. '"Arupusu no shōjo Haiji" de Takahata enshutsu ga mezashita mono' [What director Takahata aimed for in "Heidi girl of the Alps"]. *BS anime yawa*, vol. 7, 1 April 2008, 136–41.

Kaplan, Arie. *American pop: Hit Makers, Superstars, and Dance Revolutionaries*. Minneapolis: Twenty-First Century Books, 2013.

Karr, Clarence. *Authors and Audiences: Popular Canadian Fiction in the Early Twentieth Century*. Montreal and Kingston: McGill-Queen's University Press, 2000.

'Karupisu "hahaoya Tamī-chan to denwa"' [Calpis 'Mother little Tamī on the phone"]. *Broadcast Library*, 2023. Available online: https://www.bpcj.or.jp/search/show_detail.php?program=150600 (accessed 10 April 2023).

'"Karupisu" hinamatsuri purezento' [Calpis Girls' Festival Day Gift]. *Asahi*, 2023 Available online: https://www.asahiinryo.co.jp/peace/hinamatsuri/ehon/ (accessed 18 July 2023).

'"Karupisu ®" no sekigyokutekina hansoku katsudō to terebi CM no kaishi' [Calpis ® aggressive promotional activity and the start of Tv commercials]. *Asahi*. Available online: https://www.asahiinryo.co.jp/entertainment/asahiinryohistory/pdf/brand/calpis/%E3%82%AB%E3%83%AB%E3%83%94%E3%82%B904_221221.pdf (accessed 18 July 2023).

Katsura, Yuko, 'Red-haired Anne in Japan'. *Canadian Children's Literature / Littérature canadienne pour la jeunesse* 34, no. 5 (1984): 57–60.

Kawana, Sari. *The Uses of Literature in Modern Japan: Histories and Cultures of the Book*. London: Bloomsbury Academics, 2018.

Kawashima, Takashi. 'Translation History of Heidi in Japan - A Story for Girls?' [Paper presentation]. *Heidi from Japan: Anime, Narratives, and Swiss Receptions*, Zurich, 29–31 August 2019.

Keaveney, Christopher T. *The Cultural Evolution of Postwar Japan. The Intellectual Contributions of Kaizō's Yamamoto Sanehiko*. New York: Palgrave Macmillan, 2013.

Keiei chōsa kenkyūkai [Management research institute], *Nihon o sodateru shidōsha no kiroku: Keizai-hen [Memoirs of leaders who nurture Japan: Economy]*. Tokyo: Keiei Chōsa Kenkyūkakai, 1973.

Keith, Elizabeth M. *Kaneko Misuzu and the Development of Children's Literature in Taisho Japan*. MA thesis, University of Hawaii, 2002.

Kido, Misaki C. 'Interview: Eiichiro Oda'. *Viz*, 2 April 2012. Available online: https://www.viz.com/blog/posts/interview-eiichiro-oda-466 (accessed 14 April 2023).

Kimbrough, Keller R., 'Bloody Hell!: Reading Boys' Books in Seventeenth-Century Japan'. *Asian Ethnology* 74, no. 1 (2015): 111–39.

Kimura, Tomoya. 'Business and Production: Development and Politics of Outsourcing'. In *Japanese Animation in Asia: Transnational Industry, Audiences, and Success*, edited by Marco Pellitteri and Wong Heung-wah, 71-92. Abingdon: Routledge, 2022.

Kirkland, Janice. 'Frances Hodgson Burnett's Sara Crewe Through 110 Years'. *Children's Literature in Education* 28, no. 4 (1997): 191-203.

'Kōdansha no Dizunī ehon' [Kōdansha's Disney picture books]. Tokyo: Kōdansha, 1961-4.

'Kōdansha no ehon' [Kōdansha's picture books]. Tokyo: Kōdansha, 1946-58.

Kohlbacher, Florian and Michael Prieler. *Advertising in the Aging Society: Understanding Representations, Practitioners, and Consumers in Japan*. Basingstoke: Palgrave Macmillan, 2016.

Kojima, Kiyoshi. 'Iwanami Publishing House'. In *The Encyclopedia of Contemporary Japanese Culture*, edited by Sandra Buckley, 222-24. London and New York: Routledge, 2006.

'Komento' [Comment]. *Ghibli Museum*, 10 October 2009. Available online: https://www.ghibli-museum.jp/batta/comment/ (accessed 7 February 2023).

Koppes, Phyllis Bixler. 'Tradition and the Individual Talent of Frances Hodgson Burnett: A Generic Analysis of Little Lord Fauntleroy, A Little Princess, and The Secret Garden'. *Children's Literature* 7 (1978): 191-207.

Kornicki, Peter. 'Review of Adaptations of Western Literature in Meiji Japan by J. Scott Miller'. *Monumenta Nipponica* 57, no. 3 (2002): 392-93.

Krummel, John W. M. 'The Symposium on Overcoming Modernity and Discourse in Wartime Japan'. *Historická Sociologie* 13, no. 2 (2021): 83-104.

Kubiak, Ho-Chi Beata. 'Aesop's Fables in Japanese Literature for Children: Classical Antiquity and Japan'. In *Our Mythical Childhood ... The Classics and Literature for Children and Young Adults*, edited by Katarzyna Marciniak, 189-200. Leiden and Boston: Brill, 2016.

Kurokawa, Fumio. 'Little Princess Sara Staff Interview'. In *Shōkōjo Sēra*, DVD booklets, Japan: Bandai Visual Co., LTD, 1999.

Ladd, Fred with Harvey Deneroff. *Astro Boy and Anime Come to the Americas. An Insider's View of the Birth of a Pop Culture Phenomenon*. Jefferson: McFarland & Company, 2009.

Lamarre, Thomas. *The Anime Machine: A Media Theory of Animation*. Minneapolis: University of Minnesota Press, 2010.

Laski, Marghanita. *Mrs. Ewing, Mrs. Molesworth, and Mrs. Hodgson Burnett*. New York: Oxford University Press, 1951.

Le Blanc, Michelle and Colin Odell. *Studio Ghibli: The Films of Hayao Miyazaki and Isao Takahata*. Harpenden: Kamera Books, 2009.

Lebra, Takie Sugiyama. *Japanese Patterns of Behavior*. Honolulu: University of Hawaii Press, 1976.

Lefebvre, Benjamin. *Textual Transformations in Children's Literature: Adaptations, Translations, Reconsiderations*. New York: Routledge, 2013.

Lewis, Catherine C. *Educating Hearts and Minds: Reflections on Japanese Preschool and Elementary Education*. New York: Cambridge University Press, 1995.

Lindberg-Wada, Gunilla. 'Japanese Literary History Writing: The Beginnings'. In *Literary History: Towards a Global Perspective: Volume 1: Notions of Literature Across Cultures*, edited by Petterson Anders, 111-34. Berlin: Gruyter, 2006.

McCarthy, Helen. *Hayao Miyazaki: Master of Japanese Animation: Films, Themes, Artistry*. Berkeley: Stone Bridge Press, 2002.

McCarthy, Helen. *The Art of Osamu Tezuka God of Manga*. Lewes: Ilex, 2009.

McDonough, John and Karen Egolf (eds). *The Advertising Age: Encyclopedia of Advertising*. Chicago: Fitzroy Deaborn Publishers, 2002.

McDrury, Janice and Maxine Alterio. *Learning Through Storytelling in Higher Education: Using Reflection and Experience to Improve Learning*. London and New York: Routledge, 2003.

McKee, Robert. *Story: Substance, Structure, Style, and the Principles of Screenwriting*. New York: ReganBooks, 1997.

MacWilliams, Mark W. 'Introduction'. In *Japanese Visual Culture: Explorations in the World of Manga and Anime*, edited by Mark W. MacWilliams, 3-25. Abindgon and New York: Routledge, 2015.

Madej, Krystina and Lee Newton. *Disney Stories: Getting to Digital*. Cham: Springer, 2021.

Matsumoto, Masashi. *20 Seiki terebi dokuhon sekai meisaku gekijō taizen* [*20th century TV reader World masterpiece theater encyclopedia*]. Tokyo: Dōbunshoin, 1999.

Mazur, Dan and Alexander Danner. 'The International Graphic Novel'. In *The Cambridge Companion to the Graphic Novel*, edited by Stephen E. Tabachnick, 58-79. Cambridge: Cambridge University Press, 2017.

Meade, Ruselle. 'Juvenile Science and the Japanese Nation: Shōnen'en and the Cultivation of Scientific Subjects'. *Japan Review* 34 (2019): 113-137.

Mehl, Margaret. 'Women Educators and the Confucian Tradition in Meiji Japan (1868-1912): Miwada, Masako and Atomi Kakei'. *Women's History Review* 10, no. 4 (2001): 579-602.

Mitsui, Hideko. 'Uses of Finland in Japan's Social Imaginary'. In *Reflections on Imagination: Human Capacity and Ethnographic Method*, edited by Mark Harris and Nigel Rapport, 161-76. London: Routledge, 2016.

'Miyazaki Akira (1934-2018)'. *IMDb*. Available online: https://www.imdb.com/name/nm0594496/ (accessed 19 April 2023).

Miyazaki, Hayao. *Starting point: 1979-1996*. Transl. by B. Cary and F. Schodt. San Francisco: VIZ Media, 2010.

Miyazaki, Kenji. 'Kataritsugu oyako kiete "sekai no meisaku" wa hyōgaki' ['Parents and children who pass down their stories disappear and the "World masterpiece" is ice age']. *Asahi Shimbun*, Tokyo morning edition, 27 March 1997.

Monden, Masafumi. 'A Dream Dress for Girls: Milk, Fashion and Shōjo Identity'. In *Shōjo Across Media: Exploring "Girl" Practices in Contemporary Japan*, edited by Jaqueline Berndt et al., 209-32. Cham: Palgrave Macmillan, 2019.

Montenero-Plata, Laura and Marie Pruvost-Delaspre. 'Shaping the Anime Industry: Second Generation Pioneers and the Emergence of the Studio System'. In *A Companion to Japanese Cinema*, edited by David Desser, 215-46. Malden: Wiley, 2022.

Morgan, Michael et al. 'Growing up with Television: Cultivation Processes'. In *Media Effects: Advances in Theory and Research*, edited by Jennings Bryant and Mary Beth Oliver. New York: Routledge, 2009.

Mori, Yasuji. *Mogura no uta – Animētā no jiden* [*Song of a mole: Autobiography of an animator*]. Tokyo: Tokuma Shoten, 1984.
Mueller-Vollmer, Tristan and Kirsten Wolf. *Vikings: An Encyclopedia of Conflict, Invasions, and Raids*. Santa Barbara: ABC-CLIO, 2022.
'Mūmin' [Moomin]. *Asahi gurafu* [*Asahi Graph special edition*]. 15 March 1978, 63.
Munroe Hotes, Catherine. 'Tora-chan, The Abandoned Kitten (すて猫トラちゃん, 1947)'. *Nishikata Film Review*, 5 June 2010. Available online: https://www.nishikata-eiga.com/2010/06/tora-chan-abandoned-kitten-1947.html (accessed 7 February 2023).
Murakami, Saburo. *Anime in TV. Storia dei cartoni animati giapponesi prodotti per la televisione* [*TV anime. A history of Japanese cartoons for television*]. Milan: Yamato Video, 1998.
Muramatsu, Yasuko. 'Gender Construction Through Interactions Between the Media and Audience in Japan'. *International Journal of Japanese Sociology* 11 (2002): 72–87.
Myojo, Kiyoko. 'The Functions of Zenshū in Japanese Book Culture: Practices and Problems of Modern Textual Editing in Japan'. *Variants* 10 (2013): 257–67.
Napier, Susan. *Miyazakiworld: A Life in Art*. New Haven: Yale University Press, 2020.
Nardy, Deanna T. 'Tarzan and Japan: Racial Portraits of a Nation in Boy Kenya'. In *Japanese Visual Media. Politicizing the Screen*, edited by Jennifer Coates and Eyal Ben-Ari. Abingdon: Routledge, 2022.
National Diet Library. 'Part 2 The Dowa Era: From the Launching of Akai Tori to the Pre-War'. *Japanese Children's Literature*, 2017. Available online: https://www.kodomo.go.jp/jcl/e/section2/index.html (accessed 28 February 2023).
Naughton, Leonie. *That Was the Wild East. Film Culture, Unification, and the 'New' Germany*. Michigan: The University of Michigan, 2022.
Newswander, Lynita K. et al. 'Mormonism'. In *The Routledge Companion to Religion and Popular Culture*, edited by John C. Lyden and Eric Michael Mazur. Abingdon and New York: Routledge, 2015.
'Nihon jidō bunko' [Japanese children's library']. Tokyo: ARS, 1927.
Nikolajeva, Maria. 'The Changing Aesthetics of Character in Children's Fiction'. *Style* 35, no. 3 (2001): 430–53.
'Nippon Animation Co., LTD'. *Variety*, 11 October 1989.
'Nippon Animation Co., LTD'. *Variety*, 7 October 1991.
'Nippon rongusērā kō. Carupisu: Oishī omoide o tsukutte 84-nen' [Thoughts on Japan's long-selling products. Calpis: 84 years of making delicious memories]. *COMZINE*, July 2003. Available online: https://www.nttcom.co.jp/comzine/no002/long_seller/index.html (accessed 18 July 2023).
Novielli, Maria Roberta. *Floating Worlds: A Short History of Japanese Animation*. Boca Raton: Taylor & Francis, 2018.
Odell, Colin and Michelle Le Blanc. *Studio Ghibli*. Harpenden: Kamera, 2009.
Oehlkers, Peter. 'Johnny Chuck in Japan'. *Thornton W. Burgess Research League*, 8 March 2010. Available online: https://twbresearchleague.blogspot.com/2010/03/johnny-chuck-in-japan.html (accessed 10 April 2023).
Okamoto, Ippei. *Jidō manga shū* [*Children's manga collection*], 'Shōgakusei Zenshū'23. Tokyo: Kōbunsha, 1927.

Okano, Kaori and Motonori Tsuchiya. *Education in Contemporary Japan. Inequality and Diversity*. Cambridge: Cambridge University Press, 1999.
Okuyama, Yoshiko. *Japanese Mythology in Film. A Semiotic Approach to Reading Japanese Film and Anime*. Lanham: Lexington Books, 2015.
O'Neil, Paul. 'Green Meadow. At 86, Thornton W. Burgess Endures as Classic Tale-Teller'. *Life*, 14 November 1960, 112–24.
Ono, Kosei. 'Takahashi Shigeto, Nihon ni okeru terebi CM to TV anime no sōsō ki o kataru (TCJ kara zuiyō e no rekishi' [Takahashi Shigeto talks about the early days of TV commercials and TV animation in Japan (History from TCJ to Zuiyo)]. *Kyōto seika daigaku kiyōdai* [*Journal of Kyoto Seika University*] 26 (2004): 189–213.
Onoda Power, Natsu. *God of Comics: Osamu Tezuka and the Creation of Post-World War II Manga*. Jackson: University Press of Mississippi, 2009.
Ortabasi, Melek. 'Brave Dogs and Little Lords: Some Thoughts on Translation, Gender, and the Debate on Childhood in Mid Meiji'. *Review of Japanese Culture and Society* 20 (2008): 178–205.
Ørvig, Mary. *Children's Books in Sweden, 1945–1970: A Survey*. Vienna: Austrian Children's Book Club, 1973.
Oshima, Kazuyoshi. 'Dokura Fujio'. *Patrasche.net*, 20 May 2010. Available online: http://www.patrasche.net/nello/human/09.html (accessed 10 April 2023).
Osmond, Donny. *Life Is Just What You Make It: The Autobiography*. London: Orion, 2006.
Patrasche, a Dog of Flanders – Made in Japan. D. Volckaert and A. van Dienderen [crs]. Belgium: Ghent University and Vlaam Audiovisueel Fonds, 2007.
Pellitteri, Marco. 'Ad est di Oliver Twist' [East of Oliver Twist], In *Con gli occhi a mandorla. Sguardi sul Giappone dei cartoon e dei fumetti* [*With almond-shaped eyes: Looking at Japan through its comics and cartoons*], edited by Roberta Ponticiello and Susanna Scrivo. Latina: Tunué, 2005.
Pellitteri, Marco. *Mazinga Nostalgia: Storia, Valori e Linguaggi della Goldrake-generation dal 1978 al Nuovo Secolo* [*Mazinger Nostalgia: History, Values, and Languages of the Grandizer-generation from 1978 to the New Century*]. Latina: Tunué, 2018.
Pellitteri, Marco. *The Dragon and the Dazzle: Models, Strategies, and Identities of Japanese Imagination—A European Perspective*. Latina: Tunué, 2010.
Pellitteri, Marco. 'Cultural Politics of J-Culture and "Soft Power": Tentative Remarks from a European Perspective'. In *Mangatopia: Essays on Manga and Anime in the Modern World*, edited by Timothy Perper and Martha Cornog, 209–29. Santa Barbara: ABC-CLIO, 2011.
Perez, Louis G. *Tokyo: Geography, History, and Culture*. Santa Barbara: ABC-CLIO, 2019.
Piel, L. Halliday. 'Loyal Dogs and Meiji Boys: The Controversy Over Japan's First Children's Story, Koganemaru (1891)'. *Children's Literature* 38 (2010): 207–22.
Pincus, Leslie. *Authenticating Culture in Imperial Japan. Kuki Shuzo and the Rise of National Aesthetics*. Berkley: University of California Press, 1996.
Poitras, Gilles. 'Contemporary Anime in Japanese Pop Culture'. In *Japanese Visual Culture: Explorations in the World of Manga and Anime*, edited by Mark W. MacWilliams, 48–67. London: Routledge, 2015.

Prandoni, Francesco. *Anime al Cinema: Storia dell'Animazione Giapponese 1917-1995* [Anime cinema: History of Japanese animation 1917-1995]. Milano: Yamato Video, 1999.

Raffaelli, Luca. *Le anime disegnate. Il pensiero nei cartoon da Disney ai giapponesi e oltre* [Drawn souls. Schools of thought in cartoons from Disney to the Japanese and beyond]. Latina: Tunué, 2018.

Raskin, Jonah. *Mythology of Imperialism*. London: Random House, 1971.

Resler, Johanna Elizabeth. 'Sara's Transformation: A Textual Analysis of Frances Hodgson Burnett's Sara Crew and A Little Princess'. MA diss., Indiana University, 2007.

RICMANIA. 'Sekai meisaku dōwa 14 – Arupusu no shōjo'. 26 December 2017. Available online: http://ricmania.com/index.php?module=blog&act=printview &eid=10698&date=2017-12 (accessed 17 February 2023).

Rubio, Mary. 'Subverting the Trite: L.M. Montgomery's Room of her own'. *Canadian Children's Literature / Littérature canadienne pour la jeunesse* 65 (1992): 6-39.

Russell, John. 'Race and Reflexivity: The Black Other in Contemporary Japanese Mass Culture'. In *Rereading Cultural Anthropology*, edited by George E. Marcus, 296-318. Durham: Duke University Press, 1992.

Saito, Mino. 'The Power of Translated Literature in Japan: The Introduction of New Expressions Through Translation in the Meiji Era (1868-1912)'. *Perspectives* 24, no. 3 (2016): 417-30.

Sand, Jordan. 'The Cultured Life as a Contested Space. Dwelling and Discourse in the 1920s'. In *Being Modern in Japan: Culture and Society from the 1910s to the 1930s*, edited by Elise Tipton K. and John Clark, 99-118. Honolulu: University of Hawai'i Press, 2000.

Sandler, Kevin. 'Limited Animation 1947-1989'. In *Animation*, edited by Scott Curtis, 75-102. New Brunswick: Rutdgers University Press, 2019.

Sano, Akiko. '*Chiyogami*, Cartoon, Silhouette. The Transitions of Ōfuji Noburō'. In *Japanese Animation: East Asian Perspectives*, edited by Masao Yokota and Tze-yue G. Hu, 87-97. Jackson: University Press of Mississippi, 2013.

Sano, Shinichi. *Nihon eiga wa, ima – Sukurīn no uragawa kara no shōgen* [Cinema of Japan now: A testimony from behind the screen]. Tokyo: TBS Britannica, 1996.

Sato, Motoko. 'Japanese Adaptations of 19th Century and Early 20th Century Western Children's Literature'. In *Reconstructing Cultural Memory. Translation, Scripts, Literacy*, edited by Lieven D'Hulst and John Milton. Proceedings of the XVth Congress of the International Comparative Literature Association "Literature as Cultural Memory". *Studies in Comparative Literature* 31, no. 7 (2000): 145-54.

Satō, Toshihiko. 'Hans Christian Andersen's "The Improvisator" in Japan'. *Museum Odense*, 1 January 1963. Available online: https://museumodense.dk/artikler/hans-christian-andersens-the-improvisator-in-japan/ (accessed 24 March 2023).

Schodt, Frederik. *The Astro Boy Essays: Osamu Tezuka, Mighty Atom, and the Manga/Anime Revolution*. Berkley: Stone Bridge Press, 2007.

Schumann, Fred R. *Changing Trends in Japan's Employment and Leisure Activities: Implications for Tourism Marketing*. Singapore: Springer, 2017.

Schwerin, Horace S. 'Cartoons, Used Well, Can Fill Big Niches'. *The Billboard*, 10 October 1953.
Seaton, Philip. 'Taiga Dramas and Tourism: Historical Contents as Sustainable Tourist Resources'. *Japan Forum* 27, no. 1 (2015): 82-103.
'Sekai meisaku anime zenshū' [World masterpieces animated complete works series]. Tokyo: Kadokawa, 1987-8.
'Sekai meisaku bunko' [World masterpiece library]. Tokyo: Kaisesha, 1951-6.
'Sekai meisaku zenshū' [World masterpieces complete work series]. Tokyo: Kōdansha, 1950-60.
'Sekai meisaku dōwa zenshū' [World masterpiece children's stories complete works series]. Tokyo: Kōdansha, 1950-5.
'Sekai meisaku dōwa zenshū' [World masterpiece children's stories complete works series]. Tokyo: Poplar, 1963-5.
'Sekai meisaku monogatari' [World masterpiece stories]. Tokyo: Poplar, 1950-55.
'Sekai no meicho' [World famous books]. Tokyo: Poplar, 1967-9.
'Sekai shōjo shōsetsu zenshū' [World girls' novels complete works series]. Tokyo: Kōdansha, 1957-8.
Sekiguchi, Sumiko. 'Confucian Morals and the Making of a "Good Wife and Wise Mother": From 'Between Husband and Wife There is Distinction' to 'As Husbands and Wives be Harmonious"'. *Social Science Japan Journal* 13, no. 1 (2010): 93-113.
Shamoon, Deborah Michelle. *Passionate Friendship: The Aesthetics of Girls' Culture in Japan*. Honolulu: University of Hawai'i Press, 2012.
Shiraishi, Saya. 'Doraemon Goes Abroad'. In *Japan Pop. Inside the World of Japanese Culture*, edited by Timothy J. Craig. London and New York: Routledge, 2015: 287-308.
Shively, Donald H. 'The Japanization of the Middle Meiji'. In *Tradition and Modernization in Japanese Culture*, edited by Donald H. Shively. Princeton: Princeton University Press, 1971: 77-120.
'Shōgakusei zenshū' [Elementary school children's complete works series]. Tokyo: Kōbunsha and Bungei Shunjūnsha, 1927.
'Shōnen shōjo sekai no meisaku' [Boys' and girls' world masterpieces]. Tokyo: Shōgakukan, 1972-5.
Sims, Richard L. *Japanese Political History Since the Meiji Renovation 1868-2000*. New York: Palgrave, 2001.
Somers, Emily. 'An no shinjō [Anne's Feelings]. Politeness and Passion as Anime. Paradox in Takahata's Akage no an'. In *Textual Transformations in Children's Literature. Adaptations, Translations, Reconsiderations*, edited by Benjamin Lefebvre, 155-74. New York and Abingdon: Routledge, 2013.
Soothill, William Edward and Lewis Hodous. *A Dictionary of Chinese Buddhist Terms*. Delhi: Motilal Banarsidass, 1977.
Speare Triant, Diane. 'The Curious Tale of Peter Rabbit'. *Cape Cod Life*, November/December 2018. Available online: https://capecodlife.com/the-curious-tale-of-peter-rabbit/ (accessed 7 April 2023).
Standish, Isolde. *A New History of Japanese Cinema. A Century of Narrative Film*. New York and London: Continuum, 2005.

Steinberg, Marc. 'Immobile Sections and Trans-Series Movement: Astroboy and the Emergence of Anime'. *Animation: An Interdisciplinary Journal* 1, no. 2 (2006): 190-206.
Stensel, Peter. *Design & Technology. Design for Life*. Singapore: Pearson Longman, 2007.
Stevenson, Deborah. 'Classics and Canons'. In *The Cambridge Companion to Children's Literature*, edited by M. O. Grenby and Andrea Immel. New York: Cambridge University Press, 2009: 108-26.
Stoffman, Judy. 'Anne in Japanese Popular Culture'. *Canadian Children's Literature / Littérature canadienne pour la jeunesse* 91-92 (1998): 53-63.
Sugawa-Shimada, Akiko. 'Shōjo in Anime: Beyond the Object of Men's Desire'. In *Shōjo Across Media. Exploring "Girl" Practices in Contemporary Japan*, edited by Jaqueline Berndt et al., 181-206. Cham: Palgrave Macmillan, 2019.
Suzuki, Michiko. *Becoming Modern Women: Love and Female Identity in Prewar Japanese Literature and Culture*. Stanford: Standford University Press, 2010.
Taira, Koji. 'Education and Literacy in Meiji Japan: An Interpretation'. *Explorations in Economic History* 8, no. 4 (1971): 371-94.
Takahashi, Mizuki. 'Opening the Closed World of Shōjo Manga'. In *Japanese Visual Culture. Explorations in the World of Manga and Anime*, edited by Mark W. MacWilliams, 114-36. Abindgon and New York: Routledge, 2015.
Takahata, Isao. *Eiga o tsukurinagara kangaeta koto* [Thoughts while making movies]. Tokyo: Tokuma Shoten, 1991.
Takahata, Isao. *Jūniseiki no animēshon: Kokuhō emakimono ni miru eiga teki anime teki narumono* [Twelfth century animation: Seeing the cinematic and anime-like aspects in the national treasures, emakimono]. Tokyo: Tokuma Shoten, 2008.
Takahata, Isao. 'Akage no An o kataru Takahata Isao kantoku' [Director Takahata Isao talks about Red-haired Anne]. *Ghibli Museum*, 2010. Available online: https://www.ghibli-museum.jp/anne/kataru/takahata/006227.html (accessed 18 April 2023).
Takita, Yoshiko. 'Wakamatsu Shizuko and "Little Lord Fauntleroy"'. *Comparative Literature Studies* 22, no. 1 (1985): 1-8.
Tanaka, Yukiko. *Women Writers of Meiji and Taishō Japan. Their Lives, Works and Critical Reception 1868-1926*. Jefferson: McFarland & Company, 2000.
Taneda, Kazuko. 'Fūgawarina shōjo 'shōkōjo' no hensen: Wakamatsu Shizuko kara itō sei made' [Transformation of 'Queer' (the otherness in) Little Princess: Transition of 'Shokojo' from Wakamatsu Shizuko to Itoh Sei]. *Fuji joshi daigaku kokubungaku zasshi* [Fuji Women's University Japanese literature magazine] 99-100, no. 3 (2019): 21-37.
Tatar, Maria. 'What Is a Fairy Tale?'. In *Teaching Fairy Tales*, edited by Nancy L. Canepa, 15-23. Detroit: Wayne State University Press, 2019.
Thorn, Rachel Matt. 'Shōjo manga - Something for Girls'. *Japan Quarterly* 48, no. 3 (2001): 43-50.
Thornton, Richard S. *Japanese Graphic Design*. London: Lawrence King, 1991.
Thwaite, Ann. *Waiting for the Party: The Life of Frances Hodgson Burnett, 1849-1924*. London: Faber and Faber, 1994.

Tipton, Elise K. and John Clark. 'Introduction'. In *Being Modern in Japan: Culture and Society from the 1910s to the 1930s*, edited by Elise K. Tipton and John Clark. Honolulu: University of Hawai'i Press, 2000.

Toadette. 'Rintarō, 'New Moomin' (1972), and the Last Days of Mushi Pro'. *On The Ones*, 23 March 2023. Available online: https://ontheones.wordpress.com/2023/03/23/rintaro-new-moomin-1972-and-the-last-days-of-mushi-pro/ (accessed 24 March 2023).

Toritamari, Asuka. 'Shōjo' wo sagashite: "Shōkōjo" ni miru risō no shōjo' [Looking for the 'Girl': The Ideal Girl in 'A Little Princess']. *Machikaneyama ronsō. Bunka dōtai-ron-hen* [*Machikaneyama essays. Cultural dynamics*] 46 (2012): 39–57.

Travis, Catherine. 'Omoiyari as a Core Japanese Value: Japanese-style Empathy?'. In *Speaking of Emotions: Conceptualization and Expression*, edited by Angeliki Athanasiado and Elżbieta Tabakowska, 55–82. Berlin: Mouton de Gryyter, 1988.

Truby, John. *The Anatomy of Story: 22 Steps to Becoming a Master Storyteller*. NewYork: Faber and Faber, 2008.

Tsugata, Nobuyuki. 'A Bipolar Approach to Understanding the History of Japanese Animation'. In *Japanese Animation: East Asian Perspectives*, edited by Masao Yokota and Tze-yue G. Hu, 25–33. Jackson: University Press of Mississippi, 2013.

Tsurumi, Patricia E. 'The State, Education, and Two Generations of Women in Meiji Japan, 1868–1912'. *English Supplement* 18 (2000): 3–26.

Uchiyama, Akiko. 'Akage no An in Japanese Girl Culture: Muraoka Hanako's Translation of Anne of Green Gables'. *Japan Forum* 26, no. 2 (2014): 209–23.

Uda, Kaoru. 'On Location with Heidi's Japanese (grand)fathers'. *Swissinfo*, 17 September 2019. Available online: https://www.swissinfo.ch/eng/culture/anime-heidi_on-location-with-heidi-s-japanese--grand-fathers/45230948 (accessed 13 April 2023).

Usui, Kazuo. *Marketing and Consumption in Modern Japan*. London: Routledge, 2016.

Vähäkylä, Liisa. *Nordic Animation: Balancing the East and the West*. Abingdon: CRC Press, 2013.

Venuti, Lawrence. *The Translator's Invisibility: A History of Translation*. Abingdon: Routledge, 2012.

Wakabayashi, Judy. 'Foreign Bones, Japanese Flesh: Translations and the Emergence of Modern Children's Literature in Japan'. *Japanese Language and Literature* 42, no. 1 (2008): 227–55.

Watanabe, Yasushi. 'The Japanese Walt Disney: Masaoka Kenzo'. In *Japanese Animation: East Asian Perspectives*, edited by Masao Yokota and Hu Tze-yue G. Hu, 98–115. Jackson: University Press of Mississippi, 2013.

Wells, Paul. *Understanding Animation*. Abingdon and New York: Routledge, 1998.

Wells, Paul. *Basics Animation 01: Scriptwriting*. Switzerland: AVA Publishing SA, 2007.

White, Merry. *The Japanese Educational Challenge. A Commitment to Children*. New York: Simon & Schuster, 1988.

Wierzbicka, Anna. *Semantics: Primes and Universals*. Oxford and New York: Oxford University Press, 1996.

Wittner, David G. *Technology and the Culture of Progress in Meiji Japan*. Abindgon and New York: Routledge, 2008.
Wright, Jean Ann. *Animation Writing and Development: from Screen Development to Pitch*. New York: Routledge, 2005.
Xiao, Jason. 'When Advertising Meets Japan'. *Medium*, 24 June 2019. Available online: https://medium.com/@zx548/why-japanese-advertising-stands-out-6488158d5e10.
Yamaguchi, Yasuo. *Nihon no anime zenshi: Sekai o seishita Nihon anime no kiseki* [*The complete history of anime: How Japanese animation conquered the world*]. Tokyo: Ten Books, 2004.
Yamamura, Takayoshi. 'Travelling Heidi: International Contents Tourism Induced by Japanese Anime'. In *Contents Tourism and Pop Culture Fandom: Transnational Tourist Experiences*, edited by Takayoshi Yamamura and Philip Seaton, 62–81. Bristol: Channel View Publications, 2020.
Yoshimi, Shunya. 'Japanese Television: Early Development and Research'. In *A Companion to Television*, edited by Janet Wasko, 540–57. Malden: Blackwell, 2005.
Zahlten, Alexander. 'Before Media Mix: The Electric Ecology'. In *A Companion to Japanese Cinema, edited by* David Desser, 471–92. Malden: Wiley, 2022.

INDEX

A Pro 73, 97
adaptation
   faithfulness 73, 157–8, 191, 214
   in Japanese literature 8, 27, 31
   literature-to-anime 43–4, 71–2, 82, 100, 108
   manga-to-anime 55, 66
   studies 38–9
advertising 22–7, 57–63, 71–9, 103–13, 246–9
Aesop's Fables 7, 11, 29, 44, 61, 89
Ai no wakakusa monogatari 124–7, 146, 162, 175, 179
Ai shōjo Porianna monogatari 123–7, 144, 153, 172, 215
Ajinomoto 106, 142
Akage no An 105, 126, 130, 146, 156, 183, 190–214
Alcott, Louisa May 34, 125, 132, 134
American Occupation 21, 28–35, 47–51, 223
Andersen, Hans Christian
   The Little Match Girl 48, 88, 240–1
   reception 8, 16, 29, 44, 85
   The Ugly Duckling 85, 87, 164
Andersen stories, *see Anderusen monogatari*
Anderusen monogatari 84–8, 91
animal characters
   in animation 58, 68, 109, 113, 180
   anthropomorphic 45–9, 80, 87, 89–90
   insects 45–7
   in literature 9, 20, 34, 88, 220, 239
   realistic 89–90, 92, 101, 180

animation
   animetic 40–3, 54–69, 78, 106
   cel animation 40, 42, 47, 51
   cinematic 41–3, 48–50, 80, 98–101, 109
   stop motion 42, 52
animerama 68, 81, 85–6
Annette, *see Arupusu monogatari watashi no Annetto*
Arabian Nights 31, 44, 47, 51, 68, 223, 239, 242
Araiguma Rasukaru 113–16, 161, 170, 180
ARS 22–4, 26–7
Arupusu monogatari watashi no Annetto 120–2, 143–8, 172, 174
Arupusu no shōjo Haiji 97–121, 172, 180, 198–9, 220
Ashida, Iwao 45, 47, 50, 62
Ashida Manga 62–3, 69
Atom, *see Tetsuwan Atomu*
autobiography 113, 122, 131

Bambi 31, 47, 79
Bible 31, 124
biography 9, 26, 29, 31, 33–5, 110
Bologna Children's Book Fair 107, 120, 136
Bonsels, Waldemar 34, 64
Burgess, Thornton W. 88–91, 99
Burnett, Frances 8, 12, 34, 215–18, 221–41
Bushbaby, *see Daisōgen no chīsana tenshi busshu beibī*

Calpis 74–82, 87, 91–4, 103–14, 180
Calpis Theater 77–84, 88, 91, 93–8, 105–8
canon
  of Japanese children's stories 16–17, 45, 51, 110
  resulting from zenshū 24, 34, 68, 141
  of Western children's books 8, 15, 32, 44, 51, 141
Carroll, Lewis 8, 213
childhood
  dōshin shugi (child-mind) 16–17, 27
  motherhood 12–13, 85–7, 245–6
  qualities 91–4, 156, 171, 177, 232
China 6, 35, 70, 75
Chinese literature 25, 31, 43, 49
Chīsana baikingu Bikke 94–8, 249
Chūshingura 43, 54
Cinderella 129, 164, 218–19, 224, 239–41
comedy 79, 86, 91, 123, 128, 192, 206
coming-of-age 80, 91, 113, 146, 183, 252
co-production 94–8, 108–10, 186, 249
Cuore (De Amicis) 26, 35, 111–12
cute
  animals 45–51, 80, 180–2
  children 93, 178
  girls 99, 124, 140, 146, 193
CX, see Fuji Television
cyclical time 91, 201–2

Daddy Long-Legs (Webster) 129, 141
Daisōgen no chīsana tenshi busshu beibī 131–3, 142, 154, 179
Dax International 109–10
Defoe, Daniel 8, 117
Dentsu 79–81, 91, 104, 113
Dezaki, Osamu 81, 88
Disney
  animation style 40–2
  business strategies 47, 51, 67, 95
  influence 37, 42, 62–3, 80, 87, 246–8
  works 85, 109, 113, 141

A Dog of Flanders (Ouida) 27, 103, 110
Dokura, Fujio 93, 103, 110–11
Dororo 78–82
drama 58–60, 77–81, 112, 118, 164–75, 226

education
  in animation 49, 89–91, 96, 109–10, 170–1, 228–32
  in children's literature 8–11, 17, 25–6, 71, 117, 139
  girls' and women's 12–14, 189, 208–13
  kyōyōshugi (culturalism) 23, 177
empathy 101, 143, 156, 176, 196, 230
  omoiyari (fellow feeling) 209–11
encyclopaedia 26, 35
Endō, Masaharu 90, 95, 113
English literature 31–2, 141, 205
enpon 22–30, 109, 245
exotic
  fascination 101, 107, 174, 236
  location 50, 68, 113, 118, 167, 236

fairy tales
  adaptation 43–5, 50–1, 71, 84, 109–10, 240–1
  dōwa 16–19, 32, 44
  Western 8–16, 47, 68–71, 216–38
family
  ie (multigenerational household) 12, 169
  nuclear 12, 93, 168, 187
Flanders, see Furandāsu no inu
Fleischer brothers 46–7, 60, 68
Flone, see Kazoku Robinson hyōryūki fushigina shima no Furōne
Folk tales 6–11, 43–9, 80, 110, 175
Fuji Television 55–7, 77–80, 107–8, 142
Fujiko, Fujio 65–6, 155
Furandāsu no inu 110–11, 153, 158–9, 167, 175, 235

gag manga 65–6, 155
Golden time, see primetime

Greek mythology 35, 205
Grimm brothers 8, 10–11, 14, 29, 218, 244

Haha o tazunete sanzen ri 111–13, 152–3, 169, 183
Haikara-san ga tōru 106–7
Hakubunkan 9, 11, 118
Hakujaden 49–50, 53
Hanna & Barbera 47, 60, 89
Heidi, see *Arupusu no shōjo Haiji*
Heidi (Spyri) 31, 35, 69–70, 97–100
Hodgson, *see* Burnett, Frances
Hollywood 31, 44–8, 141, 165, 168, 224
House Food 106–7, 135

Ie-naki-ko Remi 139–40, 144, 148, 153, 172
Ioka, Masahiro 103, 116, 118, 121
Ishii, Momoko 32, 35
Iwanami Shoten 25, 30, 32–4, 157
Iwaya, Sazanami 9–11, 14, 45

Jansson, Tove 71, 73, 84, 89
The Jungle Book 67, 106

Kadokawa 113, 142
Kaisesha 33–4
kamishibai 42, 196
karma 161, 244
Katabuchi, Sunao 135, 139
Katō, Kikuzō 79–80, 104
Katri, *see Makiba no shōjo Katori*
kawaii, *see* cute
Kazoku Robinson hyōryūki fushigina shima no Furōne 117–20, 128, 144, 146, 152
Kikuchi, Kan 22, 24, 26, 128
Kitahara, Hakushu 17, 22, 76
Kitayama, Seitarō 43
Kōbunsha-Bungei 22–4, 26–7
Kōdansha 19, 25, 30–4, 49, 71, 122, 141
Kōndo, Yoshifumi 126, 183, 193–4
Kotabe, Yōichi 98, 100, 103, 145, 249
Koyama, Akiko 103, 126, 128

Kuroda, Masao 111, 155, 158–9, 167
Kurokawa, Fumio 125–6, 215, 223–7
Kusuba, Kōzō 121, 123–39, 143, 146, 151–6, 172

Little House on the Prairie (Ingalls) 29, 120, 158
A Little Princess (Burnett) 15, 34, 126, 141, 215–26
location hunting 97, 101, 108, 167–8, 194, 225
love
  familial 85, 114, 156, 173, 206
  first love 75, 119, 148
Lucy, see *Minami no niji no Rūshī*

magazines
  for boys 10–11, 19–20, 79
  for children 10–12, 17–20, 185–6, 216
  for girls 12–13, 99
  for women 12–13, 15, 18
mahō shōjo 58, 65, 69, 227
Makiba no shōjo Katori 121–4, 147–9, 158, 177–8, 220–1
Malot, Henry 34, 114, 139
marriage 13, 146
Masaoka, Kenzō 44–6, 48–50, 111, 247
masterpiece 26, 33, 70, 106, 192
Matsudo, Takaji 108, 117–18
Maya the Honeybee 63, 69, 96
media mix 57, 61, 66, 79–80, 246
Meiji Seika 57, 63, 66
Meiken Rasshī 58, 137–9, 150, 167–8
melodrama 59, 148, 153, 161–2, 234–8
merchandise 50, 57, 63, 87, 108, 113–14, 117, 180
Mickey Mouse 34, 46
Minami no niji no Rūshī 118–22, 144–7, 152–3, 182
Mirai shōnen Konan 109, 115, 117
Miyazaki, Akira 114–17, 155–7, 221
Miyazaki, Hayao 41, 47, 97–103, 115, 168, 183

Momotarō 10, 43, 45–6, 54, 191
Montgomery, L.M. 34, 183–213, 218
Mori, Yasuji 50–1, 90, 103–4, 116, 180, 215
mukokuseki (non-nation specific) 29, 172
Mūmin 71–4, 81–5, 128, 221
Muraoka, Hanako 190–2, 200
Mushi Production 55, 57, 68, 79, 83–90

Nagagutsu haita neko 51–2, 67
Nakajima, Junzō 90, 98, 108, 111, 194, 215
Nanatsu no umi no Tiko 134–6, 149, 170, 174, 180
narration
  comic relief 86, 159, 175, 180, 225, 244
  digression 163–4
  Hero's Journey 80, 176, 196
  horizontal 86, 91, 101, 159
  rags-to-riches 126, 161, 218, 226
  subplot 120, 125, 157, 159
  travelling angel 144, 188, 238
  vertical 86, 96, 109, 159
narrator 160, 164, 186, 196, 225
nationalism 10, 16, 20, 27–8, 45, 170
nature
  and children 17, 134, 180
  harmony 71, 90, 174, 189
  ideas about 173–4
New Thought 216, 231
Newbery Medal 33, 113
NHK 59, 107, 115, 120, 158
Nichidō Eigasha 49–50, 62
Nikkatsu 42–3, 235
Nippon Animation 96, 104–10, 183, 220
NTT 106

Ōfuji, Noburo 42, 47
oil crisis 53, 99
Ōishi, Ikuo 45–6
Okawa, Hiroshi 49–51, 53, 62, 67, 80
Onishi, Kiyoshi 62–3

orphan (trope) 48, 97, 123, 170, 176, 217–19
The Osmonds 93–4, 131
Ouida 34, 110–11
outsourcing 52, 72, 94

PEI, see Prince Edward Island
Perīnu monogatari 114–17, 146, 157, 159–61, 164
period drama 79, 113
Perrault, Charles 51, 218
Perrine, see *Perīnu monogatari*
Peter Pan, see *Pītā Pan no bōken*
Pinocchio 41, 47, 52, 108
Pippi Longstocking 97, 130
Pītā Pan no bōken 128–30, 132
Pollyanna (Porter) 123–4, 141, 191, 222
Popeye 46–7, 60
Poplar 30, 34
Porter, Eleanor H. 123–4
primetime 58, 60, 78
Prince Edward Island 184–5, 189, 194–5, 197, 201
Proletarian literature 19, 27, 29
propaganda 19, 28, 45

Rankin/Bass 52–3, 109
Rascal see *Araiguma Rasukaru*
realism
  animation 49–50, 90–2, 99–101, 108, 164–7, 193, 236–8
  literature 16, 19–20, 88–9, 219
religion
  Buddhism 15–16, 43, 80
  Christianity 14–15, 86, 98, 172–5, 230–7
  Shintō 76, 80, 173
Remi, see *Ie-naki-ko Remi*
Rocky Chuck, see *Yama nezumi Rokkī Chakku*
romance 87, 129, 147, 193
Romeo, see *Romio no aoi sora*
Romio no aoi sora 136–40, 150–2, 162–3
Rupan sansei 83, 86
ryōshin (conscientious) 29, 100, 102

Saitō, Hiroshi 95, 115, 155–6, 221
Saiyūki 43, 51, 54–5
Sakurai, Michiyo 126, 128
Sans Famille (Malot) 27, 67, 139–41
Sanzen ri, see *Haha o tazunete sanzen ri*
Satō, Shōji 90, 107, 142, 155, 220–1
Satō, Yoshiharu 124, 134, 137
Scandinavia 31, 82–5, 122, 174, 221
science-fiction 57, 100, 135
Seki, Shuichi 87, 95, 117–18, 122, 132–3, 179
Seo, Mitsuyo 45–6, 48–9, 54
Seton, Ernest 89, 109
Shakespeare, William 152, 205
Shimada, Michiru 137, 139
Shin Mūmin 83–4
Shirato, Sanpei 69, 72–3, 79
Shōgakukan 34–5, 66
shōjo (girl)
    concept 13, 192–4, 222
    manga 13–14, 106, 193
    novels 34, 99, 190, 223
    style 100, 140, 194, 227, 252
Shōkōjo Sēra 4, 105, 123, 160, 215, 221
Shōkōshi Sedi 126–8, 150, 153, 173
slapstick 60, 86, 89, 91
spokon 65–6, 81
Stevenson, Robert Lewis 29, 68
Studio Ghibli 39, 47, 97, 100, 134–5, 139, 173
Supreme Commander of the Allied Powers (SCAP) 29–30, 47–8
Swiss Robinson (Wyss) 117–18, 141
Switzerland 97, 100, 136, 141, 151, 158, 167
    Alps 97, 101–3, 116, 131, 157, 198–9

Taiga drama 59, 107, 250
Taiyō no ōji Horusu no daibōken 51, 94
Takahashi, Shigeto 69–74, 81–90, 97–104, 140

Takahata, Isao 41, 51, 97–103, 155–6, 183, 191–208
Tamī-chan 92–3
Tarzan 28, 44, 67
TBS 66, 77–8, 110
Television Corporation of Japan (TCJ) 62–73, 81, 87
Tetsujin 28-go 63, 69, 73
Tetsuwan Atomu 55–60, 63–6, 78–9
Tezuka, Osamu 21, 47, 54–7, 60–4, 68, 79–86
Tico, see *Nanatsu no umi no Tiko*
Tōei 48–55, 66–73, 80–2, 109–10
Tokyo Movie 66, 72–3, 83, 97
Tom Sawyer, see *Tomu Sōyā no bōken*
Tomu Sōyā no bōken 115–17, 146–7, 158, 161, 167
Tora-chan 48–9, 111
Torappu ikka monogatari 131–4, 146, 149–50, 170–1
translation 32
    adaptation 8–11, 26–8, 31
    domestication 8, 14, 32, 112, 117, 223
    faithfulness 32, 157–8, 191, 252
    foreignization 2, 8, 222
Trapp, see *Torappu ikka monogatari*
Twain, Mark 28, 115, 158, 179, 218

United States of America
    illustrators 90, 117
    influence 31–2, 47
    representation 48, 115, 126, 167
    television 53, 58, 91, 106, 118, 120
    writers 44, 90, 113, 115, 117, 129

Verne, Jules 8, 34, 108, 134
Vicke, see *Chīsana baikingu Bikke*

Wakakusa, see *Ai no wakakusa monogatari*
Wakakusa monogatari Nan to Jō sensei 132–5, 144–5, 170
Wakamatsu, Shizuko 15, 222–3
war
    First World War 18, 75, 113, 123

Opium Wars 6, 70
Second World War 20, 45–7, 55, 59, 73
Watashi no Ashinaga ojisan 129–30, 146–7, 171–2, 178
womanhood
 angel in the house 12, 222, 228–9
 ryōsai kenbo (good wife, wise mother) 12, 223
Wyss, Johann David 34, 117–18

Yama nezumi Rokkī Chakku 88–92, 94–6, 108, 113, 180, 242
Yamamoto, Sanae 48, 61
Yasuda, Michiyo 103, 194
yōkai 66, 79

zenshū 22–8, 30–5, 68–70, 109–10, 142
Zuiyō Eizō, *see* Zuiyō Enterprise
Zuiyō Enterprise 72–3, 85–101, 108–11, 157, 224

Capacitación inicial

Haga un análisis inicial de las necesidades de capacitación. Esto debería hacerse en una fase temprana, y abarcar cuestiones como:

i) ¿Cuáles habilidades ya tiene el/la estudiante?

ii) ¿Qué otras habilidades necesita? (por ejemplo, recopilación y gestión de datos, registro, mantenimiento y almacenamiento de documentos, habilidades informáticas y de comunicación —TICs)

iii) Especialmente en áreas bíblicas, aunque también en otros campos teológicos e históricos, puede necesitar otros idiomas —alemán, francés, latín— e incluso mejorar su hebreo y/o griego.

iv) Las/los supervisores necesitan saber qué oportunidades y recursos hay para ayudar con el aprendizaje de idiomas. ¿Hay cursos específicos?

v) ¿En qué momento del programa será mejor que haga el aprendizaje de idioma(s), para contar con esas habilidades cuando las necesite?

vi) ¿Hay otros cursos, talleres o programas de capacitación a nivel posgrado, disponibles en el seminario/universidad, que serían de beneficio para él/ella?

vii) Las/los supervisores deben ser conscientes de lo que hay disponible y de lo que será beneficioso. No debe simplemente confiar que sus estudiantes lo puedan averiguar por su cuenta.

viii) ¿Hay financiación disponible para estas necesidades adicionales de capacitación?

ix) ¿En qué momento del programa será necesaria la capacitación adicional? Esto debe ser acordado entre supervisor/a y estudiante, e incorporado al plan de investigación.

x) Las necesidades de capacitación deben ser evaluadas por lo menos una vez al año —a medida que se desarrolla o cambia el proyecto, pueden cambiar también las necesidades de investigación.

Preguntas de reflexión

¿Qué habilidades específicas de investigación necesitó usted para su doctorado?

¿Cómo accedió a esas habilidades?

¿Cuáles son las necesidades de su actual estudiante de doctorado?

De esas habilidades de investigación que él o ella necesita, ¿cuáles puede proveer usted y cuáles tendrán que proveerse externamente?

Objetivos clave para las/los estudiantes en los primeros meses de supervisión

i) El problema de investigación debe quedar claramente establecido.

ii) El diseño de la investigación debe ser claro. La propuesta de investigación debe haber sido revisado, y si no fue aprobada lo debería estar ahora.

iii) Los métodos de recopilación y almacenamiento de datos deben quedar establecidos.

iv) Los asuntos de ética investigativa relacionados con el proyecto deben ser entendidos y acordados.

v) El acceso adecuado a los recursos de la biblioteca (en la institución o en otros sitios) debe haber sido negociado.

vi) Podría necesitarse un estudio piloto.

Iniciación a la escritura

Las y los estudiantes necesitan desarrollar sus habilidades de escritura lo antes posible. Esto es vital, no solo para su tesis sino también para otros aspectos de su trabajo a nivel de doctorado, incluyendo la preparación de informes, ponencias de seminarios, presentaciones de conferencias y documentos académicos.

Es importante que en una etapa temprana comiencen a documentar sus ideas y resultados de investigación para que más adelante los puedan desarrollar más. Esto significa que hay que ponerles a escribir lo antes posible. Aunque sus estudiantes ya tendrán experiencia con diferentes formas de escribir, es bueno que escriban piezas cortas que luego se convertirán en trabajos de nivel de doctorado.

Desde el inicio las/los supervisores deben requerir de sus estudiantes altos niveles de ortografía, gramática, edición y uso de referencias, con el fin de fortalecer sus habilidades y definir las expectativas. Si se empieza con esto desde temprano y se adquiere práctica en el ejercicio de estas habilidades, entonces la edición de la versión final será un proceso más simple y menos largo.

Las y los supervisores tienen diferentes políticas en cuanto a la corrección del lenguaje y la gramática de lo que escriben sus estudiantes, pero se entiende que el valor académico de un trabajo es más difícil de apreciar cuando el texto está lleno de errores ortográficos o gramaticales o no se entiende. Cuando un/a estudiante no está escribiendo en su primer idioma, debería recibir ayuda de un corrector experimentado para fortalecer su estilo y su forma de expresarse. Debe quedar claro que este apoyo no implica "ayuda" ni "corrección" de cuestiones de contenido o argumento.

Además de desarrollar las habilidades de la prosa escrita, las/los estudiantes también deben seguir ejercitando las habilidades de planificación de textos y de producción de bosquejos funcionales. Necesitan desarrollar formas de construir introducciones y títulos de capítulos para sacarle el mayor provecho a su material.

También necesitan desarrollar habilidades para revisar su propio trabajo escrito y distinguir entre lo que es bueno y lo que no.

Preguntas de reflexión

¿Qué cree usted que añadirá a la investigación de su estudiante una revisión de la vanguardia/los últimos avances en su área temática?

¿Cuáles son las fortalezas de hacer esto al iniciar el proyecto de investigación, y cuáles son las fortalezas de hacerlo hacia el final?

Revisión de Literatura

Un enfoque útil para que sus estudiantes escriban pronto es pedirles que produzcan reseñas breves (200-500 palabras) de textos clave en su área temática. Estas piezas se pueden luego incorporar como parte de la revisión de la literatura, así sus estudiantes sienten que aun su trabajo inicial está contribuyendo a la tesis.

Localización de fuentes

En las etapas iniciales, las/los supervisores necesitan orientar a sus estudiantes sobre cuáles son las fuentes que necesitan leer para desarrollar su investigación. Algunos puntos de partida:

i) Los textos clave de los principales eruditos deben contener amplias bibliografías de material publicado e inédito.

ii) Las revistas académicas tienen artículos y también reseñas de libros. Algunas producen una lista anual de libros, artículos y tesis en áreas temáticas específicas.

iii) Los catálogos de las bibliotecas son una fuente esencial y ahora muchos están disponibles en línea, incluyendo bibliotecas tan importantes y amplias como la Biblioteca del Congreso (de Estados Unidos) y la Biblioteca Británica (del Reino Unido).

iv) Los sitios de búsqueda en línea albergan muchas bases de datos de revistas académicas y ofrecerán lo mejor de los recursos recientes.

v) Las/los estudiantes de doctorado deben consultar las bases de datos de tesis recientemente publicadas —es esencial que estén al tanto de las últimas investigaciones.

vi) Contactos personales y diálogo con otros eruditos. Esto puede ocurrir en conferencias, mediante correspondencia personal, etc.

Las investigaciones deben establecerse en el contexto de la erudición más amplia

La 'literatura' que hay que revisar (y reseñar) son las contribuciones eruditas en el campo de investigación, que incluye libros, artículos de revistas, ponencias de conferencias y seminarios (algunas inéditas), revistas electrónicas, sitios web académicos, debates en línea e informes de conferencias.

Las revistas académicas y las ponencias de conferencias suelen tener material que está a la vanguardia investigativa, y es crucial que sus estudiantes de doctorado las consulten. A menudo este es el ámbito en donde las y los estudiosos 'piensan en voz alta' y donde primero presentan los resultados de sus investigaciones —con vista a recibir la retroalimentación inicial de sus pares académicos.

Algo que es útil para las/los estudiantes es leer las reseñas de obras clave, escritas por otros eruditos y publicadas en las revistas académicas. Esto les ayudará a ver los enfoques que toman los eruditos ya establecidos y las fortalezas y debilidades que han identificado en esas obras. Se puede animarles a que evalúen y critiquen estas reseñas. Sin embargo, no debe sustituir que lean por sí mismos la obra y formen su propia evaluación crítica.

El propósito de la revisión de literatura en la tesis

Los examinadores de una tesis doctoral querrán saber si el/la estudiante:

i) tiene un conocimiento amplio del tema.

ii) ha hecho una revisión crítica de otros materiales académicos que son medulares para el campo de estudio. El/la estudiante necesita demostrar que sabe exactamente lo que se está haciendo en el campo (en cuanto a los enfoques y avances más recientes). La tesis doctoral debería poder, de alguna manera, generar cambios en el campo.

iii) ha logrado una buena percepción de cómo su investigación es diferente, y no solo una réplica, de otras en el campo.

iv) siguió leyendo desde que inició la tesis. En los tres, cuatro (o más) años que lleva escribir una tesis, el campo pudo haber cambiado de maneras significativas. Si la revisión de la literatura se hizo tres años atrás, y no se actualizó, puede contener importantes vacíos.

v) siguió leyendo entre la entrega y el examen de su tesis, para estar al tanto de otras investigaciones y/o tesis que es están publicando y presentando.

vi) ha demostrado la relación entre su trabajo y el resto del campo, a fin de establecer conexiones entre sus propios resultados de investigación y los avances más recientes.

Las formas de la revisión de literatura

i) Un sondeo inicial del material importante en el campo.

Esto produce una lista de los textos de 'lectura obligada' en el campo. En su forma inicial, aparecerá en la propuesta de investigación.

ii) Un resumen del conocimiento actual de base en el campo y un análisis de los tipos de investigación que otros han utilizado en el campo.

Esta revisión más completa demostrará una comprensión de las principales escuelas de pensamiento y establecerá lo que se investiga en la actualidad, especialmente lo que se ha investigado recientemente. Se podrán apreciar cuáles son las áreas bien trabajadas en el campo y también en cuáles áreas hay vacíos importantes. El/la supervisor/a puede animar a su estudiante a desarrollar su investigación en esas direcciones para que sea una "contribución original al conocimiento".

Esta dimensión de la revisión de la literatura establece las preguntas clave de investigación que habrá que plantear o probar, y es conveniente definirlas en una etapa temprana de la investigación.

iii) Una revisión de las metodologías

La revisión de la literatura también establece las principales metodologías en el campo, y la forma en que han surgido diferentes posiciones académicas. Una vez más, el valor de hacer este trabajo temprano en el proceso de investigación es evidente. Ayudará a que el/la estudiante identifique y defina el enfoque que usará, y a que tenga conciencia de sus fortalezas y debilidades.

iv) La determinación de los límites

Con la revisión de la literatura, puede delimitar el campo que está por abordar. Es el momento propicio para establecer límites y definir lo que abarcará.

Las revisiones de literatura sirven también para otros propósitos

- Crea interlocutores

    Esto es esencial para la participación en la discusión académica. Los escritos de otras y otros estudiosos se convierten en interlocutores, proveyendo material para desarrollar, respaldar, desafiar o revisar.

- Un chequeo de nivel

    La literatura académica con la que interactúan las y los estudiantes de doctorado les permitirá conocer no solo lo que otros están diciendo sobre su mismo tema, sino también el nivel al que están escribiendo. Al principio sus estudiantes pueden sentir que nunca lograrán ese nivel, pero a medida que ganan confianza comienzan a reconocer maneras en las que están escribiendo al nivel de sus pares e interlocutores académicos.

    A medida que progresan en su programa de doctorado, deberán poder criticar el trabajo de otros de manera eficaz. Con el tiempo deberían ser capaces de decir, si el trabajo de este académico fuera presentado como tesis doctoral, ¿sería aprobado?

    De lo contrario, ¿por qué no?

- "¿Están pensando lo que yo estoy pensando?"

    Los escritos de otros académicos se convierten en una "caja de resonancia", en la cual se mide la resonancia de las propias opiniones.

    Lo que se está diciendo, ¿se sostiene ante la evaluación de otros/as? ¿Están pensando de la misma manera? Si no, ¿por qué no? Las ideas propuestas, ¿son brillantes y originales, o son insostenible e incluso disparatadas?

Esto hace que la revisión de la literatura sirva de control de seguridad, permitiendo la comparación de ideas y niveles.

- "Esto es importante"

    Un amplio diálogo con la literatura en su campo permite que él/ella pueda ver la necesidad y legitimidad de su estudio, y facilita articular un argumento claro sobre su importancia. Su investigación debe originarse a partir del sondeo del campo y "enlazarse" con él en puntos apropiados. La revisión de la literatura hace más que simplemente sentar las bases. A lo largo del resto de la tesis, él/ella necesita remitirse a, y estar en diálogo con, la literatura clave. Uno de los peligros que amenaza a muchas reseñas de literatura es que quedan como capítulos sellados poco relacionados con las otras secciones de la tesis, en lugar de ser una parte central del flujo narrativo y lógico.

La revisión de literatura debe actualizarse constantemente

La erudición está cambiando. Las y los estudiantes deben alimentar sus borradores —sus documentos de trabajo 'en desarrollo'— con material nuevo donde sea oportuno.

El alcance de la revisión de literatura

Una duda que surge con frecuencia es acerca de cuánto, o qué tan poco, material se necesita para una revisión aceptable de la literatura.

El proyecto que el/la estudiante lleva a cabo puede ser muy innovador y puede haber poca literatura secundaria en el campo específico. Esto, sin embargo, no debe impedir que se haga una revisión. Habrá literatura en campos relacionados o integrados con material que es relevante y puede servir de contexto para el trabajo. También habrá una serie de fuentes que se pueden explorar que permitirán llevar a cabo un estudio comparativo.

Si el alcance de la literatura secundaria en el campo específico es demasiado vasto para hacer una revisión, quizás signifique que el proyecto es demasiado amplio y debe ser reducido.

Preguntas de reflexión

¿Cómo aconsejaría a un/a estudiante cuando le informa que hay poco material secundario en su campo elegido?

¿Qué temas paralelos, o enfoques metodológicos pueden considerarse?

Las responsabilidades de las/los supervisores

Todo esto confiere una fuerte responsabilidad sobre la supervisión.

Las y los supervisores necesitan conocer bien el campo de investigación. Necesitan conocer a fondo la literatura secundaria para poder identificar los vacíos en el trabajo de sus estudiantes. Es importante no supervisar estudiantes fuera del propio campo de investigación o área de competencia, para asegurar que no estén en desventaja por carencias en esa profundidad de conocimiento. Cuando un proyecto contiene elementos significativamente ajenos al campo de investigación del supervisor, se debe reforzar el equipo de supervisión con miembros que tengan esa especialización, o se debe asignar el proyecto a otro/a supervisor/a que tenga los conocimientos específicos necesarios.

Es un requisito esencial que las y los supervisores estén activamente investigando y escribiendo, de esa manera estarán a la vanguardia del campo en que están supervisando.

No es posible darle a las y los estudiantes una experiencia de supervisión adecuada únicamente en base al conocimiento y la experiencia investigativa obtenida diez o quince años atrás cuando su supervisor/a obtuvo su doctorado.

Para leer más

Murray, R. *How to Write a Thesis*. Maidenhead: Open University, 2002.

Phillips, E. M. y D. S. Pugh. *How to Get a PhD: A Handbook for Students and Their Supervisors*. Maidenhead: Open University Press, 2010. (Disponible también para Kindle)

Potter, S. *Doing Postgraduate Research*. Londres: Sage, 2006.

Smith, K. *Writing and Research: A Guide for Theological Students*. Carlisle: Langham Global Library, 2015.

Taylor, Stan y Nigel Beasley. *A Handbook for Doctoral Supervisors*. Nueva York: Routledge, 2005.

8

Cómo enmarcar las preguntas de investigación y la propuesta de investigación

"Para tener éxito debemos aprender a hacer las preguntas correctas" —Aristóteles

La capacidad de hacer preguntas está en el corazón del pensamiento crítico (juicio reflexivo). No cualquier pregunta, sino las correctas. Hacemos preguntas con el propósito de adquirir conocimiento y comprensión.

Hace poco tiempo mi hijo y yo estábamos trabajando en el motor de un viejo tractor que había estado en desuso durante muchos años. Llegamos a un punto en el armado del carburador donde no podíamos ver dónde cabía una de las piezas. ¿A quién le podríamos preguntar? Mi padre lo sabría, pero lamentablemente ya no está vivo. Así que mi hijo encontró el número de la pieza, el modelo y la marca, y los buscó en Google. Y, sorprendentemente, encontró un video de Youtube de algún viejito en su patio desmantelando y volviendo a armar el mismo viejo carburador que teníamos nosotros. Problema resuelto. La solución estaba en el "conocimiento de muchos" que nos ha abierto el Internet.

Pero esa solución solo fue posible porque ingresamos los detalles correctos e hicimos las preguntas correctas.

Las y los estudiantes de doctorado necesitan entrenamiento en cómo hacer las preguntas correctas. El desarrollo de preguntas específicas de investigación,

- nos permite entender lo otro (es decir, lo que aún no se conoce).
- nos ayuda a hacer uso de nuestra racionalidad y capacidad de reflexión crítica.
- nos inicia en un emocionante viaje hermenéutico.

Preguntas de reflexión

Recuerde su propio estudio de doctorado.

¿Cuáles fueron las tres preguntas más importantes que necesitaba hacer?

¿Cómo fue que llegó a identificar esas preguntas?

Hay una relación estrecha entre ser buenos investigadores y saber hacer las preguntas correctas. Como ya hemos visto, es útil recordar la imagen del abogado en la corte. Muchas veces la capacidad de sondear y cuestionar, de mirar las cosas desde perspectivas inusuales y cavar bajo de la superficie con preguntas incisivas logra exponer la verdad —que quizás estaba oculta u ocultada. Del mismo modo, las y los estudiantes de doctorado necesitan ser buenos pensadores críticos y demostrar que pueden emitir juicios deliberados y reflexivos acerca de qué creer o hacer, en respuesta a —o sobre la base de— observaciones, experiencias, argumentos y expresiones verbales o escritas

Las y los pensadores críticos necesitan demostrar un uso eficaz no solo de la lógica, sino también de habilidades intelectuales como la precisión, la relevancia, el análisis, la síntesis, y el equilibrio académico.

Estas habilidades se demuestran en la tarea vital de concebir el conjunto de preguntas —de investigación— correctas.

La dimensión comunitaria

El proceso de formular preguntas puede ser difícil de hacer en solitario. A veces surgen con más naturalidad mediante la discusión y el diálogo. A menudo, la necesidad de articular las cosas en un debate, de explicárselas a otras personas, ayuda a "ver" los temas con mucha más claridad.

Como supervisoras y supervisores, servir de interlocutores informados es una ayuda vital para nuestros/as estudiantes. Permite:

- una fusión de los horizontes —las perspectivas del supervisor sirven para refinar o mejorar las del estudiante.
- la reflexión dialógica. Puedo recordar muchos casos en los que un estudiante de investigación que he supervisado pareció quedarse atascado en cierto punto de su reflexión, y no progresaba. Pero 'hablar del problema' lleva a la claridad. No necesariamente significa que el supervisor le dirá al estudiante cuál es la solución. Que el estudiante llegue a 'ver' la solución por sí mismo es mucho mejor como experiencia de aprendizaje. Sin embargo, a veces hace falta un poco de dirección para que encuentre esa solución.
- el diálogo con otras áreas temáticas, que también pueden plantear preguntas profundas y aportar nuevos conocimientos.

Las grandes preguntas

A veces las preguntas más grandes se expresan con muy pocas palabras —especialmente las que son medulares. ¿Por qué?, ¿qué?, ¿cómo?

Tengo una caricatura que a veces muestro a mis estudiantes para ilustrar esto. Es de un niño que se acerca a su padre y le dice, 'Papá, ya sabes que siempre tengo preguntas... ¿Por qué?"

La pregunta '¿por qué?' prepara el camino para el análisis y la evaluación de ideas y los acontecimientos. Investiga las razones detrás de un problema.

La pregunta '¿qué?' ofrece una manera de diagramar y describir la naturaleza del campo temático y los problemas que plantea. Ayuda a abrir y delimitar la investigación y las hipótesis que se explorarán.

La pregunta '¿cómo?' invita a explorar cómo funciona, cómo está compuesto, cómo se organiza o cómo se ve. Conduce a cuestiones metodológicas —la forma en que se interpretan los datos. El uso del método correcto ayudará a obtener los resultados más útiles.

Persistencia

Las y los estudiantes de doctorado necesitan ser tenaces e implacables en su capacidad de plantear preguntas y rastrearlas, dejando a un lado las respuestas simplistas y explorando más y más profundo. En las sesiones de supervisión, especialmente en las etapas iniciales de un proyecto de doctorado, es importante que sus estudiantes logren aclarar cuáles son las preguntas que su investigación está diseñada para responder. Por lo tanto, el/la supervisor/a necesita ser implacable con sus preguntas —¿sobre qué basó este argumento? ¿por qué aparece en este punto de este capítulo? ¿por qué ha elegido este enfoque? ¿cómo llegó a esta conclusión? ¿hacia adónde nos lleva esto? Son preguntas que buscan pulir y afilar. Están diseñadas para que él/ella tenga que pensar y volver a pensar, cada vez con más profundidad. Tendrá que articular sus razones en la tesis y, más adelante, ante sus examinadores. Por eso es bueno que tenga la experiencia de hacerlo de forma verbal en las primeras etapas de su trabajo.

La lectura crítica

Los pensadores críticos necesitan leer los textos con atención, y luego escribir sobre ellos con efectividad.

Al leer los textos clave y las fuentes primarias, deben examinarlas con una serie de preguntas. Estas deben ser,

- preguntas de importancia vital, formuladas con claridad y precisión;
- diseñadas para cosechar información pertinente;

- creadas para ayudar a sus estudiantes a usar el andamiaje teórico del campo más amplio a fin de elaborar interpretaciones efectivas;
- capaces de producir conclusiones y soluciones que se pueden comprobar;
- diseñadas para facilitar que sus estudiantes mantengan su mente abierta a soluciones alternativas;
- capaces de producir resultados y soluciones que se pueden comunicar de manera eficaz;
- un medio para formar hipótesis nuevas o alternativas, o desafiar las conocidas.

Al hacer esto las/los estudiantes están en efecto poniendo a otras y otros académicos —y sus escritos— en el banquillo e interrogándoles a fin de encontrar respuestas más profundas.

En cierto sentido la investigación es 're buscar' (en inglés, 'RE' + Search) en cuanto a menudo implica repasar ideas y recorrer caminos que otros han transitado, pero haciéndolo con nuevos ojos, con técnicas nuevas y mejoradas, y haciendo conexiones que no se habían hecho antes.

Es sorprendente cuánta literatura secundaria se basa en resúmenes de otras publicaciones secundarias, sin haber leído las fuentes originales. En su tesis, el/la estudiante debe demostrar su familiaridad —de primera mano— con los escritos de las figuras más importantes en su campo, y dar evidencia de que ha interactuado críticamente con ellos. Los examinadores pueden exigir que se reescriban partes de la tesis en donde no se han usado fuentes primarias y la tesis depende de fuentes secundarias.

Un resumen del proceso

Hacer(le) las preguntas correctas (pensamiento crítico)
    a las fuentes correctas
        de la manera correcta (metodología)
            con el fin de recolectar información
                que puede ser interpretada y registrada con una perspectiva fresca
                    y conducir hacia recomendaciones y acciones creativas
                        conforme a la voluntad de Dios y para su gloria. (cf. Fil 1:9-11)

Ejercicio

Haga una lista de las habilidades básicas que usted piensa que se necesitan para desarrollar las preguntas de investigación correctas.

Formas de desarrollar las preguntas clave

Las y los estudiantes deben aprender a:
- Estar atentos al estado actual de la disciplina.
- Escuchar a sus fuentes —sus voces deben ser escuchadas y respetada, y no leídas a través de otros/as intérpretes que pueden haber equivocado su valoración.
- Escuchar a Dios —la investigación es un aspecto de glorificar a Dios con nuestra mente, por lo que debe incluirse en el proceso. La oración puede mover montañas, y puede ayudar a mover obstáculos en el camino del investigador.

En una etapa inicial las/los estudiantes deben trabajar con su supervisor/a en:

1) Buscar una pregunta clave que se puede desglosar y reelaborar como una serie de preguntas complementarias

2) Reflexionar sobre las preguntas que han propuesto:

   i) ¿Las preguntas van lo suficientemente profundo?

   ii) ¿Son capaces de abrir y esclarecer el campo de investigación? Si no, ¿son demasiado estrechas?

   iii) ¿Se pueden responder? Si no, ¿son demasiado amplias?

   iv) ¿Cuáles de estas preguntas clave son las que se pueden ser usar como el foco central de la tesis/disertación?

Controles y equilibrios: problemas a evitar

1. 'Ya sé cuáles son las respuestas'.
Esto produce una investigación 'cerrada'. El/la estudiante ha decidido cuál será el resultado de la investigación antes de llevarla a cabo. En vista de ello, es probable que la evidencia no sea evaluada de manera objetiva. Las fuentes tenderán a leerse de una forma que apoye su teoría.

2. "Dios me proveerá las respuestas".
Este es un enfoque híper espiritual. Martin Lutero se lamentaba que había cristianos cuya noción de la providencia de Dios era tal que creían que si tenían hambre solo tenían que abrir la boca y vendría volando un pollo frito. Como docentes cristianos, creemos que Dios puede dar respuestas y, de hecho, las da. Pero normalmente lo hace a través de diversos medios, como el uso debido de la razón dada por Dios, el estudio esmerado, la recopilación de evidencia y su cuidadoso análisis. ¡Hay que hacer más que solo abrir la boca!

3. La investigación no cambiará nada.

Esto sugiere una falta de motivación para emprender el proyecto. Dedicar de tres a cinco años a un doctorado de investigación requiere de ímpetu y propósito. Si el tema parece irrelevante para las necesidades actuales o futuras, sus estudiantes se pueden desmotivar y perder interés.

Los siguientes son algunos valores clave que sirven de motivación para la investigación, y que pueden animar a las y los estudiantes cristianos que está supervisando:

- esto se hace para el honor y la gloria de Dios;
- esto ayudará a que sus estudiantes se desarrollen como siervos y siervas de Cristo;
- las y los estudiantes que se someten a este proceso trabajoso y detallado lograrán un modo de pensar más profundo;
- esto les permitirá contribuir a la misión de Dios porque sus voces serán escuchadas en el campo académico;
- esto les dará habilidades de investigación y otras capacidades que les servirán para sus trabajos futuros.

Preguntas de reflexión

Cómo supervisor o supervisora de estudiantes de doctorado, ¿cuál puede ser su mayor aporte para que desarrollen sus preguntas de investigación?

PREGUNTAS CORRECTAS E INCORRECTAS

En 1 Crónicas 21:1-17 se describe un proyecto de investigación que ciertamente fue muy interesante, pero que no agradó a Dios.

¿Cuál era el problema con la motivación de David?

¿Qué habrá pensado David que podría lograr con esa investigación?

¿Cómo pueden las y los supervisores ayudar a que sus estudiantes eviten trabajar temas poco útiles o infructuosos?

La propuesta de investigación

Como hemos visto en un capítulo anterior, el pensamiento crítico es el ejercicio de un juicio deliberado y reflexivo en torno a cuestiones complejas. Implica decidir qué hacer en respuesta a —o sobre la base de— observaciones, experiencias, expresiones verbales o escritas, o argumentos que encontramos. El pensamiento crítico exige la formulación de preguntas claras, precisas, relevantes, profundas, amplias, importantes e imparciales.

La propuesta de investigación es donde se desarrollan las preguntas que impulsan el proyecto de investigación. Este es un ejercicio importante que se lleva a cabo antes del inicio formal de la investigación de la tesis. Es un trabajo escrito que debe tener una extensión considerable, y debe incluir una bibliografía bien desarrollada que respalde la propuesta.

Para muchos estudiantes este puede ser un momento de crisis, y puede tomar mucho más tiempo de lo esperado. Es especialmente difícil si no han escrito un trabajo extenso de investigación independiente a nivel de maestría, o si vienen de contextos educativos donde no se fomenta la reflexión crítica.

Las habilidades del estudiante todavía están en una etapa temprana, y el/la supervisor/a necesita encontrar un delicado equilibrio entre dejar que su estudiante revolotee en la incertidumbre y la falta de dirección, y ser excesivamente directivo/a al punto de prácticamente redactarle la propuesta. A fin de cuentas, es el proyecto de su estudiante.

Lo que sigue bosqueja una propuesta de investigación. Es un ejemplo que ha sido útil para algunos y podría servir como marco de referencia para sus estudiantes de doctorado.

Bosquejo para una Propuesta

1) Tema o título de la investigación.

2) Objetivo de la investigación —una declaración de las preguntas para las cuales la investigación proveerá respuestas.

3) Lo que le motiva a emprender esta investigación . . .
   - en relación con sus propios estudios e investigaciones hasta el momento,
   - en relación con el estado actual de la investigación en este campo,
   - su interés personal.

4) ¿Qué compone el núcleo de su material de investigación?

5) ¿Cuáles son las principales ideas y áreas de estudio en este campo? Esto debería incluir las temáticas y los problemas que espera tratar en el desarrollo de su tesis. Haga referencia a trabajos académicos y fuentes clave.
   - Nombre dos o tres académicos que tienen trabajos publicados que son importantes en este campo.
   - ¿Cómo podría desarrollar sus ideas o desafiar su perspectiva?
   - ¿Cuáles son los vacíos en el conocimiento?
   - ¿En qué se distingue el enfoque que piensa tomar?

6) Esboce una serie de capítulos provisionales, con un párrafo breve que explique los temas que espera explorar en cada capítulo.

7) ¿Cuáles serán los enfoques (métodos) principales que se discutirán en la investigación, y cuáles los que va a usar?

8) Bibliografía (detalle al menos treinta libros académicos que son clave para su tema de investigación y que espera usar).

9) ¿Qué espera que su investigación, cuando la haya terminado, contribuya a la teología y a la misión de la iglesia en su país de origen?

Evaluación formal de la propuesta de investigación

Cada institución debe definir las expectativas para el desarrollo y la defensa de la propuesta para la tesis/disertación. Hay diferentes maneras de hacerlo. En algunos programas la propuesta se completa antes de la inscripción o matrícula formal, en otros hacerlo lleva una buena porción del primer año de investigación y es parte de la revisión de fin de año para poder progresar en el programa. Por lo general, las/los estudiantes no pueden avanzar a los siguientes años sin haber establecido un claro bosquejo de su investigación y un plan para la tesis. Para las disertaciones más conceptuales, la propuesta puede ser bastante corta, donde el/la estudiante ofrece evidencia de un vacío importante en la literatura de investigación que podría ser de gran utilidad para la iglesia si se suple. Además de mostrar por qué es necesaria esta investigación, el/la estudiante también debe demostrar que ha podido identificar los campos de investigación relevantes que deberá explorar para abordar los problemas identificados, y que tiene acceso a los recursos necesarios para llevar a cabo el estudio. Tanto el argumento lógico para el estudio como la metodología propuesta y los recursos necesarios para abordar las cuestiones a investigar son fundamentales para el éxito del esfuerzo. No basta con mostrar la necesidad, el/la estudiante debe demostrar cómo la abordará y que se puede suplir.

Para las disertaciones que contienen una investigación empírica, es posible que la propuesta sea mucho más larga, y que escribirla requiera una inversión de tiempo mucho mayor. Este tipo de propuesta debe explicar por qué es necesario el estudio y los beneficios potenciales de llevarlo a cabo, e incluir: una revisión exhaustiva de la literatura —del campo de las ciencias sociales— sobre la fundamentación teórica e investigaciones relevantes que informan la propuesta investigativa; preferiblemente algún tipo de revisión teológica relevante al tema; y un plan detallado para la investigación —enfoque, métodos, muestra, recopilación y análisis de datos. Ya que la revisión de la literatura es la tarea inicial, las propuestas para este tipo de disertaciones pueden extenderse cien o más páginas, y tomar hasta un año o más para desarrollar y defender antes de que el/la estudiante emprenda su propio trabajo de investigación empírica.

La defensa de la propuesta de tesis/disertación en los doctorados de tipo estadounidense

En este tipo de programa, el supervisor/presidente del Comité de Disertación supervisa el proceso del desarrollo de la propuesta, lo cual conduce a una defensa formal de la misma. También se asegura que los miembros del Comité tengan la oportunidad de revisar los borradores de las distintas secciones de la propuesta y de ofrecer retroalimentación a la presidencia y al estudiante sobre cualquier área que vean que necesita más trabajo. A menudo la presidencia trabaja con el/la estudiante para completar los borradores iniciales y determinar cuándo están lo suficientemente desarrollados como para compartirlos con los otros miembros del Comité para su revisión. Este proceso se repite hasta que las revisiones necesarias sean cada vez menos extensas, lo cual indica que con un poco más de trabajo la propuesta puede estar lista para ser defendida. Cualquier preocupación importante debe ser compartida con la presidencia y con el/la estudiante y resuelta en el proceso de desarrollo de la propuesta, y no relegada hasta la reunión de defensa de la propuesta. Si el/la estudiante presta atención a la retroalimentación de todos los miembros del Comité, la defensa debería ser una experiencia de afirmación y una oportunidad para pulir la propuesta, en vez de una discusión acerca de si debe avanzar o no.

Después de que el documento de la propuesta ha sido presentado a los miembros del Comité, y como parte de la preparación para la reunión de defensa, la presidencia debe reunirse con el/la estudiante para discutir cómo deberá prepararse para la defensa. En esta reunión se debe discutir cómo él o ella hará la presentación, cuánto tiempo le dedicará, qué información relevante habrá que incluir, si se compartirán materiales impresos con los presentes (por ejemplo, diapositivas, documentos), y el tipo de preguntas que debe estar preparado/a para abordar en la interacción con los miembros del Comité (por ejemplo, preguntas típicas para el tipo de investigación que propone la disertación). Además de este tipo de orientación, siempre es apropiado apartar un tiempo para orar juntos por una reunión fructífera. Este es un tiempo para aprender y asegurar que el plan para la investigación es robusto. A menudo, en una revisión final de la propuesta, surgen cuestiones que pueden darle más fuerza, lo cual también presenta una oportunidad para afinar la propuesta.

Antes de empezar la reunión de defensa puede servirle a la presidencia reunirse brevemente con los otros miembros del Comité. Es el momento oportuno para mencionar las principales cuestiones que piensa que se deben explorar en la defensa, y para definir quién tomará la iniciativa de plantearlas y discutirlas luego de la presentación de la propuesta. Aunque no es algo crucial para la defensa, esto puede ayudar a la presidencia a prepararse para guiar la sesión de manera que cada miembro del Comité pueda ser escuchado, y que los problemas críticos reciban la atención necesaria.

Es típico que una reunión de defensa en el contexto estadounidense sea un evento público, abierto a otros miembros de la comunidad académica, tanto miembros de la facultad como estudiantes. Se suele compartir un anuncio de la defensa con la comunidad académica y se puede dejar una copia de la propuesta de la disertación en la oficina del programa de doctorado para quien quiera revisarlo. La reunión de defensa puede comenzar con una presentación oral de la propuesta, seguir con una discusión de la propuesta entre los miembros del Comité y el/la estudiante, y luego se puede abrir el espacio a preguntas y comentarios de los demás presentes. La reunión puede durar un par de horas. La presidencia del Comité de Disertación debe guiar el proceso con cuidado, asegurando que la discusión se mantenga enfocada en la propuesta y en cuestiones que puedan ayudar a que sea más clara, más completa y más fuerte para la realización de los objetivos de la investigación.

Una vez concluida la discusión, el Comité puede despedirse de las y los estudiantes, los miembros de la facultad y demás invitados presentes para poder tener sus deliberaciones finales antes de tomar una decisión acerca de la investigación propuesta. Las opciones a menudo se dividen en cuatro categorías: (1) Aprobada sin reservas, (2) Aprobada con revisiones menores, (3) Necesita revisiones mayores y otra defensa, o (4) No aprobada. Las opciones 1 y 4 son muy infrecuentes. La mayoría de las defensas resultan en la opción 2 o, en escasas situaciones, la opción 3. En este caso, el Comité debe decidir qué revisiones son necesarias, y quién del Comité será responsable de revisar y aprobarlas. En algunos casos, todos los miembros del Comité pueden querer ver la revisión; en otros casos la lectura y aprobación puede quedar en manos de la presidencia o de otro/a lector/a.

Después de la propuesta de defensa, y una vez que el/la estudiante ha recibido la decisión del Comité, normalmente la presidencia se reúne con él o ella para repasar las revisiones solicitadas, establecer una línea de tiempo para abordarlas, e identificar quién los revisará y aprobará. La decisión también se aclara en cuanto a la prioridad de las cuestiones que se deben abordar y lo que el/la estudiante debe completar antes de seguir avanzando en el trabajo de investigación.

Caso de estudio

Rosa produjo un sólido trabajo escrito a nivel de maestría, y ha aplicado para estudiar a nivel de doctorado. Hubo algo de discusión en el comité de admisiones en cuanto a si ella era capaz de producir reflexión original, pero se decidió darle la oportunidad. Rosa ahora está trabajando en su propuesta de investigación, pero no parece tener ideas claras sobre lo que quiere investigar dentro de su campo general. Como su supervisor/a, usted tiene muchas ideas al respecto, pero no sabe si es correcto compartirlas con Rosa. Usted sabe que necesita ser su propio proyecto de investigación.

Preguntas

¿Qué cuestiones generales plantea esto?

¿Cómo debería ayudar a Rosa?

Para leer más

Murray, R. *How to Write a Thesis*. Maidenhead: Open University, 2002.

Phillips, E. M. y D. S. Pugh. *How to Get a PhD: A Handbook for Students and Their Supervisors*. Maidenhead: Open University Press, 2010. (Disponible también para Kindle)

Potter, S. *Doing Postgraduate Research*. Londres: Sage, 2006.

Smith, K. *Writing and Research: A Guide for Theological Students*. Carlisle: Langham Global Library, 2015.

Taylor, S. y N. Beasley. *A Handbook for Doctoral Supervisors*. Nueva York: Routledge, 2005.

Wisker, G. *The Good Supervisor: Supervising Postgraduate and Undergraduate Research for Doctoral Theses and Dissertations*. Nueva York: Palgrave MacMillan, 2005.

9

La gestión de las sesiones de supervisión doctoral

Los detalles de la relación de supervisión se negocian directamente entre supervisor/a y estudiante, pero los programas de doctorado deben contar con lineamientos apropiados que establecen la frecuencia normal y la duración esperada de las sesiones de supervisión. Esto evita malentendidos sobre el nivel de apoyo disponible, y crea expectativas realistas.[1]

La frecuencia de las reuniones variará según si el/la estudiante está a tiempo completo o parcial, y acorde a la fase del programa que ha alcanzado. En una fase temprana con estudiantes a tiempo completo puede ser necesario reunirse cada semana para establecer el proceso de supervisión y fijar la dirección inicial del proyecto. Luego, para el resto del primer año, es usual reunirse al menos una vez al mes. En el segundo año las reuniones serán menos frecuentes, pero normalmente no deberían espaciarse más de dos meses.

Para estudiantes a tiempo parcial, la expectativa es que se reúnan tres o cuatro veces al año. Cuando la distancia geográfica es un factor limitante, las reuniones presenciales se pueden complementar con otros formatos como videoconferencias, Skype, etc. La dinámica es diferente, pero en muchos casos estos formatos han sido eficaces.

Defina la agenda

En una fase temprana, defina con el/la estudiante:

- ¿Con qué frecuencia esperan reunirse? Debe haber directrices institucionales, pero es importante establecer por escrito cómo se hará en la práctica con cada estudiante. Habrá variaciones, pero al menos debería haber una frecuencia de referencia.

---

1. Shaw, *Principios y mejores prácticas*, Sección 16.

- ¿Cuál será el foco de las reuniones? No siempre es necesario esperar a que su estudiante entregue un trabajo para agendar una reunión de supervisión. También debe haber oportunidades para seguimiento, evaluación y resolución de problemas.
- Además necesita establecer el procedimiento a seguir cuando usted (como supervisor/a) no se siente bien o está de viaje o de licencia de investigación.

Contacto entre reuniones formales

Como supervisor/a, necesita definir en una fase temprana qué tipo de contacto será permitido entre las sesiones formales de supervisión. ¿Permitirá o fomentará el contacto informal?

- ¿Cómo será esa interacción? ¿Tendrá horas de oficina o le puede contactar 24/7? ¿Cuáles serán los límites?
- ¿Qué métodos de contacto serán aceptables? ¿Correo electrónico, texto, teléfono? ¿Puede él o ella 'pasar' por su oficina en cualquier momento?

El patrón para las reuniones de supervisión

1. Cómo empezar

Cuando empiece a supervisar a un/a estudiante, aclare sus expectativas de lo que debe suceder durante las reuniones de supervisión. Es necesario encontrar un equilibrio entre dirección y libertad para que su estudiante se desarrolle como investigador/a independiente.

Cuando yo era estudiante de investigación, y tuve mi primera reunión con mi supervisor, no estaba seguro si estaba permitido tomar notas durante la reunión. Aclare ese tipo de asuntos con sus estudiantes.

A veces, el/la estudiante pregunta si puede hacer una grabación del audio de la reunión de supervisión. Usted tendrá que definir su propia política al respecto, pero cualquier grabación que se haga solo se puede hacer con su permiso, y quizás usted querrá dar instrucciones sobre cómo puede, o no, ser usada.

2. Defina las directrices

Establezca las directrices sobre cuándo el/la estudiante debe entregar trabajos para su revisión —con suficiente tiempo para que usted lo pueda leer y hacer comentarios significativos. Algunos estudiantes tienen expectativas poco realistas. La mayoría de las/los supervisores no podrán leer, comentar y dar directivas sobre un texto de 20 000 palabras si se entrega la noche antes de una reunión de supervisión. Las/los estudiantes no siempre entienden eso. Aclare con qué antelación deben entregar el trabajo y el tipo de aviso que usted requiere.

3. Retroalimentación

Las y los supervisores ofrecen retroalimentación de diversas maneras.

Necesita explicarle a sus estudiantes de qué manera(s) va a responder a los trabajos escritos que le entreguen. ¿Redactará un informe completo, escribirá notas en el manuscrito, enviará comentarios electrónicos, etc.? La mejor práctica es dar retroalimentación en forma escrita —la retroalimentación verbal puede reforzar lo escrito, pero no es suficiente por sí misma.

También necesita explicar lo que usted espera que hagan con los comentarios que les ha dado. ¿Deben volver y revisar lo que entregaron hasta que hayan atendido a todos los comentarios o sugerencias, o quedan para más adelante?

Sus estudiantes pueden querer pasar rápidamente a otra cosa; quizás les parezca tiempo muerto hacer revisiones de los borradores. Sin embargo, si no hacen las revisiones cuando tienen el tema fresco en la mente, fácilmente se pueden olvidar de ellas, o dejar cosas sin atender. Además, si los primeros borradores están bien revisados y actualizados, se reduce el tiempo necesario para "reescribirlos" al final de la investigación. Puede ser muy frustrante para el/la supervisor/a recibir un borrador posterior del capítulo y encontrarse con todos los mismos problemas identificados anteriormente, que su estudiante no ha atendido y que ahora necesitan la misma retroalimentación que antes.

¿Escuchan lo que les está diciendo?

Hay importantes cuestiones culturales y comunicacionales que afectan las relaciones entre estudiantes y supervisores. En algunas culturas, los supervisores serán muy directos y francos, hasta bruscos, con sus comentarios. Algunos estudiantes aprecian esta claridad. Pero otros se sienten desanimados, despreciados, y hasta se pueden ofender.

En otras culturas, el lenguaje académico es más mesurado. Este es especialmente cierto en Inglaterra donde yo he hecho mucha supervisión, y donde las y los estudiantes tienen que 'leer entre líneas', y detectar las pistas.

Así, por ejemplo, un supervisor podría decir:

- "Creo que hay cierta disparidad en la calidad de algunas secciones de su trabajo", lo que significa: "En realidad necesita mejorar la calidad de esas áreas porque no es buena".
- "Necesita mirar más de cerca lo que dice ese autor —que significa, "Ha malinterpretado por completo lo que ese autor dijo".
- "Esta sección necesita ser más clara" —que significa, "Esta sección no está clara, está confusa y no tiene sentido".
- "Le aconsejaría que busque la ayuda de un corrector" —que significa, "Su trabajo está lleno de errores gramaticales y ortográficos y los examinadores lo reprobarán si lo entrega así como está".

Los problemas ocurren cuando chocan las culturas de supervisor/a y estudiante, y el/la estudiante no capta bien las señales. Me llamó la atención oír de un estudiante estadounidense que pidió a su supervisor —un señor ingles, de la vieja escuela— que opinara de su proyecto de tesis que estaba casi completo.

— 'Bien, señor' —dijo el estudiante, 'sea franco conmigo, ¿es basura o no? (pudo haber usado una expresión menos delicada, que no repetiré) Solo quiero saberlo'. A lo que el amable caballero respondió: 'Creo que hay algunas áreas que necesitan algo de atención'.

En vez de leer esto como una advertencia de que todavía era necesario que trabajara bastante, el estudiante norteamericano entendió que solo necesitaba hacer algunas revisiones menores, las cuales hizo. Presentó su tesis, pero fue desaprobada.

Tenga cuidado y preste mucha atención a lo que le está comunicando a sus estudiantes, y a cómo lo están recibiendo. Asegúrese de que su instrucción y sus directivas sean claras, y que sus estudiantes no necesiten 'leer entre líneas'. Esto es especialmente importante cuando se trabaja con estudiantes de otras culturas. Posiblemente tenga que pedirles a sus estudiantes que le repitan lo que entendieron de lo que dijo. Las cuestiones que está comunicando son demasiado importantes para que se malentiendan.

4. Mantenga un registro de las discusiones y los comentarios

Debe mantener un registro del cuándo y el dónde de cada reunión de supervisión, aun si es informal, y de los consejos y las directivas principales dadas. Servirán para hacer los informes. También son un registro importante en caso de presentarse alguna queja sobre la naturaleza de la supervisión.

Ahora es común pedirle al estudiante que elabore un informe de la reunión —con los temas discutidos, las decisiones tomadas y las directivas dadas–, y que se lo envíe a usted. Esto sirve como registro y también como un chequeo para asegurar que su estudiante entendió lo que se le ha pedido.

Los tipos de reuniones de supervisión

1. Reuniones circunstanciales (ad hoc)

Suelen ser breves y enfocadas en un asunto específico. Quizás su estudiante necesita revisar una referencia u obtener alguna información básica. Pueden ocurrir al final de un seminario, o incluso en el corredor. No hay necesidad de mantener un registro de estas reuniones.

2. Reuniones informales

Pueden tomar la forma de una discusión general o de una puesta al día del progreso, sin que incluya una discusión de un trabajo escrito. Quizás haya un trabajo en proceso, y hace falta considerar algunos aspectos. Estas reuniones se pueden hacer por Skype, correo electrónico, teléfono, etc.

Se debe mantener un registro escrito de estas reuniones, y el /la estudiante puede redactar algunas notas para ser confirmadas por su supervisor/a. Estos registros servirán para los informes más formales.

3. Reuniones formales

Sirven de foro para la retroalimentación formal a un trabajo escrito.

Reuniones de este tipo pueden hacer falta para ayudar a el /la estudiante a prepararse para una etapa específica de revisión o para progresar a otra etapa. Tiene valor, en algunas reuniones formales, dar un paso atrás para observar partes del texto desde una perspectiva más amplia y evaluar tanto el avance en general como los planes para su finalización. Para el último año de estudio, ya debe haber un plan establecido y acordado para la conclusión de la tesis.

4. Revisiones de progreso

En la mayoría de los programas normalmente habrá por lo menos una reunión formal al año donde se trata el progreso y la continuación del estudiante en el programa, se resuelven asuntos relacionados con la progresión o transferencia de la matrícula, o se otorga permiso para que él o ella presente su trabajo para ser examinado. Supervisor/a y estudiante deben preparar los informes de estas reuniones. Estas reuniones incluirán otros participantes, y es probable que esté presente el director del programa o el jefe del departamento. Debe mantenerse un registro formal de las decisiones que se toman, y estas se deben comunicar por escrito al estudiante.

La definición de los estilos de supervisión

Es importante que el/la estudiante entienda su estilo de supervisión temprano en su programa. Me he encontrado con algunos supervisores que adoptan como política "un mismo estilo para todos", y que en efecto dicen, "este es mi estilo, o se adaptan o buscan otro supervisor". Aunque queremos usar nuestras habilidades y experiencia de maneras que nos resultan cómodas, no siempre es útil tomar una postura inflexible. Hay ocasiones en que la capacidad de adaptación es una virtud.

Repito, es bueno discutir su estilo de supervisión con sus estudiantes en una etapa temprana.

Preguntas de reflexión

Reflexione sobre su propio estilo de supervisión. ¿Cómo lo describiría?

¿Qué aspectos está anuente a cambiar?

¿En qué aspectos no está dispuesto/a a cambiar? Si no, ¿por qué no?

¿Hay ocasiones en las que ha usado diferentes estilos con diferentes estudiantes?

¿En qué eran diferentes esos estilos, y qué problemas estaba buscando abordar con su estudiante?

Estilos de supervisión de uso frecuente

1. Activo y directo

Este es un estilo en que las/los supervisores se involucran mucho con sus estudiantes, indicándoles detenidamente lo que deben hacer y lo que no en cada etapa. El proceso está cuidadosamente controlado y las y los estudiantes saben exactamente lo que se espera de ellos. Aunque esto puede ser útil para estudiantes que carecen de confianza o que tienen poca experiencia trabajando de forma independiente, crea un fuerte sentido de dependencia que juega en contra de la creatividad y la independencia que requiere el proceso de doctorado. Al final del proceso sus estudiantes deben poder aprender de manera autogestionada. Es poco probable que este enfoque lo logre. Puede ser necesario adoptar este enfoque en etapas tempranas de un proyecto o con estudiantes más débiles que están teniendo dificultades, pero exige mucho de quien supervisa.

2. Activo e indirecto

En este enfoque hay más interacción con el pensamiento propio de las/los estudiantes. Se les involucra más conscientemente en la planificación de las próximas etapas de su trabajo. Se les pregunta regularmente, ¿cuál piensa que es el siguiente paso que debe tomar? Se les invita a revisar y evaluar su propio trabajo y progreso. Se les pregunta —¿en qué áreas cree que hace falta desarrollar el trabajo? La persona que supervisa está claramente guiando el proceso, pero se asegura que sus estudiantes aporten respuestas y soluciones.

3. Pasivo e indirecto

Aquí las/los estudiantes claramente toman la iniciativa, y el rol de quien supervisa es apoyar, escuchar y responder cuando se le pregunta. Las/los estudiantes suelen llegar con una serie de preguntas o respuestas para las que buscan asesoramiento y apoyo, o bien con ideas e hipótesis que desean probar o evaluar. En estas instancias se están convirtiendo en estudiantes autogestionados, y usan el asesoramiento académico con discernimiento y mesura. Quienes supervisan necesitan seguir "dirigiendo" el proyecto por el camino correcto en caso de que parezca desviarse, o si no está avanzando lo suficientemente rápido, pero la iniciativa y autogestión de sus estudiantes es alta. Con algunos estudiantes que son muy activos y tienen mucha energía, la intervención que necesitan de sus supervisores es que les digan que intenten menos, que delimiten más estrechamente el campo y que no sean demasiado ambiciosos.

4. Pasivo

En este enfoque las/los supervisores se limitan a responder y ofrecen poca o ninguna dirección. El proyecto es del estudiante, quien debe dirigirla. Quien supervisa solo responde si se le envía trabajo para revisar. En mi experiencia de apoyar a estudiantes de doctorado en una variedad de contextos, este es el enfoque del que más se quejan los estudiantes y qué más les cuesta manejar, especialmente temprano en su proyecto. Cuando conversan de los posibles campos a explorar, el/la supervisor/a simplemente dice 'es su proyecto, depende de usted', o 'no es mi rol ofrecer ese tipo de dirección'. Algunos estudiantes han presentado propuestas de investigación solo para que se les diga, "eso no funcionará, intente con otro enfoque", sin que se les ofrezca ninguna dirección en cuanto al enfoque que deberían tomar. En algunas instituciones y contextos académicos, sorprende lo común que es este enfoque. Sin embargo, hay muchos casos en que no funciona, y produce altos niveles de insatisfacción, e incluso resentimiento, en las y los estudiantes -"¿por qué estoy pagando tanto cuando mi supervisor no me da ninguna idea de lo que debería estar haciendo?". He visto a algunos estudiantes abandonar su proyecto ante la pasividad extrema de su supervisor, que a menudo parece más indiferencia. En las etapas posteriores del doctorado el modo de supervisión bien puede orientarse más a dar respuestas que a ser directivo, pero generalmente quedarse esperando que los estudiantes entreguen algo y solo responder a lo que se envía no es un buen modelo para todo el período de la redacción de la tesis.

Yo promovería un estilo que se adapta y cambia a medida que se desarrolla el proyecto. Por lo general, el estilo puede progresar de más a menos directivo. Sus estudiantes van a trabajar de diferentes maneras y a diferentes ritmos, e incluso en el doctorado tendrán diferentes niveles de habilidades.

Si ve que un/a estudiante no está avanzando en su proyecto, no le deje a la deriva por mucho tiempo. Si un estilo o enfoque no funciona, entonces pruebe con otro.

Preguntas de reflexión

A partir de su propia experiencia, ¿cómo fue el estilo de su supervisor/a de doctorado?

¿Cuáles fueron las tres cosas más efectivas que hizo su supervisor/a en las sesiones de supervisión?

¿Cuáles fueron las tres cosas menos efectivas que hizo?

Cómo educar a los estudiantes para obtener el máximo beneficio de la supervisión

Las "reglas de interacción" para la supervisión doctoral deben ser claras.

Para que sus estudiantes pueda obtener el máximo beneficio de la supervisión, algunos factores son importantes:

i) Hay que ayudarles a ver que la supervisión es un esfuerzo colaborativo. No se trata solo de que ellos reciban retroalimentación suya, sino de que usted y él o ella trabajen juntos.

ii) Sus estudiantes deben aprender a ser independientes. A medida que se desarrolla el proyecto hay que animarles a tomar la iniciativa. Al final del proceso de doctorado no siempre deberían estar preguntando, '¿Y ahora, qué debo hacer?'.

iii) Permita que la relación crezca y se desarrolle. Con el tiempo su estilo debe volverse menos directivo y más dialógico. Al final del proceso serán socios y pares académicos, y quizás algún día colegas.

iv) Asegúrese que sus estudiantes entiendan la necesidad de presentar trabajos bien editados para que el tiempo no se desperdicie trabajando en asuntos básicos de presentación y estilo, y cuestiones ortográficas y gramaticales.

v) Sus estudiantes necesitan saber cuáles son sus responsabilidades respecto a la puntualidad, la comunicación, la preparación y el flujo de información.

vi) Tenga en cuenta que, así como las y los supervisores administran la relación de supervisión, habrá aspectos de la relación que las/los estudiantes necesitan 'administrar'. En mi propia experiencia de ser supervisado, había elementos del enfoque de mi supervisor a los que yo tenía que 'encontrarle la vuelta' para que la reunión de supervisión lograse lo que yo necesitaba.

EL libro de E. M. Phillips y D. S. Pugh, *How to Get a PhD*.[2] es una guía muy accesible al proceso de doctorado. Incluye muchos ejemplos útiles y también desafiantes. También tiene un capítulo sobre cómo 'manejar' a su supervisor/a. Es bueno que tanto estudiantes como supervisores lo lean a fin de entender mejor la dinámica de la relación.

La relación que desea establecer

Una pregunta clave que debe hacer: ¿Es esta una relación transaccional o una relación de amistad?

Esto afecta el tipo de retroalimentación que ofrecerá y la forma en que llevarán adelante las reuniones. Afectará cómo se dirigen la palabra usted y el/la estudiante. ¿Usará su nombre de pila, o "Dr. Shaw"? La cultura nacional e institucional influenciará cómo lo maneja. Mi supervisor era una figura muy reconocida y estaba por retirarse, y nunca sentí que era apropiado usar su nombre de pila para dirigirme a él.

Vale recordar que puede haber una buena supervisión aun si no se lleva bien con la persona que está supervisando. El respeto profesional y el deseo de hacer aflorar lo mejor de la otra persona es más importante que lo que sentimos. Pero también vale recordar que de una buena supervisión pueden brotar amistades duraderas y relaciones de mentoreo. Usted está edificando a la próxima generación de eruditos y eruditas. A través del proceso sus estudiantes se deben entusiasmar e inspirar, y deben sentirse cuidados y valorados.

La dimensión pastoral de la supervisión

En el capítulo 3 describí algunos aspectos del estilo de supervisión que más apreciaron las y los estudiantes de doctorado con los que hablé. Entre esos aspectos, le dieron mucha importancia a la dimensión pastoral. El/la estudiante que tiene delante suyo consiste en mucho más que el trabajo que está presentando y discutiendo. Su bienestar emocional, físico y espiritual afectará su capacidad de funcionar bien en sus estudios. Habrá asuntos de su vida familiar que impactan en su trabajo de investigación. Asimismo, habrá tensiones y desafíos en su comunidad. Trabajé con un estudiante que estaba estudiando lejos de su hogar, y su país fue invadido por fuerzas hostiles en medio de su doctorado. El país de otro estudiante sufrió un golpe militar, y el de otro un tifón devastador. En instancias como estas, la capacidad de mostrar una verdadera preocupación pastoral por ellos como personas completas es muy importante.

Es muy importante que el/la supervisor/a de doctorado tenga un corazón pastoral y capacidades pastorales, como se destaca en el libro *Principios y mejores prácticas* de ICETE. Pero no es el pastor o la pastora de sus estudiante, ni su rol principal es ofrecer

---

2. Phillips y Pugh, *How to Get a PhD*.

consejos pastorales. Aunque es importante mostrar sensibilidad y preocupación pastoral, para consejería o apoyo pastoral más profundo es mejor referirlos a la capellanía o a profesionales de consejería, o al personal pastoral de su propia iglesia. Por lo general, no hay suficiente tiempo en las reuniones de supervisión para ofrecer un apoyo pastoral amplio, y existe el peligro de que esto interfiera con los aspectos académicos y formativos de la supervisión. La sensibilidad pastoral es vital, pero cuando surgen problemas pastorales importantes, es conveniente remitir al estudiante a las/los especialistas correspondientes.

En los primeros minutos de una sesión de supervisión suelo preguntar cómo está él o ella y cómo está su familia, prestando atención a cualquier asunto que pueda afectar su progreso o necesitar más atención —y asegurándome de que conozcan los mecanismos de apoyo correspondientes en caso de que necesiten alguna ayuda. Pero esto no debe prolongarse más de lo necesario, y debe mantenerse el enfoque principal de la supervisión académica. Muchos supervisores comienzan y/o terminan la sesión de supervisión con oración, pidiendo la ayuda y bendición de Dios sobre el/la estudiante y el siguiente paso en sus estudios.

Muchos estudiantes han agradecido la oportunidad de visitar a su supervisor/a en su casa para tomar café o compartir una comida. La hospitalidad y la apertura personal hacia los estudiantes son formas de modelar la formación espiritual que buscamos. Pero tiene que haber límites adecuados, y a algunos supervisores les preocupa que demasiado contacto personal fuera de las reuniones de supervisión pueda afectar su capacidad de hacer una crítica objetiva y detallada del trabajo de sus estudiantes. Hay que mantener las cosas bajo control y con el equilibrio adecuado.

Áreas problemáticas de las sesiones de supervisión

1) **El/la supervisor/a habla demasiado.**
En esta situación, la sesión de supervisión se convierte en una cátedra, sin diálogo. No hay espacio para que el/la estudiante interactúe, ni oportunidad para que desarrolle iniciativa o liderazgo propio.

¡Hay solo una persona que puede corregir esta situación!

Reflexione sobre su propia práctica, y evalúe el equilibrio en sus reuniones entre las contribuciones de su estudiante y la suya. ¿Hay algo que cambiar?

2) **El/la estudiante habla demasiado.**
Esto es igual de problemático, porque quien supervisa no puede comunicar información vital ni dar dirección. Tampoco es una buena práctica si más adelante el/la estudiante tendrá que someterse a un examen oral. Sus examinadores se frustrarán mucho si su estudiante no puede responder a las preguntas con claridad y precisión, y habla todo el tiempo. Se necesita de buena dirección y trato claro para asegurar un equilibrio adecuado.

3) **El/la estudiante se resiste a decir mucho, o a preguntar y responder preguntas.**
Este silencio puede ser un problema propio del estudiante y no de su supervisor/a.

En estos casos, hace falta ayudarle a aprender a hablar con confianza y de manera clara acerca de su propio trabajo. Una vez más, esta es una habilidad vital que las y los estudiantes deben aprender para un examen oral, y para presentaciones académicas o futuros roles docentes.

Con instrucciones preparatorias —sobre lo que se les pedirá discutir o responder preguntas en una próxima sesión de supervisión-, se puede crear expectativa y confianza en él o ella.

4) **El/la estudiante viene, pero no está preparado/a.**
Esto puede suceder ocasionalmente, pero si se convierte en un patrón que se repite debe ser cuestionado. Cuando un/a estudiante no está preparado/a, las reuniones de supervisión se deben mantener breves y reorganizarse para cuando lo esté. Es irrespetuoso que su estudiante agende una reunión y use el tiempo de su supervisor/a sin haber dedicado tiempo a prepararse o sin tener la cortesía de contactarle con antelación para reagendar la reunión.

Los problemas que enfrentan las y los estudiantes de doctorado varían de un supervisor a otro, y de una institución a otra. En el modelo europeo de doctorado, la relación de supervisión suele vincular estrechamente al estudiante con una o dos personas. En el modelo estadounidense de doctorado, el vínculo suele ser con un comité. En esta situación los desafíos son diferentes.

Desafíos comunes con respecto a los comités de disertación (del modelo estadounidense de doctorado) y maneras de abordarlos
Desacuerdo entre los miembros del Comité

No es inusual que los miembros del Comité de Disertación tengan ideas y estándares diferentes para el trabajo que esperan del estudiante. Por esta razón es importante que, temprano en el proceso, el presidente del Comité converse con los otros miembros acerca del enfoque de investigación propuesto por el/la estudiante, y trate de llegar a una comprensión compartida del producto de investigación que anticipan recibir. Cuando es posible, es útil tener una reunión del Comité completo con el/la estudiante —también, temprano en el proceso— para una discusión inicial de la investigación propuesta y de lo que pueden esperar. En esa reunión cada miembro puede opinar del proyecto y expresar lo que piensa que sería importante considerar o incluir.

A medida que se comparten los borradores de partes de la disertación con los varios miembros del Comité, es importante que el presidente reciba cualquier retroalimentación antes de que sea compartida con el/la estudiante. Esto permite que el presidente identifique si hay áreas de conflicto en las expectativas y pueda hablar con los demás miembros del Comité para resolver las áreas de desacuerdo o las diferencias en perspectiva. El objetivo debe ser que los miembros del Comité puedan resolver juntos estos asuntos, sin involucrar al estudiante en sus conflictos. Un proceso minucioso de revisión de los borradores debería dejar en evidencia cualquier diferencia importante entre los miembros del Comité, lo cual da tiempo para abordarlas antes de una defensa pública de la propuesta o de la defensa final.

Si surgen desacuerdos importantes al principio del trabajo del Comité, y no se pueden resolver, debe haber una forma en que un miembro pueda abandonar el Comité discretamente y se reclute a otra persona. El presidente querrá discutir este tipo de situación con el director del programa de doctorado para asegurar que se maneje de una manera que preserve las buenas relaciones laborales. Si se produce un desacuerdo importante durante la defensa final de la disertación, y no se puede resolver dentro de la reunión, puede ser conveniente retrasar el voto de los miembros. Eso da tiempo a que el Comité tenga otra reunión (con o sin el/la estudiante) para tratar de resolver sus problemas. Esto debería ser extremadamente infrecuente. No debería suceder si hay buena comunicación y si se hace una buena revisión.

Respuestas lentas de los segundos y terceros lectores

Las instituciones deben establecer expectativas en cuanto al tiempo que pueden tomar los miembros del Comité para la revisión de los borradores que se les envía. Esta expectativa se debe comunicar con claridad tanto a los miembros de la facultad que sirven en los Comités como a los estudiantes. Así los estudiantes sabrán cuánto tiempo deben esperar antes de preguntar sobre una revisión, y los miembros de la facultad sabrán los plazos en que deben presentar sus comentarios.

Si el presidente ve que un miembro del Comité acostumbra tomar más tiempo de lo esperado para completar las revisiones y enviar comentarios, y esto está retrasando el trabajo del estudiante, debe ponerse en contacto con ese miembro del Comité para discutir la causa de los retrasos y volver a enfatizar la importancia de la retroalimentación oportuna y los plazos estipulados. A menudo hay cosas fuera del control del miembro del Comité que pueden estar creando dificultades. En esos casos habrá que ser pacientes. En otros casos, el miembro del Comité puede simplemente haber perdido registro de la fecha límite y un simple recordatorio le volverá a poner en marcha. El presidente del Comité puede ayudar a que no se estanque el proceso de revisión, lo cual reduce el estrés que siente el/la estudiante por los retrasos.

Percepciones de las/los estudiantes de doctorado acerca de la supervisión eficaz

La siguiente lista viene de estudiantes que han expresado su apreciación por diversos aspectos de la supervisión, y sirve como un inventario de prácticas y actitudes a las cuales aspirar. Cada supervisor/a desarrollará su propio estilo, pero la lista ofrece algunos de los indicadores clave:

1) Sabe adaptarse a cómo se desarrollan o evolucionan las necesidades de sus estudiantes en diferentes etapas del proyecto.

2) Sabe adaptarse a los diferentes estilos de aprendizaje de sus estudiantes.

3) Tiene la capacidad de percibir bien lo que dicen y lo que necesitan sus estudiantes. Si pregunta: '¿Ahora qué hago?', el/la supervisor/a debe preguntarse: ¿he fomentado demasiada dependencia o será que necesita más apoyo del que le ha dado?

4) Tiene la capacidad de establecer límites en cuanto a lo que él o ella puede hacer y lo que no.

5) Tiene la habilidad de proveer estructura para el trabajo y el progreso de sus estudiantes, asegurando que se lleve a cabo una planificación adecuada.

6) Es capaz de descubrir y aprovechar las fortalezas de los demás integrantes del equipo de supervisión.

7) Respeta a sus estudiantes y muestra interés por su trabajo.

8) Tiene la habilidad de ofrecer retroalimentación que sus estudiantes pueden entender y a la que pueden responder con acciones apropiadas.

9) Muestra su disposición a darle una capacitación más amplia a sus estudiantes y a apoyarles como mentor/a, por ejemplo, con oportunidades para dictar clases, corregir monografías, etc.

10) Ofrece instrucción en cuestiones específicas tanto metodológicas como de ética investigativa.

11) Crea un ambiente en el que se pueden intercambiar y debatir ideas.

12) Enseña a sus estudiantes a ser autocríticos con su propio trabajo.

13) Puede desarrollar una visión global y metas a largo plazo a partir de objetivos a corto plazo.

14) Mostrar que ha leído el trabajo de sus estudiantes —con un comentario o una marca al final de una página— evita los comentarios que hacen los estudiantes de que sus supervisores no se molestan en leer su trabajo.

15) Cuando sus estudiantes enfrentan problemas, les dirige hacia el apoyo institucional apropiado, por ejemplo, la biblioteca, la administración, el área de finanzas, etc.

16) Ayuda a sus estudiantes con la redacción y preparación de ponencias para conferencias

17) Estimula la moral. Muestra confianza en el trabajo de sus estudiantes y elogia las señales de progreso, con lo cual hace frente al desánimo y la desmotivación.

18) Mantiene un adecuado juicio (crítico) profesional —cuando a un/a estudiante le está costando avanzar, prolongar la agonía del fracaso no le hace ningún favor, ni siquiera si es una persona muy simpática.

19) Tenga en cuenta que usted es una referencia, un modelo a seguir. ¡Lo que usted le hace a sus estudiantes, bien pueden hacérselo a otros!

Para leer más

Eley, A. y R. Murray, *How to Be an Effective Supervisor*. Maidenhead: Open University Press, 2009.

Gatfield, T. 'An Investigation into PhD Supervisory Management Styles', *Journal of Higher Education Policy and Management*, Vol. 27, No. 3, Noviembre 2005, 311-325.

Murray, R. *How to Write a Thesis*. Maidenhead: Open University Press, 2002.

Phillips, E. M. y D. S. Pugh. *How to Get a PhD: A Handbook for Students and Their Supervisors*. Maidenhead: Open University Press, 2010. (Disponible también para Kindle)

Shaw, I. *Principios y mejores prácticas para Programas de Doctorado*. Carlisle: Langham Global Library, 2025.

Taylor, Stan y N. Beasley. *A Handbook for Doctoral Supervisors*. Nueva York: Routledge, 2005.

Wisker, Gina. *The Good Supervisor: Supervising Postgraduate and Undergraduate Research for Doctoral Theses and Dissertations*. Nueva York: Palgrave MacMillan, 2005.

10

La Excelencia en la supervisión de la investigación académica y la formación espiritual

Los estudios de doctorado en una institución cristiana evangélica se basan en una comprensión del conocimiento que es más que académica. En la Biblia, adquirir y practicar la sabiduría implica una combinación de fe, razón y acción. Requiere:

- *creer lo correcto y estar comprometido con confiar en el Dios viviente ("el temor del Señor es el primer principio de la sabiduría"),*
- *emplear de manera creativa y humilde la racionalidad que Dios le ha concedido a los seres humanos creados a su imagen, y*
- *vivir en el mundo de una manera que refleje el llamado de Dios a ser partícipes en la misión de Dios.*

ICETE, *Estándares de Beirut*, Preámbulo

En cualquier contexto que se lleve a cabo, el estudio de un doctorado tiene que ver con aprender y con ser. El estudio doctoral es un aspecto del aprendizaje transformador, y la tarea de crear significado (en el doctorado, a partir de las fuentes y datos que encontramos mediante la investigación), está conectada con nuestra espiritualidad de manera intrínseca. La investigación es más que un frío ejercicio de análisis racionalista. Más bien se nutre de la imaginación, la intuición y la emoción, incluso en los contextos más seculares. El estudio doctoral debe tener un impacto en las dimensiones cognitivas, sociales y afectivas de la persona. En las instituciones evangélicas, las y los supervisores necesitan crear un entorno en el que sus estudiantes interactúen con (y a) todos estos niveles. El crecimiento personal que esto produce va mucho más allá del análisis académico de conceptos teológicos. A partir de la experiencia de ser supervisados, las y los estudiantes van a salir con una autovaloración más firme, con habilidades para construir significados y conocimientos más profundas. Los *Principios y mejores prácticas* de ICETE lo expresan así:

Los programas de doctorado deben ayudar a que los estudiantes reconozcan la conexión entre el trabajo de investigación y la formación espiritual. Deben ser investigadores capaces de integrar la excelencia académica y la espiritual, que se comprometen con el objetivo superior de la transformación de todo el pueblo de Dios a la imagen de Cristo y su misión en el mundo.[1]

Junto a la capacidad de reflexión teológica avanzada, las y los estudiantes de doctorado necesitan seguir creciendo en su sensibilidad espiritual, juicio moral, sabiduría, madurez de carácter y comprensión de su comunidad de fe. Muchos estudiantes de doctorado se están preparando para trabajar en una facultad teológica, un seminario o un instituto bíblico. Otros asumirán roles de liderazgo estratégico en el ministerio cristiano. Promover la formación espiritual debe ser un aspecto prominente del propósito misional de las y los supervisores, y debe moldear cómo nos acercamos a nuestra tarea de formación doctoral. Eso hace que este capítulo probablemente sea el más importante de este libro.

La formación espiritual se ha definido como "los procesos intencionales por los cuales se forman e integran las marcas de una auténtica espiritualidad cristiana".[2] El corazón de la espiritualidad cristiana no es simplemente saber acerca del Dios eterno, sino conocerlo de cerca a través del Señor Jesucristo. El proceso de preparar a una persona para un aspecto del ministerio cristiano, incluyendo el liderazgo estratégico en la educación teológica o en la iglesia, debe servir para profundizar ese conocimiento de Dios. A la par del progreso académico, el proceso de emprender estudios doctorales en una institución evangélica debe estar permeado por un compromiso más profundo con Cristo, una mayor reverencia y fidelidad a su Palabra, una apreciación más fuerte por nuestro prójimo, y una integración más profunda en la comunidad eclesial. Lamentablemente, para algunos estudiantes, el resultado del proceso de estudios doctorales parecer ser lo contrario. En el doctorado de investigación, donde el estudio académico es del más alto nivel y las presiones son muy intensas, es fuerte la tendencia a marginar la búsqueda de una fe vital e integral.

Para las y los estudiantes de teología, el contacto constante con las cosas de Dios conlleva el mismo peligro que enfrentaron los sacerdotes y levitas en el Antiguo Testamento: que lo sagrado se volviese ordinario y habitual. La Biblia está llena de ejemplos de lo peligroso que era esto —¡solo hay que preguntarle a Uza! El privilegio de interactuar con lo más profundo de las cosas nunca debe tomarse por sentado. Así lo expresó uno de los grandes teólogos de Princeton hace más de un siglo:

> Con este contacto constante con las cosas divinas, ¿están creciendo en santidad, volviéndose cada día más y más [personas] de Dios? Si no, ¡se

---

1. Shaw, *Principios y mejores prácticas*, Sección 8.
2. S. Amirtham y R. Pryor, editores, *The Invitation to the Feast of Life; Resources for Spiritual Formation in Theological Education* (Ginebra: World Council of Churches, 1991).

están endureciendo! Nunca prosperarán en su vida religiosa en el seminario teológico hasta que su trabajo en el seminario teológico se convierta, para ustedes, en un ejercicio religioso a partir del cual día a día agrandan su corazón, elevan su espíritu y se deleitan en su Creador y Salvador.[3]

La cultura de la educación teológica

Debido al deseo de que las facultades teológicas y los seminarios evangélicos alcancen credibilidad académica, y que sus estudiantes se gradúen de sus programas con cualificaciones y credenciales, necesariamente se han enfatizado las dimensiones académicas de la teología. Este énfasis en el entrenamiento de la mente llevó a que Leslie Newbigin hablara de la "Cautividad babilónica de la educación teológica", ejecutada por el mundo académico, que ha exiliado a la teología de la vida y de las necesidades de las iglesias.[4] Se pueden emprender estudios bíblicos o teológicos minuciosos que tienen poca relevancia para la comprensión más amplia del texto bíblico, o de la persona de Dios, o para la iglesia o el testimonio y la vida cristiana.

La tendencia de estudiantes y supervisores de doctorado a concentrarse en cultivar la mente, y la falta de integración con la necesidad continua de formación espiritual, pueden dejar a las y los estudiantes con una profunda sensación de desconexión entre su trabajo académico y su relación personal con Dios, o su conexión con su comunidad de fe local. Ellas y ellos anhelan tener buenos modelos a seguir en esta área.

Modelos para promover la formación espiritual

Nuestro modelo del educador teológico perfecto es, por supuesto, Jesús. Dedicó unos tres años a la formación de sus discípulos. Les inculcó sus enseñanzas, pero también el patrón de cómo vivir y pensar, de cómo 'ser' sus seguidores, y de cómo integrar todo eso. Les enseñó sobre la coherencia entre creencia y práctica. Pedro podía proclamar audazmente su perpetua lealtad a Jesús, pero lo que realmente importaba era cómo se comportaba en las circunstancias cotidianas de la vida de fe. Después del arresto de Jesús, se produjo en Pedro una seria desconexión entre proclamación y práctica, y fue interrogado alrededor de la fogata por una serie de personas, incluyendo una sirvienta. Sin embargo, en su increíble sermón de Pentecostés demostró una fuerte conexión entre creencia y práctica. Aquellos tres años invertidos en la educación teológica de los discípulos produjeron un grupo de seguidores que no solo estaba dispuesto a desvivirse por, y ser usado para, un extraordinario

---

3. B. B. Warfield, *The Religious Life of Theological Students [La vida religiosa de los estudiantes de teología]*, discurso pronunciado en la Conferencia de Otoño en el Seminario Teológico de Princeton, el 4 de octubre, 1911.
4. Citado en David Heywood, 'A New Paradigm for Theological Education?' *Anvil* 17, no. 1 (2000): 19.

período misionero que, antes de que murieran, no solo alcanzó la mayoría de los países del Medio Oriente y la cuenca mediterránea, sino que también trasmitió fielmente a la siguiente generación la más profunda expresión de la doctrina y la práctica del maestro.

Su propia experiencia de ser mentoreado/a en la excelencia académica y la formación espiritual

Como vimos, cuando consideramos los enfoques de supervisión, solemos recurrir a nuestra propia experiencia como modelo para nuestra práctica. Si hicimos nuestros estudios doctorales en el contexto de una universidad secular, quizás no sea tan fácil derivar un modelo repetible a partir de nuestra experiencia, aunque hay supervisoras y supervisores evangélicos en esos contextos que encuentran maneras de modelar los principios que buscamos fomentar.

Preguntas de reflexión

¿Cómo modeló su supervisor/mentor la conexión entre la investigación y la formación espiritual?

¿En qué aspectos falló su supervisor/mentor como modelo de esta conexión?

¿Cuáles son las lecciones clave que usted deriva de su experiencia?

La experiencia de otros

Durante los seminarios de capacitación que he dirigido para supervisores de doctorado, a menudo pregunto a las y los participantes qué entienden por "formación espiritual". Estas son algunas de sus respuestas:

- la preocupación por toda la persona
- la integración del conocer y el ser
- adoración
- el desarrollo de valores
- la formación de la cosmovisión
- la relación con Dios

Preguntas de reflexión

¿Qué piensa de estas respuestas?

¿Qué piensa usted que es la mejor definición de la formación espiritual?

Las cosas que se elogian cuando las y los supervisores promueven la formación espiritual

En los seminarios de capacitación también pregunto qué cosas que hicieron sus supervisores de doctorado para promover la formación espiritual fueron buenas, y qué cosas no hicieron tan bien.

Las cosas buenas . . .

- fueron cristianos sinceros y comprometidos;
- estaban involucrados en el ministerio de la iglesia;
- mostraban respeto por las personas;
- respetaban las opiniones de otros, incluso si no estaban de acuerdo;
- su integridad académica era un reflejo de su integridad como personas;
- demostraban ser personas "genuinas";
- mostraban humildad ante la verdad.

Cosas no tan buenas. . .

- "No oraba conmigo";
- "Muy reservado";
- "Nunca se convirtió en una amistad";
- No compartía de su propia vida espiritual.

Luego les pregunto cómo quisieran promover la integración de la formación espiritual y la excelencia académica. Estos son algunos de sus comentarios:

- enfatizar que la excelencia académica glorifica a Dios;
- enfatizar que la excelencia académica refleja la espiritualidad;
- el corazón, la mente y el alma necesitan involucrarse en el estudio;
- el trabajo académico es una expresión del servicio y el amor a Dios;
- debemos ser humildes;
- la búsqueda del conocimiento es un acto espiritual;
- ayudar a que las y los estudiantes aprendan desaprendiendo, y dejando de lado los prejuicios;
- no evitar las preguntas grandes y difíciles;
- la teología es acerca de la vida —es un verbo— hay que vivirla, practicarla;
- hay que asegurarse de que haya algún servicio relevante para la iglesia o la comunidad.

Preguntas de reflexión

Tome nota de lo que siente acerca de este tipo de respuestas.

¿Qué le sorprende?

La pregunta clave que las y los supervisores necesitan abordar es, ¿cómo hacemos esto, o cómo lo hacemos mejor?

Lo que buscamos formar en nuestros estudiantes de doctorado

John Stott identificó la importancia clave de la formación del profesorado de instituciones teológicas evangélicas para el futuro de la iglesia, una preocupación que lo llevó a fundar el programa de Becas de Langham Partnership: 'Los miembros de la facultad son el personal clave del seminario porque influencian, para bien o para mal, generación tras generación del futuro liderazgo de la iglesia. Lo que se necesita, entonces, es un flujo constante de nuevos docentes que combinan la excelencia académica con la piedad personal'.[5]

Entonces, ¿qué aspecto tiene esta 'piedad personal' que las y los supervisores deben inculcar?

1. Fidelidad a Cristo

Esto, por supuesto, es lo que hizo Jesús con sus discípulos, para que después de tres años con él estuvieran preparados no solo para poner al mundo patas arriba, sino también para morir por él. La futura facultad teológica debe ser entrenada para ser cristocéntrica —para honrar y agradar al Señor Jesucristo en todo.

> Hagan lo que hagan, trabajen de buena gana, como para el Señor.
> (Col 3:23)

Dietrich Bonhoeffer, en *Vida en comunidad* (su modelo para el seminario teológico), dice que el trabajo, que ocupa la mayor parte del día, adquiere sentido y unidad cuando se hace en el nombre del Señor Jesús.[6]

2. Fidelidad a la Palabra de Dios

> *Las y los investigadores deben ser fieles tanto a la Palabra de Dios como a las exigencias de su disciplina.*[7]

---

5. John Stott en una carta a varios amigos, Marzo de 1994.
6. D. Bonhoeffer, *Vida en comunidad* (Salamanca, Sígueme, 1982).
7. Shaw, *Principios y mejores prácticas*, Sección 8.

Como señala Dietrich Bonhoeffer, solo en las Escrituras aprendemos a entender correctamente la realidad. Nos sentamos a los pies del Señor, prestamos atención a su voz y hacemos nuestra su agenda.[8] El estudio teológico debe, con regularidad, volverse doxología.

3. Fidelidad en la oración

Las y los estudiantes de doctorado necesitan ser, continuamente, personas de oración. Necesitan, metafóricamente, estudiar de rodillas. No deben avergonzarse de orar por aspectos de su investigación. De hecho se les debe alentar a pedir que Dios sea parte de la dinámica de lo que están haciendo. La conversación con Dios puede ser un lugar para la crítica autorreflexiva y el discurso crítico. Así es como B. B. Warfield se expresó sobre este aspecto de la integración:

> Si nos enfrentamos a la tremenda dificultad del trabajo que tenemos ante nosotros, ciertamente nos hincará de rodillas; y si estimamos el poder del evangelio que nos ha sido encomendado, ciertamente nos mantendrá de rodillas.[9]

Bonhoeffer llamó a sus estudiantes a encomendarse unos a otros a las manos de Dios, implorando su bendición, paz y protección… y pidiendo perdón por los males cometidos.[10]

4. Fidelidad a la comunidad

> *Los programas de doctorado deben reconocer el importante papel que desempeña la comunidad en la formación de eruditos.*[11]

Mucha de la espiritualidad moderna es individualista, en contraste con el énfasis del Nuevo Testamento en la comunidad. Tendemos a enfatizar lo que nosotros pensamos que significa "comunidad", y olvidamos que a través de ella estamos entrando en algo que Dios ha creado. El cristianismo significa comunidad por causa de Jesucristo y en Jesucristo. Aparte de Cristo, la comunidad cristiana no existe y no tiene ningún propósito. Dios invita a las y los cristianos a ser partícipes en lo que está haciendo en la comunidad de su pueblo. Como lo expresa Bonhoeffer, "Si podemos ser hermanos es únicamente por Jesucristo y en Jesucristo".[12] Los cultos de adoración son una expresión, y el resultado, de ser comunidad,

---

8. Bonhoeffer, *Vida en comunidad*, 56
9. Warfield, *Theological Students*, 192.
10. Bonhoeffer, *Vida en comunidad*, 65-66.
11. Shaw, *Principios y mejores prácticas*, Sección 4.
12. Bonhoeffer, *Vida en comunidad*, 13.

y deben participar tanto docentes como estudiantes en instituciones evangélicas donde se ofrecen programas de doctorado.

Los estudios de doctorado se deben realizar en comunidad Esto implica:

1) Escuchar, paciente y atentamente a las demás personas. Esto sucede en discusiones, seminarios de capacitación, durante presentaciones académicas, etc. Es un aspecto del amor al prójimo y del amor a la comunidad. Las y los supervisores deben enseñar a respetar las opiniones ajenas, incluso si no están de acuerdo. Sus estudiantes, eruditos en formación, necesitan modelos de cómo debatir y disentir con cortesía, consideración y un espíritu humilde y dispuesto a aprender. Las y los estudiantes de doctorado deben apoyar a sus compañeras y compañeros en la comunidad académica, alentándolos con su asistencia cuando hacen presentaciones en seminarios de investigación y haciéndoles buenas preguntas. Necesitan darse cuenta que fallas académicas como el plagio son faltas de amor al prójimo.

2) La virtud de la disponibilidad (o servicialidad). En comunidad, las y los estudiosos aprenden a trabajar con y para los demás. Ya sea para un problema informático, una referencia que falta o una fuente que no se encuentra, es vital contar con una red de apoyo mutuo. Quizás los cónyuges de algunos/as estudiantes quieran y puedan compartir el cuidado de sus niños. La disposición a ayudar, tanto en cosas pequeñas como grandes, es necesaria.

3) Sostener las cargas. En el programa de doctorado que dirigí, regularmente teníamos almuerzos comunitarios de investigación y tiempos de oración. La disposición de las y los estudiantes a compartir y orar unos por otros era elogiable. Si uno estaba con dificultades o por tirar la toalla, o alguien tenía un familiar enfermo, el resto del grupo podía alentarles y orar por ellos.

Como dice Pablo en 1 Tesalonicenses, todo esto es reflejo del amor mutuo.

> En cuanto al amor fraternal... Dios mismo les ha enseñado a amarse unos a otros... No obstante, hermanos, los animamos a amarse aún más. (1 Tes 4:9-10)

5. Fidelidad a la iglesia

Warfield observó que a través del compromiso con una iglesia local y la adoración de la comunidad dentro de la institución, los estudiantes encontrarían "apoyo e inspiración para su vida religiosa personal que no hallarán en ningún otro lugar, y que no pueden permitirse perder."[13]

---

13. Warfield, *Theological Students*, 189.

6. Fidelidad a su llamado

B. B. Warfield le recordaba a sus estudiantes la razón de sus estudios:

> Ustedes están reunidos aquí para un propósito religioso, en preparación para el más alto servicio religioso que los hombres pueden realizar: guiar a otros en la vida religiosa... como estudiantes para el ministerio, mantengan siempre ante sus mentes la grandeza de su llamado, es decir, estas dos cosas: la inmensidad de la tarea que tienen por delante, y la infinidad de los recursos a su disposición...[14]

Preguntas de reflexión

¿Cómo desafían las 'demandas de la disciplina' su compromiso personal con la fidelidad bíblica?

¿Cómo ayudaría a estudiantes de doctorado a reconciliar esa tensión?

¿Qué enfoques o abordajes usará para modelar y fomentar la formación espiritual?

¿Cuál es el objetivo de desarrollar comunidad entre las y los estudiantes de doctorado?

¿Por qué las/los estudiantes de doctorado a menudo no participan en cultos de adoración de la comunidad académica, y en cambio se aíslan?

La formación espiritual implica integración

> Pero la erudición, aunque indispensable, no es lo más indispensable para un ministro. Antes y por encima de ser erudito, un ministro debe ser piadoso. Sin embargo, nada sería más letal que contraponer estas dos cosas... ¿Por qué debería uno apartarse de Dios cuando se acerca a sus libros, o sentir que debería abandonar sus libros para volver a Dios?[15]

Es importante enseñarle a las y los estudiantes de doctorado cómo evitar la separación entre su disciplina académica y el resto de la vida, que tan a menudo caracteriza al estudio avanzado.

---

14. Ibid., 188.
15. Ibid., 182-183.

Preguntas de reflexión

Como supervisor o supervisora de doctorado, reflexione sobre la relación entre su propia vida académica y su desarrollo espiritual personal.

¿Le resulta satisfactorio cómo interactúan? ¿Qué querría cambiar?

¿Qué dificultades en esta área ha visto entre sus colegas?

¿Cómo busca integrar la excelencia académica y espiritual en su trabajo con sus estudiantes?

¿De qué manera piensa que su rol como supervisor/a e investigador/a contribuye a llevar a cabo la misión de Cristo en el mundo?

Se necesita a todo un seminario evangélico para formar a un estudiante de doctorado

Hay que subrayar que la formación espiritual es responsabilidad de todo el programa de doctorado, no solo del supervisor. Además, las y los estudiantes deben estar plenamente comprometidos con su necesidad de crecer en la integración de la formación académica y espiritual. Este debería ser un criterio para quienes solicitan ingresar al programa de doctorado. La expresión "se necesita a todo un seminario para entrenar a un estudiante" es tan cierta aquí como en otros ámbitos. Los miembros de la facultad, el personal y los estudiantes están involucrados en esto como parte de una comunidad de aprendizaje y apoyo, de manera que el proceso se vuelve recíproco, y la facultad y el personal también crecen espiritualmente a través de la interacción.

Una de las razones por las que un/a estudiante escoge un seminario evangélico como contexto para sus estudios de doctorado debería ser su compromiso con la formación integral de lo académico y lo espiritual. Esto mismo es lo que motiva a las y los supervisores a querer trabajar en este contexto y no en otro. Si no hay un compromiso con la formación espiritual de las y los estudiantes, bien podrían estudiar en un contexto universitario secular. El compromiso con la formación espiritual debe realzar el compromiso con ser un contexto de investigación académica de alta calidad. El seminario evangélico, como contexto académico, debe estar al mismo nivel de lo que hay en el ámbito secular, sin perder de vista su propósito de crear también un contexto para el crecimiento avanzado en lo espiritual.

El carácter del supervisor de doctorado evangélico

No debe aislarse el desarrollo espiritual de la formación académica; más bien, "debe ser una perspectiva que incide en todo el proceso educativo".[16] Esto se debe reflejar en la manera en que las y los supervisores se desenvuelven. Los atributos clave incluyen:

1. Humildad

> En tanto que los programas de doctorado deben esforzarse por la excelencia académica, también deben estar arraigados en la necesidad absoluta de la humildad y la total dependencia de Dios. La inteligencia humana autónoma —sin depender del Espíritu de Dios— puesta al servicio de la búsqueda de conocimiento, no honra a Dios. Los estudiantes de doctorado deben buscar la ayuda de Dios en todos los aspectos de su vida y su educación.[17]

Como dice el Apóstol Pablo: "Nadie tenga un concepto de sí más alto que el que debe tener" (Rom 12:3). En palabras de Dietrich Bonhoeffer, 'El que quiere aprender a servir, debe aprender ante todo a tenerse en poco'.[18] Como escribió Thomas á Kempis en *La imitación de Cristo*, '¿De qué te sirve discutir profundamente de la Trinidad si no eres humilde y, por lo tanto, no agradas a la Trinidad?'[19]

Quienes conocieron al gran erudito del Nuevo Testamento F. F. Bruce a menudo comentaban de su brillante conocimiento del griego y el hebreo, pero también de la humildad con la que compartía sus ideas.

Preguntas de reflexión

Dé ejemplos de eruditos de primer nivel que usted ha conocido y que han demostrado esa humildad.

¿Cómo manejamos la tensión entre ser líderes académicos, mentores y guías, y a la vez 'tenerse y reputarse de nada'?

---

16. B. J. Nicholls, 'The Role of Spiritual Development in Theological Education,' *Evangelical Review of Theology* 19, no. 3 (1995): 231.
17. Shaw, *Principios y mejores prácticas*, Sección 8.
18. D. Bonhoeffer, *Vida en comunidad*, cap. 4.
19. T. A Kempis, *La imitación de Cristo* (Bogotá, San Pablo, 2010), 14.

2. Veracidad

Los programas deben inculcar los valores de la honestidad y el rigor intelectual, un compromiso con la verdad dondequiera que conduzca, y una humilde disposición a reconocer errores, malentendidos, prejuicios y presupuestos, y a valorar su corrección.[20]

Preguntas de reflexión

Como supervisor/a de doctorado, ¿cómo puede modelar la honestidad y el compromiso con la verdad, dondequiera que conduzca?

Como líderes académicos, ¿cuáles son las dificultades de reconocer errores, malentendidos y presupuestos?

3. Coherencia ética e intelectual

Las y los estudiosos y supervisores deben evidenciar un compromiso con investigaciones que serán profundas y rigurosas y que demuestran coherencia ética e intelectual.[21]

Preguntas de reflexión

¿Qué ejemplos ha visto donde la investigación y la enseñanza han carecido de consistencia ética e intelectual, y qué ha aprendido de ello?

¿En qué áreas ha sentido la tentación de incurrir en comportamiento poco éticos o en laxitudes intelectuales?

4. Autenticidad

Las y los educadores teológicos deben ser personas íntegras que han sabido integrar bien su propia espiritualidad. Deben estar dispuestas a practicar lo mismo que esperan de quienes supervisan. Las y los estudiantes rápidamente reconocen inconsistencias.

En 1992, ACTEA requirió que los docentes de seminario tuvieran 'una participación activa en la vida y el culto de la institución… no es meramente decorativo sino bíblicamente

---

20. Shaw, *Principios y mejores prácticas*, Sección 8.
21. Shaw, *Principios y mejores prácticas*, Sección 8.

esencial que todos los miembros del cuerpo educativo —tanto personal como estudiantes— no solo aprendan juntos, sino que también jueguen, coman, adoren y trabajen juntos".[22]

Para resumir, las cualidades que las y los supervisores necesitan demostrar e inculcar en otros incluyen espiritualidad personal (la pasión por Jesús y por la piedad personal), visión (y la capacidad de inspirar e inculcarla en otros), dones pastorales, habilidades comunicativas, una erudición emprendida con mentalidad de servicio, transparencia personal, amor por la iglesia y amor por la gente.

El rol de capacitar a las y los futuros líderes cristianos es digno de honor y profundamente exigente. En América del Norte, un informe de 1972 de la Asociación de Escuelas Teológicas (ATS, por su sigla en inglés) sobre la formación espiritual concluyó que "la facultad debería estar activa en su propia formación y desarrollo espiritual... el desarrollo espiritual y la formación de los estudiantes comienza con, y depende de, la espiritualidad de la facultad".[23]

Una buena parte de lo que aprenden las y los estudiantes acerca de la formación espiritual viene de maneras implícitas a través de la música, el temperamento, las actitudes y los comportamientos de los miembros de la facultad. La relación entablada entre docentes y estudiantes en un curso teológico contribuye al proceso de formación espiritual. Las actitudes de desconfianza y frialdad pueden socavar los esfuerzos positivos. En un seminario de capacitación que dirigí, un recién graduado del doctorado de una importante institución evangélica en América del Norte habló abiertamente sobre la discontinuidad entre lo que los miembros de la facultad enseñaban en el aula y cómo se criticaban mutuamente fuera del aula.

La espiritualidad se forma de manera constante, a través de las interacciones con las y los estudiantes —ya sea en sesiones formales de supervisión o en seminarios, en cultos de adoración o en excursiones, en retiros, días de oración o comidas comunitarias. Cómo vivimos y compartimos la fe en estos contextos como supervisores y supervisoras es vital para las y los estudiantes, especialmente cuando vienen de culturas diferentes.

La meta final

Así es como Warfield resume el objetivo y el increíble privilegio de todo esto:

> Un ministro debe ser erudito y religioso. No es una cuestión de escoger entre los dos. Debe estudiar, pero debe estudiar como si está en la presencia de Dios, y no

---

22. Accrediting Council for Theological Education in Africa, *Standards and Procedures for Accreditation at Post-secondary level,* 5a edición (Kaduna, Nigeria: ACTEA Continental Office, 1992).
23. D. Babin, E. Briner, L. A., Hoon, P. W., Martin, W. R., Smith, T., Van Antwerp, P. J. Whitney, *Voyage-Vision-Venture: A Report by the Task Force on Spiritual Development* (Dayton: American Association of Theological Schools, 1972), 9, 27.

en un espíritu secular. Debe reconocer el privilegio de emprender sus estudios en un ambiente donde Dios y la salvación del pecado son el aire que se respira.[24]

Tanto estudiantes como supervisoras y supervisores son llamados a crecer "en la gracia y en el conocimiento de nuestro Señor y Salvador Jesucristo" (2 Pedro 3:18). El rol de las y los supervisores de doctorado en una institución evangélica incluye nutrir un contexto en el que eso se pueda llevar a cabo —donde las cosas de Dios y la salvación son "el aire que se respira". Esto requiere un abordaje educativo tanto integral como integrado, y no uno estrictamente enfocado en el crecimiento cognitivo y el logro académico. El crecimiento espiritual de las y los estudiantes de doctorado no debe ser una contingencia— algo que puede resultar o no— de ese abordaje, sino un aspecto esencial e integrado del mismo. Las y los supervisores deben esforzarse por presentar, al final del programa de doctorado, a un/a estudiante que está unos cuántos pasos más cerca de la madurez y la semejanza a Cristo. Nuestra meta es presentar a cada persona 'madura en Cristo' (Col 1:28).

Preguntas de reflexión

Como resultado de haber leído este capítulo, ¿qué hará de manera diferente en su próxima reunión con sus estudiantes?

¿Qué dos cambios harán a la manera en que evalúa el progreso de sus estudiantes?

¿Qué ideas debe adoptar su institución para avanzar en la formación espiritual de sus estudiantes de doctorado?

Para leer más

Bonhoeffer, D. *Vida en comunidad*. Salamanca: Sígueme, 1982.

Cannell, L. 'Theology, Spiritual Formation and Theological Education: Reflections Toward Application', en *Life in the Spirit Life in the Spirit: Spiritual Formation in Theological Perspective*, editado por J. P. Greenman y G. Kalantzis. Downers Grove: IVP, 2010.

Cheesman, G. 'The Spiritual Formation of Students—A Personal Selection from the Literature.' *The Theological Educator*, Marzo 2007 (2.1).

Nicholls, B. J. 'The Role of Spiritual Development in Theological Education.' *Evangelical Review of Theology* 19, no. 3 (1995): 231.

Shaw, I. *Principios y mejores prácticas para Programas de Doctorado*. Carlisle: Langham Global Library, 2025.

Warfield, B. B. *The Religious Life of Theological Students, Lecture given at Autumn Conference at Princeton Theological Seminary, October 4, 1911*. Repub. Nueva Jersey: Presbyterian and Reformed, s.f.

---

24. Warfield, *Theological Students*, 189.

11

La supervisión y el desarrollo de una cultura de investigación

Los estudiantes de doctorado solo deben ser admitidos a un entorno donde se ofrece apoyo para aprender sobre la investigación y llevarla a cabo, donde la investigación ya se está llevando a cabo, y donde existe una cultura de investigación.[1]

Yo vivo en una zona del hemisferio norte que es bastante fresca y húmeda. Disfruto de cultivar plantas, pero muchas no crecen con vigor en frío y humedad, y aun les cuesta hacerlo en mi invernadero. Sin embargo, cuando viajo a partes de África y Asia veo que estas mismas especies florecen sin ayuda artificial, simplemente porque están en su entorno natural. Las cosas florecen y crecen cuando están en el contexto correcto. Lo mismo es cierto para estudiantes de doctorado.

El doctorado de investigación ha sido reconocido universalmente como,

i) la máxima expresión de la erudición;

ii) un galardón custodiado por los guardianes de la disciplina, con respetados tenedores de dicha condecoración fungiendo como examinadores;

iii) un producto orientado a la investigación, elaborado por un investigador individualmente responsable, por el que se adquieren conocimientos especializados, y que se posiciona en el contexto de la erudición universal.

Para llevarse a cabo con éxito, la investigación doctoral debe emprenderse en el contexto apropiado. El foco de atención en el pensamiento educativo ha tendido a desplazarse del doctorado a la "educación doctoral" —el marco de referencia más amplio dentro del cual se llevan a cabo los estudios de doctorado. Esta atención a las actividades y relaciones que se requieren como respaldo del trabajo de doctorado ha producido un énfasis mucho

---

1. Shaw, *Principios y mejores prácticas*, Sección 11.

más saludable en las dimensiones personales de los estudios de doctorado. Ahora hay un mayor reconocimiento de la importancia de comprender las pedagogías, los procesos y las instalaciones que se requieren para formar, y apoyar las necesidades de, las y los estudiantes de programas de doctorado.

El propósito de la educación doctoral es producir 'estudiantes/aprendices autogestionados'.[2] Este es un objetivo mucho más grande que ayudar a alguien a producir una pieza única de investigación con la que obtiene un doctorado. Más bien implica preparar a las y los estudiantes de doctorado para toda una vida en el ministerio de la investigación y el trabajo académico. Además de suponer una relación entre supervisor/a y estudiante, también es una experiencia en un contexto educativo público. Lograr esto requiere mucho más que los mejores esfuerzos de supervisión, aunque el desarrollo de habilidades profesionales de investigación y supervisión es un aspecto clave.

Desarrollar un programa de doctorado en una institución no significa simplemente agregar otro programa al perfil institucional, o agregar un nivel de enseñanza más alto a lo que ya se ofrece. Hacer que una institución sea un entorno propicio para la investigación implica un cambio significativo en el enfoque de su trabajo, y un cambio en su cultura. Significa hacerse preguntas de fondo acerca del propósito de la institución. Este es un paso que requiere de una cuidadosa reflexión, una cuantiosa inversión y el ejercicio de la oración y la imaginación.

Así es como se expresa en *Principios y mejores prácticas* de ICETE:

> Solo se deben implementar programas de doctorado dónde se haya establecido una cultura de investigación, y donde se impulsa la investigación. Este es el contexto idóneo para el aprendizaje basado en la investigación.[3]

1. Aspectos clave de una cultura de investigación

La decisión de implementar un programa de doctorado dentro de una institución académica evangélica implica una discusión sobre qué tipo de institución va a ser. Es una decisión que necesita el apoyo y la adhesión total de la comunidad académica más amplia. La decisión de ofrecer programas de doctorado de investigación es una declaración de que la institución no solo está comprometida con tener estudiantes de doctorado, sino también con producir investigaciones y generar interacción crítica a un nivel avanzado. La institución está declarando su intención de ser un lugar de reflexión y aprendizaje teológico serio y de vanguardia. Este es un componente vital de un entorno en el cual los programas de doctorado van a sobrevivir. Implica una inversión seria en los debidos

---

2. J. Stephenson, 'Managing Their Own Program,' *Studies in Continuing Education* 28, no. 1 (2006): 17-32.
3. Shaw, *Principios y mejores prácticas*, Sección 17.

procesos académicos y en capital intelectual. Quienes fungen como supervisores/as necesitan tener el tiempo y los recursos para supervisar, ser investigadores activos y hacer su propia contribución a la conversación académica de vanguardia.

En algunos contextos académicos, especialmente en las universidades más importantes, la investigación es incentivada con generosas becas de investigación y tiempo para investigar. Sin embargo, en la mayoría de las instituciones evangélicas los recursos para esto son mucho más limitados. Aun así, que la disponibilidad de recursos sea menor no disminuye su importancia, y se deben implementar medidas positivas para lograrlo.

A las y los estudiantes de investigación de doctorado se les pide que desarrollen respuestas originales y creativas a preguntas de investigación que son vitales. Necesitan ser supervisados por docentes que son investigadoras e investigadores activos, que tienen un historial de investigación bueno y actual, que funcionan bien dentro de su disciplina, y que participan en el diálogo con sus pares en conferencias y foros académicos. Necesitan modelar lo que esperan de sus estudiantes de investigación. La institución en la que las y los supervisores enseñan, y donde las y los estudiantes de doctorado investigan, debe demostrar claramente sus intenciones de facilitar estas oportunidades, y de ponerlos a disposición de sus estudiantes de investigación.

Preguntas de reflexión

¿Qué significa para usted el término "cultura de investigación"?

Enumere tres características de una "buena" cultura de investigación.

Describa una situación que experimentó donde había una cultura de investigación "favorable" y "habilitante".

Describa una situación que experimentó donde había una cultura de investigación "pobre".

¿Qué se puede hacer para desarrollar una mejor cultura de investigación en su institución?

2. La creación de una cultura de investigación

La investigación florece en entornos que la nutren. Esto incluye la presencia de programas de maestría de alta calidad que tienen un componente de investigación y que desarrollan las habilidades de investigación de futuros estudiantes de doctorado (ver caps. 4 y 5). El contexto institucional también debe fomentar la reflexión y la investigación, para que estas se destaquen como valores clave en la identidad de la institución. Esto implica comprometerse a facilitar que los miembros de la facultad investiguen en sus campos de especialización y mantengan un diálogo fructífero y continuo con sus pares académicos. A su vez, ello nutre la capacidad de llevar a cabo investigaciones personales y supervisar a estudiantes de investigación, e impregna la docencia a los niveles de maestría y de grado.

Una cultura de investigación no es solo un lugar donde se llevan a cabo investigaciones. Es un aspecto de una cultura de aprendizaje crítica y reflexiva, donde la capacidad de pensar ideas frescas y acoger conocimientos creativos se convierte en un valor central.

Una cultura de investigación es una cultura de ideas, que fomenta los enfoques y las perspectivas frescas de estudiantes y supervisores. Estas se consideran un recurso vital para la comunidad eclesial más amplia, en cuanto ayudan a la reflexión sobre cómo vivir y pensar en su propio contexto y, además, son una manera en que las y los eruditos evangélicos contribuyen a la conversación académica global.

El seminario de investigación

El seminario de investigación desempeña un papel clave en:

i) el desarrollo de una cultura de investigación,

ii) mejorar las instalaciones de investigación disponibles,

iii) apoyar la formación de estudiantes al nivel de la investigación doctoral.

Las y los estudiantes de doctorado necesitan un foro apropiado en donde presentar sus ideas y escuchar las de sus pares académicos. El seminario de investigación sirve de punto focal para el debate académico inter pares y facilita la discusión en torno a las ideas de vanguardia. Ofrece a las y los estudiantes de investigación la oportunidad de adquirir experiencia en la presentación de sus ideas y de aprender las habilidades necesarias para dirigir y participar en discusiones académicas.

El seminario debe proveer oportunidades para que la facultad y el estudiantado participen en la interacción crítica con las ideas de académicos visitantes.

El seminario de investigación puede tomar varios formatos —un solo trabajo escrito y luego una discusión, o una serie de escritos cortos o informes de investigaciones en proceso que luego se discuten. Lo ideal es que los trabajos escritos se distribuyan por adelantado para ayudar a la reflexión crítica, aunque a menudo no es factible.

Un seminario de investigación tiene éxito cuando tanto supervisores como estudiantes se comprometen a dedicarle tiempo. Funciona mejor llevarlo a cabo de forma regular —idealmente por lo menos una vez al mes.

Algunas de las maneras en que un contribuye a la cultura de la investigación:

i) Anima a que las y los supervisores se mantengan frescos y estimulados para contribuir regularmente a nuevas reflexiones, y eso les mantiene equipados para la investigación y la enseñanza.

ii) Como muy pocas veces los temas coincidirán exactamente con el campo de investigación del estudiante, el seminario de investigación alienta a supervisores y estudiantes de posgrado a pensar por fuera de sus horizontes inmediatos y de manera interdisciplinaria. Esto puede aportar creatividad a los enfoques de investigación y entendimientos más amplios.

iii) Ofrece un entorno seguro en el que tanto estudiantes de postgrado como supervisores/as pueden probar sus ideas y recibir retroalimentación de sus pares. Estas pueden ser ideas originales de investigación o preguntas que surgen de la discusión académica actual. La oportunidad de expresarlas en un marco formal, seguido de un respetuoso diálogo académico, ayuda a mejorar la autoestima intelectual de las y los estudiantes.

iv) Es oportuno invitar a académicos visitantes a presentar trabajos, para exponer la comunidad académica local a ideas o enfoques nuevos y a la discusión académica más amplia a nivel regional o global.

v) Ayuda a la facultad académica y a las y los estudiantes a crecer intelectual, relacional y espiritualmente en torno al valor medular de formar mentes cristianas creativas.

La conducción del seminario

Se debe procurar una postura flexible y usar enfoques imaginativos. El seminario necesita una moderación adecuada que fomente conversaciones de amplio alcance. Si como supervisor/a usted asume el papel de moderador, es importante asegurar que las y los estudiantes puedan encontrar su voz, y no quedarse en silencio mientras los miembros de la facultad dominan el diálogo. Los trabajos que se presentan necesitan ser entendibles para los presentes. Si son interdisciplinarios, deben ser accesibles a los que no son expertos en campos específicos, sin perder su rigor académico.

Los trabajos pueden compartirse de antemano para su revisión, presentarse brevemente y luego discutirse, o bien presentarse en su totalidad en el seminario y luego abrir espacio para preguntas y debate. Se pueden desarrollar presentaciones más breves, de veinte minutos, sobre investigaciones en curso.

Otro enfoque productivo consiste en tomar un texto clave —primario o secundario— que todos leen a fin de discutirlo. Puede ser de un campo de investigación específico o relacionarse con desarrollos educativos.

Para tener éxito, el seminario necesita del compromiso institucional. Tanto supervisoras y supervisores académicos como sus estudiantes de investigación necesitan comprometerse por un par de horas cada vez que se lleve a cabo. Es una cuestión de cortesía y respeto asistir y apoyar a quienes están presentando trabajos. El seminario de investigación ayuda a construir apoyo mutuo, aprendizaje compartido y estímulo académico.

Preguntas de reflexión

¿Su institución tiene un seminario de investigación?

¿Qué tan efectivo le parece como espacio para el debate académico a nivel de pares?

¿Qué puede hacer para mejorar su eficacia?

¿Cómo puede ayudar a sus estudiantes de investigación a sacarle el máximo provecho?

3. Desarrollo de la biblioteca y sus recursos

A pesar de la creciente disponibilidad de acceso remoto a recursos de estudio y bases de datos electrónicos, la biblioteca es aún el "corazón" de la institución académica. La provisión de un entorno adecuado para que la investigación prospere requiere una cuantiosa inversión en recursos bibliográficos. Las y los supervisores deben tener un rol importante en este esfuerzo, participando activamente en la recomendación de textos y recursos clave para ser adquiridos por la biblioteca, y trabajando para mantener la biblioteca actualizada en su campo de investigación. El presupuesto de la biblioteca se debe usar de maneras creativas para apoyar individualmente a cada estudiante en su necesidad de acceder a recursos de investigación de alta calidad. Para esto es esencial el puesto de bibliotecario/a. No debe ser visto como un papel administrativo menor, sino como un aspecto central del trabajo de enseñanza e investigación de la institución. En el seminario donde enseñé, el bibliotecario era miembro de la junta académica.

4. Espacios de estudio designados para estudiantes de investigación

Los estudiantes que emprenden investigaciones necesitan espacio para libros, notas y materiales de investigación. Es frustrante tener que transportar un gran número de libros a un escritorio de uso general de la biblioteca y tener que llevárselos al final del día. Algunos seminarios y universidades han creado salas de estudio para estudiantes investigadores o designado un área de la biblioteca. Otros ofrecen pequeñas oficinas o cubículos designados para sus estudiantes. Todo esto mejora la capacidad de las y los investigadores de seguir con su trabajo. Si lo que se provee es una sala de investigación designada, esto ayuda a que las y los investigadores tengan un sentido de identidad, y allí puede surgir una comunidad de investigación de apoyo mutuo.

5. El tiempo de supervisión como parte de la carga laboral de la facultad

Algunas instituciones deseosas de introducir programas de doctorado no hacen ninguna provisión especial para la carga horaria de quienes estarán involucrados. De alguna manera, esas instituciones esperan que se integre con todo lo demás. Las reuniones de supervisión llevan tiempo, también leer y comentar el trabajo de las y los estudiantes de investigación, por lo que esa falta de provisión no es una buena práctica.

Por consideraciones acerca de la calidad de la supervisión, se debe garantizar que esta no se ponga en peligro por asignar responsabilidades excesivas a supervisores individuales.

Si le piden que asuma la supervisión de estudiantes de investigación, es importante acordar con el liderazgo de su institución la asignación de suficiente tiempo, dentro de su carga laboral regular, para las reuniones de supervisión. Su institución debe contar con directrices en cuanto al número máximo de estudiantes de investigación (incluidas las investigaciones a nivel de maestría) que se pueden supervisar en un momento dado. Las cargas académicas y administrativas deben ajustarse para reflejar las cargas de supervisión.

> *Una estimación razonable del tiempo que necesita un supervisor para supervisar a un estudiante de doctorado de investigación a tiempo completo es de 60-90 horas de trabajo al año.*

Esto puede variar ya que se requiere más tiempo en las primeras etapas del programa de un estudiante y menos en el segundo año. Para supervisoras o supervisores con mucha experiencia, es posible que el tiempo necesario sea ligeramente menor. La previsión de este tiempo como parte de su carga laboral debe ser parte de sus discusiones anuales con su jefe de departamento o Decano Académico. No debe sobreextenderse aceptando demasiados estudiantes de doctorado para supervisión. Sería perjudicial para su trabajo, para la experiencia de sus estudiantes y para su salud en general.

6. Desarrollo profesional del personal de supervisión

A muchos supervisores se les pide asumir el rol sin ningún entrenamiento formal ni preparación para llevarlo a cabo. Sin embargo, siendo tan importante una buena supervisión para el éxito del trabajo de investigación, las instituciones que ofrecen programas de doctorado deben establecer oportunidades apropiadas para el desarrollo de su facultad y proveer capacitación para las y los supervisores doctorales. La lectura de este manual es un primer paso, y el Comité de Doctorado de ICETE también ofrece seminarios de capacitación para supervisores. Algunas universidades locales también los ofrecen. Es importante que quién dirige su programa de doctorado entienda lo importante que es esto, y se le debe animar a regularmente poner estas oportunidades a disposición de la facultad. Se pueden organizar seminarios de discusión en torno al contenido de este manual.

Debe asegurarse que los planes de desarrollo institucional incluyan disposiciones para la identificación y capacitación de futuros supervisoras y supervisores académicos. Necesitan ser mentoreados en el trabajo que emprenderán. Este proceso puede requerir tiempo suyo, si usted tiene amplia experiencia supervisando y se le pide mentorear a otros.

7. La actividad investigativa y su actualización

Las instituciones que ofrecen programas de doctorado necesitan crear estructuras que faciliten que la facultad académica que se dedica a la supervisión doctoral pueda mantenerse actualizada a nivel investigativo, y estas necesitan ser parte de las oportunidades provistas para el desarrollo de la facultad,

Esto debe resultar en que las y los supervisores, regularmente, produzcan trabajos investigativos y artículos de revistas en su área temática, y participen y presenten trabajos en conferencias académicas. Esto no es fácil si tienen una fuerte carga administrativa o docente, y las tareas urgentes desplazan a las importantes actividades de investigación. La inversión de su tiempo en estas actividades de investigación es esencial para mantener su aptitud para supervisar. Cuando esto resulta imposible, su capacidad de mantenerse al día en lo académico disminuirá rápidamente y ya no deberían seguir supervisando.

La tarea de las y los profesores de mantenerse actualizados debe ser apoyada por la institución con la provisión de días de estudio y períodos sabáticos libres de responsabilidades docentes y administrativas. Es importante manejar su tiempo con disciplina, para poder hacer pleno uso de estas provisiones y no permitir que se llenen con otras tareas. La investigación activa nutre la buena supervisión, la docencia inspiradora y la capacidad de examinar el trabajo de otros.

La institución necesita ver que la inversión en su liderazgo académico requiere de una inversión en capital intelectual, y de la provisión de oportunidades para que sus líderes académicos crezcan en su madurez espiritual.

Preguntas de reflexión

¿Cuáles son las principales preocupaciones que surgen en su propia institución a partir de estos planteos?

¿Cuáles son las principales áreas en su propio trabajo que necesitan atención?

Identifique tres pasos clave que se deben tomar para abordar las áreas identificadas.

8. Conferencias

Es importante que las y los supervisores de estudiantes de doctorado se mantengan actualizados en lo académico. Esto implica, entre otras cosas, asistir a conferencias académicas —ya sean nacionales, regionales o internacionales— y, siempre que sea posible, presentar trabajos. Esto les permite interactuar con las tendencias más recientes en el campo y formar redes con sus pares académicos. Siempre que sea posible, los trabajos presentados deben ser trabajos de investigación. La necesidad de preparar y exponer trabajos académicos ayuda a enfocar la mente en los resultados de la investigación.

En todo esto hay un costo. Los recursos de las instituciones son limitados. Los presupuestos para el desarrollo del personal suelen ser los primeros en ser recortados, pero esto puede rápidamente socavar el compromiso de la institución con la enseñanza orientada a la investigación. Muchas conferencias ofrecen subsidios para los costos de traslado de quienes asisten, y se debe aprovechar lo más posible esta oportunidad.

Otra posibilidad es que las instituciones periódicamente organicen sus propias conferencias sobre temas clave. Se pueden convocar varios oradores invitados y complementarlos con académicos locales y estudiantes cuya investigación está en una etapa avanzada. Las y los supervisores debe hacer todo lo posible para fomentar el desarrollo de estas oportunidades para el beneficio de sus estudiantes de investigación, de la institución y de su propio perfil como investigadores.

Las conferencias se pueden organizar a nivel local para beneficio de los líderes y pastores de las iglesias locales, ayudándoles a entender las perspectivas académicas sobre cuestiones de su contexto local. Esto contribuye al compromiso de promover el aprendizaje contínuo y de por vida entre los líderes eclesiales, y permite que el seminario sirva a la iglesia local y promueva la reflexión sobre las necesidades y los problemas contextuales.

9. Publicaciones

Las universidades orientadas a la investigación no solo fomentan la actividad investigativa, también valoran su publicación. La actividad investigativa suele medirse según estándares externos de referencia, a fin de determinar su posición relativa dentro de la comunidad de revistas arbitradas. En algunos contextos las publicaciones investigativas se corresponden con una remuneración adicional.

Es posible que los recursos para esto sean más limitados en instituciones teológicas evangélicas, pero el ethos debe ser el mismo. La buena investigación debe ser compartida, discutida y difundida ampliamente. Aunque es posible que los trabajos académicos y las revistas arbitradas no alcancen un número muy grande de lectores, por lo general son leídos por los protagonistas clave en el debate académico. Por lo tanto, hacer un aporte estratégico que contribuye a moldear la trayectoria de la erudición es algo muy importante. Contribuir una perspectiva distintivamente evangélica a esta discusión académica es un aspecto de la misión cristiana. También existe la necesidad de escribir y publicar materiales que beneficien tanto a estudiantes como a líderes de la iglesia. Esto conecta la academia con la iglesia, y ayuda a que sirva al trabajo y al testimonio más amplio de esas iglesias.

Se debe animar a las y los estudiantes de investigación a publicar sus trabajos de investigación, no solo como monografías de investigación. También pueden desarrollar artículos a partir de capítulos de sus tesis, o sobre temas relacionados con sus investigaciones. O pueden producir otras versiones que responden a las necesidades de los líderes eclesiales del contexto.

Resumen

El programa de doctorado no debe existir como algo aislado, sino que debe integrarse con el trabajo de toda la institución. Las y los estudiantes no deben sentirse aislados de otros estudiantes ni de la comunidad en general.

Las y los supervisores de investigación deben desempeñar un papel importante en la cultura de investigación y en su promoción dentro de toda la institución. Deben hacer esto con la convicción de que:

i) La investigación nutre la buena docencia —hay una fuerte sinergia entre ambas.

ii) Las buenas ideas de investigación se propagan a través de la comunidad académica y elevan la calidad de la reflexión y la discusión académica entre colegas.

iii) La interacción con la conversación académica entre pares desde una perspectiva evangélica es un aspecto de la misión cristiana.

iv) Los recursos desarrollados beneficiarán a otros programas y se fomentará el intercambio académico.

v) Lo que contribuye una cultura de investigación bien desarrollada a una institución no se puede medir meramente en términos económicos, sino que debe ser visto como una manera de brindar más profundidad, madurez y riqueza a la tarea de capacitar a las y los líderes y pensadores cristianos para el contexto.

Preguntas de reflexión

¿En qué medida la cultura de investigación en la que hizo su investigación doctoral mejoró su experiencia investigativa?

¿Qué se podría haber hecho para mejorarla?

¿Cómo es la cultura de investigación en el contexto donde usted actualmente enseña?

Haga una lista de las cosas que usted hace que contribuyen a la cultura de investigación allí donde usted actualmente enseña.

¿Qué ideas tiene para seguir construyendo la cultura de investigación en su institución?

Si su institución está empezando a construir una cultura de investigación, y tiene fondos limitados, ¿dónde empezaría?

¿Cómo puede ayudar a sus estudiantes a contribuir y a beneficiarse de la cultura de investigación?

Caso de estudio

En el seminario teológico donde trabaja Paolo, y donde él dirige el programa de investigación, se ha introducido un seminario de investigación. Los primeros seminarios van bien, pero Paolo nota que la facultad académica tiende a dominar los debates, y las y los estudiantes de investigación contribuyen muy poco. Después de una de las presentaciones, la discusión se agita mucho y hay un fuerte intercambio de opiniones entre dos miembros de la facultad, lo que deja sintiéndose incómodos a los estudiantes presentes. Cuando Paolo conversa de esto con los dos miembros de la facultad, ambos dicen que es imposible argumentar a favor de una posición en particular sin hacerlo de manera apasionada. Paolo teme que las emociones están nublando los argumentos.

Preguntas

¿Qué cuestiones plantea esto?

¿Qué debería hacer Paolo para ayudar a mejorar la atmósfera en los seminarios, y para modelar una buena práctica académica?

Para leer más

Eley A. y R. Murray. *How to Be an Effective Supervisor*. Maidenhead: Open University Press, 2009.

Quality Assurance Agency, 'Doctoral Degree Characteristics.' www.qaa.ac.uk/en/Publications/Documents/Doctoral_Characteristics. pdf

Shaw, I. *Principios y mejores prácticas para Programas de Doctorado*. Carlisle: Langham Global Library, 2025.

12

Cómo lograr que sus estudiantes de doctorado escriban (y sigan escribiendo)

Lo escribo, lo vuelvo a escribir, y lo escribo por tercera vez... Entonces tomo la tercera versión —y literalmente lleno la página con correcciones para que otra persona no lo pueda leer— y lo vuelvo a escribir bonito para la imprenta. Luego lo dejo a un lado. Lo vuelvo a mirar. Empiezo una vez más a corregir. No sirve. Las modificaciones se multiplican. Las páginas se reescriben. Frases y trazos se cuelan entre las líneas y pasean por la página. Toda la página está desfigurada. Lo vuelvo a escribir. No puedo decir cuántas veces se ha repetido este proceso. No puedo más que comparar todo este asunto con un quehacer muy doméstico: lavar una esponja para quitarle la arenilla y el olor a mar.[1]

Así escribió John Henry Newman, uno de los teólogos ingleses más famosos del siglo diecinueve. Si el proceso de escribir, de poner las palabras correctas en el orden correcto, le pareció tan difícil a él, ¡no es ninguna sorpresa que piensen lo mismo nuestros estudiantes de doctorado!

El reto de escribir

Pocos estudiantes de doctorado entran a programas de doctorado como escritores capaces, con alto nivel de confianza y totalmente formados. La redacción académica es una habilidad que debe ser perfeccionada y desarrollada a lo largo de todo el proceso del estudio del doctorado. Ya que el examen final del doctorado se centra en la evaluación escrita de una tesis, son esenciales las habilidades de redacción. Las y los estudiantes de doctorado

---
1. J. H. Newman, *Letters and Diaries of John Henry Newman*, Vol. VI (Oxford: Clarendon Press, 1961), 188-189.

tienen que empezar a escribir desde una etapa temprana. El viejo modelo del estudiante de doctorado que se sienta y lee por varios años, y luego 'redacta' una tesis en los últimos pocos meses, se reconoce ahora como insatisfactorio. De hecho, que un estudiante no escriba regularmente y no cumpla los plazos para entregar sus trabajos escritos, es un indicio de que hay problemas. Los estudios han detectado que la dificultad para comenzar a escribir es, con frecuencia, una de las razones por las que no se presenta una tesis, o se presenta una tesis que requiere mucha revisión y corrección.[2] Por ende, es vital y necesario integrar la enseñanza del proceso de redacción académica en la etapa inicial del estudio de doctorado.

Escribir es diferente de hablar o predicar en público, aunque tiene similitudes. El orador recibe retroalimentación inmediata y rápidamente puede remediar la falta de claridad. Puede agregar material, cambiarlo o corregirlo según la reacción de su audiencia. Cuando se escribe, la retroalimentación es más remota y tarda más en llegar al autor —las reseñas de libros pueden publicarse varios años después de que salió el libro. La forma escrita es más fija, más abierta a ser evaluada de una manera diferente a cómo se evalúa el habla. Las respuestas a lo escrito pueden ser más formales, menos personales, y como no se pueden explicar y matizar de la misma manera en que se hace con respuestas verbales, pueden parecer más frías y aun más duras.

La expresión '*Escribir la tesis*' puede sonar bastante relajado y sugiere que la investigación está en gran medida completa y todo lo que queda por hacer es ensamblar algunos capítulos para ya completar la tesis. Pero no, escribir es difícil. Implica un esfuerzo concentrado y profundo de reflexión. Requiere que el autor exprese pensamientos complejos de manera lógica y lúcida, y que los fije en un manuscrito. Exige que el escritor sustancie por escrito los enunciados de la tesis.

Poner por escrito lo que uno entiende en su mente no es tarea fácil. Algunos estudiantes pueden ver un tema de manera conceptual, y tal vez puedan explicarlo verbalmente, pero cuando se trata de escribir, no logra encontrar las palabras.

Escribir es construir significado con el lenguaje. Es parte de un proceso de negociación entre quien escribe y los miembros de la comunidad dialogante para quienes escribe. Todo lo que el o la estudiante de doctorado escriba será examinado detenidamente al final del proceso. Debe estar a la altura del rigor de esa evaluación —¿tiene sentido? ¿es comprensible para los demás? Tiene que ser cuidadosamente pensado, reflexionado y reevaluado. Las y los estudiantes necesitan aprender a examinar lo que escriben para asegurarse de que transmite lo que pretenden, porque otros leerán, interpretarán y construirán significado a partir de lo que han escrito. Deben considerar si cada frase es informativa, si tiene la información apropiada y pertinente, sin ambivalencias ni ambigüedad. ¿Se fundamentan todos los argumentos y se consta toda la evidencia? Es poco probable que el/la estudiante

---

2. E. Rudd, *A New Look at Postgraduate Failure* (Guildford, Surrey: Society for Research into Higher Education, 1985).

pueda producir el producto terminado en su primer intento. La práctica de redactar varios borradores permite que un escrito madure y pueda pulirse, con múltiples oportunidades para resolver problemas, en lugar de tener que enmendar y ensamblarlo todo a último minuto. Esperamos que el proceso no sea tan escabroso como le pareció a John Henry Newman, ¡pero podría llegar a serlo!

Obstáculos que impiden la escritura

Los escritores tienen fama de ser propensos a la procrastinación. Escribir no es un proceso "natural" como lo es hablar. Sus destrezas necesitan ser aprendidas y desarrolladas constantemente. Muchos escritores adolecen de una sensación de fracaso a causa de su trabajo. Incluso novelistas reconocidos hablan de lo difícil que es enfrentarse a una hoja —o pantalla— en blanco, al comienzo del día. También hablan de sentirse 'bloqueados', cuando simplemente no encuentran las palabras. Escribir es una actividad individual, y puede aislar a quien lo hace.

Preguntas de reflexión

Reflexione sobre sus propios sentimientos en torno a la escritura.

¿Cuáles son los principales retos que ha enfrentado?

Piense en las cosas que ha escrito. ¿Cuál ha sido su experiencia más exitosa?

¿Qué hay detrás de ese resultado exitoso?

La importancia de que sus estudiantes escriban secciones pequeñas de manera regular

Insistir con que sus estudiantes escriban secciones pequeñas con regularidad es importante por varias razones:

i) Les permite reflexionar sobre dónde les ha llevado su reflexión, y hacia dónde se dirigen. Esto crea momentos en el proceso formativo que sirven como hitos.

ii) El acto de escribir puede ser una forma poderosa de generar ideas y recordar información.

iii) Discutir acerca de un trabajo escrito que luego integrará la tesis/disertación permite recibir retroalimentación. Aunque no se califica formalmente, el/la supervisor/a puede percibir el nivel del trabajo de su estudiante, y ofrecer comentarios, correcciones y orientación.

iv) La producción de trabajos evaluados suele ser un requisito institucional para las revisiones de progreso, etc.

¿Por qué sus estudiantes se resisten a entregar sus trabajos? Hay varias causas:

i) Una tesis siempre está en proceso de constituirse, de "llegar a ser". Sus estudiantes sienten que el producto no está terminado y se resisten a presentar lo que parece estar a medio terminar.

ii) Sienten que sus habilidades no están bien desarrolladas y se resisten a mostrar su trabajo a sus supervisores.

iii) En sus estudios anteriores no se les enseñó a escribir trabajos largos.

iv) Les atormenta el miedo al fracaso, o a ser "juzgados" prematuramente.

Preguntas de reflexión

¿Cuáles fueron sus propias razones por las que se resistía a escribir?

¿Qué tareas le dieron sus supervisores para que empezara a escribir?

¿Qué estrategias ha usado para que sus estudiantes escriban?

Obstáculos específicos que impiden la escritura

La dificultad para escribir no se debe simplemente a fallas o debilidades académicas. Si un/a estudiante tiene dificultades para escribir, su supervisor/a debe explorar las posibles razones.

Estrés: Redactar una tesis es muy estresante. A medida que crecen las presiones por los plazos y la dimensión del trabajo, algunos estudiantes sienten que su capacidad de escribir decrece. Algunos estudiantes pueden padecer fuertes dolores de cabeza. Otros pueden pasar mucho tiempo frente a la pantalla con la mirada perdida. Si se vuelve algo extremo, es posible que algunos necesiten asistencia médica por síntomas relacionados con estrés o depresión severa.

Falta de organización: Algunos estudiantes no pueden establecer un tiempo y un lugar para escribir. Tal vez sus notas no estén bien ordenadas o no son fácilmente accesibles. Se necesita mucha disciplina personal y mental para lograr que todos los elementos necesarios para escribir de manera sostenida estén en el lugar y el momento adecuados.

Demasiadas distracciones: Escribir requiere de una profunda concentración, y las constantes interrupciones de correos electrónicos, mensajes y llamadas telefónicas o pedidos familiares o pastorales les hace difícil enfocar en sus pensamientos. Ante estas presiones surge la necesidad de retirarse a un lugar tranquilo para concentrarse en escribir.

Escribir no tiene prioridad: Para muchos estudiantes la investigación original y la expansión de las fronteras de un área temática son actividades excitantes y estimulantes. En comparación, escribir puede parecer algo insulso. Sin embargo, la fase de 'rendir cuentas' y documentar la investigación es tan importante como la recolección de la evidencia.

Algún discapacidad del aprendizaje: Es posible que algunos estudiantes hayan llegado a la etapa del doctorado con una discapacidad de aprendizaje no diagnosticada, como la dislexia. Cuanto más crece el reto de leer grandes cantidades de texto, y luego de escribir largos, concentrados e intensos trabajos escritos, más puede acentuarse un problema de fondo. Si se evidencian dificultades serias, podría ser necesario referir a la persona a una evaluación profesional para ver si existe una causa, y si la hay recibir consejos sobre estrategias apropiadas para afrontarla. No hay que desanimar a las personas que tienen estas discapacidades ni disuadirlas de emprender el estudio a nivel de doctorado. He supervisado a estudiantes con dislexia que han tenido éxito a niveles de maestría y doctorado. Con el apoyo adecuado de especialistas, estudiantes que enfrentan estas cuestiones pueden tener éxito en sus estudios avanzados.

La comprensión y la enseñanza del proceso de escribir

La tarea de escribir implica el uso de habilidades de planificación y de construcción de contenidos. También incluye la capacidad de comprender el proceso y la disposición a recibir crítica.

Planificación

Las y los estudiantes de doctorado deben entender la importancia de dedicar tiempo a producir un bosquejo inicial de un trabajo escrito. Es necesario enfatizarlo. Algunos supervisores piden ver el bosquejo antes del inicio de cada etapa de redacción. El plan o bosquejo es el esqueleto del capítulo o la sección, y la evidencia y la argumentación son la carne que se le agrega.

El plan debe establecer la estructura del escrito y demostrar la claridad del argumento propuesto. Los puntos principales del plan de la sección se convierten en los títulos y subtítulos del escrito.

A algunos estudiantes les resulta útil usar estrategias de preescritura —como la lluvia de ideas y los mapas mentales— para generar y organizar sus ideas antes de esbozar el plan de la sección.

El primer borrador

Después de la planificación, comienza la redacción. Es bueno que los estudiantes escriban de manera planificada en la etapa inicial, y que permitan que sus ideas fluyan sin pasar mucho tiempo puliendo los aspectos técnicos —que pueden interrumpir la generación de ideas. Se debe esperar aproximadamente un día antes de pasar a la revisión del primer borrador.

Revisión

El/la estudiante debe leer cuidadosamente el borrador, buscando repeticiones, falta de claridad e imprecisiones. Luego de hacer estas correcciones, debe dedicar otro espacio de tiempo para revisar el estilo, la gramática y la ortografía.

Las frases deben ser de una extensión apropiada. Cuando se extienden mucho y divagan, hay que señalarlo y resolverlo. A veces son tan cortas que dificultan seguir un argumento. Por lo general es más interesante cuando las oraciones varían en extensión y forma.

A continuación se deben corregir los aspectos técnicos como las notas a pie de página.

En una etapa temprana de la redacción, él/ella debe adoptar y apegarse luego a una de las guías de estilo académico (como el *Manual de Estilo de Chicago*[3]). Su supervisor/a deberá hacer recomendaciones en cuanto a las guías de estilo que acepta la institución.

Se debe insistir en el uso de altos estándares de redacción y presentación, aun para los primeros borradores. Se están aprendiendo y consolidando habilidades que a futuro serán clave.

El estilo de escritura

El estilo debe ser apropiado para el nivel y el área temática. Las y los supervisores deben dar consejos sobre el "lenguaje discursivo" y el uso correcto del lenguaje técnico correspondiente al tema específico. Sin embargo, aun cuando se emplea lenguaje técnico, la prosa no debe volverse inaccesible ni tedioso.

El flujo y la secuencia lógico

Los capítulos y las secciones deben tener una introducción que sirve de orientación para lo que sigue. Si hay subsecciones, las principales se deben indicar aquí. La introducción debe atraer al lector, despertar su interés y hasta generar un poco de intriga. Una cita que estimula a pensar o el argumento de otro erudito pueden servir para atraer al lector. Aun en la introducción se debe tener en cuenta la conclusión —hacia dónde va todo esto.

---

3. *The Chicago Manual of Style* (16th Edition, University of Chicago, Chicago, 2010).

El argumento global

Una tesis debe tener un argumento integrador —una meta-narrativa. Cada capítulo también.

Un buen ejercicio para evaluar el flujo lógico de un trabajo es leer la introducción e ir a la conclusión, sin mirar lo que está entre medio, y ver si hay conexión entre el comienzo y el final del trabajo. ¿Se responden las preguntas o cuestiones que se plantearon en la introducción?

Estructura

Dentro de la tesis, cada sección debe tener una estructura clara —con una introducción breve, postulados y argumentaciones apropiadas y una conclusión que resume hasta dónde ha avanzado el argumento. Esto sirve como puente a la siguiente etapa clave del argumento global.

El contenido principal

El cuerpo principal del capítulo o la sección debe concentrarse en justificar o fundamentar el argumento o la evidencia clave. Aquí lo central es *describir* y *explicar*.

Su estudiante necesita construir un espacio de debate erudito y discusión académica, que él o ella entiende y en el cual toma un rol arbitral. Debe emplear las habilidades críticas y discursivas de su área temática, con argumentos a favor y en contra de las diversas posturas. Es común usar un abordaje dialéctico. Idealmente el trabajo construye una síntesis a partir de una tesis y una antítesis, que lleva a una nueva tesis que conlleva nuevos paradigmas de comprensión.

Debe enfatizarse el uso de palabras y frases como *aunque, sin embargo, en contraposición, asimismo, por otra parte, por último, por un lado... por el otro* que construyen argumentación académica. Frases como *por lo tanto, se deduce que, se desprende que, entonces, por ende* son herramientas importantes que se deben usar en las conclusiones de los capítulos y de la tesis en sí.

La conclusión

La conclusión es la culminación del argumento. Debe enfatizar las partes más importantes, reconocer las áreas que son más débiles y afirmar la "tesis" que se ha sido presento en forma sostenida a lo largo del trabajo. A menudo contiene ideas para trabajos adicionales que se necesitan sobre el tema, que el/la estudiante u otras personas podrán emprender más adelante.

El amigo crítico

Es recomendable aconsejar a sus estudiantes a que busquen un amigo crítico que lea algunos de sus trabajos y pueda 'ver' los errores que pudieron habéreseles escapado. Sin embargo, deben ser claras las reglas. El 'amigo crítico' no debe hacer más que marcar problemas de presentación, estilo y gramática, y no debe 'mejorar' el trabajo del estudiante en otros aspectos. Un buen corrector ortográfico y de estilo en un procesador de texto debería eliminar muchos de estos problemas. Si sus estudiantes no están trabajando en su primer idioma, es importante que tengan acceso a un buen nivel de apoyo en esta área.

Presentación final

Las y los supervisores deben inculcarle a sus estudiantes la importancia de seguir altos estándares de presentación en la redacción de su tesis. Desde el principio se les debe dar instrucciones sobre tamaños de fuente y márgenes apropiados, espaciado interlineal, etc. El espaciado interlineal doble hace que la revisión sea más fácil.

Se deben incluir y numerar secuencialmente todas las tablas, figuras, listas de referencias o apéndices.

La escritura académica debe ser precisa y clara. No se le puede dar lugar a los malentendidos o a las malas interpretaciones. En la defensa de la tesis, su estudiante no debería tener que decir: "En realidad lo que quise decir es. . .".

Preguntas de reflexión

¿Cuál es la mejor manera de estimular estas habilidades en sus estudiantes de doctorado?

¿Qué manual de estilo usa y recomienda?

¿Qué ejemplos de escritura académica puede usar que demuestran estas habilidades?

¿Cómo evalúa usted la legibilidad y la comprensión de un escrito?

Cómo fomentar la creación de estructura y significado —Algunos puntos específicos a tomar en cuenta (desde la supervisión)

i) ¿Es clara la intención de cada sección o capítulo?

ii) ¿Es claro el argumento/análisis?

iii) ¿El/la estudiante ha respetado las convenciones de escritura de la disciplina?

iv) Los puntos planteados, ¿se han sido respaldados con evidencia?

v) ¿Se distinguen y expresan claramente las conclusiones?

vi) ¿Se han trazado de manera clara los vínculos entre este y otros trabajos?

Preguntas de reflexión

¿Qué estrategias de escritura han funcionado bien con sus estudiantes?

¿Cuáles no?

¿Qué ideas o técnicas recomienda para empezar a escribir temprano en el día?

Cuando su estudiante requiere un fuerte estímulo para que avance más rápidamente con su redacción:

¿Puede él o ella cambiar su modo de trabajo?

¿Puede subir el ritmo y aumentar su producción?

Puede ser útil compartirles sus propias estrategias de redacción y los altibajos de su progreso. Algunos escritores recomiendan que la manera de empezar a escribir al principio del día es dejar una oración inconclusa en la página al final del día anterior. Al día siguiente la primera tarea es completar esa oración, y así retomar la redacción.

La importancia del cierre

El "cierre" le pone fin a algún aspecto de la investigación. Significa limitar, concluir, ultimar. No necesariamente significa que un trabajo escrito haya alcanzado su forma final, pero está en una etapa en la que por el momento se puede dejar de lado y, más adelante, volverlo a revisar. Escribir es crear una serie de pequeños cierres. En estos puntos, estudiantes pueden seleccionar, priorizar y descartar ideas que no van a desarrollar.

Preguntas de reflexión

¿A qué puntos de cierre ha llegado él o ella en lo que ya ha escrito?

¿A qué puntos de cierre necesita llegar ahora?

Un socio a quien responder —el diario de investigación

Es una recomendación de muchos de los manuales de escritura de tesis. Algunos programas de doctorado lo consideran un requisito y forma parte del perfil de desarrollo personal de sus estudiantes. En este diario de redacción se debe registrar:

i) Los progresos logrados, las reuniones celebradas, lo que hizo el/la estudiante y cuándo lo hizo.

ii) Es importante que sus estudiantes calibren su progreso, que ajusten su redacción y reflexión según cómo están progresando.

iii) Observaciones sobre el avance de su reflexión y las ideas que se están desarrollando. Debe haber espacio para hacer lluvia de ideas y para anotar nuevas ideas clave a medida que se desarrollan. Allí se deben registrar los principales problemas que se preveen y los momentos 'eureka' cuando las soluciones se vuelven más claras.

iv) Reenfoque —qué queda por hacer y cuándo y dónde se hará

v) Planificación —los estudiantes tienden a ser poco realistas en sus evaluaciones de cuánto tiempo se tarda en escribir un trabajo académico bien desarrollado. Pídales que calculen cuánto tiempo les lleva escribir quinientas palabras de texto académico bien desarrollado. Luego, les puede pedir que esbocen un plan de redacción (aproximado) para el siguiente año en función de ese ritmo de redacción.

El curso de redacción de postgrado

Los cursos cortos de redacción pueden ser útiles para desarrollar las habilidades de escritura académica. Los que más sirven se centran en la producción de texto, y no meramente en la organización de las ideas antes de ponerlas por escrito. Incluyen aportes de expertos en escritura académica, y generan oportunidades para que las y los estudiantes puedan criticarse sus trabajos unos a otros.[4]

---

4. M. S. Torrance y G. V. Thomas, 'The Development of Writing Skills in Doctoral Research Students,' in *Postgraduate Education and Training in the Social Sciences. Processes and Products*, ed. R. G. Burgess (Londres: Jessica Kingsley, 1994), 105-123.

Preguntas de reflexión

Durante sus propios estudios de doctorado, ¿asistió a un curso de redacción? ¿Le fue útil?

¿Qué cursos de apoyo de este tipo ofrece su institución a nivel de posgrado?

Si se ofrece un curso así, ¿qué elementos clave se deben incluir?

Si no, ¿qué libros de autoayuda sobre redacción de tesis puede recomendar?

La retroalimentación como parte del proceso de capacitación

En un estudio de cuarenta y cinco estudiantes de doctorado se encontró que preparar y recibir críticas de profesores y otros estudiantes era percibido como *"el elemento que más influyó en ayudarles a entender el proceso de escritura académica y en producir un trabajo mejor escrito"*. En el desarrollo de su autoconfianza como escritores académicos, resultaron esenciales *"la retroalimentación cara a cara y personalizada y el aspecto contínuo o reiterativo de las críticas recibidas"*. Sin embargo, los estudiantes también reconocieron que el proceso de crítica era *"altamente emocional y a veces frustrante"*. El estudio concluyó que es vital facilitar que los estudiantes aprendan tanto a recibir como a dar retroalimentaciones útiles.[5]

Esto significa que la retroalimentación de las y los supervisores es muy importante en el proceso de capacitación académica. Es necesario pensar con cuidado cómo hacerlo. Las y los supervisores necesitan desarrollar formas de facilitar que sus estudiantes reciban, y se beneficien, de la retroalimentación, ya sea de su supervisor/a, de sus pares en un seminario académico o de revisores académicos externos.

Preguntas de reflexión

¿Qué tipo de retroalimentación ofrece usted a sus estudiantes —por escrito, de forma oral, por adelantado, el mismo día?

¿Cuánto tiempo tarda en darla después de recibir un trabajo escrito?

¿Cómo comunica la retroalimentación negativa?

---

5. R. S. Caffarella y B. G. Barnett, 'Teaching Doctoral Students to Become Scholarly Writers: The Importance of Giving and Receiving Critiques,' *Studies in Higher Education* 25, no. 1 (2000): 40-43.

Estilos de retroalimentación

La retroalimentación permite que sus estudiantes entiendan los estándares que deben adoptar para obtener un doctorado, y que puedan medir si las están alcanzando o no. Esto es importante porque tienen pocas oportunidades para medir cómo les está yendo.

Hace muchos años me llamó la atención lo que dijo uno de mis estudiantes de investigación. Había entregado un trabajo largo y en general bueno, el cual yo comenté de manera extensa con observaciones mayormente positivas y con muchas palabras de aliento. Pero el estudiante respondió que, porque había escrito mis comentarios en tinta roja, parecía que la retroalimentación era toda negativa. Fue una lección simple pero importante. Pregúntese, ¿qué mensajes no deseados está transmitiendo mediante las distintas formas en las que ofrece retroalimentación?

Escribir es un acto muy personal —implica pensar y reflexionar en voz alta, de forma semi permanente. Por lo tanto, los sentimientos de autoestima de las y los estudiantes como investigadores y escritores están estrechamente vinculados a este proceso de recibir críticas públicas por su trabajo. Los momentos de retroalimentación crítica pueden ser emocionalmente difíciles. Pueden plantear preguntas profundas sobre la capacidad de escribir, e incluso puede llevar a que una persona cuestione si debería continuar en un programa de doctorado.

En las siguientes citas, que aparecen en estudios publicados, varios estudiantes describen su experiencia de recibir retroalimentación:

> *"Mi primera reacción, si tienen muchas sugerencias, debería ser de profundo alivio, porque tengo a alguien en mi vida que será honesto conmigo y me ayudará a lograr el mejor trabajo que soy capaz de hacer. Pero mi primer pensamiento es, 'Bueno, lo siento, pero ya no podemos ser amigos, porque debes tener una mala personalidad para escribir así sobre mi trabajo. Y un mal carácter'.*
>
> *"A veces no logro que salgan palabras de mi boca porque estoy tan decepcionado".*

Preguntas de reflexión

¿Cómo se sintió cuando algo que escribió recibió retroalimentación negativa?

¿Cómo habría dado usted esa retroalimentación de manera diferente?

¿Cómo quisiera que sus estudiantes respondan a su retroalimentación?

¿Qué haría usted si cuestionaran sus comentarios?

El manejo de las sesiones de retroalimentación

Es importante manejar bien la relación de supervisión en los momentos clave en que se ofrece retroalimentación. La mayoría de las y los estudiantes intuitivamente sabe que debe tratar de no ponerse a la defensiva cuando recibe retroalimentación y que tiene que aprender a recibir retroalimentación negativa con amabilidad y respeto.

- Como supervisor/a, antes de empezar a dar retroalimentación, considere bien el proceso. ¿Qué quiere que su retroalimentación logre y cómo quiere que su estudiante reaccione?
- En su orientación inicial debe darles instrucciones detalladas a sus estudiantes de cómo les dará la retroalimentación y de cómo espera que la reciban. Cada tanto tendrá que reforzar estos puntos.
- Sus estudiantes necesitan aprender cómo manejar instancias en las que reciben retroalimentación contradictoria de diferentes supervisores. En lo posible, estos conflictos se deben resolver entre los supervisores antes de que se reúnan con el/la estudiante, y no exteriorizarse en su presencia, de lo contrario podrían generarle confusión y angustia.
- Los supervisores necesitan considerar cuidadosamente qué es lo que quieren lograr con el proceso de crítica, y deben preparar materiales para sus estudiantes que les ayuden a incorporar este proceso a su práctica de aprendizaje.
- Hay que reconocer que para la mayoría de las personas recibir críticas es un proceso tanto racional como emocional. Las y los estudiantes de investigación son juzgados y evaluados por lo que escriben. Es mucho lo que está en juego, pues se comprometen e invierten mucho en su trabajo.
- Tratar de transmitir una sensación de progreso —la retroalimentación debe mostrar lo que se ha logrado, además de lo que hay que mejorar. No alcanza con decir "escríbalo mejor". Es mejor decir "esto es lo que ha hecho bien y así es como puede escribir mejor . . .".
- En el proceso de dar retroalimentación por el trabajo académico, es importante enseñar a sus estudiantes a ser críticamente reflexivos con su propio trabajo. En el futuro, cuando sirvan como maestros, eruditos y escritores, tendrán que ejercer su propio juicio profesional e independiente. Esta es una habilidad que tienen que aprender paulatinamente. Sus estudiantes lo aprenderán a partir de su experiencia de recibir críticas por su trabajo y de criticar el trabajo de otros. Hacer esto en un ambiente en el que reciben apoyo es de lo más útil.

> **Caso de estudio**
>
> Noé ha presentado un trabajo lleno de expresiones poco claras, errores ortográficos e imprecisiones gramaticales. El trabajo necesita una revisión extensa, pero el plazo para la presentación es muy corto, y como su supervisor usted sabe que pedirle que haga las correcciones llevará mucho tiempo. Está considerando revisar el trabajo y resaltar todos los problemas usted mismo, aunque sabe que llevará tiempo. Pero también sabe que hacerlo ayudará a asegurar que Noé logre terminar el trabajo a tiempo.
>
> **Preguntas**
>
> ¿Qué debería hacer?
>
> ¿Qué no debería hacer?

Para leer más

Caffarella, R. S. y B. G. Barnett. 'Teaching Doctoral Students to Become Scholarly Writers: The Importance of Giving and Receiving Critiques.' *Studies in Higher Education* 25, no. 1 (2000): 39-52.

Chicago University Press. *A Manual for Writers of Term Papers, Theses and Dissertations* (7a edición). Chicago: Chicago University Press, 2010.

Cutts, Martin. *Oxford Guide to Plain English*. Oxford: Oxford University Press, 2009.

Kamler, B. y P. Thomson. *Helping Doctoral Students Write: Pedagogies for Supervision*. Abingdon: Routledge, 2006.

Murray, R. *How to Write a Thesis*, 2ª edición. Maidenhead: Open University Press, 2006.

Seely, J. *Oxford Guide to Effective Writing and Speaking*. Oxford: Oxford University Press, 2005.

Swan, Michael. *Practical English Usage*. Oxford: OUP, 1996, para EFL (inglés como idioma extranjero).

Torrance, M. y G. Thomas. 'The Development of Writing Skills in Doctoral Research Students.' en *Postgraduate Education and Training in the Social Sciences. Processes and Products*, editado por R. G. Burgess, 105-123. Londres: Jessica Kingsley, 1994.

Torrance, M., G. Thomas y E. Robinson. 'The Writing Experiences of Social Science Research Students.' *Studies in Higher Education* 17 (1992): 155-167.

———. 'Training in Thesis Writing: An Evaluation of Three Conceptual Orientations.' *British Journal of Educational Psychology* 63 (Febrero 1993): 170-184.

13

El sostén administrativo del proceso de doctorado

Aunque la supervisión y las instalaciones sean buenas, fácilmente pueden ser desvirtuadas si hay deficiencias en las oficinas de finanzas o registro, o en los procesos administrativos. Cuando hay complejidades y/o retrasos en estas áreas pueden obstaculizar el progreso investigativo de los estudiantes, y perjudicar sobremanera su experiencia académica. La excelencia debe reflejarse en todos los niveles y en todas las dimensiones de la institución.[1]

Los programas de doctorado deben tener procesos administrativos y financieros que funcionen bien. Aun así, conozco pocos colegas académicos a quienes realmente les gusta la administración, aunque algunos lo hacen muy bien y tienen un don muy especial en esta área. La mayoría lo ve como un fastidio, y otros como un asunto de baja prioridad. Parece entrometerse en la vida académica 'verdadera' —que es enseñar, investigar, escribir e interactuar personalmente con las y los estudiantes. Sin embargo, para que haya un buen proceso académico es vital mantener registros, escribir informes, asegurar que los formularios se completan a tiempo y asistir a reuniones. Estoy regularmente involucrado en el apoyo a estudiantes de doctorado que sienten mucha frustración porque sus supervisores no completan los formularios o no escriben los informes requeridos. Puede retrasar su progresión, sus exámenes y los tiempos de finalización de sus programas. Puede significar que desperdician recursos vitales de tiempo y finanzas mientras esperan que se complete el debido proceso. He sabido de estudiantes que quedaron meses a la espera de los resultados oficiales de sus exámenes o reenvíos, simplemente porque alguien no completó un formulario o un informe, o no se había convocado una reunión. Esto es muy estresante e injusto para un estudiante. Puede causar grandes problemas con las agencias

---

[1]. Shaw, *Principios y mejores prácticas*, Sección 14.

de financiación y patrocinio y puede, potencialmente, llevar a que se retenga o se deniegue la financiación.

La excelencia tiene que ser el sello distintivo de la supervisión doctoral, y la atención a los detalles del proceso es parte de ello. Ayuda a asegurar que la experiencia es buena tanto para el/la estudiante como para su supervisor/a.

Este asunto tiene dimensiones espirituales

El Apóstol Pablo lo expresa bien en Colosenses 3:23: "Hagan lo que hagan, trabajen de buena gana, como para el Señor y no como para nadie en este mundo". Debemos recordar que el trabajo fiel, aun estas tareas rutinarias, que se hace para el Señor es una dimensión de la adoración. Como lo expresó el poeta cristiano George Herbert en el siglo diecisiete:

> Enséñame, mi Dios y mi Rey,
>   a verte a ti en todas las cosas,
> Y sea lo que sea que haga,
>   que sea como para ti:
>
> Un sirviente con esta disposición
>   lo banal lo hace divino:
> Quién barre una habitación,
>   para tu ley, sigue el buen camino.

Para muchos académicos, hacer tareas administrativas, completar formularios, compilar informes y asistir a reuniones es tan monótono y ordinario como barrer una habitación. Sin embargo, como servicio fiel ofrecido al Señor, son una manera de encauzar nuestras vidas como actos de sacrificio vivo.

De la misma manera, en el famoso himno *"Llena de alabanza, Señor mi Dios, cada parte de mi ser"* compuesto por Horacio Bonar en 1866, la adoración se infiltra en todos los aspectos y las circunstancias de la vida, como lo expresa en la tercera estrofa:

> Alabanza en las cosas comunes de la vida,
> en sus salidas y entradas;
> alabanza en cada deber y quehacer,
> no importa cuan pequeño u ordinario.

Debemos hacer todas las cosas, incluyendo las tareas administrativas pequeñas y rutinarias, como para el Señor.

La importancia de la gestión de la calidad

En todo el mundo los programas luchan contra la inflación de las calificaciones (o su de inflación), y el inflamiento de las credenciales académicas. Las y los supervisores necesitan desempeñar su papel de garantizar que un doctorado sea un doctorado donde sea que se haga.

Esto significa que se deben establecer mecanismos para asegurar la calidad de la implementación y la evaluación tanto del nivel como del éxito de los programas de doctorado.

Como parte de su atención a la excelencia, las y los supervisores deben considerar cómo se deben medir la implementación y la eficacia de los programas. Deben jugar un papel clave en garantizar que las instituciones monitoreen el éxito de sus programas de investigación de posgrado de acuerdo con indicadores y objetivos adecuados, tanto internos como externos. Cuando esto no sucede, deben esforzarse por establecer los sistemas que habiliten hacerlo.

Las normas académicas se deben definir y mantener

Las instituciones que ofrecen programas de investigación deben tener maneras de definir los estándares académicos de sus programas de doctorado. Los criterios y procedimientos con los que se evalúan los programas de investigación deben aclararse tanto para estudiantes como para supervisores y examinadores externos. Los logros de las y los graduados en sus cursos de doctorado deben quedar registrados. La calidad del trabajo de las y los estudiantes de doctorado también se debe evaluar con estándares externos, especialmente con respecto a la calidad del trabajo de estudiantes de doctorado en otros programas.

Preguntas de reflexión

Como supervisor/a de doctorado, califique de uno a diez la utilidad de las siguientes opciones para asegurar que se lleve a cabo la gestión de la calidad y la evaluación según estándares externos (benchmarking):

i) formar parte de equipos de supervisión en otras instituciones,

ii) evaluaciones externas,

iii) invitar a examinadores externos a evaluar las tesis de sus estudiantes,

iv) leer tesis doctorales escritas por estudiantes de otros contextos.

¿Qué problemas presenta esto para su práctica personal?

Evaluaciones: procedimientos, reglamentos y códigos de conducta

Deben ser elaborados por las juntas académicas o comités de estudios de posgrado —según corresponda–, e implementadas por el liderazgo del programa de investigación. Sin embargo, las y los supervisores individuales deben desempeñar un papel activo en mantenerlas y aplicarlas.

Los procedimientos de evaluación deben ser claros y se deben poner en práctica de manera rigurosa y justa. Su uso debe ser consistente entre todos los miembros de la institución. Los reglamentos se deben complementar con lineamientos accesibles y específicos para cada área a nivel de la facultad de profesores, la escuela o el departamento.

Debe haber códigos de conducta y prácticas claras aplicables en toda la institución para el comportamiento tanto del personal como de las y los estudiantes, y deben estar a disposición de todas las personas involucradas en los programas de investigación de posgrado. Estas se deben implementar y revisar periódicamente.

Es responsabilidad del programa asegurar que cada año las y los estudiantes reciban copia de estos reglamentos y códigos de conducta y prácticas, y que los entiendan. Las y los supervisores también, cada año, deben releer y familiarizarse con los reglamentos y lineamientos, para que puedan responder adecuadamente a las preguntas de sus estudiantes y ofrecerles asesoramiento.

Preguntas de reflexión

¿Cuándo fue la última vez que leyó los reglamentos de su institución?

¿Qué tipo de asesoramiento le piden más frecuentemente sus estudiantes de doctorado?

¿Quiénes son las personas clave en su institución que proveen la información que necesitan sus estudiantes?

Asuntos de acreditación y validación

La mayoría de los programas de doctorado trabajan con agencias de acreditación o validación. Estas organizaciones externas a la institución participan en la auditoría y en asegurar que se siguen los estándares internacionalmente aceptados. El objetivo es lograr la equivalencia académica entre programas, aun si se imparten de maneras diferentes, para asegurar que los títulos de doctorado sean creíbles, aceptables y transferibles entre contextos académicos internacionales. Aunque es posible que las y los supervisores no estén involucrados directamente en estos asuntos, parte de lo que se informa y evalúa regularmente es su desempeño, y los informes que escriben y el apoyo estudiantil que ofrecen son aspectos esenciales de este proceso. Por eso es importante, por el bien de la institución y de sus estudiantes, contribuir a este proceso de manera eficiente y sin reservas.

Preguntas de reflexión

¿Cómo asegura la institución la calidad del programa de doctorado que ofrece?

¿Qué formas externas de medición usan?

Cuando surgen problemas, ¿cuál es el mecanismo acordado para abordar y resolverlos?

El proceso académico y su seguimiento

Aun cuando usted no tenga un rol administrativo o de liderazgo en la institución, habrá puntos en los que interactuará con el proceso académico formal, por lo general a través de un comité, o de un directivo que supervisa los programas de doctorado. Es importante que usted y sus estudiantes tengan una buena comprensión de este proceso y del papel que desempeñan las y los supervisores. Usted y sus estudiantes necesitan saber cuál es el punto focal para la toma de decisiones académicas en su institución en lo que se refiere a los estudios de doctorado.

Preguntas de reflexión

¿A quién acude usted para lo que atañe a problemas en el programa de doctorado, ya sean cuestiones académicas o del bienestar de sus estudiantes?

¿Cómo se les comunica esta estructura a sus estudiantes?

¿Qué representación estudiantil incluye esta estructura?

¿Hasta que punto tienen poder de decisión en este proceso sus estudiantes de investigación y el personal? Si es necesario cambiar algo, ¿dónde más le gustaría ver esos cambios?

El seguimiento del progreso del estudiante

La institución necesita contar con mecanismos claramente definidos para monitorear y apoyar el progreso de sus estudiantes, y necesitan ser comunicados a las y los estudiantes y al personal pertinente. Las y los supervisores de doctorado deben estar actualizados con respecto a estos procesos institucionales y conocerlos bien a fin de llevar a cabo dicho seguimiento. Las y los supervisores son el principal punto de contacto entre sus estudiantes y estos mecanismos de seguimiento y, como tal, periódicamente deben mantenerlos al tanto de cualquier asunto relevante.

En el ámbito de la educación doctoral de varios países se han planteado preocupaciones respecto al progreso y la deserción de estudiantes. En muchísimos casos los estudiantes pasan demasiado tiempo trabajando en su tesis, lo cual retrasa la graduación mucho más allá de lo originalmente anticipado. Un asunto relacionada es la preocupación por la cantidad de estudiantes que entran en la fase de disertación pero no completan su programa de estudio. Uno de los retos que enfrentan los directores de programas de doctorado, y los presidentes de los comités de disertación, es cómo animar a sus estudiantes a mantener en movimiento sus proyectos de investigación, con progreso sostenido y sin permitir que se estanquen la investigación y/o la escritura. Una de las mejores maneras de lograrlo es que el/la estudiante agende interacciones periódicas. Las y los supervisores deben pedir a sus estudiantes que estén en contacto cada dos semanas con una breve actualización, aun si no han logrado mucho en ese tiempo. Las conversaciones periódicas impiden que sus estudiantes se aíslen en su trabajo, y pueden ayudar a que las cosas vuelvan a ponerse en movimiento si se paralizaron. La interacción frecuente permite monitorear el progreso de sus estudiantes y determinar si hay obstáculos que necesitan ser superados.

Informes de supervisión

Durante la fase de investigación de sus programas, las y los estudiantes de doctorado a menudo sienten incertidumbre en cuanto a su progreso, y eso puede crearles inseguridad y frustración. Habrán venido de niveles anteriores de trabajo académico donde se estipulan con precisión las tareas, se entregan según el plazo y se recibe una calificación. Presentar trabajos escritos y recibir comentarios detallados sin ninguna calificación (como es habitual en el trabajo de doctorado), es una experiencia nueva.

Las instituciones deben implementar una serie de revisiones formales de progreso, en diferentes etapas, para ayudar a que sus estudiantes progresen en su programa. Esto provee una estructura para su trabajo, establece estándares apropiados y asegura que las expectativas sean realistas. Estas revisiones formales involucran a supervisores y estudiantes. Debe haber asesoramiento para estudiantes, supervisores y cualquier otra persona que esté involucrada en el seguimiento del progreso y el proceso habitual de revisión. Es importante mantener un registro detallado de los resultados de estas revisiones. Si un/a estudiante no está trabajando a un nivel apropiado o no está progresando lo suficientemente bien, se le debe informar de ello para que pueda hacer los ajustes necesarios.

Desempeñar un papel activo en esta área es una parte muy importante de la supervisión de estudiantes de doctorado, aunque implique llenar formularios o completar informes.

Muchos supervisores le dan poca prioridad a esto, y necesitan que se les recuerde repetidamente que hay que completar estos informes y no dejarlos desatendidos en su bandeja de entrada. No es justo para sus estudiantes, ni para el liderazgo del programa, ni para las organizaciones que patrocinan a las y los estudiantes.

Completar formularios e informes no debe ser un simple ejercicio de "marcar casilleros"; sino que debe proveer un registro formal de progreso, logros y preocupaciones. En la mayoría de los casos serán una celebración de los logros, pero en otros serán un registro claro, un "rastro en papel" de las preocupaciones expresadas, las soluciones propuestas y las oportunidades ofrecidas para corregir el rumbo. Esto es importante en caso de llegar al final del proceso sin un resultado exitoso para el/la estudiante.

Revisiones formales

El progreso de las y los estudiantes de doctorado normalmente debe ser monitoreado de manera formal por lo menos cada seis meses o, para estudiantes a tiempo parcial, una vez por año. Estas revisiones formales deben ocurrir en momentos clave de la progresión de sus estudiantes, cuando se necesitan tomar decisiones clave sobre su continuidad en un programa de doctorado y su progresión a la siguiente etapa. Tanto sus estudiantes como la facultad académica deben estar preparados para cuando se lleven a cabo estas revisiones.

Documentación escrita

Esto es vital para sostener el proceso de doctorado. Tanto estudiantes como supervisores deben mantener un buen registro de sus reuniones, de los temas tratados, la orientación dada y el trabajo presentado. También deben preservar muestras del trabajo presentado. Todas las personas involucradas en las revisiones y el seguimiento de progreso (estudiantes, supervisores, etc.) deben recibir orientación sobre cómo documentar estos procesos y cómo conservar lo registrado.

Estos registros deben referirse al progreso personal y documentar el desarrollo de la investigación y el logro de otras habilidades.

Seguimiento de la respuesta del Equipo/Comité de Supervisión

A veces no son sus estudiantes, sino las/los supervisores o los miembros del comité de doctorado que no están al día con el calendario previsto para su trabajo de revisión. Si usted supervisa o preside el Comité de Disertación, y hay estudiantes que están a la espera de respuestas atrasadas de los miembros del comité, anímeles a que le avisen si perciben algún patrón en los retrasos, así usted puede hacer las averiguaciones apropiadas y ver cómo se puede volver a poner en marcha el proceso de revisión. Si ve que hay lectores/as en su Comité que necesitan un amable recordatorio para mantenerse al día con su trabajo, no deje que sus estudiantes tengan que resolverlo por su cuenta. Intervenga como colega y busque cómo abordar la situación.

Preguntas de reflexión

¿Qué documentación mantiene regularmente de las reuniones con sus estudiantes, y cómo los presenta a la institución?

¿Qué informes completa para juntas de revisión de progreso y agencias externas?

¿Cuáles son las etapas de revisión de su programa de doctorado?

¿Cómo se documentan estas etapas de revisión?

¿Cuáles son los problemas que enfrenta más frecuentemente para obtener respuestas de los miembros de su Comité de Doctorado?

Retroalimentación estudiantil

> *Las instituciones que ofrecen programas de doctorado deben contar con mecanismos apropiados para responder a las expresiones formales e informales de retroalimentación de los estudiantes sobre la supervisión, incluyendo mecanismos oficiales para la presentación y el manejo de quejas. En caso de disputas que no se pueden resolver, debe haber provisiones para apelar a una instancia final que sea neutral y externa a la institución, y que entienda el proceso académico.*[2]

Las instituciones que ofrecen programas de doctorado deben recoger, revisar y, cuando sea apropiado, responder a comentarios y retroalimentación de todas las personas que intervienen en los programas de investigación de posgrado. Las y los estudiantes necesitan tener plena confianza en que su retroalimentación será tomada en cuenta. Todos los procedimientos relacionados con la retroalimentación deben ser justos, claros para todos los interesados y aplicados de forma consistente. Las y los estudiantes necesitan saber que sus comentarios son valorados y tomados en serio. Deben recibir información sobre las respuestas a su retroalimentación y las acciones que se han tomado.

Es fácil tomar por sentado que todo está progresando bien si no hay mayores quejas o evidencia de descontento estudiantil. Sin embargo, puede haber asuntos importantes irresueltos o problemas con el programa de los que la facultad necesita enterarse. Se

---

2. Shaw, *Principios y mejores prácticas*, Sección 16.

deben tomar las medidas necesarias para evitar que perjudiquen el desarrollo de las y los estudiantes.

Los programas de doctorado deben tener un sistema formal para obtener retroalimentación periódica de sus estudiantes acerca de su experiencia en el programa, por lo menos cada doce meses, preferiblemente cada seis meses. Esto puede ser mediante un cuestionario, aunque se puede hacer de forma oral en una reunión con personal independiente. Lo ideal es incluir las dos modalidades, porque las respuestas escritas permiten un análisis cuantitativo pero también hay oportunidad para recibir comentarios (orales) más abiertos y discursivos. Los asuntos a tratar deben incluir la calidad de la experiencia investigativa, las instalaciones disponibles (incluyendo la biblioteca, los recursos informáticos y el apoyo tecnológico), la satisfacción con la supervisión, la participación en la cultura de investigación, la vida comunitaria, el cuidado pastoral, la formación espiritual, etc. Los formularios de retroalimentación suelen completarse de forma anónima. Permiten que las y los estudiantes identifiquen problemas o preocupaciones. En la institución donde enseñé, cada estudiante de doctorado tenía una reunión con una persona externa que tenía un puesto de Decano académico (de Humanidades) en una importante universidad de investigación local, y que era un cristiano evangélico. Para los estudiantes, ambos mecanismos eran útiles. Las entrevistas individuales les permitían abordar los problemas de forma informal, lo cual iba más allá de la retroalimentación escrita.

La forma de estas revisiones debe ser tal que pueda abarcar la retroalimentación de las y los estudiantes respecto de la calidad de la supervisión que han recibido. Esta retroalimentación es útil para el desarrollo del estilo de supervisión. Además, como practicantes reflexivos, las y los supervisores deben acogerla y agradecer la oportunidad de aprender y desarrollar su propia práctica.

No siempre es fácil ser "evaluados" por sus estudiantes de esta manera. Sin embargo, en pos de la excelencia, a veces aprendemos mejor cuando las cosas van menos bien o cuando recibimos críticas. Las y los supervisores deben discutir lo que surge de la retroalimentación con otros líderes académicos para ver qué acciones se deben tomar, qué enfoques cambiar o mantener, etc. En los apéndices 1 y 2 se incluyen ejemplos de formularios de retroalimentación anual y de fin de programa.

Preguntas de reflexión

¿Cómo reacciona usted a la retroalimentación de sus estudiantes?

¿Qué cosas importantes ha aprendido y cambiado como resultado de la retroalimentación de sus estudiantes?

Informes de fuentes externas

Periódicamente se recibirán informes de auditores, agencias de acreditación y examinadores externos. Deben ser leídos cuidadosamente por el personal de supervisión, así como por el liderazgo del programa. Las y los supervisores deben tener plena participación en el desarrollo de cualquier respuesta a esta retroalimentación. De esta manera, los supervisores de doctorado están activamente involucrados en el esfuerzo por hacer que la institución sea una comunidad caracterizada por el aprendizaje autorreflexivo y el crecimiento.

Representación estudiantil

Es buena práctica tener una representación estudiantil formal en los comités académicos que se ocupan de los estudios de nivel de doctorado. El estudiantado debe elegir a su representante, y él o ella deben reunirse y comunicarse regularmente con otros estudiantes. Vienen a ser el canal formal para dar a conocer las preocupaciones de las y los estudiantes, y son un recurso vital para determinar el punto de vista del estudiantado acerca del programa y de posibles mejoras o cambios. Como supervisoras y supervisores, es importante animar a las personas que considera idóneas para ese rol.

Quejas

Las instituciones que ofrecen programas de doctorado deben contar con mecanismos apropiados para responder a las expresiones formales e informales de retroalimentación de los estudiantes sobre la supervisión, incluyendo mecanismos oficiales para la presentación y el manejo de quejas. En caso de disputas que no se pueden resolver, debe haber provisiones para apelar a una instancia final que sea neutral y externa a la institución, y que entienda el proceso académico. Si como supervisor/a se encuentra en la desafortunada situación de ser objeto de una queja estudiantil, es importante manejarla con profesionalismo y con madurez espiritual. Debe cooperar plenamente con el proceso, y escuchar la queja y lo que hay detrás. Entre académicos puede existir la tentación de "cerrar filas", pero si un/a estudiante tiene una preocupación se le debe escuchar con atención y el asunto debe tratarse sin parcialidad. Si se han cometido errores, entonces es responsabilidad del supervisor cristiano ofrecer las disculpas apropiadas y buscar el perdón. Debemos esforzarnos por remediar cualquier problemas que se haya identificado. Si se encuentra que la queja no tiene fundamento, eso también se debe manejar con la madurez espiritual apropiada, y con un espíritu dispuesto al perdón. Si usted va a seguir trabajando con el/la estudiante, no debe permitir que el proceso ensombrezca o impida mantener una buena relación de trabajo.

Las responsabilidades de las y los supervisores

La institución que ofrecen programas de doctorado debe contar con orientación escrita sobre cuáles son las responsabilidades de quienes supervisan estudiantes de investigación.

Elección del supervisor o la supervisora

La asignación de estudiantes a las/los supervisores es una decisión institucional, pero debe hacerse en consulta con ambas partes. El factor crucial debe ser una estrecha correspondencia entre el campo de investigación del estudiante y el área de competencia investigativa del supervisor. Cuando esto no se da, hay que escoger otra persona como supervisor/a. La asignación no debe hacerse sobre la base de quién tiene la menor carga de supervisión —y que entonces tiene más disponibilidad–, ni debe basarse en una cuestión de quién es más popular. En algunas culturas los miembros de la facultad con más seniority —en edad y experiencia— escogen para sí los mejores estudiantes. Si bien la seniority merece ser respetada, la mejor asignación sera la que encuentra una relación óptima entre la necesidad de cada estudiante y las áreas en las que brilla el talento de el/la supervisor/a. En estas situaciones, dependiendo de su rol en el proceso de asignación, es posible que deba armarse de paciencia y amabilidad.

Es importante entender y respetar el proceso de la institución para la asignación de supervisores. Lo más conveniente y beneficioso para las/los estudiantes es que pueda identificar lo antes posible un probable supervisor para una tesis/disertación. A veces construyen una relación con un probable supervisor durante el proceso de aplicación, y luego pueden frustrarse cuando se les asigna una persona diferente cuando reciben la aceptación. De manera similar, un/a supervisor/a puede dedicar bastante tiempo a trabajar con un/a potencial estudiante para darle forma a su enfoque, para luego enterarse de que se le ha asignado a otra persona. Eso es decepcionante. Para evitar estas eventualidades, es muy importante mantener la claridad y la transparencia del proceso y la comunicación.

Equipos de supervisión/Comités de disertación

Normalmente, estudiantes que emprenden el componente de tesis de un programa de doctorado tendrán más de un supervisor. En tal caso las y los supervisores trabajan juntos como parte de un equipo de supervisión o, en programas de estilo estadounidense, hay un Comité de Disertación. Para evitar confusiones en torno a lo que se espera de los miembros del equipo de supervisión/Comité de Disertación, las instituciones deben asegurarse de que las responsabilidades —de supervisores de investigación, presidentes de comités y segundos y terceros lectores— se comuniquen claramente a supervisores y estudiantes mediante una guía escrita. Estas responsabilidades deben ser acordadas por todos los supervisores y firmadas por ellos, el liderazgo del programa y el/la estudiante.

La creación de equipos de supervisión/comités de disertación significa que el/la estudiante tiene acceso a la mejor variedad de pericia y especialización, especialmente si el proyecto tiene elementos interdisciplinarios. También asegura la continuidad del apoyo al estudiante si un miembro del equipo está de licencia de investigación o no está disponible por un período de tiempo, ya sea por enfermedad u otras razones. Los equipos de supervisión pueden incluir segundos supervisores/lectores que no estén doctorados. Tales personas deben ser docentes con amplia experiencia a nivel de posgrado y con conocimiento profundo y actualizado de su especialidad. Su tarea es apoyar el trabajo de el/la supervisor/a principal.

Normalmente, el supervisor principal/presidente del Comité de Disertación debe ser miembro de la facultad académica en la institución donde se ofrece el programa de doctorado, pero a veces los equipos de supervisión incluyen miembros de otras instituciones académicas. Si usted es el/la supervisor/a principal o preside el Comité de Disertación, es importante que asegure un buen flujo de información entre los demás miembros del equipo.

Como supervisor de doctorado, he servido como supervisor principal, y también en ocasiones como segundo supervisor. Para cada caso se requiere un enfoque diferente. Colaborar en un equipo de supervisión es un aspecto del trabajo académico que puede ser de enriquecimiento y beneficio mutuo. Es un privilegio trabajar estrechamente con otros colegas, algunos de los cuales han sido líderes mundiales en su campo, y de quienes se puede aprender mucho. Pero es una relación que requiere respeto, confianza, comprensión, humildad y sensibilidad mutua. Hay casos en los que un miembro del equipo 'toma el mando', y eclipsa a otros. A veces se toman decisiones y se dan consejos sin informar a los demás miembros del equipo de supervisión.

Algunos supervisores pueden sentirse amenazados o perjudicados por ser parte de un equipo. El valor de cada miembro del equipo se debe afirmar regularmente. Con respeto y comprensión mutua se pueden evitar estas situaciones. Es esencial que la comunicación sea clara y que haya un proceso bien establecido en el que todos pueden confiar. El primer supervisor/presidente del Comité de Disertación debe asegurar que la comunicación entre los miembros del Comité sea clara y regular.

La necesidad prioritaria es que las y los estudiantes tengan una experiencia de supervisión positiva y enriquecedora. Lamentablemente, como demuestran los comentarios de estudiantes de una variedad de contextos, esto no siempre sucede.

Sin embargo, también es necesario gestionar las expectativas y el comportamiento de las y los estudiantes de doctorado cuando su supervisión la lleva adelante un equipo. Algunos estudiantes intentarán crear rivalidades entre unos y otros supervisores/lectores del equipo a fin de lograr estándares menos onerosos u obtener el consejo que les gustaría recibir. Por esta razón, se deben incluir a todos los miembros de un equipo de supervisión en la correspondencia entre el supervisor primario y el/la estudiante, y los comentarios sobre el trabajo deben ser compartidos de manera similar. Las decisiones sobre dirección y métodos clave y las recomendaciones sobre asuntos de progresión deben ser decisiones de todo el equipo, alcanzadas mediante la discusión y la búsqueda de consenso.

Recuerde el privilegio que es la supervisión

Este capítulo ha cubierto muchos asuntos rutinarios y de proceso. Entre todas las exigencias administrativas que acompañan la supervisión de la investigación, nunca se olvide del privilegio que es supervisar a estudiantes de investigación. Recuerde siempre estar emocionado/a porque:

- alguien ha escogido emprender una investigación en su área.
- alguien le ha escogido para supervisar su trabajo de investigación, reconociendo que usted es una eminencia en este campo.

A medida que emprende este proceso, reflexione sobre cómo puede, entre todas las exigencias del proceso, supervisar a sus estudiantes de tal manera que se vuelvan tan entusiastas, dispuestos a trabajar duro y deseosos de enseñar en esta área temática como lo es usted. ¿Qué hará para que sus estudiantes de investigación amen el tema tanto como usted lo ama?

Caso de estudio

Es bien sabido por usted y por sus colegas académicos que un cierto miembro de la facultad que es supervisor es muy incumplidor a la hora de completar los informes y formularios de progreso. Quedan en su escritorio, y sin completar, por meses, a pesar de los reiterados pedidos de que las entregue. Por lo demás, es un buen profesor y un colega dispuesto. Las juntas de revisión se retrasan porque él no ha completado la documentación. Un formulario importante solo se completó porque el director de Estudios de Posgrado se le quedó al lado mientras lo hacía. Se ha convertido en un asunto de quejas verbales por parte de los estudiantes.

Preguntas

¿Qué cree usted que es la raíz de este problema?

A fin de mejorar la experiencia de las y los estudiantes, ¿qué pueden hacer usted y sus colegas para ayudar a remediar esta situación?

Para leer más

Eley A. y R. Murray. *How to Be an Effective Supervisor*. Maidenhead: Open University Press, 2009.

Phillips, E. M. y D. S. Pugh. *How to Get a PhD: A Handbook for Students and Their Supervisors*. Maidenhead: Open University Press, 2010. (Disponible también para Kindle)

Shaw, I. *Principios y mejores prácticas para Programas de Doctorado*. Carlisle: Langham Global Library, 2025.

Taylor, S. y N. Beasley. *A Handbook for Doctoral Supervisors*. Nueva York: Routledge, 2005.

Wisker, Gina. *The Good Supervisor: Supervising Postgraduate and Undergraduate Research for Doctoral Theses and Dissertations*. Nueva York: Palgrave MacMillan, 2005.

14

Áreas problemáticas

A veces la relación de supervisión se desarrolla sin tropiezos y la experiencia es positiva. Sin embargo, pueden surgir problemas, y es bueno haber desarrollado una serie de respuestas apropiadas antes de enfrentarlos. Lo que sigue describe algunas de las problemáticas más comunes que surgen en el trato con estudiantes de doctorado.

Área problemática 1: el plagio

> *El reglamento institucional y los lineamientos del programa deben establecer con claridad que todo material fuente necesita ser reconocido y referenciado por completo. También se debe definir la forma en que dichas referencias serán presentadas. El plagio no solo refleja debilidades académicas, sino también delata fallas morales y espirituales. Las advertencias contra el plagio deben resaltarse en el reglamento institucional y en los lineamientos del programa, junto con detalles de las sanciones a ser impuestas si el plagio es detectado en una tesis/ disertación de doctorado.*[1]

Aun a niveles de maestría y doctorado, se debe advertir sobre el plagio y estar alerta para que no suceda. La tesis doctoral debe ser una "contribución original al conocimiento". Es serio cuando el trabajo de un/a estudiante consiste en parte, o incluso en su totalidad, de material de otras fuentes que no son reconocidas. No solo revela fallas académicas, sino que deja entrever debilidades en el método educativo y también en la formación espiritual. El plagio es robo académico, y algo que tanto estudiantes como supervisores evangélicos necesitan tomar en serio.

---

1. Shaw, *Principios y mejores prácticas*, Sección 19.

1) ¿Qué implica el plagio?

El plagio es el uso de materiales de una fuente escrita por otra persona, sin reconocer su origen. La fuente puede ser un libro, un artículo, una fuente de Internet u otra tesis. Todas las fuentes que las/los estudiantes usan deben ser plenamente reconocidas, incluso cuando no se citan directamente, y su uso debe apoyarse mediante las referencias apropiadas.

Cuando se citan o reproducen las palabras exactas de una fuente esas palabras se deben colocar entre comillas, y se debe indicar la referencia. Las comillas deben encapsular toda la cita textual, de lo contrario se da la impresión de que el resto de la cita es trabajo propio de el/la estudiante.

Cuando se resumen o parafrasean ideas de otra fuente, incluso si no se citan directamente, la referencia debe ser clara, para indicar su origen. Estas no son las ideas propias del estudiante, sino un resumen de las ideas de otra persona.

2) Formas de plagio

El plagio puede manifestarse de diversas maneras:

i) **Involuntaria.** Puede ser el resultado de la cultura académica en la que han sido entrenados las/los estudiantes, y entonces no se dan cuenta que es un asunto serio. Necesitan entender que la referencia es una señal de buena práctica académica, no de mala dependencia o debilidad académica. Deberían celebrar la amplitud de sus lecturas y demostrarlo en las síntesis, alusiones, citas y referencias que usan. Serán elogiados por ello. Es posible que aun académicos experimentados, que han tomado notas de sus lecturas, descubran que un tiempo después, cuando van a usar sus notas para escribir un artículo o un libro, no están completamente seguros de cuáles fueron las palabras de su fuente y cuál su propia reflexión personal sobre la misma. Por eso es de suma importancia ser diligentes en hacer ese tipo de distinción cuando se hace la recopilación de fuentes. Otros quizás copian material de una fuente, especialmente una electrónica, y se olvidan de incluir una referencia a su origen. Sin embargo, la precisión en la toma de notas y la identificación de todas las fuentes con un buen registro de su referencia sigue siendo un aspecto medular de la buena práctica académica, y toda persona que escriba debe revisar bien este aspecto de su trabajo.

ii) **Puede ser deliberado.** Lamentablemente, aun en contextos evangélicos, algunos estudiantes pueden verse tentados a intentar engañar deliberadamente a sus supervisores y examinadores, haciendo pasar parte de lo que entregan —o en casos extremos todo— como si fuera su propio trabajo, cuando en realidad es de otros. Algunos casos de plagio son intentos de engaño muy cuidadosamente planeados.

Puede incluir la obtención de materiales en línea, o incluso la contratación de escritores externos para que redacten un trabajo por encargo. Aunque es menos probable que esto suceda al nivel de un doctorado en investigación, donde las y los supervisores interactúan regularmente con la evolución de los trabajos de sus estudiantes, sigue siendo posible, y las/los supervisores deben mantenerse alerta. Los programas de doctorado que no incluyen un examen oral con al menos un evaluador externo —en donde los examinadores tienen la oportunidad de asegurarse de que el trabajo es propio del estudiante-, necesitan estar especialmente alerta.

Es más común el plagio de tipo "copiar y pegar", en donde un trabajo incluye una gama de materiales no atribuidos tomados de recursos electrónicos, sitios web o, a la antigua usanza, de libros y artículos.

iii) **Variable en grado, y en sanciones.** Los ocasionales deslices y las referencias inadecuadas se pueden confrontar sin que se requiera una sanción seria. Sin embargo, si los incidentes son recurrentes y a gran escala hay que recurrir a sanciones más serias. Estas se deben estipular en el reglamento académico de la institución.

3) *El plagio tiene diversas causas*

Las y los estudiantes recurren al engaño por todo tipo de razones. Con tanto material disponible en línea, es una falta cada vez más fácil de cometer, y las y los supervisores necesitan estar siempre alerta.

Puede ser el resultado de la falta de tiempo. Bajo presión, un/a estudiante puede encontrar grandes cantidades de material en otra fuente y, para ahorrar tiempo, simplemente lo repite. Con recursos electrónicos esto es muy fácil.

Puede ser el resultado de una mala formación académica. Algunos estudiantes vienen de entornos académicos en los que no se presta mucha atención al asunto del plagio, y sus supervisores necesitan esforzarse por inculcarles las habilidades bibliográficas apropiadas.

Puede reflejar cuestiones culturales. Para estudiantes que fueron educados en una cultura de aprendizaje basada en la memorización, donde hay un alto respeto por la figura del docente y una aversión a disentir, puede resultar difícil entender qué es lo que tiene de malo el plagio —podrían pensar que copiar el trabajo de un erudito es honrarlo. Una vez más, esto debe ser confrontado y corregido.

Puede ser el resultado de flaquezas académicas, o falta de confianza. Una fuente académica aborda un tema de una manera que el/la estudiante siente que no puede mejorar, así que simplemente la repite palabra por palabra. Las y los supervisores necesitan mostrarles a sus estudiantes cómo encontrar su propia voz académica.

En lo más profundo también es un asunto espiritual. Es fraude académico. Es tomar algo que no les pertenece —las ideas y el trabajo investigativo de otra persona— y usarlo sin permiso y para su propio progreso. Es una forma de robo, y quiebra el octavo de los Diez Mandamientos. Demuestra una falla en el amor al prójimo y en el respeto por su propiedad (intelectual). Por motivos de formación académica y espiritual, estas acciones deben ser confrontadas en etapas tempranas del desarrollo del estudiante, y él o ella debe comprender la gama de sanciones que merece.

4) *Las y los estudiantes necesitan aprender sobre la forma correcta de parafrasear, resumir y sintetizar*

Los estudios sugieren que una cuidadosa instrucción y orientación sobre el plagio reduce su incidencia. Es más, los que tienen la mayor inclinación a cometer plagio son los más propensos a abandonar sus estudios.[2]

Las y los estudiantes necesitan conocer la diferencia entre parafrasear y resumir, y copiar una porción continua de texto sin comillas o referencia. Necesitan aprender a mezclar paráfrasis y citas directas, y a indicar las referencias correspondientes en los lugares adecuados. Pero la diferencia entre pobreza de estilo y un engaño deliberado puede ser difícil de evaluar

Si un estudiante parafrasea material de una fuente pero no la cita directamente, y luego no da una referencia, esto todavía es plagio. Las y los estudiantes necesitan reconocer y atribuir cada instancia en la que usan trabajo, ideas, materiales de investigación y estadísticas que no son suyas. Algunos estudiantes simplemente sustituyen una o dos palabras en un texto que copiaron y ya piensan que lo pueden considerar trabajo propio, pero esto todavía es inaceptable.

5) *La forma correcta de indicar las referencias*

Muchos estudiantes entran en sus programas de doctorado con una comprensión inadecuada del método correcto de indicar referencias, y de su razón de ser. Por una serie de razones de "buenas prácticas", necesitan ver la importancia de usar referencias adecuadas:

- Indica las fuentes que han utilizado, evitando así acusaciones de plagio.
- Ayuda al lector a localizar fácilmente la fuente que el/la escritor/a ha usado (si la desea consultar).
- Muestra que los argumentos presentados se sustentan en una base adecuada de lectura, y que el/la escritor/a interactúa con las fuentes al nivel correcto. Las/los estudiantes necesitan mostrar que están familiarizados con el lenguaje de

---

2. M. E. Earman Stetter, 'Teaching Students about Plagiarism Using a Web-Based Module,' *Journal of Further and Higher Education* 37, no. 5 (2013): 675-693.

la discusión académica en su campo, y las referencias y la bibliografía sirven para demostrarlo.
- Muestra respeto por el capital intelectual de otros. Ya que el trabajo académico se está convirtiendo cada vez más en propiedad intelectual monetizable, las/los estudiantes necesitan mostrar respeto por sus pares académicos, y a cambio esperan que se respete su propio trabajo.

6) *Bibliografías*

Las bibliografías deben contener todo el material que se haya consultado y evaluado durante la redacción del trabajo, y no solo lo que se cita. Insistir con esto asegura que las/los estudiantes están mostrando los materiales con los que han trabajado, y ayuda al lector a rastrear el uso deliberado o involuntario de material no atribuido, y a detectar omisiones intencionales.

7) *Guías de estilo*

Si bien es necesario proveer orientación inicial, se puede derrochar mucho tiempo de supervisión innecesariamente corrigiendo las citas y referencias de las/los estudiantes. Es mejor pedirles que sigan la guía de estilo al pie de la letra, y luego señalar dónde han fallado en hacerlo. Las/los supervisores deben exigirles a sus estudiantes que en una fase temprana obtengan una buena guía de estilo, como el *Manual de Estilo de Chicago*, que provee orientación detallada sobre citas, referencias y bibliografías para una gran variedad de material de investigación.

8) *La detección del plagio*

i) Software de detección de plagio

De a poco la tecnología se está poniendo al día respecto de las oportunidades para el plagio. Aplicaciones como *Turnitin* exigen que las/los estudiantes entreguen trabajos electrónicamente. La aplicación los procesa y califica su originalidad en relación con su base de datos compuesta de otros trabajos académicos. Esto ayuda a las y los estudiantes a identificar dónde su trabajo depende excesivamente de otras fuentes.

Qué se mide:
- el porcentaje total de material copiado, o el número de palabras copiadas textualmente, dividido por el número total de palabras en el trabajo.
- el número de cadenas de palabras copiadas textualmente.
- la sección más larga de texto copiado.

Este sistema exige que todos los materiales se entreguen electrónicamente. Puede ser bastante engorroso hacer esto en las etapas iniciales del trabajo de doctorado, pero cuando se trata de borradores más completos puede ser útil para resaltar áreas problemáticas. Si hay un problema importante —una sección que depende excesivamente del trabajo de otros–, es mejor detectarlo temprano, en lugar de descubrirlo en la etapa final de la presentación, cuando ya es demasiado tarde para cuestionar, y solo queda la opción de aplicar una sanción seria.

ii) Limitaciones

Sin embargo, aun estas medidas pueden tener que complementarse con formas cualitativas de evaluación. El uso de software de detección de plagio no elimina el 100% del plagio. La tecnología de Internet facilita el uso del copiado y pegado para la redacción, y las/los estudiantes pueden parafrasear y/o reorganizar el material para evadir el software de detección de plagio. Así que la formación y la sensibilización siguen siendo vitales.[3]

Además, un/a estudiante puede citar material de otro idioma o tener acceso a tesis de maestría o doctorado que no se han incluido en la base de datos del software de detección. En estos casos las fuentes plagiadas pueden no ser detectadas. Hay que ingresar otras disertaciones y trabajos de investigación al software de detección, para ampliar los materiales que usa para las comparaciones, y eso no siempre ocurre.

En algunos contextos académicos, se anima a que las y los estudiantes presenten su trabajo en un idioma local o regional. Puede haber mérito en esto, si se pueden encontrar examinadores con un alto grado de competencia en esos idiomas. Sin embargo, la mayoría de los sistemas de detección de plagio solo funciona con los idiomas principales del contexto académico mundial.

iii) Cómo detectar el plagio

Aun con la disponibilidad de ayudas electrónicas, las y los supervisores necesitan permanecer en alerta y atentos a señales de advertencia, además de familiarizarse con el estilo de redacción natural de sus estudiantes. Al interactuar con sus estudiantes, usted debe prestar atención a la evolución de sus habilidades y su enfoque.

Esté alerta a:

- Cambios repentinos de estilo. Si usted está familiarizado con el 'estilo natural' de un/a estudiante, y de repente aparece una sección con un estilo muy diferente, debe investigar.
- La aparición de ideas y resultados que parecen fuera de lo que usted esperaría que el/la estudiante haya logrado en ese punto.

---

3. J. Warn, 'Plagiarism Software: No Magic Bullet!' *Higher Education Research and Development* 25, no. 2 (2006): 195-208.

- Material bien escrito, pero que no es directamente relevante al punto en discusión.
- Ausencias largas y sin explicación de parte del estudiante, seguidas por la aparición repentina de un trabajo bien desarrollado.

9) *Sanciones por plagio*

Las instituciones deben contar con declaraciones claras sobre el plagio y lo que constituye, las sanciones que se aplicarán si se detecta y, en lo posible, sobre el uso de recursos electrónicos para identificar los casos en que ha ocurrido. También deben ofrecer capacitación adecuada para ayudar a sus estudiantes a evitar el plagio.

Las sanciones deben ajustarse al carácter de la ofensa. Pueden variar, desde pedir que se vuelvan a escribir ciertas secciones hasta presentar advertencias formales, o incluso la posibilidad de un 'no aprobado'. Si se detectan problemas menores, se deben indicar y se deben corregir rápidamente. Si estos persisten a medida que se entregan los borradores de la tesis, debe ser reportado al liderazgo del programa de estudio, y cuando sea necesario a la junta académica pertinente.

Para los programas de doctorado que incluyen cursos académicos, en cada etapa se deben indicar claramente las sanciones por plagio y se deben aplicar de manera consistente.

Si se detecta un caso de plagio mayor, por ejemplo que una gran parte de la tesis no es el trabajo del propio estudiante, está dentro de la capacidad de los examinadores desaprobar de una vez la tesis.

Cuestiones clave

En estudios recientes[4] se destaca la importancia de:

i) Tener un diálogo abierto sobre el tema con grupos de estudiantes de investigación, y ayudarles a identificar posibles áreas de problemas.

ii) Clases e instrucción sobre cómo parafrasear, con pruebas prácticas para que puedan demostrar cómo han aplicado la instrucción.

iii) Orientación sobre las formas correctas de citar y referenciar materiales.

iv) Orientación clara sobre el uso de materiales electrónicos y de Internet.

v) Discusión de la cuestión moral de reconocer las fuentes —cómo el plagio es un robo intelectual, pero también un fracaso espiritual.

---

4. E.g. F. Duggan, 'Plagiarism: Prevention, Practice and Policy,' *Assessment & Evaluation in Higher Education* 31, no. 2 (2006): 151-154; R. Sharma, 'A Step-by-Step Guide to Students: How to Avoid Plagiarism,' *Journal of Education Research* 4, no. 2 (2010): 143-153; A. L. Walker, 'Preventing Unintentional Plagiarism: A Method for Strengthening Paraphrasing Skills,' *Journal of Instructional Psychology* 35, no. 4 (2007): 387-395.

Preguntas de reflexión

¿Cómo se ha sentido cuando ha detectado plagio en el trabajo de sus estudiantes?

¿Qué métodos y/o recursos ha utilizado para identificar el plagio? ¿Qué es lo que funciona mejor?

¿Qué puede hacer para asegurar que sus estudiantes de doctorado no cometan este error?

¿Cómo aborda cuestiones culturales, educativas y espirituales que podrían estar detrás de este problema?

Área problemática 2: ¿Hasta qué punto debe un/a supervisor/a corregir errores gramaticales y ortográficos?

Es una pregunta que se formula repetidamente en los seminarios que dirijo para supervisores de doctorado. Las respuestas varían mucho entre supervisores y culturas. Las faltas ortográficas y la mala gramática, aun en trabajos presentados temprano en un programa de estudio, pueden dificultar la lectura y hacer que el argumento sea difícil de seguir. La forma en que se presentan los trabajos constantemente distrae la atención de las y los supervisores.

Al evaluar la medida en que se ofrece este tipo de apoyo, es importante tener en cuenta que,

i) Al final, la tesis es y debe ser el trabajo de su estudiante.

ii) La tarea principal de el/la supervisor/a es evaluar el contenido, la estructura y los estándares académicos, no ser corrector/a profesional de ortografía y gramática.

iii) La mayoría de las/los estudiantes de posgrado necesitan ayuda para escribir. Por eso las instituciones deben ofrecer cursos de capacitación para ayudarles.

iv) La mayoría de las/los supervisores hacen correcciones básicas en la primera entrega de un trabajo. Si entregas posteriores necesitan correcciones extensas, y repiten los mismos problemas, es habitual que esos trabajos se devuelvan para ser corregidos antes de avanzar a revisiones más completas.

v) Es útil para las/los estudiantes contar con un amigo crítico que pueda leer sus primeros borradores, siempre y cuando solo comenten la ortografía, la puntuación, la gramática, la claridad y no el contenido.

vi) Es bueno dedicar tiempo a apoyar a sus estudiantes de doctorado en la preparación de los informes periódicos de progreso que les exige la institución. El tiempo que dedica a asesorarles en temas de presentación de estos informes puede ser una buena inversión.

Área problemática 3: ¿qué es trabajo original?

A veces el trabajo original no es bienvenido.

> El "teléfono" tiene demasiadas deficiencias para ser considerado seriamente como un medio de comunicación. El dispositivo no tiene ningún valor para nosotros. (Memorando de Western Union, 1876)
>
> Pero, ¿quién va a querer escuchar que los actores hablen en las películas? (HM Warner, Warner Brothers, 1927)

La originalidad puede ser una preocupación importante para los estudiantes de doctorado. En los *Estándares de Beirut* de ICETE, el trabajo a nivel de doctorado se describe como una "contribución creativa y original... que extiende las fronteras del conocimiento".[5]

A veces no es claro qué significa 'original' —y en algunos campos es difícil ser original cuando ya se han investigado todos los temas clave. Los *Estándares de Beirut* amplían la referencia a lo "creativo y original", y lo explican así: -"o desarrolla nuevas perspectivas para la articulación y la relevancia contextual de la tradición cristiana, algunas de los cuales ameriten ser publicadas a nivel nacional o internacional en revistas arbitradas".

La originalidad puede ser un concepto bastante amplio, y se puede demostrar de diversas maneras. Puede ser simplemente "escribir sobre algo que nadie ha escrito antes", o puede ser una nueva síntesis, o una nueva interpretación de las ideas de otros. Puede consistir en aplicar un cierto enfoque en un contexto en el cual nunca se ha intentado antes, o en reutilizar una técnica conocida a un nuevo campo académico. El/la estudiante puede querer evaluar el conocimiento actual de una manera original, o desarrollar una idea de investigación de otra persona y llevarla más allá y en nuevas direcciones. Puede consistir en aportar nuevas evidencias respecto de un tema antiguo. Los enfoques interdisciplinarios pueden abrir nuevos campos y conocimientos.

---

5. 'Estándares de Beirut,' en *Principios y mejores prácticas*, ed. I. Shaw, Sección 1, Estándar 4.

Preguntas de reflexión

¿Cuáles fueron las dimensiones originales de su propia tesis?

¿Qué aspectos de originalidad ve usted en el trabajo de sus actuales estudiantes de investigación?

Si la investigación de un/a estudiante es en gran parte trabajo derivado, ¿cómo puede usted ayudarle a mejorar el nivel de originalidad de su trabajo?

Área problemática 4: Apoyo a estudiantes que trabajan en idiomas que no son sus propios idiomas

Esta es otra área que regularmente se plantea y se discute en seminarios de capacitación doctoral, y que crea importantes retos para supervisores. Cuando un/a estudiante lucha con la comunicación oral o escrita en el idioma en que se implementa el programa, y en el cual deberá escribir la tesis, para su supervisor/a esto implica una importante carga extra de trabajo y estrés.

Debe haber un acuerdo muy claro sobre políticas y prácticas entre quienes admiten a los estudiantes al programa de doctorado y quienes lo llevan adelante. A veces las y los supervisores sienten que les dejan 'recogiendo los pedazos' cuando la institución ha admitido a estudiantes que carecen de las habilidades lingüísticas exigidas.

Los programas de doctorado deben operar según el principio de que todas y todos los estudiantes deben ser tratados de la misma manera, aun cuando el programa no se ofrece en el idioma primario del estudiante. Si un/a estudiante ha elegido estudiar en un programa cuyo idioma principal es inglés, alemán, francés, chino, etc., no debe esperar que se le otorguen derechos especiales o normas académicas inferiores si no es su idioma primario.

Las y los estudiantes necesitan contar con las habilidades orales y escritas en el idioma del programa para poder progresar y superar con éxito los exámenes. Sus examinadores deben poder entender lo que están escribiendo, o diciendo si existe un componente oral.

Algunos principios útiles:

i) Debe haber estándares respecto de los niveles de idioma aceptables para la admisión al programa, y deben aplicarse de manera consistente. Por lo general, se establecen según las calificaciones obtenidas en exámenes de idioma reconocidos internacionalmente.

ii) Las y los supervisores deben mostrar simpatía y comprensión con quienes trabajan y escriben en un idioma que no es el propio, pero no se deben autoimponer cargas excesivas en pos de ayudarles a lidiar con su déficit lingüístico, y no deben comprometer los estándares académicos. Cuando hace falta un nivel más alto de apoyo, se les debe referir a cursos de capacitación profesional en los idiomas apropiados.

iii) Una vez que un/a estudiante es aceptado/a y ha aprobado los criterios de admisión, es responsabilidad de la institución darle la ayuda que necesita. Por lo tanto es vital que el estándar exigido sea apropiadamente riguroso. Las y los supervisores también deben tener un rol importante en la admisión de las y los estudiantes que supervisarán, asegurándose que desde el principio cuenten con las habilidades lingüísticas necesarias para tener éxito.

iv) Las y los supervisores deben encontrar cuáles son las formas de comunicación culturalmente más aceptables y adaptar su estilo teniéndolas en cuenta.

v) Ayude a sus estudiantes que vienen de otros idiomas y otras culturas educativas a ver que la cultura de aprendizaje que se espera a nivel de doctorado significa que como supervisor/a el apoyo que puede ofrecerle es limitado.

vi) Cuando supervisa a estudiantes que vienen de otro trasfondo lingüístico, anímeles a preguntar. A veces necesitará pedirles que repitan sus instrucciones para asegurarse de que han entendido lo que usted pidió. Si se quedan en silencio o hacen muy pocas preguntas, no significa que entendieron por completo, y a veces sucede exactamente lo contrario.

vii) Anímeles a debatir y dialogar con otros estudiantes en el idioma del programa, y a presentar su trabajo en forma oral cuando puedan. Trate de ofrecer retroalimentación en estas ocasiones. Haga hincapié en la importancia de la claridad y la audibilidad —mejor quinientas palabras audibles que mil que son inaudibles o incoherentes. Sus estudiantes necesitan saber cuántas palabras (de un texto escrito) pueden presentar en el tiempo asignado, y deben practicar su estilo de presentación.

Área problemática 5: Finanzas

Como vimos en el capítulo 6, hacer un doctorado es un emprendimiento muy costoso. Una de las mayores causas de abandono es la falta de financiación para terminar el proyecto. A veces se retira un patrocinador, o se agota el tiempo estipulado para la financiación antes de que se haya terminado el proyecto. Muchos estudiantes tienen expectativas poco realistas del costo de los estudios de doctorado, e incluso no tuvieron los suficientes fondos para empezar, lo que hace que el capítulo en este libro sobre planificación y revisión sea muy importante.

También está la dificultad de medir cuánto tiempo se tardará en completar la investigación y la redacción de una tesis, especialmente en temas que requieren de extensas investigaciones de campo o de archivos. La falta de fondos causa mucho estrés, y puede llevar a que el/la estudiante busque trabajo adicional remunerado para compensar el déficit, lo que restringe aún más el tiempo para sus estudios.

Las y los supervisores reaccionan de diversas maneras a estos problemas. He conocido supervisores que han hecho grandes esfuerzos para encontrar más fondos para sus estudiantes, e incluso conozco casos en que han pagado facturas de electricidad de sus propios bolsillos para ayudar a que sus estudiantes sigan adelante. ¡Por supuesto que esto es cuestión de decisión personal, y no un requisito del rol de supervisión!

Preguntas de reflexión

¿Qué previsiones institucionales existen para ayudar a estudiantes que enfrentan necesidades financieras?

¿Cómo cambia la supervisión que ofrece si un/a estudiante está enfrentando problemas financieros?

¿Qué medidas preventivas pueden tomar usted y su institución para evitar que sus estudiantes enfrenten problemas financieros graves?

Área problemática 6: Problemas familiares y de salud

En un programa de doctorado que dura cuatro años o más, sucederán muchos 'eventos vitales', y las y los supervisores necesitan estar preparados para estas eventualidades.

Las y los estudiantes de doctorado y sus familias tienden a ser jóvenes, por lo que puede haber miembros adicionales de la familia que nacen durante el período de estudio. Esto resultará, por lo menos, en algunas noches sin dormir y gastos adicionales para comida, ropa y educación. Pero el nacimiento de una criatura puede ser un evento de mucho estrés, que puede interrumpir de manera considerable los estudios de doctorado. Para las mujeres, en particular, será necesario suspender los estudios por un período hacia el final del embarazo y después del nacimiento. El impacto en los estudios puede ser considerable. Algunas mujeres se adaptan a estos desafíos adicionales sin grandes dificultades, pero en otros casos pueden ocasionar largas pausas de estudio, o incluso al abandono del programa de doctorado. Puede ser útil conversar de estos temas honestamente al comienzo del programa, como parte del cuidado pastoral de las y los estudiantes, y en ese ámbito plantearse delicadamente el tema de la planificación familiar.

El cuidado de los niños puede ser un gran desafío para estudiantes que estudian lejos de su hogar o en otra cultura. Sin las estructuras típicas de apoyo familiar, puede ser muy difícil coordinar el cuidado de los niños cuando no están en la escuela, o llevarlos a la escuela.

Esta dificultad crece cuando el o la cónyuge trabaja. Sus estudiantes necesitan ayuda para lograr un balance adecuado. Que no tengan un empleo remunerado no significa que están libres para asumir el cuidado de los niños a tiempo completo, además de llevar adelante sus estudios de doctorado. De hecho, el doctorado debe verse como un trabajo a tiempo completo. Otros estudiantes están tan dedicados al estudio que apenas tienen tiempo para sus familias, que comienzan a sentirse descuidadas y a resentirse. Es útil hablar de estos problemas de vez en cuando con sus estudiantes.

La mayoría de sus estudiantes tendrá parientes ancianos. En algunas culturas la responsabilidad de cuidarlos personalmente es muy fuerte. También se presentan retos cuando familiares se enferman gravemente, y puede haber fallecimientos que enfrentar. Las y los supervisores debe estar preparados para acompañar a sus estudiantes cuando sucedan estos tipos de eventos en su vida, y atentos a hacer los ajustes apropiados y aconsejarles.

Emprender un programa de doctorado puede ser extremadamente estresante, y a veces las/los estudiantes necesitan ser asesorados y animados a buscar ayuda médica para ello. El estrés se suma a las presiones físicas sobre el cuerpo. Muchos estudiantes experimentarán un período de enfermedad durante sus estudios. Los regímenes de supervisión deben ser lo suficientemente flexibles como para tomar en cuenta las interrupciones periódicas por enfermedad, y deben disponer de los procesos adecuados para cuando eso ocurra.

Preguntas de reflexión

¿Qué provisiones institucionales existen para apoyar a sus estudiantes cuando enfrentan problemas vitales como los que se han descrito?

¿Está familiarizado con los procesos estipulados para pedir una suspensión de los estudios por salud, parto, duelo, etc?

¿Cómo cambia el tipo de supervisión cuando se presentan estos tipos de problemas vitales?

> **Caso de estudio**
>
> Ha sido muy difícil agendar reuniones regulares de supervisión con Samuel, para su tesis de maestría. Cuando le pregunta qué está haciendo, habla de su investigación en términos generales, pero no entrá en ningún detalle. Ha producido una introducción corta, que no fue un trabajo muy fuerte, y el bosquejo de otro capítulo. La fecha de entrega se acerca rápidamente, y el resto de los capítulos no ha aparecido. Cuando logra reunirse con él, balbucea que pronto tendrá algo listo, y luego desaparece por varias semanas. Sus amigos no saben dónde encontrarlo, solo saben que está fuera de la ciudad. Al llegar la fecha de entrega aparece con una disertación completa, que parece estar bien presentada, pero el título es un poco diferente a lo que se había discutido y la introducción ha sido modificada. Hay tres nuevos capítulos, que son mucho mejores que la introducción original, pero el estilo en el que están escritos parece diferente del que Samuel ha usado en la introducción. El argumento de la disertación no sigue una secuencia lineal. Cuando le pregunta dónde ha estado, dice que encontró algunas buenas ideas en la biblioteca de un seminario a cierta distancia, y a partir de esas ideas la tesis tomó forma rápidamente.
>
> Cuando piensa en esta situación, algo no parece estar bien.
>
> **Preguntas**
>
> Analice la evidencia del caso.
>
> ¿Qué debe hacer usted como supervisor/a en esta situación?
>
> ¿Qué debe hacer su institución en un caso como este?
>
> ¿Qué le debe decir a Samuel?

Para leer más

Duggan, F. 'Plagiarism: Prevention, Practice and Policy.' *Assessment & Evaluation in Higher Education* 31, no. 2 (2006): 151-154.

Embleton, K. y D. S. Helfer. 'The Plague of Plagiarism and Academic Dishonesty.' *Searcher* 15, no.6 (2007): 23-26.

Lancaster, T. y F. Culwin. 'Preserving Academic Integrity—Fighting Against Non-Originality Agencies.' *British Journal of Educational Technology* 38, no. 1 (2007): 153-157.

Nitterhouse, D. 'Plagiarism—Not Just an 'Academic' Problem.' *Teaching Business Ethics* 7, no. 3 (2003): 215-227.

Sharma, R. 'A Step-by-Step Guide to Students: How to Avoid Plagiarism.' *Journal of Education Research* 4, no. 2 (2010): 143-153.

Walker, A. L. 'Preventing Unintentional Plagiarism: A Method for Strengthening Paraphrasing Skills.' *Journal of Instructional Psychology* 35, no. 4 (2007): 387-395.

Warn, J. 'Plagiarism Software: No Magic Bullet!' *Higher Education Research and Development* 25, no. 2 (2006): 195-208.

15

Apoyo y desarrollo integral de estudiantes de doctorado

Las y los evangélicos tienen un fuerte y perdurable compromiso con la persona y obra de Cristo, y dan especial énfasis a enseñanzas claves acerca de él y de la revelación de Dios en la Biblia. La esperanza de las y los supervisores de investigación evangélicos es que a través de los estudios de doctorado, el compromiso de sus estudiantes con estas creencias se fortalezca, se profundice y se enriquezca.

Sin embargo, John Stott solía insistirles a los estudiantes evangélicos que emprendían estudios de doctorado que era necesario crecer en "excelencia académica y piedad personal al mismo tiempo". Les advertía del peligro de regresar a la iglesia o al seminario después de tres o cuatro años como 'un exitoso académico pero un fracaso espiritual, un "doctor" (cualificado para enseñar), pero ya no un "discípulo", sin ninguna nueva visión, poder o santidad'. Le gustaba citar las palabras del Obispo Handley Moule, "Desconfíen de una devoción no teológica y de una teología no devocional". Stott también les señalaba a los estudiantes la reflexión de T. F. Torrance sobre el estudio teológico como una forma de "intensa comunión intelectual con Dios, en la cual nuestras mentes son cautivadas por su amor y llegamos a conocer a Dios cada vez más a través de él mismo". Animaba a los estudiantes de doctorado evangélicos a convertirse no solo en profesores de teología competentes, sino también en personas que "verdaderamente conocen y adoran al Dios del que hablan".[1]

Tristemente, algunas de las personas que tienen la oportunidad de investigar las Escrituras más profundamente, o de explorar asuntos teológicos clave, han descubierto que lo que leen desafía su profunda fe. Algunos han abandonado las convicciones teológicas evangélicas que alguna vez estimaban y han abrazado la teología liberal, o han fracasado en sostener patrones de vida y moralidad que son reconociblemente evangélicos.

---

1. 'An Admonition from John Stott,' *Fellowship of Langham Scholars Newsletter,* no. 2, Abril 1996. Ver también las notas personales del autor del curso de orientación de Langham Scholars, Oxford Centre for Mission Studies, septiembre de 1993, al que asistió el autor como becario del Instituto Whitefield.

Esto pone un énfasis significativo en que las y los supervisores evangélicos de estudiantes de doctorado sean maestros, consejeros y amigos sabios, a fin de que la interacción con los desafíos de la teología académica no resulte en una deconstrucción de la fe personal de sus estudiantes de doctorado.

Libertad académica y compromiso personal de fe

La libertad académica para investigar y explorar áreas clave sin restricciones ni limitaciones artificiales, que se encuentra en el corazón de la labor investigativa a nivel de doctorado, puede crear desafíos para quienes tienen un compromiso personal con una posición confesional ortodoxa, o que trabajan en un contexto donde la ortodoxia confesional está cuidadosamente definida. Es importante que cada institución tenga una declaración claramente definida sobre la libertad académica, y que las y los supervisores la entiendan y trabajen dentro de sus parámetros.

La "libertad" académica es la apertura a someter todas las ideas a una investigación honesta. La posibilidad de realizar una genuina investigación intelectual y la libertad de expresión para comunicar sus frutos son esenciales en una institución de educación superior. Crear un contexto de "libertad académica" significa producir un entorno en el que todas las ideas, aun las más apreciadas dentro de una tradición teológica, están abiertas a discusión. En una institución que ofrece estudios de doctorado y promueve una cultura de investigación, es necesario fomentar y apoyar la más amplia gama posible de erudición. Las y los estudiantes de investigación y las y los miembros de la facultad que se dedican a la investigación necesitan tener la libertad de hacer esto según sus propias convicciones y conciencia. La libertad de investigar y practicar el juicio crítico individual según lo que dicta la conciencia ante Dios, un valor que fue tan importante para la Reforma protestante, sigue siendo importante para el crecimiento espiritual y la responsabilidad personal.

Si este ejercicio de juicio individual produce opiniones que son nuevas, o que discrepan de las perspectivas tradicionales, no deben ser "censuradas" o penalizadas. Más bien deben ser evaluadas exhaustivamente para ver si han sido presentadas con rigor intelectual, argumentos sólidos y la debida apelación a las evidencias, y para constatar si están basadas en una interpretación correcta de las Escrituras. Si fallan estas evaluaciones, deben ser desafiadas con imparcialidad y gracia como parte de un serio compromiso con la tarea de comprender más claramente la mente de Dios sobre el asunto. En términos populares, se pueden lanzar cometas teológicos para ver hasta dónde llegan, pero los estudiantes deben hacerlo con una actitud abierta a que se les indique si hay fallas en su argumento o en su apelación a la evidencia, o si no han manejado apropiadamente las Escrituras. De hecho, deberían apreciar y agradecer que se les muestre dónde están los puntos débiles.

Por otro lado, es importante que se reconozca que la investigación académica no debe emprenderse de manera aislada. Tanto para estudiantes como supervisores/as, la actividad investigativa debe ejercerse responsablemente junto con las tareas del cuidado profesional y pastoral de otros estudiantes, la pericia académica en la enseñanza y la investigación, y la disposición a someter el propio trabajo a la evaluación de otros. Si el/la estudiante está realizando su investigación en una institución cuyo propósito es la capacitación de personas para el ministerio cristiano, entonces no debe ignorar la necesidad de preservar y defender su ethos y sus valores. Esto significa que en instituciones con fundamentos confesionales, la libertad académica necesita operar a la par de la responsabilidad confesional. La libertad académica puede crear tensiones con el compromiso personal —nadie es absolutamente neutral. Sin embargo, aun intelectuales con motivaciones confesionales o apologéticas pueden llevar a cabo investigaciones académicas y construir una tesis que usa la argumentación académica apropiada, al igual que los abogados que, aunque pueden tener sus propias opiniones sobre un asunto, constantemente investigan casos usando procesos judiciales adecuados para probarlos. Debemos estar dispuestos a someter nuestros compromisos teológicos a ser examinados y evaluados con honestidad según el estándar de las Escrituras mismas. Se debe permitir que la investigación académica corra su curso. Sin embargo, quienes se empeñan en emprender investigaciones que estén directamente en desacuerdo con el propósito y los compromisos teológicos de la institución que les acoge, podrían sentirse más a gusto haciéndolo en otro contexto. Este tipo de problema debe ser identificado por el equipo de admisiones y los posibles supervisores cuando las/los estudiantes son entrevistados o entran en diálogo antes de ser aceptados, a fin de asegurar que encajarán bien en cuanto a sus trasfondos y expectativas. En algunos casos, las/los supervisores podrían aconsejar a posibles estudiantes que busquen un contexto en donde un determinado tema o enfoque cabría más naturalmente.[2]

El contexto apropiado para los estudios teológicos —la iglesia más amplia

John Stott no hizo un doctorado en investigación, pero el alto mérito académico de su profunda erudición bíblica y teológica le valió el grado de Doctor en Divinidad del Lambeth Palace. Stott combinó la erudición con un cálido y sincero compromiso evangélico con Cristo, la Biblia, y la profunda integridad de una fe personal. Consciente de cómo el estudio académico de la teología desafía a la fe, Stott habló extensamente de la tensión entre apertura y compromiso.

---

2. Este resumen se basa en la declaración de Moore College, una institución anglicana de formación teológica en Sydney, Australia.

Tenemos que animar a los estudiosos cristianos a ir a las fronteras y a participar en el debate y, a la vez, mantener una participación activa en la comunidad de creyentes. Sé que es una cuestión delicada, y no es fácil definir las relaciones correctas entre la investigación libre y la fe asentada. Sin embargo, a menudo me ha intranquilizado la soledad de algunos eruditos cristianos. Ya sea que se hayan alejado de la comunidad de fe, o que la comunidad haya permitido que queden a la deriva, su aislamiento es una condición insana y peligrosa. Como parte de su propia integridad, los eruditos cristianos necesitan preservar la tensión entre apertura y compromiso, y aceptar alguna medida de responsabilidad mutua unos a otros, y unos por otros, en el cuerpo de Cristo. En una comunidad de cuidado mutuo, creo que podríamos ver menos bajas por un lado y más creatividad teológica por el otro.[3]

Las y los supervisores evangélicos y sus estudiantes/investigadores de doctorado deben encontrar formas de vivir dentro de esta tensión de estar en las "fronteras" del debate académico, y participar activamente en la comunidad de fe. Las y los estudiantes de doctorado necesitan la libertad para discutir estos asuntos, y necesitan buenos ejemplos a seguir. Las palabras de John Stott destacan el peligro del erudito a la deriva, lejos de la comunión de la iglesia. Lamentablemente hay momentos en que esto le ha sucedido a estudiantes de investigación evangélicos. Estoy convencido de que Stott tiene razón, que el arraigo en la comunidad de la iglesia resultará en más creatividad teológica y menos bajas. Esta cuestión debe ser abordada seriamente por las y los supervisores. El erudito 'llanero solitario', que carece del apoyo y la responsabilidad mutua que ofrece una iglesia local, está en una situación peligrosa.

Me llamó la atención recientemente la respuesta categórica al respecto que me ofreció un estudiante de doctorado en un departamento teológico de una universidad sudafricana predominantemente liberal:

> Tengo gente piadosa en mi país de origen que ha dado sacrificialmente de su tiempo y dinero para invertir en mí, y mi deber a ellos es volver firme en la fe y sin haber cedido a este liberalismo.

Lo que es aún más angustioso es ver supervisores de doctorado, a quienes estos estudiantes tienen como modelos, que se han alejado de la participación en una iglesia local, e incluso han dejado de asistir regularmente. Hablan abiertamente de que están totalmente desilusionados con la iglesia. Esto es más común de lo que uno se imagina.

Si bien esto es una grave anomalía —que algunos de los que preparan a otros para el liderazgo en la iglesia han optado por apartarse de la vida de la iglesia local-, me alegra haber visto que lo contrario también sucede. Conozco a académicos reconocidos, de

---

3. J. Stott, *I Believe in Preaching* (Londres, Hodder and Stoughton, 1982), 87.

instituciones teológicas muy prestigiosas, que sirven fielmente como ancianos y diáconos, toman su turno en la rotación de predicadores, dirigen grupos de estudio bíblico en su casa y se comprometen con entusiasmo a compartir el evangelio con niños y jóvenes.

Para teólogos académicos y talentosos puede ser difícil escuchar la predicación de ministros que saben mucho menos que ellos, cuyos sermones no están bien desarrollados teológicamente o que no manejan el texto bíblico tan a fondo como podría desearse. Puede ser un desafío relacionarse con creyentes laicos, cuya comprensión de su fe es muy simple o aun simplista. Cuando sus estudiantes teológicos se quejaron de la vida poco excepcional de la iglesia, Martín Lutero observó:

> La gente no puede tener ministros exactamente como los quisieran... deben agradecer a Dios que tienen la palabra pura y no deben exigir que San Agustín y San Ambrosio se lo prediquen. Si un pastor agrada al Señor Jesús y le es fiel, no hay nadie tan grande y poderoso que no deba estar también complacido con él.[4]

Tal vez la iglesia local no es el lugar donde las y los supervisores de doctorado encontrarán la enseñanza profunda que todos anhelamos. Sin embargo, la Escritura es clara en este asunto, y es aplicable tanto a un profesor de seminario cristiano como a un fontanero cristiano o a un limpiador de ventanas cristiano —"No dejemos de congregarnos, como acostumbran hacer algunos, sino animémonos unos a otros, y con mayor razón ahora que vemos que aquel día se acerca".[5] Como subraya el autor de *Hebreos*, pertenecer a la iglesia local implica mucho más que recibir una enseñanza profunda y desafiante, por más anhelada que esta sea. La iglesia local ofrece apoyo mutuo en la oración, el amor, el ánimo y la bondad de los creyentes, que de hecho es una gran riqueza. Pero también hay oportunidades de servicio y de dar aliento y ánimo a los demás. Los pastores de iglesias local pueden ponerse nerviosos por tener profesores de teología en sus congregaciones, y necesitan recibir ánimo y apoyo. Los enfermos necesitan que se les visite, las visitas necesitan hospitalidad. No hay razón alguna para eximir a una supervisora de doctorado o a un estudiante de investigación de liderar un grupo casero, enseñar una clase de escuela dominical, servir el café o ayudar con una jornada de limpieza en la iglesia. Todo lo contrario. Nuestro modelo es Cristo, que debatió con los escribas en el patio del templo, pero también le lavó los pies a sus discípulos.

---

4. Lutero, citado en Warfield, *Theological Studies*, 190.
5. Hebreos 10:25.

Preguntas de reflexión

¿Cómo evaluaría su compromiso con una iglesia local?

¿Qué oportunidades tiene para servir en la comunidad local?

Cuando era estudiante de investigación, ¿Cuál era el área más problemática de su relación con la iglesia/comunidad local?

¿Cómo le ha ayudado en su vida académica y cristiana estar arraigado/a en una iglesia local?

¿Qué es lo que más le gustaría cambiar?

El manejo de áreas problemáticas en las disciplinas teológicas

Es importante que las y los supervisores de doctorado sean abiertos con sus estudiantes en cuanto a las cuestiones problemáticas de su disciplina. A veces hay un extraño silencio al respecto por parte de las/los supervisores, que deja a sus estudiantes preguntándose si no se deben mencionar, y si hay permiso para hacerlo. Esta reticencia les deja mal equipados para manejar estos temas en el futuro, y sin el lenguaje discursivo apropiado para tratarlos.

Claridad acerca de las Escrituras

Muchos estudiantes evangélicos que estudian la Biblia a nivel de doctorado no tienen una doctrina clara de las Escrituras. Aunque trabajan muy de cerca con los textos bíblicos, mantienen este trabajo bastante separado de sus puntos de vista doctrinales. Eso parece extraño.

Preguntas de reflexión

¿Cuál es su propia doctrina de las Escrituras?

¿Cómo es moldeada por su contexto institucional, y qué tensiones crea ese contexto?

¿Cómo le explicaría esto a un/a estudiante de doctorado que está explorando sus propias perspectivas en torno a las Escrituras?

Cómo enfrentar los problemas difíciles

John Stott reflexionaba abiertamente sobre los desafíos que había enfrentado al estudiar teología en el ambiente predominantemente liberal de la Universidad de Cambridge en la década de 1940. Stott a menudo vio que era el único evangélico en toda la clase cuando los profesores exponían sus enfoques liberales con confianza y seguridad. Esto le supuso a Stott un severo "dolor mental", porque trataba de encontrar respuestas a esos argumentos y, a la vez, sostener con rigor intelectual su posición evangélica y demostrar —para su propia satisfacción— que era acertada. Se consideraba un "milagro" que alguien estudiara teología en un contexto así, y sobreviviese con sus convicciones evangélicas intactas. Así fue con Stott. Lo que lo sostuvo fue su implacable certeza de que para desafiar a aquellos que socavaban la comprensión evangélica del evangelio había que responderles al mismo nivel de erudición. Cada vez que se topaba con un tema que lo dejaba perplejo o desafiaba su fe, trabajaba y oraba sin descanso hasta encontrar lo que creía que era una solución satisfactoria. También le ayudo tener un amigo cercano con quien compartía y discutía los temas, Douglas Johnson, quien llegó a ser un líder clave en InterVarsity Fellowship, luego conocido como UCCF.[6]

Las cuestiones pequeñas no deben anular las grandes convicciones

En algún punto del proceso, el estudio teológico de alto nivel planteará profundos desafíos. Es crucial la forma en que el/la estudiante de investigación reacciona en esas instancias. Hablando en la Consulta de Langham Scholars en la Universidad de Cambridge en 2011, un reconocido erudito bíblico se refirió a los desafíos que enfrentaba al investigar y escribir en su propia disciplina:

> Hay momentos en los que encuentro algo en el estudio de las Escrituras que desafía mis convicciones evangélicas. En ese momento tengo que escoger. ¿Exploro este tema que potencialmente puede socavar mis convicciones profundamente arraigadas, o escojo conscientemente decidir que mi fe y mi posición doctrinal son más grandes que este tema, y lo dejo, aunque sin resolver, hasta que pueda entenderlo mejor? La persistente preocupación por ese pequeño tema puede resultar en que sobreamplifico su importancia, y en última instancia me puede causar un daño espiritual. Sin embargo, si tengo el valor de dejarlo de lado por ahora, a menudo, con tiempo y con la maduración de la reflexión y el estudio, encuentro que el Señor de verdad tiene cómo traer iluminación fresca, y a futuro se me va aclarando una solución satisfactoria.

Conozca las consecuencias de cruzar fronteras

Otra imagen que a veces he oído que se usa para entender el equilibrio entre la libertad académica y las convicciones personales confesionales, es la de una piscina. Las convicciones

---

6. T. D. Smith, *John Stott, The Making of a Leader* (Downers Grove: InterVarsity Press, 1999), 180-203.

cristianas y las declaraciones confesionales históricas sobre doctrina y estilo de vida crean límites o bordes seguros dentro de los cuales se puede nadar. Dentro de esos límites hay libertad para moverse en muchas direcciones y explorar muchas opciones. Sin embargo, cuando se toca el borde de la piscina, ya sea en una cuestión doctrinal o incluso moral o de estilo de vida, el/la intelectual ahora tiene que decidir qué hacer. O vuelve para atrás y usa su libertad para moverse en otra dirección, o la usa para salirse de la piscina. Muchos eligen nadar en otra dirección. Posteriormente regresan a ese punto y, con reflexiones frescas, descubren que ya no es tan problemático —su entendimiento ha cambiado y pueden verlo de una manera diferente o más madura. A veces las personas eligen salirse. Muchos que así deciden se alejan de los valores centrales de la fe. Uno de los pioneros modernos de los estudios críticos del Nuevo Testamento, David F. Strauss, tomó esa decisión y perdió por completo su fe personal, y al morir rechazó un entierro cristiano. Las filas de eruditos liberales son periódicamente ampliadas por evangélicos que han renunciado a sus creencias fundamentales. De vez en cuando, en los momentos límite "al borde de la piscina", pueden surgir nuevas perspectivas que conducen a nuevos entendimientos acerca de la piscina, como cuando Martín Lutero logró superar las limitaciones confesionales del catolicismo medieval e impulsar la Reforma protestante.

El apoyo a estudiantes en momentos críticos

Una de las tareas que las y los supervisores evangélicos deberían estar dispuestos a abrazar, es apoyar a sus estudiantes en estos momentos críticos. Muchos evangélicos han tomado decisiones potencialmente significativas o devastadoras sin contar con un interlocutor que les acompañara. En el espíritu del compromiso con la investigación académica abierta, no se debe prohibir la discusión de asuntos complejos que pueden desafiar la fe, como sucede en algunas tradiciones eclesiales. Más bien se debe apoyar con sabiduría y discernimiento. A las y los eruditos se les debe conceder la oportunidad de considerar bien las implicaciones de cualquier decisión de este tipo que puedan enfrentar. Puede ser vital contar con una perspectiva externa sobre lo que les está preocupando profundamente. ¿Es este un momento como el de Lutero, o como el de D. F. Strauss? Esto implica apoyarles no solo en lo intelectual, sino también en explorar cómo estos asuntos impactarán la fe personal, las relaciones con su comunidad de fe local, incluso la familia y las amistades. Y a lo largo de este proceso, por supuesto que el/la supervisor/a debe orar para que la fe de su estudiante no sea debilitada, sino fortalecida por el proceso.

Preguntas de reflexión

¿Qué espacio ofrece en las sesiones de supervisión para hablar de las áreas problemáticas de la disciplina?

¿Qué tan cómodo/a se siente compartiendo con sus estudiantes los problemas que estas áreas problemáticas plantean para su fe?

Si es algo que prefiere evitar, ¿cómo explica su renuencia?

¿Qué necesita para cambiar en esta área?

Cuándo funciona y cuándo no

Vivir en esta tensión entre "apertura y compromiso" tiene, por supuesto, sus peligros. Es posible que, a pesar de su apoyo y oración, un/a estudiante pueda tomar decisiones que le lleve a renunciar a las convicciones evangélicas fundamentales. Pero también es peligroso no permitir que se planteen cuestiones difíciles y rehusarse a discutirlas de manera franca. Eso puede conducir a una fe oscurantista, o a una fe impregnada de una profunda dicotomía entre la mente y los asuntos de la fe. Sus estudiantes pueden verse abrumados por una profunda ansiedad, causada por grandes preguntas que quedan sin abordar ni resolver y que pueden, por sí mismas, socavar la fe. En estas cuestiones las y los supervisores son importantes como puntos de referencia, y deben estar preparados y equipados con respuestas, lo que significa que usted misma/o necesita haber reflexionado sobre los potenciales problemas. No es una buena práctica capacitar personal médico solo dejándoles ver pacientes que están sanos y sin problemas; aprenden de los casos difíciles. Lo mismo sucede con las y los teólogos. Ser desafiadas y desafiados en las áreas difíciles debería llevar a un nivel más profundo de comprensión y compromiso con la fe.

Esto hace que la supervisión de estudiantes de doctorado sea uno de los mayores privilegios y desafíos del trabajo académico. La estrecha interacción con las y los estudiantes y sus habilidades de aprender, de alguna manera, hacen que este sea uno de los enfoques pedagógicos más cercanos al modelo de discipulado de Jesús. Él es un ejemplo muy eminente a seguir, y hacerlo puede producir algunos de los resultados más satisfactorios y duraderos.

Preguntas de reflexión

Haga una lista de los libros y artículos que recomendaría para estudiantes que están luchando por reconciliar sus convicciones evangélicas con problemas bíblicos o teológicos específicos.

¿Qué persona (aparte de usted) recomendaría como mentor/a y socio de diálogo para un/a estudiante que está enfrentando desafíos de este tipo?

Si su seminario tiene un capellán, ¿qué rol podrían desempeñar en el abordaje de los temas discutidos en este capítulo?

¿Cómo pueden las y los supervisores ayudarse mutuamente a responder a las preocupaciones de fe de sus estudiantes?

Medición y evaluación del desarrollo integral de estudiantes de doctorado

Las y los supervisores evangélicos querrán medir el "éxito" de sus estudiantes de doctorado en términos más que meramente académicos.

Preguntas de reflexión

¿Cuál es su mayor esperanza para sus estudiantes de doctorado?

¿Cómo va a medir el éxito, o la falta de éxito, aparte de si aprueban o no los exámenes?

Evaluación de progreso y de habilidades y logros clave

La visión para las y los supervisores de doctorado en instituciones evangélicas comprende la tarea de producir estudiantes de doctorado que están motivados y empoderados por una profunda apreciación de la tradición cristiana evangélica y que tienen: una mayor comprensión y aplicación del pensamiento y las prácticas de un discipulado fiel y piadoso; una base más extensa de conocimientos; una mayor capacidad de investigación y enseñanza; y una mayor capacidad para la reflexión original. Si nuestros estudiantes de doctorado se convierten en docentes, queremos que tengan la capacidad de comunicar eficazmente lo que han descubierto en las aulas y los entornos profesionales, y que puedan trabajar a la vanguardia del pensamiento cristiano. Cuando han completado un doctorado, queremos que sean capaces de seguir sirviendo a Cristo fielmente y de crecer profesionalmente.

Cada estudiante es diferente, con un conjunto único de fortalezas e intereses.

El Apéndice 3 es un listado de referencia que contiene aptitudes y habilidades clave que se puede utilizar como "registro de aprendizajes" para cualificar el progreso y discutirlo a medida que el/la estudiante avanza a otra etapa.[7] Las y los estudiantes que ingresan a un programa de doctorado deben tener claro que su progreso general será evaluado según estas áreas.

Caso de estudio

Alba es una estudiante muy capaz, que reflexiona con profundidad. Su tesis doctoral integra áreas del estudio del Nuevo Testamento y la filosofía. Al profundizar más en el lado filosófico de sus estudios, que disfruta muchísimo, se concentra cada vez más en los enfoques filosóficos y comienza a plantearse preguntas importantes sobre su enfoque de las Escrituras. Luego comparte con usted que ha dejado de leer su Biblia devocionalmente, porque no siente la necesidad de hacerlo, y su asistencia a la iglesia se ha vuelto más irregular. Esto está causando tensión con su marido que desea mantener con regularidad los tiempos devocionales familiares. Usted comienza a sentir que aunque le está yendo bien académicamente, ella no está progresando en su fe personal, y eso a usted le preocupa cada vez más.

Preguntas

¿Qué asuntos importantes plantea esto?

¿Qué puede hacer, como su supervisor/a, para ayudarla?

¿Qué debe hacer la institución en un caso como este?

---

7. Un muy buen ejemplo de la implementación de una lista de este tipo es este *PhD Mastery Checklist* de la McMaster Divinity School, amablemente compartida con el autor por miembros de su facultad.

16

Cómo preparar a las y los candidatos al doctorado para ser examinados

La culminación del proceso de supervisión se da cuando el trabajo del candidato a doctorado es presentado para ser examinado por un panel más amplio de expertos. Esto puede ser un momento emocionante, pero también estresante, tanto para el/la estudiante como para quien le supervisa. Él o ella debe recordar que lo que se está examinando es el trabajo del candidato, y no el suyo. Sin embargo, también hay una sensación de que para que le vaya bien, quien le supervisó debe haber hecho un buen trabajo. Si el/la estudiante falla, su supervisor/a se hará preguntas importantes acerca de si ofreció la clase correcta de supervisión. La mayoría de las formas de evaluación doctoral incluyen oportunidades para revisar y reescribir lo presentado después del proceso de evaluación. Esto permite corregir algunos de los problemas, pero como supervisor/a uno quiere que todo vaya bien.

El momento óptimo para entregar la tesis

Como parte de la supervisión regular, es importante definir para cuándo es probable que la tesis esté lista. A medida que el programa de doctorado se acerca a su fin, el/la estudiante comenzará a preguntarle, "¿cree usted que la tesis está lista para ser presentada?" Los últimos meses y semanas de la supervisión de un/a estudiante de investigación pueden ser muy intensivos para el/la supervisor/a.

Él o ella debe leer cuidadosamente el borrador final y hacer sugerencias de revisiones adicionales antes de que se entregue. Este es un tiempo para que su estudiante pula, revise y reescriba. Su estudiante no debería estar pensando que "quizás los examinadores no se den cuenta" si hay deficiencias o discrepancias. ¡Se van a dar cuenta, ese es su trabajo!

Ante la pregunta de su estudiante sobre cuándo es el mejor momento para presentar una tesis, la respuesta apropiada es 'cuando esté lista'. Sin embargo, la realidad puede ser más compleja. La fecha de entrega puede estar influenciada por la línea de tiempo del programa —habrá una fecha límite para la presentación de la tesis. El/la estudiante puede tener un trabajo al cual debe regresar o una visa que se vence, lo que puede adelantar la fecha límite. Los fondos de los que depende su estudiante probablemente se están agotando, lo cual exige que no se retrase la presentación. Las y los supervisores deben tratar todas estas cuestiones de forma regular con el/la estudiante, para que cualquier fecha límite y/o circunstancias se mantengan claramente a la vista.

Si usted no tiene mucha experiencia supervisando estudiantes de doctorado, es una buena práctica consultar con los demás miembros del equipo de supervisión, o con algún colega senior más experimentado, para obtener retroalimentación en cuanto a si la tesis está lista para su presentación. Las revisiones anuales deberían haber examinado cuidadosamente los conceptos básicos, la metodología y la intención del estudio a fin de asegurar que el proyecto avanza en la dirección correcta, y en ese momento se debería haber identificado cualquier problema importante. Sin embargo, es importante hacer una evaluación final antes de la presentación. En ese punto algunas instituciones tienen una sesión "pre-viva" o una "confirmación de estatus", oportunidad en la cual otros miembros de la comunidad académica pueden revisar un borrador completo de la tesis e identificar cualquier asunto clave que requiera revisión.

El proceso académico difiere según la institución, pero por lo general se requiere que, de alguna manera, el/la supervisor/a dé su aprobación para la presentación, lo cual es luego confirmado por la persona o el comité que supervisa el programa de investigación. Cuando el/la supervisor/a da su consentimiento a la propuesta de presentar la tesis, deben tener claro que,

- Se ha producido un trabajo de investigación sustancial y original.
- El/la estudiante ha seguido todas las normas requeridas en cuanto a la presentación y el formato.
- Hay una tesis defendible y lista para los examinadores.
- Él/ella cuenta con la preparación necesaria para la defensa, en términos de su desarrollo personal y académico.

La defensa oral cuando hay un Comité de Tesis/Disertación

En muchos aspectos, el proceso de preparación para la defensa final de la disertación en los programas del tipo estadounidense es muy similar al proceso de preparación para la defensa de la propuesta. El supervisor/presidente del Comité habrá usado la retroalimentación de la defensa de la propuesta para guiar al estudiante en el desarrollo del documento de la disertación, ofreciéndole retroalimentación de los primeros borradores de capítulos o secciones de capítulos, y determinando cuándo le parece apropiado compartir los borradores más completamente desarrollados con los demás miembros del Comité para su revisión. Cuando se ha recibido la retroalimentación de todos los miembros del Comité y esta se ha resuelto e integrado al desarrollo de un documento de defensa, llega un momento en el que el presidente del Comité y el/la estudiante están de acuerdo en que la disertación está lista para una defensa final. No se debe avanzar con la defensa si hay miembros del Comité que aún sienten que alguno de los borradores de las secciones que revisaron necesitan una cantidad significativa de trabajo adicional.

Hay que estar completamente seguros

Una vez que se entrega la tesis, no hay vuelta atrás, por lo que el/la estudiante y su supervisor/Comité de disertación deben, en lo posible, tener confianza de que la tesis está lista. No es una buena práctica que el/la estudiante sea humillada por la experiencia de presentar una tesis que está irremediablemente mal. Tampoco lo es que los examinadores estén obligados a dedicar su tiempo a examinar una tesis que no tiene ninguna posibilidad de ser aprobada.

En algunos sistemas existe la posibilidad de que él o ella presente una tesis en contra de los consejos de sus supervisores/as. Esta es una situación que hay que evitar, pero en algunos casos excepcionales, donde la relación con su supervisor/a se ha dañado (ver cap. 3), él o ella puede reclamar el derecho a que su tesis sea defendida. En esos casos, el examen se debe llevar adelante con la misma imparcialidad y rigor que en cualquier otra situación. Si es posible, no se le debe informar a los examinadores, ni antes ni durante el examen, que la tesis fue presentada sin la aprobación del supervisor, para asegurar que el trabajo sea evaluado por sus propios méritos.

Examen sin defensa oral[1]

No todos los programas de doctorado tienen un examen oral, y en algunos se examina solo la tesis.

Cuando la tesis se somete a examen sin defensa oral, el proceso exacto debe ser explicado a las y los estudiantes. Deben tener claro quién(es) va(n) a leer la tesis y cuánto tiempo tomará el proceso. Si los examinadores solicitan correcciones o revisiones, se debe explicar cómo se harán y cuáles son los plazos para hacerlas. Debe quedarles claro el punto en el cual la tesis será considerada firme y validada. Aunque no haya una defensa oral, los examinadores deben quedar satisfechos con la misma variedad de cuestiones que hubieran exigido en un examen oral.

---

1. ICETE y el autor recomiendan que, siempre que sea posible, la defensa oral sea parte del examen de la tesis.

El examen oral

Cuando se lleva a cabo un examen oral, es una parte muy importante del proceso y requiere de una buena preparación. Las razones por las que se usa un examen oral son, esencialmente:

- Asegurar que la tesis es el trabajo propio de cada candidato/a; él o ella debe ser capaz de hablar al respecto con conocimiento y en persona. El examen oral constituye así una de las protecciones contra el plagio en la tesis.
- El/la candidato/a demuestra su capacidad para discutir y "defender" su trabajo académico, que es una dimensión esencial del diálogo académico.
- Ofrecer la oportunidad para explicar y expresar ideas más allá de lo que está escrito.
- Él/ella puede explicar y justificar el enfoque adoptado y responder a cualquier pregunta que pueda surgir al respecto.
- Permite una base más amplia que solo el texto para las decisiones de los examinadores.
- Puede resultar en oportunidades de empleo o en ideas que se pueden publicar.
- Por lo general juega a favor de el/la estudiante. Una tesis que está en el límite puede ser compensada con un buen examen oral, pero no una tesis pobre, aunque se le puede dar oportunidad de hacer revisiones si la defiende bien.

El panel examinador

Esto variará de una institución a otra, y según el programa. El/la supervisor/a debe explicarle claramente a su estudiante lo que eso implica y el rol que desempeñará como supervisor/a. Normalmente el panel incluye un examinador externo cuya función es aportar una evaluación objetiva y facilitar que el trabajo sea evaluado según estándares comparables en otras instituciones de vanguardia.

En algunos programas se consulta al estudiante sobre la elección del examinador. El/la supervisor/a también debe tener un rol en la recomendación de los nombres más apropiados para el panel, aunque la designación final la suele realizar la institución. Académicos que son importantes en el campo, autores con cuyo trabajo el/la estudiante ha interactuado en su tesis y aquellos que entienden el contexto, son todas personas clave. Deben ser líderes académicos en el área temática.

La fecha del examen

Por lo general, la institución define la fecha del examen, pero el/la supervisor/a puede preparar el camino interactuando con los examinadores y el/la estudiante para establecer un rango de fechas de mutua conveniencia. No siempre es fácil hacer esto en épocas del año académico con mucha actividad. Pero el/la estudiante no debe tener que esperar muchos meses para que se lleve a cabo el examen.

En los programas de doctorado de estilo estadounidense, a medida que crece el tamaño del Comité de Disertación, también aumenta el reto de agendar una reunión para la defensa. Es importante que el presidente del Comité le aconseje al estudiante que planifique con mucha anticipación y no espera hasta el último momento para buscar posibles fechas para una defensa. En general, los miembros del Comité serán muy flexibles —donde lo pueden ser–, pero sus agendas pueden estar muy llenas y eso dificulta agendar una defensa. Puede ser útil contar con un asistente de oficina para contactar a los diferentes miembros del Comité, explorar opciones para una reunión de defensa y coordinar la planificación del evento y su anuncio dentro de la institución.

La preparación del estudiante para el examen oral

Para muchos estudiantes, la defensa oral de su tesis doctoral es una escena de pesadilla. Lo ven como un interrogatorio implacable. Tal vez se imaginan que incluso habrá focos brillantes alumbrándoles, con examinadores esperando para atacarles por cada error que cometan, por más leve que sea. La defensa pública, el aspecto central del examen oral en algunos contextos, con un panel de expertos que debaten la tesis adelante de una audiencia —que puede ser bastante numerosa— de miembros de la facultad, otros estudiantes, e incluso público general, puede ser un gran tormento. He participado en un número de exámenes de doctorado, a veces en el papel de examinador, a veces como observador pero sin participar, y a veces apoyando a los estudiantes hasta el momento en que comienza el examen. La realidad es bastante diferente al mito, y las y los estudiantes necesitan estar adecuadamente preparados con una buena comprensión de lo que podría suceder y de por qué es una parte necesaria del proceso en la mayoría de los sistemas de doctorado.

Las y los supervisores siempre deben animar a sus estudiantes de doctorado a ver el examen como algo positivo:

- Esta es una oportunidad para hablar largo y tendido sobre el tema que ha sido el centro de su vida y su reflexión en los últimos años.
- Algunos eruditos de verdad han leído su tesis, ¡y están interesados en lo que dice!
- Es una ocasión para que él o ella demuestre lo mucho que sabe. Puede haber mucho más material de lo que pusieron en la tesis, y les dará la oportunidad de hablar sobre su experiencia más amplia.
- Aquí hay una oportunidad para que el/la estudiante demuestre que es experto/a mundial, e incluso puede conocer el campo mejor que sus examinadores.

- La tesis será leída por otros expertos que pueden hacer recomendaciones de correcciones y revisiones que la mejorarán antes de su publicación.
- Los examinadores pueden hacer recomendaciones acerca de la publicación de la tesis completa o de partes de ella. Se pueden sugerir revisiones importantes antes de que el documento sea finalizado y publicado. Una defensa oral de pesadilla solo ocurrirá si la tesis es pobre y el/la candidato/a no se ha preparado lo suficientemente bien.

Preparación para el día del examen

Una vez entregada la tesis, el/la estudiante de doctorado no debe dejar de trabajar. Debe seguir leyendo y refrescando su pensamiento —nuevos artículos y libros pueden publicarse luego de la fecha de entrega, y se le puede preguntar al respecto.

Las y los estudiantes necesitan aprender a prepararse para el examen oral tal como lo harían para cualquier otro examen.

Ejercicios útiles para la preparación

En preparación para las preguntas que el/la estudiante enfrentará, se le puede pedir que,

- Resuma en una oración el tema clave de la tesis —a menudo los examinadores piden esto temprano en el examen.
- Resuma en unas pocas oraciones los puntos principales del argumento de la tesis, y explique cómo un punto construye sobre el anterior de una forma lógica.
- Resuma en unas pocas oraciones la contribución singular que piensa que aporta su tesis al conocimiento.

Las y los estudiantes también necesitan evaluar críticamente su propio trabajo, ver en dónde su trabajo ha tenido éxito, y en donde es menos exitoso. Es útil tener una reunión de supervisión antes del examen en el que se consideran los problemas que podrían surgir en el examen, y se exploran áreas como,

- Las limitaciones de la tesis;
- Dónde, a futuro, se necesita más trabajo;
- En dónde no se desarrolló la investigación o no resulto de la manera esperada.

Antes del examen, el/la estudiante debe,

- Releer la tesis cuidadosamente. Debe considerar cada sección y capítulo, evaluar si está a la altura del nivel de doctorado, y decidir qué preguntas le podrían plantear los examinadores.

- Aprender a ser su propio/a examinador/a:

    i) ¿Está claramente expresada la tesis de la investigación?

    ii) El argumento de la tesis ¿muestra conocimiento de la literatura relevante?

    iii) ¿Se citan correctamente las fuentes relevantes?

    iv) El argumento principal, ¿es coherente y lógico? ¿está bien expresado?

    v) ¿Hay una línea de desarrollo clara a lo largo de cada párrafo, sección y capítulo de la tesis?

    vi) ¿Cuáles son los puntos débiles de la tesis? Los examinadores tienen experiencia en localizar las áreas en donde el argumento no es fuerte.

    vii) ¿La conclusión tiene el respaldo de la evidencia recolectada?

Él o ella puede preparar algunas notas en las que resume la tesis e identifica cuáles son las preguntas clave que espera que se le pregunten. Luego puede,

- Reducir su contenido principal a unas pocas páginas de notas;
- Incluir una explicación de la parte más compleja de la tesis;
- Aprenderse definiciones breves de términos y conceptos clave que usa, para poder hablar de estos con confianza y conocimiento;
- Mostrar que es experto/a en su propia investigación;
- Tener confianza en sus conclusiones.

La explicación del proceso

Al estudiante se le debe explicar claramente lo que sucederá en el examen. A menudo el proceso del examen está rodeado de misterio, y entre las y los estudiantes circulan muchos rumores extraños acerca de lo que sucede! Deben saber qué es lo que sucederá, y tienen que poder practicar de antemano las habilidades que van a necesitar.

En instituciones que tienen defensas abiertas se permite que otros estudiantes asistan. Se debe alentar o exigir que las y los estudiantes de doctorado asistan a por lo menos una defensa de tesis antes de tener la suya.

El día del examen

Las y los estudiantes deben asegurarse de estar bien descansados antes de un examen oral, porque es un proceso muy exigente. Mientras se hayan hecho los anteriores preparativos, la mejor opción es una buena noche de sueño, en vez de una última y febril lectura de la tesis que dura hasta la madrugada.

La duración del examen puede variar. Una hora sería un examen corto; dos horas sería más normal; más de tres es inusual.

Los paneles de examinadores varían. Puede haber desde dos examinadores hasta un gran número de miembros de la facultad y examinadores visitantes. Esto significa que la forma de hacer preguntas puede ser muy variada, y el/la estudiante necesita estar preparado/a para interactuar con esos diversos abordajes.

La mayoría de los programas de doctorado permiten que el/la estudiante tenga consigo una copia de su tesis, a la que pueden referirse durante el examen.

Para que sea más fácil localizar capítulos o secciones, puede usar indicadores de colores u otro tipo de señalización. De esa manera no perderá tiempo en ubicar la sección correcta. Sin embargo, normalmente no se permite que él o ella ingrese al examen con otros documentos o libros aparte de la tesis. Se puede preparar una fe de erratas (errores ortográficos y tipográficos, problemas gramaticales y errores fácticos que el/la estudiante ha identificado después de la entrega) y mostrársela a los examinadores al final del examen. Si él o ella desea, puede pedir permiso para incluirlo en la versión final revisada, pero esta no debe incluir nuevas secciones de texto.

Preparación para la reunión con los examinadores

El/la supervisor/a debe ayudar a preparar al estudiante para el momento en que se reunirá con quienes revisarán la tesis en el examen. Él o ella puede haber participado en las discusiones sobre la selección de examinadores, pero también debe estar preparado/a para los enfoques metodológicos y académicos que puedan tomar los examinadores y las preguntas que pueden plantear.

El/la estudiante debe hacer un poco de "revisión" de sus examinadores. Si han escrito en el área de la tesis debe leer esos textos, o releerlos. El/la estudiante necesita estar al tanto de diferencias de enfoque y conclusiones entre su propio trabajo y el de los examinadores, y poder explicar y justificar esas diferencias.

Si su trabajo es interdisciplinario, debe ser capaz de orientar a los examinadores que no son especialistas en el tema.

Preparación para hablar bien sobre la tesis

Algunas instituciones ofrecen una experiencia pre-viva, o una simulación del examen. Esto puede ser útil para preparar al estudiante para lo que vendrá, permitiéndole practicar cómo responder a preguntas que no conoce de antemano, y escucharse a sí mismo/a dando las respuestas. Toma tiempo, ¡y algunos estudiantes piensan que duplica el nivel de estrés! Si el/la supervisor/a es parte del panel de examinadores, entonces no debe participar en un examen simulado. De lo contrario puede ser útil que se involucre, o que sugiera otros docentes que podrían ayudar.

El/la estudiante necesita aprender a expresarse con brevedad y precisión, y con ejemplos apropiados. Debe responder sin dar vueltas ni "divagar" y desviarse del punto. Tampoco debe incluir demasiado material que no responde a una pregunta. Los examinadores se exasperan cuando un/a estudiante tarda mucho en responder una pregunta simple. Hay un número limitado de preguntas que se pueden hacer en el tiempo estipulado para el examen, y no desean malgastarlo. Si el/la estudiante no sabe la respuesta a una pregunta, es mejor que lo admita, en vez de dar vueltas sin responderla.

Ayude a sus estudiantes a que lleguen al examen con una postura relajada, mostrando interés y entusiasmo (¡pero no entusiasmados de manera extravagante!), dispuestos a ser abiertos y autocríticos con su trabajo y listos para una discusión académica madura entre pares.

Se les debe explicar el código de vestimenta apropiado para la ocasión, de manera que no sientan vergüenza por llegar con vestimenta muy formal o demasiado informal.

Preparación para las preguntas

Si el/la supervisor/a no forma parte del panel de examinadores puede, con base en su experiencia, dedicar tiempo a conversar con él o ella sobre algunas de las preguntas que podrían plantear los examinadores.

La primera pregunta sirve a menudo para "romper el hielo" y relajar al candidato. Podría ser algo como, '¿por qué eligió investigar este tema?'. Esto puede permitir que él o ella hable de su motivación personal, pero también necesita luego asegurarse de pasar a responder con el rigor académico apropiado. Debe haber en el campo una pregunta de investigación clave que necesita de una respuesta.

Las y los estudiantes necesitan saber cuáles podrían ser las preguntas probables, y poder "leer" las preguntas para entender el tipo de habilidad sobre el que se le está pidiendo que hable. Estos son algunos ejemplos:

i) En un par de oraciones, ¿cuál es su tesis? (él o ella no puede responder, "¡Ah, será que no lo ha leído!").

ii) ¿Cuál es la contribución original o importante de la tesis? (esta pregunta va al corazón de la definición clásica de la investigación).

iii) ¿Cree que ha cubierto todas las cuestiones abarcadas por su título? (esta pregunta evalúa el contenido).

iv) ¿Cuáles fueron sus preguntas/hipótesis de investigación? (esta pregunta aborda los métodos de investigación que se usaron).

v) ¿Qué otros enfoques consideró para su investigación? ¿Por qué escogió este? (esta pregunta también considera los métodos de investigación).

vi) Si estuvieras haciendo la investigación de nuevo, ¿qué haría diferente?

vii) Muéstrenos cómo es su metodología usando una de las secciones de la tesis. ¿Cree que sus conclusiones son justificadas? (él o ella debe indicar exactamente donde ha mostrado esto).

viii) ¿Cómo ha verificado sus conclusiones? ¿Cómo se sostienen?

ix) ¿De qué manera deberá cambiar la erudición como resultado de su tesis? (es otra pregunta sobre la originalidad de la contribución).

x) ¿Cuál de sus conclusiones le sorprendió más?

xi) ¿Cuál cree que fue su conclusión más importante? (considera la importancia de la investigación).

xii) ¿Cuál es la relevancia, o cuáles son las implicaciones de la tesis para. . . ? (considera la importancia de la investigación).

xiii) ¿Qué otros temas de investigación surgen de su trabajo?

xiv) ¿Cómo compara su tesis con el trabajo de. . . ? (esta pregunta requiere que esté al día con investigaciones similares y con la literatura secundaria pertinente).

xv) ¿Cuál es la mayor debilidad en su enfoque? (la autocrítica y la defensa apropiada deben estar en equilibrio)

xvi) ¿Hasta que punto está satisfecho/a con su investigación?

xvii) ¿Cuál será su próximo trabajo de investigación? (¿hacia dónde lleva su tesis?)

Las y los estudiantes también necesitan aprender a responder usando los argumentos apropiados, y cuando no hay una respuesta clara, reconocerlo. Si los examinadores señalan deficiencias en la tesis, él o ella debe defender su trabajo —cuando sea apropiado–, pero cuando los examinadores claramente demuestran deficiencias o que se han cometido errores, no debe tomar una postura defensiva sino aceptar la necesidad de revisión. El debate y la discusión académica son importantes, ¡pero no un altercado acalorado con los examinadores! ¡Tampoco tratar de defender lo indefendible! Los buenos académicos reciben la crítica con aprecio. Quieren aprender de ella y que contribuya a mejorar su trabajo.

Anime a sus estudiantes a disfrutar de la experiencia tanto como sea posible. Es un aspecto del rito del rito de pasaje a su carrera como académico/a, en el que debaten con seriedad con quienes serán sus pares académicos.

Preparación para lo que sucede después del examen oral

Debe repasar los potenciales resultados del examen con el/la estudiante, de modo que sepa exactamente cuáles son las posibilidades y lo qué pueden requerir. Si hay disposiciones para que los examinadores requieran revisiones o correcciones, debe conversar de lo que implicarían para que él o ella esté bien preparada.

Ha sido mi rutina estar presente el día en que mis estudiantes son examinados. Para ellos es un momento estresante y necesitan apoyo antes y después. Algunos estarán eufóricos por el resultado, y otros profundamente decepcionados. Les puede ser difícil recibir retroalimentación o instrucciones en ese momento. Algunos están emocionalmente muy vulnerables. Por lo general, organizar una celebración por adelantado no es la mejor idea. Si no le ha ido bien, no es fácil lidiar con amigos y familiares que están esperando con flores, chocolates y celebraciones preplaneadas. Nada es seguro o predecible hasta que los examinadores hayan terminado su trabajo. De lo contrario habría poca necesidad de tener exámenes. Es mejor animarles a esperar hasta que se confirme el resultado exitoso antes de preparar el festejo.

Caso de estudio

Lidia es una estudiante brillante que escribe bien y es claro que tiene habilidad para la investigación. Usted sabe que es capaz de escribir una tesis que será aprobada sin problemas. Sin embargo, sufre mucho nerviosismo en situaciones públicas. La presentación de su investigación salió muy mal. Estaba tan nerviosa que habló muy rápido y en forma casi inaudible para la audiencia. Se extendió más del tiempo estipulado y la persona que presidía la reunión tuvo que detener la presentación. Lidia terminó llorando. Ella le ha dicho que cuando está bajo estrés su nerviosismo la puede hacer enfermar físicamente.

Preguntas

¿Cómo se puede preparar a Lidia para su examen de tesis?

¿Cómo puedes ayudarla a poder hacer presentaciones orales, que serán esenciales para la carrera académica que emprender en el futuro?

Para leer más

Lovitts, B. E. 'Making the Implicit Explicit', en *The Assessment of Doctoral Education: Emerging Criteria and New Models for Improving Outcomes*, editado por P. L. Maki y N. A. Borkowski, 163-187. Sterling, VA: Stylus, 2006.

Murray, R. *How to Survive Your Viva: Defending a Thesis in an Oral Examination*. 2ª edición. Maidenhead: Open University Press, 2009.

Pearce, L. *How to Examine a Thesis*. Maidenhead: Open University Press, 2005.

Phillips, E. M. y D. S. Pugh. *How to Get a PhD: A Handbook for Students and Their Supervisors*. Maidenhead: Open University Press, 2010. (Disponible también para Kindle)

Tinkler, P. y C. Jackson. *The Doctoral Examination Process: A Handbook for Students, Examiners and Supervisors*. Maidenhead: Open University Press, 2004 —basado en el sistema del Reino Unido, pero con principios valiosos.

17

El examen de la tesis doctoral: preparativos previos al examen

Es un gran honor ser invitado o invitada a examinar una tesis doctoral. Implica el reconocimiento de su condición de "guardián de la disciplina". También implica una gran responsabilidad, y mucho trabajo. La forma en que se lleva a cabo un examen de doctorado y los roles que desempeñan los examinadores varía según el programa. En *Principios y mejores prácticas* de ICETE se hace hincapié en la necesidad de que las y los examinadores entiendan con seguridad en qué consiste su trabajo antes de comenzar el proceso de examen:

> Los examinadores deben entender claramente cuál es su rol en el proceso de examen de doctorado, y cómo han de llegar a decisiones finales sobre el otorgamiento del título académico. La institución debe disponer de lineamientos y procedimientos claros para cuando exista desacuerdo entre los examinadores en torno al resultado de un examen de doctorado.[1]

Preguntas de reflexión

¿Cuál fue su propia experiencia del examen de doctorado?

¿Qué fue lo más útil?

¿Qué fue lo menos útil?

¿Qué tres cosas considera usted que son las más importantes para examinar una tesis doctoral?

---

1. Shaw, *Principios y mejores prácticas*, Sección 20.

Los examinadores

> Las instituciones deben garantizar que los paneles examinadores para títulos de doctorado estén compuestos por miembros con competencias que aseguren una equivalencia de los estándares del sector de enseñanza superior/universitaria a nivel nacional e internacional. Por esta razón, las instituciones deben contar con procesos de evaluación para títulos de doctorado que normalmente incluyen representación externa en los paneles examinadores.[2]

Las y los examinadores deben estar debidamente cualificados. Deben contar con un título de doctorado en investigación y ser capaces de demostrar que están actualizados y activos como investigadores. Se deben escoger por su conocimiento especializado del área temática y su comprensión de los estándares y parámetros apropiados para la titulación a nivel de doctorado. Además deben estar activos en la investigación y en la supervisión de estudiantes de doctorado.

Siempre hay algún elemento de subjetividad en la evaluación de un trabajo escrito, y contar con un panel de examinadores ayuda a contrarrestar eso, pero todos los involucrados en el proceso de examen deben usar criterios apropiados de evaluación académica.

> Los examinadores externos nombrados a un panel examinador deben: contar con los conocimientos especializados requeridos, ser académicos con prestigio internacional, estar activamente involucrados en actividades investigativas y contar con publicaciones importantes y actuales en el campo que se está examinando.[3]

Una cuestión importante es asegurar que el panel examinador esté compuesto no solo por expertos académicos, sino también por especialistas en el tema y personas que entienden los enfoques que estudiantes en un contexto evangélico pueden tomar. Los examinadores deben ser escrupulosamente imparciales y calificar positivamente el buen trabajo académico, aunque estén en desacuerdo con algunos de sus contenidos teológicos. Sin embargo, no hay que agregar obstáculos innecesarios en el camino del candidato. No deben nombrarse examinadores que se sabe que son hostiles a tal o cual metodología o enfoque teológico que se haya tomado. Tampoco se le debe dar una ventaja especial, por elegir examinadores que podrían ser demasiado solidarios con la perspectiva del candidato. Debe haber un adecuado rigor académico y un equilibrio entre las y los examinadores.

Así es como se indica en *Principios y mejores prácticas* de ICETE:

---

2. Ibid., Sección 21. Un examinador externo es alguien que no es empleado regular de la institución donde se ha llevado a cabo la investigación doctoral, y que no ha participado en la supervisión del estudiante de investigación.

3. Shaw, *Principios y mejores prácticas*, Sección 21, e.

> *Cuando los exámenes de doctorado se llevan a cabo en contextos académicos evangélicos, la institución debe asegurarse que los paneles examinadores estén compuestos por miembros que tengan: un entendimiento de la perspectiva teológica de la institución y del candidato; y la capacidad de garantizar que la tesis/disertación en sí sea examinada puramente según sus méritos académicos.[4]*

Cuando se pide que alguien examine una tesis, el principio de integridad e imparcialidad académica implica que debe dejar de lado sus preferencias personales para centrarse en la calidad del trabajo académico presentado.

Otro asunto importante es que se debe practicar una adecuada ética académica e informar de cualquier interés personal en el/la candidato/a. Si usted planea contratar al candidato, publicar con él o ella, o si tienen o han tenido alguna relación cercana (personal o familiar), normalmente no debe formar parte del panel examinador.

Preguntas de reflexión

¿Cuál es el proceso para seleccionar examinadores en su institución?

¿Quién los escoge?

¿Qué materiales se le proveen?

¿Qué entrenamiento o inducción reciben?

El examinador externo

Es un honor especial ser invitado/a a desempeñar este rol, y también una gran responsabilidad. El examinador externo (o lector) es una persona externa a la institución, seleccionada para que aporte una medida de calidad y objetividad externa, que proviene de una universidad o un seminario local, o de la comunidad académica global. Su tarea consiste en asegurar que una tesis doctoral alcanzaría un grado de reconocimiento similar si fuera presentada a nivel de doctorado en un seminario o universidad en un lugar diferente. Su rol es actuar especialmente como parte desinteresada y guardian de la disciplina. En algunas instituciones los lectores externos fungen como asesores de los examinadores internos. Ofrecen comentarios sobre la tesis desde su área específica, sin actuar formalmente como examinadores. Por lo general, los examinadores/lectores externos son parte de un panel de examinadores, y su rol es asegurar que el candidato no sea ni sobrevalorado ni infravalorado con respecto a comparaciones externas. El examinador externo debe ser

---

4. Ibid.

remunerado por la institución que lleva a cabo el examen. Todas las gestiones relativas a su nombramiento y remuneración deben ser hechas por la institución.

El/la supervisor/a en el panel de examinadores

Algunos programas de doctorado permiten que el/la supervisor/a sea parte del panel examinador. Esto le ofrece la oportunidad de explicar al resto del panel algo del esfuerzo que está detrás de la tesis y las razones de los enfoques tomados. Sin embargo, también debe haber equilibrio y objetividad. El trabajo debe ser evaluado por sus méritos académicos, y no según los sentimientos personales hacia el/la candidato/a. Puede existir la tentación de 'lograr que su estudiante pase' después de muchos años de trabajar duro juntos, pero si la tesis no tiene el mérito suficiente no debe ser aprobada. También existe la tentación de ponerse a la defensiva si el trabajo es criticado. El examen es una evaluación del trabajo propio de el/la estudiante, y el panel está evaluando eso y no a quien le supervisó.

Preguntas de reflexión

¿Cuáles son sus sentimientos acerca de que le pidan ser examinador/a?

¿Cómo ha velado por la imparcialidad y el juicio independiente cuando ha tenido que evaluar trabajos?

Si usted es examinador (lector) externo, ¿cuál es la mejor manera de orientarse sobre la institución en donde examinará y acerca del tema del candidato?

Preparación para examinar una tesis

Se debe seguir un proceso detallado antes de realizarse un examen de doctorado. Ya se debe tener en mente quiénes podrían ser los examinadores cuando el/la estudiante da su aviso formal a la institución de que presentará su tesis. Esto ahorrará largos retrasos luego de entregarse la tesis, mientras se definen los examinadores y se confirma su disponibilidad. Una vez que se entrega la tesis, estos deben ser formalmente contactados y nombrados.

Al decidir si acepta o no la invitación a ser examinador/a, tenga en cuenta lo siguiente:

i) La tesis, ¿es sobre un tema que es central para su propia área de investigación? Si no lo es, el/la candidato/a no obtendrá la mejor evaluación y retroalimentación. No es buena práctica examinar una tesis que está fuera de su área de conocimiento.

ii) ¿Tiene tiempo para emprender la tarea? Hacerlo correctamente, lleva bastante tiempo —tendrá que dedicarle por lo menos tres o cuatro días de su tiempo de trabajo. Además puede haber un examen oral al que deberá asistir, que se puede llevar a cabo a cierta distancia de su hogar. Hacerlo es un gran honor y es un servicio para la comunidad académica más amplia, pero hay que reconocer que requiere bastante tiempo, hasta una semana.

iii) ¿Puede llevar a cabo la evaluación en un tiempo razonable? Es injusto que los candidatos tengan que esperar por meses hasta que se encuentra una fecha adecuada. En campos que cambian rápidamente, la investigación puede perder vigencia pronto. Además, el período de espera puede ser extremadamente estresante, y el retraso en la realización del examen puede significar que él o ella no puede ocupar un puesto académico o regresar a su país de origen.

iv) ¿Hay alguna razón personal por la que usted no debe ser examinador/a, como una relación cercana con el/la estudiante?

Qué hacen los examinadores antes de un examen

¡Es vital leer la tesis con mucho cuidado! Esto puede parecer obvio, pero he estado en exámenes en donde los examinadores no parecían tener un conocimiento detallado de la tesis, lo cual es muy mala práctica. También es injusto e irrespetuoso hacia el/la estudiante.

Se necesitan al menos uno o dos días enteros para leer y evaluar de manera integral una tesis de 80.000 palabras (350 páginas), y se debe leer por lo menos dos veces.

El/la examinador/a debe tomar notas detalladas, anotar comentarios y preparar una lista de posibles preguntas. Puede ser necesario consultar materiales relevantes u otras tesis en la materia. Se debe revisar y comprobar un buen número de las referencias a otras fuentes. Habrá que producir un informe y hacer una lista de las correcciones que se recomendarán. Hacer este trabajo de valoración y evaluación de manera rigurosa toma tiempo, y el examen mismo también.

Normalmente, el informe inicial se produce independientemente de los demás examinadores. Este informe se presenta antes de reunirse con los demás examinadores, para asegurar un elemento de imparcialidad.

Programas sin examen oral

Los programas de doctorado en los que solo se examina la tesis no le dan a los examinadores ninguna oportunidad de reunirse con el candidato, y no es posible la discusión e interacción personal. Esto tiene una serie de ventajas. Reduce los costos y tiende a hacer que el proceso sea más rápido. Centra la evaluación en la tesis, que es el producto final del proceso de doctorado, y no se distrae con una evaluación personal del candidato, sino solo el trabajo que ha producido.

Sin embargo, al no tener la oportunidad de discutir seriamente la tesis con el/la candidato/a, no permite que los examinadores puedan determinar si es su propio trabajo. Tampoco permite que los examinadores sondeen con más profundidad y hagan preguntas sobre lo que está detrás de lo escrito. No permite que el/la candidato/a "defienda" o explique más su razonamiento en la tesis, ni que interactúe y discuta como par con colegas académicos.

La recomendación en *Principios y mejores prácticas* (de ICETE) es que siempre que sea posible se haga una defensa o un examen oral de la tesis.

Programas con examen oral

El examen oral, o *en vivo* permite a los examinadores determinar si la tesis es el propio trabajo del candidato, ya que pueden pedirle que responda a preguntas sobre la misma y que discuta seriamente lo que ha escrito. Ofrece una oportunidad para que los examinadores sondeen más profundamente para encontrar la historia detrás de lo que ha escrito, de su selección de métodos y de cómo funcionó el proceso, incluyendo los desafíos que surgieron durante el proceso de investigación y los cambios de enfoque que se necesitaron. Permite que el/la candidato/a "defienda" o explique más su razonamiento en la tesis, que aclare ciertos puntos y justifique su enfoque y sus resultados.

El examen oral permite una base más amplia que solo el texto para la toma de decisiones de los examinadores. Permite que el/la estudiante de doctorado participe en la conversación académica, como par, con colegas académicos, lo cual es un importante atributo como graduado/a del doctorado y marca su entrada en la comunidad académica de expertos y expertas en el campo.

El examen oral tiene algunas desventajas. Puede ser un tormento para los candidatos. Puede penalizarles si son personas nerviosas o si tienen poca habilidad para presentaciones orales. Si están siendo examinados en un idioma que no es el propio pueden estar en desventaja. El aspecto oral aporta un elemento personal, y por ende más subjetivo, al examen. A veces esto puede funcionar a favor del candidato y a veces en contra. Estos factores pueden atenuar que la evaluación se haga exclusivamente sobre la base del trabajo mismo, y es necesario darles su debido lugar.

Cuando la distancia es un factor limitante para los examinadores o los candidatos, es posible llevar a cabo un examen por teléfono o por medios electrónicos/videoconferencia, siempre y cuando el desempeño del candidato no se vea perjudicado por el uso de estos medios. Es ciertamente menos satisfactorio que una reunión en persona, pero a veces se hace necesario por cuestiones prácticas.

Preguntas de reflexión

¿Qué tipo o formato de examen se usa en su programa de doctorado?

¿Cuáles son sus fortalezas y sus debilidades?

El resto de este capítulo enfoca en el componente oral del examen, que es la forma más común y la que se recomienda en los *Principios y mejores prácticas* de ICETE. No obstante, los principios que sustentan el enfoque que se debe adoptar pueden aplicarse también a los programas que no tienen examen oral.

Tipos de exámenes orales

¿A puerta cerrada o foro abierto?

Incluso con los exámenes orales, hay gran variedad entre los diferentes programas de doctorados.

En algunas situaciones el examen es privado, y solo asisten el/la estudiante, los examinadores y un presidente.

A veces el/la supervisor/a participa en el examen; en otros sistemas solo puede observar.

En algunos contextos el examen es un evento muy público, al que asisten otros académicos, a veces otros estudiantes, familiares, amigos, y el público general.

Si le invitan a examinar una tesis, es importante entender qué tipo de formato se usará para el examen.

¿Celebración o inquisición? —El propósito del examen oral

Una vez más, hay variedad entre los sistemas. En algunos casos, gran parte del trabajo del examinador se ha hecho antes de realizarse el examen oral. La defensa oral se convierte entonces en una presentación pública del trabajo emprendido y la celebración del logro. El resultado no está en duda.

En otros contextos, aunque los examinadores han hecho mucho trabajo antes de la defensa oral, los examinadores no toman su decisión hasta que termine el examen oral. El examen es para eso precisamente, y durante el examen los examinadores deben quedar convencidos de que la tesis escrita alcanza los estándares doctorales, que es el trabajo propio del candidato, y que él o ella merece el reconocimiento doctoral. No deben anunciar sus conclusiones hasta que tengan claro que estas cuestiones se han demostrado.

Montaje del recinto para el examen oral

Si un examen oral va a ser parte del proceso, debe considerarse cuidadosamente la ubicación y el tamaño del recinto. Si el examen es un gran evento público, es necesario contar con una sala de conferencias o un salón de reuniones grande. Debe haber suficiente espacio para la audiencia. Los examinadores y el/la candidato/a necesitan ser vistos y escuchados claramente, sin que los espectadores abarroten el recinto. Se debe disponer de micrófonos y equipo de amplificación, y deben estar en buen estado.

Si el examen no es un evento público, un recinto más pequeño es más propicio —una sala de seminarios o una oficina. Las sillas se deben acomodar de una manera que facilite la comunicación, y se deben proveer mesas donde el/la estudiante y los examinadores pueden poner sus papeles y copias de la tesis.

Todos los lugares deben contar con cierto equipamiento considerado esencial: un reloj, agua para el/la estudiante y los examinadores, ventilación adecuada, y un mínimo de ruido exterior. Se debe pedir que todas y todos los participantes apague sus teléfonos celulares. Un rótulo de 'No entrar' en la puerta es un agregado vital, para impedir interrupciones innecesarias.

Y luego empieza el examen. . .

Caso de estudio

Ester ha estado dando cátedra por unos años desde que completó su doctorado. Ha supervisado algunas tesis de maestría y las ha evaluado. Su Decano Académico se le acerca para preguntarle si está dispuesta a servir en el panel examinador de uno de los estudiantes de doctorado en el departamento. El tema está en un campo en el que ella ha publicado dos artículos, así que es un área en el que tiene experiencia. Ester conoce bastante bien al estudiante, y han tomado café juntos un par de veces. Durante sus conversaciones ha surgido el tema de la tesis del estudiante, y Ester ha hecho algunas sugerencias sobre qué cosas leer. Ella siente que es un honor que se lo propongan, pero se pregunta si puede ser verdaderamente imparcial si ya conoce al estudiante. Además, es muy consciente de lo recientemente que ella misma fue estudiante de doctorado, y no se siente muy calificada para examinar a otros.

Preguntas

¿Debería aceptar la invitación?

Ya que conoce al estudiante, ¿es lo suficientemente neutral y objetiva en esta situación para asumir la supervisión?

¿Cómo le aconsejaría sobre sus sentimientos de insuficiencia para asumir esta tarea?

Para leer más

Lovitts, B. E. 'Making the Implicit Explicit', en *The Assessment of Doctoral Education: Emerging Criteria and New Models for Improving Outcomes*, editado por P. L. Maki y N. A. Borkowski, 163-187. Sterling, VA: Stylus, 2006.

Murray, R. *How to Survive Your Viva: Defending a Thesis in an Oral Examination*, 2nd edition. Maidenhead: Open University Press, 2009.

Pearce, L. *How to Examine a Thesis*. Maidenhead: Open University Press, 2005.

Tinkler, P. y C. Jackson. *The Doctoral Examination Process: A Handbook for Students, Examiners and Supervisors*. Maidenhead: Open University Press, 2004 —basado en el sistema del Reino Unido, pero con principios valiosos.

18

El examen de la tesis: el examen en sí

Porque es necesario que todos comparezcamos ante el tribunal de Cristo para que cada uno reciba lo que le corresponda, (2Co 5:10)

Examínense... pruébense a sí mismos... Espero que reconozcan que nosotros no hemos fracasado. (2Co 13:5-6)

La noción de enfrentar exámenes y evaluaciones es algo de lo que toda persona cristiana es consciente. Las Escrituras son claras: tendremos que rendir cuentas de cómo hemos vivido y de lo que hemos hecho. También sabemos que el juez de toda la tierra hará lo correcto, que será absolutamente imparcial en su evaluación, y que la justicia será aplicada con gracia en el juicio. Las y los examinadores de tesis necesitan aplicar los mismos principios. Ya sea que solo examinen la tesis, o que esta sea apoyada por una defensa oral, su tarea es la misma. Deben decidir si la tesis cumple o no los criterios de evaluación. El examen debe llevarse a cabo de manera rigurosa, imparcial, justa y compasiva. Una tesis nunca será perfecta.

El examen oral

En el inicio, los examinadores deben explicarle a el o la estudiante exactamente lo que sucederá en el examen. Él/ella necesita saber lo que está sucediendo y lo que se le va a pedir que haga. Los procedimientos de evaluación deben haberse aclarado de antemano, y deben ser aplicados de manera rigurosa, justa y coherente. Los miembros externos de un panel también necesitan entender exactamente cuáles son los procedimientos en la institución. A menudo el examen es presidido por un miembro independiente de la facultad académica, a fin de asegurar el debido proceso.

Duración

No hay una duración fija para los exámenes orales. Un examen de menos de una hora no da mucho tiempo para un análisis profundo. Si dura más de tres horas puede convertirse en un tormento para el/la estudiante, y la mayor parte de las deliberaciones deberían haberse hecho antes de que transcurra ese tiempo. Una duración de alrededor de dos horas es más normal.

Un/a examinador/a debe tener en cuenta que entre la reunión preparatoria, el examen en sí, las discusiones y la redacción posterior del informe, el proceso completo le tomará al menos medio día. Esto se suma a los varios días que ya ha dedicado a leer y evaluar la tesis.

Preguntas

Los examinadores deben reunirse antes del inicio del examen para discutir la lista de preguntas que les gustaría que el/la candidato/a responda, y asignarlas a los diferentes miembros del panel. Debe haber una variedad de preguntas que abarquen temas de toda la tesis, y ningún examinador debe dominar la discusión, aunque el examinador externo debe tener un rol prominente.

Preguntas de reflexión

¿Cuál sería una buena pregunta para 'romper el hielo' al comienzo de un examen oral?

¿Qué tipo de preguntas se pueden usar para explorar si el/la candidato/a ha identificado correctamente una pregunta o problema que sustenta o está detrás de la tesis?

¿Qué preguntaría para que él o ella hable de su metodología?

¿Qué hace si él o ella no puede responder a una de sus preguntas (que usted piensa que debería poder responder)?

¿Qué tipo de preguntas le puede hacer para confirmar que su trabajo es propio?

¿Qué preguntas se pueden usar para explorar si una tesis es una "contribución original al conocimiento"?

Cuestiones clave en la sesión de preguntas

- Es importante dar lugar a que el/la candidato/a exprese el corazón de la tesis en sus propias palabras. Sin embargo, es importante insistir que se enfoque en responder a las preguntas.
- Si él o ella habla largo y tendido sin responder a una pregunta, se le debe advertir al respecto.
- El/la estudiante debe tener la oportunidad de "defender" la tesis.
- Las preguntas deben ser claras, precisas y agudas (perspicaces), pero no deben ser hostiles. El propósito es desarrollar una discusión académica respetuosa a nivel de pares.
- Se debe buscar que él/ella piense, y las preguntas deben ser retadoras, pero no es justo someterle a una implacable 'inquisición'.
- La persona que preside el examen tiene un rol importante. Debe intervenir si siente que el tono de la discusión es contraproducente o si el trato le parece injusto.

La evaluación de la tesis

La pregunta clave que se deben hacer los examinadores es, ¿qué cualidades de nivel de doctorado deben haberse demostrado en la tesis a fin de considerarla sostenida, para así poder aprobarla?

Esto aplica si se examina solo el texto de la tesis o si hay un examen oral. En el contexto de un examen de doctorado en una institución teológica evangélica, los *Estándares de Beirut de ICETE*[1] establecen las cualidades que un candidato de doctorado debe demostrar. Será útil usar estas como una especie de lista de control para evaluar los logros del candidato.

Estas habilidades son:

> **Estándar de Beirut 1: Comprensión integral,** *[haber] demostrado: un entendimiento amplio y sistemático de un campo de estudio que es relevante para la comunidad de fe cristiana; y el dominio de las habilidades y los métodos de investigación adecuados para ese campo de estudio.*

Los examinadores deben estar convencidos de que el/la estudiante tiene un entendimiento "profundo y sistemático". ¿Qué preguntas se pueden usar para que demuestre que su comprensión de su campo de investigación responde a este criterio?

¿Qué busca un examinador en una tesis que demuestre que el/la estudiante domina las habilidades y métodos de investigación apropiados para ese campo?

---

1. 'Estándares de Beirut,' en *Principios y mejores prácticas*, ed. I. Shaw.

En un contexto evangélico, es apropiado explorar la relevancia de la investigación y sus conclusiones para la comunidad de fe cristiana. ¿Qué preguntas se pueden usar para esto?

Estándar de Beirut 2: Habilidades críticas, ejercidas en el marco de la fe, *demostradas por: la capacidad para el análisis crítico, la evaluación independiente de fuentes primarias y secundarias, y la síntesis de ideas nuevas e interconectadas empleando argumentaciones coherentes; y el compromiso a practicar dichas habilidades sobre la base de la fidelidad bíblica a Jesucristo y su iglesia.*

¿Cómo puede evaluar el nivel de estas habilidades académicas de análisis crítico, evaluación independiente, síntesis y argumentación coherente?

¿Qué aspectos del trabajo de un/a candidato/a indican que es capaz de escribir con rigor e integridad académica, y que tiene la habilidad de hacerlo de manera sostenida dentro de su perspectiva de fe?

Estándar de Beirut 3: Investigación seria con integridad, *[habiendo] demostrado la capacidad de concebir, diseñar e implementar un proyecto sustancial de investigación y hacerlo con integridad cristiana y académica, dando como resultado una tesis sostenida y coherente.*

Esto lleva al examinador al corazón de la tarea de evaluar las capacidades de investigación de un candidato y los métodos que ha utilizado. La capacidad de "concebir" un proyecto, y de luego llevarlo a su término, es fundamental para su vida futura como docente e investigador académico. El examinador debe juzgar qué tan efectivamente lo ha hecho.

¿Son adecuados los métodos de investigación? ¿se aplican de forma coherente? El/la estudiante debe mostrar la capacidad de formular juicios informados en campos complejos. En esencia, la tesis doctoral tiene que demostrar que el/la estudiante se ha convertido en experto/a en su campo, con la aceptación de sus pares. Después de obtener un doctorado debe ser capaz de continuar y emprender su propia investigación de una forma independiente, autogestionada y autosostenida, sin el apoyo de un supervisor. La capacidad de desarrollar y adaptar la investigación para tomar en cuenta evidencias o resultados inesperados es la insignia de la investigación académica.

La palabra "integridad" pone de relieve la necesidad de coherencia entre la erudición y la profesión cristiana. La falta de coherencia, como cuando se detecta el plagio o si las fuentes no han sido manejadas de manera imparcial o transparente, es un fracaso de la integridad cristiana y de la erudición. Los examinadores deben explorar esta área cuidadosamente en todos los casos.

¿Qué tipo de preguntas en el examen oral permiten explorar estas áreas?

Estándar de Beirut 4: Contribución creativa y original, *demostrada por haber producido, como resultado de tal investigación disciplinada, una contribución que extiende las fronteras del conocimiento, o desarrolla nuevas perspectivas para la articulación y la relevancia contextual de la tradición cristiana, algunas de los cuales ameritan ser publicadas a nivel nacional o internacional en revistas arbitradas.*

La tesis necesita demostrar que el/la candidato/a tiene muy buenas habilidades para la "creación e interpretación" de conocimientos. Esto nos lleva al área de "originalidad", que es el sello distintivo de una tesis doctoral.

Los resultados de la investigación, ¿son producto del trabajo propio de él o ella? Los *Estándares* se refieren a extender "las fronteras del conocimiento" pero también hablan de "desarrollar nuevas perspectivas". El campo de investigación no necesita ser completamente nuevo. De hecho, gran parte de las áreas de ciencias bíblicas y teología ya han sido bien investigadas. Sin embargo, la posibilidad de que la contribución implique el desarrollo de "nuevas perspectivas" permite considerar como originales las nuevas interpretaciones de material existente.

También se señala un punto de referencia externo: el trabajo debe ameritar su publicación "a nivel nacional o internacional en revistas arbitradas". Si la tesis sirve como rito de pasaje del investigador, este es el estándar aceptado para su entrada a la comunidad académica, y el nivel al cual se le debe considerar capaz de trabajar de aquí en adelante. Al final del examen, los examinadores a menudo recomendarán maneras en las que se podría publicar la tesis o parte de ella.

Los examinadores deben valorar que el trabajo sea de nivel "D" —nivel académico de doctorado— y que esté a la vanguardia de la disciplina académica. Esta es la razón por la que un panel examinador debe incluir examinadores cualificados que sean ellos mismos investigadores activos. Por medio del examen, los guardianes de la disciplina deben determinar si el/la estudiante ha alcanzado el nivel apropiado para llevar a cabo investigaciones de manera independiente y estar calificado/a para supervisar a otros a nivel de doctorado.

Estándar de Beirut 5: Relevancia contextual *evidenciada —durante su programa de doctorado y en las expectativas para su futuro potencial— por su capacidad de interacción crítica y bíblicamente informada con las realidades de su contexto cultural.*

Esto es particularmente importante para investigaciones llevadas a cabo en un contexto teológico evangélico. El/la candidato/a debe poder expresar la razón por la que ha llevado a cabo su investigación y su posible relevancia para el contexto con el cual ha tratado, o el ámbito en el cual trabajará.

Para repetir, los examinadores en instituciones evangélicas están buscando que haya integración entre la capacidad académica y las bases escriturales, y que está se evidencie en la "interacción crítica y bíblicamente informada" con su contexto.

> **Estándar de Beirut 6: Habilidad comunicativa,** *evidenciada por su capacidad de comunicar e interactuar en torno a su área de especialización con audiencias de su mismo nivel académico y, donde y cuando corresponda, con no especialistas en comunidades cristianas locales y en la sociedad en general, mediante modalidades culturalmente relevantes, por ejemplo a través de la enseñanza, la predicación o la escritura, e incluyendo su lengua materna.*

Los examinadores deben determinar si el/la candidato/a tiene la capacidad de comunicar ideas a audiencias de su mismo nivel académico y audiencias no especializadas. La audiencia académica obviamente se refiere a los mismos examinadores, aunque el/la estudiante también puede escoger dedicarse a una carrera de docencia, por lo que debe mostrar las capacidades comunicativas conducentes a ello.

El requisito de evidenciar la capacidad de comunicación con audiencias de no especialistas tiene como objetivo asegurar que los resultados de la investigación se difundan lo más ampliamente posible, en vez de limitarse a los ámbitos más restringidos de la comunidad académica. Estas ideas, ¿cómo cambiarán o confirmarán el conocimiento y la reflexión en el contexto más amplio, en las iglesias o entre los líderes cristianos, además de en la disciplina académica. Una forma de evaluar esta habilidad es pidiéndole a él o ella que describa cómo le explicaría su trabajo a alguien que no es especialista, alguien de su iglesia o a una persona en un autobús. Esto no solo demuestra las habilidades básicas de comunicación, también revela algo mucho más profundo. Como supuestamente dijo Albert Einstein, 'Si no puedes explicar algo de forma sencilla, es que no lo has entendido bien'. Para explicar algo de forma sencilla hace falta entenderlo profundamente.

Obviamente es difícil evaluar la capacidad de enseñar o predicar durante un examen de dos o tres horas. Estos aspectos del desarrollo de un/a estudiante deben, en lo posible, ser evaluados por otros medios a lo largo de su programa de estudio, y deben ser parte del desarrollo integral de habilidades que pretende el programa —como se describe en el capítulo 15.

> **Estándar de Beirut 7: Impacto misional,** *habiendo demostrado su compromiso a utilizar el fruto de sus estudios de doctorado, las habilidades aprendidas y las oportunidades que brinda, para promover el reino de Dios y prosperar la misión de la iglesia (tanto local como global) mediante un servicio transformador según el modelo de Jesucristo y para la gloria de Dios.*

Esto aborda el área de los resultados a largo plazo y considera preguntas acerca de qué habilidades ha desarrollado el/la estudiante durante sus estudios de doctorado.

- ¿Muestran indicios de la capacidad de relacionar las habilidades académicas que ha desarrollado con un propósito misional, y promover el reino de Dios?
- ¿Es publicable el proyecto? ¿Él o ella ha reflexionado sobre cómo su trabajo prosperará la misión de la iglesia?
- Los materiales producidos, ¿son capaces de abrir una discusión más amplia en torno a temas diferentes pero relacionados?
- ¿Él o ella entiende las implicaciones de su investigación para este y otros campos relacionados, y para sus contextos eclesiales?
- ¿Qué investigación futura generará el proyecto, y cómo podría eso promover el reino de Dios? Es bueno que, durante un examen oral, los examinadores exploren estas cuestiones potenciales —lo que está 'debajo del iceberg'. ¿El/la candidato/a tiene mucho más material de investigación que no ha usado? Si es así, ¿cómo lo va a usar en nuevos proyectos de investigación o escritura?
- ¿Qué potencial muestra como futuro/a investigador/a?
- ¿Muestra evidencia de habilidades docentes? Con el tiempo el/la estudiante puede convertirse en maestro/a de otros, o supervisor/a de estudiantes de doctorado, usando las habilidades que ha adquirido. A veces se pide a los examinadores que sirvan de árbitros cuando estudiantes que examinaron se presentan para un puesto de trabajo, o se les pide una recomendación laboral para un puesto afín, por lo que es bueno evaluar cómo comunican conceptos e información clave durante el proceso de examen.

El resultado

Los Estándares de Beirut abarcan el conjunto de logros que deben demostrarse en la tesis doctoral y el examen. Habrá alguna variación en las habilidades demostradas según estos Estándares clave, y lo que los examinadores están buscando es un buen 'promedio' general. Una tesis puede demostrar excelencia en todos los Estándares, pero puede no ser comunicada muy bien durante la defensa oral. Es poco probable que un candidato así sea desaprobado. Por otro lado, si una tesis es brillantemente comunicada, pero es débil según todos los demás Estándares, no sería aprobada, y requeriría una revisión importante.

Entonces, ¿cuáles son los posibles resultados?

En general los examinadores disponen de una gama de resultados académicos, aunque puede variar según la institución. Además algunos sistemas tienen un simple aprobado o desaprobado sin niveles adicionales estipulados, otros tienen un rango de grados dentro del aprobado, como *Cum Laudae* o *Magna Cum Laudae*.

Dependiendo del sistema, estos son algunos de los posibles resultados:

- Tesis aprobada (a veces con una calificación) y otorgamiento directo del título.
- Aprobación pendiente de correcciones menores.
- Aprobación pendiente de correcciones mayores y reescritura (sin reexaminación).
- Correcciones mayores, con nueva entrega y un segundo examen oral.
- Otorgamiento de un título de menor grado (por ej., MPhil).
- No se otorga un título.

El resultado se debe comunicar de manera clara y eficiente al estudiante, junto con las explicaciones adecuadas.

Normalmente, cuando el resultado ha de ser confirmado por un comité de titulación superior dentro de la institución, cualquier decisión comunicada por el panel examinador es solo provisional. Por lo general, los examinadores solo pueden indicar que están recomendando al candidato para cierto título. Usualmente el título es conferido formalmente por el máximo órgano académico de la institución, o por un organismo externo de validación.

Las instituciones deben disponer de políticas claras sobre la relación entre el panel examinador y el órgano superior que confirma la titulación, y de un reglamento para resolver disputas. Las instituciones deben asegurarse que estos procesos operen sin contratiempos, y que las decisiones se comuniquen prontamente al candidato.

Comunicación de los resultados al estudiante y su supervisor

Debido a la considerable energía intelectual y emocional que el/la candidato/a ha invertido en el examen oral, puede resultarle difícil escuchar y entender completamente el resultado que se le comunica al final del examen. El resultado obtenido y lo que significa (especialmente si se necesitan más revisiones o correcciones) se le debe explicar cuidadosamente.

La retroalimentación oral debe ir seguida de comentarios escritos e instrucciones detalladas enviadas al candidato/a unos pocos días después del examen para permitir que él o ella emprenda rápidamente las revisiones.

Se debe alentarles a ver que las correcciones y enmiendas que reciben tienen como propósito asegurar que su trabajo se ajusta al nivel y a los criterios académicos. La tesis tendrá que ocupar su lugar en la literatura académica al nivel adecuado, y se debe enfatizar que la copia final y permanente de la tesis que se presenta después de la revisión tendrá que estar disponible para ser revisada. Las/los estudiantes querrán asegurarse de que sea de la más alta calidad posible.

Por lo general, las/los candidatos reciben el apoyo de su supervisor y/o del presidente del Comité de Disertación para el proceso de hacer las revisiones necesarias. Es importante que todas las correcciones y revisiones estipuladas por los examinadores se completen antes de que se vuelva a considerar la aprobación de la tesis. Usualmente, un miembro del panel de examinadores de la institución del candidato tiene esta responsabilidad, pero si el examinador externo hace recomendaciones especiales él o ella puede hacerse cargo de asegurar que sean implementadas. Si la tesis se va a publicar, se debe realizar una revisión minuciosa de la ortografía y la gramática antes de dar el permiso para su publicación.

La siguiente lista enumera los asuntos clave que deben considerar los examinadores:

i) ¿La tesis hace una contribución original y distintiva al conocimiento?
   - ¿El/la candidato/a es ahora capaz de realizar investigaciones independientes?

ii) ¿El/la candidato/a tiene un buen conocimiento del campo?
   - ¿La bibliografía y las referencias reflejan el estado actual de la erudición?
   - ¿Él/ella entiende el alcance y los límites de su contribución?
   - ¿Él/ella ha realmente demostrado un dominio de la literatura clave y mostrado dónde en ella cabe su contribución?
   - ¿Él/ella ha hecho conexiones entre su revisión de la literatura y el resto de su trabajo —mostrando cómo su estudio surge de problemas o lagunas en el debate académico más amplio?
   - ¿Él/ella hace conexiones entre las conclusiones de su investigación y la literatura académica clave a lo largo de toda su tesis —mostrando cómo su trabajo interviene en el debate o cambia el campo?

iii) ¿La tesis es un trabajo original?
   - ¿El/la estudiante ha demostrado que hizo el trabajo?
   - ¿Él/ella escribió toda la tesis?
   - ¿Qué hará si sospecha que parte del contenido ha sido plagiado?
   - ¿El/la candidato/a es consciente de su propio posicionamiento respecto al tema de la investigación?
   - ¿De qué manera se demuestra la "originalidad" en el contenido, los métodos, los resultados y las propuestas para futuras investigaciones?

iv) ¿Se han utilizado y entendido los métodos apropiados?
   - ¿Se han respetado los procedimientos adecuados en materia de ética investigativa?
   - ¿El/la estudiante es consciente de los límites de confiabilidad de estos métodos?
   - ¿Son válidos estos métodos para esta investigación?

- ¿Cuáles fueron los criterios para la selección de los textos y las fuentes usadas?
- ¿Se pueden extrapolar las conclusiones apropiadas usando estos métodos?

v) ¿El argumento de la tesis sigue un hilo claro y lógico?
- ¿Los capítulos principales se desarrollan a partir de la introducción y se conectan con la revisión de la literatura?
- ¿Los capítulos se conectan entre sí y siguen una secuencia apropiada?
- ¿En cada capítulo se establecen las direcciones clave al principio y se dan las conclusiones al final?
- La conclusión, ¿se desarrolla sobre la base de la tesis? ¿Reune en un mismo lugar los diferentes aspectos del debate que se consideran en cada capítulo? ¿Responde a las preguntas de investigación planteadas en la introducción?
- ¿La conclusión concluye el trabajo, o es material nuevo y un nuevo argumento que se introducen de repente y van en otras direcciones?
- ¿Todo lo que está en la conclusión pertenece ahí?

vi) ¿El estilo literario y el estándar de presentación son adecuados para una tesis doctoral que se debe poder publicar a nivel accadémico internacional?

vii) ¿Toda o parte de la tesis merece ser publicada?

viii) ¿El/la candidato/a explicó y presentó bien su trabajo en el examen oral?
- ¿Él/ella es capaz de defender el trabajo y la tesis con confianza en discusión con sus pares académicos?

Áreas problemáticas

Las instituciones deben disponer de políticas claras sobre la relación entre el panel examinador y el órgano superior que confirma la titulación, y de un reglamento para resolver disputas.[2]

Decisiones empatadas

Ya que los examinadores traen un elemento de subjetividad al proceso de examen, no siempre logran ponerse de acuerdo en un resultado. Cuando los examinadores no logran llegar a una decisión, el reglamento institucional debe indicar el procedimiento a seguir.

¿Es posible un veredicto por mayoría? ¿Qué sucede si el examinador externo está en la minoría? ¿Él o ella tiene voz y voto?

---

2. Shaw, *Principios y mejores prácticas*, Sección 13, f.

En algunas instituciones, en caso de que los examinadores no pueden acordar una decisión, se procede a constituir un nuevo panel de examinadores para reexaminar la tesis.

El/la estudiante se queja del resultado

Una vez más, los reglamentos institucionales deben ofrecer orientación clara sobre los motivos por los que él o ella puede apelar la decisión, y sobre el proceso correcto a seguir para todos los casos.

La presencia (en el panel de examinadores) de un presidente independiente puede ayudar a aliviar los posibles motivos de algunas quejas. Como presidente es su deber asegurar que el/la candidato/a recibe un trato imparcial y que se sigue el proceso apropiado. También debe asegurar la redacción y el procesamiento correcto de los registros e informes, que inicialmente son elaborados independientemente por los examinadores.

Por lo general, el/la estudiante no puede quejarse de una supervisión inadecuada —como causa de su fracaso académico— después de que ha sido examinada la tesis. Ese tipo de queja debe presentarse antes del examen, y debe haber lineamientos establecidos para responder de manera adecuada. La institución necesita comunicar dichos lineamientos a sus estudiantes regularmente. Algunos estudiantes pueden dudar de quejarse por temor a posibles consecuencias que podrían afectar su continuidad en el programa y su graduación. Este es un asunto importante que hay que atender cuidadosamente y que debe ser explicado claramente a las y los estudiantes. Es importante que tengan la mejor experiencia posible a lo largo de todo su programa, en vez de que los problemas se ventilen al final del período de estudio cuando ya es demasiado tarde y han afectado negativamente el resultado. La existencia de mecanismos de retroalimentación regulares y robustos también debería evitar que los problemas pasen desapercibidos.

Hacia el futuro

Es habitual que se pida a los examinadores que apoyen al estudiante en el desarrollo de su futura carrera académica. Se les puede pedir que brinden referencias para puestos laborales. Suelen recomendar cómo se podría publicar una tesis. Todo esto es apropiado una vez que haya terminado el examen y que la aprobación de la tesis haya sido confirmada. En cierto sentido, el trabajo de los examinadores nunca está completo, pero es un gran privilegio darle la bienvenida y ayudar al tenedor o la tenedora de un nuevo doctorado a integrarse a la comunidad académica, y ver con interés su desarrollo como investigador/a erudito/a. ¡Algún día incluso puede pedirle que examine a uno de sus propios estudiantes de doctorado!

Preguntas de reflexión

Si los exámenes de este tipo son algo nuevo para usted, ¿cuáles son los tres datos más importantes que necesita pedir de la institución antes de examinar una tesis de doctorado?

¿A quién se lo puede preguntar?

Si usted tiene experiencia como examinador/a, ¿qué tres lecciones quisiera compartir con sus colegas académicos menos experimentados sobre el proceso del examen de doctorado?

Caso de estudio

Juan es un examinador novato. La primera tesis para la cual forma parte del panel examinador es una que le interesa, y él ha trabajado en este campo, Sin embargo, siente que la tesis es bastante débil en áreas clave de conocimiento y método, y espera que otros examinadores estén de acuerdo, Se sorprende al escuchar que muchos de los comentarios de los demás panelistas son positivos, y que no ven ningún problema que impida aprobar la tesis. El examinador externo también tiene una evaluación positiva, aunque Juan se da cuenta que la tesis realmente no está en su área principal de conocimiento.

Preguntas

¿Qué cuestiones institucionales plantea este asunto?

¿Qué debe hacer Juan?

¿Qué hace usted si no está de acuerdo con los demás examinadores en un examen de doctorado?

Para leer más

Lovitts, B. E. 'Making the Implicit Explicit', en *The Assessment of Doctoral Education: Emerging Criteria and New Models for Improving Outcomes*, editado por P. L. Maki y N. A. Borkowski, 163-187. Sterling, VA: Stylus, 2006.

Pearce, L. *How to Examine a Thesis*. Maidenhead: Open University Press, 2005.

Tinkler, P. y C. Jackson. *The Doctoral Examination Process: A Handbook for Students, Examiners and Supervisors*. Maidenhead: Open University Press, 2004.

Conclusión

Este manual ha tratado de demostrar que la supervisión de estudiantes de doctorado es un gran privilegio, una gran responsabilidad y ademas una oportunidad muy significativa para invertir en la formación de algunos de los líderes cristianos más estratégicos del presente y del futuro. Es, sin duda, un proceso de aprendizaje. Trabajar con algunos/as estudiantes de doctorado demuestra ser una tremenda bendición, pero en otros casos puede decepcionarnos porque no logran todo lo que esperábamos. Sin embargo, es mejor no juzgar el valor de la inversión de tiempo por la experiencia de supervisar a solo uno o dos estudiantes, sino tomar una perspectiva más a largo plazo.

Cada estudiante que supervisa le requerirá una inversión de varios cientos de horas de trabajo. Sin embargo, en términos de "valor agregado", la formación de estudiantes de doctorado tiene una estimación muy alta. La supervisión doctoral tiene que ver con facilitar la extensión del conocimiento y de la conciencia bíblica y teológica, y con trabajar en el desarrollo de respuestas de vanguardia a algunos de los temas más importantes que actualmente enfrenta la iglesia. También implica asegurar que las y los estudiantes desarrollan habilidades de investigación y escritura de acuerdo a los más altos estándares, lo cual beneficiará a la iglesia por muchos años. Las y los estudiantes de doctorado a menudo se convierten en educadores teológicos. Invertir tiempo en su formación implica trabajar con quienes entrenarán a futuras y futuros predicadores, maestros y líderes cristianos.

La supervisión de estudiantes de doctorado también tiene implicaciones mucho más allá del ámbito local. En el actual contexto globalizado, el doctorado nunca puede ser un programa académico aislado y local. A través de su trabajo con estudiantes de doctorado, las y los supervisores están ayudando a fomentar la cooperación internacional y el trabajo colaborativo, lo cual puede derribar barreras y ser una fuerza que robustece las alianzas en la educación teológica a nivel global. Como tal, es un recurso vital tanto para la iglesia local como para la global.

Este manual ha fomentado la reflexión sobre la práctica, sirviendo para mejorar el buen trabajo que ya se está realizando y promoviendo cambio donde se necesita. Las y los supervisores deben estar siempre abiertos a nuevos aprendizajes y enfoques, a fin de responder a las necesidades de sus estudiantes y poder adaptarse a las circunstancias y oportunidades cambiantes. Este manual ha pretendido aplicar una serie de principios clave, también descritos en el libro *Principios y mejores prácticas,* de ICETE, al trabajo de las y los supervisores evangélicos.

- La supervisión en contextos teológicos evangélicos implica más que desarrollar habilidades académicas. También requiere invertir en la formación espiritual de las y los supervisados. En cómo se lleva a cabo la supervisión y en lo que se espera de las y los estudiantes, debe haber una estrecha integración entre la formación académica y la formación espiritual. La formación espiritual deseada se basa en la convicción de que la Biblia es fundacional para la fe y la práctica. Las y los supervisores de doctorado deben fomentar una integración bíblicamente informada de la erudición y la vida. Todos los aspectos de la relación de supervisión deben reflejar los más altos estándares de integridad ética y moral, y demostrar coherencia en la búsqueda de la excelencia académica y espiritual.
- Las y los supervisores de doctorado en disciplinas teológicas deben tener un abordaje misional de su labor. Sus estudiantes de doctorado necesitan ser equipados con una amplitud de conocimiento, entendimiento y habilidades de pensamiento crítico que les preparará para ser las y los futuros líderes de la educación teológic, y para hacerlo con una perspectiva global. El propósito misional de la educación doctoral en las disciplinas teológicas significa que el doctorado no debe ser visto como un fin en sí mismo, sino como una manera de servir a la iglesia mediante la formación de formadores —de aquellas personas que prepararán la próxima generación de predicadores, pastores, maestros y líderes cristianos. Las habilidades que se desarrollan a través de la educación doctoral también deben ser aquellas que ayuden a sostener un futuro ministerio de docencia, investigación y escritura en la educación y el liderazgo teológico.
- Las y los supervisores de doctorado deben esforzarse por vencer la desconexión entre la academia y la iglesia local, especialmente cuando ocurre en los niveles más altos de estudio. Deben modelar el compromiso activo con la iglesia local como expresión del cuerpo de Cristo, y fomentar un compromiso similar en sus estudiantes.
- Los estudios de doctorado se deben realizar en comunidad. Tanto las y los supervisores como sus estudiantes deben desempeñar roles plenos y activos en las dimensiones espirituales y académicas de una comunidad. La formación ofrecida también debe facilitar la colaboración con hermanas y hermanos en Cristo de la comunidad académica global, construyendo redes y asociaciones internacionales que fortalezcan el trabajo de la educación teológica como un aspecto de la misión de Dios.
- Las y los supervisores de doctorado deben fomentar investigaciones que sean contextualmente relevantes. Debe haber un compromiso de parte de las y los supervisores de servir a la iglesia mediante el apoyo a estudiantes de doctorado que no solo son excelentes en lo académico, sino que también tienen

las habilidades que más se necesitan en su contexto y que abordan temas que apuntan a resolver los desafíos teológicos, sociales y misiológicos que enfrenta la iglesia.

- Las y los supervisores de doctorado deben asegurarse de que sus estudiantes sean plenamente capaces de participar en el discurso académico global y de interactuar con la naturaleza global de la iglesia. Deben animar a sus estudiantes a participar plenamente en la conversación teológica global y, cuando sea posible, pasar parte de su tiempo de estudio en otro contexto u otra cultura. Las y los supervisores también deben hacer su parte en la promoción y la práctica de la educación teológica en diversos contextos y culturas. Por tanto, deben comprometerse a capacitar a las y los "teólogos del mundo", quienes contribuyen a la iglesia mundial y comprenden la dinámica global y las implicaciones locales de su erudición. También deben traer las riquezas de ese contexto local a la conversación teológica global.

  Esta alianza debe estar orientada a reducir la "fuga de cerebros" de las mejores mentes teológicas del Mundo Mayoritario hacia Occidente, e intencionalmente trabajar para desafiar la desigualdad en la distribución global de recursos teológicos. Esto implica un compromiso con compartir información, datos y recursos.

  Las y los supervisores de doctorado deben desempeñar un rol activo en la formación de una cultura investigativa y un entorno institucional que apoya el desarrollo y el florecimiento de las y los estudiantes de doctorado. Esto implica facilitar que sus estudiantes puedan acceder a los mejores recursos académicos. También implica crear una cultura de ideas donde la creatividad del pensamiento y la reflexión pueda ser nutrida de una manera piadosa, articulada con claridad, examinada a la luz de las Escrituras, evaluada según lo mejor de la erudición contemporánea y aplicada de manera relevante.

- Las y los supervisores deben ser modelos de buenas prácticas en el trabajo en equipo y en la colaboración con otros supervisores y supervisoras. Si bien han de mantener un fuerte énfasis en sus disciplinas principales, deben mostrarse abiertos a emplear enfoques interdisciplinarios cuando sirven a los proyectos de sus estudiantes.
- Las y los supervisores de doctorado evangélicos deben comprometerse a aplicar normas internacionales de excelencia y gestión de calidad en la educación doctoral. Deben participar plenamente en los debates en torno a la educación teológica, a fin de hacer su parte para lograr un consenso internacional sobre lo que es la educación doctoral, las competencias que requiere y los resultados

que se esperan. Las y los supervisores deben modelar la excelencia académica e inculcarla en las y los estudiantes que supervisan.
- Las y los supervisores de doctorado deben promover estructuras académicas que funcionan bien. Debe haber un compromiso de su parte por lograr fuertes indicadores de eficacia, como altas tasas de finalización, tiempos de finalización cortos, altos niveles de empleabilidad y compromiso con el servicio a la iglesia.
- Cuando sirven como examinadores, las y los supervisores deben asegurar que la evaluación y examinación de las/los candidatos de doctorado sea rigurosa y apropiada para el nivel más alto de trabajo académico.

Mi oración es que la educación teológica evangélica global sea enriquecida a través de lectoras y lectores de este manual que toman en cuenta y aplican estos principios clave y la variedad de otros consejos y sugerencias que contiene.

¡Espero con anticipación poder leer en los próximos años acerca de las contribuciones clave al discurso teológico evangélico global que producirán sus estudiantes!

Apéndice 1

Formulario de retroalimentación anual de estudiantes de doctorado

Fecha _____

1. Las reuniones de supervisión con mi principal supervisor/presidente del Comité de Disertación han sido lo suficientemente frecuentes.

1	2	3	4	5

Muy de Acuerdo   Muy en Desacuerdo

¿Con qué frecuencia se ha reunido o ha tenido contacto con su supervisor/a?

Comente sobre la idoneidad de esta frecuencia.

2. Mi principal supervisor/presidente del Comité ha estado disponible para contactarle informalmente fuera de las reuniones formales de supervisión.

1	2	3	4	5

Muy de Acuerdo   Muy en Desacuerdo

Comentarios:

3. El apoyo y los consejos que he recibido de mi principal supervisor/presidente del Comité de Disertación han sido satisfactorio.

1	2	3	4	5

Muy de Acuerdo   Muy en Desacuerdo

Comentarios:

4. El apoyo y los consejos que he recibido de mi segundo supervisor/lector han sido satisfactorio.

1	2	3	4	5

Muy de Acuerdo   Muy en Desacuerdo

¿Con qué frecuencia se ha reunido con su segundo supervisor/lector?

Comente sobre la idoneidad de esta frecuencia.

Otros comentarios.

5. El programa de inducción y capacitación continua para investigadores/as de posgrado ha sido satisfactorio.

1	2	3	4	5

Muy de Acuerdo   Muy en Desacuerdo

¿Qué oportunidades se ofrecieron?

¿Cuáles aprovechó?

Comentarios:

6. El apoyo administrativo durante los procesos de aplicación, matrícula y adecuación financiera ha sido satisfactorio.

1	2	3	4	5

Muy de Acuerdo   Muy en Desacuerdo

Comentarios:

7. La biblioteca ha provisto los recursos adecuados para la investigación de posgrado, incluyendo el acceso a otras instituciones cuando ha sido apropiado.

1	2	3	4	5

Muy de Acuerdo   Muy en Desacuerdo

Comentarios:

8. El Seminario de Investigación ha resultado útil para fomentar una comunidad de investigación y estimular la reflexión.

1	2	3	4	5

Muy de Acuerdo   Muy en Desacuerdo

Comentarios:

9. Si ha presentado un trabajo en el Seminario de Investigación, ¿cómo le ayudó a desarrollar sus habilidades de investigación y reflexión? (Si no, escriba "No corresponde")

1	2	3	4	5

Muy de Acuerdo   Muy en Desacuerdo

Comentarios:

10. El programa de doctorado ha provisto oportunidades adecuadas para la integración con la vida comunitaria.

1	2	3	4	5

Muy de Acuerdo — Muy en Desacuerdo

Comentarios:

11. Mis supervisores/as y la institución han ofrecido apoyo y oportunidades adecuadas para mi cuidado pastoral y la formación espiritual.

1	2	3	4	5

Muy de Acuerdo — Muy en Desacuerdo

Comentarios:

12. La institución ha provisto un ambiente de aprendizaje apropiado para la investigación, y el desarrollo de habilidades para mi futuro ministerio en la docencia y la escritura académica.

1	2	3	4	5

Muy de Acuerdo — Muy en Desacuerdo

Comentarios:

13. Estoy generalmente satisfecho/a con la experiencia de investigación que se me ha provisto.

1	2	3	4	5

Muy de Acuerdo — Muy en Desacuerdo

Comentarios:

A continuación, por favor agregue otras observaciones que tenga sobre cómo la institución puede mejorar o desarrollar más su apoyo a estudiantes de posgrado.

Apéndice 2

Formulario de retroalimentación estudiantil al finalizar el doctorado

Instrucciones: Por favor, responda a las siguientes preguntas y comparta con nosotros lo mejor que pueda su apreciación y evaluación de su experiencia como estudiante de tesis en nuestro programa de doctorado. Sus respuestas a estas preguntas son anónimas; por lo tanto, no incluya ninguna información en sus respuestas que le identifique a usted o al tema de su disertación. ¡Gracias por su ayuda con esta encuesta!

Disponibilidad de Supervisores y Lectores

Dado que los miembros de la facultad tienen una variedad de responsabilidades y roles en el programa de doctorado (por ejemplo, supervisar disertaciones, enseñar, corregir, asesorar, administrar, investigar y escribir):

1. En general, ¿qué tanto siente que su primer supervisor/presidente del Comité de Disertación estuvo disponible para discutir su trabajo y sus planes para la disertación? (Marque su respuesta con un círculo)

5	4	3	2	1
Siempre	Casi siempre	Por lo general	A veces	Pocas veces

Si enfrentó algún problema en esta área, explíquelo brevemente.

2. En general, ¿qué tanto siente que su segundo y tercer supervisor/lector estuvieron disponibles para discutir su trabajo y sus planes para la disertación? (Marque su respuesta con un círculo)

5	4	3	2	1
Siempre	Casi siempre	Por lo general	A veces	Pocas veces

Si enfrentó algún problema en esta área, explíquelo brevemente.

El aprovechamiento del tiempo de reunión

3. Cuando se reunió con su supervisor/a o presidente del Comité, ¿sintió que la interacción le ayudó a comprender mejor cómo abordar los aspectos de su trabajo que se reunieron para discutir? (Marque su respuesta con un círculo)

5	4	3	2	1
Siempre	Casi siempre	Por lo general	A veces	Pocas veces

Si enfrentó algún problema en esta área, explíquelo brevemente.

4. Cuando se reunió con su segundo y tercer supervisor/lector, ¿sintió que la interacción le ayudó a comprender mejor cómo abordar los aspectos de su trabajo que se reunieron para discutir? (Marque su respuesta con un círculo)

5	4	3	2	1
Siempre	Casi siempre	Por lo general	A veces	Pocas veces

Si enfrentó algún problema en esta área, explíquelo brevemente.

Orientación práctica

5. Como usted sabe, la tesis/disertación requiere diferentes tipos de trabajo en diferentes etapas del proceso. Al reflexionar sobre su experiencia con su Comité de Disertación, por favor evalúe qué tanto le ayudaron con retroalimentación y orientación para navegar con éxito estos aspectos de la disertación. Use la siguiente escala para sus respuestas: (marque sus respuestas con un círculo)

	Muy útil	Bastante útil	Algo útil	No muy útil
El proceso de enfocar el tema	4	3	2	1
La revisión bibliográfica	4	3	2	1
El trabajo de integración teológica	4	3	2	1
La planificación del abordaje y los métodos de investigación	4	3	2	1
El análisis de los datos	4	3	2	1
Las conclusiones e implicaciones	4	3	2	1
Documentos de apoyo (Apéndices, etc.)	4	3	2	1

Si enfrentó problemas en alguna(s) de estas areas, expliquelo(s) brevemente:

Retroalimentación oportuna

En nuestro programa, les decimos a las y los estudiantes que cuando envían un documento a un miembro del Comité, deben permitir hasta dos semanas para que revise el material y envíe sus comentarios.

6. ¿Cómo caracterizaría su experiencia de recibir retroalimentación de su supervisor/presidente del Comité? (Marque su respuesta con un círculo)

5	4	3	2	1
Siempre a tiempo/plazo	Casi siempre a tiempo	Generalmente a tiempo	A veces a tiempo	Pocas veces a tiempo/plazo

7. En esta misma área, ¿cómo caracterizaría su experiencia con su segundo y tercer supervisor/lector? (Marque su respuesta con un círculo)

5	4	3	2	1
Siempre a tiempo/plazo	Casi siempre a tiempo	Generalmente a tiempo	A veces a tiempo	Pocas veces a tiempo/plazo

Aliento y apoyo

8. ¿Cómo describiría la calidad del aliento y el apoyo que ofrecieron su supervisor/presidente del Comité durante el proceso de disertación? (Marque su respuesta con un círculo)

5	4	3	2	1
Excelente	Buena	Más o menos	Débil	Pobre

Si enfrentó algún problema en esta área, explíquelo brevemente.

9. ¿Cómo describiría la calidad del aliento y el apoyo que ofrecieron su segundo y tercer supervisor/lector durante el proceso de disertación? (Marque su respuesta con un círculo)

5	4	3	2	1
Excelente	Buena	Más o menos	Débil	Pobre

Si enfrentó algún problema en esta área, explíquelo brevemente.

Preparación para la defensa

10. Cuando llegó el momento de prepararse para la defensa de su propuesta y/o de la disertación, ¿recibió el asesoramiento adecuado de su supervisor/presidente del Comité sobre cómo prepararse? (Marque su respuesta con un círculo)

5	4	3	2	1
Excelente	Bueno	Más o menos	Débil	Pobre

Si enfrentó algún problema en esta área, explíquelo brevemente.

Seguimiento después de la defensa final

Después de la tesis final/defensa de tesis, generalmente hay que hacer trabajo adiciónal de revisión.

11. ¿Recibió la orientación adecuada de su supervisor/presidente del Comité para hacer las revisiones finales necesarias para que la disertación fuera aprobada. (Marque su respuesta con un círculo)

5	4	3	2	1
Excelente	Buena	Más o menos	Débil	Pobre

Si enfrentó algún problema en esta área, explíquelo brevemente.

Preguntas finales

12. Dada su experiencia de investigación, si estuviera empezando ahora con su tesis/disertación, ¿Querría trabajar con el mismo supervisor/presidente del Comité y demás miembros del equipo de supervisión/Comité? (Marque su respuesta con un círculo)

3	2	1
Sí.	No	No estoy seguro

Si respondió "Sí", ¿cuáles son las principales razones por las que querría las/los mismos supervisores/miembros del Comité?

Si respondió "No", ¿cuáles son las principales razones por las que querría que al menos algunos miembros del Comité de disertación fueran otras personas?

Si respondió "No estoy seguro", ¿cuáles son las principales razones que le hacen dudar?

13. Sabiendo que diferentes estudiantes pueden responder de manera diferente a los enfoques y procesos de supervisión de tesis de un miembro particular de la facultad, ¿qué clase de estudiante cree que se beneficiaría más de los enfoques que tomó con usted el presidente de su Comité de disertación?

Gracias por tomarse el tiempo para responder a estas preguntas y por ayudarnos en nuestro esfuerzo por que el proceso de supervisión de tesis/disertación sea el mejor posible.

Apéndice 3

Lista de control de progreso para estudiantes de investigación

1. Capacitación en métodos y habilidades de investigación

Forma de capacitación _____
Temas tratados _____
¿Cómo se evaluó? _____
Áreas que requieren capacitación adicional en los próximos doce meses _____
¿Cuándo se considerará que se han logrado las habilidades clave? _____

2. Propuesta de tesis/disertación

Borrador inicial _____
Borrador completo _____
Fecha de aprobación formal _____

3. Requisitos específicos de idiomas

Cursos completados _____
Otros cursos que se requieren _____
Otros idiomas que se consideran deseables _____
Confirmación de competencia lingüística apropiada _____

4. Oportunidades de ministerio cristiano

¿De qué maneras el/la estudiante de doctorado se ha involucrado de forma sostenida en otros aspectos del ministerio y servicio cristianos en los últimos doce meses?

¿De qué maneras el/la estudiante de doctorado se ha involucrado de forma sostenida en otros aspectos del ministerio y servicio cristianos a lo largo de su programa de estudios doctorales?

¿De qué maneras han reflexionado el/la estudiante y su supervisor/a sobre esto y sobre su integración con sus estudios?

¿Qué cuestiones o problemáticas clave han surgido?

¿Están satisfechos (estudiante y su supervisor/a) de que son apropiadas para la fase actual del progreso académico, y que no afectan el tiempo de estudio?

5. Participación en la iglesia local

¿El/la estudiante ha demostrado una participación constante en la vida y el testimonio de una iglesia local?

Ubicación: _____
Nivel de participación: _____

Lecciones aprendidas en torno a la integración de la fe y la erudición:

6. Asistencia a eventos de adoración comunitaria dentro de la institución

¿El/la estudiante ha demostrado una participación constante en las instancias en que la institución académica se reúne como comunidad para adorar

Indique cualquier problema o dificultad que haya surgido.

¿Qué cambios y/o avances se han acordado para los próximos doce meses?

7. Compromiso con la comunidad de aprendizaje institucional

¿El/la estudiante ha demostrado una participación activa en la comunidad de aprendizaje de la institución? Esto incluye:

Asistencia regular a seminarios de investigación y conferencias académicas formales, incluyendo las impartidas por académicos visitantes.

Participación en las discusiones y debates de los seminarios, demostrando escucha participativa, preguntas informadas, manejo cortés de los desacuerdos y trabajo en equipo con otros.

8. Presentación en un seminario

¿El/la estudiante ha hecho una presentación formal en un seminario académico en el último año?

¿Demostró las siguientes cualidades?

   i) Habilidad para comunicar materiales y conceptos complejos de manera accesible e interesante.

   ii) Capacidad de responder preguntas de manera informada y pertinente.

   iii) Capacidad de sostener puntos de vista justificables frente a preguntas y cuestionamientos; pero también de cambiar sus perspectivas cuando es apropiado.

   iv) Capacidad para manejar las críticas con cortesía.

¿Él/ella ha recibido retroalimentación formal por su presentación en el seminario? Si es así, ¿cuáles fueron los puntos clave notados?

¿Cuáles son los planes para los próximos doce meses?

9. Conciencia teológica

¿Qué cuestiones teológicas clave se han identificado durante los últimos 12 meses como áreas en las cuales prestar más atención y crecer?

¿Qué otras áreas se deben considerar?

¿Se han detectado "áreas problemáticas" específicas? ¿se han abordado de forma satisfactoria tanto para el/la estudiante como para su supervisor/a?

¿Él o ella es capaz de explicar cómo su programa de doctorado ha moldeado su perspectiva teológica a lo largo de los últimos doce meses?

10. Práctica docente

¿Qué oportunidades se aprovecharon para adquirir experiencia docente?

    Clases dictadas _____

    Seminarios presentados _____

    Tutoriales dirigidos _____

    Oportunidades de enseñanza en línea _____

¿Qué oportunidades ha tenido el/la estudiante para diseñar y calificar diferentes formas de evaluación de estudiantes?

Retroalimentación sobre la experiencia docente

    ¿Qué tan eficaz fue él/ella en comunicar el material clave del curso a un nivel apropiado para sus estudiantes?

    ¿Hasta qué punto demostró que puede usar eficazmente una variedad de métodos y tecnologías de comunicación?

    ¿Fue apropiada la retroalimentación que él/ella dio a sus estudiantes?

    ¿Cuáles son los objetivos para los próximos doce meses?

11. Integración con la comunidad académica más amplia

Conferencias académicas a las que asistió el año pasado _____

Presentación de trabajo investigativo en una conferencia académica o de una asociación profesional

    Conferencia: _____

    Título de la presentación: _____

    Material académico (revisión de un libro, artículo, etc.) aceptado para publicación _____

¿Cuáles son los planes para los próximos doce meses en este ámbito?

12. Examen doctoral

Discusión sobre posibles examinadores, incluido un experto externo _____

Nombramiento del panel examinador _____

Examen de tesis doctoral _____

Revisiones de tesis completadas _____

Recomendaciones hechas para su publicación _____

13. Desarrollo Profesional Continuo

¿El/la estudiante y su supervisor/a de doctorado han discutido formas de comprometerse con su desarrollo profesional continuo post-doctorado y con la continuidad de sus actividades de investigación.

Plan para los siguientes años 1-2 _____

Plan para los años 3-4 _____

Plan para los años 5-6 _____

14. Desarrollo de carrera

¿El/la candidato/a al doctorado ha preparado un currículum profesional y un curriculum vitae? _____

¿Se le ha dado orientación sobre la redacción de cartas de solicitud de empleo? ¿y sobre entrevistas?

Nombres de personas dispuestas a ofrecer referencias pastorales y académicas.

Nombre, título, institución

1.

2.

3.

Global Hub for Evangelical Theological Education

ICETE es una comunidad global, patrocinada por nueve redes regionales de instituciones teológicas, dedicada a fomentar la interacción y colaboración internacional entre todos aquellos que intervienen en el fortalecimiento y el desarrollo de la educación teológica evangélica y del liderazgo cristiano alrededor del mundo.

El propósito de ICETE es:
1. Promover el mejoramiento de la educación teológica evangélica alrededor del mundo.
2. Servir como foro para la interacción, asociación y colaboración entre quienes intervienen en la educación teológica evangélica y en el desarrollo de liderazgo evangélico, para su mutua asistencia, estimulación y enriquecimiento.
3. Ofrecer servicios de apoyo y asesoramiento para asociaciones regionales de instituciones evangélicas de educación teológica alrededor del mundo.
4. Facilitar, para las redes regionales, la promoción de sus servicios entre las instituciones evangélicas de educación teológica dentro de sus regiones.

Las asociaciones patrocinadoras incluyen:

África: Association for Christian Theological Education in Africa (ACTEA)

Asia: Asia Theological Association (ATA)

Caribe: Caribbean Evangelical Theological Association (CETA)

Europa: European Council for Theological Education (ECTE)

América Latina: Asociación Evangélica de Educación Teológica en América Latina (AETAL)

Medio Oriente y Norte de África: Middle East-North Africa Association for Theological Education (MENATE)

América del Norte: Association for Biblical Higher Education (ABHE)

www.icete-edu.org

Langham Literature y sus sellos editoriales son parte del ministerio de
Langham Partnership.

Langham Partnership es un comunidad global que trabaja para actualizar la visión que el Señor confió a su fundador John Stott —la visión de

facilitar el crecimiento de la iglesia en madurez y en semejanza al carácter de Cristo por medio de la mejora de los estándares de la predicación y la enseñanza bíblicas.

Nuestra visión es que las iglesias del mundo mayoritario sean equipadas para la misión y crezcan hacia la madurez en Cristo por medio del ministerio de pastores y líderes que creen, enseñan y viven de acuerdo a la Palabra de Dios.

Nuestra misión es fortalecer el ministerio de la Palabra de Dios:
- fortaleciendo movimientos nacionales de predicación bíblica
- favoreciendo la creación y distribución de literatura evangélica
- elevando el nivel de la educación teológica evangélica, especialmente en países donde las iglesias carecen de recursos.

Nuestro ministerio

Langham Preaching se asocia con líderes nacionales que estimulan movimientos locales de predicación bíblica para pastores y predicadores laicos en el mundo entero. Con el apoyo de un equipo de capacitadores provenientes de diversos países, se desarrolla un programa de talleres a diversos niveles que proveen capacitación práctica, seguido de un programa que busca formar facilitadores locales. Los grupos locales de predicación (escuelas de expositores), que son redes nacionales y regionales, se encargan de dar continuidad a los programas y de impulsar su desarrollo con el fin de construir un movimiento sólido y comprometido con la exposición bíblica.

Langham Literature provee a los pastores, académicos y seminarios del mundo mayoritario libros evangélicos y recursos electrónicos mediante su publicación y distribución, y por medio de becas y descuentos. El programa también auspicia la producción de literatura evangélica autóctona en diversos idiomas mediante becas para escritores, con apoyos para casas editoriales evangélicas, y por medio de la inversión en proyectos importantes de literatura en las regiones, como por ejemplo los comentarios bíblicos a un solo volumen como el *Africa Bible Commentary* (Comentario Bíblico Africano) y el *South Asia Bible Commentary* (Comentario Bíblico del Sureste Asiático).

Langham Scholars provee respaldo económico para estudiantes evangélicos del mundo mayoritario a nivel doctorado, de modo que, cuando regresen a su país de origen, puedan formar a pastores y a otros líderes cristianos por medio de la enseñanza bíblica y teológica. Este programa forma a los que más adelante formarán a otros. Langham Scholars también trabaja en colaboración con seminarios del mundo mayoritario para fortalecer la educación teológica evangélica. Un número creciente de becados de Langham estudia programas doctorales de alta calidad en instituciones del mundo mayoritario. Además de enseñar a una nueva generación de pastores, los graduados del programa de becas Langham ejercen una influencia considerable a través de sus escritos y su liderazgo.

Para conocer más acerca de Langham Partnership y el trabajo que realizamos visita **langham.org**